CONSTRUCTIVE LIBERALISM

THE ROLE OF THE STATE

IN ECONOMIC DEVELOPMENT

IN GEORGIA TO 1860

STUDIES IN ECONOMIC HISTORY

Published in coöperation with

the Committee on Research in

Economic History

Constructive Liberalism

THE ROLE OF THE STATE

IN ECONOMIC DEVELOPMENT

IN GEORGIA TO 1860

Milton Sydney Heath

HARVARD UNIVERSITY PRESS

CAMBRIDGE, 1954

Distributed in Great Britain by
GEOFFREY CUMBERLEGE
Oxford University Press
London

Library of Congress Catalog Card Number: 54–8627
Printed in the United States of America

To the Memory

of

ELIZA HASTINGS HEATH

and

JESSE J. HEATH

PREFACE

This study is an effort to present the record of public action in its setting of social ideas during the early history of a key Southern state. There is no intent to minimize the influence of natural, ethnological, and technological forces on social processes, and their effects are given some consideration; but primary concern with causal relationships is confined to the links between public policy and that body of ideas known as liberalism. This doctrine, particularly in its religious, political, and economic evolutions, has been the dominant ideological force in American development. There has always been wide variance in emphasis, or interpretation, as to its meaning among its exponents and the doctrine has passed, in practice, through varying phases and cycles with the changing course of our dynamic society. Certain of these permutations define and characterize the time period chosen for this study.

Much the greater part of the study is taken up with the record of public action. The basic data were taken from the records of legislative and administrative activity. Judicial records also were studied whenever available, but they are quite inadequate for the years prior to the establishment of the Supreme Court in 1846. Concern has been restricted to what transpired in Georgia or was immediately relevant thereto. No broad claims are made for uniqueness or originality in the record. Much of what happened doubtlessly was duplicated repeatedly elsewhere. The study was undertaken solely with the hope that it might add to a better understanding of the role of government in early American economic life and, hence, of the groundwork of American economic institutions.

I am indebted to many persons and institutions for assistance during my research and the preparation of this study, particularly since its roots reach back into extended earlier research in the history of public enterprise in the Southern states as a whole. I wish to thank especially Miss Ella May Thornton, State Librarian, and the staff of the Georgia State Library; Mrs. Louise F. Hays, former Director, and the staff of the Georgia Department of Archives and History; Mr. Wymberley Wormsloe DeRenne, Archivist, University of Georgia; Mrs. Lilla M. Hawes, Director, Georgia Historical Society; Professor William Sumner Jenkins, Department of Political Science, University of North Carolina, Collector and Compiler of the Microfilm Collection of Early State Records; Miss Lucile Elliott, Librarian, and the staff of the Law School Library, University of North Carolina; Miss Mary Thornton, Librarian, North Carolina Collection, and the staff of the Library, University of North Carolina; Mrs. Richard Fitzgerald (Allene Ramage), Montgomery, Alabama, former Director, Newspaper Collection, Duke University Library; the staff of Duke Law School Library; Miss Elizabeth Cullen, Librarian, Bureau of Railway Economics, Washington, D. C.; and Mr. Wyllis Eaton Wright, Librarian, and the staff of Williams College Library. Much of the earlier work was done in Congressional Library, Washington, D. C., where the highly competent staffs of the divisions of public documents, newspapers, and collected correspondence supplied me with every facility possible.

Mr. James Houstoun Johnston read the chapters on Internal Improvements and Railways and made a number of helpful suggestions; and he and his publishers, the Georgia Public Service Commission, kindly permitted the use of data from two tables in his *Western and Atlantic Railroad of the State of Georgia.* Professor Edmund Steel of Limestone College read the chapter on the State Railway System and generously gave me the benefit of his knowledge gained from recent research in a related area. My daughter, Miss Elizabeth Hastings Heath, read the entire manuscript and contributed inestimably to the likelihood of intelligible communication between the author and his readers.

An appointment by the University of North Carolina as Research Professor of Economics in the Institute for Research in Social Science gave me sufficient freedom from teaching to complete the manuscript. I am deeply appreciative of the coöperation and assistance rendered by Professor Gordon Blackwell, Director, and members of the staff of the Institute; particularly am I grateful to Mr. William Kelvey Hubbell, Graphic Arts Supervisor, for his excellent maps.

I am indebted above all to the Committee on Research in Economic History for its support and constant encouragement; especially do I owe a great debt to its chairman, Professor Arthur H. Cole, for his counsel, many helpful suggestions, encouragement and every possible assistance in bringing this study to its conclusion.

I have followed Professor Coulter's example (*Georgia: A Short History*) of including a Table of the Chief Executives of Georgia as a helpful reference outline for the period under study. I used Rand-McNally state outline maps and leaned heavily on the maps in Ulrich B. Phillips, *Georgia and States Rights,* for early county boundary lines in working up the data from which Mr. Hubbell produced the maps for this study.

MILTON S. HEATH

Chapel Hill, N. C., 1953

CONTENTS

MAPS

TABLES

CHARTS

INTRODUCTION

LIBERAL THOUGHT AND PUBLIC POLICY

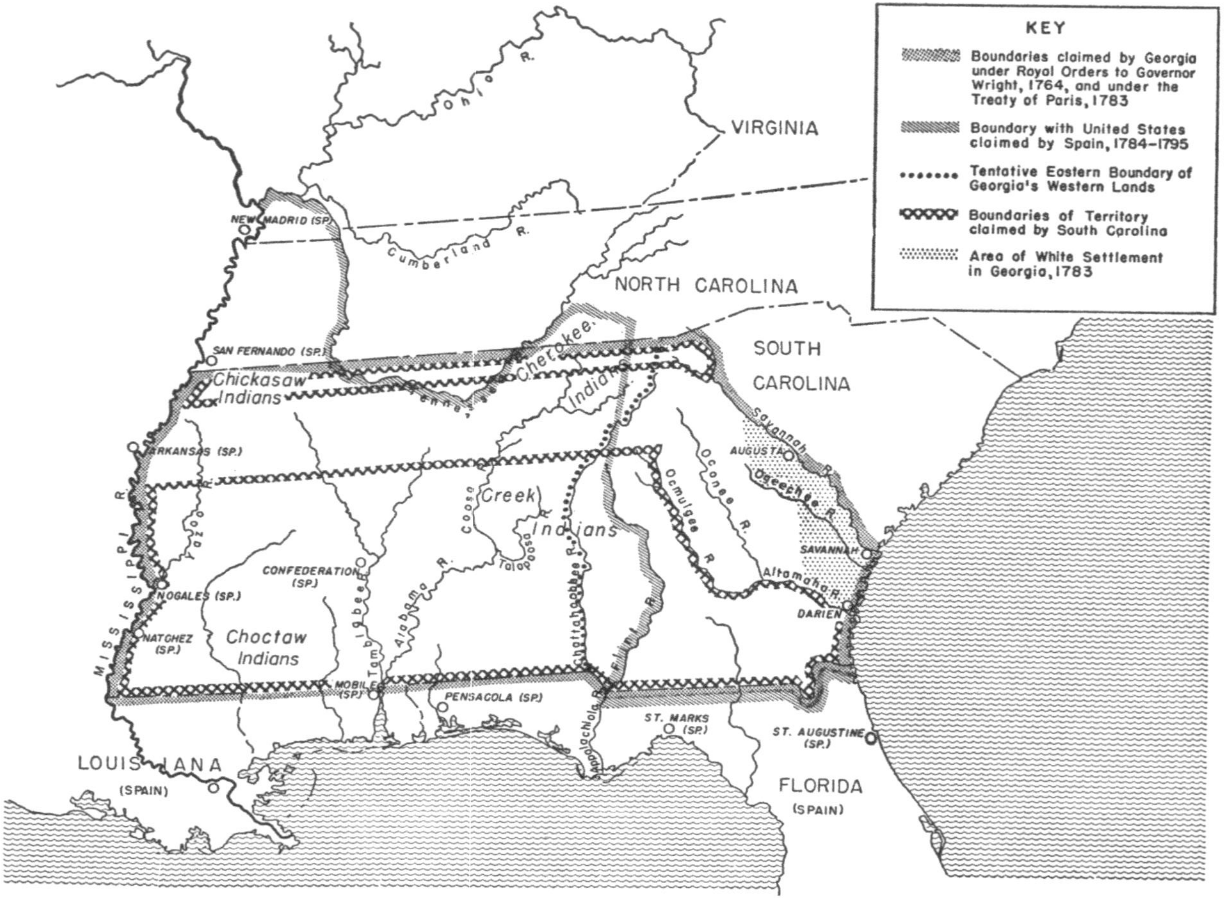

Georgia Territory: 1783–1802

CHAPTER I

PLANNING FOR ECONOMIC FREEDOM

Economic policy derives its objectives ultimately from a body of postulates, or hypotheses, concerning the fundamental nature and purposes of man, or what is commonly known as a philosophy of society. The degree of effectiveness in achieving its aims is limited by the quantity of natural agents, labor, capital, and entrepreneurship, and by technology and organization. The unit of organization may be either an individual or a group and the *modus operandi* either private or public. Instrumental forms and procedures are commonly defined in positive law; but the latter derives its sanction ultimately from some underlying body of principles of society.

1. Foundations of Liberal Thought

Eighteenth-century social thought in Georgia, as elsewhere in America and, generally speaking, in western Europe, contained little that was fundamentally original. It stemmed from the recrudescence of natural law principles in the seventeenth century, which probably reached its zenith of social interpretation in the writings of John Locke. Leading eighteenth-century applications in political theory are found in the works of Montesquieu, Rousseau, Madison, and Jefferson and, in economics, in those of the Physiocrats and Adam Smith. According to the doctrine, man is a rational purposive being whose end is happiness. All psychological action is an aspect of nature, and men are equally endowed with both the capacity for rational action and the capacity for happiness. The highest happiness is attainable only in society. Hence society is a natural state, and the positive laws which are enacted for its governance must derive their sanction from natural law, if they are to serve their fundamental purpose of facilitating the maximum of human happiness.

The most common criteria, or principles, of natural law, accepted as guides to the formulation of positive law, were the rights of freedom of choice,[1] equality in society, property in one's own labor, and free access to the common heritage of nature. These principles emphasized the primacy of the individual, but likewise embodied correlative social obligations: a social state was one of reciprocity and restraint as well as of freedom and equality. The latter qualities, in their fullest measure were products of the former and, hence, their true justification. Consequently government, the basic organizational form of society, existed always and solely for the greater benefit of the governed, and government by the will of the governed was the first law of natural society. Such in substance was the philosophy of political and economic liberalism in which Georgia and other American communities were schooled.[2]

Impediments to the attainment of human happiness were considered to be chiefly of two sorts: those imposed by nature and those contrived by man himself. Nature's limitations, it was admitted, could not be avoided but, nevertheless, should be understood; but man-imposed restrictions could and should be removed. Natural law theorists from Thomas Hobbes to the nineteenth century were deeply concerned with what they considered to be the basic relationship between man and nature, between the two "primary factors of production." Nature was limited, whereas man could increase his numbers and even possessed an irrational propensity to do so. Nature alone produced very meagerly; hence man was credited with creating the greater share of their joint product. But the more eagerly man labored, or the more he multiplied his numbers who must gain a livelihood from the soil, the less readily did nature respond to man's efforts. In Hobbes's words, man perforce must bargain with nature with his labor but the more labor he offered the less, relatively speaking, nature exchanged in return. Nature consistently drove a hard bargain. This in essence was the classic law of diminishing returns.

Recognition of these basic relationships was a sobering note in the new liberal theory of social organization. There was no panacea; man must continue to earn his sustenance by the sweat of his brow. In the background there was always a somewhat disturbing bogey of a mature society brought to a standstill, despite the perfection of positive laws, by the limitation and niggardliness of nature. But eighteenth-century theorists called equal attention to the many man-made restrictions which operated like nature's laws to thwart man's productiveness. First, there were land systems that created idle land holdings and idle owners, that prevented the free entry of labor and capital, thereby adding artificial limitations to those already imposed by nature upon agricultural production. Then there were tariffs, trade regulations, settlement laws, and monopolies that oppressed freedom of enterprise in commerce and industry. The theory of rational freedom found itself confronted by a stubborn nature on the one hand and a thick web of restrictive positive law on the other. The eradication of human restrictions would do much to release man's ingenuity for the struggle with nature. Through expansion of markets, division of labor, invention, savings, and industry, temporary respites at least could be won.[3]

It is small wonder that eighteenth-century philanthropists, bent upon constructive benevolence and inspired by the natural law ideas of Locke, should have chosen to send poor English laborers to the free lands of Georgia in quest of happiness. There, amidst nature's abundance of resources, protected by wise laws and distance from the monopolies and other restrictive institutions of the Old World, man's property right in his own labor could be freely joined with the common heritage of nature. America unquestionably offered a far more fertile soil for the growth of liberal institutions than did the land which gave birth to the philosophy of natural liberty. The abundance of virgin lands stimulated and attracted socially minded individuals and groups who were in search of the means of private wealth. It not only provided certain safeguards to democratic equality and freedom of individual enterprise, but also supplied the technical basis for an economical combination where labor and capital were scarce and therefore an abundance of land was a requisite for their most profitable use.

As the libertarian philosophy was translated into political and economic theory and policy during the eighteenth and nineteenth centuries, a division began to arise over the role of group action, in particular about that of the state. The earlier liberal writers unquestionably had held that restraint by the group was coequal in nature with private right. But they were engaged in a struggle against authoritarian government whose rule, they reasoned, sustained a legal structure that abridged the liberties of the people generally. They beheld government protecting the privileges of the few and the powerful. Locke's psychology of natural man, which provided the thesis of human equality, struck at the traditional defense — the incapacity of the common man — of the coalition of state and aristocratic privilege.

What Adam Smith did was to introduce this conception of responsible individual action into the theory of economic organization and process and to propose freedom of the individual as a basic postulate of economic policy. And Jeremy Bentham further developed and applied this central doctrine to the theory and practice of legislation in all societal relationships.[4] Smith developed a concept of economic organization in terms of free enterprise and free markets, in which competition in the market provided at one and the same time freedom of choice, the necessary social restraints, and a maximum of economic employment and production. Such a system appeared to afford a self-regulative mode of group action which made slight demands upon government other than the enforcement of such liberal rules as the right of private property, the sanctity of contracts, and freedom of access to the market. Actually there were two elements in Smith's social philosophy, as there had been in Locke's. The first was the principle of productive force inherent in free individual initiative. This, fundamentally, was an answer to the theories of human nature that had supported most of the previous politico-economical systems, and it supplied the positive, dynamic element in Smith's system. The second was the conception of automatic restraint provided by the free market, which assumed a kind of social harmony of effort among free men. Here Smith appeared much less certain of his ground, warning that powerful individuals and groups, unless restrained, were likely to abuse freedom and to take advantage of the weak, that employers were likely to engage in a kind of tacit collusion against workers and that landlords always loved to reap where they had not sown.[5]

Smith's system of natural liberty must be interpreted in its setting. Governmental action at the time still was weighted heavily on the side of special privilege; whereas private initiative, despite numerous public restrictions, had made rapid strides in the economic sphere and with obvious beneficial social results. Thus it is not curious that by the early nineteenth century the theory of liberalism had advanced along the postulates of free individual initiative much further than it had within the equally important and correlative realm of group action.

The theories of democratic government and free business enterprise rested upon identical foundations; yet the notion steadily gained headway that the roles of democratic government and private business were opposing rather than supporting lines of action. The antipathies of the earlier liberalism of Locke and Smith for government by special privilege were translated by many of their self-styled followers into an aversion to the rule of democracy. Smith's "obvious and simple system of natural liberty" was interpreted increasingly as a presupposition against nearly every form of public enterprise or interference. This famous doctrine of *laissez faire* became for its nineteenth-century advocates a dogma that held public action in almost every form to be hostile to private interests, contrary to nature and obstructive to progress.

Freedom of action cannot be reduced realistically to an absolute datum; it is inseparable from the behavior of the group. The group necessarily prescribes the conditions of freedom enjoyed by the individual, and the growth of personal liberty depends fundamentally upon the progress of the group. Therefore liberal policy rests necessarily upon complementary postulates of individual freedom and group action. It demands both freedom of action for the individual and a constructive public program designed to release the productive energies of all individuals and to curb those proclivities of some who would obstruct the freedom of the many. Practically speaking, the state is able to provide the only instrument of total group action and, hence, the widest possibility of representation and enforcement of the collective will. In itself government is only a means of group action just as the business unit, or any other form of organization, may serve a group purpose. Both are designed, in liberal theory, to advance the welfare of the individual — the term welfare being used in the broadest possible sense to include the creative, enterprising, and contemplative, as well as the consumptive capacities of the individual. Therefore, liberal policy can never have as its aim the aggrandizement of the state, but solely the elevation of the individual. This positive conception of liberal policy, which contemplates individual freedom and group action as complementary, and the former as the object of the latter, will be termed constructive liberalism in this study, in order to distinguish it from laissez-faire liberalism which has advocated as the guiding hand of public policy almost exclusively the constructive role of individual initiative. The latter is not in essence antithetical to constructive liberalism but rather is only a constituent part of it.

While the principle of constructive group action was always present in earlier liberal writings, it was more often implicitly than explicitly stated. Here and there during the eighteenth century it was given a trial in action; however, it was not before Bentham and Mill that it attained its full theoretical development, in which form it supplied the basis for much of the nineteenth-century reform legislation in Great Britain and America. While emphasis in the earlier phases of the liberal tradition was on individual freedom, it has shifted increasingly in later times to include the action of the group.

A major problem of constructive liberal policy has always been that of developing intelligent unity of purpose, or consensus, among the members of the group. Immediate self-interest on the one hand and the present costs of social action on the other have been much more readily visualized than long-run results. It has required more sustained thought and imagination on the part of both leaders and rank-and-file than men have been wont to give even to their own interests. As society progresses in complexity and productivity this task is likely to grow even more difficult.

It is the major purpose of the present study to trace the development of constructive liberal action in Georgia, in particular the role played by the state, from the founding of the colony in 1732 until the outbreak of the War between the States in 1861. Georgia supplies an excellent historical laboratory of practical experimentation and accomplishment during this period. Possibly it was then making a more thorough trial of liberal hypotheses, on the whole, than most democratic communities. The two contrasting notions of liberalism were in continuous struggle for the ascendancy and each left its mark upon policy and practice.

2. Liberal Policy in Georgia

Economic liberalism in Georgia was the product of convergent streams of ideas of widely divergent origins. Since the major colonial settlement, in the Savannah region, came in the main directly from the British Isles, the earlier liberal influence was predominantly British eighteenth-century politico-economical liberalism. The late settlement of Georgia — it was the only colony settled after the publication of Locke's *Treatises on Government* — meant that its original liberalism branched off from the parent Anglo-European trunk of thought at a much later date than was true of the other American colonies, whose liberal origins were rooted in the politico-religious turmoils of the previous century. This earlier American liberalism, with its strong religious strain, was represented however in the New England Congregational settlement at Midway and Sunbury southwest of Savannah. Another primarily religious type, of direct European origin, was represented in the German community at Ebenezer, a group that almost equaled the English in numbers during the Trustee period and contributed some important leaders during the Revolution. Emergent American democratic liberalism — the product of a century or more of frontier self-reliance and freedom from restraints — was just beginning to make its influence felt in Georgia upon the outbreak of the Revolution. It was represented chiefly among the immigrants from North Carolina who were settling in the upstate region around Augusta. This new immigration from the Carolinas and Virginia assumed flood proportions immediately after the Revolution and eventually supplied the dominant element in the population of the state. Obviously the problem of securing unity of purpose and action was to become a dual one — of removing the barriers to common thinking that inevitably were present between groups of such diverse liberal backgrounds, and of resolving the more basic conflicts within the general body of liberal thought.

The settlement of Georgia under the Trustees was among the earliest specific ventures by Englishmen in constructive liberalism. For despite its charitable and paternalistic features, its frequent cross-purposes, and its occasional concessions to illiberal aims, the Trustees' program was designed primarily to promote human liberty in Georgia. Its charitable and remedial bases reflected its origin in the two staunchest liberal movements of the age, organized philanthropy and prison reform; and its voluntary quasi-public direction bespoke an intention to avoid the pitfalls of direct sponsorship by a government that was far more interested in imperial adventure than in the rights of man. Ironically, as it turned out, the safeguards placed upon the colonists by the Trustees for the development and preservation of their liberties later proved, in the opinion of the colonists, to be an obstruction to those very liberties; and after twenty years of benevolent guidance, they welcomed the advent of the authoritarian Crown government as a promise of enhanced freedom.

The royal plan for Georgia was that of a model imperial colony. Internal laissez-faire policies in land and labor, designed to divert Georgians from possible competition with British traders and manufacturers, built up within the colony in an incredibly short time a wealthy planter capitalism. But liberalism came back in Georgia, from its earlier, nurtured roots, under the leadership of Noble Wimberly Jones, who rallied the common folk and many of the sons of wealthy planters against the authoritarian proclivities of the Crown government. This movement laid the basis of the Revolution in the colony, which ultimately joined the benevolently nurtured liberalism of Savannah with the puritan liberalism of Midway and the frontier liberalism of Augusta in a common, though not always congenial, alliance against the Tories and British.

The new experiment in government was launched in Georgia with large ambitions for social action. Characteristic were the constitutional and statutory provisions for a state-supported system of universal education, from primary through secondary and higher branches of the arts and sciences. But quickly developing regional and structural disagreements among the libertarians, coupled with financial debility of the government, private land hunger, and rapid changes in the balance of population, soon undermined most of the state's initial constructive social purposiveness.

During the ten years following 1785, the spirit of *laissez faire* fairly consumed the populace: administration of the all-important land and highway policies was relegated to the barely organized county governments; education, welfare, and waterway improvement were left to private or local quasi-public enterprise. The upholders of *laissez faire* backed the early liberal policy of voluntarism in opposition to state-supported education, despite the fact that the older theory and practice had become largely outmoded with the inauguration of democratic government.[6] It was a typical instance of misapplication of liberal precedent by laissez-faire liberals; nevertheless, it proved successful in setting the course of educational policy in Georgia for the better part of a century.

The climax of the disintegration of early constructive liberal policy was reached in the famous Yazoo Land Companies scandal of 1795–1796. The fight waged by a group of outstanding young liberals against the principles and corrupt practices involved in the western land deals produced a great awakening around the turn of the century. This unified for the first time the individualistic concepts and aspirations of the upstate region and the back country with the positive social ideals of the coast and forged them into an active common sense of social values.[7]

The supreme accomplishment of this liberal revival was a revolution in land policy. It also brought about reorganization in fiscal administration, sweeping reforms in the criminal code and the system of punishments, and a beginning toward a state system of internal improvements. It exercised a potent influence over the development of banking. Its chief failure was in education, although even there its effects were not entirely lacking. It established the state-supported university that had been included in the original plan of education, expanded the program of state aid to local academies, and secured the establishment of a small State Educational Fund. The movement largely spent its force, however, in the material prosperity that followed the War of 1812.

The decade of the twenties was predominantly laissez-faire in sentiment and policy. The political party founded by James Jackson and his liberal associates at the turn of the century had become increasingly conservative under the succeeding Crawford-Troup leadership. It came more and more to represent the views of the rising commercial-planting-financial aristocracy of the coast and the prospering planter society of the cotton belt. Although George M. Troup continued to advocate internal improvements, education, and even increased taxes, a majority of his party had become concerned solely about retaining control of the state's political machinery and reducing taxes that already were unbelievably low.[8] Meanwhile, an opposition party of the common folk and the settlers in the newer regions had risen under the leadership of John Clark, whom it was able to elect to the governorship in 1819. It had fallen heir to some of the more progressive ideas of Jacksonian liberalism and did not lack for public issues, but it too often proved negative in outlook and never was able to formulate a genuinely constructive program.[9]

Both political parties contained large liberal elements, which represented the constructive tradition in liberal thought in Georgia. Believing that their state was failing to provide the positive public program which advancing knowledge, technology, industrial organization, wealth, and population warranted and required, and losing hope that their respective parties would ever develop such a program, these liberal groups joined forces to form a new Union Party as a means of promulgating a constructive public program.

Union Party men occupied the governorship, except for two terms when the moderate conservative, George Gilmer, held the office, from 1827 until 1843. The crowning achievement of this period was the launching of the state's railroad system. Important advances were made also in education and welfare. State support of schools was doubled and a common school law actually was enacted; but before the latter could go into effect it fell a victim to the severe depression of 1837–1844 and the vigilant opposition of its enemies. Institutions were provided for the education of the deaf and dumb and the care of the insane, and a state medical college was established at Augusta. A valiant attempt also was made to utilize the Central Bank of the State, established in 1828, to relieve the economic distress, and to support the state's railroad construction program, which likewise encountered difficulties on account of the economic collapse.

But the spirit of constructive liberalism flagged during the early forties under the debilitating effects of depression and a growing lack of leadership in the Union Party. A mounting opposition, attacking the "statism" and "spendthrift waste" of the Union Party administration and demanding a policy of fiscal austerity and a return to the "sound principles" of individual responsibility and private initiative, was finally successful in its bid for state leadership in 1843. A laissez-faire policy was followed fairly consistently thereafter until the Panic of 1857. However, the state railroad was completed and placed in operation under public administration. The welfare program initiated by the Union Party was continued and even expanded; but public support of education was held down to a level far below that of the thirties and every effort to increase it or to introduce a public common school system was defeated. Meanwhile, the state's two chief banking ventures were liquidated.

Following the Panic of 1857 there was another revival of active liberalism under the leadership of Joseph E. Brown.[10] Support came primarily from the small farmers and other less privileged groups. Governor Brown's program called especially for state support for the completion of the railroad system, in southern and northern Georgia, and for the inauguration of a state-supported system of common schools. Large public efforts were undertaken in both fields, but the new cycle of social action was cut short by the catastrophe of civil war.

This brief summary of the history of constructive liberal policy in Georgia reveals that, while there appears to have been continuity throughout in most shades of liberal thought, the course of liberal action ran in cycles. Counting in the Trustees' program at the beginning and that under Governor Brown's leadership at the close, there were five high-level periods and four low-level ones. A full cycle — from the beginning of one period of constructive policy to the beginning of the next — averaged approximately three decades in length. Does this mean that the flow of social ideas and their effects are wave-like, or recurrent, in character? Are there definable causes for the pulsating nature of such movements? While such fluctuations are both influenced by and influence the fluctuations in business activity, there appears to be no general causal relationship between the two. For the period of this study it appears that movements in social thought and action might have been equally strengthened, or weakened, by either boom or depression.

PART ONE

BRITISH AND COLONIAL BACKGROUNDS

CHAPTER II

POVERTY AND BENEVOLENCE

The colonial years supply the principal background — the immediate past — of the period of our primary inquiry. The various groups, environmental influences, and ideas that molded the lives of colonial Georgians must be considered among the factors that shaped the course of development in the later period.

1. Men and Purposes

An unusual disparateness characterized the primary group of Trustees, Crown administrators, and colonists that fashioned Georgia's colonial history. The Trustees were all associated in some way with current philanthropic or reform movements, though they were drawn from many different fields of interest — religious, political, legal, sociological, scientific, and economic. There were Anglicans and Non-Conformists, parliamentarians, Crown officials, local politicians, nobles, country squires, middle-class gentry, ministers of the gospel, agrarians, manufacturers, traders, lawyers, and accountants. It was an unusual and able body of men and constituted one of the widest community-of-interest groups probably that has ever been brought together in the business of benevolence and reform. In this *Age of Organized Benevolence*, "The Trustees for Establishing the Colony of Georgia in America" were among the top interlocking management units of philanthropic enterprise. The most numerous and close-knit interest group in the organization was the Parliamentary Prison Reform Committee; the religious education group was probably second in number and influence; less numerous, though by no means always less influential, were groups and individuals interested in hospitals, foundling homes, Indian and Negro missions, and the relief of foreign Protestants.[1]

The Crown, or the executive department of the British government, in sharp contrast to the Trustees, was at this time a rather highly unified group in outlook, purpose, and operating practice. There had recently taken place considerable reorganization, and it had become the chief agency for the promotion of mature British colonial policy. It was in such a role that it chartered the Georgia colony and delegated to the Trustees such powers as they enjoyed in the promotion and direction of the colony; consequently, it became necessary to exercise a certain area of tolerance toward the Trustees in their developmnt of their own peculiar colonial policy.[2]

The colonists, though drawn largely from the same strata and conditions of society, represented numerous geographical and in some instances different national and linguistic origins. They came from both urban and rural localities, from northern as well as southern England, from Scotland, Ireland, Germany, Switzerland, Italy, the West Indies, tidewater South Carolina, New England, upper South Carolina, North Carolina, and Virginia. They divide rather significantly, however, into two main streams. The earlier, and chief colonial one comprised the immigrants from all of the above origins except the last three. This stream, though of many sources, was primarily European and converged upon the seacoast area of which Savannah was the center. The other and later migration came primarily from the Carolinas and Virginia: it was beginning to reach significant numbers in settlements around Augusta just prior to the Revolution, swelled to enormous proportions following the war, and eventually populated the greater part of Georgia.[3]

In estimating the weight of background factors upon later state policies it is difficult to assess influences emanating from such different origins among the settlers. Broadly speaking, all except the Germans, Swiss, and Italians had been affected more or less by the same general influences that were common to the experience and thinking of Englishmen during the seventeenth and eighteenth centuries; but particular conditioning factors among them had varied widely. It appears to have been true in general that political and commercial organization and practice and much of the early social philosophy of Georgia after the Revolution derived through the older colonial settlement; while the preponderant weight of mores and much of the spirit of extreme individualism probably traced their origin through the Virginia and North Carolina migration.

2. Organized Philanthropy

Georgia began as a planned economy. Philanthropy, mercantilism, and, to a lesser extent, militarism have been credited with supplying the basic motives and patterns. It is not our purpose to attempt to resolve the controversies over the relative weights that should be assigned to each of these motives in the intent of the founders. We are concerned only with what ideas and actions may have left a sufficient imprint upon the colony to influence policy at a later date.

Since philanthropy was the one unquestioned bond among all of the

Trustees, it seems logical to ask what was the character of the philanthropy that motivated the Georgia project? The "debtor colony" theory has largely been exploded and a much broader basis of benevolent action has been proved.[4] Yet the full significance of this charitable impetus has scarcely been revealed. The Georgia philanthropy was in fact a part of a vast organized benevolent movement in early eighteenth-century Britain, which developed a body of ideas, a theory of social action, and a network of interlocking enterprises. Generally speaking, the central ideas derived from the Christian ethic and the social, psychological, and educational theories of John Locke.[5] The chief social problem with which it concerned itself was poverty; the answer that it gave was reform through constructive philanthropy. Charity was distinctly not a sentimental matter; it was intended to be remedial, to transform the recipient into a productive member of society, to create the means of further production. It was not to be wasted upon slothful wretches and hardened criminals who could not be made industrious; such misguided benevolence would only increase their kind. The victims of misfortune, hard luck, or illness, who could make good use of another chance or could be rehabilitated through hospitalization, were the worthy objects of charity.[6] But the children of the poor, who might be rescued from unwholesome environments and trained into industrious, self-supporting citizens, were the especial objects of the benevolent program. Thousands of charity schools and hospitals were put into operation in England, Wales, Scotland, and Ireland solely through the voluntary activities and contributions of individuals and private organizations.[7]

Another part of this movement, embodying essentially the same principles, were the numerous Indian and Negro missions. It was believed that the hostile relations that existed between the American Indians and the white settlers, and likewise the harsh treatment that was meted out to Negro slaves by their masters, resulted almost entirely from the paganism and the primitive economic status of the savages. Conversion to Christianity and training in the productive arts of the white man, it was thought, would establish the only firm basis for peaceful and coöperative relations between Indians and Negroes and their white neighbors and masters. This would prove of great economic benefit to all parties, including the mother country.[8] A similar philosophy supported the extensive efforts to transplant the oppressed Protestant minorities of Germany and other European countries.

Benevolent reform was far less radical than the stirring religious and political doctrines of the sixteenth and seventeenth centuries.[9] In a considerable measure it was the product of the impact of increasing wealth upon the puritan conscience. It drew its leadership and support in the main from the middle-class devotees of puritan religious ethics.[10] It was businesslike in its methods and demanded a large measure of free, voluntary service.

Despite the prominence of religion and the strain of paternalism in the movement, eighteenth-century benevolence was an important root force in the growth of secular liberalism.[11] It filled an important role in the shift of moral philosophy toward a greater concern with social problems and their solution. Its proposals to solve the problem of poverty by equipping potential laborers with skills, tools, access to jobs and to ownership of property suggest new theories of productive labor and social value. Though still viewing philanthropy primarily as a religious duty, it breathed the atmosphere of human freedom and contained the principles of freer economic enterprise and maximization of welfare that clearly anticipate much of the social creed of the classical economists and their liberal associates. It offered the "helping hand" of liberal benevolence; whereas Adam Smith advocated reliance upon the "guiding hand" of the order of natural liberty. Admittedly the benevolent policy called for more collective planning for free enterprise than did Smith's system which relied heavily upon *laissez faire*.

Planning, according to the benevolent viewpoint, should be quasi-public rather than governmental; it should depend upon voluntarism rather than political choice. Its forms and methods should be adapted from private rather than from public business; and performance should be the equal in assiduity and faithfulness of that to be found in private occupations.[12] Thus, like Smith and the Physiocrats later, the Philanthropists were opposed to overmuch public enterprise, but they distinctly did not favor leaving the guidance of the economic system entirely to individual self-interest and the business entrepreneur. They appear to have been willing to rely upon private enterprise within large areas — possibly in a predominant measure — but they favored the introduction of quasi-public control within those areas where private enterprise failed to promote the general welfare.

3. Initiation of the Georgia Project

The Georgia colonial project was in many respects the broadest, most comprehensive, of the benevolent enterprises. Originating in Oglethorpe's mind as a single purpose scheme of relieving debtors and thus bolstering his prison reform program,[13] it was gradually transformed into a composite enterprise embodying most of the various phases of the benevolent movement: colonists were to be selected from among all worthy poor people who might apply, including the oppressed Protestant minorities of Europe.[14] The emphasis was placed overwhelmingly, to be sure, upon the rehabilitation of adults; however, charity schools were proposed for the training of orphans and of other children who might be sent over as apprentices to the colonists, and missions were to be established for the conversion and education of the Indians and the Negro slaves of neighboring regions.[15] The "Georgia Society," as Lord Percival referred to those who had joined with Oglethorpe in the colonizing scheme, brought together with the Parliamentary Committee on Jails the more prominent leaders in the benevolent movement. It revived the "Associates of Dr. Bray," which had been the primary directing force in the benevolent movement, enlarged it to include the members of the "Georgia Society," and thus placed its prestige behind the enterprise.[16] It secured the active coöperation and the financial and administrative support of two of the foremost religious and benevolent organizations of the day, the Society for Promoting Christian Knowledge, a giant benevolent holding company for charity schools, and its incorporated subsidiary, the Society for Propagating the Gospel in Foreign Parts. The former provided the means and the labors of transplanting foreign Protestants to Georgia, and the latter paid the salaries of colonial ministers and missionaries during the early years.[17]

The notion of such a colony in America was not a new one. Several schemes embodying various features of the Trustee project, and even suggesting the same name and location, were proposed during the preceding two decades.[18] Back of these proposals were the numerous speculations and investigations upon population, poverty, colonization, and trade of such writers as Petty, Temple, Bellers, Davenant, and Child.[19] Still earlier were the philosophical writings of More, Bacon, Hobbes, Winstanley, Plockboy, Harrington, and Locke, which first suggested many of the ideas embodied in the Trustee program. There were also the mercantilist tracts that had long been suggesting ways of solving unemployment, crime, and vagrancy through some form of enforced human transplanting.[20] Yet it remained for the organized benevolent movement of the eighteenth century to translate any of these ideas into concrete reality. The lack of strong institutional support, such as that which led to the settlement of other types of American colonies, probably accounts for the fact that there had been no colonization of the Georgia pattern prior to the eighteenth century.

Colonization offered an opportunity for full development of some of the cardinal principles of benevolence, and it seems clear that such possibilities constituted the appeal of the project for most of the Trustees. Behind their actions lay fundamental criticism of existing debtor and settlement laws, absentee ownership, and large aggregations and monopolies in land and trade. Their objectives embodied the removal of economic barriers to labor through provision of increased mobility, training, and freer access to natural agents, capital, and markets by means of quasi-public support, guidance, and regulation.

The colonial program of the Trustees was a combination of short-run and long-run policies. The short-run policies embodied a much larger measure of quasi-public action than did the long-run. Under the former the Trust provided transportation, subsistence for a limited period, and initial supplies of capital in addition to land; it maintained temporary public industries; it provided training and offered bounties; it supplied a currency; and it stood ready to secure additional laborers when needed. The long-run phases of Trustee policy relied more upon the regulation of a few basic institutions — land ownership, labor supply, and Indian trade — and upon individual enterprise in the movement of commodities.

The legal creation of the colony was an act of the Crown, and the Trustees administered the colony within an area defined by the charter. Since royal administration of colonial affairs had become centered largely in the Board of Trade, which had been created for that purpose in 1696, the position of the Trustees became somewhat analogous to that of the Board. Parliament's direct connection with the colony and its influence over it resulted primarily from appropriations in support of the project.[21]

The Crown's interests and objectives in the Georgia enterprise during the Trustee period are somewhat enigmatic. It was not without concern for the benevolent and religious purposes of the sponsors. Philanthropy constituted a widespread movement in Great Britain; in fact, it expressed about the only public welfare principle that had wide currency at the time. Furthermore, the Crown was likely to become interested in any movement that promised to expand and strengthen the domain of Protestantism in an age of militant war upon "popery." Conceivably it likewise hoped that the colony might serve in some fashion the nation's expanding imperialistic policy.[22]

Parliamentary motives, apart from those of the members among the Trustees, ran the gamut of national and group interests. The prime ministers and the majority were undoubtedly most concerned with the economic, military, and diplomatic aspects having a bearing upon imperialistic policy. "Protectionist" issues arose rather prominently in the parliamentary debates over appropriations, and seem to account for the stress placed so continuously by the colony's supporters upon economic advantages and, consequently, for the apparent "mercantilistic" features of the project. Even in parliamentary struggles the controlling concern was not with the older, narrow, mercantilistic objectives, but rather with the new high policy that was wont to juggle diplomatic, military, commercial, and territorial considerations in some over-all design of imperial aggrandizement. Philanthropy probably served the ministry in some degree as a screen for this policy, although such was in no sense the intention of the Trustees. In fact, one of the chief elements of friction between the ministry and the Trustees was the broad scope of powers secured by the latter which enabled them to pursue their true designs without much interference from the ministry.[23]

Whatever inducements may have secured the parliamentary appropriations, the monetary support of the government was a major factor in the survival of the colony.[24] Both through direct financial support and through large military expenditures, it provided much of the employment and income that kept the colony alive after the first year or two. It aided the development of the rudiments of a program of public roads, markets, land uses, and housing. There were offsetting drawbacks, to be sure, especially in connection with the military operations. Too large a portion of the meager energies of the colony was consumed in public works at the expense of the development of private industry; and this disproportionate allocation of labor and resources was greatly increased by the military ventures. In fact, the loss of life and the large withdrawal of colonists through fear of invasion resulting from the military campaigns came very near wrecking the colony. The heavy debt which was incurred added very grievously to its difficulties.[25]

With the relinquishment of control by the Trustees after twenty years, imperialistic objectives replaced philanthropic motives as the guiding factors in "official" Georgia policy. Georgia was converted into a "model" royal colony.[26] Parliament continued to pay the greater part of the expenses of civil government; but control became vested entirely in the Crown.

The colonists, in respect to their relationship to the Trust, were of three types: settlers who came "on the charity," that is, at Trust expense, of whom there were reported to have been 2,122 (1,096 British and 1,026 foreign);[27] settlers who came at their own expense; and indentured servants, who were brought to the colony either by the Trust or by the settlers.

It is not difficult to appraise the motives of the colonists. The charity settlers and the indentured servants almost certainly came primarily in the hope of improving their economic position. Religious motives, apparently of slight weight among the British settlers, were important among the Germans. Those who came at their own expense were chosen for their interest in the meliorative aspects of the enterprise, and therefore must have been motivated in part by benevolent impulses;[28] they were to a certain degree informal partners in the venture with the Trustees. Probably none of the colonists possessed any initial interest in imperial and military designs or, on the whole, developed any afterwards. On the other hand, it seems quite evident that substantially all who came had a genuine interest in the broader welfare designs of the project as well as in their own personal betterment. They must have believed in and wished to have a part in the development of this democratic, egalitarian, small proprietorship society. They must have looked upon themselves not merely as subjects of an experiment but as free, active participants in it. These ideas appear to be established by the wide publicity that was given to Trustee policies and by the methods used in selecting the colonists and in providing for local government in the colony. Later differences between many of the settlers and the Trustees arose not because of differences in basic objectives as much as because the Trustees failed to allow the partnership responsibilities of the colonists to grow with the development of colonial life. Nor did the Trustees ever work out any wholly satisfactory machinery of coöperation between the colonists and themselves. These were the outstanding weaknesses of Trustee policy. Even so, a large number of the colonists continued to support the policies of the Trustees, while disagreeing with them upon methods, which further testifies to their adherence to the basic principles of the enterprise.

Neither the Trustees nor the colonists possessed any previous knowledge of the character of the natural environment that they were planning to colonize. Practically nothing was known about the quality of soils or their adaptability to European crops and agricultural methods; and even less was known about the feasibility of the adaptation of the proposed semi-tropical productions. The possible effects of the hot climate and of semi-tropical diseases upon northwestern Europeans were equally unknown. In time the colonists learned about all of these matters through sad experience and they soon began to urge the need of changes in the carefully drawn plans of the Trustees. It was difficult, however, to convince an educated, upper-middle-class body of men of the errors in a system drawn upon the assumptions of the highest motives, the best of deductive logic, and a knowledge of parallels of latitude. Environmental factors, therefore, were in considerable measure responsible for the development of the first schism between absentee British governors and Georgia colonists.

Another important environmental factor was the human one. Situated at the southern extremity of British colonial settlement, with a slender contact only with South Carolina, Georgia found itself almost surrounded by Indian tribes and in close proximity to the military outposts of two powerful unfriendly foreign powers with whom Great Britain was almost constantly at war or on the verge of war. Small and weak and barely rooted to its location, isolated and dangerously exposed to potential enemies that far outnumbered it, the colony developed a sense of the need of unity within and of a strong protecting government without.

4. Philanthropic Liberalism in Action

Most of the early Trust business, as well as some of the regulations, grew out of the necessity of transporting and subsisting the colonists and supplying them with capital, labor, training, housing, public facilities, and general services during the initial stages of the enterprise. It was not expected that the colonists would remain dependent permanently upon the Trust, or even upon outside private enterprise for any of these services. It was a primary conception of the Trustees that an economic system should be developed by the colonists themselves,[29] who were selected with such a range of skills, aptitudes, and interests as was deemed likely to forward such a purpose.[30] It was for this reason, in part at least, that they discouraged the entrance of the usual industrial and commercial groups,[31] fearing that such interests would dispossess the colonists and reduce them to their former condition, thereby defeating the chief purpose of the colony.[32] This extreme policy of self-sufficiency, however, forced the Trustees into a far more extensive program of public activity than they had planned or for which they possessed resources to develop adequately. Consequently, they modified their policy somewhat, to encourage more self-supporting settlers, petty capitalists, and small partnership units to migrate to the colony.[33] They did not, however, relinquish their intention of protecting, encouraging, and guiding the colony until it had attained an internal efficiency and a stability of occupation and ownership that would enable it to survive and prosper under the normal conditions of trade. Their policy rested throughout upon the infant industry theory of protection rather than upon the usual mercantilistic notions.

It was a settled policy of the board that the Trust should retire from any activity as soon as private facilities should become available, provided they did not appear likely to threaten the welfare of the colony, and the deliberations and correspondence of the Trustees reveal a constant concern about the growth of private stores, mills, and other non-agricultural enterprises.[34] Furthermore, they were anxious that their public enterprises should be conducted in a manner that would foster private business development in the fullest degree. In fact, the Trustees are open to criticism for having placed too much reliance upon private initiative, in that they failed in some instances to supply facilities where there were no private ones, that they withdrew public operations before private means had become likely, and that they placed too much confidence initially in the capacities of the colonists to provide for their own needs.[35] This program comprised various quasi-public activities that may be grouped loosely into public businesses, public works, training programs, subsidies, and currency measures.[36] There was considerable overlapping and shifting and merging of operations in actual practice.

Public businesses were of four sorts, of which only two apparently had been contemplated in the beginning. The largest and most important group included the Trust stores, livestock herds, public gardens, sawmills, and passage services that were maintained for supplying the colonists with provisions, tools, ocean passage, and servants, and also for supporting the public works programs and the military operations. A second group included public grist mills and possibly similar enterprises of a public utility nature. A third type was in reality only a new set of functions taken on by the first group, namely, that of advancing capital, indentured servant contracts, and consumption goods to the colonists on credit terms. This was a pure merchandising-credit function as distinct from the original charity and public investment one, which placed the Trustees in competition with the few private commercial and manufacturing concerns that had become established. Lastly were attempts to convert some of the public industries into fiscal enterprises.

The stores were the most important of all the Trust businesses. There was one in each settlement, although the Savannah store received all goods from England and its manager acted as the purchasing agent of the Trustees in the colony. Consequently, the stores outside of Savannah were little more than distributing warehouses. The Savannah storekeeper, although he had no official control over the other storekeepers or over the managers of other public enterprises, was actually the business manager of the Trustees in the colony by virtue of the important position occupied by the Savannah store.[37] The stores were closed in 1740,[38] and thereafter poor relief and the subsistence of charity colonists and Trust servants were paid in cash.[39] The office of storekeeper, though continued for the purpose of transacting these latter matters, appears to have become an unnecessary one after the appointment of a colonial treasurer in 1743.[40]

Public sawmills were erected to manufacture lumber for both public and private construction. Public requirements were large — for store buildings, town halls and jails, barracks, forts, lighthouses, cowpens, fences, official dwellings, and bridges. Three or four public sawmills were operated — one at Ebenezer, one or two in the Savannah region, and one at Darien. The last became by far the most important one since, in addition to filling all other local needs, it supplied the lumber for the barracks and officers' dwellings of Oglethorpe's troops at Frederica and for the numerous forts and other military works in the southern part of the colony. Large numbers of Trust servants were employed at times at this mill.[41] There was some consideration from time to time of operating the public sawmills commercially; however, it does not appear that such was ever done; and all were abandoned after 1743 when the Trust withdrew from the employment of indentured servants.

Livestock was among the first purchases in America made by the Trust officers, since it was necessary to assure a supply of fresh meat for the use of the charity colonists.[42] Gradually several herds were accumulated, a large one near Ebenezer and two or three smaller ones in the vicinity of Savannah. Cowpens were erected on lands reserved for the public use.[43] The public livestock business, however, was a source of continuous difficulty and controversy. Indians, petty criminals, and runaway servants preyed upon the animals in the woods; some settlers, and even public officers, were accused of branding public cattle for their own; and farmers complained of the damage to crops by public herds. Capable pindars and cattle-searchers were hard to obtain, and most men who were hired for this public business were engaged in private pursuits as well; consequently, the interests of the Trust suffered. All of the herds, except the one at Ebenezer, were disposed of when the Trust closed out its farms in 1743.

It was decided, in 1745, to undertake commercial slaughtering at Ebenezer and bright hopes were entertained for financial success; but the results proved a great disappointment. Costs were exceedingly high, volume was low, and returns were small. Sales were made to the regimental quartermaster.[44] The Common Council of the Trustees, on May 24, 1751, ordered the sale of the herd to the Salzburgers.[45]

The public botanical garden was a combination nursery-experimental garden. Considerable sums of money were subscribed in England for the development in Georgia of exotic semi-tropical plants from the West Indies, Central and South America, and the Mediterranean.[46] Many such plants were contributed by interested individuals; and a botanist was sent to the western semi-tropics to gather additional specimens.[47] Ten acres of land were chosen a few miles east of Savannah as a site for the nurture of the imported plants, of which a considerable number were brought to Savannah. The garden was used chiefly, however, as a nursery for young mulberry trees. The site was poorly chosen, the succession of gardeners and caretakers showed no marked proficiency or industry, and the garden fared badly and was abandoned toward the end of the Trust period.[48]

The two public blacksmith shops, at Savannah and Frederica, were maintained to service the military and other public activities and to meet the needs of the Indians. It is probable that the shops engaged also in private business with the settlers.[49]

The transporting of indentured servants developed into a considerable business with a variety of angles. In Europe it was tied up with the search for the employment of German Protestants and numerous orphan groups in whom some of the Trustees or their associates were interested.[50] In Georgia the object was to supply labor for Trust officers, colonists, and the various Trust industries, especially the sawmills. The Trust frequently found itself with considerable numbers of surplus servants left on its hands owing to the inability of the colonists to take over their indentures; and it was led to expand some of its temporary businesses, especially in agriculture, in order to furnish work, food, and shelter for such laborers. It retired from the business of employing servants in 1743, but continued to supply them to the colonists throughout the years of its control.[51]

Little information exists about the public grist mills. It appears that they were operated on some kind of fee basis. One such, at least, is reported to have been operated at Ebenezer with the use of Trust servants.[52]

It is doubtful that the public farms had any place in the original designs of the Trustees. Various factors, and some unforeseen developments, operated severally and jointly to bring about their establishment. In the beginning the Trustees adopted the policy of reserving one-sixth of the tillable land — the two center forty-five-acre lots in each tything — as public domain, but no method of utilization was indicated. A cowpen was built upon one of these tracts at Old Ebenezer where the first livestock herd was placed. The Trust found itself with a large number of servants, especially Germans, in 1734 and 1735, for which the planters were unable to pay the charges, and sought to employ them in its various business activities and upon public works. Many were used on road and public building construction.[53] Then the idea arose of putting some of the servants upon the public domains to raise food for their own subsistence and for other public requirements. The burden of provisioning charity colonists, servants, and troops had proved a heavy one. It is not recorded who suggested the notion of Trust farms, but William Bradley memorialized the board on September 3, 1735, with a proposition to go to Georgia "to teach the people agriculture and to cultivate the Trust lands." He proposed opening a one-hundred-acre farm on which thirty Trust servants should be employed. The Trustees adopted his plan and, as compensation, granted him five hundred acres for his own use with the free services of ten servants for one year and an annual payment of £100 in produce from the public farms.[54] Bradley sailed for Savannah early in 1736. Later he was made overseer of the Trust's livestock herds, of additional public farms, and of all Trust servants at Savannah.[55] A farm established at Frederica was cultivated by a group of Dutch servants belonging to the Trust,[56] another was operated on Amelia Island under the direction of one of the military officers.[57] A mulberry grove was planted on one public lot near Savannah.[58]

The public farm which attracted the most attention, and likewise represented a still further advance in the unpremeditated plans of the Trustees, was the Bouverie Farm. Sir Jacob des Bouverie informed the Trustees in December 1736 that he wished to give them £1,000, left by his father for certain charitable objects that no longer existed, to be used for a single purpose in forwarding the designs of the Georgia colony. Just at this time the Trustees were beginning to envision the possibility of cultivating the public domain as a public business, not only as a means of supplying the extraordinary food requirements of servants and charity colonists but also for the support of the civil government. The heavy burden of provisioning the charity colonists was explained to Sir Jacob as well as the availability of forty German servants. It was proposed that the entire gift should be devoted to sending the Germans to Georgia and to opening another Trust farm in this gradually expanding public program, and Sir Jacob readily agreed.[59]

Thus the public farm program, begun as a temporary makeshift, began to emerge as a full-fledged fiscal enterprise. There were strong inducements back of this expansion besides the existence of surplus servants, reserved public domains, and Sir Jacob's gift. The colony was making poor progress and proving costly far beyond the means of the Trust, which compelled dependence upon grants from Parliament and brought the unwelcome task of going before the government annually to solicit such public funds. A self-supporting Georgia government would have freed the hands of the Trustees, which was what they desired above all things other than the success of the colony itself. This scheme embodied an idea that recurred frequently thereafter, namely, that of utilizing a part of the public domain, or the income from the lease or sale of it, for the support of government. A public-owned working force likewise was frequently an associated idea and was actually tried in one important instance later.

Another closely related, and at least quasi-fiscal, use for public farms that was felt keenly at this same time was in connection with church lands. Three hundred acres were granted originally for religious purposes at Savannah, but no use had been made of them. An unfortunate experience with the first minister, a struggle with the Established Church over title to the grant, severe criticism over lack of attention to religious matters, and a desire to control colonial ministers made the Trustees anxious to undertake the development of the church lands.[60]

The results of the farm operations were exceedingly disappointing. Most of them, according to reports, did not produce even the subsistence of the workers involved. As a rule they were mismanaged and neglected; the services of the Trust servants frequently were misappropriated to private uses.[61] Mr. Bradley's management in particular resulted disastrously for the public interest. Not only was his public management a miserable failure, but he was accused on every hand of speculation and of the appropriation of public property and servants to private uses. He was dismissed and finally indicted by the Trustees for an indebtedness to them of $7,650.[62] When employment of indentured servants was discontinued in 1743, the Trustees abandoned the operation of all farms and appropriated the lands to the uses of the magistrates and the ministers of the gospel.[63]

The supplying of goods and services on credit developed into another important phase of the public business that had not been anticipated by the Trustees. The original gifts to the charity group of subsistence, tools, and utensils proved wholly inadequate.[64] Few if any of them possessed any personal capital. The colony experienced a series of droughts, floods, and crop failures; poor soil locations caused the total loss of early labors upon numerous farms; disproportionate activity on public works retarded private improvements; many of the tools proved poorly suited to the job and of slight use; and sickness reduced many of the colonists and servants to public charges.[65]

The situation was little better among those who came at their own expense. The resources of most were consumed in reaching Georgia, whereupon they found themselves in about the same condition as the charity settlers. Generally they were unable to pay the passage money of indentured servants for the development of their lands; and if able to meet that expense were without means to subsist and clothe the servants.[66]

Thus the Trust found itself forced into performing the normal functions of the private merchandizing companies. Developmental outlays constituted one of the heaviest capital advances in American commercial agriculture, and these requirements were especially large in Georgia on account of the unfavorable soil and climatic conditions in the coastal area. The Trust found these outlays absorbing an ever-increasing proportion of its resources and of the products of its enterprises, which resulted in the extension of the life of most of its temporary enterprises for longer than any calculations had anticipated. The failure to appraise the full significance of developmental costs and their provision constituted the most serious weakness in the Trustees' economic program and the primary cause of the early difficulties and the slow progress of the colony.[67]

Public works, though normally a continuing category of public business, were closely related to the temporary initial program of settling the colony. They included in these early years the clearing of sites for town settlements and the laying out of lots and streets, the building of roads and bridges, public buildings, wells, markets, wharves, lighthouses, forts, military depots and barracks, and officers' dwellings. This public construction constituted a large part of employment and investment during the first decade.

Three aspects of the public works program — the fulfillment of charity obligations, the repayment of private loans, and the effects of military expenditures — deserve noting. The charity colonists were under obligation by agreement with the Trustees to devote a part of their time during the first year upon public works.[68] Such labor tasks may be viewed either as a form of payment for the "charity" or as a fiscal special assessment in labor service. Some historians hold the opinion that this levy was too large a tax upon the colonists' time and energy and interfered unduly with the development of private enterprise, thereby contributing to the disappointing progress of the colony.

The bulk of the loans and advances of goods and services to the colonists by the public agencies were paid off, not in products or cash credits as was customary practice in private transactions between merchants and agricultural producers, but in labor service on public works. These payments were made for the most part in servants' labor, although small farmers often worked upon the public projects with their one or two servants.[69] Thus were developed, in an unplanned and rather backhanded fashion, private investment and employment through public investment in public works. In this respect, also, these early activities of the Trust proved to be the forerunner of a later development in Georgia, and for that matter in the South generally, since such features became a considerable aspect of the later internal improvement and railroad developments.

The effects of military expenditures, of both capital and current sorts, proved highly significant since they provided extensive employment, a market for surplus products, and thereby a considerable part of the cash income of the colony throughout the Trust period.[70] The secondary, investment-employment effects, however, are difficult to calculate. Since there was such great dependence upon imports, even of food products, the chief effects must have derived through the increase of other public investment and employment and whatever effects the latter may have had upon private investment and employment; however, the leakages undoubtedly were very great.

Training was a basic policy in eighteenth-century benevolence; hence it was to be expected that training for any new occupations that promised hopeful results in the colony would be recognized as an obligation of the Trust. The Trustees selected from the large number of applicants persons skilled in the necessary familiar pursuits;[71] but they recognized that special arrangements must be provided for training in occupations other than those with which the colonists were acquainted. Silk production was selected to provide a commercial product and, since none of the colonists were familiar with its processes, public training was confined chiefly to that. Piedmontese silkworkers were hired to direct the introduction of silk production and train the colonists in its arts.[72]

The Trustees considered sending over experts to teach the business of getting out oak timber for the Royal Navy, but the estimated expenses were too great for their resources at the time.[73] Later they entertained high hopes that the operations of the public botanical garden would prove to be a means of educating the colonists in semi-tropical horticulture as well as in planting and caring for mulberry trees. And it appears that Mr. Bradley's public farm projects were undertaken in part to provide agricultural education. There is slight evidence that training schemes were effective except in silk production among the Salzburgers at Ebenezer.

Public subsidies were employed in efforts to stimulate the silk industry, food production and the establishment of certain other industries. They were most important by far in silk. Four shillings per pound were paid for cocoons until 1742, two shillings thereafter until 1749, when a schedule of bounty prices according to grades was adopted and continued until 1752.[74] A bonus of £5 each and subsistence during training were offered for a limited number of women learners in the arts of caring for silk worms and winding silk. Later this bonus was paid to all who had learned to perform these processes.[75]

Bounties on corn, peas, and potatoes were introduced in two limited areas during 1734–1736 and were made general for the year 1739 and again for 1742 and 1746.[76] The object was to relieve the necessity of importing food. Other instances of bounties were land grants and interest-free loans to secure the private establishment of a sawmill, a brick kiln, a pottery, a winery, a grist mill, potash production, vine culture, and possibly other ventures.[77]

The encouragement of the silk industry, since it took several forms and attracted so much attention to the Trustees' plans, deserves some further consideration. The reasons for the Trustees' decision to undertake its development appear to be clear. Other semi-tropical productions such as tobacco, sugar, rice, and indigo had been adapted successfully to the region and a capitalistically backed enterprise at nearby Purysburg, South Carolina, had established the fact already that silk could be developed within the area.[78] British factories that had developed the spinning and weaving of silk were dependent upon foreign sources for raw supplies. Furthermore, its culture and initial processing appeared to be peculiarly well-adapted to small-scale agriculture-industry of the sort that was contemplated in Georgia. Such a community was likely to contain large numbers of relatively idle women and children. Silkworm culture and silk winding would provide employment of this surplus labor, while the planting and care of mulberry trees would require male labor primarily at off seasons. Furthermore, it seemed desirable to remove from the minds of a number of members of Parliament the idea that Georgia was designed to become another New England colony. New England was decidedly unpopular in Parliament for a number of reasons including economic ones, and it was important for the sake of harmony to encourage occupations in Georgia that would not deepen the New England influence in America.[79]

There were good reasons for not choosing to encourage any of the established staples. Tobacco was already such a drug on the market that Virginia and Maryland growers were turning to grains, and it was reported that large numbers of the poorer settlers in these colonies had become bankrupt and disposed of their properties.[80] Sugar, rice, and indigo were large-scale plantation crops requiring large capital investments that far exceeded the resources of the poor Georgians and the Trustees; moreover they were produced universally with slave labor. The Trustees were convinced that free labor could not be maintained within a slave system.[81] Forest industries were thought to offer real possibilities and received considerable attention at first; however, interest in these slackened for no specified or obvious reason. It may have been realized that the principal market, particularly for cooperage products, was the West Indies where the chief back-haul for shippers would be rum and slaves, both of which were prohibited in Georgia. Furthermore, it was doubtful that a lumber industry would be able to compete successfully with that of other states where slave labor was used.

There is a real question about the degree of interest that the Trustees actually had in silk culture. Imperial economic advantage and military defense received a lot of attention in Parliament, where it was crucially important to obtain large appropriations, but were seldom mentioned in the deliberations of the Trustee bodies and as often critically as otherwise. Of course, they could have been genuinely interested in silk culture aside from its imperial aspects. Yet the Earl of Egmont, who kept a careful and minute record of the deliberations and conversations of the Trustees, both inside and out of meeting, does not mention silk more than half a dozen times during the first six years, and reports only one actual discussion of the silk project. From his records it would appear that the Trustees found considerable difficulty both in raising the necessary funds and in making up their minds to push the development of silk production vigorously.[82] Only 1.1 per cent of Trust expenditures of the first ten years and only 3.1 per cent for the entire period were devoted to the silk program; and almost half the total was spent during the last three years, after Negroes were introduced and there had developed a widespread feeling among the large-scale planters that silk could be produced successfully with slave labor.[83]

Although the planting of mulberry trees was one of the conditions of land ownership, few colonists complied and no penalties were ever invoked. Silk was mentioned less and less often in Parliament; and the program might have been dropped entirely had it not been for the small commitments to the Italian silk workers and the small protected interest in production that had been developed by the Salzburgers under the energetic leadership of the Reverend John Bolzius.[84] The Germans were the most industrious and prosperous group in the colony as well as the strongest supporters of Trustee policies. Since the required financial support was insignificant, the Trustees could not well afford to discontinue it. Nevertheless, they reduced the bounties drastically in the late 1740's.

It seems evident from these facts that silk did not play the important part in Georgia's plans that has commonly been attributed to it, nor did its substantial failure induce the difficulties and disappointments that the colony encountered. The Trustees seem to have had in mind all along the development of a relatively self-contained community of small proprietors in agriculture, horticulture, trade, and industry with a skilled artisan class developed out of the indentured servant group. If the silk venture should prosper, it promised to harmonize with the general pattern of the project and it would become a source of increased employment, wealth, and income and an additional assurance of the permanence of the Trustee design for the colony. The failure of silk culture may be attributed to the lack of tradition and adaptation in such occupations among the British colonists and to the operation of comparative advantage. The greater failures of the colony to achieve the high hopes that had been entertained for it by its sponsors were owing to other more fundamental faults and shortcomings of policy, to the misguided military ventures of Oglethorpe, and to the frequent lack of ability and the general lack of technical and business training and experience on the part of the colonists. It is impossible to assess proportionate blame, however, among these causes.

The history of currency under the Trustees presents another instance of a long-run policy that was conspicuous chiefly for its short-run adaptations. There can be no doubt that the Trustees assumed that Georgia's monetary needs would be met through the normal processes of production and trade.[85] Actually little specie ever reached Georgia, and the lack of exports coupled with the predominance of public business seriously impeded the development of private merchant credit operations.

It was obvious that free subsistence and tools and the practice of paying the officers and laborers in kind from the stores would greatly lessen the need for money in the colony during the first year or two. Nevertheless, the Trustees shipped over a considerable quantity of copper coins to be paid out as part of the subsistence grants in order to make sure that the needs for "small change" circulation were supplied.[86] They assumed apparently that the independent settlers and the merchants whom they induced to migrate would bring liquid funds with them.[87] Events proved, however, that these assumptions were quite mistaken. For the most part, only the uninvited Jews among the early immigrants brought sufficient funds even to procure subsistence. Any money that appeared in the colony speedily left in payment for imports. Transactions soon came to revolve almost entirely around the Trust businesses, with the Trust agent disposing of goods on account or promissory note and receiving payments of such in labor time on various public works. Some South Carolina currency circulated in Georgia, since that colony collected a small tax on rum during the years 1734–1737 and 1739–1740 as a donation to aid its new neighbor.[88] The sums were used for the most part for purchases on public account in South Carolina, but some small amounts were paid out for services in Georgia.[89]

Complaints over the lack of money soon began to grow.[90] The Trustees found themselves embarrassed by the confusion that was developing around the purchasing activities of Oglethorpe and other agents in Georgia and South Carolina.[91] The agents were buying and making independent commitments, frequently beyond the purposes specified, to be paid in South Carolina money, bills of exchange drawn on the Trustees, and certified accounts. Bills and accounts were appearing in London without any accompanying information.[92] The Trustees were faced with the dual need of a means of making payments and some method of exercising stricter budgetary control over their agents. They sought a solution that would resolve the colonial money problem as well as their own double-faced fiscal problem.

The first plan agreed upon, for the issue of six-month Georgia notes,[93] was abandoned upon consultation with the Directors of the Bank of England who advised the substitution of a form of bill of exchange.[94] It seems probable that the Bank officials looked upon the proposed note issue as an assumption of public banking functions; or they may have been expressing only the general opposition of British officials to the issue of any form of paper money in the colonies. Accordingly, the Common Council, on July 24, 1735, adopted the sola bill of exchange as a medium for remitting "cash" to the colony. It was resolved to send over £1,000 of bills immediately for circulation purposes.[95] The sola bill was a thirty-day sight draft upon the Trustees payable within six months.[96] Originally the bills were all drawn payable to Oglethorpe or his order, and it was necessary that he endorse each one individually before it could pass in payment from a disbursing officer. Later, the bills were signed by the trust accountant in England and then sent to the various disbursing officers who paid them out.[97]

The sola bills could not be made legal tender, and the council may have doubted whether they would meet the money needs of the colony; for on the day of adoption it resolved to petition the Crown for a license to ship £1,000 of silver coin to Georgia. However, the bills served the monetary requirements well enough to displace most other media and remained the basic money of the colony until the close of the Trust period. On March 21, 1737, the council countermanded a further shipment of coin,[98] and thereafter it does not appear that it forwarded any other medium than sola bills to the colony.

Two months after adopting the sola bill, the Trustees passed a resolution setting up more rigid purchase requirements and specifying the use of sola bills in all payments by their officers.[99] Beginning with the year 1736, "general directions" or "estimates" were forwarded to the colonial officers annually as a guide to their expenditures, and sola bills were shipped during the year as payments became necessary.[100] "Cash" payments in Georgia were increased considerably in 1740 upon the closing of the public stores; and the colony was placed almost entirely upon a private trading basis in 1743 with the Trust withdrawal from farming and with the disposal of all public servants.[101]

The sola bill provided no monetary panacea. Since it was a bill of exchange it tended upon emission to disappear from circulation promptly in payment for imports. In fact, its issue had been anticipated already, usually, in the creation of a foreign debt for imports. Any increase in commercial activity quickly created a scarcity of "money" and a sharp decline in demand for goods. Such scarcities were felt to be a severe handicap to the economy.[102] With the existing paucity of exports, the use of gold and silver by the Trustees would have produced no different result. The chief fault of the system was not in the sola bill, but that its issue was dependent entirely upon fiscal expenditures, rather than upon general economic requirements. The greater part of the credit advanced by the merchants was necessarily based directly upon the Trust "estimates." Thus the money supply remained ever highly inelastic. And the Trustees frequently were irregular in meeting their "estimates," to the great embarrassment of the merchants and their debtors.[103] This weakness also developed adverse cyclical and secular characteristics. When Trust expenditures declined sharply during the depression years of the early 1740's, the drop increased very greatly the severity of the contraction in trade. The burden of the mounting public debt fell upon the merchants in addition to the decline in "estimate"-based sales.

Later in the decade, fiscal expenditures developed a static or even a somewhat declining secular trend, whereas the private economy began to show a clear tendency to expand. Consequently, there developed a growing dearth of money and increasing numbers of complaints about the monetary situation.[104] One somewhat alleviating factor after 1739 was the presence of British soldiers. Their payrolls and purchases of provisions afforded a modest market for agricultural products and another source of money.[105] If there was any hankering after paper money in the colony during the Trust period it was never expressed openly. Proposals for increase in money rather took the form of suggestions that the Trust should establish commercial credits for the colonists and supply them with servants upon some sort of annual charge basis.[106] Money and short-time capital needs were closely associated.

The Trustees' monetary policy clearly centered upon adherence to the British standard. They believed firmly that production and trade in the long run would provide their own money and credit supplies. In this position they occupied a place among the forerunners of the classical theory of money. They recognized, however, that it would take more than the "normal" length of time to get a colony such as Georgia into normal production and trade, and that the Trust's developmental activities retarded the entrance of private commercial agencies. In fact, there is some question about their exact intentions. They thought that government should assist in the maintenance of an adequate and stable money system in so far as such action might be consonant with its other functions and with the principles of trade. They were more sympathetic with the colonists' complaints about money scarcities than were most British public officials. All sola bills were paid promptly by the Trust upon presentation in England; consequently their value was maintained on a par with British money.[107]

Major determining factors in the long-run policies of the Trustees, in addition to philanthropy and the character of the colonists, were previous policies and experiences of other American colonies and prevailing British commercial policies. Considerable attention has been given already to philanthropy and the colonists; and the significance of both may be summarized at this point in a sentence from an official communication of the Trustees in 1733 — "The design of our charter was, in settling the colony, to provide for the necessitous poor of our country, and not to make men of substance richer" — or in the words of Egmont — "the making numbers of poor families happy." [108]

The influence of the previous experiences in other American colonies was greater than commonly has been supposed. The compact town type of settlement appears to have been copied from New England along with the practice of granting land in blocks for such settlements. The feudal character of land tenures resembled those to be found in proprietary Pennsylvania and South Carolina; and the sizes of land grants might have been copied from either of the latter colonies.[109] The important role assigned to indentured labor must have been suggested by Pennsylvania's use of that system as the mainstay of its labor policy. Many of William Penn's benevolent, democratic, and idealistic arrangements find their counterparts in Georgia.[110]

But there were also striking departures from the policies of these other colonies. The self-determination permitted the members of the New England town group was largely omitted in Georgia. The commercial, theocratic, and aristocratic features of Penn's land policies were not only avoided, but were carefully guarded against. The feudal land tenures that had been employed in South Carolina to establish vast landed baronies were introduced into Georgia instead to prevent such land aggrandizement. In many other ways the structures of land, labor, and commercial policies, so similar in many respects to those of Pennsylvania and South Carolina, were modified with the hopes of forestalling the economic and social abuses and excesses that had developed in those colonies as well as obtaining the ends that the Trustees had in view.[111]

The Trustees were deeply concerned about adapting the plans of colonization to the realities of the actual economic world, without, however, being willing to relinquish their experiment to the controlling influences of certain overpowering factors in that world. Georgia was no exception to a certain realism that characterized benevolent reform. The plan was neither visionary nor revolutionary; yet it presumed the achievement of social values beyond the usual accomplishments of the prevailing order. Eighteenth-century benevolence was a part of a great, as yet largely unconscious, awakening to the possibilities of progress in the achievement of social welfare. It was this spirit that distinguished Georgia in conception and in administrative policy during the Trust period.

Trustee policy was essentially an over-all program of planning for social welfare. Although chief reliance was placed upon the initial charity and the long-run land and labor policies, there was a unity about the design that embraced the total of economic life which largely explains the Trustees' seeming equivocal attitude toward a number of existing institutions. Their experimental program embodied criticisms of certain of these institutions and implied the modification of the going system of economic enterprise in certain rather prominent respects.

The charter granted to the Trustees that part of the territory of South Carolina lying between the Savannah and Altamaha rivers and extending "westerly from the heads of said rivers respectively, in direct lines to the South Seas." [112] Before any settlements could take place, it was necessary to negotiate treaties with the Indians for the relinquishment of their titles. Oglethorpe's treaty with the Lower Creeks in 1733 secured the cession of all lands, except certain specified reservations, between the above rivers within the limits of tidewater.[113] Thus began a series of treaties that featured so prominently in the life of Georgia for the next hundred years, and which fixed successively the actual extent of available public domain and settlement, as distinguished from the limits of Georgia's sovereignty. Oglethorpe's second Indian treaty, in 1739, obtained the cession of the tidewater lands southward from the Altamaha to the St. John's River, clearly outside of Georgia's charter boundary, thus setting the original precedent in a long series of controversies over the extension of boundaries beyond the limits of the original charter.[114]

The charter permitted the Trustees to grant the lands to colonists according to such rules as they might see fit to establish, subject only to the limitations that no Trustee might benefit therefrom, that no person should receive more than five hundred acres, and that annual quitrents of four shillings per hundred acres should be paid to the Crown after ten years from date of each grant.[115] Trustee land policy was notable for three main features, namely, the form of tenure, the method of location, and the requirements of cultivation.

The first of these features has attracted the most attention. Lands were granted originally in *tail male,* whereby: sole ownership was retained in the King; grants remained forever indivisible and descended only through the male heir; and reversion to the Trust was the legal consequence of death without male heir or of non-compliance with other terms of the grant. It was the intention of the Trustees that every male citizen should be a life freeholder in land, either through grant or inheritance. Each male charity colonist or person going at his own expense received fifty acres; those who carried servants received an additional fifty acres for each servant up to a maximum of five hundred acres; and servants received twenty acres each when they had fulfilled their indentures. Leases were forbidden except by special permission of the Trustees.[116]

Rules covering the location of grants were designed to secure a compact settlement. Each town was laid out completely, in advance of individual grants, in three classes of lots in equal numbers — residence lots in the center, garden lots on the periphery of the residence section, and tillage lots beyond the garden plots. A residence and a garden lot together totaled five acres, a tillage lot contained forty-five acres, and the three comprised an individual grant and were commonly called a lot. The Trustees usually transferred a block of land for a town settlement to a board of three officers within the colony, which in turn did the actual granting. Surveyors and their assistants were appointed by the Trustees.[117]

The following conditions were designated to be filled by the grantee: those receiving fifty acres must clear and cultivate same within ten years and plant one hundred mulberry trees per ten acres as cleared; those going at their own expense and carrying servants must clear one-fifth within ten years and an additional three-fifths during the succeeding ten years and plant one thousand mulberry trees per hundred acres as cleared, except that in the case of masters of ten servants with maximum grants of five hundred no time limits for clearing were fixed beyond ten years.[118]

Differences over land tenure developed early between the colonists and the Trustees. The exclusion of widows and daughters from inheritance drew criticism from the original colonists even before they left England.[119] This soon grew into general objection to the entire system of entailed estates, particularly upon the grounds that mercantile credit could not be obtained without the power to hypothecate lands freely, and generally upon the basis of the inherent inequities in such a land system. A change from *tail male* to *tail general* would not suffice; titles must be given in fee simple. The opposition reached its climax in a famous remonstrance, in 1738, signed by 121 landholders, mostly residents of the Savannah area. The Germans at Ebenezer and the Scots at Darien did not support the remonstrance, in good part because it also demanded the admission of Negro slavery.[120] The Scots later voiced equally vigorous opposition to the land tenure.[121]

The Trustees themselves were divided over land tenure. A few opposed the chosen form from the beginning.[122] Oglethorpe and some of his intimates remained adamant against any changes, holding that to permit *tail general* would decrease the numbers of males available for the militia and thus threaten the security of the province, and to grant lands in fee simple would invite all of the abuses of land aggrandizement of South Carolina as well as the depopulation of the colony.[123] Some of the Board's ablest members took a middle position in favor of gradual modification, and this latter group was beginning to win out by 1738.[124] Inheritance was liberalized in that year;[125] in the following year, *tail general* was substituted for *tail male;*[126] the limit on total individual holdings was increased to two thousand acres and leases for three years duration were permitted in 1740.[127] An attempt was made in 1742 to allow grants in fee simple to persons carrying over servants, but this was disallowed by the Board of Trade because it would have permitted two forms of tenure in the colony.[128] Finally, in 1750, the Trustees met the colonists' demands by granting a form of tenure that amounted substantially to title in fee simple.[129]

The chief objection growing out of the compact mode of location related to the poor soils that were often received. There was much unevenness in the qualities of soils in all of the settlements, and consequent great inequalities among the settlers in the qualities and quantities of desirable land which they received. Much of the land was hopelessly poor. The entire tract of the original Ebenezer location proved to be of such inferior quality that the town site had to be relocated. This "poor land" problem generated some friction between colonists and Trustees, but when there was merit in a complaint it was usually remedied; the problem was a major factor no doubt in the gradual change after 1741 to the plantation type of land grant location.[130]

The requirements of clearing, cultivating, and planting mulberry trees were rarely, if ever, met and no attempt was made apparently to enforce them strictly. Unevenness of soils, unfavorable climate, weeds, lack of capital and labor, sickness, inefficient tools, poorly adapted crops, droughts, and floods were the principal deterrents to fulfillment other than the sociological ones.[131]

Labor policy constituted the core of general Trustee policy and its most difficult problem. There were three possible choices as to types of labor — Negro slaves, indentured servants, and free laborers. There was considerable doubt at the time concerning the availability of the last, and nobody believed that a colony could be established solely upon that type of labor resource. It was still scarce in the old colonies; and insuperable factors prevented its free movement into a new colony. The landowner and his family were likely to constitute the only free labor supply for some time.

The Trustees decided to prohibit Negro slavery because they thought that it would undermine the kind of society that they had in mind: it would reduce the wages of free labor to the level of Negro hire and assuredly keep it from immigrating into Georgia and drive out any that might be there already; and it would lead to concentrations of land ownership of the better lands and force the small farmers onto poorer soils or out of the colony entirely. The only economic opportunities for free men in a slave economy were as masters or slave overseers: the poor lacked both the capital and ingenuity to become masters, and so could look forward only to becoming overseers.[132] Nor did the Trustees possess sufficient funds had they desired to conduct the slave trade; and they desired above all things else to keep the colonists out of the clutches of the slave merchant who might be willing to supply slaves on the security of lands. Here it may be noted that the land policy, as originally formulated, constituted added insurance against slavery.

All of the early discussions of plans for the settlement of Georgia stressed an intention to use indentured servants.[133] As the design of the colony developed in the minds of the Trustees, it seemed to become modeled in this respect somewhat along the lines that had been pursued quite successfully in Pennsylvania. Indeed the success of the latter colony was often attributed to the combination of encouragement given to small and medium sized landholders and the wide use of indentured labor. Those with little or no capital who should settle Georgia should be given similar opportunities to succeed. It was never intended that Georgia should become a peasant society and, while there was no disposition to supply the charity colonist in the first instance with more than the land and sufficient tools to secure a satisfactory living for himself and family, yet the major objective probably was that the industrious and able should always be supplied with the requisites to improve their economic situation. In order to rise economically it was deemed necessary to become an employer of labor and capital.[134] Land which the Trustees possessed to give away would constitute the primary fund of capital; besides, they undertook to supply indentured servants.

It is possible now to perceive somewhat more clearly the outlines of the kind of society that the Trustees envisioned. Every male citizen in this society should have at least the full command of his own labor, fifty acres of land, and sufficient tools to enable him with reasonable industry to obtain an adequate minimum livelihood. It was expected undoubtedly that this minimum standard of living would be higher than the prevailing mercantilist notion of subsistence or the later conception of Ricardo of what was "necessary to enable the laborers, one with another, to subsist and perpetuate their race, without either increase or diminution." [135] The primary object in transplanting the "poor" to Georgia was to enable them to earn a better living than was possible in England.

The Trustees' original conception included apparently a second minimum type of free productive unit — the artisan-landholder. Servants under indenture temporarily were not included in the category of adult male citizens. When out of their time, however, they were to receive twenty acres of land. It would appear that the object of this provision was to encourage part-time agriculture and gardening combined with working for hire, skilled trades, or independent handicraft pursuits. It was a mixed labor-land-industry unit that was designed to develop a free labor supply out of the indentured group. Land ownership it was thought would lend stability, security, and status to this group and tie it to the community. The minimum standard of living of such a group should equal that of the 50-acre planters.

To all those who lived frugally and industriously and thereby "got ahead," or should migrate with sufficient private means, the Trustees undertook to grant additional lands without charge and to supply indentured servants at out-of-pocket transportation costs. A limit was fixed upon the land holdings of the individual capitalist, however, in order to prevent the growth of land aggrandizement, monopolization, and excessive inequalities of wealth and income, and to permit the widest possible diffusion of economic opportunity consistent with the maintenance of reasonable inducements to frugality and industry. This was no scheme for a regimented, dead-level equalitarianism; the desire for self-advancement was to be given ample encouragement and opportunity; but the inequalities that were likely to arise from unrestricted self-interest were to be guarded against and discouraged. The moderate group among the Trustees seem to have had in mind no fixed pattern, but rather one designed to provide immediately wider economic opportunities for the less privileged and the less capable in the economic world as it existed, subject to modification as experience and later policies might require. The Trust policy has much in common with the later American homestead policy and may be counted as one of the first positive developments in the evolution of that policy.

The board began almost immediately to transport indentured servants to Georgia for the use of its colonial officers and the independent colonists.[136] The former received them as part compensation for public service, but the latter were expected to pay the costs of transportation in exchange for the indentures. In order to avoid the criticism of withdrawing from the British labor supply, the Trust recruited its first groups of servants from the streets of London — from the "unemployables" rather than from the "unemployed." [137] This practice turned out disastrously for both the colonists and the Trust businesses in Georgia and contributed greatly to the early failures.[138] The German servants, very much favored by officials in England, proved almost equally unsatisfactory during the early years, largely on account of language and custom barriers.[139] Heeding the insistence of leading colonists, the Trust turned more to tough Scottish highlanders and rural English and Welsh youths who were accustomed to arduous labors and possessed of a knowledge of agriculture.[140] As time passed and as adaptations were made, the Germans increased in popularity and, in the end, were favored over all.[141] Correspondingly larger numbers of them were sent over during the later years. The close relations of some of the Trustees and such of their officers as the Wesleys, Whitefield, and Habersham with the charity schools might have suggested the recruiting of labor from these sources; but actually very few pupils from these institutions were sent to Georgia.[142] The sending of child servants was opposed by most of the Trustees on humanitarian grounds, and only a few who were apprenticed with their parents were sent.[143] The experience in sending female servants was unfavorable;[144] there was little demand other than as wives for the soldiers and Germans.

The experiences with indentured servants varied from feeble success to outright failure, even though there were some evidences of improvement in results toward the end of the period. Some of the causes of failure may be adduced from what has already been said. Additional reasons were the lack of capital, experience, and administrative ability of the masters and the harsh, disagreeable, and unhealthy character of the labor tasks.[145] There are strong grounds for doubting that commercial agriculture could have been developed in the region at that time except with forced labor. Alternative opportunities for the immigrant from northwestern Europe, whether free or indentured, were so much more inviting — in other occupations, in more salubrious locations, and in higher real incomes — that it is difficult to conceive of the success of any other than a slave system.[146] The location was most unfavorable to the kind of colonial experiment that had been designed.

Despite gradually improving results from the use of indentured servants and an actual increase in demand for them,[147] the sentiment for Negro slavery spread and grew steadily more insistent. The blame for all misfortunes and frustrations that befell the colony was charged against land tenure and lack of slaves jointly until the former was changed, after which it all was placed upon the latter. Although relatively few had favored slavery at first, by 1748 there were few who opposed it.[148] The use of Negroes in defiance of the law began surreptitiously on out-of-the-way plantations along the Savannah River; then it was introduced more or less openly under various forms of evasion. Some attempts were made to enforce the prohibition, but these appear to have broken down completely by 1748, when it was reported authoritatively that the use of Negroes had become fairly general.[149]

The Trustees were more nearly unanimous in opposition to slavery, probably, than on any other issue. Egmont states in 1740 that not a single member of the Board favored slavery. The anti-slavery law was the cornerstone of Trustee policy; every condition and objective rested upon it, and to abandon it was to permit Georgia to become simply another South Carolina.[150] Consequently, the Trustees were still resisting the colonists' demands in March, 1748.[151] But in August they capitulated and asked the colonial leaders to advise upon the conditions for the admission of slaves. The president and assistants and the common councilmen met in Savannah on January 10, 1749, and drew up such a statement, and on May 16, 1749, the Trustees voted to petition the Crown for the repeal of the anti-slavery law. The petition was granted, and the law was repealed on August 8, 1750.[152]

The first slave code, under which legal Negro slavery was introduced into Georgia, was the product of the Trustees' suggestions as amended by the colonists.[153] It was a relatively humane set of rules and was adopted "enthusiastically." One white servant, capable of bearing arms, must be kept for each four Negroes; artificers were forbidden to take Negroes as apprentices, and it was not allowed to hire them out except for certain specified purposes; owners should not be allowed to exercise unlimited powers over slaves; all slaves must be registered; examination and quarantine were required for imported slaves; Negroes should not be obliged, or even allowed, to work on the Sabbath, but should be instructed on that day by the Protestant ministers of the colony in the natural obligations of marriage and the worship of God; intermarriage with whites was forbidden; one female Negro for each four males should be trained in silk-winding; and import duties on slaves were limited to one-half those of South Carolina as an inducement to slave merchants and a subsidy to commerce.[154]

It is doubtful that the Trustees placed much faith in the efficacy of such rules in restraining the harsher features of slavery in Georgia.[155] Similar codes had been adopted originally in South Carolina and other slave states, but had seldom been observed. The most ardent opponents of the institution among the members of the board had become inactive or had died, and the practice of accommodation had grown steadily in board action. The colony was being supported entirely by parliamentary grants and it was destined to be returned to the Crown in four years. For some time there had existed almost a constant threat of its return to Spain, and an almost equal likelihood of its being reannexed to South Carolina if the population continued few and unable to support an independent government.[156] In any case, the introduction of slavery in time appeared certain. Possibly the board's repeal of the anti-slavery statute was designed chiefly to preserve the independent existence of Georgia; and it may have had such an effect.

The admission of slavery stimulated growth almost immediately. There was an unusual increase in land grants during 1749 and 1750; and for the first time there were large numbers of immigrants from the other British colonies, both mainland and island ones. South Carolinians were especially numerous and they brought by far the greatest number of slaves. Rice and indigo culture and trade were soon advancing notably.[157]

Physical planning was a significant part of the over-all design of the Trustees and its imprint remained as a permanent influence in Georgia's development. It related primarily to the laying out of towns and roads and their location with respect to natural waterways and other commercial facilities and to the needs for military defense.

Town sites were chosen and the towns were laid out in advance of settlement. Wide allowance was made for future growth wherever such appeared likely. Savannah, for example, as originally planned covered 37,500 acres, inclusive of tillage lots, although the number of original freeholders was only some thirty-five and the total population about one hundred and twenty.[158] The Trustees granted only five thousand acres in the first instance, but the boundaries of the town were wide enough to accommodate twenty-five hundred to three thousand souls.[159] About one-sixth of the total area, in tillage lots evenly distributed throughout, was reserved originally for public use; but this practice was discontinued in 1743, and thereafter lots were so reserved only for specific public purposes.[160]

The entire scheme provided a central town unit of dwellings grouped about the public market, churches, and other public buildings and private merchandizing and shipping facilities, with streets leading outward to the garden and tillage lots, whose locations radiated from the central village unit. Despite emphasis on compactness, there was no crowding. Ample public grounds were provided around the market and public buildings. The main avenues were made of unusual width and, with numerous connecting streets, were constructed upon a geometric pattern. Small public parks in the main streets at frequent and regular intervals constituted a striking feature of the design.

Internal improvements occupied a prominent place in the physical plan. The first instructions sent to Oglethorpe included the admonition "to take care in setting out lands to reserve necessary roads to church, to markets, and to rivers," and, consequently, roadways in the neighborhood of towns, and even between towns, appear to have been included among the "works for the common good" that were to constitute the first year of public labor agreed upon between the colonists and the Trustees. Such labors appear not to have extended much beyond the clearing of roadways, and, among the various public enterprises, the construction of roads and bridges probably lagged most.[161]

A conflict early developed between Oglethorpe and the other Trustees over both design and order of purposes of the physical planning of the colony. Defense was stressed generally in the beginning as a primary object in forming the compact settlement. This emphasis may have been necessary to obtain the backing of a large and influential group in Great Britain as well as the support and coöperation of South Carolina: the military purpose was assigned as one of the three major objects of both the colony and its particular location.[162] The Trustees naturally were concerned, under all of the circumstances, with the colonists' ability to defend themselves in their exposed position. However, the far greater weight of evidence clearly suggests that they were motivated in all of their physical plans chiefly by economic and social objectives, such as access to markets and shipping, economical use of both public and private resources, support of their land and labor policies, encouragement of the silk industry, preservation of friendly relations with the Indians and with the Spanish in Florida, accommodation to the urban background of the colonists, and the prevention of that notoriously troublesome frontier phenomenon, the squatter.[163]

As Oglethorpe's idea of "colonizing the poor" in conformity with the principle of "agrarian equality" became transformed in his imagination into a phase of unified military operation against Spain and France in America, his conception of the military aspects of colonial settlement underwent a corresponding broadening of design. Military strategy became the chief desideratum: a compact settlement must be located at or near each strategic military position as well as at regular intervals along the principal military routes, in order that immediate civilian and militia support might be given to armies and garrisons; a network of primary and secondary roads, with especial view to military operations, should connect settlements, garrisons and forts, major regions, and probable theaters of action; and especially must settlements be located along the Spanish border, which he considered to be the number one theater of military operations.[164] The other Trustees became alarmed over these projects and ordered an end to them,[165] but Oglethorpe proceeded with his southern settlements and with the construction of forts and military roads, upon which he expended large sums of the Trust funds.[166] These actions led to a virtual reprimand by the Trustees and ultimately to a complete break with Oglethorpe. His later activities in southern Georgia and South Carolina were under commission from the Crown and with parliamentary financial support, and not in conjunction with the regular business of the colony;[167] albeit his military operations had many repercussions in the colony.

The theory of internal improvements that gradually developed among the colonial leaders appears to have been shaped by a conviction that Georgia was destined to develop around water transportation. Few regions of the earth, they thought, were better supplied with natural water channels or so well adapted to utilize water transport.[168] This notion, strengthened by the fact of deep water location of practically all early settlements, probably accounts for the slight attention given to roads during the Trust period. For that matter, little was done publicly to encourage the use of waterways, by the clearing, surveying, charting, and marking of channels or the construction of public docks and wharves. The Trust purchased and rented small craft for public use and, upon occasion, supplied them for outlaying settlements until they could build or purchase their own.[169] A crude lighthouse was built on Tybee Island at the mouth of the Savannah River in 1735 and provision, which proved wholly inadequate, was made for pilot boats at Savannah and Darien in 1741.[170] Of eleven grievances presented to the Trustees by the first Provincial Assembly, in 1751, five were concerned with inadequacies of the existing system of water transportation.[171]

Data upon the administration and progress of road construction are meager. Most of it relates to the execrable condition of roads and bridges or their absence. The single most important achievement was the construction of the Western Road, connecting Savannah and Fort Argyle on the Ogeechee River, at a cost of £700 in addition to extensive labors of Trust servants and of others in payment of debts to the Trust.[172] Roads in the southern part of the province were constructed chiefly by the military forces.[173] The Trust maintained a road supervisor and caretaker at times and also placed certain roads under the jurisdiction of other Trust officers.[174] When the province was divided into two counties, public roads in the northern county of Savannah came under the president and assistants of that county in their capacity as a county court, as is found to be the case in later county administration of roads in Georgia.[175] It is not clear whether Savannah streets were under the supervision of the president and assistants or of the inferior court. Nor is it evident what happened regarding road administration after the abolition of counties in 1743. The first general road law was not adopted until 1755, or three years after the close of the Trust period.

No Trustee policy is more difficult to summarize or estimate than commercial policy. The Trustees seemed of two minds about trade. In the abstract they took it for granted, yet their actions frequently obstructed its free operations. They appeared to want merchants to supply the necessary markets, money, and credit, if for no other reason, to reduce the burdens upon the Trust; nevertheless, they feared that the free operations of merchants in Georgia would encourage rice production, slaves, and rum. They apparently assumed dependence upon free commercial enterprise, but refused to accept the realities of the system. This seeming paradox is resolved partially by their theory of the relation of trade to the balance of the economy. They held a view of trade similar to that developed later by the Physiocrats, in that they believed that if the government saw to it that the physical facilities of roads and market centers were located conveniently to the main routes of trade and if landholders would apply their efforts faithfully to production of commodities, the merchants would come to serve the producers. Production of goods was primary and trade was a secondary process resulting from the needs for exchange that grew out of production of commodities. Trade should serve, not dominate, a community.

The Trustees doubtlessly were aware of the central role played by the capitalist merchant in the prevailing system. There are evidences that they accepted this as a part of the developing character of economic life, as a tendency toward the centralization of power in the hands of the shrewd and capable, as evidence of the superior resources and bargaining power of the merchants and their control over government. They tended, however, to emphasize the evils of the system rather than the general dependence upon it. They saw how Southern planters everywhere became indebted to the merchants, how they lost their lands, and how this led to land aggrandizement and depopulation of the colonies, as free farmers and artisans emigrated and were replaced by Negro slaves. In prosperous times there was over-extension of credit, unhealthy expansion, and speculation; in bad times, bankruptcy, suffering, and population displacement.[176] For these reasons land tenures in *tail male* and similar restraining policies were introduced. The Trustees did not want land granting to "become a bubble in change alley" or to be turned "into a trade of stock jobbing."[177] They sought to protect the colonists against what they believed to be the overwhelmingly superior bargaining power of the slave merchant.

The Trustees were following an experimental policy of social welfare that was at odds with prevailing practices of commercial interests. They recognized this conflict between business values and the social values that were their own criteria of action. In their minds was the practical certainty that if their policies failed, Georgia would sink into bondage to the merchant capitalists.

Yet the Trustees never succeeded in developing a positive policy to fill the place of the one whose effects they sought to avoid. They sought to achieve a satisfactory commercial policy largely by indirection — through the policies discussed above — with primary dependence upon a few major restraints. They invited merchants to settle, but at the same time effectively discouraged them by other policies. As a result of such policies and of the colony's unpromising economic prospects, merchants came largely to sell charity goods to the Trust officers or consumption goods to the colonists for drafts on the Trustees or for cash. Few remained to become a permanent part of the colony's economic life.[178] The Trustees restricted Indian trade in their territory to Georgia residents in order to create trade for Georgia merchants; thus they alienated South Carolina and probably created more difficulties for the colony than they removed.[179] While the Trust carried on almost every other sort of business, it steadfastly refused to enter into trading operations, despite insistent appeals to do so from some of its strongest supporters in the colony;[180] nor did it attempt to sponsor any such venture as the "Free Society of Traders" that Penn had instituted in Pennsylvania.[181]

The greatest shortcoming of the Trust's policy was the failure to provide capital and credit for developmental purposes. The argument that trade would follow production presumed the prior existence in producers' hands of a fund of capital with which to establish production. These developmental requirements were enormous, relatively speaking, especially in labor costs. It so happened that in commercial agriculture, production followed trade, rather than the reverse. And trade in general followed the slave merchant, because the advance of slave labor to the planter for the development of production was everywhere outside of Georgia the *sine qua non* of economic activation and growth.[182] As was noted above, the Trustees did unintentionally become involved in modest capital advances to the planters, usually of only bare subsistence. These had little effect in promoting development. True, the Trustees made a valiant attempt to dispense with the dependence upon the slave merchant by supplying indentured servants, but they did not give the colonists as liberal terms as was customary in the slave trade. Over and over again there were appeals for better trading, credit, capital and labor terms, and facilities. The Trustees' slender resources prevented their meeting this need, made even greater by the universal poverty among the colonists. The excuse of a lack of resources, however, does not alter the fact that the Trustee program had nothing to offer in this controlling area that was filled normally by the private merchant. Some of the ablest leaders in Georgia attributed the failures of the Trust period to this weakness of commercial policy.[183] And finally, it may be recalled that Trustee monetary policy, though in some respects the most successful of all their policies, nevertheless reflected something of the same indecisiveness that characterized other phases of commercial policy. Anchored, on the one hand, to the commercial specie standard, but tied, on the other, to narrow fiscal operations, it both aided and handicapped the private merchant in his credit operations in support of the private economy.

The ultimate collapse of the Trustees' commercial policy was inevitable. The ideas that underlay Trustee policy were novel, vague, frequently ill-formed, and sprang from divergent — often narrow and even inconsistent — assumptions and bases of action. The location of their experiment at the time was an insignificant and inhospitable little area almost completely isolated from the vast growing world of British economy of which it was nominally a part. Above all, the commercial policy was unsympathetic in many respects to the most powerful forces in the entire system — the commercial interests, that furthermore received the full support of the British government. Both Trustees and colonists were caught in the strongest currents of the rising tide of eighteenth-century merchant capitalism.

CHAPTER III

IMPERIALISM, AGRARIAN CAPITALISM, AND THE LIBERAL AWAKENING

The Trustees surrendered control of the affairs of Georgians on June 23, 1752, twenty years and fourteen days from the date of incorporation. The president and assistants, who already had become virtually the ruling power, were continued in office by the Crown until the first royal governor, John Reynolds, arrived in Savannah on October 29, 1754. The colony now entered, in a sense, upon a second era of centralized guidance, likewise emanating from Britain. It exchanged its status as a model experiment in benevolent reform for that of a model colonial unit in imperial commercial policy.[1] It was to experience less immediate interference and far more prosperity, because recent concessions obtained from the Trustees were in line with governmental policies and because the immediate opportunities for economic development harmonized with imperial ends.

1. Planning a Model Imperial Colony

The controlling ideas shaping British policy at this time were: the promotion of British commercial, industrial, and financial interests, the preparation of the military establishment for the impending showdown with France and Spain, and the better management of the growing fiscal burdens. Crown policy in Georgia was the product of the growing unification of these principal elements in general policy. Georgia was a fertile field for the consummation of a streamlined colonial policy based upon such criteria, since its apparent economic interests coincided so closely with imperial policies and since Trustee control had prevented the growth of institutions such as had brought other American colonies into conflict with the mother country.

It should not be inferred, however, that Crown policy was introduced into Georgia at one stroke, or that it ever became any too clear-cut. Full administrative control was established in the governor and other royal officers and in the Crown veto; but the various other commercial, military, and fiscal policies followed in general the history of the well-known acts and regulations that led up to the revolt of the colonies. The concrete objects of royal policy were: to develop Georgia's land and timber resources and produce thereby a flow of goods for the beneficial gains of British merchants, slave traders, shippers, manufacturers, and moneylenders; to increase quitrents and other public revenues; and to encompass better the Crown's designs for Indian policy and military defense and offense.

The more significant economic features and results of Crown policy within Georgia were: unlimited land grants, the rapid expansion of slavery, the emergence of the large plantation, and the full development of the commercial exchange-credit system. Actually all were merely different aspects of a common phenomenon which may be described as the rise of commercial agriculture. Other more or less related developments of importance were: internal improvements, regulation, Indian land cessions and territorial extensions, currency and fiscal institutions.

Rules governing the granting of lands were greatly relaxed during the Crown period. The family right system that was employed permitted grants of one hundred acres to each head of a family and an additional fifty acres for each member, inclusive of slaves.[2] The only limit to the amount that could be obtained by an individual were the size of family and number of slaves that he possessed. The governor and council could exercise their judgment as to the amount that an applicant could use productively, but this discretion was seldom practiced. Requirements of land clearing to satisfy grants were reduced considerably by the Board of Trade.[3] The Crown continued to insist upon the payment of the royal quitrents after ten years.[4]

The practice of setting aside special reserves for groups that wished to migrate to Georgia, begun during the Trustee period, was continued and extended. Such reserves were in no sense a grant to the group as a company, but only the reservation of a given tract within which individual members of the group might take out grants whenever they should arrive in Georgia. In 1766 the provincial government went much further in encouraging group migrations in an act "For Encouraging Settlers to come into the Province." If forty or more families signified a desire to come, the province for a period of three years would allot and survey a township, waive the usual fees, run and mark a road to an existing public road — all at public expense — and exempt slaves of the colonists from provincial taxation for ten years.[5]

Special grants were made to the royal governors at their own request and to certain others upon warrant or proclamation by the king.[6] Most important of the latter were the soldier land bounties granted under the Royal Proclamation of 1763 awarding land bounties to the colonial soldiers of the French and Indian War.[7] Grants were made also to churches and one of two thousand acres to George Whitefield for the establishment of a college.[8] Lands were also sold to some extent. Pine lands were sold to individuals and partnerships for the sawing of lumber, and reverted lands were sometimes sold at auction or directly to individuals.[9] The squatter problem, almost entirely absent during the Trust period, became a very troublesome one under the royal governors.[10] Registered land grants by 1765 totaled 635,000 acres and probably about three times that amount by 1775.[11]

In August 1751, the Trustees reported to the King that there were 1,700 whites and 420 Negroes in Georgia. Two years later whites numbered 2,381 and Negroes 1,066; by 1760, the figures were 6,000 and 3,578 respectively; by 1765, they had increased to 6,800 and 4,500; and in 1773, Governor Wright reported that there were 18,000 whites and 15,000 Negroes.[12] Negro slaves were brought to Georgia by both merchants and planters, with South Carolinians predominating in the latter group. Many planters also came with their slaves from the sugar islands of the West Indies. Slave-labor operations centered in rice, indigo, lumber, and naval stores in the tidewater region, and in the trade and service activities of the rising ports of Savannah and Sunbury. The North Carolinians, who were beginning to pour into upper Georgia toward the close of the colonial period, brought few or no slaves, and their region was ill-adapted at the time for profitable use of slave labor.[13]

The Georgians did not wait long to replace the humanitarian code under which the Trustees had finally permitted slavery. The first assembly that met under the Crown passed a new act, on March 7, 1755, for the governing of slaves. Copied largely from the code of South Carolina, it covered all matters that might arise concerning property in slaves, relationships between master and slaves, use and treatment of slaves, and the public aspects of the institution. The work hours of slaves were limited to sixteen out of twenty-four, and working slaves on Sunday unless absolutely necessary was subject to a fine of ten shillings; one white servant was required for each twenty slaves, two for every fifty slaves and one for every twenty above fifty. Slaves were strictly limited in the buying and selling of goods, which was further restricted to the area of Savannah and only with a license; and they could not keep any boats or raise livestock for their own benefit. The killing or maiming of slaves without cause was subject to fine and imprisonment; the failure of the master to provide adequate food and clothing was subject to fine; slaves were subject to examination by any white person, and the latter could kill a slave if assaulted. Slaves were forbidden to leave a plantation without a letter from the master or a responsible person, and not more than seven might appear on a highway without a white person in charge; a slave must not carry a weapon without a license, and not on Saturday or Sunday in any case. It was a capital offense for a slave to burn or destroy maliciously any stack of rice or grain, to set fire to any tar kiln or product of the province, to steal another slave, to administer poison to anyone, or to attempt to cause an insurrection. It was forbidden, on penalty of heavy fine, to teach a slave to read or write.[14] This rigorous law provided the basis of nearly all later code legislation.

Patrols were established throughout the province in 1757, largely for the purpose of maintaining order among the slaves and preventing cabals and insurrections.[15] A correctionary workhouse was established in 1763, which took over jurisdiction of runaways and criminals from the constables and also meted out court sentences, and masters might send stubborn and incorrigible slaves to the warden of the workhouse for punishment.[16] The basic code was reënacted in 1759 and 1765 with some increase in rigorousness and a weakening of the humane features. An attempt was made in 1770 to curb excessive license of irresponsible whites in the treatment of slaves and to secure the latter somewhat more adequate justice in capital trials.[17]

The colonists, aware that slavery discouraged the immigration of free white labor, made sporadic efforts to counteract these undesirable effects. Such was the object of the prohibitions upon buying and selling by slaves, and of slaves' enterprising in their own interest. A special act to encourage free white labor and tradesmen to settle in Georgia was passed in 1758 forbidding the employment of slaves in handicraft trade in any town except under specified conditions. A board of commissioners was appointed with power to fix maximum rates for carpenters, joiners, bricklayers, and plasterers. If artisans could not be obtained at such rates, after advertising for three days, Negroes might then be used. There was no bar to hiring slaves as shipwrights, caulkers, sawyers, coopers, porters, or ordinary laborers; and a handicraft artisan might train and use an apprentice slave. The governor and council could always order the use of slaves in time of public emergency.[18]

2. The Large Plantation, Exchange-Credit System, and Internal Improvements

The rise of the large plantation in colonial Georgia was a rapid and striking development. It was, in a considerable measure, simply the extension of the great plantation-slave units from South Carolina and the West Indies to the virgin lands south of the Savannah River, whether by actual transfer of such units or through the growth of new units in the hands of old Georgia residents or newcomers like the Crown officials. It was large-scale capitalistic enterprise, devoted primarily to rice and indigo production on the rich swampland about Savannah and Sunbury, along the Altamaha, and on the sea islands. The typical, and generally considered optimum, size was forty to forty-five slaves on 350–450 acres of land; although individual units ranged from twenty to eighty slaves and from 200 to 2,000 acres in size.[19]

Individual capitalists commonly owned and operated a number of such plantation units. Governor Wright accumulated twelve.[20] The typical size of his plantations was about 450 acres and forty-five slaves. Approximately half the slaves normally were adult male hands. These numbers correspond reasonably closely to a commonly held view that about thirty slaves constituted an optimum number for one overseer on a rice plantation. Wright owned a relatively few larger units of seventy to eighty slaves, but these appear to have been residence plantations upon which there was a high proportion of house and other miscellaneous servants. They also may have been double units. Governor Wright owned altogether between five hundred and six hundred slaves. John Graham, the largest landowner in the province, possessed at least three plantations, each of which employed about eighty slaves. It is conceivable that they were double or even triple units, were devoted in part to lumbering or shipping activities, or were residence plantations.[21] James Habersham operated a giant double unit plantation that employed two hundred slaves.[22]

The large plantation in Georgia was not an isolated phenomenon but reflected rather the crest of the development of commercial rice and indigo culture in southeastern America. The throwing open of virgin territory at this time permitted the establishment of an unusual number of great plantations in a very short time. It was the result of a combination of unlimited land grants, the movement of capitalist planters, the mobility of slave labor, and the redundancy of commercial credits.

The full introduction of the commercial exchange-credit system was the fourth outstanding development under the royal governors. Since slaves constituted fully three-fourths of the capital investment of an operating plantation, the slave trade was the heart of the commercial system in this region. A new plantation with a complement of forty-five slaves required in round numbers a $12,000 investment, of which $9,000 represented the cost of slaves; $1,500, other capital supplies commonly furnished by the merchant; $500, wages and building materials; and possibly $1,000, for all the costs of acquiring land. It required at least a year to clear, fence, and bring the plantation into production, which usually added another $1,000 to merchant advances.[23] These advances were normally for one year, although frequently two years were allowed on slaves — at least, for part of the payments — and actually merchants were often compelled to wait much longer. Planter indebtedness to merchants was the normal state. Collections were made in produce, and merchant remittances to European or West Indian commercial houses were likewise in the form mainly of shipments of produce, with some use of bills of exchange.

Commercial agencies served as the combined mechanisms of exchange, investment, and money.[24] Little money ever appeared in circulation. Imported consumer goods, especially from the northern colonies, quickly drained out whatever did appear. Rapid expansion and capital investment and rising consumption kept Georgia in a debtor position.[25] Most merchants engaged in extensive plantation investments along with their trading activities. This dual role was often enforced upon them, or enhanced, by the necessities of foreclosure. James Habersham, the colony's leading merchant and also one-time acting governor, became the third largest plantation operator in the colony.

The commercial records reflect the growth of the large plantation system. One undocumented report cites the following growth of exports: 1750, $8,900; 1753, $28,000; 1756, $75,000; 1763, $200,000; and 1773, $380,000.[26] The historian George White states that exports increased from $70,000 in 1755 to $435,000 in 1770 and to $530,000 in 1773.[27] Governor James Wright records that between 1767 and 1772, the heyday of the great plantation, exports averaged $440,000 annually and that, whereas only 45 vessels of a total of 1,604 tons cleared the entire province in 1761, 212 totaling 12,124 tons cleared from Savannah and Sunbury alone in 1772.[28] It is fairly evident that the great expansion of the plantation system came about primarily within the short period of about twelve years between 1761 and 1773.

The first general public roads act was passed in 1755. Its apparent intention was to secure the development of a complete integrated system of internal improvements "for the more direct and better convenience of the inhabitants of this province." Georgia was divided into nine districts for the purposes of administration and six leading residents in each district were named a board of commissioners for their district. Administration of the program was lodged, however, with surveyors appointed by the legislature for each district, who were to have the power and the duty to lay out main high roads, secondary roads, private paths, bridges, causeways, and water passages, and to establish such ferries as they considered to be in the public interest. The surveyors of each district were required to meet at least twice a year to plan the work, and might separate the district into divisions. All surveyors were made directly responsible to the governor and council and to the legislature when the latter was in session. They might request the appointment of additional surveyors and they were given power to choose assistants. Rather specific directions were given as to procedure with the work and its character. Primary public roads, or those designed to serve the general interest of the province, were to be surveyed and constructed, after which public roads which served the interests of a district might be developed. Public roads must be twenty-four feet in width, and trees on or near the side lines should be left to shade the road. All males between ages sixteen and sixty were made liable for work on internal improvements of all sorts, and city inhabitants were to be assessed unless they were able to supply personal services. Surveyors were empowered to appoint summoning officers and overseers. They might hire competent persons to build bridges and levy the costs upon the males of the district in money, kind, or personal services; they might establish ferries, choose their operators, supervise operations, and fix rates until the following meeting of the legislature; and it became their duty to enforce various prohibitions and penalties and to collect fines. Fines were as follows: two shillings per day for refusal to work or to allow slaves to work; five pounds for hindering work, or stopping, blocking, or altering any road, and the guilty person must also repair such act; thirty shillings upon summonsers and overseers for refusals to serve; and twenty shillings for cutting any shade tree along a road. Private paths or roads might be laid out by the public surveyors, but they must be built and maintained by the beneficiaries, in proportion to benefits when more than one were served. Surveyors were empowered to build canals between streams and might utilize the annual labor service duties for such purposes. If the interests of two districts were involved in any construction, such as a bridge over a dividing stream, the work of construction and maintenance was to be carried on jointly and all labor and other costs assessed ratably upon the males of the respective districts.[29]

The above act has been described in some detail because it affords a broad base of reference for the study of almost every step in the later development of internal improvements and transportation facilities in Georgia. It represents a plan of development of a unified over-all system of internal improvements, to be guided by the principle of the general welfare, and to be administered by professional engineers subject to appointment and control by state legislative and executive officials and to the counsel of local commissioners. Particular interests were to be served, but only secondarily and in conformity with the general interest; and a certain element of central control was implied, and likewise a certain degree of benefit in return. The criteria of the public interest were not defined in the act, but the controlling elements probably at the time were considered to be trade and access to markets, defense, and political and social considerations, ranked possibly in some such order.

It would appear from an act two years later that the general policy enjoyed wide support but that it had become evident that some primary highways were more important than others as well as more costly and, furthermore, that there were pools of labor services in places like Savannah that were entirely out of proportion to the relative needs of their districts. Consequently, Savannah labor services were partially reallocated where needed upon general public highways, but also with due consideration of the benefits of such highways to Savannah and to public and private business centering upon Savannah.[30]

Acts of 1762 and 1764 introduce some slight modifications and extensions indicative of growth and new population areas.[31] The entire law was somewhat altered and reënacted in 1766. Districts were increased to twelve, of which one of the new ones was the town of Savannah. The latter no doubt marked a step toward the separation of urban areas of streets and terminal facilities from the larger, more general, area of highways. A more significant shift toward local option within the general area itself was embodied in the enlargement of the powers and responsibilities of the district commissioners at the expense of the surveyors' administrative functions. Commissioners and surveyors in each district were empowered to carry out the general program jointly. Each board of commissioners was directed to meet annually and plan its district program; and such powers and duties as laying out private roads, working out joint operations between districts, opening ferries and fixing their rates, and collecting fines were transferred to the commissioners. In particular the commissioners were instructed to undertake the cutting of canals wherever possible and the clearing of rivers and streams. This increase in local powers was offset somewhat, however, by a growing tendency on the part of the legislature to spell out public policy and to specify, and even make separate provision for certain primary improvements.[31] It is also true that some of the duties assigned originally to surveyors were more political than technical. Labor services in Savannah and environs were commuted to an annual payment of two shillings in 1767.[33]

A general ferries act was passed in 1768 providing for the opening of five principal ones and establishing classes and scales of maximum rates and regulations for operation.[34] Another interesting act of the same year authorized the selling at public auction of a five-year lease of one of the principal ferries in the province. In addition to the franchise were included public lands and buildings adjacent to the ferry site.[35] The auctioning of ferry leases became a customary practice.

The last general internal improvement act, which renewed for the most part the previous one, was passed in 1773. Districts again were increased and special ones were created out of sections of the principal highways. Maximum labor service liability was fixed at not more than six days at any one time nor more times than two in one year. The commuted payments in Savannah were diverted for the construction and maintenance of public wells. Heavy fines and penalties for creating obstructions to waterways were adopted.[36]

3. Growth of Regulation

Public regulation, hitherto largely absent, was introduced rather widely during the Crown period. This raises the suggestion that such was simply the extension of mercantilism which was undergoing a kind of dying gasp in America. But such was not wholly, or even primarily, the case, unless it is understood that there was much regulation in the mercantilist era that was not associated with the so-called mercantilist tenets. Most of the regulations were initiated by the colonial legislature rather than by the royal governor and would appear to have been adopted to serve specific situations that emerged out of the expanding and changing economy. They may be divided into four categories: (1) public utility regulations, (2) export inspection, (3) price-fixing, and (4) miscellaneous. Instances in the first two categories were by far the most numerous and were developed most consistently.

Regulated public utilities included public markets, grist mills, taverns, wharves, warehouses, pilotage services, and ferries. The objects of public market regulation were to prevent forestalling and engrossing, to determine what goods should be sold and how they should be handled, to fix times for operations, and to supervise weights and measures. In the case of the public-owned market at Savannah the rental policies of the stalls had to be determined as well as provisions for the general maintenance of the market. Tavern regulations dealt primarily with licensing, sale of liquors, and the prevention of disorderly operations.[37] The regulation of wharfage and storage rates and weighing charges connected therewith was introduced in 1774; and the harbor master was charged with enforcement of uniform maximum rates along with the regulations against the dumping of ballast and rubbish in the rivers and other navigable channels.[38] Regulation of pilotage services covered the selection and licensing of pilots and the fixing of pilotage fees, services, and conditions of operation.[39] Ferry regulation has already been noted. In addition to the fixing of maximum rates, service, and management requirements by charter, it included general supervision and enforcement, and temporary rate-fixing, by first the highway surveyors and later the district boards of commissioners.[40] Special boards of commissioners were appointed to regulate the public market and pilotage.

The object of the numerous inspection laws was to improve the reputation and the demand for Georgia products abroad and thereby stimulate production. Such efforts began with an act of 1760 "to prevent frauds in the making of lumber." It was in the "interest of the colony," ran the law, "that all lumber exported be honestly and faithfully made." Then it proceeded to define and fix the dimensions of all kinds of lumber and lumber products, and to declare certain types to be unmerchantable and subject to confiscation.[41] Six years later, inspection was extended to beef, pork, pitch, tar, and turpentine, and included specifications of the materials and sizes of containers, standard weights, and grades of qualities and textures.[42] Leather was included in 1768 and tobacco in 1770. Inspection of the latter was introduced to encourage its culture in the province, especially in the back country where it was thought that the lands were highly suitable, and where agriculture was in a backward state owing to the lack of readily merchantable products. This tobacco inspection law set the model that was followed more or less in after years when tobacco became the leading export, and when inspection agencies and public warehouses were established throughout the length of the Savannah River valley. Every tobacco container must be opened and at least two inspectors must agree upon its satisfactory quality. If approved, the container was to be stamped with the weight, the word "Georgia," and the names of the inspectors. Inspectors fees were to be paid from the public treasury.[43]

Price-fixing was introduced in 1755 with the attempt to fix maximum interest rates "in order to encourage trade." Ten per cent was declared to be the legal maximum.[44] It was common practice in Georgia as elsewhere to charge planters interest on all accounts. These charges frequently exceeded planters' profits and, in cases of crop failures or other misfortunes, would accumulate into very heavy debts in themselves. Rates were high and exceedingly onerous. Hence, it appears that these maximum interest rate statutes grew out of the problem of agricultural dependence upon commercial banking and credit. They were a part of the movement that produced paper money, public loan banks, and depression stay laws. Maximum interest rates were reduced to 8 per cent in 1759 and made universally applicable regardless of size of loan or account or length of time. Contracts for higher rates were declared null and void and subject to fine of treble the value of the loan or the merchandize that had been advanced.[45]

Other instances of price-fixing related to consumer goods. Regulation of the price of bread began in 1768 and continued generally for over fifty years.[46] Maximum prices on liquors were set in the tavern regulations.

The fence law, first passed in 1755, was the most notable regulatory act in the miscellaneous category. Its use came to have as much social and political as economic significance. It required the fencing of all fields and gardens as a requisite to the collection of damages for trespassing livestock.[47] The question at issue was the subject of heated disputes and much litigation in colonial days as in later times. Another regulation required planters to bury or destroy all steeped indigo weed within forty-eight hours of removal from vats "because of the pernicious result of flies." [48] And finally might be included in this group the embargo on corn in 1770, which resulted from a short crop: it was to run for two years, but the governor and council were given the power to lift it if the supply situation improved sufficiently and thereafter to reinvoke it should the shortage reoccur.[49]

4. Territorial Expansion

The most significant developments in Indian relations under the Crown were the four land cessions that were negotiated by Governor Wright. A large area between Savannah and Augusta had been in dispute for some time, because the Indian tribes of this region had died or largely departed and the whites had moved in without benefit of title cession. The Creeks finally relinquished their claims to this section in a treaty at Augusta in 1763. Two years later the long-standing white claims to the tidewater lands between the Altamaha and St. Marys rivers were confirmed.[50] The largest addition of new territory for white settlement came, however, in a treaty of 1773 in the settlement of some $175,000 to $200,000 of debts owed to white traders by the Creeks and Cherokees. In liquidation of these debts the Indians agreed to cede two huge tracts, one stretching far northward and westward above Augusta and organized as Wilkes County during the Revolution, and the other lying west of the original Oglethorpe cession between the Ogeechee and Altamaha rivers.[51] The four cessions together increased the actual available lands of Georgia some five or six times over those of the Trustee period.

The expansion of the limits of territorial jurisdiction in this period was equally striking and fraught with important future consequences. In a commission to Governor Wright in 1764, the King extended the southern boundary of Georgia to the St. Marys River, thence west to the junction of the Flint and Chattahoochee rivers, thence up the latter to the thirty-first parallel and thence along this parallel to the Mississippi River; and the latter river was made the western boundary.[52] This declaration voided South Carolina's claim to a vast area south and west of the Altamaha River and placed the areas of present Alabama and Mississippi within the limits of Georgia. The dispute with South Carolina over interpretations of the charter regarding northeastern and northern boundaries, however, was not settled. But Wright's Commission of 1764 became the principal basis of Georgia's statehood claims after the Revolution.

5. Paper Money

Georgia like other colonies had its paper money history. Paper money was issued to serve four basic purposes: currency, private investment, public investment, and public deficits. Monetary and fiscal purposes were distinguished at the start, but soon became inextricably interrelated. Although such a combination of inducements presented the usual dangers of overissue and depreciation, paper money emission never got out of hand in Georgia.

Merchants supplied imported goods and slaves on credit, but specie for internal transactions continued scarce. High interest rates also created a demand for a cheaper source of capital loans. The government found itself under similar pressures owing to the rapid growth of the colony and of its defense needs. The lack of currency made tax collections difficult and large capital expenditures almost impossible. Some means of augmenting the currency became a practical necessity. Two methods of issue were employed: first, through what was virtually a public bank of issue and, second, government paper money.

The commissioners of the General Loan Office were created by an act of February 17, 1755. They were given power to emit £7,000 in bills of seventeen denominations ranging from two pence to one pound. Bills above two shillings were made full legal tender for all payments in Georgia including taxes; those of two shillings and under were made legal tender in amounts up to two shillings; and all were to be inscribed as an obligation of the province. They were declared further to be "the lawful and current money of this Province of Georgia." [53]

The commissioners were authorized to make loans up to seven years duration on mortgage security at 6 per cent; such loans must not exceed one-half the value of the security in the case of real property or one-third in the case of slaves; and they were limited to a maximum of £80 and a minimum of £10 to one person. One-fourth of the interest return should be added to principal and should be loaned also, but at the expiration of said loans, must be used together with all interest paid thereon, to retire the bills. The other three-fourths of interest payments were to be paid to the treasurer of the colony for public use as directed by the legislature. The commissioners were to be paid for their services out of the initial issue of bills and in fees levied upon the borrowers. "Since the issuing of too much paper currency," ran the language of the statute, "has had bad effects in some of the other colonies," it was ordered that no bills should be issued until the Crown had approved the law, and that no more than £3,000 should be issued during the first year. Additional issues should be subject to the approval of the legislature.

Thus was put into operation a public loan bank with limited note issue, whose obligations were guaranteed by the government. Its notes were inconvertible paper money, but were subject to gradual retirement after eight years. Notes were issued upon capital loans, rather than upon commercial transactions; hence they did not constitute a very elastic currency. Such elasticity as there was depended, apparently, upon the periodic actions of the legislature. Bills to the amount of £2,785 were printed and loaned during the first two years and interest in the amount of £172 was received, of which £129 was paid into the public treasury. The latter sum remained unappropriated, however, and in the meantime the treasury had accumulated a deficit of £767; therefore the legislature voted to apply the interest sum to the treasury deficit and also directed the commissioners of the General Loan Office to print an additional £638 of bills and pay the same into the treasury to cover the balance of the deficit; and further authorized also the printing of new bills to replace worn and defaced ones.[54]

The government began, in 1759, to borrow from the Loan Office for public capital purposes, when the legislature authorized an issue of £790 for the repair of the Savannah church and Tybee lighthouse and the construction of a powder magazine. The issue also covered a small treasury deficit of £59. The government pledged the tax on taverns for the amount spent on church repairs, and certain revenues derived from the operations of the lighthouse and powder magazine for the amounts going for those objects.[55] This emission brought the total of Loan Office note issues approximately to £4,400, of which one-third represented non-interest-bearing loans to the government.

The outbreak of the Cherokee War in 1760 marked the beginning of government paper certificate issues. The object was the construction of forts and the issue amounted to £1,100. The certificates were made full legal tender for five years; and a general property surtax, designed to raise £200 annually, was levied and pledged, along with the general tax, for their retirement in equal annual installments during that period.[56]

The General Loan Office was rechartered in the same year. The new statute, after reviewing the successful and highly useful operations of this institution and citing the steady growth of the province and consequent expanding needs for currency and credit, authorized an increase of note issue for private loan purposes to £6,500, and an additional £910 for certain temporary public purposes, or a total of £7,410. The new law was designed to go into effect in 1762 when the original loans began to fall due. The old bills then were to be replaced by new ones and new loans were to be made on substantially the same terms as previously. New loans should be made at the end of each seven years as long as the act should continue to be in force. Of the £910 for public purposes, £500 were to be used to repair Christ Church in Savannah, £200 for the cost of printing, £100 for an initial fee to the commissioners, and £10 for incidental expenses. The regular compensation of the commissioners was changed from the fee basis to an annual charge of £50 against earnings. The balance of annual interest returns was ordered to be divided as follows: £210 for the expenses of the various established churches and £130 to sink the above non-earning issue of £910. The bills continued to be full legal tender, and the commissioners were authorized to print £200 of new bills annually to replace those worn and defaced. There was no provision for any retirement of the General Loan Office issues after retirement of the £910.[57]

Thus, after seven years, the General Loan Office became a public bank of issue for dealing solely in private long-time loans. Its notes, or bills as they were called, supplied a fixed amount of currency which could be increased only by legislative act. The other form of paper currency, the government certificate, became the variable element in the money supply, although its elasticity was related to fiscal operations and exigencies rather than to conditions of the general economy. Government issues were invariably of shorter duration, of one to five years, and were automatically redeemable out of taxation. The latter feature undoubtedly was deflationary in effect, since an increase in business would increase tax collections and thereby reduce the volume of money. The government certificates were issued variously, by special commissioners appointed for the purpose, or by the treasury directly. There appears to have been an effort to adapt the denominations of the particular government issues to the current monetary needs. These operations possessed the elements of both public monetary control and public banking.

Government certificates of £650 were issued in 1765 for the construction and repair of barracks and forts;[58] again, £1,115 in 1766 to pay the expenses of settling immigrants in Georgia, and £700 in the same year for rebuilding the Savannah courthouse;[59] £2,200 in 1768 for rebuilding the lighthouse and making a coastal survey;[60] and one-year treasury certificates of £100 were issued in 1770 to pay one-third of the cost of the Savannah watch.[61] All issues carried full legal tender in Georgia, but for a limited period only; and various taxes were pledged for their retirement. A new feature was added in 1770 when tax anticipation certificates, or warrants, were issued in the amount of £2,430 against the current tax levies.[62]

A total of £5,865 of government paper money was emitted during the decade, 1760 to 1770, almost the whole of which was spent for public works. All but £1,817 had been retired by 1773. Also outstanding still were all of the tax anticipation certificates of 1770, which, with the remaining other certificates, amounted to a total of £4,247. All of these were ordered, in 1773, to be called in and replaced by a new issue of £4,299 which was to be retired from general taxes over the next three years.[63] This amounted, of course, to the monetization of a large treasury deficit, which had been incurred because of the breakdown of tax collections during the troublesome years of 1770 to 1773. The final government issue in colonial Georgia occurred in 1774, when £800 were authorized in connection with supplying protection to settlers within the new land cessions that Governor Wright had secured from the Indians the year previously. It also marks the first instance in Georgia in which land sales were pledged for the retirement of paper money.[64]

There can be little question that paper currency was handled carefully during the colonial period in Georgia. All evidence indicates that the General Loan Office in particular was well operated, that its loans were judiciously placed, and that its losses were negligible. The statement of its condition in 1773 shows that it had retired the £910 non-interest-bearing issue, covered its expenses and its annual appropriations of £210 for religious purposes, and had accumulated a net profit balance of £510.[65] The government's record with currency certificates may not appear in as favorable a light, though it was a creditable one on the whole. About 70 per cent of the certificates, on the average, were retired as scheduled; and such failures in retirement as occurred resulted from the lack of tax collections during 1771–1772 when the governor and House of Assembly were at odds.[66] In fact, an even slower rate of retirement would appear to have been advisable under the conditions of money shortage. The largest amount of paper money outstanding at one time, including both Loan Office and government issues, could never have exceeded about £11,500 (or $50,000), scarcely an excessive — and probably an insufficient — sum of domestic currency for an expanding economy of 30,000 population and annual exports of nearly one-half million dollars' value. No evidence exists that there was any depreciation of Georgia's currencies, as was true in South Carolina and elsewhere. The curriencies met an urgent need and were undoubtedly an important factor in local economic development.

Public expenditures were surprisingly low for a colony growing as rapidly as Georgia and situated in as exposed a position. Some annual appropriations by the legislature, for which the colonial taxes were levied, were as follows:[67]

1758	£ 645
1762	1,421
1769	3,047
1770	3,355
1773	3,820

These covered, in addition to the retirements of the paper certificates, the expenses of the legislature, lower courts, and various minor colonial officials, the pay and maintenance of regular troops, minor repairs to public property, and a variety of incidental items.

The salaries of the Crown officers, paid by the British Parliament, amounted to £2,400 in 1773, and fees collected in Georgia in the same year by this same group of officials for their services totaled £3,925.[68] Of the entire sum of public expenditures during this last colonial year for which records are available, Great Britain bore approximately 25 per cent and the colony 75 per cent. The notable fact is the large proportion — 39 per cent — supported through fees, representing an amount greater than that raised by taxes.

Most of the cost of internal improvements is omitted from this summary, since it was paid in labor service. Estimated at the legal rate of commutation, its value may have amounted to as much as £3,000 in 1773. Regular militia service, which included the supply of personal arms, was likewise universally compulsory without compensation.

The first general tax law in Georgia was enacted in 1755 and carried a mixture of specific and ad valorem rates, chiefly on property. These rates were low but were very unequal as between rural and urban property. One shilling was levied per slave or one hundred acres of land, and seven shillings per £100 value of urban property, merchandise, and money on loan. Nine tax districts were created and assessors and collectors were appointed in each by the legislature.[69] Rates were doubled two years later. No other significant changes were made until 1760, when rates on slaves and lands were increased by 25 per cent.[70] The persistent complaints of the merchants against the excessively higher rates on urban properties and businesses brought a reduction in 1762 of 45 per cent on general urban property and 60 per cent on urban commercial improvements. The rate on money on loans, however, was reduced only slightly. A poll tax on free colored persons of ten shillings was introduced.[71] The urban property rate still remained one and a half to twice that on land and slaves. All rates were reduced 25 per cent in 1768, except that on free colored persons, which was increased to 15 shillings.[72] All rates again were reduced 25 per cent in 1770, which brought the level close to that of the original law.[73] No tax law was passed, and no taxes were collected, in 1771 and 1772 owing to the dispute between the governor and the House of Assembly.[74] The last colonial tax statute, passed in 1773, raised the rates 67 per cent and introduced a 1 per cent income tax on all salaries paid by legislative appropriations, on all business profits and on all other incomes of public officials and professions, except ministers of the gospel. The increase in rates was intended primarily to cover a treasury deficit of £1,350 and the partial retirement of the funded tax anticipation certificates, both of which had resulted from the absence of tax collections during 1771 and 1772.[75]

Particular taxes, for both special and general purposes, were levied more or less continuously throughout this period. Tonnage duties and imposts on slaves and rum were the more common ones. Rates also were often added, both generally and locally, to the general tax or to specific classes of property, for such special purposes as the maintenance of pilotage, lighthouses, courts, the watch, religious services, and the retirement of particular issues of the government paper certificates. A schedule of fees for all public offices was adopted in 1773, primarily as a regulatory measure.[76]

Tax administration lagged in effectiveness under the royal governors though numerous efforts were made to remedy its deficiencies. Assessments and collections were always incomplete; delinquencies and defaults were frequent among both taxpayers and collectors; and evasion, especially in the listing of slaves and non-resident properties, was widespread. The situation appears to have grown worse in the closing years under the impact of the growing conflict between the colony and the British government.[77]

One remaining question concerns the effectiveness of quitrent collections in Georgia. None were collected during the Trustee period and all arrears were forgiven when the Crown took over the colony. Governor Wright estimated that arrears exceeded £2,000 in 1767; nevertheless, in 1773 he listed quitrents among the chief sources of revenues in the colony. The collector of quitrents is reported also to have received a salary of £100 and fees of £71 in that year, but no statement is given of amounts of quitrents that were collected. This information, however, together with the fact that the bulk of quitrents would have been due in the older plantation region where the owners were prosperous and where a high percentage were loyal to the Crown, argues strongly that quitrents probably were paid in Georgia about as fully as rural property taxes.[78]

6. Rise of a Landed Aristocracy

The most prominent development possibly of the two decades of royal government in Georgia was the growth of an aristocracy of Crown-appointed officials, great landlords, and wealthy merchants. The members of these classes comprised a fairly homogeneous group and many belonged to all three classes. By 1773 some sixty men owned 2,500 acres or more of land; and since 2,500 acres represented a family grant of forty-nine headrights, it may be safely assumed that each of the sixty owned at least forty to forty-five slaves, or enough for the operation of one large plantation. Actually they owned nearly one hundred slaves each on the average and not a few operated several large plantations each or one or more multiple plantation units of super proportions. Governor Wright's holdings of twelve plantations probably represented the highest number under single ownership.[79] There were twenty planters who owned more than 5,000 acres each. These were the great planters. At least four of them, and possibly eight, held more than 10,000 acres each. John Graham's 27,000 and Governor Wright's 19,000 acres topped this group, with the great merchant James Habersham's 12,000 to 15,000 probably in third place. These sixty wealthiest men, together with their business associates and the members of their immediate families, owned something like 350,000 acres. Thus it appears that less than 5 per cent of the landholders had received about 20 per cent of all lands granted by the government; and they probably possessed over half of the total of Negro slaves in the province.[80] Furthermore, their landholdings constituted the bulk of the best quality and most favorably situated lands. Most of them owned both town and plantation homes, and many of their residence plantations were elaborately developed with buildings, gardens, orchards, parks, and driveways.

The condition of the other 95 per cent of proprietors was quite different. Governor Wright reported more than 1,400 plantations in 1773 with a total of actual land under cultivation of 120,000 acres.[81] From these figures and the data on large plantations, slave ownership, and numbers of slaves employed on an average-sized large plantation, certain deductions may be made regarding the size of cultivated units among the many small planters and farmers. The large plantation group probably owned between 7,000 and 8,000 slaves, of which 6,000, it may reasonably be assumed, were employed upon large plantations. Applying de Brahm's figures upon the ratios of land and slaves on large plantations would give about 140 in this group, of two hundred acres each under cultivation, and 1,260 small plantations of about seventy acres each.[82] Evidence from actual plantation data indicates that the estimated divergence between the two groups should be greater. Some of the 140 large plantations were multiple units of much greater extent than two hundred cultivated acres and the optimum size single unit was also probably considerably larger.[83] This would reduce the average acreage of the small plantations under cultivation to between fifty and sixty acres, and it is easily conceivable that the great majority were much smaller still. Population and militia data would indicate further that there were probably two thousand additional proprietors of yet smaller farms or garden plots or unimproved properties that were not included as plantation owners. In any case the overwhelmingly greater number of proprietorship operations were small.

The creation of the landed aristocracy was entirely in harmony with British imperial policy. It kept enterprising Georgians for the most part out of shipping and other occupations in which they would be likely to compete with the British; it promoted the growth of agricultural and timber exports which fitted profitably into the imperial pattern of shipping, West Indian sugar and rum, slaves, manufacturing, merchandising, banking, and insuring; and it built up a wealthy conservative group within the colony that was sympathetic toward the British ruling class. Bound to the British government by the policies that had nurtured them and the generous financial support that kept their taxes down, they became completely "obedient" to the royal will in colonial government and to the broader imperial policy of which Crown government was a part.[84]

The great body of small proprietors benefited in no such positive way from these policies; in fact, the aggrandizement of landed estates pushed them back onto the poorer and less advantageously located soils and thereby increased the degree of economic inequality. But the opening up for settlement of extensive new public domains, as a result of Governor Wright's Indian treaties, afforded most individuals some possibility of obtaining land — even though Crown favorites might secure the lion's share or the choicer tracts; and the rapid growth of population and wealth produced a leavening prosperity which moderated the feelings of social injustice. The royal government was not entirely unmindful of the position of the small proprietor, as witness its approval of efforts to stimulate diversified exports. Governor Wright was uncommonly tactful and intelligent in administration of Crown policies, and the rank and file evidenced a large measure of contentment with their lot.[85] Enforcement of the Navigation Acts, passage of the Stamp Act, and levy of the Townshend duties, which aroused the wrathful ire of the other colonists, certainly at first produced no such resentment in Georgia, and only gradually became the basis of anti-British sentiments.

7. Growth of Opposition to Imperial Policies

It would be desirable for this study, were such possible, to determine the extent to which the rising opposition in Georgia resulted from the impact of British policies within the colony rather than from the general body of colonial policies and the growing pro-American movement in the other colonies, or even from direct instigation by the other colonies. Governor Wright attributed it almost entirely to the machinations of the other colonies.[86] Actually the answer is not so simple as that. South Carolina, to be sure, was particularly active in its attempts to stir up resistance in Georgia,[87] and the friends of liberty in Massachusetts corresponded assiduously with their Congregational brethren at Midway. But the American viewpoint already was gaining ground within Georgia — partly as a consequence of immigration, among the New England puritans at Midway[88] and the North Carolinians and Virginians in upper Georgia[89] and partly as a result of the growth of the ideas of freedom that had their root in the original scheme of settlement at Savannah and Darien.[90] Significant also were the growing complaints of the Georgia merchants against British taxes and tariffs, not only because these measures reduced trade and profits, but also because they were thought to take money out of the colony, since taxes had to be paid in specie. Now most Georgians possessed a mental complex regarding money scarcity; hence, this issue supplied a common ground for uniting the merchants and other resistance groups.

Concerted opposition expressed itself first in the Commons House of the Assembly following 1765 and developed into a virtual impasse between that body and the governor during 1770 to 1773. Leadership of the opposition came primarily from the sons of weathy planters and public officials and from the younger merchants — members of the second generation of the older communities; and support came from the small farmers, small businessmen, and artisans.[91] Among the leaders this was certainly, in part at least, a resurgence of the liberal philosophy of the Trustee period;[92] while among both leaders and followers it must have been partly a reaction to the government's illiberal policy within Georgia. The traditional ideas of freedom, however, had long since shed their dependence upon organized benevolence for the positive new experiment of political democracy. It was quite natural, therefore, that this indigenous movement should merge with the rising tide of revolt in the older colonies, particularly as increasing immigrations came from the other colonies.

PART TWO

THE NEW STATE AND THE ECONOMY

CHAPTER IV

THE PUBLIC DOMAIN AND EARLY LAND POLICY

Land was the first business of Georgians for a half century after the Revolution. Not only did it constitute the leading concern of both government and private citizen, but it also exerted a predominant influence over their other activities. The situation in Georgia was in fact unique among the several states. The other original states had disposed of the greater part of their desirable public domains, excepting their western lands, during the colonial regimes; hence they removed themselves largely from the public land business by the relinquishment of their western lands to the central government. And the new states never came into possession of any considerable quantities of public lands. But Georgia at the beginning of statehood comprised, geographically speaking, chiefly a vast unsettled territory. Over 95 per cent of its area, exclusive of its western lands, was still public domain in possession of the state. Thus it was almost inevitable that land policy should become a decisive factor in the economy of the state and its people, that it should exercise a controlling influence over fiscal and all other public policies, that it should determine largely the character and progress of migration and the composition and distribution of population, and that it should mold to a marked degree the pattern of private life — the economic productivity of the individual, his social status, his political rights, his educational opportunities, and his public duties.

The public land business in Georgia was separated into two periods by a change in policy at the beginning of the nineteenth century. Therefore the main subject matter of this chapter, early land policy, relates chiefly to the last quarter of the eighteenth century. Land policy during these years was linked to the past and to war measures as well as to the struggles of a new state in the making. Traditional elements and war experiences, however, proved rather a drag than a guide. Policy developed empirically in the main, in the midst of war, political uncertainty, fiscal weakness, financial disorder, speculation, social change, and the dire necessity for establishing law and order. The problem was complicated further by the immaturity of the state and its many other pressing public and private problems, as well as by the repeated conflicts with the Indians and the central government over territorial problems. It should prove helpful to an understanding of the state's policy to present first something of an evolutionary description of the public domain. Actually the establishment of the public domain was a twofold process of defining the state's boundaries in order that its limits might be set up and of extinguishing the Indian titles so that it might be made available for alienation and settlement. Both phases involved the state in long and acrimonious controversies that influenced land policy far beyond its merely geographical features. Few developments ever projected the state government as forcefully and persistently into a commanding position in the lives of the people. They supplied a dominant issue, in one form or another, in every political campaign for fifty years.

1. Settling the Boundaries of the Public Domain

The public lands claimed by Georgia at the end of the Revolution approximated 100,000,000 acres composed of the following categories: (1) ungranted lands in old counties, probably 4,000,000; (2) the "new ceded lands," or Wilkes County, 1,500,000; (3) Cherokee-Creek cessions of 1782–1783, 4,000,000; (4) lands owned and occupied by Indian tribes, in Georgia proper, 26,000,000; (5) "western lands," owned and occupied by Indian tribes and claimed by both Georgia and Spain and sought also by the United States, 62,000,000; (6) lands lying between the Tugaloo and Keowee rivers and claimed by both Georgia and South Carolina, 450,000; (7) lands involved in other boundary disputes, negligible amounts; and (8) confiscated loyalists' properties, 200,000 (plus some 250 town dwelling and business properties, 200 vacant town lots, and a considerable quantity of slaves and other movables).[1] This summary reveals alike the far-reaching extent of Georgia's potential public domain, the wide variety of conditions attaching to it, the uncertain status of much of it, and the equally uncertain boundaries of the state itself: a clear portent of the difficulty and vexatiousness of the land problems that lay ahead.

Of the lands secured under the Indian treaties of 1733, 1739, and 1763, something less than two million acres had been patented during the colonial period.[2] The remaining two-thirds of the original public domain were mostly useless and unattractive to settlers at the time. Governor Lyman Hall and his council in 1783 described these lands as "refuse," "barren heaths and dreary wastes," that were not wanted by anyone living in the state.[3]

"The district commonly called the new ceded lands," that had been acquired from the Indians by Governor Wright in 1773 in settlement of debts owed to white traders,[4] came into possession of the whites too late to permit extensive occupation before the Revolution.[5] It was organized into Wilkes County under the Constitution of 1777, and thus was thrown open to settlement under the wartime land laws. It constituted in effect the first virgin public domain to come under effective possession of the new state government. This fact and the large quantities of rich soils in the region made Wilkes County the first important center of settlement

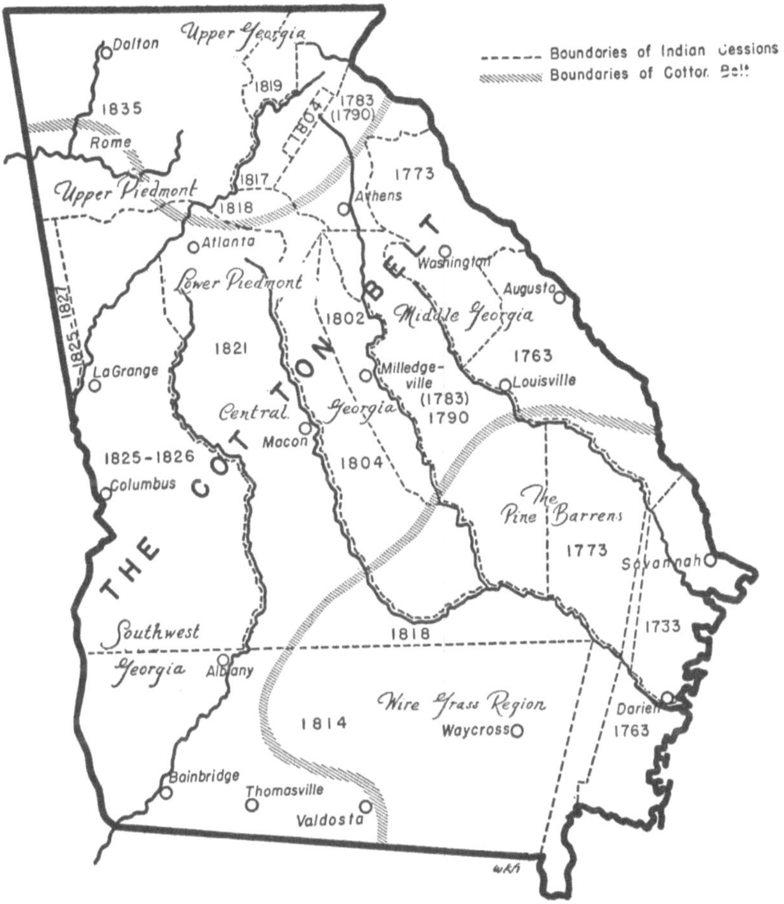

Indian Cessions and the Geographical Divisions in Georgia

of the early state period. Considerable numbers of new settlers came during the war, chiefly from North Carolina and Virginia,[6] but the flood tide of immigration was reached in the years immediately following the war. By 1790 Wilkes County contained one-third of the entire population of the state.[7]

The Cherokee and Creek cessions constituted two enormous tracts amounting together to an area almost equal to that of the whole of colonial Georgia. Both cessions grew out of indemnity claims against the Indians for wartime alliance with the Tories and British. Lying on the north and west of Wilkes County and organized in 1784 as Franklin County, the Cherokee grant contained over a million acres, and had come to the state by military and civil treaties at Augusta[8] at the close of a whirlwind campaign against these tribes in 1782. The Creek cession was effected through a treaty at Augusta in 1783 between representatives of Georgia and the leaders of friendly groups among the Creeks.[9] Another, and probably larger, body of the Creeks, led by the famous McGillivray, denounced the treaty, refused to recognize the cession, and engaged Georgia for several years in open hostilities over the matter.[10] The huge tract in dispute — 3,000,000 acres adjoining the western frontier and stretching nearly the full length of the state — was organized as Washington County in 1784 and opened immediately to settlement, even though neither its boundaries nor Georgia's rights therein had been established. Further treaties with the friendly Creeks — at Galphinton in 1785 and at Shoulderbone in 1786 — confirmed the Augusta cession, added the Tallassee territory south of the Altamaha River, and provided for running the boundary lines of the cessions.[11]

At about this juncture the central government entered the picture. The Articles of Confederation had given Congress power to regulate the trade and to manage the affairs of the Indians, "not members of any of the States." [12] With the end of British hostilities, Congress turned its attention to these matters as one of its major postwar problems, and set as its first objectives the restoration of peace with all of the Indians and the establishment of the boundaries of tribal territories.[13] It faced great difficulties, however, in the South. While considerable progress had been achieved already in the northern and middle departments, nothing had been done in the southern, and very little even was known about conditions there.[14] Furthermore, it was generally admitted that the central government was nearly estopped in the Creek-Georgia dispute since, though the Creeks were an independent tribe and not members of the state, the territory in dispute lay within the acknowledged jurisdiction of Georgia. In fact, such a touchy situation appeared likely to prevail throughout the southern department, as long as Georgia, North Carolina, and South Carolina refused to relinquish their western lands. The general government felt within its assigned powers, however, in seeking to establish effective jurisdiction over the affairs of the southern Indians; and furthermore, the alarming threats of open warfare between the Southern states and the Indians, and the evidences of growing foreign influences among the latter, urged some kind of action. Yet Congress recognized the difficulties that were involved and the need to proceed carefully. Some hope was held out that Georgia might ask Congress to intervene as arbiter of the dispute; but more reliance was placed probably upon the chance that the state would cede a sufficient quantity of its western lands "to enable the United States to contain the Indians within due bounds," and thereby to relieve the tensions. Resolutions were passed in Congress urging such a course upon Georgia, emphasizing the desirability of peace with the Creeks, and approving congressional steps designed to effect a settlement of all of the issues.[15]

The opening action of the central government was the negotiation of the Hopewell treaties, in 1785–86, with the Cherokees, Choctaws, and Chickasaws. Boundaries were defined for each of these tribal groups, and the latest Cherokee cession to Georgia was confirmed.[16] Nothing was accomplished, however, for the time being, in regard to the Creek controversy. Meanwhile, relations between the Georgians and the Creeks deteriorated steadily, and reached practically a state of war in 1787.[17] Congress resolved, that October, to negotiate treaties with all of the Southern tribes and invited the Southern states to participate jointly in the proceedings. Again Georgia was urged to cede its western lands.[18] An attempted treaty at Rock Landing, Georgia, in 1789 failed, as a result of the opposition of McGillivray and the Upper Creeks.

The establishment of the federal government in 1789 opened a new era in the administration of Indian affairs. President Washington, armed with the broadened powers over Indian affairs and foreign relations, moved firmly, if somewhat cautiously, to settle the four-cornered struggle in the South between Georgia, the Indian tribes, Spain, and the United States. The first result of his efforts was the much controverted Treaty of New York, in 1790, between the new federal government and McGillivray and twenty-three Creek Indian chiefs, by which the Creeks finally approved the land cession (Washington County) of the Augusta Treaty of 1783 in exchange for the return of the Tallassee district — ceded to Georgia by the Galphinton Treaty of 1785 —and a guarantee of ownership of all their then remaining lands to them forever.[19] The Creeks, by signing the treaty, virtually abandoned their Spanish ties and accepted, tacitly at least, the sovereignty and protection of the United States. Five years later the Treaty of San Lorenzo between the United States and Spain completed the elimination of the latter country as a factor in Southern Indian affairs and the western land issue.

The Treaty of 1790 greatly disappointed a large number of Georgians. A widespread feeling arose that the state had been unfairly dispossessed of the Tallassee country without a hearing, and there was general dismay over the guarantee of perpetual ownership of lands in Georgia to the Creeks, because it seemed to close the door to all further land cessions. Nor was the treaty entirely to the liking of the Creeks. Nevertheless, the treaty tended in time to clear the atmosphere, and border troubles declined, especially after the death of McGillivray in 1793.[20] The situation had become so accepted by 1794, that popular opinion actually rallied against the Revolutionary hero, General Elijah Clarke, and his followers in their attempted seizure of a large tract of Indian territory in central Georgia, and Governor Matthews was able to suppress this move easily with the Georgia militia, without any assistance from the federal government.[21]

Both Cherokees and Creeks continued to complain of white encroachments and injuries; consequently, the federal government agreed, at the treaties of Holston (1791) and Philadelphia (1794), to pay the Cherokees an annual sum in satisfaction of their claims against the whites. The Georgians meanwhile were becoming more determined than ever to secure further territorial cessions from the Indians within their borders. Accordingly they pressed their claims upon the central government; but the treaty arranged in consequence with the Creeks, at Colerain in 1796, gave very little material satisfaction.[22] In fact, Georgia was forced to wait until the western land cession agreement with the federal government in 1802 had laid the basis for further transfers of Indian territory. The history of succeeding Indian land cessions, therefore, falls in a later period.

Georgia's western lands had been included only by implication in the extended congressional debates which resulted at last, in 1783, in the relinquishment to the United States by Virginia and the Northern states of their rights and claims in Kentucky and the Northwest.[23] The issue was not pressed in the case of Georgia until after the Revolution, when Congress became concerned about Southern Indian affairs. Nor had Georgians hitherto given the matter any evident attention — in fact, it is doubtful if any "western territory" had become a distinct entity in their minds. Certainly there was no clear dividing line between eastern and western Georgia, and no developments, such as land company schemes or separatist movements, had occurred in west Georgia to mark it as a distinct territory. Organized Georgia itself was little more than a small pioneer settlement on the eastern border fringe of the vast land empire over which Governor Wright's administrative orders from the Crown in 1764 had established the state's sovereignty.[24] Little in fact was known even about most of the territory west of the Oconee River.

Following the Revolution, however, numerous forces both within and without Georgia, among which Indian relations probably stood foremost, operated to bring the western land issue increasingly into major considerations of public policy. Invested with independent statehood and with sovereignty over 95,000,000 acres of Indian territory stretching westward to the Mississippi, the Georgians were beginning to visualize the future possibilities of becoming a large, populous, and wealthy state.

Immediate factors alone, however, were sufficiently insistent to focus public attention upon the western lands. Land seekers were pouring into the state in an ever increasing stream; and the normal land hunger of the white man, sharpened by the lingering passions of the war and the continuing hostility of the Creeks, was fast creating a ruthless determination to remove the Indians from vast districts west of the Oconee.[25] Soldiers' bonuses, public debts, slender revenues, and currency problems supplied additional pressures. Speculators, long-practiced in their operations elsewhere and now filled with greedy anticipations by the territorial terms of the peace treaty, were beginning to invade Georgia.[26] Few state governments have ever faced more perplexing issues than this question of western lands.

The central government urged Georgia repeatedly during 1786 and 1787 to cede its western lands.[27] In 1788 Georgia responded with an offer to transfer the southern half of the territory, upon conditions that the United States could not accept.[28] The latter suggested, nevertheless, that a modified offer might prove acceptable.[29] Negotiations continued, but little headway toward a settlement was made over the next decade.

The western land issue became joined, in the 1790's, with the sharp disagreements between the state and federal governments over Creek land cessions. Georgia actually took steps both to organize counties in the territory and to sell huge sections of it to private land companies. The latter efforts culminated in the Yazoo Land Company scandals of 1796. About the middle of the decade several forces began to work toward an early solution of the problem. The successful conclusion by the federal government, in 1795, of the treaty with Spain, which defined Florida's boundaries and removed Spanish influence in Creek affairs, greatly strengthened the federal position in west Georgia.[30] Also a feeling was developing among leading Georgians that the western territories were too vast and distant for successful administration by the state and that it would be wiser to concentrate energies upon the settlement and development of the millions of acres of public domain within its more immediate borders. The willingness to pursue such a course was furthered, probably, by the somewhat embarrassing position created by the repudiation of the Yazoo land sales.

Negotiations between the two governments were accelerated notably around the turn of the century and the terms of transfer were finally completed in 1802. The United States agreed to pay Georgia $1,250,000 out of the first land sales in compensation for expenses incurred in the territory, to confirm previous land grants and to adjust certain claims within the territory, and to extinguish Indian titles to all remaining lands in Georgia as soon as it could be done peaceably and on reasonable terms.[31] Thus, Georgia exchanged the territory of the future states of

Alabama and Mississippi for the assurance of the removal of the Indians from its remaining borders and a promised financial consideration which approximated its then outstanding debt.

The land dispute with South Carolina was a revival of a long colonial quarrel between these two neighbors involving the interpretation of their respective charter grants from the Crown. Georgia was satisfied that the various issues had been settled by the rulings and ordinances of the British authorities, which had terminated with the instructions to Governor Wright in 1764.[32] South Carolina, however, as an independent state now chose to reassert its old claims. In fact, Georgia suspected even more ambitious designs. It had become deeply perturbed earlier over an official South Carolina move, during 1777 to 1779, to secure the consolidation of the two states which had been interpreted west of the Savannah as a brazen attempt at annexation.[33] This radical proposal had then been dropped by the South Carolinians; but the ensuing controversy over territory finally attracted the attention of Congress which, under the Articles of Confederation, possessed certain jurisdiction in disputes between states that could not be settled amicably by the disputants. Whereupon the central government initiated steps to resolve the matter. Under this outside pressure the two states met in convention at Beaufort, South Carolina, in 1787, and compromised their differences. Georgia gave up some 450,000 acres between the Tugaloo and Keowee rivers, and South Carolina relinquished all of its other extensive claims, which included, in addition to a large part of Georgia's western lands, all of present Georgia lying west of the St. Marys and Ocumlgee rivers and a broad strip across the northern section of the state. The treaty was ratified by Congress on July 9, 1787.[34]

Georgia's numerous other boundary disputes with its neighbors are to be noted more for their persistence and acrimoniousness than for the quantities of land that were involved. While they occurred mostly during the nineteenth century, they had their roots in the eighteenth and are closely associated with the events that we have just recounted. Conferences with North Carolina and Tennessee over location of the northern line date from this period, but dragged on for three decades before final settlement in 1818.[35] The Florida dispute was a classic one. It began with the settlement of Georgia in 1733, and involved, successively, Spain, Great Britain, Spain again, the United States, and the state of Florida. Two military campaigns at least were waged over it; harsh denunciations and uncompromising resolutions were exchanged perennially; surveys were made repeatedly; suits were carried to the United States Supreme Court; and yet the deadlock remained unbroken until after the Civil War when Georgia finally acceded to the counterclaims of Florida.[36]

With the admission of Alabama to the Union, the location of its common border with Georgia likewise came into question. Following many years of argument, an agreement was reached on the northern half of the line in 1840,[37] but dispute over the Chattahoochee River line was only resolved finally in the Supreme Court of the United States in 1859.[38]

Lastly it should be mentioned that the oldest of all of Georgia's boundary feuds was reopened by South Carolina in 1852. This concerned the respective rights of the two states to the use of the Savannah River. The Civil War ended apparently this final round of the ancient battle between the two neighbors over territorial jurisdiction.[39]

Like the other American states, Georgia confiscated the property of the Tories. This was done under two acts: the first, passed on March 1, 1778, attainted 117 persons of high treason and declared their property forfeited to the state; the second, on May 4, 1782, increased the number on the list to 279. Many of those who were thus added had only absented themselves from the state for one reason or another and later were absolved of the charge of treason.[40]

Those attainted included Governor Wright and many of the wealthiest landholders in the colony. Besides extensive tracts of the best lands, the properties included some of the most highly improved estates, large numbers of slaves, livestock, machinery, and other chattels. Much of the movable property, however, was either carried off, or consumed, or worn out, or destroyed during the war. The greater part of the lands lay in the older counties of Chatham, Richmond, Liberty, and Burke, although there were some large undeveloped tracts in the newer, recently opened regions, especially in Camden County.

Another type of action, closely associated with confiscation and administered jointly with it, was amercement of properties. Amercements were taken against many property owners, during 1782–1783, who were reputed to have been sympathetic toward the British, or less active than they might have been in the patriot cause. It amounted in effect to a capital levy of either 8 or 12 per cent — depending upon the degree of guilt attributed to the owner — of the value of the property.

It is obvious from this brief summary how many and tangled were the public issues that arose during the tortuous process of defining the extent of the public domain. Its enhancement of the role of the state has been suggested already. Of even greater weight and influence were the development and administration of public land policy, to which we shall now turn our attention.

2. Wartime Land Policy

All of the acts relating to the public domain which were passed during the Revolution were war measures primarily, intended variously to strengthen the frontier and the general defense of the state, to afford a haven for those who were driven from their homes by the enemy, to induce those who had left the state to return, to encourage the production of urgently needed goods, to punish traitors, to support the paper currency, to increase revenues, and to encourage and reward military service. Some of the objectives were partially attained, although none of the acts was administered successfully during the war. The more significant operations and results of most of the measures belong to the postwar years. The wartime land office acts were superseded by later ones, but the other wartime measures remained the fundamental laws under which large portions of the public domain were alienated during the first twenty years after the war.

The earliest land legislation pertained to soldier land bounties. On July 12, 1776, President Bullock of the Provisional Assembly issued a proclamation promising one hundred acres to all who would enter military service for three years, or until peace was declared.[41] This action preceded that of the Continental Congress by two months. The latter body offered the same bonus for enlisted men, but provided a graduated scale for commissioned officers according to rank.[42] There is no evidence that Georgia offered officers more than common soldiers at that time.

There was little military action in Georgia during the early years of the war. Yet the state was greatly worried about its isolation and defenselessness, especially on its frontiers. Consequently, on June 3, 1777 and March 1, 1778, special land bounties were offered to immigrants from other states who would settle in the interior and serve in minutemen battalions.[43] Bounties of five hundred acres were offered, in March 1779, to any who would settle in east Florida between the St. Marys and St. Johns rivers and aid the American cause, presumably in connection with the proposed Continental Army expedition against the British in Florida.[44]

As the war lengthened, Georgia, like other states and the Continental government, found it increasingly difficult to obtain enlistments for long periods of time; and in August 1778, it offered the land bounty for four-month enlistments.[45] On August 20, 1781, just four days after the reëstablishment of the state government, the assembly increased the bonus to 250 acres and added ten years of tax exemption. This was actually a militia act and as such applied to every male citizen capable of bearing arms.[46] Graduated bounties, similar to the Continental scale, also were provided for officers at this time, and were specified to be in addition to the general grant of 250 acres.[47] All rights to state bounties were over and above the United States bounties or any headright grants to which the receivers were entitled.[48] All bounty rights were also extended to "refugees." [49] Finally, an act of January 12, 1782, directed the governor to issue land bounty certificates upon presentation of certificates of service from commanding officers, and further stipulated that these claims should have priority over all others whenever a land office should be opened.[50]

One of the first measures passed by the first constitutional legislature was the general land office act of June 7, 1777. This initiated a second category of wartime land legislation. Intended to attract settlers from other states, it offered headrights of two hundred acres and fifty additional acres for each member of a family and for slaves up to ten in number. Encouragement was extended also to much needed industries: one hundred acres for each grist mill, five hundred for each sawmill, and two thousand for each iron furnace, bloomery, or bar-iron forge. The governor was directed to issue a proclamation advertising Georgia's lands and to send agents into other states to solicit immigrants.[51]

This act was amended slightly on September 16, 1777, and again on January 23, 1780, when dispossessed citizens were included under the headright privileges.[52] A considerable number of immigrants arrived in Georgia during the war, attracted by the land acts or moved by various other reasons; most of them took advantage of the land office acts.[53] Administration of these measures, however, proved exceedingly difficult and imperfect, even whenever regular government existed, which was not the case from January 1779 until August 1781. The Act of 1780, passed presumably by one of the quasi-legislative bodies of the interregnum period, was loosely constructed. Consequently, a very confused situation developed. Many warrants were issued, but never surveyed — or, if surveyed, were never recorded, or granted; titles were not passed; and most records were either removed, lost, or destroyed. Considerable numbers settled upon the public lands without benefit of warrants; and many left the state without ever fulfilling the requirements of the laws. Time limits expired, as did also the acts themselves.[54] The result was a maze of heterogeneous claims and counterclaims which presented a serious problem at the end of the war.

The third phase of wartime land legislation had to do with the properties confiscated from owners who remained loyal to the Crown. Strictly speaking, this does not belong to the general class of land legislation, since it dealt with all forms of property and necessitated special administrative procedures. Nevertheless, it bore a close relationship to both soldier bonus and headright land granting. Like the bonus, it was entirely a war measure; but it also presented an opportunity of acquiring land. In the latter respect it competed with, and produced important effects upon, general land legislation. The extensive removal or destruction of personalty and improvements of the forfeited estates further reduced this property to the status of bare land.

At the close of the Revolution, Georgia faced four problems of land policy rather than one. The most immediate, probably, was the disposal of the confiscated properties. Very urgent also, because of its bearing upon the others and on account of the returning stream of refugees and other former settlers, was the settlement of the mass of pre-war and wartime land claims. Thirdly, the land office acts having expired, the flood of immigrants pressing for admittance created an imperative necessity for a new general land office statute. Lastly, and actually already assigned priority over all of the others by law, was the matter of satisfying the bounty claims of the soldiers. Taken together, these problems presented an involved set of issues which were complicated further by the other unusual factors in the Georgia situation. Their solution was destined inevitably to have far-reaching effects upon the economic development of Georgia. The first three phases of the postwar policy will be discussed in the balance of this chapter and the history of soldier bonus grants in the following one.

3. Confiscated Property

The uses to which the state devoted the confiscated properties were both monetary and fiscal. The first act of attainder had provided that the forfeited properties should be sold for Georgia currency — part in cash and the remainder on credit — and that all receipts should be employed to sink the state debt certificates and paper currency, and to discharge the state's quota of the United States' war expenditures; and any remainder should be set aside as a fund for the future support of the state. Pending such sales, all rents and profits from the said properties were to be used to defray the current war expenses.[55] There is no record of how much property was sold under this act, but the amount was not considerable.[56] The intention to support and to sink the currency certainly failed completely. Some rents and profits (chiefly in kind) were collected and used for current war purposes. It would appear that this latter provision of the act was interpreted broadly to include the requisition or seizure of any forfeited property that could be used by the military,[57] although doubtless, these practices were prompted also by the apparent likelihood that otherwise such property would be removed by its owners or the enemy.

The emission of $100,000 of paper money, to be retired through sales of confiscated property, was authorized in January 1782.[58] Four months later the second attainder act ordered sales to begin within forty days and stipulated that payments should be made in "Mexican dollars or other monies of gold and silver"; it allowed seven years credit on realty and four on personalty, and fixed an interest rate on deferred payments of 7 per cent.[59] Both of these acts combined currency and fiscal purposes.

A large number of special legislative requisitions against the confiscated properties also were enacted during these waning months of the war. The slave property in particular was singled out for special purposes.[60] The forms of the requisitions varied: there were special issues of scrip or certificates of indebtedness to be cashed in confiscated property or out of the receipts therefrom, orders against specific items of the property, and requests upon the commissioners for special sales. The purposes served were chiefly rewards for public service and payments for urgently needed war materials. Special bounties and bonuses were awarded to various groups and individuals who participated in the final campaign against the British; some were offered even to British soldiers to induce them to desert and join the American forces. Colonel Elijah Clarke's troops were awarded one Negro to each three men, or a certificate of 20 guineas each;[61] Colonel James Jackson's dragoons were given one Negro each;[62] nine other men were voted one Negro each, to be collected in North and South Carolina whence some of this loyalist property had been moved;[63] sundry Negroes were given to "the mountain men" for aid in reducing Augusta;[64] and all officers of the Georgia line were granted certificates for 100 guineas each, payable in confiscated property.[65] Colonels Clarke and Jackson, the two outstanding Georgia officers of this campaign, were rewarded with a plantation and a house in Savannah respectively.[66] Generals Greene and Wayne were voted plantations, and certificates for 5000 and 4000 guineas were delivered to a board of trustees who then proceeded to purchase a confiscated estate for each of the popular commanders.[67] A Captain Davis was awarded one Negro, a suit of clothes, a saddle and bridle, and three hundred acres of land for discovering a conspiracy against the government.[68]

Special requisitions for regular fiscal purposes usually took the form of certificates, payable as specie for confiscated property, or redeemable out of their sales. They were issued frequently to pay the salaries and expenses of legislative and executive officers and to cover special transactions.[69] Particular parcels of property were ordered sold for specie or bills of exchange in order to meet external commitments.[70] The commissioners were instructed repeatedly to exact specie whenever possible, and to reserve from general sale any items that were likely to fetch specie.[71]

The sales of confiscated property after the war were directed almost solely toward fiscal purposes, chiefly the retirement of debt and the public support of education. However, some indirect relief for the scarcity of money was also extended in so far as the various certificates of public debt — declared redeemable in confiscated property — were employed as a medium of exchange. The general auditing act of July 18, 1783, in effect pledged the sales of the bulk of the confiscated property for the retirement of the public debt; and another act of July 18, 1783, outlined the financial procedure that was to be followed.[72] A number of special acts during 1783–1785, however, drew upon the confiscated properties for many of the current costs of the government.

Most of the confiscated property was sold from 1782 to 1785, with only some outlying tracts remaining after the latter year. However, as time passed considerable amounts reverted through the failure of purchasers to meet the terms of sale.[73] The problems of reselling and of collecting time payments (often far overdue) continued into the third decade of the next century.

After 1787 the state devoted the greater part of the remaining properties, including the ones that reverted to it, to the support of education. As early as February 14, 1786, the assembly had passed a resolution authorizing the commissioners of academies in all of the then existing counties except Camden to sell at public auction £1,000 value of confiscated or other public property for the purpose of setting up academies agreeable to the constitution and the charter of the state university.[74] There is no record that any tangible action came of this resolution, but it appears that its terms set a pattern for later action. In 1788 the assembly transferred to Chatham Academy in Savannah the rights to all income and proceeds from one of the local confiscated estates, also five thousand acres of any ungranted lands, within the county, and an additional right to purchase, without cost to the Academy, £1,000 value of confiscated property in the county.[75] The last item was the same in amount as in the previous resolution, but the procedure was altered. This right of purchase of £1,000 value of confiscated property without cost was extended to other specified academies.[76] In 1792 the right was extended to all academies within the state at the time,[77] and it was further extended repeatedly to new academies in 1802, 1810, and 1813.[78] In 1822 all remaining confiscated property in the hands of the commissioners was ordered to be distributed among the academies in such a fashion as to equalize as far as possible the results of all of the grants to the academies.[79] The total value of these grants can only be estimated. Nominally it would appear to have approached $250,000; but actually the academies almost certainly realized much less than that. The maximum sales value obtained by the state from the disposal of all of the confiscated property has been estimated elsewhere at $3,000,000.[80] This figure also is thought to exceed considerably the actual amounts realized.

The disposal of the confiscated properties involved a considerable administrative task. It partook somewhat of the character of a foreclosure and bankruptcy proceeding on an elaborate and long drawn out scale. It was necessary for the duly authorized agency of the state first to take legal possession and to make an inventory of the properties; second, to adjust all claims in favor of, or against, the properties; third, to hold, operate, or lease them pending alienation; fourth, to transfer or sell them in accordance with the terms laid down by the assembly; and, finally, to make an accounting and a financial settlement with the governor and state treasurer. Originally local county boards, or county sheriffs, were selected for this work;[81] but, in 1782, a single state-wide board was substituted, first with representation from each county, but later, in 1793, reduced to three members.[82]

If the state expected a large sum, readily collected, from the sale of these properties, it was doomed to disappointment. Much of their value was lost through wartime destruction or removal; and the costs of reassembling the movable property and conducting the sales were unexpectedly great.[83]

There was a great deal of litigation during the first postwar years, with debtors, creditors, purchasers, and former owners. Numerous properties were returned to their previous owners.[84] The assembly passed many special acts relating to the properties and made repeated demands upon the commissioners for reports.[85] Adding further to the latters' burdens was the task of collecting the levy upon the amerced properties, which involved first making a valuation of such properties. As time passed the reversions and resales of the properties of defaulting purchasers increased.

The labors of the Board of Commissioners for confiscated properties cover forty years — from 1782 until 1822. They covered not only most usual aspects of public administration, but had to cope also with currency and prices, the problems of private business, speculation, business failure, educational administration, and many other social factors. Claims involving the confiscated properties were legion and greatly entangled; the private debt structure, always resting primarily upon lands, was in chaos; the rehabilitation of coastal agriculture, a crucial factor in the value and saleability of the confiscated properties, was a costly and uncertain process and the cause of increasing numbers of defaults and reversions.

The significance of the characteristics and operations of this administrative board, or commission, has scarcely been realized. It was one of the first of a very numerous species in the public business of early Georgia. There developed many such — in other phases of public land administration, in the organization and operation of local government, in the administration of public markets and port facilities, in public education, in roads, and in other internal improvements. Generally speaking, they were public in nature, sometimes quasi-public, and in some instances private, but clothed with public functions. Altogether they embraced a large and an important body of the public business. They are also important functionally in an evolutionary respect as the forerunners of the later day administrative commission and department, and likewise for their influence upon the growth of the corporation. Their operations will be noted frequently in later chapters and will be presented in some detail in Chapter XIII.

4. The Headright System

The so-called headright system remained the basic form of land-granting in Georgia until 1802. It had its origins in the period of Crown government, although it had been known then as the family-right system. The system adhered consistently to certain rudimentary elements of *laissez faire,* such as characterized generally the development of American land policy, especially in the South. These were the ideas of free access to landed-proprietorship enterprise, free competition, and freedom of contract — a policy of first come first served. At all points in the history of the system strong clashes of economic interests arose, notably between tidewater and interior and between large planters and small farmers. More significant, however were the divergent postulates of policy which the operations of the system evoked: these concerned the nature and aims of free enterprise, and how best they might be secured and maintained. The ultimate outcome of this struggle was the abandonment of the headright system at the beginning of the nineteenth century.

The legal history of the system in Georgia after statehood is summarized in Table 1. It divides into three periods: 1775–1782, which marked the transition from colonial to state legislation and the inclusion of certain war aims; 1783–1785, which produced the final formulation of the basic pattern of the system; and 1786–1801, which witnessed only occasional and minor alterations.

Revolutionary egalitarianism in Georgia is reflected in the changes introduced into land policy in the first land office act, June 7, 1777. The headright — that is, the amount that any free white person or head of a family might receive — was doubled, from one hundred to two hundred acres; whereas the right of fifty additional acres for each slave was limited to ten slaves. Thus the amount which a man of small means might obtain was greatly increased, while the rich planter's rights to public lands were drastically curtailed. The rights of other members of a family were left unchanged. The perpetual quitrent was reduced to one year. Another significant change removed the issue of land warrants and surveying from the control of the governor's office and lodged them with local county officers. There were no changes in other administrative procedures or in administrative fees.[86] The amending act of September 1777, and the general act of 1780 reflect almost entirely the war difficulties and urgencies.[87]

Land office legislation quickly became the foremost issue in the assembly which had gathered and had elected Lyman Hall as governor on January 7, 1783. The war acts had lapsed, but had left a troublesome progeny of land claims and counterclaims; the bounty promises to the soldiers had to be fulfilled; the "new ceded" lands of Wilkes County, the recent military cession from the Cherokees, and the anticipated one from the Creeks beckoned irresistibly to the land hungry, thousands of whom outside of Georgia were already clamoring for admission; and speculators were appearing from far and near.[88]

Violent disputes over policy arose at once. The most controverted issues, probably, were free land, central *vs.* local control over administration of policy, and the proper treatment of veterans. Other lively questions were the reduction of administrative fees, limitation of sizes of grants, treatment of squatters, conditions of settlement, and proper safeguards against speculation.[89] The division of opinion was primarily a regional one, although it also reflected, at the time, the antagonism between large planter and small farmer interests. The leaders from the older, coastal communities opposed free land, reduction in fees, liberalization of the conditions of settlement, and any relaxation that might unduly encourage speculation. They advocated centralized control, severe treatment of squatters, and a moderate policy on soldiers' bounties. The representatives from the newer, upstate counties took the opposite side on most of these questions.[90]

The views of the downstate leaders were voiced in part by Governor Hall and his council in an advisory statement on the proposed land act as follows: land policy involved the disposal of "those great and invaluable sources of wealth" of the state, and should be administered therefor by the representatives of all the people "for the general welfare," and not according to the "pleasure of justices of one county"; through the local option method, urged by the younger counties, "the inhabitants of all easternmost and southernmost counties" would be "denied voice in the most consequently great and important concerns of the state"; the entire control of administration of policy should be centered in the governor and council, who represent all of the people of the state, or in a special court which should be composed of one member from each county, or in a combination of the latter and the governor and the council; such centralization would greatly reduce costs and would assure a much to be

Table 1

THE HEADRIGHT SYSTEM IN GEORGIA

Date of act	Eligibility	Number of acres	Charges		Conditions of settlement	Administration
			Price	Administrative fees		
June 7, 1777	Citizen of state; 6 months time limit on old warrants.	Headright, 200; members of family, 50 each; slaves, up to 10 in number, 50 each.	45¢ rent per 100 acres for one year.	Warrant, 85¢; survey, $3.45 plus 50¢ per 100 acres; grant, for 500 acres or under, $6.75; above 500 acres, $10.25; title, $3.00.	Must settle and cultivate within 6 months after grant; and occupy 5 years before passage of title.	Warrants to be issued by county JJ.P. courts; location and plat to be made by county surveyor; plat to be recorded by surveyor general; grant to be issued by governor and council; title to be passed and recorded by county sheriff.
September 16, 1777	Time limits on old warrants repealed.	same	same	same	same	Procedure defined more carefully.
January 23, 1780	Citizens of Georgia dispossessed by British included.	Limit on number of slaves removed.	same	same	Must bring entire family, take loyalty oath and give security to settle within 9 months.	same
February 17, 1783	Citizen of any state, if never exercised headright.	Total grant limited to 1,000 acres.	Headright free; above 200, sliding scale, 25¢ to $1 per 100 acres.	same	Must settle and cultivate for 12 months, and improve 3 acres per 100, before grant is made.	same
August 1, 1783	Old warrants extended 1 year; thereafter null and void.	No limits to amount of grants on old warrants.	Public debt certificates received as specie for one year.	same	Requirements of Act of Feb. 17, 1783 repealed.	Warrants issued and land cases tried by Board of county JJ.P., not less than five, holding court monthly.
February 15, 1784 (Applied only to Franklin and Washington counties)	Citizen of any state.	Total grant limited to 1,000 acres.	65¢ per 100 acres; ½ in 2 years, balance in 3 years, if bond given. Tax exemption for 3 years.	same	12 months limit on warrants; in order to receive tax exemption, must occupy land 12 months and cultivate 3 acres per 100 within 18 months; otherwise, no residence required.	Warrants may be issued either by governor and council or by 1 asst. judge and 2 JJ.P. of any county where applicant resides; Special Land Court — governor or president and 3 members of council — at Augusta, to make grants and hear caveats for 3 months.

February 22, 1785	All previous warrants renewed for 6 months.	No limit.	Free up to 1,000 acres; above 1,000, provisions of acts of Feb. 17 and Aug. 1, 1783 apply.	same	Warrants for use of self and family only; must give oath that have received no previous headright grant; must settle and cultivate 3 acres per 100 within 18 months.	Warrants to be issued and land disputes settled by a county court composed of 1 asst. judge of sup. ct. and 2 JJ.P.
February 13, 1786	Two-year time limit on warrants.	same	same	same	same	same
December 23, 1789	same	same	same	same	same	Any 3 JJ.P. may issue warrants; governor replaces governor and council in making grants.
December 9, 1790	same	same	same	same	same	County surveyors elected by JJ.P. in each county.
December 18, 1792	same	same	same	Warrants, 30¢; surveys, base charges of $5 for 500 and under, $5.85 for 501 to 1,000, $7.40 for over 1,000; plus 50¢ per 100 acres; grants, $5, $7.25 and $9 for 0–500, 501–1,000, and over 1,000 respectively; title, $3.	same	same
December 25, 1794	same	same	same	same	same	Action to prevent survey frauds.
January 2, 1798	same	same	same	same	same	Required processioning of boundaries every 10 years.
December 4, 1799	same	same	same	same	same	Popular election of all county officers.

desired uniformity of practice; and finally, squatters, either on public land or on Indian territory, and all those who provoke the Indians by robbery and outrage should be prosecuted "to the utmost rigors of the law." [91] The land laws, thought Governor Hall, "ought to be framed on wisest principles, to guard against monopoly, to encourage population, and also to secure the future resources of the state. In this last view, it is our opportunity, which, if once neglected, will be irretrievably lost forever." [92]

Upstate leaders emphasized the need for encouraging settlement, the poverty of the state's propertyless classes and of many of the immigrants, the superior advantages enjoyed by the wealthy landholders of the older counties and the danger that a centralized administration might be controlled by this class in the old counties. They admitted the errors, and even the frauds, committed by local courts and surveyors, and also the universal encroachments of frontier settlers, and even county officials, upon the lands of the Indians. While they acquiesced in measures designed to prevent and punish violations of laws and treaties, nevertheless they openly condoned such practices. If the potential small landowner, they argued, should wait upon the completion of treaty formalities and the slow-grinding operations of centralized administration, he was most likely to find himself circumvented by the wealthy planter, the ubiquitous speculator, and the favored insider; the complaints about the injustices of local option were not only groundless, they were a subterfuge; the doctrine of "home folks" priority was both a sound and laudable principle of social ethics.[93] Their strongest argument, unquestionably, was the unspoken, but highly realistic, one embodied in the steadily rising tide of migration into upper Georgia.

Constructive social policy was mixed with economic interest in both attitudes. The homestead tradition, for example, was strong in both regions, but in each it was interpreted and adapted according to the traditions and particular conditions prevailing within the respective region. General James Jackson, already a prominent member of the tidewater group, was the leading advocate and defender of the principle of settlement by small proprietorship. He maintained that the establishment of such a policy had been the chief purpose of the Revolution, and that it would ever remain the primary safeguard of democratic government. There can be little question that several upstate leaders held similar views.

The coastal landowners feared policies that might depress land values and, consequently, viewed with considerable apprehension any that sought to throw open the rich interior lands to easy settlement. They were afraid of a speculative boom that could decrease the values of their lands, and of competition that might lower the values of their products.

Furthermore, their primary interest in additional lands centered in the sale of the confiscated properties. Since property in the older regions bore the brunt of taxation, its owners naturally favored a policy of land alienation that would yield revenue. For similar reasons they supported a policy that would minimize the pressure against the Indians in order to avoid the heavy public expense resulting from disorders on the frontier.

The Savannah merchants were conscious of an interest in the growth of bona fide settlement and production. Most of them, however, were large landowners as well as merchants and their first interest in both capacities centered in reëstablishment of the productivity of the older agricultural areas. Their interests in the Indian trade also influenced them to favor policies that were likely to maintain peace on the frontier.[94]

The inhabitants of the interior at this time were characteristically poor; few owned any slaves, or more than one or two; and conditions of life were hard. The rapid spread of the Baptist and Methodist faiths among them, as a result of the vigorous activities of the itinerant preachers, had done much to inculcate the simple virtues, as well as an egalitarian concept of democracy.[95] They were apt to think that the downstate region was dominated by wealthy landlords, intent upon passing laws favorable to their own interests. There were those among them, of course, who likewise harbored ambitions for land aggrandizement, and some of their leaders were notorious land grabbers.[96] Speculators were active in all regions.

The first peacetime land office measure was debated at great length in the assembly. Each provision was contested hotly and all of the votes were close, since the opposing sides were numerically almost equal.[97] The older counties defeated free land,[98] the reduction of fees, and all attempts to liberalize the conditions of settlement. They also obtained a vigorous section on squatters, but they lost the fight over centralization of administration and on the soldier bounty issue.[99] The battle, however, was not over. Six months later the upstate forces secured amendments that removed the acreage limits on old warrants, that made certificates of public debt receivable as specie in land purchases for one year, and that eliminated the requirement of one year of residence and cultivation before the issue of the grant; on the other hand, an attempt was made to tighten up the local process of warrant issue.[100]

The struggle was renewed in the following year over the question of organizing the vast new land cessions from the Cherokees and Creeks. The results of this round might be termed a draw. It was provided that the Cherokee grant be organized as Franklin County and the disputed Creek session as Washington County, even though the validity of the latter cession was not recognized either by a large group of the Creeks or by the United States. Free land was again defeated, as well as a move by the upstate group to organize the territories into more than two counties. An element of centralized control was introduced for the time being — warrants for land in the new counties might be issued by either the governor and council or the justices' court of the county in which an applicant happened to reside, there being as yet no organized courts in Franklin and Washington counties — and provision was made for a temporary central land court at Augusta to handle the warrants for soldiers. A large tract was reserved specifically for the location of the soldiers' warrants; three years tax exemption was to be allowed if the grantee should settle upon and cultivate a part of the land for twelve months, but the conditions of settlement were not required, apparently, if tax exemption were not sought.[101]

The final pattern of the headright system, except for minor changes, emerged in the general act of 1785, which combined the substance of the previous general legislation with the provisions of the special act governing in Franklin and Washington counties, and inaugurated free land grants up to one thousand acres. Full local option over land warrants was reëstablished, though the composition of the local land court was changed to one assistant judge of the superior court and two justices of the peace.[102] Thus the rapidly growing upstate forces won at last on practically every point of policy.

Land legislation after 1785 dealt mostly with administrative changes or related matters. More than half of these changes resulted from alterations in other laws. For example, the governor became the sole granting officer as a result of a new constitution in 1789 which abolished the council; the county surveyor became still less responsible to central control by virtue of an act of December 9, 1790, that provided for the election of the five principal county officers by ballot of the county justices of the peace; on February 22, 1796, these county officers became elective by local popular vote and, on December 4, 1799, all county officers became elective by popular vote. In somewhat similar fashion, the bases for assessing land office fees were altered by a general act of December 18, 1792, pertaining to all fees of public officers. With respect to the land fees, it should be noted that no particular changes were made in their amount; the long and persistent movement to secure their reduction failed to attain its objective during this period.[103]

Some further description of administrative organization and procedure appears necessary in order to complete the picture of the headright system. The chief administrative bodies were: the county justices of the peace court, the county surveyor and assistants, the surveyor-general, the governor and council (until the council was abolished in 1789), and the county sheriff.

The justices of the peace served as both a land office and a court: they issued the land warrants and also tried caveats and interpreted the terms of the acts. Governor Houstoun, in an interpretation of the land laws in 1784, expressed the opinion that the effective operation of the land policy rested almost entirely with the county courts. All attempts to give the governor and council appellate jurisdiction over these local courts in land matters were defeated.[104] The superior courts, to be sure, possessed appellate jurisdiction over certain phases of the proceedings; but it was not until 1789 that an effective superior court system was established, and even then the districts were organized on regional lines.[105] The defects of the local land court were well recognized and numerous reform measures aimed at their removal were adopted, but supporters of local administration were always able to prevent its abolition.

The county surveyor was elected by the legislature prior to 1792 when the act of December 9, 1790, placing his election in the hands of the local justices of the peace, went into effect. Five years later he became elective by popular vote. He chose his own assistants. This unit likewise enjoyed a high degree of local option, which was limited only by its interpretations of the provisions of the land laws and the consciences of the individuals who composed the group. They surveyed and made a plat of the amount of land specified in each warrant.

The surveyor-general received and filed a copy of each plat. He exercised a nominal supervision over the county surveyors; but actually was little more than a recorder.

The governor and council, and after 1789 the governor alone, made the grant of the land upon the presentation of evidences of compliance with all of the above requirements. In reality even this official act of the chief executive officer was pretty much a rubber-stamping procedure, though one that was fraught with innumerable headaches because of the laxity and numerous errors of the land courts, the frequently conflicting and sometimes illegal surveys, and the innumerable conflicts among claimants. Through occasional insistence upon more adequate information from the land courts and more careful work on the part of the surveyors, the state executive department may have exerted some measure of indirect control over the operations of the headright system. Whether it was able to detect instances of illegality, except in flagrant cases, is doubtful. Even then it may be questioned whether the laws gave it authority to withhold the grant. It was certainly obligated, however, to call the attention of the legislature to observed cases of fraud and non-compliance. Such was done repeatedly during the early postwar administrations, but seldom during the decade of 1786–1795. From 1796 until 1800 the state was in the throes of a revolution in land policy that was destined to change administration entirely.

Under the headright system and the military bounty grants, to be discussed in the next chapter, all counties east of the Oconee and Altamaha rivers and the two coastal counties of Glynn and Camden were settled. Virtually all desirable lands in this area had been granted by 1800. Settlement proceeded rapidly, population more than tripling between 1783 and 1790 and doubling during the next decade.[106]

CHAPTER V

SOLDIERS AND SPECULATORS

The importance of the war veteran in the history of land distribution in Georgia can scarcely be overemphasized. He exercised a preponderant influence upon land policy determination and was its chief beneficiary for a decade or more following the Revolution.

1. Revolutionary Land Bounties

Practically every male citizen of Georgia qualified for military land bounty under one or more of the Revolutionary wartime acts. And likewise anyone from Virginia, North and South Carolina, or any other state who had served in the Georgia line during 1776–1777 was eligible for Georgia land bounties.[1] Veterans of the Georgia line were permitted also to take their United States bounties in Georgia, a privilege apparently extended to the Continental soldiers of other states who settled in Georgia.[2] Great numbers of the latter, who had become familiar with the opportunities in Georgia during the southern campaigns, came to take up land under the generous headright laws of the state.[3]

A legislative directive of January 12, 1782, required the governor to attend to soldier bounty claims before all other land business.[4] Actually, however, the veterans' rush for their bonus grants did not get under way fully until 1784, after the opening of Franklin and Washington counties. The state possessed little desirable land to offer the veterans until after the war indemnity cessions were made by the Cherokees and Creeks in 1783. The promptness with which these lands were organized into the two new counties, despite the fact that the Creek cession was still in dispute, reflects the strong pressure exerted by the soldier bounty issue. A large tract in the new counties was reserved specifically for the location of bounty warrants. Veterans were not required to accept lands within this reserve, but if they elected to take their lands within the new counties they must do so.[5]

The land bounty was distributed under the regular machinery of the headright system. The ex-soldier first was required to present a certificate of service from his commanding officer to either the governor or a local court for a land bounty certificate, which entitled him to secure his land in the usual fashion. However, his bounty grant was exempt from all of the conditions of the headright laws except the payment of the regular office fees. One special, temporary administrative arrangement was provided, however: since there were no local courts as yet in the new counties, and also because of the pressure for quick action, a special land court — composed of the governor, or the president of the executive council, and three or more other members of the council — was established at Augusta for three months for the purposes of issuing land warrants and grants and of adjusting contested claims.[6] Regular local courts were established in both counties early in 1785 which thereupon took over supervision of the land business.[7]

Table 2

REVOLUTIONARY BOUNTIES GRANTED BY GEORGIA

Rank	Continental Line: combined Georgia and U.S. bounties (acres)	Naval forces: Resolution of Feb. 17, 1783 (acres)	Minute battalions: Act of 1778 (acres)	Refugees: Resolution of Aug. 19, 1781 (acres)
Major General	2,200	—	—	—
Brig. General	1,700	—	—	1,000
Colonel	1,000	—	800	900
Commodore	—	1,000	—	—
Lieut. Colonel	900	—	700	800
Major	800	—	600	650
Aides-de-Camp	—	—	—	750
Adjutant	—	—	300	650
Chaplain	—	—	—	650
Captain	600	600	500	500
Surgeon's Mate	—	600	—	—
D.G. Advocate	600	—	—	—
Commissary	—	—	500	—
Lieutenant	400	400	400	350
Private	200	200	250	250

(A resolution of August 20, 1781 made a further bounty grant of 250 acres to each citizen as a war measure to induce settlement from other states.)

Table 2 [8] summarizes the provisions of all the various state and continental soldier bounty acts and resolutions that governed the granting of land bounties in Georgia. One feature, however, is not shown in the table. An act of February 25, 1784, commuted the ten-year tax exemption feature of the act of August 20, 1781, to fifteen acres per hundred acres of bounty grant.[9] This was added to all types of bounties as they appear in the table. It should be noted, also, that officers' bounties included the ordinary soldiers', or the citizens', bounty in addition to that allowed for the respective ranks.

The chief business of the Augusta land court, as no doubt had been anticipated, turned out to be the handling of the soldiers' claims. A tremendous rush developed, which very nearly overwhelmed the court. Under this pressure the president of the court devised a lottery system, which probably was the first use made of this device that later was to become a principal feature of the reformed Georgia land-grant system.[10] Approximately 200,000 acres were granted on bounty claims during 1784, of which 170,000 acres lay in upper Washington County — in what is now Greene and Oconee counties — and nearly all of the balance was located in Wilkes and Franklin counties.[11] Ultimately the amount greatly exceeded this figure.

It appears impossible to ascertain exactly how many became eligible for the state's military bounties, owing to the generality of some of the laws and to the lack of complete citizenship records. Some 2,500 veterans were certified for Georgia service bounties of one sort or another and it seems probable that between 1,700 and 2,000 actually received bounty grants. The total of such grants, inclusive of the United States bounties, amounted to something like 750,000 acres.[12] How much land was given, in satisfaction of United States bounty rights, to the veterans of other states who came to Georgia, is difficult to determine. Present evidence indicates that such immigrants numbered nearly seven thousand; although a considerable number did not arrive until after the bounty lands had been distributed.[13] Furthermore, the total amount given to this group must not have been large, as compared to that granted to Georgia's own veterans, since the United States bounties were less generous than Georgia's and only veterans who had served in the continental line were eligible.

In estimating the significance of the veteran's position in land distribution, account must be taken also of what he received under the headright laws. All bounties were given in addition to headright grants, and so all veterans who had not exercised the latter privileges were entitled to do so. The total amount of land granted to ex-soldiers under the headright laws must have exceeded by far the amount of the war bounties, possibly by three or four times. It seems likely, therefore, that the greater portion of the desirable lands that were distributed by Georgia during the years between the Revolution and 1800 was granted to Revolutionary soldiers under the various bounty and headright laws.

2. Creek War Bounties

Revolutionary bounties did not constitute an end of veterans' land bonuses or of their influence upon land policies; and, but for the increase of federal control in Indian affairs after 1789, they might have proved to be only a prelude. Tension between the Creeks and Georgians reached the breaking point in 1787. On the last day of that October the assembly authorized the enlistment of three thousand men, of whom half, or two regiments, were "to serve until peace (should be) established" and the other half were to be retained as volunteers in reserve. It approved also the enlistment of 1,500 Tennesseans from Sevier's "State of Franklin." This latter action resulted from a tentative plan for joint action between Georgia and Tennessee troops against the Upper Creeks. All of the troops were promised land bounties for enlistment, which were to be located *within the territories then belonging to the Creek Indians,* but which presumably should be acquired through a successful termination of the conflict. A large tract in central Georgia was reserved specifically for the Georgia troop and grants in the "Big Bent" of the Tennessee River were promised to the Tennesseans. The following scale of bounties was established: major general, 1,500 acres, brigadier general, 1,400, adjutant, 1,200, colonel, 1,200, lieutenant-colonel, 1,100, aides-de-camp, 1,000 to 1,100, major, 1,000, captain, 900, first lieutenant, 800, second lieutenant, 750, non-commissioned officer, 700, private, 640, and staff officers 250 additional for extra services. The "Franklin" troops were to be allowed additional land in lieu of rations and other claims at the rate of one-half the amounts of their bounties. The total commitment of the state in land bounties under this act amounted to approximately 1,800,000 acres or nearly three times the amount granted to all the Revolutionary soldiers.[14]

The projected joint operation did not materialize; and it appears that the state experienced considerable difficulty in recruiting even one full regiment of 750 men — it was compelled to offer additional bonuses in clothing and various other articles;[15] though no doubt the actual number of troops required were considerably reduced by the failure of the plan for the joint campaign with Sevier's group. One regiment apparently saw active service and was given bounty certificates when mustered out. The amount of such claims were reported later to have totaled 406,070 acres.[16] Since these represented promises of land within Creek territory, they were in effect voided by the Treaty of New York of 1790. Needless to say, this result greatly increased the ire and outcry of the Georgians over the treaty. No doubt it encouraged General Elijah Clarke and his followers in their seizure of Indian territory in 1794.

While repudiating Clarke's extra-legal action, the state pressed immediately for further land cessions in order to fulfill its bonus pledges and to satisfy the mounting land hunger. It directed its congressmen to seek another treaty between the general government and the Indians; and it even went so far as to provide in advance for the organization of a large area of the Creek territory into six districts, with administrative machinery, land offices, and details for the settlement of the Creek War bounty claims — all to go into effect whenever the federal government should secure the extinguishment of the Indian titles.[17] The United States acceded to Georgia's wishes by authorizing another treaty conference with the Indians. The state, "anxious to further it to the utmost of her power," appropriated a considerable sum of money and appointed three commissioners to be present at the conference.[18] Hopes ran high; but the Treaty of Colerain which followed in 1796 gave the state very little. It was still without lands with which to settle the soldiers' claims.

There were increasing evidences after 1796 that the soldier bounty issue was losing some of its force in shaping land policy. At any rate, the exposure of the Yazoo land frauds in that year was destined to change completely the course of land policy in Georgia. In 1799 the Creek War bounty warrants were recognized officially as a part of the public debt and were made exchangeable for debt certificates at the rate of 34¼ cents an acre.[19] By 1804, warrants for 384,870 acres had been exchanged for certificates, leaving 21,200 acres of claims outstanding,[20] some of which were presented in later years.[21] The certificates were made exchangeable at a set rate, in 1806, for land in the fractional surveys that remained in the government's hands under the lottery acts.[22] This law had the effect of converting the debt claims back into land bounty claims. Two years later, however, the governor was authorized to redeem all debt certificates, up to $55,000 in any one year, from any money in the treasury arising from the sale of fractional surveys.[23] Thus Georgia's final batch of soldier land bounty promises became redeemable in either land or cash. This did not end the benefactions extended to those who served in the military establishment, however, for the veterans of all wars were awarded extra chances in practically all of the state land drawings of the nineteenth century.[24]

3. Speculation

Speculation, a loosely used term in Georgia, was applied generally to any land acquisition that did not contemplate immediate settlement or use. It was frequently employed interchangeably with engrossing and monopolizing or even simply with large-scale operations. The extensive acquisitions of the planters and merchants in particular were commonly called speculations. It was a fact that planters generally acquired land holdings in excess of immediate needs; but these practices usually were related to long-range investments in new plantations or to the necessity of replacement of worn-out lands. They resulted directly from the technology of large-scale planting, or from the natural increase of slave labor, or from the ambitions of owners to expand both the size and number of plantations. Of course there was often an element of speculation in these operations, especially during boom times; and some planters engaged in outright land speculation on the side.

Merchants frequently came into possession of extensive tracts through recovery of debts. Many were also planters and/or lumber and naval stores producers; consequently, they were interested in acquiring considerable tracts of land for such operations. Eventually a small number of planters and merchants became involved in large speculative land projects, but, by and large, members of these classes were not professional land speculators.

The professional speculator did not make an appearance in Georgia until after the Revolution. Even then at first he was not a very numerous type or of significant influence. He first became an important factor around 1787; and then during the following eight years he enacted a lurid role, not only in the arts of large-scale land-grabbing but also in graft, bribery, political malfeasance, and fraud. His activities eventuated in two great scandals, the pine barrens frauds and the Yazoo land companies sales. The former passed unnoticed at the time; but the latter produced a revolution in land policy.

Many factors invited and abetted land speculation, chief among which were the large public debt, the depreciated currency, the transferability of bounty and headright warrants, the rising tide of immigration, the loosening of requirements respecting land granting, and the local administration of the land laws. The inchoate state of government and the rapid multiplication of population from outside the state, with the consequent frequent changes in public leadership and personnel, further favored speculative designs and operations. The destruction by the Revolution of the conservative party and its institutions, while it had resulted in the breakup of some large landholdings, had also removed a restraining influence.[25]

Sporadic evidences of speculation appeared shortly after the first land and soldier bounty acts of 1777; but these may have been associated with the desire to convert rapidly depreciating currency and bounty certificates into land as a more permanent and solid fund of value.[26] Joseph Clay stated that it was his opinion that a number had purchased confiscated properties during 1782 on the speculation of a new issue of paper money and its probable subsequent depreciation.[27] Clay also reports that a few soldiers of fortune of unknown backgrounds were appearing in Georgia — men like the notorious Major Washington (nee Walsh) who possessed little resources or credit and who operated on their wits by taking advantage of the confusion of the times.[28] A warning note is sounded in July 1783 in an order to county courts to scrutinize carefully all land claims for erecting mills lest these inducements to industry become the medium of "engrossing valuable lands." [29]

The fear of the spread of speculation was an important element behind the cautious attitude of Governor Lyman Hall and his supporters and their fight for centralized administration of the land laws. Irregularities appeared in Wilkes County soon after the opening of the land office there in 1783.[30] Governor Houstoun and the executive council reported fraudulent surveys in Franklin and Washington the following year, and stated that they were not only powerless to prevent them, but were equally unable to deny grants of land based upon such, owing to recent changes in the laws.[31] Not all such infractions were associated with speculators' activities, but they indicate a fertile field for such operations, and actually afford an early insight into the later *modus operandi* of the speculative clique. The way was also considerably smoothed by the growing general practice of acquiring and holding land for higher prices. There was a distinct land boom on and everyone was indulging more or less.[32]

Official reports of local land office irregularities and speculations are silent after 1785, but the records of land grants show that the activities of a small group of land-grabbers or speculators were increasing steadily. During his first term, Governor George Matthews, in 1787, granted to individuals amounts totaling variously 13,700, 14,300, 15,600, 15,800, 20,000, 21,000, 32,000, and 50,000 acres.[33] Several of these grantees already had accumulated extensive holdings during the preceding years.[34] In Governor George Handy's term, in the following year, grants included individual items of 8,300, 9,045, 9,050, 10,000, 10,362, 11,800, 20,500, and 50,675 acres.[35] The median large grant had declined, to be sure, but most of the grantees again were repeaters, and the highest one was also the top one of the preceding year.

Some twenty names recur repeatedly in the land grant records of the years 1784–1788. Besides professional speculators and their agents, the list includes politicians, merchants, planters, army officers, and, conspicuously, county surveyors. Some of the latter may have been, even at this time, professional speculators or their agents. The large individual holdings amassed during this five-year period ranged from 25,000 to 125,000 acres. It would appear, from the descriptions of many individual grants, that the purchase of soldier bounty warrants and the old unlimited headright warrants of the Revolutionary years had played an important part in these land accumulations.[36] Artifice and illegality do not seem to have been among the more significant factors, although the size of some of the grants during 1787 and 1788 suggest otherwise, as also do some of the current public advertisements.[37]

4. The "Pine Barrens" Scandal

The heyday of the speculator began, however, in 1789 in Governor George Walton's term; it extended through the succeeding administrations of Edward Telfair, 1790–1793, George Matthews, 1794–1795, and Jared Irwin, 1796–1797; and it was highlighted by an infamous blue-sky swindle, that has come to be known as the "pine barrens" frauds, and by the sensational transactions with the western land companies.[38]

The "pine barrens" frauds constitute one of the largest blue-sky operations in American history. By means of fraudulent surveys, vast tracts of fictitious lands were conveyed to a small number of men who were bent, apparently, upon peddling this non-existent property to buyers in the northeastern states. The counterfeit transactions reached their peak during Governor Matthew's second term when, in 1794 alone, no less than thirteen million acres of bogus lands were granted. One individual was granted a million and a half and another a million and a quarter acres. Both were official county surveyors! And they made the "surveys" for each other, or directly for themselves! Eighteen other persons received varying amounts ranging from a quarter to one-half million acres. And there were yet others who received in excess of one hundred thousand acres.[39] Most of the leading grantees in this speculative orgy were newcomers; the familiar names of previous years do reappear, but their grants were relatively modest ones and probably represented actual land.

These frauds received their label from the fact that the greater number of the more flagrant ones were committed in the new county of Montgomery, which had been created out of the southern half of Washington County, and which contained little other than pine barrens and wire grass wastes — almost worthless lands at the time. The spurious Montgomery County surveys, nevertheless, described the supposedly real tracts as being high quality lands of the sort that were eagerly sought for plantation culture. Fraudulent grants, however, were not limited to Montgomery County; they were common and very extensive in Camden, Effingham, Franklin, Glynn, Liberty, and Washington. Altogether, land grants during these years exceeded the total area of all the organized counties of the state by more than twenty million acres.[40]

This astounding episode of frenzied speculation, political graft, law violation, and abject fraud brings to mind a number of questions, of which few probably can ever be answered satisfactorily. What effects did the frauds have upon the state's land policy? The usual excesses of normal land booms can be explained; but this bizarre phenomenon presents something of a puzzle.

The effects of these frauds upon the operations of the headright system and actual settlement could have been only negligible. They were merely *projected* blue-sky promotions for the most part and they barely touched the life of Georgia. Their significance in land speculation has been exaggerated; they were almost purely paper transactions. They reflected a looseness in administration of the land laws, but they did not cause it. This looseness unquestionably permitted a great deal of speculation in actual lands, mostly in the years prior to the fraudulent grants. And some of this speculation in real lands also was in "pine barrens" sections.

The speculative excesses, of which the "pine barrens" frauds were doubtless a part, probably did reflect, or at least did portend, a changing tone of economic life, a New South, that was destined to take on a more commercial, pecuniary, wealth-seeking and dynamic character than had been typical of the older regions. The first display of this new acquisitive behavior came in upper Georgia, from whence it was destined to spread across the state and on into the Southwest.[41] The older section continued, at least for some time yet, to incline more toward its previous ways.

5. Western Lands

The end of the Revolution soon found the American land speculator pushing his trade from Ohio and Kentucky into Tennessee and on into the inviting but hotly contested region of west Georgia.[42] Hitherto that region's remoteness from Anglo-American settlements, its occupancy by powerful and turbulent and often unfriendly Indian tribes, and its involvement in the territorial claims and military operations of the French and Spanish had deterred for the most part private land ventures therein. However, with the conclusion of the Treaty of Paris awarding the United States all of the southwestern territory to the thirty-first parallel on the south and the Mississippi River on the west, the southwestward surge of American settlement was on. Land speculators from every state, from east and west — seasoned veterans and novitiate adventurers alike — were quick to grasp at the possibilities of fortune in west Georgia.

Preoccupation with land speculators, foreign intrigues, and the broader sectional and national issues, however, has tended to obscure some of the more significant features of Georgia's part in the multi-sided struggle over this region. Primary motives often have been lost sight of. First of all, of course, the state was anxious to secure recognition of its title to the region, which colonial statutes and ordinances, confederation agreements, and the Treaty of Paris seemed unequivocably to confirm. Secondly, the state was determined from the outset to use the western lands as a means of liquidating its heavy war and postwar obligations;

and the ensuing struggle with the Creeks increased the urgency of such a policy. And thirdly, the Georgians soon perceived that further removal of the Indians from east Georgia was inextricably interlocked with the disposition of the western territory. In the end, the struggle over the western territory produced a revolution in the state's land policy.

Georgia asserted its title to the western lands, in the general Land Office Act of February 17, 1783, on the grounds noted above. There may have been some question of Great Britain's right to transfer these lands, as far as the Mississippi River and the thirty-first parallel, to the United States, on account of Spanish conquests in west Florida and on the east bank of the Mississippi during the Revolution, but Spain did not challenge England's right at the time of the treaty.[43] Within the United States only South Carolina disputed Georgia's claim to title in 1783, and South Carolina ceded her claims in the west to Georgia in 1787.

When the central government, in 1785, first urged Georgia to transfer its western lands, the latter acceded in principle, but chose to defer further action upon the request until the question of war debts and postwar obligations had been clarified and the jurisdictional dispute with South Carolina had been settled.[44] The state was in no position to take any very decidedly active steps in the matter. It could declare its sovereign rights and policy principles, but beyond that it must play largely a waiting game.

Its fundamental policy from the outset was that the price of transfer must include equitable recognition and compensation for the state's contribution to the common cause during the Revolution. To this was added later the costs of Indian hostilities, since the central government, claiming jurisdiction over Indian affairs, had failed to quiet the Indians. And finally, after the Treaty of Washington in 1790 had guaranteed Indian land titles in east Georgia, the removal of the Indians from the latter territory was made yet another major condition to the transfer of the western lands.

It is doubtful whether Georgia possessed any alternative to the cession of the western lands. Its prompt ratification of the federal constitution committed it in principle to the national policy of creating new states out of the western territories, even if the actualities of Indian possession, administrative difficulty, geography, and the westward surge of settlement should not ultimately have forced relinquishment. The immediate possibility of organizing and developing west Georgia as an integral part of the state presented insuperable obstacles. Spain, now in possession of all of Florida and Louisiana, laid claim, by virtue of conquest from England, to all lands west of a line of the Flint and Hiwassee rivers and south of the Tennessee River, and proceeded to establish a local government at

Natchez and to fortify points on the east bank of the Mississippi as far north as the Ohio River and also at internal locations in west Georgia. The Spanish authorities likewise drew up a treaty of mutual alliance with the Indian tribes and instituted a liberal policy of encouraging American settlement under Spanish rule in Louisiana, West Florida, and the Natchez area. It seems doubtful that even the United States government at any time prior to 1795 could have forced Spain to retreat far from the position she had taken.[45]

Not only were the Americans losing influence with the Indians in favor of Spain and Anglo-Spanish merchants, but the Georgians were finding it a difficult task even to protect themselves against Indian attacks. At times there was intense fear throughout Georgia of a concerted attack by their bellicose neighbors.[46] That Georgia, with a white population far smaller than that of the Indian tribes and with a mere handful of troops that numbered only a small fraction of the total of Indian warriors,[47] could have subdued the tribes within that vast western area and could have maintained law and order there was beyond the realm of possibility. The inaction of the United States government itself in regard to the more belligerent southern tribes was not entirely a matter of indifference to the interests of Georgia.[48]

Lastly, there was the certain conflict with the central government over Indian policy and development of the western lands. Nor was the state likely to receive any encouragement from the other states for an independent course, and their opposition could be very powerful and effective.

Obviously, such a small weak community as Georgia was in the eighteenth century could not overcome such obstacles as these. There was even serious danger that it might lose whatever stake in the western lands that it actually possessed. Certainly such might happen unless the state pursued a positive policy so far as circumstances and opportunities reasonably permitted.

All of Georgia's actions involving its western lands, except possibly its dealings with the central government, seem to have stemmed immediately from speculators' activities. This does not signify, however, that speculative considerations determined the state's conduct, as will be shown subsequently. The first such instance was the project to organize the "District of Tenasee," or "Houstoun County" as it came to be called by its promoters, which originated out of a land company venture of a group of North Carolinians headed by William Blount, John Sevier, and John Donaldson.[49]

Blount and his associates contrived the idea of acquiring a large tract of land at Muscle Shoals in the Big Bend of the Tennessee River, and opening it to settlers who were spreading rapidly southwestward down the Tennessee River and its tributaries. They appear to have thought at first that the territory was in North Carolina. When they discovered that it lay in Georgia but was also claimed by South Carolina, they decided to approach both of these states for the grant. In the meantime arrangements were made for purchase of title from the Indians. Having become convinced that the territory rightly lay in Georgia, Blount appeared before its assembly early in 1784 in the interest of securing the grant.[50]

Georgia would not entertain the idea of granting land to a company, but instead passed an act creating a board of seven commissioners, to which it named three of Blount's associates, with powers to ascertain the general character of the lands within the Great Bend and to issue warrants of survey according to the general provision of the headright laws, which when properly executed should become valid for grants. The commissioners were to receive five thousand acres each for their services; but all other grantees were to be limited to one thousand acres and must pay twenty-five cents per acre. The commissioners must report to the assembly upon the completion of their task, at which time presumably the matter of organizing the region into one or more counties was to be considered.[51]

A year later, eleven justices of the peace — all but one Georgian from eastern Tennessee — were elected for the district by the assembly.[52] John Sevier, as one of the commissioners, organized a surveying party which was joined apparently by two of the four Georgia members of the board. A land office was set up, warrants were issued and surveys made apparently for some eighty or ninety potential settlers; and a representative was chosen for the Georgia assembly. Sevier soon withdrew from the project, however, either on account of the hostility of the Indians or because of the creation by the east Tennesseans of the independent "State of Franklin." [53]

The Commissioners for the District of Tennessee made their report to the Georgia assembly in 1786. The assembly refused to seat the elected representative of the district and it rejected by a close, largely sectional, vote a bill to lay out the new District of Tennessee. It likewise ordered an end to surveys within the area, but validated all that had already been made, including the grants to the commissioners and surveyors in each case where the tasks had been duly performed.[54]

The project was not entirely abandoned. One of the Georgia commissioners, Zachariah Cox, continued extremely active in its interest;[55] and it became a very lively possibility again in 1787 when a joint military operation of Georgia and "Franklin" against the upper Creeks was planned, for which Sevier's soldiers from "Franklin" were to be rewarded with land bounties in the Great Bend territory. Had this military venture materialized and met with success, it might well have put 1,200 to 1,500 families in the district within a few years.[56]

Georgia's interest in the joint venture lapsed, however, upon the appointment by the United States of commissioners for an Indian treaty.[57] The state's first concern was ever with Indian cessions in east Georgia. Its ratification of the new federal constitution also certainly reduced its desire to create new counties in the western territory;[58] and the demise of "Franklin" in 1788 and the virtual outlawing of Sevier by North Carolina likewise must have operated to discourage further pursuit of the project, since it had been largely a Tennessee venture up to this time.[59] Late in 1789 the Georgia legislature again validated the Great Bend grants, however — including those of the two Georgia commissioners; but it insisted that all of the regular grantees pay for their lands within three months or the grants were to become null and void.[60]

The second venture of this type in western territory was the launching in 1785 of the inchoate project for organizing the distant Natchez territory on the Mississippi River and west Florida boundaries into the county of Bourbon. One Thomas Green and various associates, representing themselves as already settled at Natchez, petitioned for the organization of the county, the establishment of a land court, and the right to elect delegates to the Georgia assembly. They envisioned the settlement of one thousand families within the territory in a short period of time.[61] The assembly created the county and elected eleven of the associates as justices of the peace for the new local government but declined to do more about titles than promising that those who settled there should have first claim should a land court be later opened.[62] The instructions to the justices enjoined them to notify the Spanish military authorities of Georgia's intentions but to avoid all disputes with the Spaniards, to cultivate amity and trade with the Indians, and to make no encroachments upon, or purchases of, Indian lands.[63] Georgia based its right to permit settlement in this area upon previous Indian cessions to the British before the Revolution.

The Georgia authorities must have possessed little knowledge of the actual competence and objectives of the promoters or of the status of Spanish and Indian affairs in the Mississippi area. In the light of later knowledge it appears as a jejune move. The Spaniards already were established firmly at Natchez and would not permit Green to settle there, and the non-Spanish residents were not interested in the Georgia project.[64] The state itself was in no position to support its own creation and it had no desire to incur the animosity of Spain at this time of tense relations with the Indians. The county actually never passed the paper stage; but it was abolished officially in 1788, in the legislation which embodied the first offer of the western lands to the central government.[65]

These two ventures were undertaken when there was a strong movement afoot for the extension, both territorially and politically, of local government. Millions of virgin acres were being organized into Wilkes, Franklin, and Washington counties, in the case of the latter without consent of a large body of the Creek owners. There are certainly numerous parallels between Washington County and the Houstoun and Bourbon projects of the same date. It should be noted, however, that the state was far more cautious in the latter cases. Both legislative actions were enabling measures rather than full-fledged county-creating acts. The state could recede if either venture did not pan out; yet it offered some protection to the adventures.

Georgia was conscious of the forces that were at work on the frontier — the tireless activities of speculators and the powerful, ceaseless westward movement of actual settlement, the particularism and the growing separatism among the western population, the harsh attitude of the whites toward the Indians, and the fickleness of the latter in their dealings with the whites. Georgia was a frontier state and was becoming actually more rather than less so as it filled up predominantly with the frontiersmen from other states. Its future lay with the frontier, whose forces were on its side; therefore the state must accommodate its policy to such forces as well as seek to contain them.

Georgia needed the strength of an augmented population and the support of friendly neighbors. It gave away land liberally to all who would adopt it as a home. It dealt with the seasoned speculators of other states to be sure, but it demanded conformity, in the beginning at least, to the provisions of its general land grant laws. George Matthews and his Virginia neighbors, for example, were required to take out their "reserves" in Washington County subject to the usual conditions of the headright statutes; and Blount and Green and their associates were offered substantially the same proposition in the proposed Houstoun and Bourbon counties. War veterans from Connecticut were offered identical terms with Sevier's men in the Great Bend of the Tennessee. The projection of new counties in these remote parts should be viewed as an adherence to the established constitutional procedure of erecting local governments and regular land courts, rather than as fantastic ventures of doubtful legality as they so often have been interpreted.

The western county projects may be considered also to have been attempts to uphold the state's boundary claims in two very strategic areas. And from still another and broader viewpoint they may be interpreted both as an effort to bring under control the frontier forces within its greater boundaries and as an expression of its need to make use of these forces.

It is not difficult to explain either Georgia's purposes in making its first offer, in 1788, of western lands to the central government, or the latter's reasons for rejecting the offer. The state obviously wished to coöperate upon western land and Indian policies with the general government, whose new constitution it had just adopted unanimously. At the same time, however, it was proposing to give up what was considered the least desirable half of its western territory as well as the part which contained the bulk of the Spanish forces and which was chiefly in dispute with that foreign power. It would retain the territory over which Spain seemed most likely to relinquish its claims; and it would thus wash its hands fairly clean of the dangerous Spanish question. Furthermore, if the central government should be successful in forcing Spain to retreat beyond the Mississippi and south of the thirty-first parallel, occupation of the ceded area by federal forces would separate Spain from the Indians, would weaken very greatly the position of the latter, and possibly further the efforts of merchants at Savannah and Augusta to secure the fur trade.[66] The cash consideration of $171,428.50 was designed to meet the debts that had been incurred in the Creek "War." A much higher figure might have been asked if the state had been able to estimate correctly the total cost of the Creek hostilities, and had realized that it would not be able to collect a sufficient amount from the sales of the confiscated estates to liquidate its Revolutionary debt.[67]

The central government was just as anxious to avoid an immediate showdown with Spain as was Georgia. To have accepted the cession would have forced it into a highly strained position with its foreign neighbor; and it would have been difficult also to have made any headway with the Indian problem until Spain had been dislodged. Even then, control of this region would not have given the United States jurisdiction over the most belligerent of the southern tribes, nor would it have afforded sufficient territory to make the adjustments of tribal boundaries that Georgia's demands for territory were making necessary. At any rate, the old Congress was on the way out by this time and was inclined to leave western lands, new states, Indian affairs, and Spanish claims to the new federal government. As it turned out, the latter also chose to pursue a waiting policy on Georgia's western lands and Spain's boundary claims. It concluded apparently that it could deal with both Indian affairs and Spanish claims more effectively without any immediate transfer of western lands than with the transfer of the southern half of the territory proposed by Georgia. Thus the question lapsed for another decade. Meanwhile the state began to consider other possibilities of converting these assets to a profit.

6. Western Land Companies

The following important facts should be kept in mind in any consideration of transactions with the land companies. The first was the state's fiscal condition — it was heavily in debt, the resources upon which it had counted had failed to meet expectations, and it felt that it had been unjustly treated and neglected by the central government. The second was that Georgia, up to that time, had consistently opposed the professional speculator and had held operations fairly well in check. The third was that land company operations clashed with the social opinion of a large number of Georgians of all ranks and that, consequently, strong opposition lay only beneath the surface. The fourth was the fact that immense grants to speculative groups, in one fashion or another, had been the general rule of frontier settlement — in New York, Pennsylvania, western Virginia, the Northwest, Kentucky, and Tennessee.[68]

The history of both of the Yazoo land sales has been told many times, and only those facts which seem pertinent to this study will be repeated here. The first group of companies was organized during 1788 and 1789. Two of these, the Tennessee Company and the South Carolina Company, can be traced directly to the Houstoun and Bourbon county ventures, and they sought the purchase of substantially the same tracts of land that were involved in the earlier projects. Hence their propositions were merely a return to the type of undertaking that Blount had planned originally at Muscle Shoals. A third company, the Virginia Yazoo Company, was a newcomer which had been organized by Patrick Henry and other Virginians. It sought at first a consolidation with the South Carolina Company; but failing this, it applied for a large independent grant lying between those sought by the other two companies. Still another, and unsuccessful, applicant was the Georgia Company. The Georgia legislature agreed, in 1789, to sell a total of 25,400,000 to the first three mentioned companies for $207,580. Two years later, however, the purchases were declared forfeit for failure of the companies to meet the financial terms within the specified time limits.[69]

The sale aroused a great deal of opposition within the state. A statement severely condemning the action was issued to the press by a group of fourteen leading citizens, including such outstanding persons as Joseph Habersham, John Milledge, Benjamin Taliferro, Josiah Tatnall, Seaborn Jones, Samuel Stirk, Benjamin Lanier, and Peter Winn, two of whom later became governors. The pronouncement was widely circulated and generally approved. It condemned the sales on three grounds primarily: that they were too partial, that is, they were monopolistic and privileged in their effects; that, in view of the heavy public debt, the public domain should have been alienated in such a "manner as to have made it most productive to the state"; and that the citizens of Georgia should have been given equal opportunity to purchase lands with those of other states. No opposition was expressed to the idea of disposing of the western lands for revenue; nor were any doubts expressed about the constitutionality of such action, or of the state's right to dispose of its western lands in whatever manner it might choose.[70]

The supreme test of the issues, and the controversy that convulsed the state and even the nation, resulted from the second sale, in 1795, of 35,000,000 acres — approximately three-fifths of the entire western territory — to four companies for a total sum of $500,000. One of the companies was the previous applicant Tennessee Company whose tenacious promoter, Zachariah Cox, had never ceased to labor for the development of the Muscle Shoals area since the early days of the Houstoun County legislation. Another was the Georgia-Mississippi Yazoo Company, successor of the old South Carolina Company, and the two others, the Upper Mississippi Company and the Georgia Company — the latter being the most ambitious of the lot — were entirely new organizations. The earlier Virginia Yazoo group was not a party to this transaction. In contrast to the previous groups, the companies included a great many Georgians, among them several prominent state officials as well as most of the legislators who voted for the sale. Notable participants from outside of the state were Robert Morris and James Wilson of Pennsylvania, William Blount and John Sevier of North Carolina, and Wade Hampton of South Carolina.[71]

Strong opposition had arisen even before the legislature had consummated the sale, despite the considerable secrecy that had been maintained and the speed with which the project was pushed. William H. Crawford, a relative newcomer to Georgia, but already a person of rising political influence, headed a petition from Columbia County against it and sought to persuade Governor Matthews not to sign the bill.[72] After the legislature's action became known, expressions of condemnation became general. The presentment of the Chatham Grand Jury, among these early statements, is one of the more revealing utterances and probably represents reasonably well the attitudes which prevailed in the coastal region. It should be borne in mind that it was made many months before the revelations of bribery and the sensational political campaign that followed.

The Chatham Grand Jury indicted the sale as follows: (1) it was not an opportune time for the sale, because Indian relations were still in a very delicate and unsettled state; (2) the disposal of these lands should have been as widely diffused as possible — "monopolies have ever been considered contrary to the spirit of free governments, highly injurious, and tending to enrich a few monied men to the exclusion of people in general"; (3) the government itself could have merchandised the lands, by laying out allotments, by advertising widely, and by offering them for public sale, with far greater profit to the state treasury, even to the extent of freeing the citizens from taxation forever — such a policy "would have given the poor a chance to better themselves, which should be the purpose of every public act; the minds of people could have been satisfied, and all those good consequences would have resulted which always do from measures founded upon policy and equal justice"; (4) if a public offer of bids had been permitted, the sales price would certainly have been much higher; (5) the act may not be unconstitutional, but it is inconceivable that any constitutional convention, representing the people of the state, could visualize the legislature's disposing of the public lands in this fashion; (6) it will tend unquestionably to further the operations of speculators and to make them the chief beneficiaries of the act; and (7) whenever this sort of action is perpetrated by our elected representative it becomes the duty of public bodies such as this one, however disagreeable the task may be, to take cognizance of and to condemn such acts, "otherwise one bad law after another would be passed by the Legislature, until the rights of the good people of the state would be buried in oppressions." The members of this grand jury were the foremost business and political leaders of Savannah. Their foreman was James Habersham, son of the colonial governor and merchant, and now senior member of a family of Revolutionary heroes, statesmen, educators, merchants, and planters that was probably the most outstanding in Georgia at the time.[73]

The substance of the Chatham Grand Jury presentment was repeated many times the following months.[74] Popular outcry against the acts mounted rapidly. Even so, the provisions of the legislative acts of sale might have been carried out but for the action of James Jackson, then junior member from Georgia in the United State Senate.[75]

Like most other American leaders of the eighteenth century, James Jackson espoused the natural rights theories of private property and political liberty and sought to combine them into a philosophy of social action. He held private property to be the natural right of all and equally the foundation and safeguard of democracy. Just as certainly, he thought that monopoly and aggrandizement prevented free access to ownership of property among the great body of the citizens and thereby destroyed the bases of democracy. Hence the small proprietorship supplied the bulwark of democratic institutions; and in Georgia, whose resources disposed its economy to agricultural pursuits, small landed proprietorship constituted the *sine qua non* of democracy and must ever be the peculiar object of public land policy. This general philosophy motivated Jackson in his fight against the Yazoo land sales, as it did later in his attacks upon the cotton gin monopoly.[76]

Upon the outbreak of the Yazoo storm, Jackson resigned his seat in the Senate and returned to Georgia to lead a campaign for the repeal of the unpopular law. The defenders of the act maintained that such a course would be illegal, since the legislation was a binding contract with the companies and certainly within the constitutional powers of the legislature. But the revelations of widespread corruption and apparent bribery supplied Jackson with a crushing popular argument to combine with the charge of unconstitutionality and the plea for the preservation of democracy in the person of the small landowner.[77]

The Chatham Grand Jury had suggested the charge of unconstitutionality on a sort of implied moral grounds, but Jackson pressed it vigorously as both fact and principle. He was on familiar ground; the argument was none other than that developed by the Reverend Zubly of Savannah just prior to the Revolution and adopted by the Sons of Liberty, including Jackson and most of the members of the Chatham Grand Jury. There was a glaring parallel between the acts of the British Parliament and that of the Yazoo legislature: both had exceeded their powers as vouchsafed to them by the principles of democratic government; sovereignty resided alone in the people, who should always be allowed to decide upon all major questions of policy. No legislative body could conceivably possess the constitutional right to take any action of such far-reaching effect and so patently inimical to the interests and rights of the great majority of the people. The machinery of government was an instrument of the people; it should ever be viewed by their representatives as a sacred trust. Even stupidity offered no valid excuse for violation of that trust.[78]

The issue of the campaign which had the most significant bearing upon later economic policy was the charge that such acts create monopolies and wealthy aristocracies, which in turn limit economic opportunity and thereby destroy the bases of democratic institutions. The Revolution, said Jackson, had been a struggle between aristocratic and democratic institutions;[79] and now the issue was once more joined, the victory of that great struggle itself was imperiled!

In an age of hero worship, James Jackson stirred men into action by his vehement devotion to the public trust. His gift of allegory made him doubly effective among a generation still highly susceptible to this form of suggestion: The exchangers must be driven from the Temple! The foul record of their iniquitous deeds must be consumed by the very Light of Heaven, itself! Let all the powers of darkness witness this act of judgment and take warning! As if even Divine Fire could not entirely expunge the fiendish crime, its very mention must be proscribed forever! The crusade was successful. An anti-Yazoo legislature was elected and the land sales were repealed in 1796.[80] Two years later a new constitution forbade "monopolies of land by individuals" as "being contrary to the spirit of our free government."[81]

Jackson's somewhat quixotic actions have been variously judged and his motives have been lauded, questioned, and impugned. Concentration on the personality of this controversial figure and upon the legal aspects of his victory, however, may cause one to overlook the more significant elements and effects of this famous episode. The trial of certain fundamental principles, not of a few land-grabbing legislators, was the fundamental issue. These principles had a deep root in Georgia — in the charter of the colony, in the hopes of those who came under it, in the purposes and trying experiences of the Revolution, and in the land and educational policies of the early postwar years. However, the persistent difficulties and sometime confusions that followed the war, the redundant additions of new population, and the growth of factional and sectional disputes had permitted certain individuals, who saw in the situation opportunities for large personal gain, to obtain public office and political influence. Jackson supplied the leadership to an aroused democracy that wrested public policy from the grasp of such opportunists and relaunched it upon the course of constructive liberalism.[82]

The Supreme Court of the United States later reversed the decision of the Georgia anti-Yazoo legislature and upheld the validity of the land company contracts;[83] but it could not change the decision of the people of Georgia about their own future policy; hence it altered not in the least the effects of the Yazoo affair. The controversy marked one of the most important turning points in the state's history. It signalized the drawing to a close of one era, which had begun even before independence, and the beginning of another, which was to witness the shaping of a new economic policy. The ingredients of the new policy, however, were not all new. Some have been described already and others will be noted in the summary of the aims and effects of land policy which follows and in succeeding chapters dealing with other aspects of this period.

7. Aims and Effects of Eighteenth-century Land Policy

The objectives of Georgia land policy, broadly speaking, were of two sorts: there was the usual design to stimulate growth — to increase population, wealth, and income; and there was an ever-present concern with the use of land policy as a primary means of molding social structure. The nature of the first purpose appears to be sufficiently evident, but the second may require further explanation.

The trials of various colonial land policies, based successively upon benevolent equalitarianism, middle-class progressivism, and upper-class slave ownership, have been described in Chapter II. While all of these policies were motivated and affected in some degree by both ulterior factors and immediate circumstance, each in its principal intent was designed to promote a certain type of societal structure and process. Revolutionary land policy reflected a pronounced reaction from the Crown policy which immediately preceded it, and constituted actually a return in the direction of the original Trustee ideal, omitting however the paternalistic features and the cramping limitations of the earlier policy: it offered lands to all comers at nominal prices, but limited individual grants — in particular the rights based on slave ownership — in order that public policy might not become a direct means of aggrandizement. Post-Revolutionary policy in the main followed the same principles.

The small proprietorship philosophy drew its inspiration from numerous sources and conditions. The Benevolent movement, with its faith in the common man, had left a lasting impression on Georgia; the growth of large plantations had been accompanied invariably by a rapid increase in the ratio of slaves to free men; the royalist sympathies of many of the wealthy during the Revolution had greatly increased the opposition to the great landowners, while the heroic struggles of the small landowners in defense of their homes against the incursions of the British and Tories had established the homestead right in many minds as the issue of the war and the reward of victory. This viewpoint gathered powerful, added support from the spirit of self-reliance that typified the postwar immigrant from the back country of Virginia and the Carolinas. There was ample evidence also that large grants led to huge individual accumulations, absentee ownership, speculation, the withholding of lands from use, high land prices and exclusion of persons of small means from ownership of the better lands; and the repugnance to monopoly, widespread in America, found its target in these large land holdings.

The supporters of the small-proprietorship policy often did not distinguish too clearly between monopolists, speculators, and big planters (though many of the latter were equally opposed to monopolies and speculations). They did not distinguish between large-scale operation on the one hand and monopoly and speculation on the other. They seemed not to comprehend that a limited land-grant policy would not preserve small proprietorships in a region like the tidewater area where large-scale operations were not only far more efficient but also almost a requisite for staple production. And they disliked the effects of the most efficient use of slavery, although they supported the institution as a form of labor supply. Economic interests, class antagonisms, and political alignments likewise unquestionably played important roles in determining viewpoints. At a time when antipathies to monopolies, kings, and aristocracies alike were very deep-seated, economic, political, and social democracy tended to become joined into a single concept.

How fully was the objective of economic growth attained during this period? The phenomenal increases in population — from 25,000 in 1783 to 82,548 in 1790 and 162,686 in 1800 — attest to the force of the liberal headright and bounty policies in attracting immigration.[84] This conclusion is supported by the geographical distribution of population growth: 70 per cent of the increase between 1783 and 1790, and over 90 per cent between 1790 and 1800, occurred within the primary areas of land-granting.

The connections between land policy and the growth of wealth and income, however, were neither as direct nor as apparent as in the case of population; although some allowance must be made for difficulties in securing adequate measurements of these quantities. On the slave-operated plantation, slaves normally represented 75 to 80 per cent of the value of the investment, and exports an even larger proportion of the money income.[85] If it could be assumed that the number of plantations remained a constant ratio to that of farms, that the average numbers of slaves for different sizes of units continued the same, and that there were no significant marketing or technological changes during the period, then the increases in slaves and exports would afford rough estimates of the rates of growth respectively of wealth and income.

The number of slaves only doubled between 1783 and 1790, whereas population tripled, which would indicate that total wealth did not increase as much relatively as population, and that per-capita wealth actually declined by about one-third.[86] However, the ratio of slave-operated to non-slave-operated units declined as well, and so our measurement understates somewhat the actual amount of growth of wealth. Between 1790 and 1800, slaves increased 104 per cent and total population only 97 per cent. This greater increase in slaves can be accounted for, probably, by a slight increase in number of slaves per unit; hence it is a fair inference that the number of slave-operated units maintained a constant ratio to non-slave-operated units for the decade as a whole; and consequently it appears safe to assume that wealth increased at approximately the same rate as population.[87]

Dates of available export figures do not coincide strictly with those for population and wealth; but a comparable trend may be obtained. Exports actually did not again attain the level of the colonial year 1773 until after 1787. By 1795 they still had risen only 80 per cent in value above 1773, even though population must have increased at least 400 per cent. However, between 1795 and 1800 they rose 310 per cent, while population was increasing probably 40 to 50 per cent.[88]

The failure of wealth and income to respond immediately to the liberal land policy and its induced population growth might be attributed to natural lag. But there were significant reasons for the lag, among which were shortages of currency, labor, and capital, lack of markets, and poor transportation, which could not be overcome merely by the substitution of unlimited quantities of virgin land. Production in the older coastal areas actually declined for some of these reasons; and it was only after tobacco culture had spread to upper Georgia in the early 1790's that exports again attained the colonial level and finally, toward the middle of the decade, forged ahead of it.

Marketing conditions and opportunities were generally disappointing prior to 1795. Lack of transportation, as well, restrained development in the new settlements. Colonial settlement had never extended far beyond the reaches of the natural water courses and tributary streams of the coastal area; but the settlement of Wilkes county, in this respect as in many others, marked an important change. Henceforth new settlement was to push ever farther into the interior, away from navigable water courses and more distant from the ports. Consequently, free homesteads, without adequate transportation and ready access to markets, were to become a lessening stimulus to increased production.

The phenomenal expansion of exports after 1795 resulted almost solely from the invention of the cotton gin. Cotton production increased from 1,000 to 20,000 bales, during the decade.[89] Even the increase in population at this time — especially that among planters and slaves, noted above — must have been the consequence in the main of this technological improvement.

These results do not appear to justify the high faith that the state placed in land policy alone during this period. The assumptions that market demands, transportation facilities, money, capital, and labor would seek readily the expanding population on the land proved invalid. Some supplementary steps were taken, to be sure, in connection with currency and market factors. But what actually took up the slack in land policy was the invention of the cotton gin. This revolutionary change in technology gave the new regions a staple crop that currently possessed an expanding market, that provided a basis for obtaining capital and labor, and that could be produced at costs low enough to offset the effects of inefficient transportation. A new tide of immigration immediately set in; the clamor for land rose to new heights; and the state renewed its faith for the time being in the supreme efficacy of land policy.

Did the eighteenth-century postwar land policy achieve its other primary aim of securing permanent small proprietorship in land? The period obviously is too short to provide a satisfactory answer even if the available data were less general and other factors were less numerous and influential. The question is pertinent at this point, however, for two reasons: one that it was raised forcefully in the minds of the proponents of the small proprietorship philosophy by the events of the mid-1790's; and the other that any summary of the development of policy should constitute in substance a standing interrogation of succeeding developments. A few of the outstanding trends and contributing factors are noted for what they may suggest.

The census of 1790 supplies some indications of the numbers of resident landed proprietors, as follows: the coastal counties, 1,500; the Augusta area (Burke and Richmond counties), 2,750; and the new counties, 5,600. Slaves were two-thirds of the population on the coast, one-third in the Augusta area, and one-fifth in the new counties. The relatively large number of landowners and small number of slaves in the new counties do indicate a preponderance of small proprietorships, which was quite the reverse of the well-known situation on the coast. Since the large coastal holdings had been amassed in the main under Crown policies, whereas the small holdings in the new counties were granted under the War and Postwar acts, it might be inferred that the difference in size was a consequence of the difference in policies. It seems just as likely, however, that major conditioning factors also were the character of the immigration which largely settled the region, frontier conditions, remoteness from market, and the inadaptability of the back-country at the time to the type of large-scale commercial agriculture that had flourished on the coast. The data on the Augusta area strongly confirm the latter conclusion: although settled largely under Crown grants, Burke and Richmond counties resembled the new regions in ownership characteristics more than they did the coastal section. Except for land policy, they had been influenced by the same factors as the new counties; and the somewhat higher ratio of slaves and the probable slightly larger ownership unit were doubtless consequences of greater maturity and the recent development of tobacco culture in the area.

The census of 1800 indicated: for the coast, a modest increase in the number of proprietorships, but no substantial change in the proportion of slaves to total population; for the Augusta area, an increase of 45 per cent in proprietorship units, but only 3 per cent in the slave ratio; and for the new counties, an increase of 130 per cent in proprietorships and of 8 per cent in the slave ratio. The new counties had become divided, however, rather clearly into three groups: an upland cotton belt embracing the lower Piedmont tier of counties, a vast pine-barrens region comprising what had been the southern half of Washington County, and the remaining general agricultural counties bordering the upland cotton belt on the north and south. The upland cotton belt alone now contained 6,350 proprietorships or 14 per cent more than all of the new counties combined ten years earlier, and its slave ratio had increased to 34 per cent or exactly that of the Augusta area. The pine-barrens contained only some 730 resident landowners and slaves numbering only 14 per cent of the population. The remaining new counties showed approximately 5,800 landowners, or 4 per cent more than all of the counties in 1790.

The data contained in these early censuses evidenced a developing pattern of economic life that reflected the influences of numerous factors, among which land policy held an important place. One of the dominant characteristics of the pattern was the great number of relatively small landed proprietorships that had become established in the interior. Land policy unquestionably was a leading factor in this development; but the data do not reveal its relative significance; nor do they vouch for the permanency of the small proprietorships. Some effects of the new cotton culture upon land ownership and population structure could also be discerned, even though economical production of the staple was only five or six years old. But with respect to this factor likewise, it was far too soon to discover whether cotton would create, as had rice and indigo on the coast, such a preponderant advantage in favor of the large-scale unit that the great plantations would absorb the small farms in interior Georgia and thereby undo the effects of postwar land policy.

The advocates of small ownership were far from satisfied with the accomplishments under the headright system. Many abuses had crept in, chiefly as a result of loose formulation of the laws and their faulty, at times corrupt, administration. The small homesteaders, to be sure, had received the greatest proportion of the land grants, and their actual settlements had gone far to establish a pattern of democratic equality and individual opportunity. But the speculators and the land greedy likewise had benefited, lushly and conspicuously, from the state's land distribution. The increasing evidences of large grants and extensive individual accumulations were becoming more disturbing. The Yazoo sales at this point provided the shocking proof of the growing power of the avaricious over land distribution and posed such an ominous threat to the future of land policy in Georgia that they provoked a thorough reappraisal of its basic purposes, which in the end induced a complete reform of the land-granting system.[90]

CHAPTER VI

FISCAL PROBLEMS AND THE CURRENCY, 1775–1799

While land drew the greatest share of public attention in Georgia, finance presented the most serious problem. It should be no surprise that the state suffered the usual war experience of vastly increased expenditures, inadequate revenues, public debt, paper currency, and inflation; it is noteworthy that it was able to escape complete public bankruptcy. Actually, most of the problems were familiar ones but they were greatly intensified by the war and the heavy task of reconstruction. The inadequacies of public revenues and the scarcities of currency and private capital, which had hampered the colonial economy, threatened dire consequences for the newly formed government burdened with the costly task of waging war. These difficulties were further compounded by the disruption of external commerce and credit, the disappearance of specie, and the weakness of fiscal organization.

Relatively peaceful conditions in the southern region during the first three years of the Revolution greatly aided the republican forces in Georgia, and probably prevented an early collapse of their fiscal policies. Their finances deteriorated rapidly during 1778, however, as a result of the accumulated weight of financial burdens and the increasing pressures exerted by the enemy. The government itself ceased to exist shortly after the British invasion in December of that year. The ensuing four years of bitter warfare of attrition and reprisal drove many citizens from their homes, removed a large part of the labor force, and left the land literally in ruins.

Government was not firmly reëstablished until the late summer of 1781; and control of the older section of the state and access to the sea were not wrested from the British until July 11, 1782, nine months after the surrender of Cornwallis. When at last the government was able to take up normal peacetime functions it found itself incumbered with a heavy debt, without revenues or fiscal machinery, and with only a makeshift currency. Its only quick assets appeared to be the confiscated properties. To these difficulties were shortly added a series of costly altercations with the Indians.

Private business faced no lesser obstacles. Likewise heavily in debt, its property destroyed and its trade relations broken, it stood in dire need of labor and capital with which to undertake the heavy task of rehabilitation. In an economy so largely dependent upon the export trade, an early revival of commerce was equally vital to both private and public business.

Despite the obvious impediments on every hand, the Georgians were reasonably sanguine about the outcome. It was expected that the sales of the confiscated properties would liquidate the public debt, that the recuperation of production and trade would release private debts and credits and bring about a return of specie, and that the rising tide of immigration would greatly augment production and income and correspondingly increase public revenues.

A considerable part of the war debt was retired rather quickly as was anticipated, by sales of confiscated property and through federal assumption of the external portion; but the hopes of quick recuperation, growth, and expansion of public revenues were not realized so speedily. Even the heavy retirements of war debts were offset in large measure by the growth of postwar debts. In fact, the latter represented an even more serious burden, since the sale of confiscated properties exhausted the only readily available source of debt retirement.

Business revival proved especially disappointing: the restoration of the older agricultural areas turned out to be a much more difficult and long-drawn-out process than had been anticipated; reopened markets did not come up to expectations; and the uncompromising attitude of British creditors in regard to prewar debts paralyzed the operations of Georgia merchants. Nor did the new immigration contribute significantly to business recovery; actually it would appear rather that it exerted a deterrent influence upon fiscal recovery. The general costs of government in the newly settled regions may have exceeded revenues, owing to the lack of cash products in those areas; and the rapid pushing outward of the frontier greatly increased the pressure upon the Indians, thereby producing the frictions which led to the heavy postwar military expenditures. The political influence of the newcomers was equally unfavorable. Their representatives in the assembly obtained the abandonment of a revenue-producing land policy, thwarted the early attempts to levy adequate taxes, and finally pressured the state into an emission of paper money.

Despite these numerous obstacles, within eight years of the close of the war the state had retired nearly a million dollars of internal war debt, rid itself of paper money, established a reasonably productive tax structure, and balanced its budget. It was still heavily in debt, but had come safely through its most dangerous period.

1. Public Expenditures

The financial history of the state begins with the deliberations of the Georgia Provincial Congress in July 1775. This body created a Council of Safety, endowing it with broad executive powers, including the power to issue paper money.[1] The Council of Safety, following the resolutions of the Provincial Congress and the suggestions of the Continental Congress, proceeded to purchase arms and ammunition, to commission officers in all of the parishes, and to call out the militia for active duty.[2] The immediate objective was the enforcement of the Nonintercourse Acts.[3] Units of Continental troops also were organized upon direct authorization of the Continental Congress.[4] These extensive military preparations boosted the level of expenditures some fifteen times higher than the previous colonial level.[5] This high rate of spending continued, and even increased during early 1778. Chiefly responsible were the successive attempts to invade Florida, rising prices after 1776, and the continued failure of Congress to assume the financial support of the Georgia Continental troops. With the commencement of active operations by the enemy against Georgia late in 1778, expenditures rose sharply; but the arrival of Continental funds in December removed a part of the financial burden from the state government.[6]

Although organized government largely ceased between January 9, 1779, and August 16, 1781, expenditures continued to be made in the name of the state by various patriotic groups and military officers. Most of the military personnel and a large number of the patriotic citizens, however, were engaged on fronts outside of Georgia during the greater part of this period. Almost no information is available concerning the amount of expenditures during these two and one-half years. Whatever it may have been is included, in Table 3, in the estimates for 1778 and 1781–1782. The latter figure is based upon the amount of the audited floating debt, reduced to a specie basis, at the end of the war.[7] Some of this debt was contracted as early as 1777; but there is insufficient evidence upon which to make any allocations for the years before 1781. All figures in Table 3 are in round numbers, and no claims for correctness are made beyond a reasonable degree of historical accuracy.

Public spending dropped abruptly with the close of hostilities in the fall of 1782, but by no means to the prewar level. Strained Indian relations, the expanded state of public business, and higher prices prevented such an extreme decline. A gradual worsening of relations with the Creeks eventually produced even an upward trend again after 1785. The last decade of the century, however, witnessed a return to a level that was comparable with that of the later colonial years.

During the first quarter century, taken as a whole, the state spent

Table 3

REVOLUTIONARY EXPENDITURES, GEORGIA, 1775–1782

1775	$ 100,000
1776–78	2,500,000
1779–80	([a])
1781–82	1,700,000
Total	$4,300,000

[a] Included in other years.

approximately five and one-half million dollars. Of this, 75 per cent occurred during the Revolution, 12 per cent resulted from Indian hostilities and was largely of a military nature, and only 13 per cent went to meet ordinary costs of government. The state bore most of the expense

Table 4

POSTWAR EXPENDITURES, GEORGIA, 1783–1799

Time period	Amounts	Average per year
1783–1784	$225,000[a]	$112,500
1785	100,000[b]	100,000
1786	125,000[c]	125,000
1787–1789	450,000[d]	150,000
1790–1791	75,530[e]	37,765
1792	29,190[f]	29,190
1793	24,350[g]	24,350
1794–1798	150,000[h]	30,000
1799	35,000[i]	35,000
	$1,214,070	

[a] *Georgia State Gazette*, Feb. 24, Mar. 3, 1787, "Report of Committee on Finance, Georgia Assembly.'
[b] Estimate based upon previous years and other sources; *JGA*, Feb. 19, 1785.
[c] *Ibid.*, Aug. 22, 1786; Stevens, *History*, II, 374–375.
[d] Governors' and Treasurers' Reports, 1787–1789; *JGA*, Jan. 21, Dec. 21, 1789; *Laws* (Watkins), 387.
[e] *Augusta Chronicle*, Nov. 12, 1791, Gov. Edward Telfair, "Message."
[f] *Ibid.*, Nov. 10, 1792.
[g] *Ibid.*, Nov. 7, 1793.
[h] Estimate based upon governors' messages and other sources.
[i] *SJ* (1800), 3–11, estimate based upon governor's message.

of the Revolutionary War within Georgia. The Continental Congress spent $1,100,000 in the Georgia sector,[8] for the Georgia Continental troops during 1778–1779; but much of this covered operations within adjacent areas of South Carolina.

2. Public Revenues

The state derived its revenues prior to 1800 from: taxation, fees and commissions, sales of public property, and reimbursements from the central government.

The republican forces took over the entire machinery of government on January 18, 1776, and shortly thereafter their assembly voted that all colonial laws not contravening the purposes of the new government should remain in force.[9] Presumably this included the tax statutes; yet no specific record remains concerning either tax legislation or tax collection prior to May 4, 1778.[10] On the latter date the legislature virtually reënacted the basic colonial tax structure with 100 per cent rate increases on land, slaves, merchandise, and poll taxes on free persons of color. The 1 per cent tax on salaried and professional incomes and the ½ per cent ad valorem rate on private loans were left unchanged; and a carriage tax and a poll tax on white males were added.[11] The act was designed to raise $52,000 — a highly optimistic estimate, despite the increased rates and new taxes, for the most that any colonial measure had ever raised had been about $15,000.[12] Since the government ceased operations at the end of this year, collections under this act could not have been undertaken until the fall of 1781. There are allusions at the end of the war to widespread arrearages of taxes, which suggest that some attempts had been made, or were being made, to collect the wartime levies.[13] The amounts realized, however, must have been negligible.

A special levy during 1782–1785, which was a part of the confiscation program but had the character of a tax or a capital levy, was the amercement of property of citizens who were not deemed to be traitors, but whose sympathies for the British, or lack of sympathies for the Americans, were deemed sufficient to warrant pecuniary penalties. Rates of 8 and 12 per cent of the value of properties, depending upon degree of guilt, were assessed.[14] How much revenue was raised in this fashion is not recorded, but it is doubtful that the amount was great. Some of the amerced were removed from the list for good reasons and others were forgiven.

The enactment of an adequate tax measure was urged by Governor Lyman Hall in January 1783, as the first necessity in postwar financial rehabilitation.[15] For such a policy, though the governor had the support of the inhabitants of the older sections and of most of the business leaders, he was able to obtain only a feeble response from the assembly. Upstate representatives joined with a small minority of paper money advocates in opposition to any comprehensive tax legislation. It was argued that there was not time for the study needed for legislating a broad measure; that the incomes of most of the inhabitants were so low that a general tax law would yield little revenue; that such legislation should be deferred until the following year; and that any taxes that might be approved should be restricted solely to land.[16]

A very weak law was passed finally on July 31, 1783: rates on land, slaves, and town realty were fixed at less than half the old colonial rates, which already had been extremely low; and most of the other rates, including the one on incomes, were dropped entirely. However, the law did require the tax officials to take a complete census of the state — of all lands by type and grade; slaves by age classes; town properties by descriptive classes and values (including annual rent, if rented); white persons by sex and age groups; monies, livestock, vessels, carriages, and other property — in order that the legislature might have the necessary information for devising a sound tax measure at a later date. At the same time, a 2½ per cent sales tax on auctions was imposed; and the 2½ per cent general import duty was continued, with directions for the collection of unpaid duties on importations since the reëstablishment of government.[17] Governor Hall and his supporters decried the general tax levy as disgracefully inadequate.[18]

The anticipated broad tax statute was not enacted until 1785. Generally speaking, the measure broadened the tax base somewhat and reinstituted substantially the level of the wartime act of 1778; it increased the burdens upon the better grades of land, and consequently upon plantation owners as a group; and it aimed a blow at speculators. One of the primary objectives of the act was to speed up the retirement of the public war debt; therefore it permitted one-half of any tax return to be paid in audited certificates.[19]

The yield of the new measure proved inadequate; and consequently, in 1787, all real property rates were tripled, slaves rates were doubled, and license and luxury taxes were quadrupled; penalty rates were retained, and special provisions were included to assure their collection and also collection from the numerous absentee owners of improved lands.[20] A special property surtax of 30 cents per $100 valuation, payable in army provisions, was added later in the year, after the outbreak of Creek hostilities.[21]

No further general changes were introduced during the ensuing two years of the Creek "War." The luxury tax on carriages was doubled and license taxes were increased 25 per cent, in 1788;[22] and real property rates were reduced about 15 per cent in 1789. The import duty was dropped in the latter year, on account of the provisions of the new federal constitution; but a sales tax of the same rate was imposed upon all imported goods sold by factors and brokers.[23]

Expenditures dropped precipitately in 1790, upon the return of more amicable relations with the Indian neighbors and federal assumption of more active supervision of Indian affairs, and the state, for the first time in its history, found itself with a revenue surplus. Governor Telfair estimated that the then current tax levies were producing at a rate of approximately double the normal requirements, and recommended proportionate reductions. The legislature responded promptly by cutting nearly all rates in half.[24] A year later it halved taxes again by reducing property valuations 50 per cent and making corresponding reductions in other taxes.[25] This second general slash apparently carried the process of reduction too far, because all rates were raised somewhat in 1792.[26] Two years later, however, the 1791 rates were restored throughout, except for the poll tax on free persons, which was abolished entirely.[27]

The state changed its monetary accounting from the British to the American system in 1796 and translated its tax rates into corresponding dollar terms. At the same time it made several changes in the tax structure: real property rates were cut two-thirds; the rate on slaves was increased one-third; merchandise stocks were rated at one-half of other property; the new United States stocks were taxed at ½ per cent; the luxury tax was extended to cover a number of new items; and the poll tax on free persons was reintroduced.[28] A noteworthy feature of this law was the application of the classification principle to property taxation. This was not a new practice, but this law extended the principle more broadly than had been customary.

In the following year property rates, except those on merchandise stocks, were lowered somewhat — land rates by about 12 per cent and other property rates by about 20 per cent.[29] The effect of these differential reductions was to extend the classification principle even further. Penalty double rates were reintroduced in 1798, but only on idle land holdings in excess of 10,000 acres.[30] The rate on merchandise stocks was equalized with other urban property in 1799, thus reducing by one group the range of classification of property taxes.[31] By the closing years of the century the tax system had become stabilized; it was reasonably well balanced, as well as adapted to the economic structure at the time.

Fees supplied a primary support of public services throughout the eighteenth century. The schedules instituted by the Crown were retained despite their rather widespread unpopularity. An act of 1781 approved the "customary fees of office," and ordered that they be paid in specie, or in continental currency in amounts according to the degree of depreciation of the latter.[32] Instances of overcharging, or illegal charging, apparently were not infrequent. An act of 1784 specified the exact fees of all public officers, provided heavy fines for overcharging, and required the posting of all schedules in the respective public offices;[33] and a second and similar act was passed in 1792.[34]

Fees were relatively high, which no doubt accounted for their general unpopularity. On a headright land grant of two hundred acres, for example, they added up to fourteen dollars. Fees commonly were paid directly to the officials,[35] and often constituted the primary, or even the only, source of compensation for public service. Since there were no reports upon fee collections, it is not possible to form any very significant estimate of their relative importance. However, it is clearly apparent that fees and the kindred category of commissions supplied the primary support for most ordinary services of government other than the salaries and expenses of the legislature and of a few top executive and judicial officers.

Commission payments were the rule in the sale of confiscated property and the collection of taxes. The Commissioners of Confiscated Property received, in addition to expenses, 1½ per cent of sales for their services.[36] Tax commissions were changed from time to time. Under the earlier laws the collector usually received 5 per cent of taxes actually paid; but at that time he was the sole tax-gathering official. When the receiver (assessor, or list-taker) was added, in 1785, he was allowed 1 per cent and the collector's commission was reduced to 2 per cent. Later, in the 1790's, when the receiver was made a full-time officer, the commission of each was fixed at 2½ per cent.[37]

Income from the sales of public property came almost entirely from the confiscated property. The greater part of the original sales occurred during 1782–1783. Purchase terms allowed seven years credit on realty and four years on personalty, with 7 per cent interest. From such imperfect evidence as exists it would appear that gross sales plus interest must have totaled at least $2,750,000. Properties of a value of some $250,000, probably, also were disposed of on special requisitions, bringing to $3,000,000, approximately, the total gross value of the transactions in this form of public property. Defaults and reversions, however, undoubtedly reduced the net realized figure much below this amount.[38]

Public land policy initially contemplated considerable revenues from cash sales. No records of receipts remain, however; and it does not seem likely that they were any considerable amount, since cash sales of one thousand acres or less were abolished in 1784, and payments for grants in excess of that could have been evaded by the practice of multiple grants.

The republican government, from the outbreak of the Revolution, proceeded upon the assumption that the central government would reimburse it for expenses incurred for continental troops in Georgia. Although the troops were authorized by the Continental Congress, presumably to be paid by that body, Georgia actually bore their entire expense until near the end of 1778; and it was this burden that was responsible for a large share of the paper money emissions and treasury loans.[39] Congress finally voted $400,000 in August 1777, "to sink and retire the Georgia currency";[40] but even then this sum of depreciated Continental currency did not arrive until May and June 1778. It was used to retire about one-third of the outstanding treasury certificates and their accumulated interest.[41] No further efforts were made to reimburse the state during the war; but the National Debt Funding Act of August 4, 1790, allotted $300,000 under the state debt assumption provisions.[42]

3. Public Debts

The Revolution was financed almost entirely on credit. During the first half of the war, credit operations were chiefly of two sorts: emissions of non-interest-bearing bills of credit, or paper money, and loans in the form of interest-bearing treasury certificates. The state issued paper money continuously from the outbreak of hostilities until September 1778. The total reached the neighborhood, probably, of $1,500,000.[43] It borrowed on treasury certificates some $925,000 during 1776–1778;[44] but this source of funds dried up after the heavy monetary depreciation during the closing months of 1777 had undermined the public credit.[45]

It became increasingly necessary, as public borrowing power waned and monetary depreciation made the currency less and less acceptable, to requisition army supplies on account or on officers' warrants. Troops faced the hard choice of accepting practically worthless paper or of going unpaid. These debts simply remained as outstanding claims against the government.[46] Limited amounts of Continental currency relieved the situation somewhat during the winter of 1778–1779, but this medium likewise soon depreciated to the same status as the Georgia currency. Requisitioning of goods continued throughout 1779–1781, and services generally went unrewarded.[47]

After the reëstablishment of civil government in August 1781, governor's bills were authorized as a credit medium;[48] but there is no available record of how extensively they were used. The assembly which met in January 1782, almost immediately authorized the emission of governor's certificates in the amount of $100,000, redeemable in confiscated property, to be used to pay soldiers and civilian officials and to purchase military supplies. This constituted a limited issue of paper money.[49]

Thus by the end of the war in the late summer of 1782 there had accumulated, in addition to the remaining old treasury certificates and the worthless paper money, a heterogeneous mass of other debts — purchase accounts, advances, officers' warrants, back-pay accounts, governor's bills, and the new monetized governor's certificates, which, reduced to a specie basis, totaled nearly one and one-half million dollars.[50]

Table 5

THE REVOLUTIONARY DEBT OF GEORGIA

Internal:		
Bills of credit (paper money), 1775–1778	$1,500,000	
Treasury certificates, including interest, 1775–1778	1,100,000	
Accounts payable, warrants, payrolls, advances, etc., 1777–1782	1,275,000	
Executive bills of 1781	25,000	
Governor's monetized certificates of 1782	100,000	
Total		$4,000,000
External:		
Pro rata share of Continental debt	475,000	
Pro rata share of French loans	300,000	
Pro rata share of Dutch loans	200,000	
Total		$ 975,000
Grand total		$4,975,000

The state was also incumbered, by common action and agreement, with *pro rata* shares of the Continental domestic debt and the French and Dutch loans.[51] Table 5 summarizes all of the above items of the Revolutionary debt.

Peace did not bring an end of financial deficits. High prices, extraordinary public activities, and constant Indian difficulties, coupled with the failure to levy sufficient taxes, kept the budget continuously unbalanced throughout the first seven postwar years. In effect, public obligations were met largely through the issue of governors' and speakers' orders and anticipation warrants. Sometimes, especially during 1783–1784, these commanded payments out of confiscated property sales; but typically they were orders upon the treasury and carried negotiability and legal tender for tax payments. Consequently, the treasury received little other funds than such orders and warrants. Tax levies in no year prior to 1790 equaled expenditures, which resulted in an accumulation of a large floating debt of official warrants and other claims. The Creek "War" years of 1787–1789 were especially notable for the growth of new debt.[52] The brief resort to paper money in 1786 temporarily halted the flow of warrants, presumably, but actually only added another form of debt to the collection.[53]

Net accretions to the debt in the above forms practically came to an end with the year 1790, except for certain small amounts resulting from the expenses of constitutional conventions and Indian conferences.[54]

Considerable amounts were added, however, by the conversion of Creek "War" land bounty promises into monetary obligations[55] and by the accumulations of unpaid interest on the funded portion of the debt.[56]

Table 6

POSTWAR DEBT OF GEORGIA, 1783–1799

Governors' and speakers' orders and warrants of 1783-1785, net outstanding in 1786,	$ 90,000
Bills of Credit (paper money) of 1786,	135,000
Governors' and speakers' orders and warrants, accounts payable, etc., Creek "War" period, 1787-1789,	400,000
Governors', speakers' and presidents' warrants, and treasury certificates, 1790–1799,	60,000
Conversion of Creek "War" land bounties, 1798–1799,	140,000
Accumulated interest on debt, through Dec. 31, 1799,	185,000
Total	$1,010,000

The first step in the retirement of war debt resulted from the reimbursement by Congress of $400,000 in Continental currency in 1778. As already noted, this money was used to reduce by one-third, approximately, the outstanding treasury certificates and unpaid interest.[57] Although it had been the expressed intention of Congress at the time to retire the state currency also, the funds were entirely inadequate, and no steps were taken by Congress to augment them.

Meanwhile the Georgia currency continued to depreciate rapidly, and with very oppressive effects. Despairing of further aid from Congress, the state turned elsewhere for a solution. In March 1778, following the practice of other states, it confiscated the properties of its leading royalist citizens. By the same act provision was made for the sale of these properties for Georgia currency, with the primary object of retiring the currency and the outstanding treasury certificates.[58] British invasion and subsequent breakdown of state government prevented, however, the fulfillment of this law. Nevertheless, the Georgia currency was retired in effect during the ensuing months through total depreciation.[59] The balance of unpaid treasury certificates remained outstanding until after the war.

The second half of the war, as already noted, increased the internal debts greatly, and also created sizable external ones. These were among the initial objects of consideration by the first peacetime government which assembled in January 1783. An act of February 15 directed the state auditor to receive and to audit all accounts, payrolls, and similar claims, to reduce them to a specie basis in accordance with depreciation tables which the assembly had adopted, and to issue new audited certificates accordingly.[60] The outstanding treasury certificates were not considered at this time; but two years later they likewise were ordered audited on a specie basis; and the old paper currency also was given a value of one-tenth of a cent per dollar in exchange for audited certificates.[61] The total debt at the end of the war in terms of specie amounted roughly to $2,675,000.

To attain the object of liquidating the debt, if possible, through the sale of the confiscated properties, a procedure was established by a general act of July 29, 1783, in substance as follows: all remaining confiscated property should be sold within four months; payments in audited certificates might not exceed one-half of any purchase price, including interest on deferred payments, but an option of conversion of certificates into seven-year, 7 per cent specie bonds of the state was provided; either privilege, of payment or conversion, must be exercised within one year from date of the act; sufficient amounts of private notes must be set aside, out of such as might be received through credit sales, to sink both the external debts and the new funded debt that would arise under the provisions of the act; and 200,000 acres of public lands, as well as the tax revenues of the state, were pledged additionally for the retirement of the several debts.[62]

In addition to the general war debts thus converted into claims upon the fund of confiscated properties, there were many special requisitions, usually for particular parcels of the property, which must have totaled in value at least $250,000. During the first postwar years governors' and speakers' warrants also frequently were made redeemable in these properties.[63]

The records of the financial operations under these various acts are confused, but the main outlines of what happened appear to have been somewhat as follows. The sales of the property originally grossed approximately $3,000,000, for which the state had received by 1790: in audited certificates, $770,000; in executive bills of 1781, $25,000; in certificates of 1782, $90,000; in funded specie bonds, $85,000; in governors' and speakers' warrants, $180,000; in personal notes (deferred payments), $1,600,000; and in special requisition orders (value) or specie, $250,000; some $285,000 of audited certificates were converted into specie bonds; approximately $5,000 of audited certificates were paid into the state treasury in taxes under the revenue act of 1785; and about $515,000 of audited certificates still remained outstanding, along with $10,000 of the monetized certificates of 1782.[64] Nothing whatever was done concerning the external debts; and to the remaining war debts were added some $625,000 of postwar debts.

A balance sheet of the state at the beginning of the year 1790 would have looked something like this:

Assets		*Liabilities*	
Notes payable,	$1,600,000	External debts	$975,000
		Funded debt	200,000
		Certificates of 1782	10,000
		Audited certificates	515,000
		Governors' and speakers' warrants	625,000
Total	$1,600,000	Total	$2,325,000

There was clearly a large deficit in ready assets, which required the consideration of sources in addition to the confiscated properties.

A strong movement developed in the coastal section to have the requirement of 50 per cent specie payment on confiscated property obligations reduced or eliminated entirely. This region was the chief holder of the public debt, most of which was non-interest-bearing, and almost the sole purchaser of confiscated property. Its proposal was rather hazardous, however, so long as the external and funded specie debts were outstanding. It was feared also, even by some in this section, that such a policy would unduly encourage speculations. The continued existence, however, of large amounts of outstanding audited certificates and postwar floating debt greatly enhanced the pressure for further monetization of the public debt. The governor and council ruled that public debt interest certificates should be accepted for any payment owed to the state; then the courts ruled that any claim against the government might be tendered in payment of any debt owed to the government; and finally, on January 11, 1788, the assembly resolved by a close sectional vote, that all forms of state debt should be receivable at the treasury in any payments to the state whatsoever.[65]

The Federal Funding Act of 1790 removed the entire external debt and also allotted, as previously noted, $300,000 to Georgia for the assumption of internal debts. Citizens who felt that they had borne thus far nearly the whole of the great financial and real costs of the war in their sector were keenly disappointed by the small amount of the state's apportionment; they felt, with justification it would seem, that the allotment greatly under-appraised the state's contribution to the common war effort.[66] Their efforts to secure an increase, however, do not appear to have met with success. After federal assumption, the state's remaining war debt amounted to $425,000 and its total of war and postwar debts, to $1,050,000. Thus its previous balance sheet deficit of $725,000 was transformed into a surplus of $550,000.

With the federal funding operations going forward, Governor Telfair thought the time opportune to put his state's financal affairs in order. No one knew exactly the extent of the claims against the state. Much of the debt bore no interest. The governor proposed a complete refunding in line with the program of the federal government, and including the placing of all debt equally upon one interest-bearing basis.[67] The legislature responded in 1792 by declaring that all other floating debts should enjoy the same status as the audited certificates.[68] In the following year it authorized a board, to be composed of the governor, auditor, and treasurer, which should audit all claims against the state, following as closely as possible the federal plan of debt funding.[69] The records of this auditing procedure are not clear. It would appear that some $550,000 of claims were audited, but the floating debt was not placed upon an interest-bearing basis.[70]

After the auditing measures of 1792–1793, it becomes no longer possible to separate war and postwar debts. Apparently about $350,000 of outstanding debt of one kind or another were retired during the 1790's; whereas unpaid interest on the funded debt, the conversion of Creek "War" land bounties, and the issue of treasury certificates and governors' warrants added some $385,000. Actually, since some of the arrears of interest may be credited to years prior to 1790, it seems probable that the debt remained almost stationary for the decade as a whole.[71]

Why, it may be asked, was the state not able to liquidate its debt out of the large holdings of private debts which were owing to it — an amount considerably in excess of the public debt after the federal funding act cut it in half? As things turned out, little was realized from the greater part of these private obligations. The economic recession of 1792–1793, the slow recovery of the coastal region, and the shift in speculative interest from the older region to the rich virgin lands of the interior produced wholesale defaults and reversions in confiscated properties. These properties were either resold at greatly reduced prices or, more likely, were transferred to the academies. It appears that the state did not collect much over $350,000 from this source after 1790. Although the state's accounts almost struck a balance for the decade as a whole, the periodic deficits arising out of the expenses of Indian treaties, constitutional conventions, and other extraordinary activities, and the irregularity of tax collections produced an almost continuous floating current debt in addition to the old debt. Table 7 summarizes the broad features of the history of debt retirement prior to 1800.

The final action concerning the debt during this period was the third general auditing, authorized in 1798–1799, but not completed until after 1800.[72] This was one of the first duties assigned to the new comptroller general's office, which was established in 1798, as a part of

Table 7

DEBT RETIREMENT, 1777-1799

Total Revolutionary Debt		$4,975,000
Retirements, 1777-1789:		
Treasury certificates and interest, by Continental currency, 1778	$ 400,000	
Bills of credit (paper money), by depreciation, 1777-1779	1,500,000	
Executive bills of 1781, by sale of confiscated property	25,000	
Certificates of 1782, ditto, 1782-1789	90,000	
Audited certificates, ditto, 1783-1789	770,000	
Funded debt, ditto, 1785-1789	85,000	
Audited certificates, by tax of 1785	5,000	
Treasury certificates, by reduction to specie value, 1785-1789	400,000	
Total		3,275,000
Revolutionary debt outstanding, 1790		1,700,000
Postwar debt outstanding, 1790		625,000
Total debt, 1790		2,325,000
Retirement by Federal Funding Act of 1790:		
Continental — French and Dutch loans	975,000	
Assumption of state debt	300,000	
Total		1,275,000
Total outstanding debt after federal assumption		1,050,000
Additions to indebtedness, 1790-1799	385,000	
Retirements of indebtedness, 1790-1799	350,000	
Net addition to indebtedness, 1790-1799		35,000
Total debt outstanding, December 31, 1799		$1,085,000

Governor James Jackson's fiscal reform program. No doubt the audit was intended also to supply a better factual basis for discussions with the federal government over the settlement of the western land question. The continued existence of the debt throughout the 1790's was a vital factor in the matter of western lands, in the transactions with both the central government and the private land companies. The state's attitudes and policy were in every respect identical with those of the central government: for both, the western lands presented the most likely means for the retirement of debts.

4. Fiscal Administration

Fiscal machinery remained during most of the first quarter century of statehood much what it had been under the Crown, except that there was some tendency toward decentralization of responsibility in tax administration. The state treasurer continued to be the chief receiving, disbursing, accounting, and reporting officer. Governors, speakers, and presidents of the Senate and constitutional conventions, however, regularly issued financial orders and warrants, which almost as frequently became a part of the outstanding public debt along with certificates emanating from the treasurer's office. The legislature named the tax collectors by counties for each revenue act; superior court judges appointed the tax assessors, or receivers, as they came to be called, in each county; militia officers usually were required to assist the receivers in making up the tax lists; and the clerk of the superior court in each county was required to digest the tax lists and supply copies for the collectors, the state treasurer, and the county public records. In instances of paper money authorizations, the legislature usually designated a special board, an executive committee, or the governor as the emitting agency. Such administrative boards as the Commissioners of the Confiscated Properties, the Commissioners of the Loan Fund, and the Commissioners of the State Insurance Company enjoyed a certain measure of financial autonomy.

It can readily be seen that financial administration involved a mixture of variously designated powers, *ex officio* duties, part-time activities, and divided responsibilities. Under the simple conditions that prevailed in the colony, with the controls that were exercised by the colonial governor and assembly, this conglomerate system of administration probably functioned well enough; but under the democratic processes of the new state, with its rapidly expanding territory and population, and its weighty financial problems, the traditional system responded haltingly and ineffectually.

During the Revolution, as might have been expected, the fiscal machinery proved woefully inadequate. Experienced administrative personnel were lacking, or were royalist in sympathy. Both patriot leadership and rank-and-file were spread thinly over civil and military functions, as well as over the operations of a private economy that had lost its markets and chief means of financial support.[73] The state treasurer in person constituted most of the fiscal administration. Fortunately for the republicans, their number included such able men as John Wereat and Samuel Stirk, who were willing to devote their business experience, untiring energy, and deep patriotism to wrestling with state financial problems.[74] There are no records of the collection of tax revenues; but since it had never been done very effectively under peaceful conditions and before the colony was divided, it could scarcely have been attempted seriously during the years of revolt. Purchasing and disbursing necessarily became greatly expanded tasks. Staffs could not be recruited for the performance of such functions; and they were distributed, as additional duties, among various civil and military officers. Probably there was scarcely an official of any rank, civil or military, who did not at some time perform some task of a financial character.[75]

Financial records were in a chaotic state at the end of the war. Few officers had submitted any reports of financial transactions intrusted to them, or, in all likelihood for that matter, had even kept any accounts of such transactions.[76] Many had been outside the state for long periods serving on other fronts; and records had been destroyed, lost, or sent elsewhere for safekeeping. Nevertheless, financial rehabilitation demanded as prompt and complete an accounting as possible. A general law was passed in 1784 "to compel all persons who have received public monies to account for the same." [77] Inadequate accounting and reporting, however, continued to characterize the fiscal side of government operation for several years after the war.[78] This resulted as much from administrative structure as from official ineptitude.

The weakest link in postwar fiscal administration, probably, was tax collection. Listings were extremely incomplete in the early years; and there was much evasion by both resident and nonresident property owners. Tax delinquencies and collection defaults were shockingly high, in some years almost equaling the amount of revenues paid into the treasury. Defaulting collectors presented an especially difficult problem. They were surprisingly numerous, and individual delinquencies frequently amounted to large sums, many of which were never recovered. The reporting of collections to the state treasurer was haphazard and irregular.[79] Governors repeatedly urged the legislature to remedy the situation, but obtained little effective response. The great majority of the tax officials were local politicians or petty officials of long standing in their communities, and their legislative representatives were diffident about measures that might disaffect them. Little was done until 1796–1799, when a complete overhauling of the administrative machinery finally was effected under the reform leadership of James Jackson.

Jackson advocated taking tax administration out of politics and placing it upon a purely professional basis. The employment of old, faithful political workers on part time, he contended, resulted in haphazard, desultory performances and a general inefficiency in fiscal operations. His program called for: the employment of full-time young men; the centralization of each responsibility in a single individual; the establishment of regular time schedules for the performance of all duties, including even those of the taxpayer; the provision for proper and adequate safeguards and penalties; and some measure of central executive control.[80]

The legislature of 1796, of which Jackson was a member, made a beginning by introducing provisions designed to secure better listing, reporting, and digesting of returns and imposing penalties upon listers and collectors for administrative failures.[81] A year later tax-listing was placed in the hands of a single receiver in each county, who was directed to supervise listing by the militia captains and to make up the tax digest; collectors were to be placed under bond which should be in proportion to the amount of funds that each normally handled.[82] The final changes, made in 1799, required the receiver to do the actual listing, with the aid of the militia captain; both receivers and collectors were made directly responsible to the comptroller-general of the state and to such regulations as he might deem necessary; returns were required before May 1 in each year; and taxes became in default after the following February 1.[83]

Coincident with these changes in tax administration there were instituted, during 1798–1799, equally important changes in the central executive segment of fiscal administration. The state treasurer was relieved of a large number of his general duties and was made almost solely a disbursing officer. The new office of comptroller-general was established and was given financial and accounting control over all fiscal operations of the government. Financial operations generally were separated into specialized tasks, as already noted above in regard to tax collection, with the comptroller-general's office endowed with the general supervisory function of auditing and reporting.[84] The principles and aims behind this legislation were unquestionably of the nature of those of present day budgetary control. During these four years the state moved a considerable way toward establishing a unified fiscal organization which was fashioned, in image at least, along modern functional lines.

PART THREE

THE DEVELOPMENT OF PUBLIC ECONOMIC POLICY

CHAPTER VII

THE STATE RECHARTS ITS LAND POLICY

1. The Reawakening of the Spirit of Constructive Liberalism

The Constitution of 1798 completed the transition from the old colonial system to the framework of the new democratic state. James Jackson was greatly pleased with it and was proud of the wide interest taken in it outside of the state. It contained a declaration of his cardinal principle, "that monopolies of land by individuals" are "contrary to the spirit of our free government." [1] It constituted, in his opinion, a reaffirmation of the principles of the Revolution and thereby provided a solid basis in government for individual liberty and opportunity. It was fitting that Jackson should be the first governor to be chosen under it. He was followed over the succeeding two decades by such able members of his party as Josiah Tatnall, John Milledge, David B. Mitchell, and Jared Irwin, who, with William H. Crawford and Thomas U. P. Charlton, had led the actions in the rescinding legislature and the constitutional convention.[2] Crawford, who already was second only to Jackson in influence in the state, was soon to become the foremost Georgian in national life, and Charlton was destined to guide in large measure the judicial life of the state for the next three decades. To this group of men, whose vigorous leadership and ideas in the Yazoo controversy had awakened a new social consciousness and coöperative spirit among the citizens of Georgia, was given the opportunity to formulate and guide a policy of constructive social action.

The program developed around the following primary objectives: the creation of a new land policy, promotion of education and internal improvements, establishment of a sound currency, reform of the penal laws and institutions, and development of efficient and responsible public administration. Land policy, viewed from almost any angle, was the heart of the program. In a broad sense, the full employment of land was the chief objective of all economic policy. At the same time, through the disposal of land it was hoped to secure the means to promote the balance of the program. And, finally, it was through land policy primarily that it was planned to lay the foundations for the type of society that would promote the largest measure of human welfare. The first four decades of the nineteenth century witnessed the various steps in the development of this program of constructive liberalism. Important reforms in public administration were introduced under Governor Jackson during 1798–1801,[3] the new land policy was launched in 1803, followed by some beginnings in education and internal improvements. Banking was begun in 1810, penal reforms in 1812, followed by renewed and larger efforts in education and internal improvements for a decade and a half, then the establishment in 1828 of a public bank for capital loans and, finally, in the mid-thirties, the climactic launching of the railway system.

Commencement of the program, however, almost of necessity awaited the settlement of the western land question. Consequently, Jackson opened negotiations for a settlement with the federal government almost immediately upon becoming governor. He proposed the establishment of Georgia's western boundary upon the line of the Chattahoochee River, because he believed that such a limitation of territory would enable the state to plan and execute its internal development upon a scale proportionate with its powers to achieve constructive results.[4] Negotiations with the United States lagged, however, until Jackson's election to the United States Senate in 1801; whereupon he became one of the Georgia commissioners with Abraham Baldwin and John Milledge and terms of transfer were shortly arranged between this group and the United States Commissioners James Madison, Albert Gallatin, and Levi Lincoln. Georgia ratified the treaty on June 16, 1802, whereby it transferred the territory comprising the future states of Alabama and Mississippi to the United States in return for a sum of $1,250,000, to be paid out of the receipts from land sales in the territory, and a promise from the federal government to extinguish all Indian land titles within Georgia as soon as possible.

The United States met the first installment on the latter promise during the same year through the Treaty of Fort Wilkinson, whereby the Creeks were induced to relinquish about a third of their lands between the Oconee and Ocmulgee rivers and the Tellassee region south of the Altamaha River which Georgia had long claimed under previous treaties. Thus the state found itself again with public lands that were available for settlement.

The Jacksonian Liberals were determined that the old headright system — almost as tainted with administrative laxity, corruption, and monopoly as the Yazoo land sales — should not be extended to the new territories, and their attitude appears to have met popular approval. The willingness to give up so readily a system that had become deeply rooted in the state's institutional fabric is one of the amazing facts of history and testifies to the capacity of human beings for undertaking group planning and experimentation. There was not the same agreement, however, regarding principles upon which a new policy should be drawn. The most crucial difference was the perennial one of free land versus revenue. This promised the sharpest political division, arraying the poorer counties and frontier communities against the older and wealthier sections. Furthermore, the supporters of the revenue principle were divided by differences in motives into three groups: the liberals, who were seeking sources of funds with which to carry out the complementary projects of social and economic development; the property owners, whose object was the reduction of taxes; and the holders of state debt, who sought to have debt payment recognized as the first claim upon the new lands. There was the further problem of agreement upon criteria and levels of prices. Both liberals and tax reduction advocates had in mind the conversion of public equities in land into some permanent and more convenient and manageable type of public investment that would supply a continuing stream of public revenues; hence they favored prices that would yield a substantial capital sum. The holders of public debt, on the other hand, were not concerned with any such continuing public revenue objectives. Many were speculators who had acquired public certificates of debt at greatly depreciated values with the object of purchasing public lands therewith at low prices. They favored a law that would permit direct exchange of public debts for land. If such provision were made, a cheap land policy would prove most beneficial to public debt holders. Herein lay a serious danger to land policy reform: that the free land advocates would join forces with the land speculators to produce a new version of the old headright system. Nothing would be more likely to defeat the purposes of the free land advocates than such an outcome; but it was just such a coalition that had produced the demoralization of the headright system.

The land issues crowded out all others in the legislative campaign of the summer and fall of 1802. The advocates of free and equal land grants contended that a revenue policy would exclude the poor man from land ownership and produce the very speculation and land-grabbing that the rescinding law, the Constitution, and proposed reforms sought to prevent. The revenue policy supporters countered with the argument that equal distribution would promote speculation and large holdings, because it would result in plots too small for economical use, which therefore would be sold; that public administration of such a plan would be very costly and, if land were given free, would create an intolerable fiscal burden; that reasonable prices, particularly if deferred payments were allowed, would work a hardship on no one; that the failure in the past to obtain any revenue from the alienation of the public lands had caused the state to lag far behind other American states in education and internal improvements; that the needs for such public services had become more urgent than the supplying of a part of the citizenry with free lands; and that the benefits to be derived from such services almost certainly would be more universally and equitably distributed. Much was made by landowners in the older regions of the probable adverse effects of free land upon land values in their sections. Their plea for a revenue policy as an avenue to tax reduction did not have the sympathy of the liberals, since such an outcome was likely to defeat a considerable part of the liberal program. The debt-payment proposals attracted little support other than from the debt holders themselves. It was popular belief that the principal holders were none others than the Yazoo land speculators themselves and that they were trying to perpetrate another land "deal" upon the state. It was too soon after the Yazoo scandal for the public to consent to the adoption of any policy whereby any participants in that speculation might benefit.[5]

Regardless of the equities of the public debt claims, popular opposition resulting from their supposed speculative basis strengthened the hands of the liberals in their fight for land policy reforms. One of their primary aims was the prevention of land speculation. Not only did they wish to make certain that speculators would not benefit directly from the process of land distribution but they also hoped to build a structure of land ownership that would not be conducive to land speculation in the future. To Jackson, speculators and monopolists were the eternal foes of a free society.[6] Governor Josiah Tatnall in his final message to the legislature in November 1802, urged that body, in its consideration of a policy for the new land cessions, to "guard against large monopolies in land by individuals, the baneful effects of which already (had) become all too visible in America. The histories of other nations, ancient and modern, (furnished) abundant proof of the destructive consequences of these encroachments upon the natural and common rights of man."[7] As the leading professional military member of the liberal group, Tatnall also outlined the relationship between liberal military policy and land policy. A large standing army being inconsistent with and dangerous to a democracy, reliance for protection must be placed in a militia of all the free citizens, of whom the yeoman population would always constitute the best defenders; hence the widest possible land ownership among its citizens would afford the maximum of safety to the democratic state; whereas, concentrations of wealth in land would reduce the numbers of independent land owners and correspondingly weaken a democracy, and more especially so in the South where the bulk of the population, under conditions of large landholding, would always be composed of slaves.[8]

A special session of the legislature, as previously arranged, was called by Governor John Milledge in May 1803, to deal specifically with land policy in the new cessions. In his special message, Milledge placed foremost emphasis upon the desirability of keeping the lands out of the hands of speculators. This had proved very difficult in the past in Georgia, unless title had been withheld until actual settlement and improvement of a grant had taken place. If the headright system were continued, all those who did not wish to settle would nevertheless exercise their rights to acquire land in order to sell to land companies. The legislature must "guard all avenues of private interest," if it expected to achieve a land policy that would serve the highest interests of the state and produce the maximum general welfare. With a soundly conceived land policy, Georgia, because of its strategic geographic location between north and south, east and west, interior and sea, the old Atlantic communities and the virgin soils of the southwest, might lay the foundations that would enable it to become the empire state of the union. The strength of a state depended upon the numbers of its population and their industry. Above all, Georgia must "smother in the bud all hopes entertained by individuals of accumulating in the western parts of the state a large landed interest. Let us secure the industrious poor from the grasping hand of the rich speculator."[9] Here was an appeal for the creation of a genuine homestead system that would assure a society made up predominantly of small independent landed proprietors.

2. A New Homestead Policy

The land law passed on May 11, 1803, was remarkable, in that it abandoned almost entirely every vestige of the headright system and substituted in its stead a blueprint for settlement of the entire region under a centrally administered plan which provided for mass surveying in advance, the distribution of uniform homestead grants by lottery with equal opportunity to all and the planning and laying out of a metropolitan center within the area.[10] It marked a return to the concept of planned settlement introduced into Georgia by the Trustees. Instead of small parcels of land for everybody, which was obviously impracticable, everyone was given substantially an equal chance to draw a lot that was adequate in size to permit an average family to attain a reasonably high level of income. The act as originally passed also embodied the revenue principle: lands were to be priced from 6¼ cents to $1.00 per acre according to quality, and administrative fees were to be graduated in similar fashion. The prices were extremely moderate, since the maximum charge was 20 per cent below the lowest charge for any quality of land ever made by the federal government. Fractional lots, resulting from irregularities of streams and boundaries, and islands were to be withheld from the lottery and sold at the direction of the legislature. Fraudulent draws and reverted lots were to be treated in the same manner as fractions. A tract of 3,240 acres was to be selected at or near the head of navigation on the south bank of the Oconee River and reserved for the site of a city, which should be the new capital of the state and should be named Milledgeville in honor of the governor.

The legislature carefully retained control over general policy and the appointment of commissioners, surveyors, and managers. These, however, were to serve under the direction of the governor, who was named the chief administrative officer of the new land policy, and who was empowered also to call upon various executive departments for assistance whenever necessary. Local officialdom, which had ruled supreme under the headright system, was restricted to compilation of the lists of eligible drawers. This was made the duty of the county inferior courts. Even this remaining exercise of local option was to be carefully scrutinized by state officers who were empowered to initiate action, to unearth fraud, to throw out fraudulent names, and to recover any lands obtained in a fraudulent manner. Broadly speaking the new land distribution system was to have four main administrative tasks: (1) the general surveying and platting of the new territory, (2) the operation of the lottery, including the assembling of lists, the actual drawing, the collection of prices and fees, and the issuing of titles, (3) the sale of fractions, special lots, fraudulent draws, and reverted grants, the collection of payments, and the issue of title, and (4) the selection, planning, and laying out of city sites, the disposal of lots, and the construction of public works.

The law passed the legislature by majorities of two to one with only a group of the poorer interior counties opposing it.[11] But the division was much closer in the votes on some of the cardinal issues. A proposed free land amendment failed to pass by the narrowest of margins, with the poorer counties favoring it and the richer ones opposing; and an attempt to introduce a soldiers' bounty feature obtained considerable support, though it finally was defeated. However, the efforts to introduce provisions for the exchange of lands for the public debt certificates were defeated easily.[12]

The free land principle had won additional adherents with the meeting of the regular session in the autumn of 1803, when the provisions for graduated prices and administrative fees were deleted from the law and in their place was inserted the stipulation that lands should be granted free of purchase in fee simple and subject only to a uniform fee of $4.00 per hundred acres in lieu of all customary fees of office and other charges. The revenue principle was not scrapped entirely, however, since the provisions for the sale of fractions and city lots were retained; but unquestionably the hopes of the liberals for the establishment of funds for the promotion of education, internal improvements, and welfare institutions were greatly dimmed. Even the very modest prices that had been established might have netted the state eventually between $15,000,000 and $20,000,000 out of its public land domain — a sum that might have carried the state a considerable way toward the goals set by some of its more forward-looking leaders. The rank and file of Georgians still were motivated primarily by land hunger and had not as yet become fully aware of the correlative needs of education, cheap transportation and ameliorative social services.

The law created out of the land cessions the three new counties of Baldwin, Wilkinson, and Wayne, which were to be laid off in districts and further divided into squares of 202½ acres in Baldwin and Wilkinson and 490 acres in Wayne.[13] The lines of the lots were to be run parallel to the boundaries of the districts. The lottery commissioners were to hold the drawing as soon as the numbered plats of the lots had been returned to the surveyor-general's office. Draws were to be allowed as follows: one to every free white male of twenty-one years or over, who was a citizen of the United States and a resident of Georgia, or had paid taxes, during the preceding twelve months; two draws to every such with wife and one or more minor children; two draws to every widow with one or more minor children; and one draw to every family of orphans under twenty-one years of age. The law further stipulated the procedure of the Milledgeville commissioners.

This act laid the foundation of the state's new land policy, which was to remain essentially unchanged in principle and practice thereafter. Under this policy some 26,000,000 acres, or nearly three-fourths of the area of the state, were distributed among more than 100,000 individuals or families. It constituted the leading business of the state during the first third of the nineteenth century.

3. Land Cessions, Land Lotteries, and Settlement

The history of Georgia during this period featured a succession of waves of migration set in motion by successive Indian land cessions and public land lotteries. Each wave constituted a self-generating cycle, which also initiated in large measure its successor. As one territorial cession filled up, pressure against the Indian frontiers would increase, the clamor for a new cession would grow more intense, the demands of political leaders upon the federal government for action would mount to fever pitch, Indian treaties again would be arranged, a new territorial cession would be obtained, another lottery would be run off, and a new wave of migration would thrust forward. This wave-like pattern of settlement produced successive frontiers in Georgia over a longer period, probably, than was experienced by any other American state. Georgia had a highly active frontier continuously from its founding until the outbreak of the Civil War. Its frontier reached its most mobile, wave-like character, however, after 1800.

Relatively few basic changes were made in the lottery system after 1803. The act of 1806 assigned the proceeds of the fraction sales of the cessions of 1804–1805 to retirement of the state debt. When it became

Table 8

GEORGIA: TERRITORIAL CESSIONS AND LAND LOTTERIES

Indian cession treaty	Ceded territory	Date of lottery
Fort Wilkinson, 1802	Trans-Oconee region; Tellassee region south of Altamaha River	1804
Flint River, 1804 and Washington, 1805	All remaining Creek lands between Oconee and Ocmulgee rivers	1806
Cherokee Agency, 1814	Wafford's Settlement in northeast Georgia	
Fort Jackson, 1814	All remaining Creek lands in south Georgia	
Cherokee Agency, 1817	Tract in northeast Georgia	
Creek Agency, 1818	Tract in north-central Georgia; tract south of Altamaha and Ocmulgee rivers	
Cherokee Agency, 1819	Tract in northeast Georgia	1820
Indian Springs, 1821	All remaining Creek lands east of Flint River	1821
Indian Springs, 1825, 1826, and 1828	All remaining Creek lands in Georgia	1827
New Echota, 1835	All remaining Cherokee lands in Georgia	1832 (gold) 1832

The five tracts that were ceded under treaties during 1814–1819 were lumped together in one lottery in 1820. The military treaty of Fort Jackson, which granted to Georgia the lands in the southern part of the state, was very unpopular; the lands were remote and were considered most inferior, hence there was little demand to have then distributed. Action was held up also by controversies with Florida over the boundary line between the two states.

Northwest Georgia (Cherokee Territory) was surveyed and distributed three years prior to the Treaty of New Echota, which ceded the territory to Georgia, and six years before the last Cherokees were ejected from it. Gold was discovered in the region at the time of the surveying, and so the gold lands were separated from the others and distributed through a special gold lottery.

apparent later that the returns would be insufficient for the purpose, the proceeds from the remaining fraction bonds of the previous cession also were included. Thus the original decision of 1803 was reversed. The size of the regular grant was increased to 250 acres in 1820, because of the less desirable quality of the lands in that group of tracts,[14] but again was fixed at 202½ acres in the great lotteries of 1821 and 1827, and was reduced to 160 and 40 acres respectively in the general and the gold lotteries of 1832. Successful drawers, other than war veterans, were excluded from succeeding lotteries. Eligibility for drawing was broadened somewhat in successive lotteries to include all widows, single females in some instances, idiots, lunatics, insane, deaf, dumb, and blind. Disabled veterans, and eventually all veterans, were given an extra draw, but were limited to a single draw if they had been successful in a previous lottery. The administrative fee was increased to $6.00 per hundred acres in 1806 and then was changed to a flat rate of $18.00 per grant in 1820. This was increased to $19.00 in 1821, but was returned to $18.00 in 1827. The gold lot fees were fixed at $10.00. Provisions similar to those relating to the establishment of Milledgeville were included in the laws of 1821 and 1827 for the laying out of Macon and Columbus at the head of navigation of the Ocmulgee and Chattahoochee rivers respectively. Lots 10 and 100 in each surveyor's district of the tracts distributed in 1820 were reserved for the establishment of schools for poor children. This latter policy was discontinued in later acts, but the returns from special reserves withheld by the state from the lotteries of 1821 and 1827 were assigned to poor schools. The policy of withholding special reserves, advocated by Governor John Clark, represented the introduction on a modest scale in non-urban as well as urban lands of the principle of holding back a part of the public lands for the advance in values that was expected to result from private settlement of contiguous lands. Administrative changes, with one exception, were minor. When the Central Bank of Georgia was established in 1828, the personal bonds and notes that had been received for fractions and other lot sales were transferred to the Bank for collection or conversion to a banking basis.

The lottery distribution constituted by far the most extensive and important phase of the new land policy. It proved a relatively simple and popular method of land distribution. Successful drawers were slower, however, in claiming their grants than had been anticipated and, consequently, the legislature was being importuned continuously to extend the time limits for taking out grants. The law permitted one year from the time of drawing, but extensions of time soon became a chronic action of the legislatures. It required from ten to twelve years on the average before the bulk of the grants in any lottery was taken up. These delays were caused by a variety of social and economic factors affecting the individual drawers, by the frequent isolation and remoteness of lots, by the usual percentage of poor lots, or by the desire to avoid taxation as long as possible when occupation was not anticipated at once. A severe business depression always produced widespread delays. The lottery of 1820 was peculiarly beset by practically all of these factors in a high degree: consequently, only about two-thirds of the grants were claimed during the first ten years. However, during the 1830's, as settlement and cotton production spread south and southwest and as a boom developed in land prices, the remaining grants were mostly taken up. The legislature was particularly lenient with time extensions during this period. Although the last lottery was drawn in 1832, time extensions still were being granted in the late 1840's. Finally, in 1854, it was decreed that all remaining unclaimed grants should be sold.

There is no indication of serious malfeasance in connection with the lottery distributions; though fraudulent listing at the local level persisted as a minor vexation. It was reported after the first two lotteries that many had returned names falsely, "even under oath" — either they had not been in the state the required length of time, or were under age, or pretended to be heads of families, or "alleged to be widows when they knew they were married women." [15] Certainly the temptation to have a poor memory, under the circumstances in Georgia in the early nineteenth century, must have been very strong indeed with many people. Numerous laws were passed in an effort to ferret out such misfeasances and to prevent their recurrence, but the law of averages respecting human nature seemed to run right on through all the successive lotteries. Sales of fraudulent grants reached their highest level in the 1830's.[16] Relatively speaking, however, the incidence of this type of fraud must be considered insignificant. It was restricted entirely, apparently, to isolated individual cases, as there was no evidence of collusion with local officials.

4. The State as Land Merchandiser

The fraction sales were conducted usually by special boards of commissioners elected by the legislature. They were widely advertised in Georgia and in neighboring states and were held at public auction commonly at Milledgeville shortly following the lottery drawings. Terms of sale usually were four equal yearly payments with interest, and with personal bond and mortgage upon the property in favor of the governor required. Title was not allowed to pass until payments had been completed. The state also found it necessary to introduce certain other safeguards of its interest: the government was authorized, in 1815, to bid at foreclosure sales in order to prevent collusion, and minimum prices on all fractions, according to type and grade, were legislated in 1821.

The policy of renting unsold fractions and other reserved lands was adopted in 1808. This was not an entirely novel undertaking, since the state had long engaged in the leasing of public ferries, ferry sites, and bridges. But this first venture in renting lands proved extremely troublesome and vexatious, and scarcely returned its costs.[17] Consequently, it was abandoned almost immediately and renting was not attempted again until the decade of the 1820's following the lotteries of 1820 and 1821. School lands, under the former law, and the special reserves under the latter were chiefly involved. The business was contracted to special agents and the results proved somewhat better than in the earlier experience; yet renting was a source of trouble, and uncollected rents ran high. The practice of allowing deferred payments, on the same basis as in the sale of fractions, appears to have been exceedingly unwise. This second experiment with renting ceased with the decision in 1827 to dispose of all remaining fractions, public reserves, and lots of every kind.

The state experienced much difficulty with the collection of time payments, partly as a result of official laxity, but mostly from economic reasons of one kind or another. The legislature alternately ordered foreclosure and granted relief. The extent of the latter customarily amounted to the waiving of further payments for one year provided all back interest and a part of the defaulted principal were paid. Such relief was granted very generally during 1811–1812, 1815–1819, and 1824–1829. These acts bore some resemblance to stay laws and were continued from year to year in much the same fashion. During 1824–1829, payments were waived five successive years. Relief granted in similar fashion to renters of public lands usually resulted in the loss of the rents, since the state frequently held poor security and renters were inclined to move away. Relief often came to purchasers and renters without benefit of legislative action, simply through the failure of officials to enforce collection or foreclosure. The Clark administration of 1819–1823, being strongly in sympathy with small farmers and appreciative of their difficulties, appears to have made rather feeble efforts to collect debts in a number of the newer counties.[18] Losses to the state were heavy in both this and the 1824–1829 periods.

It should not be concluded from such evidence, however, that the government was notably less efficient than private business concerns in similar transactions, or that political factors necessarily made for greater laxity in the conduct of the public business. By and large the government simply was following the common practices of the merchants, who habitually indulged hard-pressed debtors or were compelled to forego collections during hard times. Laxities in private business, furthermore, never resulted in public exposure, impeachment, or trial as sometimes did omissions and transgressions in public office. Considering the fact that the state was extending credit almost entirely upon new ventures in pioneer areas which were without established markets or transportation facilities, whereas merchants normally granted accommodation to established planters in developed regions, the public record, comparatively speaking, was a surprisingly good one. The state probably was overlenient, and lost considerable money as a result. However, a large amount of land was recovered from defaulters under foreclosure and was resold; and there is little evidence that any considerable number of purchasers ultimately escaped payments. The business was difficult owing to its scattered, local nature and to the large number of small buyers.

The merchandising of the fractions did not come off without some charges and evidences of fraud. Governor Irwin ordered resurveys in one district in 1808, because of evidence that sizable tracts were being classed falsely as fractions, apparently to accommodate large buyers.[19] Three commissioners were impeached, tried, and convicted in connection with this and similar actions, and the governor's secretary was charged with profiting out of questionable sales and illegal fees.[20] The most publicized case was the impeachment and trial of three commissioners who were appointed by Governor Clark in 1820 and later charged with withholding receipts of sales and other fraudulent actions. The legislature tried the case in 1825, but failed to convict in what appeared to be primarily a political action against the Clark forces.[21]

The business of selling fractions was most extensive under the laws of 1803 and 1806. It declined in importance under later laws mainly because of the practice of including the larger and more desirable fractions in the lottery drawings. However, the merchandising of a miscellaneous collection of old fractions, fraudulent grants, reverted lots, unclaimed lots, foreclosed lots, and various parcels of land that had been overlooked continued on as a sort of residual business for a couple of decades after the last lottery was drawn. Repeated attempts were made, from 1827 on, to wind up the business. Finally, an act was passed on December 28, 1842, which granted all claimants and debtors until July 1, 1843, to make settlement with the state, after which all lands remaining unclaimed or in default as to payments were to revert to the state and, with all other lands of any sort whatsoever in the state's possession, were to be sold immediately at public auction. Subsequently however, the deadline for settlement was extended for one year and another method of sale was substituted for the auction plan. This ingenious procedure, first used in 1814 and 1815 to dispose of remaining ungranted lands of the first two lotteries, provided a sliding scale of payments in time. Anyone could claim any tract of land remaining in the state's possession during October 1844, by paying $2,000; during November, by paying $1,500; during December, $1,000; January through April 1845, $500; May to June, $250; July to August, $100; September to December, $25; and after December, $5.00.[22] The response to this offer astonished the state officials. By the time that the $25 period approached over four thousand applications with cash payments enclosed had been received and several hundred people had arrived at the capital with the intent of purchasing land. The numbers were so great that the officials decided to run a lottery to determine the order of selection. The treasury had received $75,000 before October 1, 1845.[23] Additional lots and fractions that had never been offered to the public, were discovered later in the year, and so a second descending-scale sale was ordered for 1846–1847. An act of December 30, 1847, ordered that any fractions that reverted after November 1, 1848, should be sold by the sheriffs of the respective counties, and an act of 1854 made this rule applicable to all unclaimed lands.

5. Town and City Planning

That phase of the new land policy concerned with the laying out of Milledgeville and, later, of Macon and Columbus, unlike its other aspects, was by no means novel. The planning and laying out of cities in advance of inhabitation was the oldest and had been the most consistently practiced feature of Georgia public land policy, since it dated from the planning and surveying of Savannah and had characterized the origin of almost every town and city afterwards. It is one of the strongest links between Trustee planning and the new land policy and almost might be said to have suggested the central principle of that policy. The procedure already had become well standardized.

It was customary for the legislature to elect a board of commissioners and to endow them virtually with the powers of a public corporation for the purposes of selecting a site, planning and laying out streets, lots, squares, and parks, choosing the locations of public buildings, markets, commercial properties, schools, churches and other common facilities and premises, selling lots and issuing titles, and constructing a courthouse, jail, market, wharf, warehouse, academy, public school, or such other facilities as the particular municipality or its location should require. The legislature either granted the land for the urban site from the public domain or, if no public lands were available, authorized the commissioners to acquire a suitable tract. The commissioners invariably were constituted the governing authority of the new municipality until such time as the legislature saw fit to incorporate the town into a self-governing unit. Such incorporation, however, seldom terminated the life of the original board of commissioners: usually it continued to hold and dispose of the remaining public lots; sometimes it became the corporate body of directors of the public market, ferry, bridge, or some other public utility; but most frequently it continued in existence as the board of trustees of the local academy or public school. Such an educational institution commonly was designated by the legislature as the residuary legatee of all public lots and other public property within the limits of the municipality. Because of the importance of this early planning, selling, and public construction work, the board of commissioners for a time often overshadowed the elected town government. Not infrequently the two bodies were almost identical. Usually, the original board, in its metamorphosis from a legislatively elected planning board to the governing body of the local institute of learning, became a self-perpetuating body.

Augusta had supplied the earliest instance of urban planning under state authorization. That town, like others before the Revolution, had been planned and founded originally by the colonial government of the Trustees; but the frontier, trading character of its early life, speculation, and the Revolution had rather twisted the early plan. Consequently, a state law of 1780, after reciting the fact that lots in Augusta had been monopolized in such a way as to prevent settlement in the manner originally intended, created a board of five commissioners with powers to lay out all vacant lands above and below the town into streets and lots and to have the lots sold at public auction. The board was authorized further to straighten all streets in Augusta as well as all roads leading thereto. Minimum dimensions were specified for all houses; and they were to be built in a workmanlike fashion and placed on that part of each lot directed by the commissioners, "to the end that the town shall be regularly built." The commissioners were further empowered to reserve lots for schools, seminaries, and churches.[24] The British invasion shortly after its passage prevented any action under this law, but it was reënacted in 1783 with some additional provisions. Purchased lots were to be built upon within two years, or they should revert to the commissioners. Ten of the principal lots were reserved for public uses and one for a church. All others were to be sold at the discretion of the commissioners and all funds derived therefrom, except enough for the building of the church, were to go toward the erection and support of a seminary or academy, of which the commissioners were to be the trustees.[25] Out of this last provision of the act originated the famous Richmond Academy. The commissioners likewise operated the church and almost every other public function in Augusta for a number of years. But after the incorporation of the municipality as a second class city, their chief function became the direction of the affairs of the academy. Under their governance that institution acquired a large property endowment — in city lots, ferry and bridge leases, bank and canal stocks, and various legacies.[26]

The most prominent of these early boards of commissioners, other than the Augusta one, was that of Louisville. This board was empowered to select one thousand acres of land within twenty miles of the old trading post of Galphin's Old Town on the upper Ogeechee River and to lay out a city to be the state capital and the site of the state university. It was to reserve sufficient land in the new city for the capitol building and the university, but might sell the remaining lots as deemed desirable in the public interest. In order to obtain the necessary funds for the acquisition of the Louisville site, the board was authorized to sell the government's house and lot in Savannah. Any monies remaining from this source, and the revenues received from public lots, were to be applied to the erection of the public buildings in Louisville. In order to carry out its manifold functions, the board was given the powers to bargain, to buy and sell, to accept bonds, and to convey titles in fee simple. In every respect it was a full-fledged public corporation.[27] Other prominent early examples of town planning were afforded by Waynesboro, Sunbury, Wrightsboro, Riceboro, Washington, St. Marys, Brunswick, Springfield, Jacksonborough, Petersboro, and Greensboro.[28]

The principles governing town planning in Georgia are clear. They combined aesthetic and ethical with utilitarian objectives in an effort to achieve a balanced development of individual and community life. The city was conceived as a social community within itself, as a primary unit within the larger community of the state and, in the case of a principal commercial center, as a chief nexus between the state and the outside world. Sites were chosen with an eye to natural beauty, adaptability to expansion, health of the future population, location in regard to navigable waterways, ease of access to the hinterland, and relation to the existing or probable development of the main arteries of transportation and communication within the state. Suitability for military defense was an important consideration in some instances. Artistic achievement in the building of the city was to be joined with consideration for the convenient and efficient functioning of business life. Above all, the cultural growth of the community, in which the educational institutions would provide the solid basis, should be the crowning aim. The planning and development of the city was essentially a public function in which emphasis was placed upon group coöperation and community benefits. Private interest was not ignored but was to be harmonized with the common aims. The speculator was not to become the chief beneficiary of the increment in land values that would result from the growth of the community. Such socially created values were to be converted as far as possible, through public ownership and disposal of lots, into those public and quasi-public instruments and services which conferred benefits upon all members of the community.

The land laws of 1803, 1821, and 1827 embodied these principles, with some changes in emphasis and procedure, into the new land policy, in the provisions for the establishment of Milledgeville, Macon, and Columbus. Thus was city planning as long practiced integrated into the objectives of the broader state-designed land program. The legislature retained a greater degree of control than hitherto had been customary, or than was exercised over the planning of local towns during the same period. The boards of commissioners remained essentially state administrative units, quite separate from the local governing bodies and institutional trustees, and ceased to exist after the early phase of planning, lot-selling, and public construction had been completed. And the state treasurer or some other state fiscal agent handled the collection and disbursement of the revenues from lot sales and leases. Possibly, also, revenue was a stronger motive.

The Milledgeville commissioners selected the site and drew up the city plan in 1804 and began selling lots during the following year. Sale of lots was restricted to two in any block and to two to a person, and purchasers were required to build upon their lots within two years, otherwise lots were to revert to the commissioners. The commissioners commenced construction of the state capitol in 1806. They were given charge of all public property in Milledgeville, with powers to make rules regarding them. In 1807 they were authorized to lease public lands for periods of seven years in lots of twenty acres, which they proceeded to do to the extent of three hundred acres for an annual rental of slightly over $600. The town was incorporated in 1806 under a separate board of commissioners and raised to a second class city in 1810; thereafter, the city corporation served as the chief agency for the public lot business. It also was authorized to lease public lots pending their sale or other disposition and to use the revenues for town purposes. The legislature also made a number of direct grants: an acre to the trustees of Baldwin Academy as a site and six lots to raise funds for a building; six lots to the inferior court of Baldwin County to erect a courthouse and a jail; leases of lots for two tanyards, two public hostelries, a brewery, and a slaughter pen; and rent-free leases to various poor persons as a mode of public relief. All told, the state realized some $86,000 from its sales and rentals of Milledgeville lots.[29]

The planning of the cities of Macon and Columbus was combined with Governor Clark's policy of special reserves, referred to previously. Two such reserves — the Fort Hawkins Reserve around the head of navigation on the Ocmulgee River and the Coweta Falls Reserve at the head of navigation of the Chattahoochee River — were selected with the future sites of cities in mind. A board of commissioners was elected in 1822 to lay out Macon within the Fort Hawkins Reserve. The original site was laid out immediately and lots were sold each year through 1826. Separate town commissioners were elected by the legislature in 1823, and a year later the governor was authorized to appoint five commissioners to build a toll bridge across the Ocmulgee at Macon at state expense. When completed, the bridge was to be rented at public outcry, and a scale of maximum tolls was specified.

Steps were taken in 1827 to dispose of the balance of the Fort Hawkins Reserve in a manner reminiscent of the Trustee plan at Savannah. The governor was authorized to appoint three commissioners to lay off on the west side of the river, adjoining Macon, three successive ranges of lots of which the one bordering the town should be in lots of ten acres each, the second of twenty acres each, and the third of one hundred acres each; and on the east side of the river, a commons containing fifty acres, and then four successive ranges of lots of one, ten, twenty, and one hundred acres each respectively. The commons and the one-acre lots east of the river anticipated the extension of Macon's growth across the river. The lots were to be advertised for sale by description and price. Apparently this board replaced both previous boards, since it was authorized to convey ten Macon lots to Bibb County for the construction of a court house and other public buildings and a single lot to the Baptist Church, and also to sell the Macon bridge. The records indicate that the state received approximately $100,000 from the sale of Macon lots; and the bridge over the Ocmulgee, constructed with a part of these receipts, was sold for $25,000 to the city of Macon, which continued it as a municipal toll bridge.[30]

The governor was authorized in 1827 to appoint commissioners to lay out Columbus in the Coweta Falls Reserve. The site was to contain 1,200 acres fronting on the Chattahoochee River and was to be selected with especial reference to the "commercial progress of the town and the health of its inhabitants." The influence of the Savannah model appeared more strongly in the Columbus plan than in any other. Like Savannah, the entire plan of the city, with its streets and parks, commons, business and shipping districts, public squares, residence districts, and surrounding garden plots, small farms, and planting lots, was to be designed and mapped out in advance of settlement. Not less than five hundred half-acre building lots were to be laid out, and a square of ten acres was to be set apart for the use of Muscogee County in constructing a courthouse and jail. The lands adjoining the town limits were to be laid off in successive ranges of ten, twenty, and one hundred acre lots until the Coweta Falls Reserve should be exhausted. The commissioners were directed to advertise and sell all "said building, gardening and planting lots," the sales to be held daily at some designated place within the Reserve.[31] As a matter of fact, the commissioners did not remain long in charge of the business. The town was incorporated in 1828 and given certain rights of leasing lots as had been done previously at Milledgeville; and collections from sales of public lots were lodged with the new Central Bank of the State.

Urban planning at the local level during this period was more important, probably, if less spectacular, than that of the three major interior cotton belt cities. It followed closely the early practice, and the county seats afforded the chief examples. As each new county was created, commissioners were selected, either by the legislature, or by the inferior court of the county after legislative authorization, who were empowered to buy a tract of land and lay out the town site, to sell lots and to build a courthouse and jail, to assign lots to churches and schools, and sometimes to build bridges and other public utilities. The commissioners usually became the trustees of the county academy, and this institution almost invariably was made the residuary legatee of the public lot business. The size of tracts that were authorized varied from 10 to 250 acres, with most of them nearer the higher figure. Some of the boards achieved notable results in the designing and management of early town development, and were able to endow their academies quite amply.[32]

The degree of success, measured in monetary returns, varied not only with the managerial ability of the boards, but with the growth and productivity of particular communities and their surrounding territories. Taken as a whole this practice of urban planning contributed a significant chapter in local government. Some 230 towns and cities in Georgia were so designed and improved. The procedure produced many good results. Urban land speculation was greatly reduced and increments in land values were converted into important public institutions and services. The state was covered with towns and cities that were laid out in an orderly fashion for the most part and often with features of beauty as well as convenience. The policy developed the spirit of local coöperation and interest in the common welfare. The academy was one of its brightest achievements, and this accomplishment of local planning in education clearly outshone action at the higher state level.

6. Financial Results of the New Land Policy

The financial results of the state land policy under the lottery distribution, in so far as items of expense and revenue can be identified, are given in Table 9. Not included in the summary are the rents and sales receipts of city lots that were expended on court houses, schools, and other local public improvements and services and the values of the numerous lots that were given as sites for various public and religious structures. Lack of data necessitates their omission; but their total probably equaled the sum realized by the state. It was not possible to obtain data on expenses other than such as were credited to the individual lottery distributions, and these could not be separated for the first two lotteries. The figures given for the lottery expenses may include possibly some of the costs of disposing of items in the other classifications; but it is not likely that such amounts were considerable, since the sale of fractions, town lots, and other parcels was handled usually on a commission basis; and since commissions were deducted from gross receipts by the commissioners or agents, the revenues shown for these items in the table are largely net of expenses. Possible "hidden" expenses, such as the

Table 9

GEORGIA LAND DISTRIBUTION AFTER 1803: EXPENSES AND REVENUES[a]

Lottery or other classification	Expenses	Receipts from land fees	Receipts from sale of fractions	Total revenues
Lottery, 1804 & 1806	$114,585.32	$ 96,208.20	$601,163.77	$697,371.97
" 1820	227,930.28	178,821.50	85,965.74	264,787.24
" 1821	117,601.90	189,190.50	178,037.40	367,227.90
" 1827	183,304.24	222,427.00	5,232.30	227,659.30
" 1832	195,642.54	192,827.50	2,596.00	195,423.50
City lots				156,359.94
Collections by Central Bank[b]				477,220.72
School lands				16,333.83
Miscellaneous[c]				175,022.27
Rents				27,855.87
Totals	$839,064.28	$879,474.70	$872,995.21	$2,605,262.54

[a] Compiled from annual reports of Treasurers and Comptrollers, 1800–1860, and of Central Bank, 1829–1840.

[b] These collections cannot be allocated among the other items from the existing records; but they represented chiefly returns from sales of fractions and town lots, among the latter, principally those at Columbus.

[c] Includes fraudulent grants, forfeited and recovered lots, and fractions, reverted lots, unclaimed grants, and ungranted lands.

services of regular state officials in connection with issuing and recording grants and titles, were all pretty fully covered by fees. Yet another unrecorded expense was that incurred by the Central Bank in making collections. No allowance for any of these possible costs is made in the table.

It would appear that the state realized an average of approximately ten cents gross, or six and two-thirds cents net, per acre for the vast territory that it distributed after 1800. A comparison of these figures with the minimum price of $1.25 per acre received by the federal government for its lands during the same period testifies amply to Georgia's adherence to the principle of free land and its traditional emphasis on settlement. In these respects the new policy did not constitute any noteworthy break with the past. Consequently, the hopes of the liberals of obtaining funds from the public lands for the promotion of education, internal improvements, and other badly needed public services were largely defeated. From the net receipts amounting to $1,765,000, debt retirement absorbed $460,000; the costs of state buildings at Milledgeville, $170,000; and capital stock of the Central Bank of the State, $990,000 — leaving some $40,000 for all other purposes.[33] It is evident that the state's dominant policy of economic development during the first third of the nineteenth century was land settlement, supported chiefly, as will be shown in the next two succeeding chapters, by a policy of commercial bank credit and, after 1828, of investment bank credit. Consequently, the appropriation of land far outran the supplies of such complementary factors as transportation, technological improvements, and trained skills. However, the wide extension of settlement in time intensified the very need for such factors and thus supplied the *raison d'être* for important developments later by the state and local governments.

The social philosophy of the new land policy was predominantly the radical liberalism of the Revolution. The essence of the latter in Georgia was that individual freedom rested upon the inalienable rights to equal access to nature's productive powers and to the full product of one's labor. Private property in land was accepted as the best safeguard of both. Hence every citizen in a democracy ideally should be the proprietor of that amount of land, and no more, which would enable him to employ his industry to a maximum. Widespread proprietorship in land, therefore, was the primary aim of land policy, as the chief means of maximizing both individual and general welfare.

CHAPTER VIII

BANKING THEORIES AND POLICIES, 1800–1824

The antecedents of nineteenth-century banking in Georgia have been described at some length in earlier chapters, wherein they were shown to have been both public and private in nature. Chief of the public developments were: the efforts of the Trustees to supply the colony with currency and capital, the General Loan Office and the emission of public certificates during the Crown period, the Revolutionary bills of credit, and finally the numerous post-war issues of treasury certificates, auditors' certificates, bills of credit, speakers' certificates, and governors', speakers', and presidents' warrants and anticipation notes. Such paper monies were the forerunners of the bank note. At the same time other rudiments of banking — loans and discounts, deposit credits, and the transference of funds through checks, drafts, bills of exchange, and specie shipments — were being practiced and developed in private business by the merchants. The painful experiences with public issues of paper money during the Revolution and afterward unquestionably discouraged the introduction of local banks of issue and left the banking functions largely in the hands of private middlemen. Hence it was out of the financial operations of the merchants, in the main, that specialized banking functions emerged as a separately organized business. Offices of discount and deposit were opened as early as 1802, before any banks of issue were established in Georgia, which carried on the banking functions of deposit, loans and discounts, and domestic and foreign exchange transactions.[1] Even the immediate origins of banknote currency sprang from the practices of the merchants who learned that their paper obligations could be circulated as money. Mercantile firms, as well as offices of discount and deposit, began to conduct a common law banking business around the turn of the century. These establishments received deposits on occasion, made loans, dealt in bills of exchange, handled specie, and issued notes, scrip, change bills, and other paper obligations.[2]

1. Theories and Attitudes

Banking in Georgia prior to the Civil War falls into five definite periods: before 1810, the operations of common law private banks, the Bank of the United States and the banks of other states; 1810–1824, the incorporation of state banks and the development of branch-banking; 1825–1837, the growth of unit banking and the establishment of a public long-term bank of discount; 1837–1844, the Great Depression; and 1845–1861, the rise of country banks. Since our central point of interest is the relation of banking policies to the public programs of land distribution, internal improvements, railroads, and education, some consideration will be given first to the theories that were current in Georgia regarding banks and their functions. At least three such bodies of thought were of major importance: the hard-money, the commercial banking, and the long-term credit views. Like banking itself, they were rooted in the past, and it will be necessary to look briefly into the years before the advent of chartered banks.

The hard-money philosophy developed vigorously in the wake of the depreciated Revolutionary paper currencies and the last brief trial of government paper money in 1786. Its partisans could find no more promise of virtue in bank currency than in the public paper money. They admitted somewhat doubtfully the utility of banks in the great primary markets of world commerce where the accumulation of surplus commodities created heavy requirements for cash from the wholesale merchants, but they could see no need for banks in Georgia where the products of the farmers and laborers constituted the necessities of life and readily commanded goods and specie in exchange in the markets of the western world. The maintenance of the value of labor, therefore, was the first criterion of a sound currency, and only the precious metals could assure the necessary stability. The precious metals were natural money in an order ruled by natural law. Banks should not only be limited as to location to primary commercial centers, but their notes should be restricted to large denominations to insure that they might not find their way into ordinary exchanges, and they should be convertible into specie at all times to prevent their banishing specie and thereby further endangering its general circulation. The advocates of hard money believed that there were two dangerous tendencies inherent in banking. One was that an excess of banks, owing to the natural desire to obtain business, would lead to overextension of loans and circulation, overtrading, inflation, speculation, and an inevitable business revulsion with heavy losses to the community; and the other, that banking by its very nature lent itself to the manipulations of the rich and powerful and to the exploitation of the common people. These dangers were greatly enhanced by the displacement in ordinary exchange of specie by paper currencies. Such fears were agitated further by the corporate form of most banks, for corporations had long been associated in the popular mind with oppressive aristocratic institutions, vested interests and greedy money powers.[3]

The hard-money philosophy became almost a universal creed in Georgia during the two decades prior to 1807 and supplied the chief reason for the delay in the incorporation of banks. But the success of the first Bank of the United States finally loosened somewhat its grip upon the state, although it continued to enjoy wide acceptance in the regions less engaged in cotton production and even among the planters of the Cotton Belt. It supplied the opposing arguments to the spread of banks, and especially of their branches, into the interior and against the supplanting of specie with bank notes. During the first bank suspension period, of 1814–1816, the advocates of hard money demanded the enforcement upon the banks of their charter obligations to redeem their notes in specie. After the Depression of 1819 the tone of the hard-money sentiment shifted increasingly from suppression to regulation of banks. It flared up again throughout the state with some of its earlier flavor, however, in the late 1850's.

Commercial banking was nurtured in Georgia both by the British banking tradition among the older merchants and by the rising immigration from the states to the northeast, particularly the increasing number of larger planters among the latter. The numbers of its supporters were greatly augmented by the discreet policies and the highly successful operations of the Savannah Branch of the first Bank of the United States from 1802 to 1811, as well as by the steady growth of banking in other states. Leading arguments emphasized that banks — through the wise discretion of their officers — assembled idle funds and put them to work in the hands of the able and ambitious; that they provided a convenient money both when and where it was needed; and that they sustained the natural level of agricultural prices. It was pointed out that credit was the true basis of commerce and it was equally affirmed that a bank supplied the most efficient mechanism for providing credit that had as yet been devised; in fact, banks were said to be the product of the slow and well-tested development of commerce. The beneficial effects of banks were enjoyed not alone by merchants, but accrued to all members of society, through increased productivity, greater certainty of markets, more stable prices, and added conveniences in exchange. There was no danger in the displacement of specie by bank notes, as had been so often charged, so long as loans and circulation were based on short-term commercial paper, reserves were maintained at a level above all reasonable demands for specie, and banks were not chartered in excess of the state's needs for money as measured by the volume of trade. The most oft-repeated arguments, probably, were that banks provided a convenient currency and that they sustained prices.[4] It was asserted frequently, in reply to the hard-money claims, that a specie currency tended to have deflationary effects, that it was neither plentiful nor mobile enough to meet the monetary needs of a community that was growing rapidly, and hence that specie prices would always tend to be below the natural level, especially during times of heavy crop marketing; that it was indeed fortunate that the markets of the world were not dependent upon specie, because production and trade were increasing more rapidly than the precious metals and, were it not for the development of banks, prices everywhere would be declining. Such an occurrence would bear most heavily upon the poor.[5]

The notion of long-term credit investment through the medium of banks was less widespread in Georgia than in most of the newer agrarian states. Yet it may be clearly traced in various popular reactions and in certain trends in banking practice, as well as in the movement which finally led to the establishment of the public bank of long-term discount. The frequent outcries of interior communities against the policies and practices of the city banks, and their demands for their own banks, probably reflected some impatience with the short-term discount policies of the traditional commercial bank.[6] The development of accommodation loans and of the practice of continuous renewals indicated a growing willingness on the part of banks to meet the demands for longer term credits. All of these evidences betoken the rising pressures of the ever-growing long-term investment problem upon the banking system.[7] It is in this area that banking policy most closely parallels land, internal improvement, and railroad policies, because of the central importance of long-term investment in all of them.

Generally speaking, banking policy in Georgia after 1810 adhered pretty consistently to the commercial banking tradition. The trial of a public bank of long-term discount, between 1828 and 1842, while an important new development in banking, was not actually incompatible with the prevailing commercial principle. The existence of large frontier areas down to 1860 produced some continuous pressure for easier banking practices, but the weight of influence lay with the older communities. Furthermore, the new communities were settled in large measure from the old and strongly reflected the attitudes of the latter. Despite the high ratio of new development that was ever present in Georgia, the tone of public sentiment was predominantly that of a mature community. Commercial banking represented a middle-ground policy between the ultra-conservative hard-money philosophy and the frontier cheap-money ideas. In times of dire financial stress the hard-money and cheap-money forces sometimes united for a brief time, but their incompatibility of views and diversity of interests usually soon forced them apart. The moderate conservatism of most Georgians and the overwhelming importance of commercial crops, chiefly cotton, held the state rather firmly to the commercial banking tradition.

The first significant discussion of banking among Georgians began in Congress with the chartering of the Bank of the United States in 1791. James Jackson, already an influential political figure in Georgia, shared with James Madison the leadership of the opposition to the Bank bill.[8] In the fight on the National Bank, Jackson revealed himself, despite an expression of a limited approval of state banks, as a hard-money critic of banks in general. Banks, in his opinion, served only mercantile interests and hence possessed no social utility in the country at large. They were a profitable convenience to such primary wholesale centers as Philadelphia, New York, and Boston, but they offered no gain to the Georgia farmers. The claim that the national bank would serve the entire country was false; the only "general welfare" that it could serve was the private interest of the aforementioned commercial centers, and they were adequately supplied already with banking facilities. An excess of banking would constitute a positive danger, since it would lead to overextension of loans and circulation, overreaching, speculation, and inflation.

Jackson was one of the first Americans to raise the argument of diversity of conditions against centralized banking for the United States. First, he challenged the frequent justification of the proposed bank upon the supposed advantages of European central banks. Conditions in Europe were entirely different from what they were in America. England, Holland, and Venice were commercial-industrial countries whose economies revolved around great wholesale trading centers; whereas America was primarily an agrarian country with few important commercial cities and with relatively simple monetary needs. The occasions for banks of issue were limited. Still more important however were the regional differences within the United States itself. These made of a central monetary institution such as that proposed, with sweeping powers over the entire life of the nation, an unworkable and dangerous scheme. Especially ominous was the intended union of a great financial corporation and the central government. It would create "a monopoly of very extraordinary character" supported by public monies for the benefit of a privileged corporate group. Jackson recalled the deep-seated American repugnance to British corporations and privileged companies and denounced the bank measure as likely to raise up a national monied monopoly and to introduce a trend toward the domination of American life by powerful privileged groups. Jackson appealed frequently to Adam Smith in support of his arguments, but actually his views were narrower than those of the Scottish economist.[9] All of Georgia's representatives, who comprised an unusual number of its top leaders, voted against the bank measure.

The earliest recorded public suggestion for the establishment of banks within Georgia came from Governor George Matthews in January 1796, when he recommended that the state invest its Yazoo land sale receipts in banks, which he deemed should prove so profitable to the state in all probability that taxes could be eliminated. He justified the action further on the grounds, that became a basic tenet of commercial banking philosophy in Georgia, that banks would prevent the state's produce from ever falling "below a cash market." They "would give," he continued in a Hamiltonian vein, "a spring to the enterprising and industrious, as money on every emergency would be in his power to produce." [10] Commercial banking theories were undoubtedly current at this time among the Savannah and Augusta merchants and the upstate Virginians. The exposure of the Yazoo land scandals shortly afterwards ended abruptly Matthews' political career and possibly produced an unfavorable reaction to his banking notions. Certainly the annulment of the land company sales later in 1796 ended any possibility for the time being of investing western land revenues in banks, although later events indicate that the notion had taken root. Barely five years had elapsed since Jackson's unsuccessful attempt to defeat the national bank, when he crushed the Yazoo land companies and gained absolute political mastery of the state. His attack on the land companies paralleled closely that on the bank: they were pictured as a big "monied" group seeking dominion over the lives of the people of Georgia for purposes of private exploitation.[11] The struggle intensified Jackson's opposition to the incorporation of financial institutions of all kinds. The fight upon monopolies of every nature, even to patent rights, became a passion with him. His intimate friends and immediate successors in the governorship, Josiah Tatnall and John Milledge, were no less fervent in their devotion to Jacksonian principles than Jackson himself and the decade from 1797 to 1807 found the hard-money creed in particular almost unchallenged.

2. The First Incorporated Banks

Powerful economic forces were at work already, however, that were destined to change entirely the economic geography and life of Georgia during this decade following the Yazoo affair. The invention of the cotton gin, the extensive rich land cessions, and the immense waves of migration both from within and without created the "Cotton Belt" in middle and east central Georgia and lifted Savannah and Augusta into the status of important commercial centers.

The first incorporated bank to be established in Georgia was the

Branch of the Bank of the United States at Savannah in 1802.[12] During succeeding years, the surprising growth of the loans and discounts and circulation of this bank, as well as of the circulation of paper bills and scrip of the "private" banks and the banks of neighboring states, indicates how great had become the demand for "cash" in the wake of the expansion of cotton production in Georgia. It was the sound operation and beneficial effects of the Bank of the United States, according to William H. Crawford, that removed the old, deep-seated objections to banks.[13] The legislature approved the first charter for a bank in 1807. This instrument gave permission for the establishment of an institution with certain statewide features; the main office was to be located in Savannah, but there was to be a branch in Augusta. Its capital of $1,000,000 was to be subscribed throughout the state, and its directors were to be selected always on a state-wide basis. The bank was never organized. Three years later, in December 1810, the first state banks to be established in Georgia, the Planters' Bank of Savannah and the Bank of Augusta, were chartered. The advocates of hard money, who had opposed banks so long, were satisfied apparently that the commercial growth of Savannah and Augusta warranted the establishment of the two banks, because such opposition as arose came largely from the Milledgeville region and registered the disappointment over the failure of that city to obtain a bank.

3. The State as Investor

A sixth of the capital stock in both banks was reserved for state subscription. This was to provide profitable investment for surplus state funds, rather than to lend public encouragement to banking or to place the state in the banking business. The desire to create a source of public revenue through investment was not a novel one. It had appeared frequently in discussions of land policies, since hopes were often expressed that some kind of permanent fund might be realized out of the disposition of the vast public domain. Some progress in this direction had been made locally in connection with the academy grants. The proposed objects of state investment had been tax reduction and the promotion of education and internal improvements. No surplus revenues were realized from land alienation prior to 1810, however, because of a virtual free land policy and the continued existence of a public debt. The first modest surpluses began to accrue from the sale of land fractions about the time that the first banks were chartered; and larger ones were anticipated from the federal government's payments under the terms of the western lands agreement. It is not likely that Georgians had overlooked the lucrative returns obtained in one form or another from banks by other states, or the handsome profit that the federal government had derived from its "investment" in the Bank of the United States. As compared with the shares of other private enterprises, bank stocks offered certain advantages for public investment in addition to their general profitableness: the element of public control through incorporation and regulation, particularly the power to limit numbers and resources of banks and to dictate their location, permitted the safeguarding of the government's investment; and the quasi-public nature of banking also lent some plausibility to such investment. The amount of the state's subscription in each instance seems to have been determined by the amount of the actual or anticipated surplus revenue. Surpluses were relatively light between 1810 and 1813 and the state did not exercise its option on the Planters' Bank stock until late in 1812. The surprising increases in revenue after 1813 justified the subscription of two-fifths of the capital stock of the large Bank of the State in 1815. The even greater revenue redundancy during 1816–1818, together with the establishment of permanent Education and Internal Improvement Funds, explained the state's subscription of one-half the capital of the Bank of Darien in 1818. This prosperous state of the treasury was accounted for in large measure by the federal payments under the western lands transfer agreement. It was proposed at one time that the state invest these federal credits in stock of the Second Bank of the United States. Such action might well have gained the support of some of the private promoters of banks in Georgia, since they did not seek the public subscriptions for their banks as a rule and invariably used whatever influence they had with the legislature to have them kept at a minimum. Bank stocks were in universal demand and stocks of some of the new banks sold at a considerable premium even before the banks were organized.[14] Although Georgia refrained from the policy which was common both in Europe and America of exacting bonus payments for the granting or extending of bank charters and other privileges, the right to subscribe, in itself, was often considered to be in the nature of such an exaction. Many private subscriptions were excluded by the state subscriptions, particularly in the cases of the Bank of Augusta and the Bank of Darien. Subscription rights in both instances had a considerable market value.

The change in sentiment toward banks, evidenced by the charters and public investments just noted, was reflected also by a shift in attitude among the leaders toward the Bank of the United States. Whereas James Jackson had led the struggle to prevent the start of the Bank, William H. Crawford, Jackson's chief lieutenant in upstate Georgia after the Yazoo upheaval and co-leader of the republicans with George M. Troup after Jackson's death, became the champion of the Bank's right to continue in being. At the time of his defense of the Bank, in 1811, Crawford was the outstanding Georgian in American life and a powerful local figure, especially in the older sections of the Cotton Belt. His cogent arguments in favor of extending the Bank's charter brought him wide recognition as a student of banking and exerted a strong influence at home where, according to Crawford himself, the great majority of his constituents at the time probably were not as yet in agreement with him on the Bank issue.

Crawford completely dominated Bank debates in Congress. His arguments covered the wide range of banking functions, the nature of the banking system, and the role of a central bank. "Credit is the true basis of commerce . . . and no person, who has undertaken to discuss this question, has ventured to declare that a bank is not necessary. Every man admits, directly or indirectly, the necessity of resorting to banks of some kind." Not simply banks, but the necessity of a banking *system* was equally obvious. Congress must decide what kind of system America should have: One that should hold a checkrein upon state banks, provide a convenient and uniform currency, and enable both private individuals and governments to manage their businesses efficiently? Or one in which each unit, or group of state or local units, should be left free of responsibilities to one another, with powers to create local currencies, to issue notes recklessly, and to bring confusion and irreparable losses upon the business community? Crawford questioned the effectiveness of state regulations. "The check which one bank has upon another is, in fact, the only substantial check which can be devised against excessive discounts and emissions by state banks." The Bank of the United States had provided just such a check.[15]

George M. Troup, also in Congress at the time, opposed the extension of the Bank's charter as vigorously as Crawford defended it, and on virtually the identical grounds that Jackson had taken against the Bank twenty years earlier.[16] In fact, it may be noted here, parenthetically, that the leaders of the dominant party in Georgia were to remain divided on the National Bank as well as on other banking issues. Crawford, Forsyth, Wilde, and Bibb supported a central bank, while Troup, Gilmer, and Cobb were always opposed to it in principle. Lumpkin was favorable toward it for a while, but later changed his mind and became strongly opposed. The latter four men always possessed something of a hard-money inclination that ever prompted them to a doubtful attitude toward powerful central banks and to a questioning acceptance of banks in general. A majority of the rank and file of the Republican Party were long opposed to the Bank of the United States and only very gradually shifted over in favor of it after the Party became identified with the national Whigs in the late 1830's.[17]

The rapid expansion of the Cotton Belt, which began around 1800, was notably marked in the western part of the state after 1810, where the growing needs for capital in the production and marketing of the staple created a widening interest in banks. This interest was stimulated further by rising prices, the suspension of specie payments in 1814, and the move to establish a second Bank of the United States. Simultaneously a cleavage also began to develop over banking policy between the new regions and the older commercial-planting communities represented by Savannah and Augusta. The chief causes of this difference seem to have been the questions of location and organization of banks and the development of new types of banking operations. There developed also at this same time a very bitter controversy over stay laws that divided the state along somewhat similar lines. Since this latter phenomenon has been credited with considerable significance in the rise of American banking in newer regions, it seems wise to attempt to estimate its influence in Georgia.

4. Stay Laws

The Revolutionary and post-Revolutionary laws staying executions against debtors have been discussed in earlier chapters. They were revived in 1808 under somewhat similar circumstances when the Embargo prostrated the economy of Georgia and visited severe financial distress upon debtors. This measure, like its predecessors, was viewed at the time of passage as a temporary stopgap; but it was reënacted by every subsequent legislature through 1814. It became a political habit that few politicians dared to relinquish; although as time passed and war prices and general prosperity placed debtors in an exceedingly favorable position, the law would appear to have lost all moral validity. Merchants, bankers, and other creditors — predominantly residents of the larger cities and the older and wealthier communities — became more and more incensed over what they considered a rank injustice.[18] When the legislature reënacted the law for another year in 1814, Governor Peter Early sent a sharp veto message to that body, which initially rallied enough support apparently to assure an end to the law; but inclusion in the measure of special exemptions to soldiers who were in the army and some last-minute logrolling rallied the necessary two-thirds vote to override and retain the law for another year.[19] Thereupon a test case was brought in the superior court of the Augusta district, upon which sat by special agreement the superior court justices of all the judicial districts in the state. There being no supreme court as yet in Georgia, it was the intention that the decision of this special court would constitute in effect a final decree upon the stay law question. In that decision they held that stay laws contravened the sanctity of contracts on both legal and moral grounds, and hence were in violation of both the Constitution of the United States and the Constitution of Georgia.[20] The fact that the decision was unanimous seemed to assure that it would have binding effect upon all courts in the state. There were immediate outbursts of approval and criticism from the respective sides;[21] the stay law supporters in the House of the next legislature, led by Benjamin Williams of Putnam County, were able to carry a resolution of censure upon the superior court justices;[22] but the majority was only three doubtful votes. The state as a whole appeared ready to accept the decision and eventually the leg-

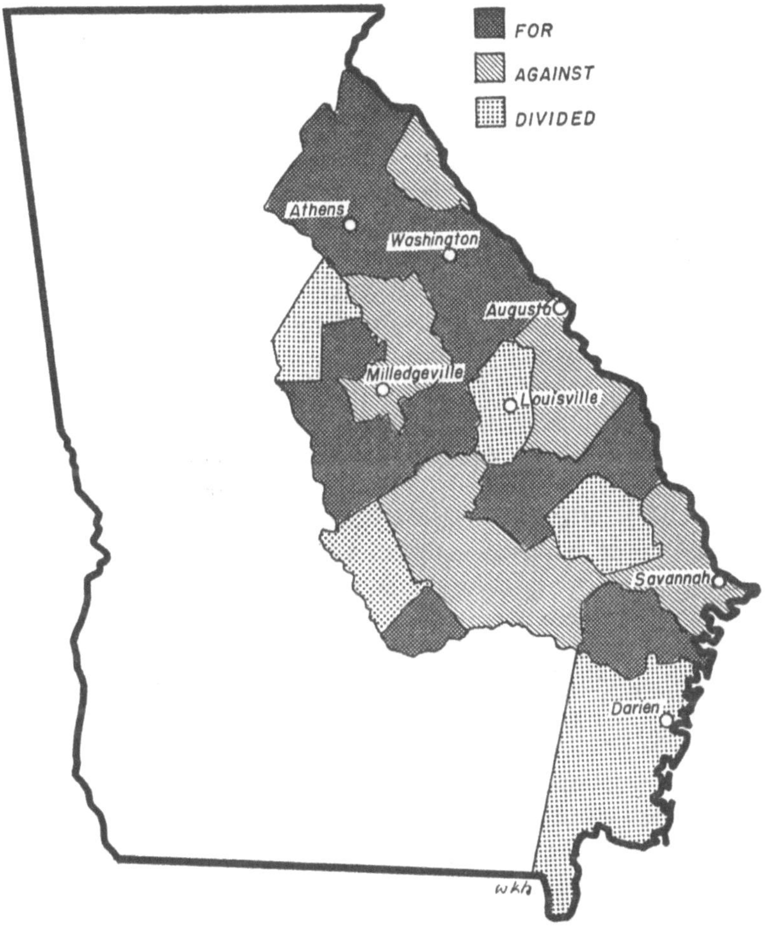

Georgia Stay Law: Composite Vote of House and Senate, 1814

islature repealed all laws permitting stays of execution except in questions of equity.

The popularity that stay laws had continued to enjoy in the new and underdeveloped regions, long after the cause of their introduction had been removed, undoubtedly reflected in some degree a shortage of capital funds in those areas and hence raises the question of whether or not they were causally related to the banking movements that were developing in those regions, as was the case apparently under similar conditions in other states.[23] The evidence does not indicate that such was the case. Four major bank projects came out of the interior during the decade, 1810–1820: (1) the Milledgeville bank project, (2) the proposal for a public bank of long-term discounts, (3) a projected agricultural bank, and (4) the Bank of Darien. The supporters of the projected bank at Milledgeville were one of the three major groups who opposed the stay laws. They sought a commercial bank in the interior, and stay laws were especially pernicious to commercial banking that was steadily expanding into accommodation loans. Of the eighteen counties that fully supported the stay laws in 1814, only eight voted for the public bank of long-term discounts; eight voted against it, and two were divided. Of the nine counties that partially supported the stay laws, only two voted for the public bank; two were divided, three voted against it, and two did not vote. And of the twelve counties that opposed the stay laws, four voted for the public bank. The agricultural bank project received even less support from the stay law localities: only five of the eighteen counties of the first group voted favorably, and only three of the other nine gave partial support; in fact, the stay law counties voted overwhelmingly against the agricultural bank. Numerically there appears to be a somewhat closer relationship between the Darien Bank and the stay law votes; but a careful scrutiny raises strong doubts about the significance of the higher correlation. The nine southern counties that partially or fully supported the stay laws voted for the Bank of Darien because it was a south Georgia project. They were adjacent to the port of Darien or the Altamaha-Oconee-Ocmulgee river system which emptied at Darien. In the same area, four other southern counties that voted solidly against the stay laws voted just as solidly for the Bank of Darien, as did Baldwin County (Milledgeville) in central Georgia which had been a stronghold of opposition to the stay laws. On the other hand seven of the ten counties in the largest single stay law block, in northeast Georgia, voted against the Darien Bank and the other three gave only partial support. The old block of stay law counties on the western border of the Cotton Belt voted for the Darien Bank because they preferred to be served by a banking institution based at Darien than one in either Savannah or Augusta.

Thus it is difficult to identify stay laws with banking in Georgia, even though they undoubtedly have some common roots. The stay law votes represented debtor communities. The two chief strongholds were the western Cotton Belt, whose leader was Williams of Putnam County, and the northern small farm area where Daniels of Madison was the chief spokesman. The poorer counties in the south — in the piney woods and coastal sections — were almost evenly divided in sentiment. The primary centers of opposition to the stay laws were the three large cities of Savannah, Augusta, and Milledgeville and their adjacent areas. The stay law movement was primarily an anti-urban movement. In respect to currency questions it actually contained two diverse elements — the supporters of investment credit and easier money from the newer sections of the Cotton Belt, and the hard-money advocates of the interior regions to the north and south of the Cotton Belt. The former were willing to support any and all banks that offered a promise of ample credits, whereas the latter usually opposed all banks unless sectional interests outweighed their monetary predilections.

5. Sectionalism and Branch-Banking

In contrast to this diversity and division of opinion on banks in the interior, the Savannah-Augusta axis had become thoroughly committed to the British commercial banking tradition as a complete answer to the credit and currency needs of the state. The planters in the interior Cotton Belt also accepted the commercial banking theory, but they wanted their own banks or more lenient terms than the Savannah and Augusta banks were always wont to give, and they had great need of investment credits. Long-term capital funds were exceedingly scarce in the new regions and the planters who were inclined to expect the banks to furnish such frequently became irritated by the policies of the city banks. Savannah and Augusta were intent upon retaining control of the banking operations; but the rising inland cities, supported by their planting communities, were equally anxious to have their own banks. In the contest between maturity and youth, the hard-money communities, which lay outside the domain of cotton production and traffic, were destined often to wield the balance of power.

The earliest interior bank movement centered around Milledgeville which had become the first major interior market west of Augusta as well as the latest capital city of the state. A petition of citizens of Milledgeville was turned down by the legislature in 1813 and another attempt the following year was deferred, doubtlessly by the general bank suspension which dampened the ardor of Georgians temporarily for banks. Milledgeville came back in 1815, however, with renewed determination; whereupon the older cities countered with a proposal instead for another bank in Savannah. After much maneuvering by both sides, in and out of the legislature, a compromise was effected which was the charter of the Bank of the State of Georgia.[24] This provided for the establishment of a large branch-banking institution, probably suggested by the form of the first United States Bank and of the proposed new one then before Congress,[25] with a capital of $1,500,000 and with the main office in Savannah and branches in Augusta and Milledgeville and wherever else the directors should see fit to locate them. Two-fifths of the capital stock was reserved for state subscription and the remaining, private shares were apportioned one-half to Savannah and Augusta and one-half among eight interior centers. The state also reserved the right to increase the capital stock at any future date to $3,000,000, or any other figure, and to subscribe one-half or more of any such increase. Thus the two older cities secured the main bank and one of the two chief branches, and they prevented the inauguration of a policy of creating individual country banks, while the interior folk obtained one branch bank and a promise of others. The new regions hoped furthermore, through control of the legislature, to be able to name the six public directors and so, with power to select one-half of the private directors by virtue of stock ownership, to dictate the bank's policies.

It should be pointed out that the Bank of the State was not, as the name might imply, in any respect an agency of the state, but was a private commercial bank to all intents and purposes. It differed from the two earlier banks solely in regard to the branch-banking structure. There seems to have been a prevalent notion, however, that such a statewide institution, in which the public directors constituted a large minority, might exert a significant influence for uniformity of the currency and other banking policies within the state resembling that which it was confidently expected the Second Bank of the United States would exercise between the states. The strongest argument for the bank, nevertheless, was the commercial one of the rapid growth of production and trade that was taking place and the consequent need for an expansion of the currency.

The proposal for a bank of long-term discounts to be founded upon the consolidated funds of the state, introduced into the legislature in 1813, was of a quite different character from the banking projects that led up to the incorporation of the Bank of the State. This proposed a public bank that would loan the surplus funds of the state government in small amounts for long-term periods and at moderate rates of interest to producers throughout the state.[26] The project originated wholly in the new regions and sprang from their widespread investment needs. It possessed the important virtue of proposing a separation of the business of long-term capital loans from that of short-term commercial credits. The charter of the bank passed the Senate by the narrow margin of two votes, but failed by six votes in the House, where the basis of population still slightly favored the older counties. The hard-money counties in the northeast and south joined with Savannah and Augusta to defeat it.[27] Had the measure been adopted it would have marked a significant change in the state's policy of investing its surplus funds. Fiscal income would have ceased to be the sole, or possibly even a primary, purpose, and the chief aim would have become to supply the permanent capital needs of the thousands of agricultural producers to whom the state had distributed unimproved lands. Public investment policy thereby would have become correlated more directly with public land and internal improvement policies. But the state was not ready as yet for such a step and fifteen years were to elapse before it adopted such a course.

6. Suspension of Specie Payments

The suspension of specie payments by the two Georgia banks in 1814, following the stoppage by the Philadelphia banks, introduced the first period of inconvertible bank paper in the state, which lasted for almost three years and produced some important reactions in the banking movement. The latent hard-money opposition came to active life immediately in a legislative motion proposing that the legislature express the judgment that the banks *should* resume.[28] The resolution failed to pass, only to be introduced a year later in the imperative form that the banks *be required* to resume. Its sponsors again met with failure, but they obtained some measure of satisfaction in the passage of a resolution calling for an investigation of the directors of the Bank of Augusta.[29] This bank had incurred widespread ill-will in consequence of its vigorous curtailment and collection policies. The Planters' Bank in Savannah was currently in considerable favor as a result of having extended to the state a non-interest-bearing loan to construct war defenses at Savannah; in fact, this patriotic act did much to temper public opinion on the suspension question.[30] Actually, both banks were in strong positions and continued to discount commercial bills and loans and to issue notes. The notes circulated freely without redeemability and seldom bore a discount, because rising cotton production and prices maintained a steady balance of trade in favor of Georgia. This prevented unfavorable exchanges which were the only serious occasion normally for a demand for specie. Nevertheless, the long duration of suspension produced concern among many besides the hard-money people about the banks' seeming lack of concern over their charter obligations to redeem their notes.

The banks did not want for defenders, who insisted on the folly of any other course than that which the banks had pursued, and who challenged their foes to produce evidence of failure of the banks to serve the needs of trade to the limits of their capacity.[31] The insufficiency of currency, so frequently proclaimed, was owing to the need of additional banking facilities according to this view. That the attitude of the state as a whole was highly favorable to banks despite the suspension, appears to be amply borne out by the chartering of the Bank of the State during this period. The confidence in the two existing banks was greatly strengthened also by their coöperation in establishing the Bank of the State. The latter's charter required stock payments of $250,000 in specie actually paid in before the bank could be organized and opened for business. The state made a large payment on its subscription in notes of the other banks and the governor appealed to the banks to redeem the notes in specie in order to enable the Bank of the State to open; whereupon the other banks readily complied with the request.[32]

Despite the freedom from any serious consequences, the suspension period produced a significant change in attitude toward banks in Georgia. The state's caution in the creation of banks had proved wise. Its banking capital in 1814 was only one-third that of either North Carolina or Louisiana, one-sixth of Virginia's, and less than one-sixth of South Carolina's; although its production was nearly equal or greater than that of all except Virginia.[33] Economic conditions also had been exceptionally favorable. But could the state always expect to escape so easily? What was happening in other states, where banking excesses had ended in chaos, had not gone unobserved. Furthermore, even with proper limitations upon numbers of banks, could Adam Smith's notion of a redeemable bank paper be made to work satisfactorily on a purely state basis? Were there not inherent dangers in such great displacement of specie, since it was the only factor that held the heterogeneous paper currencies in some kind of operating relationship? Such questions and doubts explain the conversion of large numbers of Georgians to William H. Crawford's views concerning the insufficiency of local banking systems and the necessity of a central bank.

7. Georgia Supports a Second Bank of the United States

Georgia's members of Congress, with one exception, worked indefatigably from beginning to end for the establishment of the Second Bank of the United States. For the third time on as many occasions, they were among the leaders in the struggles over the national bank question. John Forsyth in the House and William Bibb in the Senate became the wheelhorses of the Bank forces; Thomas Telfair of Savannah was one of the most effective speakers for the Bank; and Wilson Lumpkin, though more busily engaged with Indian affairs and internal improvements, was a consistent Bank supporter. Only Bolling Hall, a Clark Democrat and the lone representative of the hard-money sentiment in Georgia, withheld support of the Bank, and proposed instead a limited public specie bank in the District of Columbia, that incidentally suggested some of the principal features of the later Independent Treasury System.[34] Crawford was not in Congress at the time, having resigned from the Senate in March 1813, to become Minister to France. He returned in June 1815, however, to become Secretary of War and, shortly thereafter, Secretary of the Treasury, and is credited with having had a large hand in getting the Bank charter past the last major obstacles.

The Georgians took the ground that the primary functions of a national bank were to maintain a stable and uniform currency and to facilitate the government's fiscal operations, and not merely those of an ordinary commercial bank. These proper central banking functions were identical with the purposes of the government's rightful and constitutional control over money — which principles were first applied in regard to the minting of money but now extended to banking, since, with the development of commerce, bank currency had become the principal medium of exchange, hence provided sufficient purpose and authorization for the government's establishment of the Bank. The proposed partnership of government and private individuals seemed especially suitable to the nature of the objectives, since it would insure the performance of the general welfare functions and, at the same time, would secure the driving force and greater vigilance of private interest.[35] Fears of erecting a dangerous "monied" monopoly — so disturbing to the minds of earlier Georgia Congressmen — appear not to have worried this group, since one of their chief concerns was that Congress should approve of a bank with sufficient resources to perform its weighty functions effectively. In the long fight over size, on which the northeast held out for a small bank, the Georgians were the most tenacious supporters of the "big bank" policy, and only acquiesced reluctantly in the eventual compromise that set the capitalization half way between twenty and fifty million dollars.[36]

The years 1814 through 1818 were a period of great prosperity and growth in Georgia. Cotton prices held steadily in the range between twenty-five and thirty-five cents per pound — the highest level attained during the nineteenth century — and production more than doubled during the decade as a whole. The Bank of the State was organized at Savannah immediately after its incorporation in 1815 and branches shortly were opened at Augusta and Milledgeville and subsequently at Washington, Athens, Eatonton, Greensboro, and Macon. It quickly became and remained throughout the ante-bellum period the largest banking institution in the state. The Second Bank of the United States opened a branch in Savannah on May 26, 1817, amidst expressions of welcome and good will from both the people and the state banks, since it was expected that it and its branches would assure the maintenance of specie payments, the equalization of the exchanges, and the institution of sounder banking practices generally. The business of the Savannah Branch grew rapidly, reaching a million dollars of loans within the first year.[37]

8. The Bank of Darien

The great increase of settlement in the interior, especially in the frontier region bordering the Ocmulgee River, gave rise to renewed efforts to obtain banks in the western part of the state. The east again proposed instead the addition of banks in Savannah and Augusta.[38] A further powerful stimulus for new banks — as a medium for public investment — was created by the previously cited redundancy of the public revenues and establishment of the education and internal improvements funds. The governor was authorized to invest the principals of the latter in stocks of existing banks or other equally profitable corporations. Actually bank stocks were about the only available attractive securities, but they were selling at such high premiums that successive governors refrained from exercising the authority given to them.[39] There were proposals that the capitals of existing banks be increased with reservations for state subscription, and several groups came forward seeking charters that would allow state subscription up to 50 per cent. The movement for more banks or banking capital came to a head in the legislature of 1818. The eastern cities backed a number of unit bank proposals; Augusta, in addition, sponsored an agricultural bank; while the west supported a proposal of the small port of Darien for the establishment of a second great state-wide branch-banking institution with headquarters at Darien. Every one of these proposals anticipated permitting the state to make a large stock subscription.[40]

The agricultural bank scheme was the only novel one, although some of its sections were copied from the original Planters' Bank charter of 1807. It provided for a single large bank with a capital of $1,000,000 — $350,000 reserved for the state — to be located in Augusta. The private stock subscriptions were to be sold throughout the state and the directors were to be elected regionally. The directors were authorized "to advance money, or make loans, on deposit of produce, pledge or transfer of the stock of a corporation, or any other country security, which in their opinion (would) effectually secure the bank against ultimate loss, and at the same time promote the accommodation of persons resident beyond the limits of the city of Augusta." The state could declare the charter forfeit for "failure to redeem notes with specie equal to any other bank in the state."[41] Despite the suggestions of easy credit facilities, the measure attracted almost no support from either the Cotton Belt or the coastal agricultural region. Advocacy came chiefly from the poor piney woods section in the south and the small farming region north of the Cotton Belt. The agricultural bank proposal reflected several of the traditional complaints of the back country against the city banks; but its greatest significance lay in the fact that it inaugurated the movement to secure commercial banking that would provide loans on industries other than cotton and rice production, or on products other than the staples. This movement was destined to gain ground with the rise of north Georgia and of manufacturing and more diversified commerce, of cities such as Atlanta, and to be opposed rather bitterly by the traditional banking interests and their supporting Cotton Belt and staple-marketing centers.

The Darien bank project was inspired by Darien's freshly awakened commercial ambitions and the renewed demands for more banking facilities in the west. Darien's enthusiasm was a product of the current water-

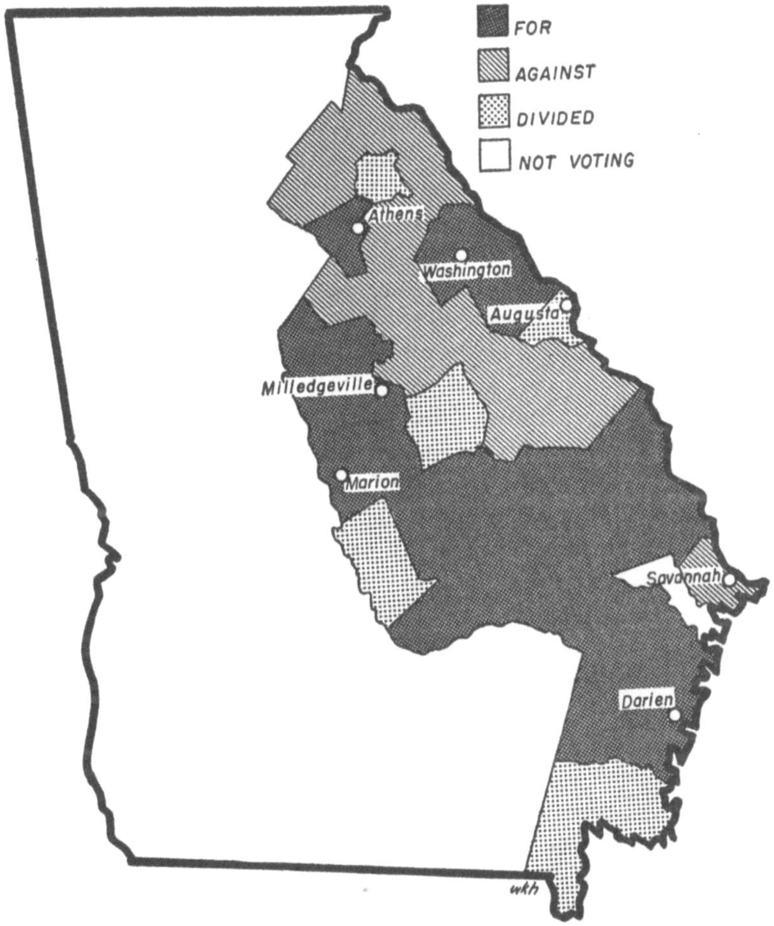

Georgia: Vote on Bank of Darien (House), 1818

way improvement fever and, in particular, of the grand Altamaha-Oconee-Ocmulgee riverway project.[42] The bank proposal envisioned the likelihood that such an institution, with its head office in Darien and its branches throughout the Cotton Belt, would bring the trade of central Georgia down the improved water route to the port of Darien at its mouth. Central Georgia likewise was fired by the vision of cheap water transportation to the sea, such as the eastern Cotton Belt of middle Georgia enjoyed from the Savannah River leading to Savannah; and its long-standing differences with the older cities must have disposed it strongly in favor of a system of banks under the leadership of Darien capitalists rather than the further creation of banks in Savannah and Augusta. Darien, with its immediate interest in the development of connections with the interior, was likely to be much more sympathetic to its needs. The plan received almost the solid support of central and south Georgia, as well as most of the votes of the agricultural bank advocates, and passed both houses of the legislature by heavy majorities. The agricultural bank, on the other hand, was defeated by almost identical majorities and the unit bank bills mustered even far less support. The legislature was not inclined to experiment with the agricultural bank nor to add to the state's banking capital beyond the amount provided for the Darien bank.

The authorized capital of the Bank of Darien was $1,000,000 of which one-half was reserved for state subscription. A branch was to be opened at Milledgeville within six months after the organization of the home bank, another within two years at some location on the Ocmulgee River, and additional ones thereafter at other places as the directors should see fit. Private subscription rights were apportioned: fifteen hundred shares to Darien, five hundred to Milledgeville, and three thousand among fourteen other interior localities; and the Darien subscription committee, which included the chief promoters of the Bank, was empowered to take steps to open the Bank immediately. There was a rush to subscribe for the shares, because bank stocks were still booming in early 1819 despite the business recession and the decline in cotton prices. The legislature exercised the state's five thousand share option just two days after the chartering of the Bank. When the subscription books were opened two weeks later in Darien, its allotment was immediately oversubscribed by 30 per cent and in Milledgeville subscriptions equaled four times the apportionment.[43] The main bank was opened early in 1819 and the branches at Milledgeville and Marion (the Ocmulgee location chosen) shortly afterwards. The legislature which met that fall directed the governor to invest $100,000 from each of the School and Internal Improvement Funds in the shares that had been reserved for the state and also appropriated $175,000 additionally from the general fund for the same purpose. Since only 65 per cent of the stock payments were ever called by the management the state invested only $325,000 in the Darien Bank.[44]

The Darien Bank structure was modeled closely upon the Bank of the State and, like the latter, was strictly a commercial bank. A couple of provisions in the charter, to allow reserves in cash funds instead of in specie and to permit the drawers and endorsers of short-term notes to be residents outside of the banking city, were relaxations of traditional commercial banking requirements in Georgia;[45] but some other features of the charter regulations appear to have been more restrictive than had been customary. The legislature, for instance, reserved the sweeping power of exercising control over the bank at all times and of suspending its charter for failure to comply with any provision of the act. Hence, there was little to distinguish the bank, actually, from the other three in the state, except possibly the matter of judgment about its location and any ulterior purpose there may have been involved. Darien was a small undeveloped port with poor physical facilities at the mouth of an undeveloped watercourse. Isolated from established commercial and financial centers, its capitalists were inexperienced in commerce and finance. It might be doubted that there was any great amount of liquid capital in Darien or in any of the centers in which it was contemplated to locate branches, and other uncertain and highly speculative factors were present. There is the further question concerning the wisdom of granting banking facilities as a device to attract trade to a locality that had been lacking apparently in the requisite facilities to develop commerce. Such an act undoubtedly had elements of protection or subsidy. Granting the desirability of a protective policy, was banking its proper instrument, especially in view of the uncertain and speculative nature of the results? It does not appear, however, that opposition was voiced on any of these grounds. Savannah belittled Darien's commercial possibilities, to be sure, but believed in the feasibility of the improvement of the Altamaha-Oconee-Ocmulgee system and feared Darien's competition for the western trade. Its capitalists were still pouring money ten years later into a Savannah–Altamaha canal that was designed to bring the traffic of the state's central river system to their city. It had been the traffic on the Savannah River that had caused the growth of Savannah and Augusta, and the faith in improved waterways, inspired by the Erie Canal, had become unbounded. These and the steady expansion of cotton production southwestward, together with the general acceptance of a "need for additional banking capital" at the time, must have amply justified the incorporation of the Bank of Darien in the minds of most Georgians. General feeling in the matter was similar to that which had prevailed three years earlier when the Bank of the State had been chartered. The state was growing at an amazing rate; it had just opened up fresh lands to settlement in the central region and was anticipating the opening soon of far greater areas in the west and southwest. Even the fact that a depression was already enveloping the country did not appear as a serious deterrent to Georgia's inevitable prosperity.

That the likely success of the Darien Bank was scarcely questioned seems borne out by the attitudes upon the state subscription. The sponsors and supporters of the Bank made a strong effort to have the state's subscription reduced to 30 per cent, but their conservative opponents from the older and wealthier sections mustered sufficient strength on this issue to retain the 50 per cent allotment to the state.[46] The fact that the acceptance of the state as an equal partner in ownership was forced upon the Darien promoters and their western associates by the representative from the strongholds of *laissez faire* in eastern Georgia would seem to indicate that there was little question in the minds of either group regarding the Bank's probable success, and it should remove also any impression that may have been gained that the Bank was either a "rag money" or a socialistic venture inspired by "cheap money" agrarians. It was not of the genre of wildcat public banking that flourished in some of the younger states at this time. It was expected that it would be run as the other banks in the state were operated and, like them, would yield a high return on the state's investment.

9. The Banks and the Depression of 1819

The recession that began in mid-1818 and deepened into a major depression during the following year brought Georgia's first experience with banking in economic crisis. By the middle of 1819, cotton prices had dropped more than half and a prolonged period of unfavorable exchanges had begun. Banks, whose loans and note issues had swollen enormously during the long period of prosperity and rapid economic growth, were forced to adopt a policy of drastic curtailment and vigorous collection of loans. Note circulation declined over 75 per cent during 1819–1820. Such deflationary operations were painful indeed; but even so, Georgia escaped the financial debacle that was visited upon so many of the southern and western states, and that was generally attributed to the growth of unsound banking and the issue of bank "rag money." The Georgia banks did not suspend specie payments and there were no bank failures; in fact, they weathered the depression surprisingly well.[47]

10. Controversy with the Second Bank of the United States

Public concern over the banks became focused after 1819 almost entirely upon a single outgrowth of the depression — the struggle that developed between the state banks in Savannah and the Bank of the United States over changes in clearing policy introduced late in 1819 at the Branch of the Bank of the United States in Savannah. Prior to this time the Branch had adapted its operations to the clearing customs that prevailed generally among Southern banks and which had resulted from the seasonal nature of the Southern producing-trading economy. Trade being confined largely to the export-import season from September to June, discounts and circulation were heavy only during eight or nine months and declined to very low figures during the balance of the year. It was customary among banks to accept one another's notes during the active season and pay them out as cash. Exports normally paid for imports and federal taxes; circulation contracted automatically toward the end of the season; and banks settled their inter-bank balances in due time with drafts on various exchange balances. The Branch of the Bank of the United States at Savannah, as a depository of federal revenues, commonly received large amounts of Georgia bank notes during the active trading season from the Savannah Customs House and Alabama land sales. It had been in the habit of paying them out as cash in discounting loans or purchasing exchange, or of accepting exchange drafts for them at the convenience of the issuing banks. Frequently it had held large amounts of notes in its vaults for considerable periods. The Branch also issued its own notes during the trading season as the opportunity for increasing its discount business beyond the volume of federal deposits warranted. The federal treasury had likewise followed the practice of accommodating its fiscal operations in the South to the seasonal character of the economy.[48]

Exchanges almost invariably became adverse to the South during the off season; but in normal times this proved no serious burden, because of the lack of any great need to make external payments. It was only when a business revulsion, a crop failure, a late harvest, a low price, or an unusual occurrence in the international money market prolonged the period or created an exceptional condition of adverse exchanges that the situation became acute and complaints arose. Such occasions were frequent enough, and the premiums on exchange charged in such demand markets were high enough, to make the exchange question one of the persistent public issues in the South. Blame was heaped primarily upon Northern and foreign banks, merchants, speculators, and bill brokers and "shavers"; but since Southern banks were the chief suppliers of exchange, they likewise came in for a great deal of criticism. The "equalization of exchanges" had been one of the primary objects and hopes, in the minds of Georgians, in the establishment of the Second Bank of the United States. Actually the Bank had done very little toward any real solution of the problem. It had followed the Southern custom in clearance practices and it had protected itself against adverse exchanges by instructing its Southern branches not to issue any notes when exchanges were adverse, in order to prevent their being used as bills of exchange to escape the payment of premiums.

The severe decline in cotton prices during 1818–1819 produced the most prolonged period of adverse exchanges that Georgia had experienced since the days of the embargo. The Bank of the United States, pursuing its usual policy regarding circulation, stopped note issue entirely at its Savannah branch; but, as depression deepened, both the treasury and the

Bank changed their policies regarding drafts and clearances in Savannah. Late in 1819 the Branch was instructed by the parent office in Philadelphia to institute daily clearings with the Georgia banks; accordingly, it presented a large amount of notes, recently received, to the Planters' Bank and the Bank of the State in Savannah for immediate redemption. The ensuing controversy was marked by increasingly bitter charges, countercharges, and occasional truces, until finally in June 1821 the Planter's Bank virtually refused to pay any more of its notes presented by the Branch. It declared that the Bank's refusal to issue its own notes had increased greatly the pressures of the hard times upon the state banks and had thrown upon them the entire burden of maintaining the currency; and it charged bad faith behind the clearance policy and a sinister design to use federal funds and the business revulsion to destroy the state banks. The Branch demanded an immediate settlement and issued circulars charging the Planters' Bank with suspension of specie payments. The legislature, thoroughly aroused against the Bank of the United States, passed an act virtually denying its right to recover specie from the state banks; whereupon the Bank brought suit in the federal courts against the Planters' Bank. The Supreme Court of the United States handed down a decision in favor of the Bank of the United States in 1824, whereupon Georgia repealed its anti-bank law.[49]

The Bank controversy revived against the Second Bank of the United States much of the old opposition and bitterness that had prevailed in Georgia toward the First Bank during its early life. While still professing their belief in the utility of a central bank, the Georgians accused the Second Bank of failure to perform the functions for which it had been created; that its actions, on the contrary, had been guided entirely by the selfish motives of an ordinary commercial bank, and had worsened and lengthened, rather than relieved, the effects of the depression; and that it had abused its depository privileges and had actually used them in an effort to destroy sound state banks.

Neither side gained anything from the struggle. Some writers have maintained that it cost Georgia heavily in unfavorable exchange rates for many years.[50] Certainly the Bank of the United States paid a heavy price for victory. It lost the support of a state that had been its staunchest advocate; and the business of the Savannah branch slumped to half its former level and remained virtually stationary for many years despite a doubling of production in Georgia and an increase of banking business of four- or fivefold. Even during the boom of the 1830's it only partially regained its previous volume. It built up its dealings in exchange and, for a brief two months early in 1835, actually attained its 1818–1820 level in total volume of business; but it lost ground rapidly after September of that year and thereafter maintained little more than a nominal existence until its demise in November 1837.[51] Probably the most important consequence of the Bank controversy was that after 1824 the policies of the state banks and the state government became the dominant monetary factors within Georgia.

11. Financial Troubles of the Bank of Darien

Shortly after the Planters' Bank decision, the state's attention was abruptly diverted from the activities of the Bank of the United States to the troubled affairs of one of its own banks — the Bank of Darien. The first authentic intimation that the Darien Bank was in financial difficulty came when it failed to resume specie payments with the other banks in the winter of 1824–1825.[52] Although it had opened business in 1819 amid general economic depression, it had launched at once upon a liberal loan policy, aided materially no doubt by the government's payment of $325,000 on its stock subscription. Having no immediate problems of curtailment or liquidation, such as beset other banks, it had been able to increase its loans and discounts while they were reducing them; consequently, its notes had steadily supplanted those of the other banks and in time had become the principal circulating medium of the state.[53] Darien notes had appeared at other banks in such ever-increasing quantities that the latter had instituted the practice of redeeming their own notes one-half in Darien notes in order to save themselves the expense of carrying notes to Darien to exchange for specie.[54] Darien had not escaped sizable demands for specie redemption, particularly from the Bank of the United States, but had been able to meet all such up to the time that the Bank suit and a further decline in cotton prices forced a general suspension in 1822. Darien had enjoyed certain favorable factors no doubt, such as its isolation and the low velocity of money in western Georgia; furthermore, the United States Treasury had entered into an agreement with it whereby it had replaced the Branch of the Bank of the United States at Savannah as the depository of federal revenues from southern Georgia, Alabama, and Florida, and had been permitted to meet out-of-state treasury drafts with New York or Philadelphia exchange.[55] This arrangement relieved Darien of the pressure from the Branch at Savannah. It also indicated that the Darien Bank enjoyed a favorable public regard which it seems to have retained reasonably well up to the time of the resumption of specie payments by the other banks. Whatever difficulties it hitherto may have been encountering had remained undisclosed to the public.

As soon as it became apparent that Darien would not resume, the value of its notes dropped precipitately and, since they constituted the greater part of the circulating medium, involved the state again with a depreciated paper currency.[56] The bank's troubles centered primarily in the Marion branch. Located in a frontier region, this unit had loaned freely, only to find that its assets had become frozen when further price declines, slow recovery, lack of markets, and poor transportation caused the planters to default on their debts. Furthermore, Marion had proved an unwise choice of location, as Macon began to show unmistakable evidence of becoming the commercial metropolis of central Georgia.[57]

The state found itself doubly embarrassed by the depreciation of the Darien notes: it held large quantities in the treasury and was the virtual owner of the bank. It had been accumulating gradually another large surplus and the far greater proportion of this was in Darien Bank notes.[58] The situation became even more serious during 1825, under the operation of a law requiring the treasury to receive the notes of all banks that were reported sound by the Joint Legislative Committee on Bank Inspection. This committee had made its investigation and report in 1824 prior to general resumption and had approved the condition of all of the banks including the Bank of Darien. When the true condition of the latter became apparent early in 1825, every one indebted to the state became intent upon paying in Darien notes. There could not be another Joint Committee report until November 1825, and the legislature ruled that the treasurer must receive Darien money, if presented, in payment of any tax or other debt owing the state that had been incurred prior to November 1825. Consequently, the state found itself with approximately $600,000 of Darien money and little of any other sorts when the legislature met in November.[59] That body ordered that all current obligations should be paid one-half in Darien notes; but even so, all other monies in the treasury were soon exhausted leaving only Darien bills in the surplus account.[60]

The state's proprietorship relation to the bank presented a no less complicated problem. The original one-half ownership had become a four-fifths ownership during the depression through no action on the part of the state. Private stockholders originally had paid in, at least nominally, $326,000 to match the state's $325,000; but a large number of the private subscribers, having become heavily indebted to the Bank and unable to pay, had transferred back to the Bank in settlement some $231,805 of its own shares, thereby reducing the capital to $419,195 and the privately owned portion to approximately one-fifth of the total. Numbers of directors had been reallotted, four to the state and one to the private stockholders, and so the bank had become not only largely the property of the state, but also presumably was being controlled and operated by the state's majority of the Board of Directors.[61]

A third important public aspect of the situation created by the Darien default soon became evident. The spirit of internal improvements had been reviving with economic recovery and the state was displaying a mood to inaugurate some kind of comprehensive statewide system. Large public expenditures no doubt would be required. The treasury surplus was the most likely source, but the depreciation of the Darien notes threatened to wipe it out. A large part of the Internal Improvement Fund was invested in Darien Bank stock, which certainly would yield no return for some time and eventually might also be entirely lost. Approximately three-quarters of a million dollars of potential internal improvement funds, therefore, were tied up with the fate of the bank; furthermore, as four-fifths owner of the institution, the state was proportionately liable for other outstanding debts of the bank, which could become a first claim against the solvent revenues of the state. A large quantity of the depreciated notes and certificates of deposit still remained in the hands of private individuals.

It was under such public and private pressures that the legislature faced the Darien Bank problem in 1825. Three alternatives were presented: it could allow matters to take their course under the present directors, aided possibly by some palliative measures, hoping that time would enable the institution to work out of its unfortunate condition; it could take over the bank and liquidate it; or it could attempt to restore the bank's solvency under outright public operation.[62] There was a strong presumption that the legislature had little choice under the terms of the bank's charter other than to take steps to liquidate it, but such a course posed some embarrassing possibilities. In the position of receiver, the state would be under the necessity of taking action against itself and a small private minority of stockholders and the defaulting debtors. From this last group, chiefly planters, it could only seize lands which would then have to be sold; but already, in its efforts to collect the purchase prices of lands sold under recent lottery acts, it had found these procedures very difficult and of little gain. Furthermore, such a course promised to have political repercussions. Hence, a policy of liquidation possibly meant not only the loss of the bank's notes in the treasury, but also the assumption by the state of most of the other outstanding liabilities of the bank.

Each of the three possible lines of action had strong support. The other banks and their friends and many of the hard-money people wanted to see the bank liquidated. Equally opposed to such a course were many friends and customers of the bank, representing wide political influence in the interior and in south Georgia, who generally favored allowing the bank to continue operations under the existing management. There was also a growing revival of sentiment for a State Bank, sparked no doubt by Governor John Clark's recommendation two years earlier for a public bank that should be organized upon the treasury surplus and stock investments of the state. Clark also recommended that the Darien Bank be moved to Milledgeville. While there was no suggestion by Clark that the two institutions should be combined, the bank's later difficulties and the multiple involvement of the state in its affairs seem to have suggested the notion of absorbing the bank into some kind of state banking institution. Those who favored continuance of the existing management and operations, however, were still largely opposed to public banking. They were also the chief proponents of internal improvements and deeply concerned about the recovery of the values of the state's surplus and Internal Improvement Fund. The will of this group prevailed and the officers of the bank were given the opportunity of trying to work the bank out of its troubles. The legislature authorized the removal of the Marion branch to Macon and recommended that the public directors seek some kind of arrangement for relief in the Marion situation that might remove that unit's influence upon the main bank and its other branches. An effort was made a year later to have the main bank moved to Milledgeville, but the necessary approval of the stockholders was never secured.[63]

The condition of the bank had improved sufficiently by 1827 to enable it to undertake to redeem its notes in the treasury at the rate of $75,000 semi-annually, which obligation was met regularly thereafter, payments being made to the Central Bank of the State after the treasury funds were turned over to that institution in 1828.[64] It was reported officially in 1829 that the Darien Bank had regained public confidence and was making new emissions on a limited scale.[65] In the following year, however, the legislature accepted the House Finance Committee's recommendation that the bank's charter should not be renewed upon its expiration in 1835, but that its affairs should be wound up and the state's investment therein transferred to the capital stock of the Central Bank.[66] This action resulted apparently from the wide popularity of the Central Bank's capital loan policy and from the belief in some quarters that the Darien Bank's recovery was more apparent than real.[67] The governor was authorized to ascertain upon what terms private stockholders would agree to sell to the state, as a possible mode of closing out the bank's affairs. Semi-annual dividends were resumed in 1831 and a petition for rechartering was presented in 1833.[68] The bank had recovered upon a considerable part of its old loans, had retired the state-held notes, and regained a profitable operating basis. Consequently, the legislature reversed its previous decision and extended the charter for twenty years. Permission was given to increase the privately owned capital stock by $100,000, primarily to enable the bank to open a branch at Dahlonega, in the center of the then current gold rush in north Georgia. The state's equity was established at seven-tenths and a new total of ten directors were so apportioned between the state and the private stockholders. Moreover, the state was accorded the privilege of selling its stock whenever it desired.[69] The bank expanded operations greatly during the subsequent three years until, by April 1837, its loans and discounts had reached $1,300,000 and total assets,

$1,800,000, which placed it with the other three early banks in the top group of the financial institutions of the state.[70]

12. Bank Regulation

One further important result of the Depression of 1819, to which the Bank controversy and the Darien Bank experience added momentum, was the rise of a regulatory movement. In the main this represented a shift in the policy program of the adherents to the hard-money philosophy. The old demand for a specie currency and the opposition to banks was becoming transformed into a cautious acceptance of bank currency subject to strict regulation of the issuing banks. Two other important factors, which produced a feeling of the need for closer public supervision, were the concern over the state's large investment in bank stocks caused by the depression and the Darien episode, and the increasing evidence of control of policies and practices of country branch banks by their parent offices in the large cities.

Prior to 1820, bank regulation had been confined almost entirely to charter regulation. Other than this, banking acts had dealt only with particular situations or individual banks. Charter regulation covered the usual organizational procedures, the rights, obligations, and duties of stockholders and officers, the corporate privileges and liabilities, specie requirements, limitations on note issues and other debts, records and reports, and penalties for violation of charter provisions. Typically they included the following regulations: the voting rights of stockholders should vary with the number of shares held individually, but less than proportionately and with a maximum limit for any individual stockholder; special meetings could be called at any time with proper notice by any small minority of stockholders — minimum number specified — holding as much as 2 per cent of the total shares; stockholders might inspect the books; and they were proportionately liable for the debts of the bank to the full amount of paid-in capital. Directors and appointed officers must not hold official positions with any other bank, or be associated in any firm with any person who might be so connected; they must supervise all of the business of the bank, keep records, and render regular reports to the stockholders. The amount which any director or other officer or stockholder could borrow from the bank was limited. The bank was forbidden to engage in insurance or in any commercial transaction whatsoever other than in bills of exchange, notes, and bullion, except to recover debts owed to it; it could own only sufficient real property for the transaction of its proper business, except such as might be acquired and held temporarily as a result of judgments and executions in cases of indebtedness to it; it must have specie or specie funds in its vault to the amount of 25 per cent of its capital stock before opening for business and it must redeem all of its notes on demand in specie under penalty in case of failure of forfeiture of charter; total indebtedness must not exceed three times capital paid-in, over and above deposits of specie for safekeeping; and dividends must never exceed the amount of actual realized profits.[71]

Banking acts of a particular nature included those dealing with unchartered banks, resumption of specie payments, and special investigations. An act of 1816, designed to prevent the circulation of other than notes of incorporated banks, prohibited the issue of notes resembling bank notes in denominations of two dollars and over; permitted the recovery of three times the face value of "change" bills in denominations under two dollars; required the declaration and payment of a 20 per cent tax on all outstanding bills of non-incorporated banks; and imposed heavy fines upon violators. Another section of the same act required the incorporated banks to resume specie payments whenever the Bank of the United States and the banks of neighboring states should do so, and to redeem their notes under five dollars after February 20, 1817, in specie or in one dollar notes; and failure to meet either of these requirements should subject any bank, upon protest, to a tax of 25 per cent per annum until paid. This tax was repealed in 1820 upon notes presented by the Bank of the United States, and entirely in the following year. "Change" bill legislation was a frequent occurrence for many years.

The first general regulatory act was passed in 1820 and required that all state banks must report annually to the governor on the first day of October the amount of specie in vault, circulation, deposits, and total debts owed to others and owing to each.[72] The reports made proved too general, however, to serve any useful purpose; while such occurrences as the Bank Controversy, suspension, bank note depreciation, and heavy exchange premiums raised widespread questioning about the policies, purposes, and attitudes of banks. Consequently, in 1823, a much stronger act was passed: henceforth, reports must be much more detailed; they must present the true condition of the banks; they must show in each case, in addition to the information previously required, notes in suit, bad and doubtful paper with names of drawees and endorsers and the number of times renewed, and all items of real and personal property held by a bank together with the cause of acquisition in each case, its cost, and current market value. A permanent Joint Legislative Committee was established, whose duty it should be to investigate thoroughly these bank reports each year and to make a full report to the legislature with judgments and recommendations. The state treasurer was forbidden to receive the notes of any bank whose condition was found by the Joint Committee to be unsound or whose actions were not in full compliance with its charter.[73]

CHAPTER IX

BANKING POLICIES, 1825-1860

The resumption of specie payments by the Georgia banks in 1824–1825 marked the beginning of another upsurge in banking growth. The ensuing twelve years, designated as the third period in banking development, witnessed a multiplication of commercial banks chiefly of the unit type and the establishment of a public bank upon the consolidated funds of the state. Twenty new private banks were chartered and banking capital was increased from three to twelve million dollars. Commercial banking continued to inhabit solely the regions of cotton production and marketing, advancing into Milledgeville, Macon, and finally Columbus as the Cotton Belt spread from middle Georgia southwestward across the state. As cotton became king, bank notes became the universal medium of exchange. Few banks were located outside of the primary cotton marketing cities, and, as late as 1837, nineteen of the twenty-five state banks and thirteen of their seventeen branches were located in the commercial cities of Savannah, Augusta, Milledgeville, Macon, and Columbus. Savannah and Augusta led in banking capital; but Macon, near the geographical center of the Cotton Belt, led in number of banks with five unit and six branch banks, followed by Augusta with four unit banks and three branches, Savannah with three parent banks, one unit bank and two branches, Columbus with four unit banks and one parent bank, and Milledgeville with one unit bank and two branches. Athens, with a parent bank and one branch, was the only other city with more than one bank. Five other cities — Darien, Hawkinsville, St. Marys, Rome, and Brunswick — possessed single banks and three cities — Washington, Eatonton, and Greensboro — had a branch each.

1. Rise of Unit Banking

The new banks brought no changes in the fundamental practices of commercial banking that had prevailed previously. Nor did the public bank, though organized on different principles, challenge in any respect the predominant position of the private commercial banks in the banking system. The only notable change in the commercial banking field —

structural rather than functional — was the relative decline in branch-banking. There were no duplications of the Bank of the State and the Bank of Darien. The troubles of the latter may have accounted in part for the trend away from branch-banking, but even prior to that episode there had developed strong opposition to state branch-banking quite similar to that expressed against the Bank of the United States and possibly in part resulting from the unpopularity of the latter. Branch-banking at the state level had certain parallels to that on the national scale and produced almost equal dissatisfaction. Parent offices were accused of dictating the policies and practices of the branches solely in the interest of the home banks rather than the purposes of the communities in which the branches were located, and there was always the feeling that such policies were ultimately determined by the weight of external elements that were alien to the domestic economy, and that the repercussions from such extraneous factors were transmitted by the branch banks into the naturally more stable domestic agricultural economy with effects highly detrimental to it.[1] Much of the trying experience with credit restriction, suspension, and debt collection between 1818 and 1825 were laid first at the door of the Bank of the United States and second upon the state branch-banking institutions. The opposition was then intensified after 1824 by the experience with the Bank of Darien and its depreciated notes. Hence there developed a pronounced preference for unit banking. Whereas *only* branches had been located in the earlier interior cities of Milledgeville and Macon prior to 1825, not a single branch was established in Columbus which developed into a commercial center after that date. Branch-banking, however, was not forbidden; in fact most of the new charters explicitly permitted it on a limited scale, often a single branch at some specified point; and after 1830 charters customarily allowed a maximum of three branches, but stipulated invariably that the consent of any city must be secured before a branch might be located therein. Likewise the purposes of branch-banking underwent some change. Branches were established with an eye to convenience in dealing with correspondence, collections, clearings, and exchange transactions of the parent bank; country banks found it advantageous to have branches in Savannah or some other primary center; and the railroad banks found it convenient to have offices at more than one point on their respective company lines. Yet only five of the twenty-one new banks actually exercised the privilege of opening branches — four established a single branch each and one established two branches.[2]

2. The Central Bank of Georgia

The incorporation of the Central Bank of Georgia on December 22, 1828, was undoubtedly the most singular step ever taken in the state's banking history and it is not without considerable significance, as well, for American banking history, notwithstanding the slight attention that has been given to it by monetary historians. The preamble of its charter recites that it was "deemed expedient and beneficial both to the State and its citizens, to establish a bank upon the funds of the State, for the purpose of discounting paper, and making loans upon terms more advantageous than has been hitherto customary." [3] The bank was to be a public corporation owned entirely by the state and operated by three directors appointed annually by the governor. The capital stock was to include all unappropriated monies in the treasury, all bank stocks owned by the state, all bonds, notes, specialties, and judgments due to the state, all monies arising from sales, past or future, of land fractions and town lots and all other debts and monies at any time due to the state. The bank was made the depository for all taxes and other monies received by the state; and, in fact, was to serve as the state's fiscal agent. No officer or member of the operating staff could be a director in any other bank, or a business partner of any person who was such a director; nor could he borrow, or endorse for any borrower, from the bank. The bank was authorized to discount bills of exchange and long-term notes on two or more good securities or endorsers as the officials judged necessary. All accommodation notes, however, must be renewed at least every six months and interest thereon must be paid in advance. No limitation was placed upon the number of renewals, but the directors could require that a maximum of 20 per cent of principal be paid annually and that additional security be given whenever it should be deemed necessary. Thus it was made possible for the bank to extend, either at its own option or that of the borrower, loans of a wide variety of terms ranging from a minimum of six months to five or more years. Obviously it was intended to be a bank of intermediate and long-term credit, though the borrower had the option of retiring his loan at the end of any six-month period. Loans were to be distributed throughout the state by counties on the basis of population as nearly as possible, and the amount loaned to any one person, corporation, society, or group of persons must not exceed $2,500. Note issue was permitted, but circulation must never exceed the amount of specie and notes of specie-paying banks held in the bank's vault; and the total of debts of the bank must not exceed its capital.

The notion of a bank for relatively long-term capital loans had numerous antecedents in Georgia history. In fact, the first bank, the General Loan Office of 1755, was just such an institution; and the governmental certificate issues of the same period were made for public capital purposes. The need for developmental capital was widely evidenced in the complaints of the agricultural borrowers against the commercial banks and in the steady growth of accommodation loans and renewals. The Central Bank differed materially from all previous developments, however, in that it was a loan office for existing capital funds, whereas they represented the use of bank or governmental credit for capital purposes. The first attempt to charter a capital-loan bank upon the consolidated funds of the state, in 1813, had barely failed; but the demand for such a bank had been eased appreciably by the high cotton prices, the commercial bank expansion, and the growth of accommodation loans during the long period of prosperity that followed. The Depression of 1819 and the opening of extensive new territories, however, revived the idea. Governor Clark proposed, in 1823, that a State Bank be established for the purpose of making long-term loans at moderate rates of interest and that the state invest in it the existing surplus of over $400,000 and all future net revenues from land sales, and that it sell its bank stocks and add the proceeds likewise to the bank's capital.[4] Clark was a hard-money man in the James Jackson tradition and opposed any further extension of commercial banks, especially of the branch-banking type. He favored restricting commercial banks to primary marketing cities and requiring strict convertibility at all times. His policy, though never very clearly enunciated, appears to have favored a system of banking and currency made up of three elements: commercial banks for the sole purpose of supplying the cash needs of wholesale merchants; specie for general circulation; and some instrumentality for making long-term loans to producers. Clark believed that the profits of a public capital loan bank, such as he recommended, would enable the state to develop internal improvements, improve educational facilities, and reduce taxes. The latter result would prove an additional direct aid to farmers. He did not favor permitting such a bank to make loans to internal improvement companies or even to the state for internal improvement or other capital purposes. Nothing came, however, of Clark's proposals at the time.

Historians have seemed puzzled to explain the reasons behind the sudden decision, in 1828, to incorporate the Central Bank. Nothing appears to have foretold the action. Both political parties have been given credit for it. Actually, the vote, nearly two to one in favor of the measure, disregarded old party lines almost completely. It followed in a general way the outlines of the new Union Party — composed of the liberal elements from both the Troup and Clark parties — that was beginning to take shape during this legislative session, although it does not appear clearly that the bank was entirely a part of the program of that group. Governor Forsyth, who was to become one of the outstanding leaders of the Union Party, opposed the measure.[5] The core of its support came from the new regions. All but five counties in the seven land districts that had been settled after 1818 voted for the Central Bank and all but one in the most recent land opening — west of the Flint River. But a large core of the state's most productive counties in central Georgia, around Milledgeville, likewise supported the act and the supposedly Whig-controlled Athens region gave a considerable vote

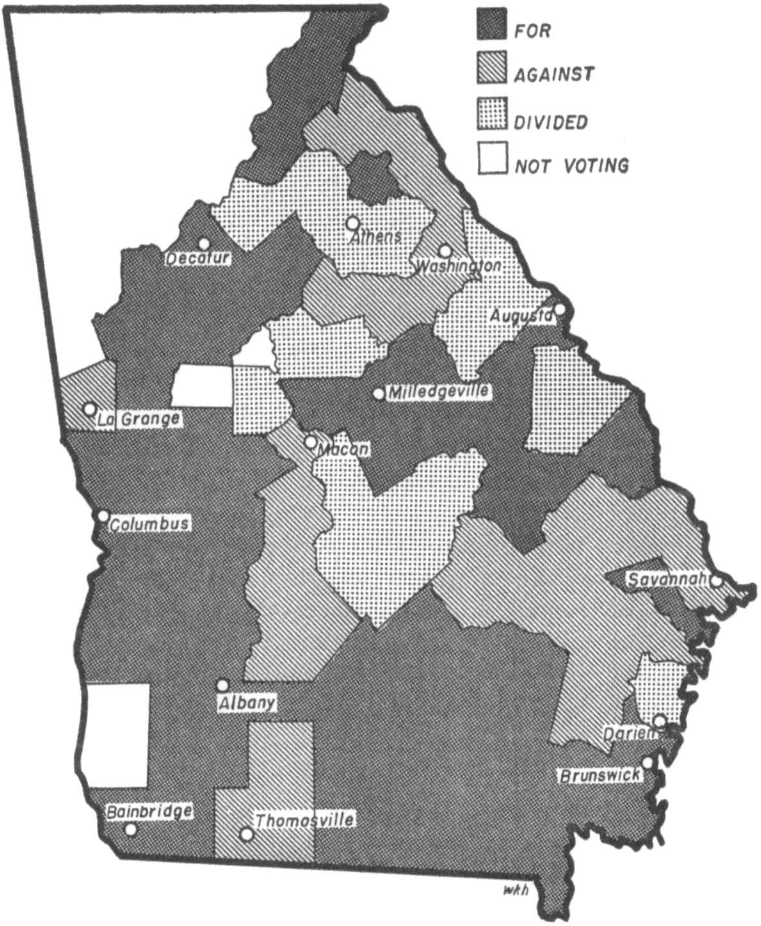

Georgia: Vote on the Central Bank (House), 1828

for it. The opposition came chiefly from the commercial banking centers of Savannah and Macon and from a few traditional strongholds of both the Troup and Clark parties. It was a somewhat curious company that united against the Central Bank — supporters of commercial banking joined advocates of hard money and delegates from old wealthy communities banded together with the representatives of the piney woods sections. There were notable exceptions among such groups however:

Augusta voted for the bank; McIntosh County, home of the Darien Bank, divided on the question, as did Burke County, one of the most conservative communities in the state, and Putnam County, the center of the earlier stay law movement. An important factor in the division of the vote was the resolution passed at this session to cease further appropriations for internal improvements until a better system could be devised than that, chiefly waterways, upon which the state had been spending its monies. Some rather extensive poorer regions, that stood to lose heavily by the abandonment of waterways and to benefit little from loans distributed on the basis of population, voted against the bank. Governor Forsyth, a strong adherent of William H. Crawford's views in favor of a central bank of issue, apparently still believed that banking reform should take that direction rather than experiment with innovations such as those suggested by the Central Bank charter. He may have feared that such an institution would encourage the kind of local credit laxities that most needed curbing. His position exemplifies the wide differences in opinion upon major public issues that prevailed among Georgia leaders even within the same party groups.

The creation of the Central Bank resulted in the main from the demands of the planters and farmers for long-term capital at reasonable rates of interest. The powerful expansionist forces released by Georgia's new land policy had created a situation in which capital had become the most urgently needed factor in the state's economy. In two decades over one-half the state's entire area had been distributed among many thousands of prospective agricultural producers; consequently there had been created an insatiable need of capital — for investment in labor, equipment, and improvements on land and in internal improvements and other marketing facilities. Traditional commercial bank loans provided, strictly speaking, only short-term operating credits; although such loans very generally were extended, by one device or another, to cover some intermediate term purposes. The development of the accommodation loan and the practice of continuous renewal, in particular, achieved the latter end and, during such prolonged boom periods as that of 1814–1818, no doubt came to serve many of the purposes of long-term capital loans. But the shortcomings of such policies were glaringly revealed by the depression of 1819 and the commercial fluctuations of the following decade.

While the Central Bank was designed primarily as a bank of long-term discount, such was not intended to be its sole function. At least three others — the revenue, regulatory, and fiscal agency functions — were assigned to it in greater or lesser degree. It was something of an omnibus measure, rather than an integrated central-banking plan; it had commanded the support of widely varying groups, who saw in it the opportunity to further one or more of these various purposes. It was not given adequate powers to carry out any of these functions except possibly the discounting one, and the diversity of opinion as to its proper functions, together with the high degree of control retained by the legislature, were to result in bitter controversy and confusing changes in policy.

The perennial urge to invest idle state funds in some form that would create a non-tax source of public revenues was enhanced by the abandonment of the policy of waterway improvements. Governor Clark had emphasized that relief from taxes was as important to agricultural producers as relief through long-term discounts. Governor Forsyth likewise stressed this point in 1829 when urging careful management of the bank and the payment of its revenues into the treasury as it prospered.[6] James Camak, chairman of the board, first president of the Central Bank, and a prominent member of the Troup Party, stated specifically that one of the two primary objectives of the legislature in chartering the Bank was to create a major source of public revenue.[7] There seemed little immediate likelihood that the Bank would be able to contribute greatly to appropriable revenues since its earnings probably would be absorbed in new loans to meet the demands which far exceeded its existing capital, but the long-run prospects seemed favorable, especially if the debts to the state could be collected and added to capital. Camak looked forward confidently to the day when the bank would supply the entire annual revenue of the government; when the state would become a self-supporting, going concern, with the Bank paying all public expenditures out of the earnings of its multi-various investments.

The somewhat nebulous regulating provisions in the Bank's charter were inspired from three sources: the long-prevailing sentiment in Georgia for some kind of centralized control of the currency, the hard-money hankering for a currency that would be independent of commercial bank notes, and the rising regulatory movement. The over-all objective was the creation of a uniform, dependable currency which Camak listed as the second primary purpose in the establishment of the Bank. To this end the Bank was empowered to issue notes on 100 per cent reserve of specie or specie funds, to create, it was hoped, a circulating medium of the utmost soundness that should serve as the foundation of the state's monetary system. The Central Bank note would have, in addition to 100 per cent specie reserve, something more than 100 per cent of producers' paper behind it. It was expected that the bank's circulation should be independent of the commercial bank currency and should supply the relatively constant hand-to-hand money needs. Commercial bank notes then would afford the elastic element in the currency that was required during the marketing period of greatly expanded trade. Specie would serve solely as bank reserves, with much higher ratio requirements imposed upon the Central Bank, behind its basic widely used currency, than upon the commercial banks, behind their more elastic circulation. The privilege of dealing in exchange was expected to serve three main purposes, all of which should complement the currency function: to permit profitable employment of idle funds, to facilitate the bank's clearing functions, and to enable it to protect its reserves and its currency.[8]

The fiscal function was twofold, one part of which was expected to be transitional and the other the normal conduct of the government's financial operations. The transitory phase was the collection, or refinancing, of the vast quantity of debts owed the state on land sales, rents, and related agency operations. There existed several thousand of these individual debts totaling approximately $360,000 as well as some $100,000 of delinquent taxes. The state previously had made its collections variously through the treasurer, the comptroller, the county sheriffs, and special agents. In cases of land purchases, it had withheld title until payments had been made in full and had, as a consequence, become involved in endless litigation on account of the numerous defaults. The entire business had become extremely muddled during the 1820's, collections had broken down, and much legislation, seeking both to enforce and to defer payments, had been passed. In turning the entire business over to the Central Bank, it was hoped that the mass of debts could be placed on a banking basis. It was intended that each individual debt either should be collected or should be converted into a regular long-term interest-bearing loan on the same basis as obtained for the other capital loans of the Bank. Upon such disposition of the debt, title should be allowed to pass and a source of constant complaint be thereby removed. It was hoped that this inducement would facilitate greatly the eventual collection of the debts.

The Central Bank was to hold all of the funds of the state and serve in a general capacity as its financial agent. Its duties, other than the payment of all warrants, were not too clearly defined, however, and became the subject of dispute and subsequent legislation. Such was the case, for example, in the matter of loans to the state and of loans contracted for the state.

The Central Bank opened for operation in June 1829. Table 10 itemizes the groups of assets that were turned over to it by the state, and Table 11 presents the balance sheet report at the end of the first six months, December 6, 1829. The original capital of the Bank included the funds released to it for permanent use in making loans and the $1,005,000 of bank stocks. The old debts owed to the state did not become actual capital until they were either paid or converted into Bank loans; although they were credited to capital stock in the Bank reports. The capital could be augmented in three additional ways: by annual surpluses of state revenues over expenditures, from net earnings of the Bank, or from extraordinary sources. Declarations were made annually or semi-annually by county allotments of the total amounts of new loans to be made. These were called distributions or dividends. The first such distribution was in the amount of $400,000.[9] There were 9,000 requests for loans on the first day that the Bank was open; and over seven-eighths of the original distribution was quickly taken. The conversion of $120,000 of the old debts into loans and the exchange of $50,510 of the depreciated Darien Bank notes for debts owed to the Darien Bank brought to approximately $550,000 the total volume of capital loans during the first six months of operation.[10] Discounts of domestic bills of exchange exceeded $90,000. Circulation of $263,409 equaled only two-thirds the amount of specie and specie funds in the vault of the Bank.

Table 10

STATE FUNDS TRANSFERRED TO CENTRAL BANK OF GEORGIA, January 29, 1829

Bonds and receipts for sale of confiscated property	$ 20,987.30
Bonds for fractions sold, 1807–1810	26,343.86
Notes for town lots, 1811	1,786.14
Bond for sale of Louisville State House	262.83
Notes for fractions sold, 1821	1,372.58
Notes for rents of reserved lands	766.12
Notes for rents of fractions, 1822, 1824, 1827–1828	24,792.32
Bonds for Macon lots, 1824–1827	40,656.25
Notes for rent of property at Fort Hawkins	16,911.87
Notes for rent of property at Indian Springs	685.00
Notes for rent of Macon bridge, 1828	4,918.00
Bond for Macon bridge	22,500.00
Bond of Unicoi Turnpike Co.	3,000.00
Bond of Savannah, Ogeechee and Altamaha Canal Co.	50,000.00
Receipts for bonds for Indian goods	649.14
Bonds and receipts for university lands	34,067.67
Bonds and receipts from collection agents	105,898.82
1,000 shares of Bank of Augusta @ $100 each	100,000.00
1,000 shares of Planters' Bank @ $80 each	80,000.00
5,000 shares of Bank of State @ $100 each	500,000.00
5,000 shares of Bank of Darien @ $65 each	325,000.00
Notes of Bank of Darien	310,261.00
Specie and notes of specie paying banks	202,840.77
TOTAL	$1,873,699.67

Source: Journal of the Senate (1829), 358–359.

The item "Deposited in Georgia banks, $46,311.18," is highly significant. This included balances created through domestic exchange operations in a half dozen state banks and the branch of the United States Bank. Such operations enabled the Bank to earn a profit on surplus current cash, chiefly notes of other Georgia banks, and also to build up the credit balances in the other banks for purposes of clearing, or redeeming, its own notes that might be presented at such banks. Since its notes were distributed widely throughout the state by long-term discounting operations, they turned up in considerable amounts at the other banks. The purchases of exchange and the establishment of clearance bal-

Table 11

BALANCE SHEET OF CENTRAL BANK OF GEORGIA, December 10, 1829

Assets		Liabilities	
Bank stocks	$1,005,000.00	Capital stock	$1,959,922.87
Bonds, notes, etc. received from state	282,900.88	Interest account	14,843.46
Notes discounted (long-term)	547,382.74	Discounts account	19,217.54
Bills discounted	91,499.04	Discounts on bills	1,878.54
Miscellaneous credit accounts	6,392.20	State deposits	84,743.62
Deposited in Bank of U.S.	4,558.24	Individual deposits	32,858.77
Deposited in Georgia banks	46,311.18	Notes in circulation	263,409.00
Current bank notes and specie	392,829.52		
	$2,376,873.80		$2,376,873.80

Source: Journal of the Senate (1829), 239.

ances prevented any considerable drains of specie from either the private banks or the Central Bank; and they enabled the latter to protect its currency. The Bank exercised great care to avoid undue pressures upon the commercial banks. It made a minimum demand for specie upon them when it opened, but none thereafter; and relationships during the early years remained cordial and coöperative. The policy of the Bank was to seek to exert a stabilizing influence upon the currency through these open market operations and clearance supports of its own currency rather than through direct demands upon the banks or through any sort of independent-treasury type of operations.[11]

The operations of the Central Bank six years later, near the peak of the prosperity of the 1830's, are reflected in Table 12. Capital stock had been increased by $630,000 although not as greatly as had been anticipated, because of a series of fiscal deficits that actually had trenched upon the Bank's capital. Long-term loans had doubled and exchange dealings were up a half, but circulation and specie and specie funds had declined

Table 12

BALANCE SHEET OF CENTRAL BANK OF GEORGIA, December 22, 1835

Assets		Liabilities	
Bank stocks	$1,005,000.00	Capital stock	$2,591,952.58
Stock of Sav., Ogeechee and Alta. Canal Co.	98,500.00	Interest account	51.92
Bonds, notes, etc., received from state	190,413.30	Discount on notes	1,799.60
Notes discounted	1,107,807.77	Discount on bills	1,023.33
Bills discounted	138,790.06	Deposits by other banks	538.24
Credit accounts	473.49	Deposits by state	43,416.00
Balances in other banks:		Deposits by individuals	37,246.51
Bank of U.S. at Sav.	6,628.77	Circulation	172,700.00
Planters' Bank	4,567.49		
Bank of Augusta	6,560.49		
Bank of State	3,269.16		
Bank of State at Augusta	39,208.75		
Central Bank of Florida	391.60		
Union Bank of Florida	1,805.00		
Insurance Bank, Columbus	5,219.25		
Current bank notes	135,948.00		
Specie	104,145.05		
TOTAL	$2,848,728.18	TOTAL	$2,848,728.18

Source: *Laws* (1835), 300–303.

a third, retaining the same ratio to each other as six years earlier. The balances in other banks were about one-fifth higher and the banks are listed individually. Balances had been created in two Florida banks, indicating that the Bank's notes were circulating in the bordering areas of that neighboring state, which had recently become a region of active settlement by emigrating Georgians.

The operations of the Bank prior to the Great Depression of 1837–

1844 appear to have given general satisfaction to the citizens of the state; even its more irreconcilable opponents offered no noticeable complaints. It fulfilled its first object of extending modest capital loans to producers throughout the state with equity and with substantial efficiency, despite other numerous and onerous duties placed upon it. Profits averaged 5 per cent on capital, which was remarkable in view of the limitations on loans and note issue, the 6 per cent interest rate, and the large expenses not associated with income-yielding operations. Commercial banks, with a three times greater legal loaning capacity and higher interest rates, averaged slightly under 8 per cent for the same period.[12] There was a rather disturbing increase in delinquencies in note payments and renewals at the bank toward the end of this first period. Of $1,103,111 of notes outstanding in December 1836, $46,924 were in suit and $211,058 were past due and unpaid.[13] Most of the latter group, to be sure, did not represent actual default, but only the exigencies of distance, communication, weather, and crop marketing.

The services which the Bank rendered the government were not inconsiderable. It was only moderately successful, to be sure, in liquidating the old outstanding debts owed to the state, chiefly on account of their poor character, but also because of the difficulties and expense involved and the inadequacy of staff. The balance sheet of 1835 showed over $190,000 still uncollected. It asked to be relieved of the burdens of suing and foreclosing on the balance of these old claims, but the legislature turned a deaf ear. In addition to acting as the depository for the state's current funds, meeting treasury drafts, and supplying exchange, the Bank when called upon extended short-time loans to the state. From one such loan eventuated a fiscal policy that soon had profound effects upon the Bank. In 1831 the legislature appropriated $75,000 over what it provided in income and Governor Lumpkin, faced by the consequent deficit the following year, borrowed the necessary amount from the Central Bank.[14] The succeeding legislature thereupon decided to liquidate the loan by requiring the Central Bank to debit its capital account in that amount, a power the legislature possessed, since the Central Bank was a public corporation belonging entirely to the state.[15] But the legislature also directed the Central Bank to cover any deficit that might arise during 1833 in the same fashion, without going through the formality of granting a loan to the state. Thus the state entered upon a policy of disinvestment as a method of paying current appropriations, because, although such overdrafts did not exceed the Bank's earnings, according to its charter earnings automatically became a part of the Bank's capital stock. A continuation of fiscal deficits obviously threatened to dry up the Bank's two normal sources of growth — state surpluses and its own profits. During the first four years, the state's deficit demands upon the Bank, while large, probably did not greatly exceed the Bank's earnings. However, after the remission of all taxes to the counties in 1835 and the further decline in state revenues after 1837, the state's deficits grew larger, posing the far more serious possibility of gradual liquidation of the Bank. Insofar as such deficit appropriations were for the purchase of securities of canal companies or the construction of the state railroad, the policy represented merely a transference of state investment; but for the most part the appropriations were for ordinary expenses, particularly after the Crisis of 1837. Paradoxically, the groups that voted the appropriation deficits were most often likewise strong advocates of increasing the Bank's loaning powers.

Considerable doubt may be entertained concerning the effectiveness of the Bank's currency policy. President Camak reported during the early years of operation that the directors believed that the currency objective was being "accomplished, *so far as the charter permitted*." [16] The later decline in circulation must have disproved even this qualified endorsement of success. The absolute decline in circulation in the face of the large growth in the Bank's business and the even greater expansion of production and trade and of commercial banking credit must necessarily have reduced greatly the influence of the Bank's circulation. The decline resulted no doubt from the deficit appropriations which so reduced the Bank's specie funds that it could not both maintain a considerable volume of circulation and conduct the exchange operations that were the only effective means of supporting its circulation and its reserves. The scheme of circulation and its supporting open-market operations were almost certain to prove ineffective sooner or later without a large permanent reserve and, probably, some supplementary method of exerting pressure upon the commercial banks. Some of the Bank's stanchest supporters already were becoming convinced that currency control could not be achieved with a currency tied to long-term loans and 100 per cent specie reserves.[17] Unless some more effective basis could be established, it would be better to pay out specie and current bills, thereby saving the added expense of printing what amounted to little more than warehouse receipts for specie and specie funds. Even before the appropriation deficits gave an additional powerful boost, a movement was beginning which favored granting the Central Bank the same note-issue powers enjoyed by the commercial banks; this did not achieve any great headway until the years of the depression.

3. Railroad Banks

The group of banks, whose association with railroad projects will be discussed later, requires brief consideration to indicate its relationships to banking developments. Since all were chartered during 1835–1836, they mark substantially the closing new development of this period. This was not the first instance in which banking in Georgia was combined with other business, for mercantile firms earlier carried on banking under the common law, and later, in a few instances, insurance companies were granted banking privileges. On the whole, however, sentiment had been against such practices. The public nature of the railroad projects and the likelihood of the launching of a state railroad to unite these municipally sponsored enterprises into a state system, together with the withdrawal from the state of the Bank of the United States, undoubtedly led to the unusual act of granting banking privileges to the railroads. Such privileges were not granted indiscriminately as seems to have been the case in some states; they were restricted to five companies that had undertaken to construct three continuous trunk lines into the interior of the state. The banking provisions contained in the acts followed faithfully the traditional pattern of commercial banking policy. It was never suggested that the railroad banks should create money for the construction of railroads. Even the earnings of the banking operations were to be paid out to the stockholders as dividends. Their charters were justified as a public necessity on the grounds that the closing of the Bank of the United States in Georgia had created a vacuum in existing banking facilities. This was the long-accepted volume of trade theory.

The railroad banks bore some resemblance, in the nature of their objectives and in their history, to the Bank of Darien. There was a like element of intended subsidy, or encouragement, to a public purpose and there were like questions about the wisdom and feasibility of associating banking with any other purposes than those of currency, deposit, exchange, and investment. Assuming that a need for new banking resources had been created, could it be met most effectively by granting a franchise at a location determined by the situation of a single other enterprise? Was the duality of purpose thus established likely to lead to misdirection or abuse of banking functions? Was it not a particularly unsound step in public policy to unite currency-creating institutions with non-monetary enterprises, even though the latter were likewise and equally affected with a public interest? It is difficult to answer these questions upon the basis of empirical evidence. The railroad banks, like the Bank of Darien, were launched on the brink of a great economic revulsion that obliterated all possibility of objective trial. Governor Gilmer's vigorous opposition in 1838 to any further conferring of banking privileges upon companies chartered for any other purpose than banking must have reflected, nevertheless, the conclusions of a majority of Georgians upon these questions, because no further grants of banking privileges of this sort were ever made.

4. Banks and Business Fluctuations

The effects of business fluctuations upon banking operations during this period attracted much public attention. The strong upward turn late in 1824 was featured by a mania of cotton speculation that carried the price from thirteen cents to thirty cents per pound; but the sudden collapse of the boom in the summer of 1825 dropped cotton to nine cents and produced severe bank curtailment and extreme hardship among debtors. Some revival set in during early 1826, but slackened toward the end of the year. Prosperity returned through 1827 and early 1828 only to run into a money crisis late in 1828 that brought trouble to many American banks and had its repercussions in Georgia. The years 1829 through 1832 witnessed a major boom, with a steep rise in cotton production and exporting, large inflows of specie, and a parallel increase in both numbers and resources of banks. There was a moderate recession late in 1832 attended by the first bank failures — two in number — in Georgia's history. Recovery came again in 1833 and another strong upward swing began which carried, save for a mild reaction in 1835, to the great break in 1837. Except for the two cases mentioned, where bad management and flagrant violation of the laws rather than economic conditions were responsible, Georgia banks weathered the commercial and financial storms of this period successfully,[18] but their policy of expansion and curtailment of credits with the swings of the business cycle produced painful repercussions and widespread criticism. Southern banks often found themselves caught in seasonal gold movements and exchange fluctuations, induced by external causes or variations in the size or timing of crop movements, and were forced into credit curtailment, collections, and premium charges on exchange that appeared to the layman, especially the debtor, to have no reasonable basis. Attitudes about such bank actions became sharply divided. Those favoring the banks absolved them of blame, commended them for necessary and salutary action, and contended that their practices reduced the severity of the economic fluctuations and protected the values of property in the community, and that public meddling reduced the banks' abilities to cope with difficult situations.[19] The other side agreed that business fluctuations were not of the Georgia banks' making, but believed that, left to their own devices, all banks followed selfish interests, that their actions were designed to protect themselves rather than the public. They contended that banks by nature should be a public utility; hence Georgia banks should be so ordered and regulated that they would serve and protect first and foremost the interests of the people of Georgia.[20]

The recession of 1832 with its credit curtailments, the rather shocking circumstances surrounding the failure of the Bank of Macon in that year, and a growing uneasiness over the rapid multiplication of banks and bank currencies produced a widespread demand that a tighter rein be placed upon all banks. Governor Lumpkin devoted a prominent portion of his annual message to an analysis of the public nature of banking functions. He warned of the dangers of overissue, removal of specie, and downright fraud inherent in a banking system that was conducted almost entirely as a private industry. The behavior of the Georgia banks had been commendable, as compared with banks elsewhere, for the evils of unregulated banking were nationwide. This was all the more reason why Georgians should be on their guard, to prevent the generality of banking abuses from working harm upon them. He advocated much stricter regulation of the state's banks. Subsequently, the legislature passed "an act more effectively to secure the solvency of all banking institutions in this state." After citing the great amount of banking capital chartered, the dependence of the state upon bank currency as money, and the great need for public knowledge about bank conditions as a safeguard against receiving depreciated or doubtful paper, the act went on to require semi-annual detailed reports from all banks in the state. The notes of any bank failing to make a report should not be received by the treasury or the Central Bank and its name should be published throughout the state; a statement of individual stock ownership and of amounts paid upon stock also must be included in the report; personal notes and discounts transferred from one bank to another should remain payable in notes of the bank of origin.[21] Additional legislation during the same year subjected all banks to penalties of 10 per cent, in addition to the customary rate of interest, for failure to redeem in specie, and prohibited the issue of bank notes in denominations under five dollars. The failure of a second bank in 1833 moved the legislature to seek better protection for noteholders by authorizing the governor to publish the bank reports in as many newspapers as he deemed necessary to afford adequate publicity concerning the condition of each bank. In 1836, Governor Lumpkin's successor, William Schley, who represented the Clark hard-money wing of the Union Party, was even more urgent in seeking banking reforms. He advocated basing note issue upon specie reserves rather than nominal capitals, a change which he thought would assure convertibility and prevent the frequent wide expansions and contractions of currency. Suspension could not be justified, only excused under the inherent weaknesses of the existing banking system. He further proposed that banking profits in excess of a reasonable return should be recaptured and held in the treasury to be paid back to the banks at such times as they might fail to earn a fair return. No steps were taken, however, on any of these recommendations.

5. Private Banks and the Great Depression of 1837–1844

The country's first "Great Depression" began in mid-1837, although its severity was not begun to be felt in the South generally until 1839. It lasted eight years. A mild decline of cotton prices in 1836 had been offset by higher production and, when in 1837 the cotton price broke sharply to nine cents per pound, even this was offset in considerable measure by the largest crop thus far on record — nearly one-third above that of the previous year. The suspension of specie payments by the Northern banks was followed by similar action by the Georgia banks. There was a considerable revival in the South in 1838, but the downward trend began anew in 1839 and continued almost uninterruptedly through 1840–1842, which marked the depth of the depression. Conditions remained largely stagnant through 1843–1844, although agriculture, trade, and banking by that time had passed through the worst phases of bankruptcy and liquidation. Actually, recovery did not become pronounced until 1846, when a rise of nearly 100 per cent in cotton prices gave the South, despite a rather short crop, its first taste of prosperity in nearly a decade.

The depression focused the attention of Georgians upon their banks as never before. This economic revulsion had been preceded by two decades of phenomenal expansion of both the area and the volume of agricultural production. Approximately two-thirds of all the land in the state had been distributed for settlement in that brief time, cotton production had increased from 50,000 bales to 300,000, and banking resources had undergone a corresponding growth in response to the obvious expansion in need for credit accommodation. The prosperity and solvency of the entire economy had come to depend upon the cotton crop and its price. A pronounced decline in either produced a downward spiral of falling incomes and values, bank curtailments, defaulting debtors, and bankruptcy sales. The intensity and long duration of the economic collapse of 1837–1844 brought the activities and failures of the banks into bold relief against the general background of depreciated money, low prices, debts, and general economic prostration. Two heated controversies developed — one around the policies of the private banks and the other around the activities of the public Central Bank.

There were twenty-one commercial banks and sixteen branches in operation in Georgia, with a combined capital of $8,850,000; loans and discounts of $17,000,000; circulation of $8,700,000; deposits of $3,110,000; and specie reserves of $3,175,000 in April 1837, just prior to suspension of specie payments. They were in a relatively strong specie position. Banks in only one or two other states had more favorable ratios of specie to demand liabilities.[22] In fact, the ratios of the Georgia banks had risen somewhat over the two previous years. Suspension in 1837 resulted from the action of the Northern banks and all but one resumed when conditions eased in 1838. All of the banks and their branches, with approximately the same capital as in 1837, were still in operation in April 1839. Loans and discounts were down only one million dollars. However, both

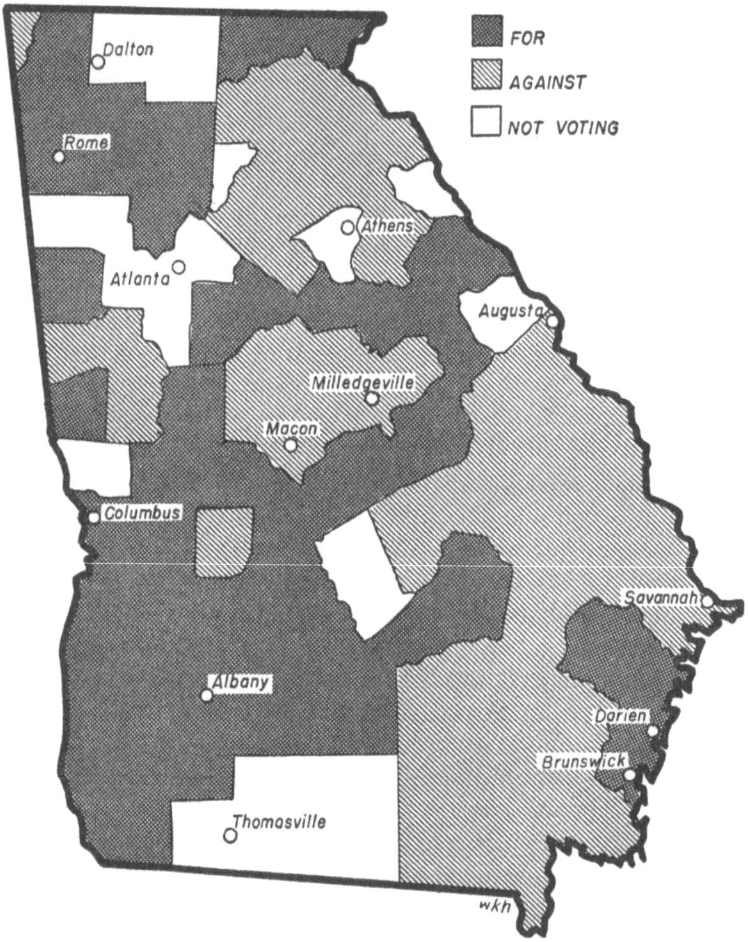

Free Banking Vote (Senate), 1838

circulation and deposits were down one-third, and, since specie reserves had declined less than one-fourth, specie ratios to demand liabilities had risen nearly 25 per cent.[23]

No new banks had been incorporated after 1836, but, with the return of favorable conditions in 1838, on December 26 the state adopted a free banking law. This statute permitted the organization of joint stock banking associations with powers to make loans and issue notes upon deposit with the state of 5 per cent bonds of Georgia or other approved state bonds or bonds of the federal government, or of 6 per cent first mortgages upon real estate or Negroes not in excess of 50 per cent of the value of the same, to the full value of the notes issued. A commission was provided, composed of the state comptroller and two members to be elected annually by the legislature, whose duties were to prepare and issue the notes to the banking associations in exchange for the bonds and mortgages and to hold the latter as security. It was empowered further to sell said security for purpose of redemption of the notes of any association that failed to redeem its notes upon demand. These banking associations were required to hold 25 per cent specie reserves at all times against bills and notes in circulation, and were subject to all of the rules and laws governing incorporated banks in the state. An association could come into existence by establishing intention of compliance with the provisions of the act through the filing of a certificate with the clerk of the superior court in the district where the office was to be established and by recording a copy of same with the state comptroller. The life of an association was limited to twenty years.

The measure was backed predominantly by the new regions of the southwest and northwest, with the support of half the counties in the older cotton belt and a few of the counties in the piney woods–coastal section. The opposition came from the southeast, the northeast, and a group of wealthy counties in the center of the Cotton Belt. The regions of the major commercial banking centers of Savannah, Augusta, Milledgeville, and Macon all voted against the law. Two banks — the Exchange Bank of Brunswick and the Bank of Ruckersville — were organized under the act during 1840 or 1841.[24] The former failed and was closed during the depression; the latter maintained an existence until 1854, when it notified the state that it had redeemed all of its notes and was petitioning for the right to cease operations; whereupon the commission was authorized to release the securities deposited with it and the Bank was given permission to close.[25]

The deepening of the depression in 1839 and the steady drain of specie to the North caused all of the Georgia banks to suspend anew. This second suspension, accompanied by depreciation of bank notes, adverse exchanges, a short cotton crop, and growing pressures upon debtors gave rise to steadily mounting complaints against the banks. Governor Gilmer, though a Troup-Crawford Party standard bearer who had defeated Schley in 1837, was almost as critical of the banks as his two Union Party predecessors. He insisted on enforcement of the principle of strict convertibility: although the brief suspension of 1837 might be excused, since it was forced by the action of the Northern banks, the suspension of 1839 was wholly without justification and revealed the slight control that the obligation of contracts had over bankers; convertibility was essential, except under the most extraordinary circumstances, for the settling of balances when exchanges were unseasonable and for maintaining reasonable rates of domestic and foreign exchange; legislation ought to be adopted, therefore, to prevent excessive note issues, speculation in cotton, and the selling of specie, and to force resumption at an early date and liquidation of all banks that were unable to resume.[26] Gilmer's Union-Democrat successor, Charles McDonald, who held office through the worst depression years — from 1839 to 1843 — blamed the private banks for the disorders of the currency, to which he attributed much of the distress of the period. The banks had flouted the laws and their charter contracts with the public, and they should be required to resume or to submit to liquidation. He suggested the establishment of a single bank in Savannah with branches throughout the state as a possible step toward better banking; however, he later expressed the "firm conviction . . . that banks of all descriptions (were) injurious to the people," that all the talk about the "public need" for banking capital was sheer deception, and that the only sound argument for banks was the saving of the cost of transporting specie. This cost, he believed, was a small price to pay for sound money.[27] These hard-money attitudes came increasingly to the fore throughout the state as economic conditions worsened.[28] Their revival was especially pronounced in the small farming regions. It was argued over and over that banks were the cause of business fluctuations and instabilities: bank currency begat overreaching and speculation, enhanced values unduly in good times, and increased the severity of price declines in bad; it was a local, fluctuating, and unsafe medium in which to estimate the values of labor and produce.[29] Some writers and speakers expressed themselves as opposed to the banking system and its great abuses, but were not certain that banks could be eliminated from the modern commercial economy. They inclined to the old position of James Jackson, that commercial banks should be restricted to wholesale trade and that some independent currency — either specie or possibly the currency of the Central Bank — should be maintained in the customary exchanges among artisans, retail merchants, and farmers.[30] It was especially notable that there were widespread complaints among the merchants against the banks. Numerous meetings were held in the interior towns. A large meeting of merchants in Columbus in 1841 censured the private banks severely and held them solely to blame for the depreciation of the currency.[31]

The banks' defenders countered the attacks of the critics with arguments that bank curtailment and suspension were results and not causes, that in protecting their own resources the banks were also protecting the resources of the community, and that the bank actions actually alleviated rather than enhanced the widespread economic distress and suffering. Such steps were necessary in order to preserve and safeguard the credit system upon which the very existence of both public and private business rested. The distressing effects of a few bank failures were as nothing compared to the evils that would result from the replacement of the credit system with a hard-money system; such a change would be highly deflationary in its effects, it would increase the burden of all debts at least threefold, which could only benefit the wealthy and fall with the most cruel effects upon the poor; poverty was everywhere greatest in the specie-using countries and least where credit mechanisms had been developed. Furthermore, to strike at banks, to abridge their right of action, to subject them to control, was to threaten "the very destruction of our liberties," to strike at "the primary springs" of the free institutions upon which democratic government rests.[32]

Many who were favorable to banks admitted, however, that suspension created hardship and that resumption should take place as soon as possible; but they accused the leading advocates of resumption of seeking to destroy the private banks or of playing politics with the bank question.[33] Other bank men thought that resumption was unwise, if not virtually impossible, as long as all governments were running deficits and producers were heavily in debt to the merchants and banks. Specie would soon be drained out entirely, foreign exchanges would become increasingly unfavorable, cotton prices would be depressed further, and general economic conditions would deteriorate still more;[34] the banking system had been built up with care and by slow degrees and should not be sacrificed to a condition that fundamentally it had not caused and could not have prevented. One of the wisest observations from either side came from a pro-bank writer, who concluded that "the currency question (had) put at fault the first and most experienced minds." [35]

The defenders of the principle of convertibility mustered sufficient strength in 1840 to pass a law requiring the banks, upon a proclamation by the governor, to resume specie payments on February 1, 1841. The proclamation was issued, but a number of the banks either could not or did not comply, and a year of grace was extended to them. This act of 1840 was destined to remain a cardinal ordinance of public policy down to the Civil War. Under it any bank failing to redeem its notes upon presentation, except in case of special act of the legislature, was subject at once to suit for foreclosure and liquidation. Of the banks that were in operation earlier in the depression, eleven banks and eight branches resumed in 1841 or 1842. These included all of those in Augusta and Savannah except two branches of the Darien Bank and a branch of a Columbus bank, two banks and three branches in Macon, and the Bank of Milledgeville. Although this group comprised just over half the total number of banks, it represented over three-quarters of the total banking resources of the state exclusive of those of the Central Bank. The remaining ten banks and eight branches and the Central Bank were unable to resume. Their notes, totaling nearly $3,500,000, consequently depreciated in varying degrees depending upon likelihood respectively of recovery or failure. Among the more prominent issues, those of the Georgia Railroad Bank at Athens soon declined 15 per cent, of the Central Bank, 10 to 15 per cent, of the Bank of Darien, 20 to 25 per cent, and of the Monroe Railroad Bank, 30 to 50 per cent.[36] The solvent banks, between 1839 and 1842, reduced loans and discounts from $11,155,650 to $5,074,-300, and circulation from $3,582,500 to $1,046,800; and meanwhile, specie reserves had declined from $1,668,450 to $583,000. The ratio of reserves to demand liabilities had risen steadily and a third of the banks actually held specie equal to or greater than their circulation.[37] Some of this drastic contraction had been forced by the law of 1840; but the most of it was the result of the depressed state of business and prices and the conservative policies of the banks.

The year 1842 marked a low point in commercial bank operations, and the banks began expanding loans again in 1843, when they almost doubled both circulation and specie holdings. Improvement in cotton prices and large retirements of Central Bank notes were the major factors facilitating this upward turn in bank activity. Conditions were somewhat less favorable in 1844, but improved again in 1845; and in 1846 loans and discounts passed $6,500,000 and circulation $3,000,000. The important Georgia Railroad Bank at Athens and the free banking association at Ruckersville ultimately surmounted their financial difficulties; so the survivors of the Great Depression finally numbered thirteen banks and nine branches of the total of twenty-four banks and sixteen branches. The solvent banks, however, represented 80 per cent of the commercial banking capital and had conducted approximately the same proportion of the banking business of the state prior to the depression. The casualties included the Bank of Darien and its four branches, all of the banks in Columbus and the two branches of one of them, the Monroe Railroad Bank, the Branch Railroad Bank, and the Ocmulgee Bank — all of Macon, the western Bank of Rome, and the Exchange Bank of Brunswick. With the exception of the Darien Bank, all of the failures were recently established institutions, located in newly settled western sections of the state. All except the Darien Bank and one of the Columbus banks also were relatively small. As suggested already, it was the large institutions, as well as those located in the older centers, that weathered the storm. The governor, as required by their charters and a special act of December 13, 1842, appointed three receivers for each defunct bank, except the Bank of Darien, to liquidate and distribute its assets.[38]

6. The Role of the Central Bank in the Depression

The role played by the Central Bank during the depression became the subject of one of the most heated controversies in the state's history. The Bank was drawn by a chain of circumstances at the very beginning of the economic revulsion into a central position in the financial affairs of the state, which it continued to occupy until near the end of the depression. The federal government in 1836 announced its intention to distribute its surplus revenues among the states. Georgia's share was indicated to be $1,401,896.12 and the Joint Finance Committee of the legislature took under advisement the disposition of this sum. A majority of the committee favored distributing it among all of the commercial banks on temporary loans and investing it ultimately in railroads. The minority arguing that the federal government might ask for it back and that bank investment was the most profitable urged that it be added to the capital of the Central Bank for the purpose of long-term discounts.[39] The legislature followed the advice of the minority, specifying that it should be kept in a separate capital account in case the central government should call for it. The Central Bank went ahead with plans for distribution of the full amount of the state's anticipated share of the surplus; but the federal government subsequently paid only three-fourths of it. Meanwhile, the business contraction of 1837 had begun, banks and other creditors were pressing collections, and requests to the Central Bank for loans were mounting. When the legislature met again, in the fall of 1837, it authorized the Bank to discount loans in the full amount of the state's share of the surplus on the questionable assumption that the federal government would pay the remaining fourth, and to borrow $150,000 in order to complete the distribution as planned. The state also faced a certain revenue deficit that was likely to be greatly increased by proposed expenditures on the Western and Atlantic Railroad, just then being placed under construction. The legislature passed this onerous fiscal problem to the Bank by directing it to pay all appropriations and to negotiate loans of three-quarters of a million dollars to cover the Western and Atlantic requirements.[40] Under these authorizations the Bank negotiated two sterling loans through New York — one through the Phoenix Bank for $263,000, which was used mostly for the loan distribution, and the other through Reid, Irving and Company, which was applied to construction of the Western and Atlantic.[41] Thus the Bank became the primary agency of financial relief for both the state and its citizens.

The question of rechartering the Central Bank came up in 1838. Lines became drawn substantially as on the original bill for incorporation ten years earlier — the newer capital-hungry sections favoring extension of the Bank's life and the older wealthier regions opposing.[42] The addition since the previous vote of northwest Georgia and its ardent support of the Bank more than offset some increase of opposition among the planters of the Cotton Belt, and the charter was extended to May 1, 1850. The limitations on the Bank's privilege of dealing in short-term discounts and bills of exchange were waived on remittances on the public debt outside

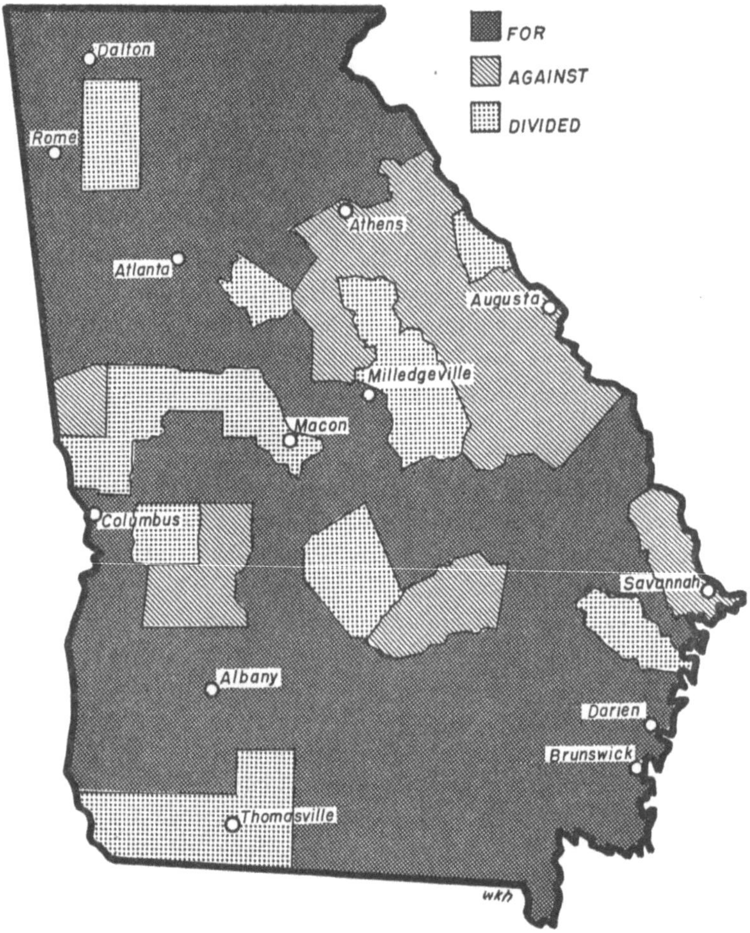

Georgia: Vote on Rechartering the Central Bank, 1838

of the state, to enable the Bank to pay interest and principal on the sterling loans in New York.

The economic situation deteriorated rapidly during 1839. Distress increased among the debt-burdened agricultural producers, depreciation of the bank currency followed the second suspension, fiscal deficits grew while demands for tax reduction arose on every hand, and consequently the strains upon the Central Bank multiplied. Demands for new long-term loans and for the renewal of old ones increased. Meanwhile, collections became steadily more difficult, state deficits — reaching an average of approximately a half million dollars annually — continued to reduce the Bank's active capital, and the steady depreciation of Darien Bank notes, which clogged the Central Bank's vaults, depleted its liquid funds.[43] The Bank obviously had reached the limits of its capacity under its charter to support the state's credit and revenue needs and to extend private relief. Its backers were intent upon finding a way of easing the extraordinary pressures upon it and of enabling it again to extend much sought after loans. The long present sentiment for giving the Bank the full note-issue powers enjoyed by the commercial banks gathered increasing support. This proposal met bitter opposition, particularly in the older sections of the state. Such an action, it was maintained, would increase the state's debt and correspondingly weaken its credit, would necessitate eventually an increase in taxation which would work the inequitable result of taking wealth from one group and giving it to another. The opposition was unable, however, to rally sufficient strength to prevent adoption of the measure; for the Bank was authorized on December 21, 1839, to issue notes up to twice its capital and to make a loan distribution of $750,000. The Bank's enemies made much of the fact that most of its capital, not tied up already in loans or in private bank shares, was composed of uncollectible obligations owed to the state. In order to relieve the pressures upon the Bank somewhat, it was authorized to sell uncommitted state-owned bank shares, at not less than par, to pay off the sterling debts in New York.

Having been defeated in their efforts to block the granting of note-issue powers to the Bank, the opposition, led by George W. Crawford, drew up a "protest" against such "perversion and debauchery of the public powers." Its fifty-four signers included such prominent names as Robert Toombs, Alexander Stephens, A. H. Chappell, Charles Jenkins, W. Daniel, and J. W. M. and T. M. Berrien, representing both commercial banking and hard-money points of view. According to this protest, the extension of relief through the Bank rested upon the "outrageous proposition that public credit is to relieve popular wants and will end with the certain necessity of universal and heavy taxation, in order to redeem that public credit"; it constituted "an inversion of the role of all proper government . . . people should support government and not look to government to support them"; furthermore, it violated the basic principle of a sound money system that "there must be some established standard of value," which, "among all commercial nations . . . is regulated by the precious metals"; lacking such a means of "easy and immediate convertibility," the Bank's "currency must necessarily depreciate . . . Mere credit cannot supply capital"; governments require abundant and appropriate checks upon their powers, and most particularly so regarding the regulation of money; but this law leaves to the discretion of the Directors of the Bank matters that "should be controlled by certain and positive law." Finally, the protestants voiced their opposition to the Bank as a mode of investing the state's funds and reaffirmed their preference for investment in private bank stocks, since the Central Bank over the preceding decade had earned barely 5 per cent, while bank stocks had yielded 8 per cent. Thenceforth this document became the platform and rallying cry of the anti-Bank forces in their war on the Bank.[44]

Clothed with its new powers, the Bank proceeded at once to make a distribution of $750,000 (actually only $705,000 in notes, since one year's interest was charged in advance) in small loans to several thousand little borrowers, who thereby were enabled to pay creditors who would not wait. It also supported the financing of the Western and Atlantic Railroad construction by accepting nearly $100,000 of scrip which the commissioners had issued when they found it was impossible to negotiate the state's bonds. But otherwise the Bank's pathway became increasingly rough. The adverse effects of the depression upon the security and exchange markets hampered both the Bank and the state in their financial operations more and more as time went on. The Bank was able to dispose of only $300,000 worth of bank stocks under the par sale requirement; it had to pay heavy premiums on exchange for servicing the external debt; the state's deficit drafts for the year totaled over $406,000; and collections of old loans became ever more difficult. As a result of its operations during 1840, the long-term loan account was increased to $1,800,000, exchange purchases to $325,000, and circulation from $65,000 to over $1,000,000.[45] The notes suffered the inevitable depreciation of inconvertible bank notes under such circumstances, because the Central Bank could maintain no reserve with which to support its circulation in the face of the prevailing adverse exchanges.

The Central Bank controversy reached its climax during 1840–1842. The legislature met in November 1840 under a cloud of gloom. It had been a year of poor crops as well as low prices, of a sharp decline in public revenues, of continued bank suspension and increasing bank note depreciation. It was now becoming clearly evident that there would be a number of bank failures. The depreciation of the Central Bank's notes was a cause of general worry. Friends of the Bank agreed with its opponents that it was a vicious circle to continue to load the Bank with state deficits, thus forcing it to make larger emissions that would inevitably cause still further depreciation; but they differed from them sharply in their appraisal of the Bank's activities. The Democrats, led by Governor McDonald, were lavish in praise of what the Bank had accomplished in the relief of distress, in meeting the state's large deficits and in preventing stoppage of work on the Western and Atlantic Railroad. They blamed the private banks for much of the distress, accusing them of selfishness and of failing to meet their legal obligation to maintain the currency on a specie basis; they proposed to require the banks to resume or forfeit their charters; and they favored a levy of heavier taxes upon property in order to balance the budget and remove the fiscal pressures upon the resources of the Central Bank.[46]

The Whigs, conversely, placed almost entire blame for the financial troubles of the state as well as of private individuals upon the Democratic-controlled Central Bank. To their way of thinking, the Bank was the chief vehicle of the financial folly of their opponents. They charged that, in three brief years, Democratic policies had converted a government surplus of between two and three million dollars and a sound currency into a government debt of a similar amount and a depreciated currency. The Central Bank, in their opinion, had been the instrument of this sad transition in the public economy. The attack on the Bank was centered upon its new note-issue powers. The Whigs claimed not to have opposed the Bank — some even laid claim to its founding — so long as it had remained a "loan office for present capital," although its task had been a hopeless one in their opinion; but the conversion into a public credit bank threatened the "very foundations of free society." The union of government and banking, always dangerous, had in this instance become a means of increasing the public debt in order to buy votes to maintain the Democratic Party in power. It took wealth from one group to support another; it robbed the industrious to debauch the impecunious. "A State should be just before she was generous." Such abuse of state credit invited "people to lean on the government, when, rightfully, the government should be supported by the people." "Industry and economy" were the only sound measures for relief. They proposed that the affairs of the Central Bank be wound up and banking policies and operations returned to the private banks, that spartan retrenchment be practiced in public expenditures, and that taxes be reduced.[47]

Neither party accomplished its full aims in the legislature of 1840, but, owing to the critical state of the times, each was able to secure the adoption of important parts of its program. The Democrats secured the law requiring the private banks to resume specie payments on February 1, 1841, on penalty of forfeiture of charter for noncompliance. The Central Bank was directed to buy the scrip issued by the commissioners of the Western and Atlantic Railroad and to pay the state's New York debts. To meet the latter obligation, it was authorized to sell bank stocks at 10 per cent discount for specie or its equivalent, after all other available funds had been exhausted. The Whigs obtained the passage of laws preventing the making of loans by the Central Bank that might involve any further issue of the Bank's notes, and authorizing the governor to redeem the outstanding notes of the Bank through the sale of the state's 8 per cent bonds to an amount not in excess of $1,000,000. The effect of these laws, if carried out fully, would be to return the Central Bank to its status before the note-issue act of 1839. The Whigs claimed a great victory; but Governor McDonald was scarcely opposed to the second measure, because he was apprehensive about overissue and consequent depreciation, and actually hoped that redemption of the Bank's notes through bond sales would support their value.

The attempt to reduce the Bank's circulation at this time failed; in fact, the exact reverse happened. State bonds, even bearing 8 per cent interest, could not be sold at all for the lack of any market; still heavier premiums and other costs of obtaining exchange greatly increased the burden of the obligation to pay the principal and interest of the external public debt; and the state ran still another large deficit, of $221,600. As a consequence, note circulation rose to nearly $1,500,000.[48] Since the solvent private banks curtailed their note issues drastically prior and subsequent to resumption and since the issues of the insolvent banks disappeared from circulation, Central Bank currency became practically the sole circulating medium of the state, except for the likewise irredeemable notes of the Georgia Railroad Bank that continued to circulate in the Athens-Augusta region.[49]

Opposition to the Bank gained headway steadily after 1840. An act of 1841 forbade the Bank to make any additional loans with its existing notes until they should be maintained at par with notes of specie-paying banks; and the governor was authorized to exchange the state's 8 per cent bonds directly for notes of the Bank, said bonds to be payable as to principal and interest by the Bank. This amounted in essence to requiring the Bank to pay interest upon its inconvertible paper money, which presents an interesting contrast to the policy toward the private banks. Critics of bank suspensions long had sought to have private banks required to pay interest upon outstanding notes during periods when they refused to redeem them; but friends of the banks had always successfully opposed such moves. Now the latter were insistent upon imposing upon the Central Bank's inconvertible paper the maximum legal rate of interest, even though the Bank had violated no provision of its charter and the notes had been issued to meet public needs. Also another of the state's problems was thrown upon the Bank in this same year, as the assets of the Darien Bank were ordered transferred to the Central Bank for liquidation.

The Bank's powers of active operation were terminated in 1842; and the fiscal business was transferred back to the treasury, along with liability for payment of all state debts except the 8 per cent bonds, which remained an obligation of the Central Bank. The latter was to make no further loans of any sort, although it was to be permitted to renew outstanding ones; nor was it to issue any more new notes, or to reissue old ones.[50] Its chief business henceforth was to be the collection of its outstanding loans and the redemption of its obligations, chiefly comprised of circulating notes and the 8 per cent bonds. The law required further that all surplus state revenues should be used to retire the Central Bank notes. Under this act, circulation was reduced during 1843 from $1,453,583 to $680,922 as follows: by debt collections, $381,186.40; by exchange for 8 per cent bonds, $291,154.60; and by notes on hand, $100,320.00. The Bank's liabilities then stood: circulation, $680,922.00; 8 per cent bonds, $520,144.60; and deposits, $100,888.15; total, $1,301,954.75.[51]

Under the ensuing administration of Governor George W. Crawford, inveterate foe of the Bank and the person most responsible for its overthrow, liquidation continued apace. Total liabilities were reduced during 1844–1845 to $840,609.64, of which only $67,750 were represented by remaining notes in circulation; and Crawford estimated that probably between $40,000 and $50,000 of these had been lost and would never be presented for payment.[52] A special legislative commission investigated the remaining assets of the Bank in 1845 and concluded that ultimate losses would be $364,223.93, which would leave the state with a final deficit in excess of $200,000.[53] The process of liquidation was continued under a skeleton force for another ten years. The remaining 8 per cent bonds, falling due in 1848 and 1849, were refunded into new 7 per cent ones. The operations of the Bank were declared at an end on February 16, 1856; and the remaining $296,000 of its 7 per cent bonds became a part of the state debt and an obligation of the treasury. The residue of $312,650.53 of assets, considered to be largely worthless, was turned over to agents for whatever collections might be possible.[54]

These concluding financial items scarcely provide a final balance, either quantitatively or qualitatively, of the accounts of the Central Bank with the state and its people. Unfortunately, complete records of the financial history of the Bank are lacking and reliance must be had too often upon summaries made by other state officers and committees. In Table 13, upon the basis of available records, an attempt is made to summarize in balance sheet form the major items in the Bank's financial history.[55] As the record indicates, the Central Bank began operations as a means of investing state and, later, federal surplus revenues, or savings — derived largely through public land sales — in small, long-term capital loans to individuals. Then, after a few years, the state began to draw back the Bank's capital for the purposes of meeting current expenses and constructing the Western and Atlantic Railroad. As a result of this depletion of its capital assets, on the one hand, and of increasing private

Table 13

FINANCIAL HISTORY OF THE CENTRAL BANK OF GEORGIA, 1829–1856

Debit Account: Capital and Other Liabilities—	
Assets transferred to Central Bank originally, 1829:	
12,000 shares of bank stocks	$1,005,000.00
Bonds, notes, and receipts—owed to the state	355,597.90
Specie and bank notes	513,101.77
Additional bonds and notes transferred to Bank for collection after 1829	477,220.72
Sale of public slaves, 1834	158,195.16
U.S. Surplus Revenue, 1837	1,051,422.09
Sterling loans, 1837–1838	703,000.00
Note issue for loans, 1839–1840	705,000.00
Note issue for other purposes, 1839–1842	977,573.00
Eight per cent bonds exchanged for notes in circulation, 1842–1845	730,000.00
Net Income, 1829–1843	640,414.34
Deposits (estimated maximum figure)	150,000.00
Profit and loss, 1844–1856	118,430.70
	$7,584,955.68
Credit Account—	
Treasury warrants charged against capital, 1831–1841	$2,333,356.65
Purchases of Western and Atlantic RR. obligations, 1839–1842	680,001.70
Other payments for state purposes:	
Poor School and Academy Funds, 1830–1842	80,076.09
University of Georgia, 1831–1842	73,000.00
Augusta Medical College, 1834	10,000.00
Brunswick Canal Company stock, 1836	50,000.00
Penitentiary and Governor's Mansion, 1842	6,653.96
Paid into Treasury after 1847	27,303.09
Miscellaneous—	100.00
Bank stocks withdrawn, 1840–42	417,700.00
Bank stocks withdrawn, 1844	262,300.00
Sterling loan assumed by state, 1842	440,000.00
Macon Bridge bond	14,354.53
Loss in operation, chiefly interest on 8 per cent bonds, 1844–1847	85,716.13
Darien Bank stock, total loss	325,000.00
Darien Bank notes, total loss	54,170.00
Retirement of note circulation, through collections, 1841–1855	907,573.00
Retirement of note circulation, through exchange for 8 per cent bonds, 1842–1845	730,000.00
Notes lost in circulation (estimated)	45,000.00
Retirement of 8 and 7 per cent bonds, 1846–1856	434,000.00
Uncollected assets, largely worthless, 1856	312,650.53
Seven per cent bonds assumed by the state, 1856	296,000.00
	$7,584,955.68

and public needs for funds, owing to the depression, on the other, the Bank was authorized to issue notes against its remaining capital assets, largely debts owed the state and the Bank. Under its new powers, the Bank issued a million and a half dollars of circulating notes, divided about equally between loans to private individuals and payments of the state's drafts and other obligations. The virtual exhaustion of its active capital and the depreciation of its circulating notes, together with the strained financial condition of the state, finally enabled the Bank's opponents to secure the termination of its active life and provision for its liquidation. In the end the state took over the Bank's remaining assets, largely worthless, and assumed an approximately equal amount of the Bank's bonds that remained outstanding.

It was asserted frequently in later years that the state had suffered heavy losses in its Central Bank venture. Just how real were these "losses"? For various purposes the Bank paid the state at least $680,000 of net earnings and saved it another $37,925 through absorption of losses on Darien Bank notes, for which the state as chief stockholder of that institution was seven-tenths liable. Subtracting $296,000 — the amount of Bank bonds assumed by the state — from the sum of these two amounts would leave $421,925 as the state's net income from the Bank's operations. Furthermore, over half the remaining $312,650.53 of uncollectible assets were debts to the state that had been turned over to the Bank for collection. Considering the huge volume of the Bank's business, the type of loan that it had made, and the severe and prolonged depression, the relatively small amount of its ultimate losses is remarkable. It is very doubtful whether any private bank was able to match its performance. In addition to actual earnings realized for the state, the Bank collected nearly one million dollars of debts owed to the state at a possible savings in the neighborhood of one hundred thousand dollars in commissions or other expense; and it rendered fiscal services also of no inconsiderable pecuniary value. Another important fact that was overlooked was that the Bank, during liquidation, paid some $550,000 of interest on its circulation — in the form of interest charges on the bonds which were exchanged for its notes. Not only did the state and the public benefit from this action through prevention of depreciation of the Bank's circulating notes, but likewise private banks and wealthy enemies of the Bank were thereby enabled to convert their holdings of Bank money into investments yielding the maximum legal rate of interest. Had the Bank been allowed to pursue the customary course of private banks in liquidation, it not only would have saved such interest payments but might have returned to the state ultimately a profit equal to the earnings paid out by the private banks on the par value of their shares.

What of the charges that the state lost approximately 3 per cent annually as a result of investing its surplus through the medium of the Central Bank instead of in private bank stocks as the Bank's opponents claim to have proposed? In the first place, the simple comparison veils the fact that the "loss" was distributed widely in the form of a gain in lower interest rates upon loans. Of course, the equities of such an interference with the natural "laws" of market costs and income distribution may be debated; yet the lower return on Central Bank loans was adopted definitely as a positive public policy; and hence the argument should have been directed against the virtues of the latter policy rather than against the foregoing of a possible higher dividend yield. But weighty facts of a purely pecuniary sort likewise were ignored. Had the state chosen instead to purchase private bank stocks, inevitably it would have invested the greater portion of its funds in newly chartered banks. This conclusion is justified not only by its previous history and an understanding of the operation of political forces, but also by the facts that older banks opposed sharing new stock issues with the state and that the purchase of old shares of such banks at high premium prices reduced actual yields far below the "customary eight percent" and discouraged their purchase. Any considerable purchase of outstanding bank shares by the state during the early thirties would have forced their prices to very high levels. The bank failures of the depression were confined chiefly to the newer banks; hence state purchase of bank stocks in all probability would have resulted in total loss of much of the investment as well as income and, also, in yet further losses through the state's liability as a stockholder — as it turned out in the Darien Bank case — for indebtedness of the banks. Heavy state investment in commercial banking might well have caused far greater overextension of short-term banking facilities than actually took place and consequently greater public and private losses than was the case. Assuming even that the state might have been able to invest solely in solvent banks, dividend reductions and stoppages during the depression would have cut off income at the very time when the state needed it most and the collapse of the securities' market would have caused the state heavy capital losses in the liquidation of its holdings of bank stocks, the greater, of course, the higher had been the premium prices paid for the stocks. As it was, the Central Bank, by means of gradual collections and the issue of notes, transferred the entirety of its active capital back to the state treasury or to the state's railroad construction without serious loss. Incidentally, the heaviest losses were suffered in the sale of the state-owned private bank stocks.

Political considerations loomed so large in the eyes of the Bank's antagonists that many of the weighty economic factors were overlooked. The most important of these are not measurable probably in accounting terms. The Bank proved itself to be the most stable factor in the financial situation. Its relief of private producers and its support of public works and the state treasury undoubtedly supplied an important counter-cyclical force in the depression. Its inconvertible paper money, never an excessive amount, enabled it to extend loans that did afford the intended relief to thousands of small producers who were caught in the debacle of price and credit prostration. "Industry and economy," as one close observer who was a private banker reminded the foes of the Central Bank, would not meet executions.[56] It was far easier for the wealthy than for the poor to practice such virtues during a depression. In fact, the "industry and economy" of the more fortunate often enabled them to profit from the distress of the "less industrious," by acquiring properties at bankruptcy sales. Nor was it strictly true that the issue of notes by the Bank was simply a case of increasing the state's debt and hence eventually also taxation. The notes for the most part were exchanged either for self-liquidating assets in the form of individual producers' notes, or for outstanding obligations of the state, or for exchange funds to pay the state's external debts. In the case of the first, though slow maturity may have increased the Bank's difficulties, the Bank's notes were retired eventually by the payment of principal and interest — they were self-liquidating debts; while in the other cases the Bank's debt replaced the state's debt, a transaction that could scarcely be labeled correctly as an increase of state debt.[57] Many of the opposition arguments appear to have been posited upon the assumption that the Bank's long-term loans during the depression would largely be lost. There was no necessary reason to assume that such would be the case, despite the inevitability of considerable banking losses during a severe depression and in the face of the long-standing curtailment policies of individual commercial banks. The question of the Bank's solvency does not appear to have been too different from that of the commercial banks during the long suspension periods of 1814–1817 and 1821–1824, so long as loans were selected carefully and note issue was kept within reasonable limits. The chief danger lay always in the continuation of state deficits.

The depreciation of bank currency in Georgia, generally speaking, was related to export-import balances and the resulting price of exchange. A very large part of all income ultimately was spent upon imports. The purchase of exchange was an everyday fact among merchants and farmers and, when export balances failed to cover the payments required for imports, exchange rose to a premium and bank currencies declined to a corresponding discount. When such a situation continued for some length of time, as in a major depression, the discounts on bank notes might become considerable and differences in the amount of discount among the notes of various banks might also become general. The financial burdens placed upon the Central Bank by the state during 1839–1842 forced it to become a heavy purchaser of exchange and to extend its note issue correspondingly. At the same time, the solvent banks were curtailing their circulation drastically; hence most of the force of the adverse exchange situation fell upon the note issue of the Central Bank. Foes of the Bank charged that heavy losses were visited upon the public by the depreciation of the Central Bank notes; but such charges appear to have confused cause and effect. The depreciation reflected in the main the adverse debit-credit situation in the economy during depression.

Finally, the Central Bank's policy undoubtedly must be credited with creating some increases in employment and real income. Such increases cannot be measured for lack of data, and they easily may be overestimated through failure to allow for heavy leakages in debt payment and hoarding. Above all, it must be kept in mind that employment was conditioned largely by institutional forces and by the external factors that governed export-import relationships; whereas the effects of the Bank's actions were limited to variable operations of an intra-state nature. The greatest stimulus to employment from its actions probably was felt in the public works program, and that not alone in direct employment upon the Western and Atlantic Railroad, but likewise in employment in railroad construction and related industries in other regions. The state project stimulated very greatly the continuation of construction upon the major municipal-private projects of other areas.

The foes of the Central Bank appear to have overlooked, or poorly visualized, the public nature of banking, especially in times of extreme economic emergency. Their theory of banking was still largely the notion of a specialized phase, or extension, of the merchant's activities; to too great an extent, they viewed banks as simply another form of private business. Actually many Georgians, possibly a majority, had lost sympathy with this notion; but the complexity of banking problems defied understanding. The course of economic events whose causal forces reached far beyond state boundaries actually decided the fate of the Central Bank, rather than the relative validities of the arguments of the opposing parties to the controversy.

The Bank of Darien, after the Central Bank, was the most prominent casualty of the depression. It stood third in size among the commercial banks, with nearly two million dollars of assets, at the outset of the depression. Its act of suspension in 1837 with the other banks afforded no concern; but when it suspended again early in 1839, before the other banks did, and shortly thereafter stopped making loans, it became evident that it was in serious trouble again. It never reopened for active business. The causes of the bank's failure lay in great overextension of loans during the boom years of 1834–1836 and poor management generally. Governor Gilmer attributed its condition to control by state directors, who lacked interest in safe and proper management, and he recommended either that the institution be liquidated or the state's seven-tenths ownership be sold to private capitalists.[58] It soon became obvious that the latter was not possible and equally clear that, although the bank had been operated as a private business, as a bankrupt its debts for the greater part became the obligations of the state as the major stockholder. Since the state's shares were a part of the capital of the Central Bank, the Darien assets were turned over to it for liquidation. This process required fifteen years, and a considerable part of the loan assets ultimately had to be written off as uncollectible. In the final settlement of claims the courts fixed the remaining obligation of the state as $48,500, which was paid on July 1, 1855, in state 6 per cent bonds. Thus ended the troubled life of this famous institution, like that of the Central Bank, as an item in the public debt.[59]

The solvent banks resumed specie payments during 1841–1842, as required by law, but their operations remained at a low ebb through 1843 and 1844. They expanded modestly during the good price years of 1845 and 1846, although their combined loans and discounts of $6,000,000 and circulation of $3,000,000 still remained far below the levels of 1840. A severe dip in cotton prices through 1847–1848 arrested further expansion for the time being. But the recovery of 1849–1850, which carried cotton prices to their best level since 1838, initiated a broad upward trend in business prosperity and a new period of bank expansion.

7. Rise of Country Banks

Not a single bank had been incorporated in Georgia in a span of fourteen years, but in half that time, from 1850 through 1856, thirty-three new banks were chartered, three in 1850, three in 1852, eight in 1854, and nineteen in 1856. The Panic of 1857 abruptly ended this rapidly growing new bank movement and no additional banks were created during the remaining ante-bellum years. Seven of the new banks were located in Savannah, two each in Macon, Columbus, and Atlanta, and one in Augusta; the remaining nineteen were country banks.[60] As compared with earlier Georgia banks, the new ones were small in size — typically $200,000 capital, except for five of the Savannah banks and one each in Macon, Dalton, and Albany. The total capital of all thirty-three, amounting to $12,000,000, approximately equaled the combined capitals of the eleven old banks that had survived the depression. The other conspicuous difference between this and the earlier bank movements was the predominant trend toward country banks. Among the older cities only Savannah, whose high rate of growth between 1840 and 1860 — as a result of the Central of Georgia Railroad system — carried it to a leading position among Southern ports, figured prominently in this last bank movement.[61]

8. Panic of 1857 — Suspension

The Panic of 1857 brought a return of bank suspensions although most Georgia banks were in a relatively strong specie position. It was reported that the average ratio of circulation to specie for all Georgia banks was 3.74 to 1 as compared to 8 to 1 in South Carolina. The country banks in particular had low ratios: all but two were under 3 to 1 as compared with typical ratio of 10 to 1 and 15 to 1 in neighboring states.[62] Since the act of 1840, requiring banks to redeem their notes in specie, was still in force, the suspension made the banks subject to loss of their charters. They appealed to the legislature for relief and were granted a suspension of the 1840 act until November 15, 1858. Several conditions were included in the relief measure. Banks were forbidden during suspension to send capital out of the state for the purchase of notes, to charge in excess of 7 per cent interest on notes, and 1 per cent premium on bills of exchange, to sell any exchange other than sight drafts, or to pay above 7 per cent dividends; officers were required to sign affidavits as to the truth of the semi-annual bank reports; and damages of 10 per cent in addition to the lawful rate of interest were made recoverable on notes that were not redeemed after November 15, 1858. Governor Joseph E. Brown vetoed the measure on account of its leniency toward the banks. In a strongly worded message, he assailed the banks bitterly for their actions and demanded the immediate enforcement of the law of 1840; but the legislature passed the act over the veto by majorities of three to one in the Senate and two to one in the House.[63]

The matter did not come to rest, however, with the passage of the relief measure. Suspension revived many of the old bank questions. As so often previously, the blame for the panic and the suspension was laid initially upon Northern rashness and speculation. Those who supported the temporary relief measure were confident that on this occasion it was only necessary for the Georgia banks to protect themselves against Northern drafts until the new crop began to move. The recession appeared to be wholly of Northern making, since the European cotton market and cotton prices reflected only a moderate reaction at the time.[64] Georgia banks were warned, however, not to take advantage of the situation to charge high premiums and to indulge in speculation. Such friendly critics directed their attack against the prevailing system of banking relationships that permitted Southern banks and the Southern economy to be preyed upon by the capitalists and financial institutions of another section. James Jackson's old arguments regarding regional diversity were revived and amplified. As Georgia derived its income largely from cotton which enjoyed a wide international market its real income represented the imports that were received in exchange for cotton. This export-import exchange of the basic necessities of life was a direct, simple, and relatively cheap marketing operation; therefore planter and merchant accommodations should be among the least costly and most stable in the world. The Northern economy was a different one. It was based upon agriculture, manufacturing, and trade: agriculture was much more diversified than in the South and was dependent upon both local exchange and the manufacturing-trading market areas. Such an industrial economy was more complex and interdependent than that of the South, subject to much wider fluctuation of activities and values and to a great deal of speculation. The Southern economy, oriented to world markets whose primary center was European, was not actually mutually interdependent with the Northern economy. However, if Georgia's banks were to be allowed to continue their ties with Northern ones, or to imitate them, it could be expected that all of the fluctuations of Northern origin would be reproduced gratuitously within Georgia. Southern banking laws should be adapted to serve Southern economy; then fluctuations in prices and prosperity, though they would never cease entirely, would be neither so great nor so erratic. Northern domination of banking was a twin brother of the protective tariff. Northern control of exchange caused Southern banks to default and produced the depreciation of Southern bank notes; the latter increased the cost of domestic exchange and added another burden upon the South, since Southern merchants ultimately had to pay for their goods with Northern exchange. The result was a general depression of Southern cotton prices, wages, employment, and property values. Banks were necessary to the South, but their operations should be restricted to the business of cotton marketing and the maintenance of a uniform currency at all times.[65] The new and stricter banking laws of Louisiana, whose banks had not suspended during 1857–58, drew much attention and many favored the enactment of similar legislation in Georgia.[66]

After Governor Brown's veto message, and especially after the failure of Georgia banks to resume with the New York banks in December 1857, criticism turned chiefly upon the Georgia banks themselves. They were charged with breaking their "contract with the State," with "abusing their privileges," with "making the public good subservient to their own emolument," with converting their premises into "shaving offices" and "broker shops," with conducting "swindling transactions," with speculating in exchange and in their own depreciated currencies, and with coercing the legislature and assuming an arrogant attitude toward the public; banks had so dinned into the minds of everyone the notion that cotton prices depended upon bank notes, that many of the people and their legislative representatives were cowed by the fear that enforcement of the act of 1840 would bring a debacle of cotton prices; and so banks were able to use this bogey of disaster as a shield behind which they broke their contracts with impunity. Setting aside the law of 1840 for a year amounted virtually to passing a "stay law for banks." Other debtors enjoyed no such immunity, least of all those who were indebted to the banks. Why not at least require the banks to pay interest upon their demand liabilities until they resumed? If banks were forced to resume or forfeit their charters and cotton prices should fall in consequence, would it not be better to hold cotton rather than bank notes until conditions became righted, not knowing which banks eventually might fail and involve their noteholders in complete loss? [67] The true issue, according to the editor of the Milledgeville *Federal Union*, was: should banking laws make banking essentially a private interest, or should they control it in the public interest? The case stood: the banks *versus* the common people.[68] Defenders of the banks replied that nobody actually had lost through the depreciation of the currency, since the average person could do no more with gold than with bank currency; neither farmer nor laborer had genuine need of gold. To which the *Federal Union* answered that the bank men did not go beneath the surface facts; the increased costs of exchange were added to prices by the merchants, which affected adversely the interests of all laborers and debtors and property owners.[69]

Governor Brown launched his attack upon the banks through the following chain of arguments: "labor produces all," hence "all capital is the result of labor." A private individual can loan only saved capital, the product of his own labor, and is restricted by law to a maximum return of 7 per cent; but banks are granted an exclusive privilege of loaning their notes at interest. Since upon one dollar of investment of actual capital they are privileged to loan three dollars of notes, they are allowed actually to earn 21 per cent on saved capital; while in fact, through note shaving, premiums on exchange and extra fees, they often realize 30 or even 50 per cent. This system of legalized monopoly, whereby banks are enabled to enrich themselves by taking from the laboring masses the income of their labor, "is not only unjust, but is contrary to the genius and spirit of our government." In return for this privilege of exploitation, the banks had promised to maintain a sound currency which they now not only refused to honor, but used as the means of further gain. Suspension had been judged by immediate causes, but men should go behind the immediate to the underlying causes, which will be found to be speculation and over-extension of credit. The question which faced Georgians it was said was: shall the banks govern the people, or shall the people govern the banks? "The richest corporation should be made to obey the law as promptly and explicitly as the humblest citizen." Brown proposed the requirement of a one-third specie reserve behind bank notes, the redemption immediately of all notes of small denomination and a gradual increase in the minimum lawful size to twenty dollars after 1860, a maximum charge for exchange in line with the legal rate of 7 per cent, forfeiture of charter for violation of any provision in either charter or banking law, and the establishment of a state sub-treasury system and specie collections at the state treasury.[70]

The old hard-money notions flared up anew throughout the state under the stimulus of Governor Brown's pungent veto message. Anti-bank meetings were held in great numbers, especially in the country districts, at which resolutions endorsing the veto message and condemning the banks were adopted.[71] The proposal for a state sub-treasury received wide support, since many seemed to feel that such an institution would bring about the general circulation of specie and thereby remove the dependence upon bank currency in ordinary exchange transactions. In the popular mind the existing banking system imposed a danger to the sovereign rights of the people; much stricter banking laws, with heavy penalties and rigorous enforcement, were needed; and even the recapture of excess bank earnings appeared desirable to some.[72] The age-old feeling against the corporate form of business began to revive once more and banks were referred to as "soul-less corporations." [73] "All corporations are dangerous," ran one anti-bank meeting resolution, "as they favor the interests of the few by taking from the interests and pockets of the many. They are privileged orders in the community, and tend to the dividing of the people into the high and the low — into an aristocracy of rich and poor; they should be tied down strictly to their contracts." [74] A constitutional amendment to forbid the chartering of new banks or the renewal or extension of the charters of existing banks was proposed in some quarters.[75]

Some of the banks refused to report to Governor Brown in 1858 as required under the act of the previous year, whereupon the governor issued a proclamation forbidding the acceptance of the notes of such banks at the treasury. For this action Brown was accused by the pro-bank papers of making war upon the banks.[76] The tension eased somewhat toward the end of 1858 as cotton prices rose and most of the banks resumed specie payments.[77] Legislative enactments during 1858 and 1859, however, reflected a continued widespread desire for stricter controls over the banks. An 1858 statute subjected all banks that failed to make semi-annual reports with proper affidavits to a tax of 2 per cent on capital stock from date of delinquency. Another law in the following year provided that a noteholder could recover principal, lawful interest and 25 per cent damages against any bank that failed to pay specie upon demand; and juries must find for plaintiff in any such case. The regulations governing exchange, however, were eased a little: the price of foreign exchange could include an interest charge of 7 per cent per annum plus the cost of shipping specie from the point where the bill was payable, but it must be a *bona fide* bill of exchange and not a loan or accommodation designed to evade the legal interest rate. Maximum premiums on both domestic and foreign exchange were established in 1860, but the restriction that limited banks to the use of sight drafts was removed. The appearance of war clouds already had started a drain of specie, making suspension a probability again; and the legislature granted the right to suspend until December 1, 1861, but stipulated that if any bank in Savannah, Augusta, or Atlanta should suspend, the collection of all private debts and actions relating thereto should likewise be stopped during the period of suspension; and no suspended bank should be permitted to charge in excess of 1 per cent premium on foreign exchange. Thus the ante-bellum period closed, as it began, on the familiar notes of hard money and stay laws.

The discussion of this and the preceding chapter may now be summarized:

Banking policy in Georgia throughout the ante-bellum period adhered rather strictly to the commercial banking tradition. This may be attributed largely to the overwhelming predominance of commercial agriculture, chiefly cotton, and the central roles of merchant and planter in the economic development of the state. A relatively high proportion of the capital needs of commercial agriculture, with virtually free land, was short-term, and such needs could be supplied through merchant advances and bank commodity loans and discounts. The growth of accommodation loans and renewals expanded the coverage of credit needs to include as well a considerable part of the longer-term capital requirements. The chief controversy over policy determination arose between the proponents of commercial banking and the advocates of hard money, with the former gradually winning the state to the acceptance of commercial banks and the latter forcing the adoption of bank regulation. Both groups were essentially conservative in outlook. Both believed in the desirability of stable prices and that the necessary quantity of currency for maintaining stable prices was determined by the volume of trade. Conversely, the doctrine of easy money gathered relatively few followers and must not be identified with the investment banking theory that developed strong support in the state.

Saving and investment in the staple economy were predominantly united in the individual producer, and eventuated in the main through devoting some portion of family labor hours to making improvements upon the land, or through exchanging a part of the annual produce for capital goods and slaves. Bank and merchant loans and advances permitted substantial amounts of investment in anticipation of savings; in the case of slaves, credit commonly was allowed for two years, and for other capital goods, one year.

As a community matured and its wealth increased, its dependence upon capital advances declined. Many of the older communities of Georgia had attained considerable maturity before the advent of banks. The newer communities, however, were always short of capital and usually found the commercial bank accommodations inadequate and, in times of business depression, a cause of severe embarrassment. The extent of new producing territory and, consequently, the volume of demand for permanent investment capital were multiplied tremendously by the rapid land distribution and settlement of the first three decades of the nineteenth century. The experience of the Darien Bank proved in part the inability of the commercial banks to meet the situation. This insatiable demand for capital and the existence of a considerable state treasury surplus afforded the grounds for the establishment of the Central Bank of the State for the purpose of making small capital loans to producers. It was the fact that the public surplus was the only pool of saved funds in the state, other than the capitals of the commercial banks and merchants, which were tied up in short-term advances, rather than any popular demand for public banking, that led to the chartering of the Central Bank.

Public investment banking was complementary rather than antithetical to commercial banking; it was also a logical corollary of the new land lottery policy whose aim was to secure the permanent establishment of large numbers of small landed proprietorships. Governor Gilmer's notion of using the state's credit to obtain capital funds from abroad for investment in Georgia was a further extension of the principle embodied in the Central Bank,[78] and a limited application of this notion was tried in connection with the Western and Atlantic Railroad construction; but the collapse of state credit during the Great Depression and the inherent conservatism of most Georgians prevented any further development of investment banking on the basis of public credit.

Two theories of regulation obtained especial prominence: the doctrine of statutory control, sponsored by the hard-money group, and the theory of a quasi-public central bank, advanced by certain supporters of commercial banking. Both theories stressed the important element of public purpose inherent in the monetary function of banking. The advocates of the statutory method stressed the twofold obligation of each individual bank, to maintain a sound currency and to serve the regional interest of the state. The expounders of the central bank theory conceived of banking as an interdependent system in which banks controlled one another by their respective actions, but in which primary responsibility for safeguarding and promoting the public interest would be lodged in a national quasi-public bank of discount and issue with ample coercive operative powers over the state banks.

Banking history in Georgia reveals the economic transitions from local to state to national bases. State banks developed directly from local mercantile banking operations and, in lesser degree, from public currency experiments; and they achieved their dominant position because of their adaptation to an economy that was bounded still by the geographical limits of the state. Any interpretation of the state bank movement merely as an assertion of "states' rights" is entirely too narrow. In fact, the states-rights party in Georgia was sharply divided on banking policy. The state banks represented a higher degree of maturity, in the regional stage of banking evolution, than did the United States banks at the national level. Federal monetary standards were little more than a recognition of established monetary practices in international trade; and the federally established banks behaved more after the fashion of state banks than as quasi-public central banks. As an internal regulatory force, federal monetary policy was in its infancy. William H. Crawford saw its true possibilities. So also did Wilson Lumpkin in 1816, but later he decided that the federal interstate powers were too fragmentary and undeveloped to supply an adequate instrument of bank regulation. The situation actually left responsible control of the currency largely to the states. It was not so much a case of their attempting to usurp the national monetary powers. The bounds of the problem, however, already had grown far beyond the boundaries of a single state and only a partial solution could be found through state regulation. Georgia created banks with uncommon care and commendable restraint upon number; it attempted consistently to enforce sound banking practices and convertibility, although it never adopted the superior reserve requirements of the Louisiana policy. But the difficulties that beset banking frequently transcended the powers of the state.

CHAPTER X

DEFINING A SYSTEM OF INTERNAL IMPROVEMENTS: WATERWAYS AND ROADWAYS

The development of internal improvements in Georgia was influenced strongly by particular conditions of physiography, geographic position, and settlement as well as by the general factors of advancing technology, agriculture, industry, and trade. A study of public policy, therefore, must consider the effects of economic isolation, distance, natural facilities and barriers, sparse settlement, slow removal of the Indians, and the difficulties of establishing effective state and local government, as well as the course of general development and the requirements of an expanding economy. The history of public policy falls roughly into three periods: (1) 1777 until the end of the War of 1812, during which the provision of transportation facilities was left almost entirely to local governments and private individuals and companies, (2) the years following the second war with England, to 1833, which marked the introduction of state support and efforts to determine upon an effective system of internal improvements; and (3) 1833 to 1861, a period which featured the joint promotion and construction of the railroad system by cities, the state, and private individuals and groups. This chapter deals with the first two periods and the following one with the public railroad movement.

Earliest settlement in Georgia began at the ports of Savannah and Darien and spread along the coastal sounds and estuaries and up the lower reaches of the Savannah, Ogeechee, and Altamaha and various tidewater rivers. The lack of adequate harbors at the mouths of practically all of these streams and the shallowness of the coastal waterways prevented the movement of ocean vessels to the settlements and private wharves of planters, and products had to be assembled for export at one or two usable ports. This characteristic of Georgia's natural waterway facilities was to remain a dominant factor in the development of transportation to the Civil War. Charleston, South Carolina, served as the chief entrepôt for Georgia's commerce in the beginning, but the industry of Savannah merchants after 1745 gave a home commercial port. This started a fierce rivalry between these two cities for the trade of the interior that continued unabated throughout the period covered by this study.

The coastal region was swampy and difficult to penetrate with roads; back from the coast lay a pine barrens that discouraged settlement and hence did not give rise to a need for roads. Consequently, produce and merchandise in the coastal area were moved largely by small boats and rafts upon the shallow inland water courses. Waterways likewise supplied the chief mode of transportation from the interior. The principal stream of inland settlement moved up the Savannah River valley. Augusta was established at the head of navigation by Oglethorpe in 1735 as a military and trading post in the interests of protection and the promotion of trade with the Indians by the Georgia colony. It soon became, and long remained, the principal inland trade center of Georgia, and the Savannah River afforded the chief means for traffic between the interior and the coast. Georgia developed as an agricultural state, and the demand for transportation largely remained that of getting out bulky agricultural raw products for export and bringing in consumers' and agricultural producers' goods. For more than a hundred years, transportation, both from convenience and necessity, utilized predominantly the watercourses.

The settlement of Wilkes County following the Revolution marked a change in the direction of settlement and of population movements that likewise forecast a significant turning point in the history of transportation. Thenceforth Georgia was to be populated primarily from North Carolina, Virginia, and South Carolina, and the flow of settlement was to be across the state from the northeast rather than inland from the coast. The new immigration first filled up the upper Savannah River valley and then thrust southwestward across central Georgia and on into the Flint and Chattahoochee river valleys and, lastly, fanned out northwestward into the upper piedmont and mountain regions. The chief rivers of the state flowed from the interior across the pine barrens to the coast; but only the Savannah possessed an adequate port. Use of the others necessitated transshipment from their mouths, and the Flint and Chattahoochee flowed into the Gulf of Mexico at a point that was inaccessible to foreign shipping before the advent of steamboats upon those waters. Most of the rivers were badly clogged with logs and with sand bars and other natural obstructions and all were closed to traffic for varying and frequently long periods by low water. Nevertheless, the rivers supplied the principal routes for the movement of produce and heavy manufactured articles until the advent of the railroad in the late 1830's and early 1840's. The Savannah River long held the predominant position. Goods were wagoned to and from Augusta at the head of navigation, for distances as great as 150 miles. But traffic on the Oconee, Ocmulgee, and Altamaha increased with the westward movement of settlement despite the difficulties of navigation and the necessity of transshipment. Cotton was floated down in boxes, and salt and other heavy articles poled back, during the 1820's. Construction of the steamboat had been adapted to Georgia rivers by the thirties and river traffic developed to large proportions.

Realization of the need for improved forms of transportation also grew steadily. Prior to the end of the War of 1812, most of the population lived in close proximity to the navigable reaches of the major water courses; but thereafter increasing numbers settled above the heads of navigation and on lands more distant from water courses and in northern Georgia where the streams mostly were too rapid or shallow for navigation. Consequently, the need for transportation on land increased greatly.

1. Early Internal Improvements

Public policy from the Revolution to the end of the second war with England was characterized by private and local government responsibility for the provision of transportation facilities, with the state in the role of regulator. The general road laws of 1777 continued in force, in substance, the Act of 1773, requiring annual labor services on the roads by all males, white and Negro, aged sixteen to sixty, defining road districts, electing road commissioners, and prescribing procedures, rules, fines, penalties, and road specifications. An act of 1785 placed the road system under the supervision of the superior courts and required the grand juries to supply the courts with all necessary information. In 1791 the roads were transferred to the jurisdiction of the inferior courts of the respective counties and road construction and maintenance became almost entirely a local matter. Owing to the wide variety of statutes applying to various roads, a general act was passed in 1799 which provided for uniformity of county administration throughout the state. This was one of Governor Jackson's moves for reform in public administration. An exception to the act was made in 1803 for the six southeastern coastal counties, since they were faced by needs and problems that were peculiar to the area.

Much complaint arose around the turn of the century about the bad condition and lack of roads.[1] The dissatisfaction appears to have resulted from the rise and spread of cotton culture and the growth of trade, because it was especially marked in Augusta and its vicinity. This city levied a special poll tax in 1799 for the repair and upkeep of roads. The tax was extended to property in 1801 and a special tax on lumber delivered at the city wharves was included, because the wagons hauling from nearby sawmills were especially destructive to the roads and streets.[2] In response to constant complaints about the lack of attention on the part of counties to through roads, the legislature ordered the counties, in constructing roads, to observe the shortest possible distance between major cities. This rather certainly was a hollow act. Governor Milledge lamented that little was being accomplished by the county road system,[3] and Governor Mitchell uttered severe criticisms of the existing methods and practices in his messages of 1810 and 1811.[4] In Mitchell's opinion, the county system had been a total failure: the inferior courts were too local in their point of view, lacked the knowledge of how to construct modern highways, and by and large were not interested in the work; the main highways should be constructed and maintained by the state, at state expense and under state administration; the local roads could be left to the counties. The response of the legislature was the passage of a general law in 1811 which provided some tightening up in procedures and enforcement and required the appointment of interested citizens as commissioners in charge of bridge work and the location of new roads, but which made no fundamental change in the system.

An important road, at least from the viewpoint of later history, was constructed at state expense shortly after the beginning of the century. This was the Georgia-Tennessee road through the Cherokee territory in northwest Georgia. Tennessee had approached Georgia about the desirability of building a road that would connect the two states, and middle Georgia planters, already becoming specialized in cotton production, could see the advantages of a supply of livestock, grains, and food products from eastern and central Tennessee. If a road should be built through the Indian territory joining at the southern end with the roads and rivers in the new cotton-growing region, Tennessee planned to build a number of feeder roads from various sections of that state to the northern terminus. It was hoped that the federal government could be induced to construct the main trunk road, but it pleaded a lack of funds. However, it did obtain the consent of the Cherokees, who in return were given the right to operate the toll ferries along the route; and Georgia built the road, at a cost of approximately $5,000, during 1804 and 1805.[5] This was a prophetic step in the history of internal improvements in Georgia, because it was the forerunner of the Central Canal scheme of the mid-1820's which was designed to unite the Tennessee River and the western waters with the Atlantic Ocean by way of the Georgia rivers, and of the Western and Atlantic Railroad of 1836, which ultimately did connect the railroads of Tennessee, the Southwest, and the Northwest with the Georgia railroads at Altanta and thereby with the south Atlantic ports.

Ferries and bridges, though obviously a part of the highway system, were not provided in the same manner as were the public roads. Ferry rights almost invariably were leased by acts of the legislature to private individuals or partnerships, usually adjacent property owners, and bridge rights likewise were very commonly so disposed of. Bridges also were built by the counties, acting either individually or jointly; although they were not normally constructed with labor service, but instead were contracted and paid for out of county funds or special levies. Tolls were charged on all ferries and private bridges; but public bridges were usually free, except those over larger streams that had involved a heavy cost. There were also a few toll roads, both public and private, during this early period.

Waterway improvement policies prior to 1815 varied greatly but were uniformly ineffective. An attempt was made soon after the Revolution to extend the roadwork system to the rivers, by requiring those males living within a given distance of certain specified streams to work at clearing channels instead of on the public roads. Special river commissioners were selected to supervise the work. This method was tried on various rivers and creeks until about 1805 and appears to have proved wholly ineffective. It was never tried on the Savannah River where, it was generally agreed, the task required tax levies and the hire of specialists and skilled artisans. A tax was levied for this purpose in 1786 on adjacent property and on South Carolina tobacco moving on the river; but the property tax was repealed a year later, as unduly oppressive, and the tax on South Carolina tobacco probably never was enforced. A $4,000 lottery was authorized in 1796 for work on the Savannah above Augusta. In the same year an omnibus arrangement was authorized to raise funds for work on the Ogeechee River and Brier Creek. The legislature elected commissioners whom they empowered to receive any monies from either the state or local governments that might be appropriated, to take private subscriptions for gifts or donations, to conduct a $1,500 lottery, to levy a special tax on adjacent lands, and to use timber free of charge from adjacent lands. The legislature appropriated $1,150 and $450 respectively for work on the two streams, which constituted the extent of direct state support of waterway improvements during this thirty-year period. The voluntary principle of private subscriptions of gifts and regular contributions for public purposes, embodied in the above project, was widely exploited throughout this period, and large sums were reported frequently to have been raised in this manner. Most famous example was the Oconee Association — organized late in this period, it operated for a number of years and was reputed to have accomplished more for the improvement of the Oconee River than all other and far more expensive efforts combined; and later it was subsidized to some extent by the state. Lotteries also became a common device for raising money for waterways, as for many other public purposes. They were authorized for the Altamaha, Oconee, Broad, and Canoochee rivers, as well as for various canals, between 1798 and 1802, and one of $10,000 for the Oconee as late as 1814.

Since most of the methods employed prior to 1800 had produced meager results, the state was induced to try still another — the chartered navigation company. It incorporated the first of these, the Savannah Navigation Company, in 1799 with authorized capital of $40,000, to clear the channel of the Savannah River between Augusta and Petersburg until a stipulated depth of water was obtained, after which it could charge tolls on all traffic moving upon this section of the river. Similar companies were chartered over the next ten years for the Ogeechee, Broad, and upper Oconee rivers. In reality, this device was merely an extension to river improvements of the principle of granting ferry and bridge rights to private individuals and partnerships, except that the undertaking was on a much larger scale. The life of the charter also was relatively short, as was true with ferry and bridge grants. The navigation company was expected to supply a waterway for passage of vessels of commerce and in return was permitted to charge tolls for the service. The companies failed to live up to expectations, however, and their charters were seldom renewed.

An attempt also was made at this time to establish a public navigation company for the lower Savannah. The cities of Savannah and Augusta were authorized to select three commissioners each, who were to unite with any similar group of commissioners elected by the state of South Carolina to form a body corporate. The relation between river improvements and tolls in this instance, however, was to be reversed: the commissioners were given power to charge tolls on all traffic on the river and to use the funds to carry on the work of improvement of navigation. Apparently South Carolina did not see fit to coöperate in this venture, since nothing more was heard about the "Board of Commissioners for the Improvement of the Savannah River."

There were numerous provisions in early statutes authorizing internal improvement commissioners to cut artificial waterways between various coastal water courses, but the first genuine canal project appears to have been the Brunswick Canal. Even this originally seems to have been deemed as little different from previous projects. In 1798 the trustees of Bryan Academy, who owned confiscated lands in the area, were authorized to construct a canal from the Altamaha River through their property to Brunswick harbor. This was the launching, apparently, of what was to become one of Georgia's perennial canal projects, designed to connect the largest river system of the state with the only deepwater harbor south of Savannah. That the job appeared a simple one to the legislature is attested by its permission granted to the academy trustees to sell confiscated property to the amount of $1,250 to raise the necessary funds for construction of the canal. The trustees, of course, were to be allowed to charge tolls. Further investigation, however, revealed that the undertaking was a more ambitious one than had been calculated, and in the following year a $35,000 lottery was authorized for the purpose. This was the largest sum of money provided for any internal improvement project up to that time. But little was accomplished. Other canal projects for coastal Georgia were discussed, but the canal movement did not make much headway until the 1820's.

The accomplishments of this first period were notable chiefly for the heterogeneity of methods and devices employed and the paucity of results. The state government authorized nearly every conceivable suggestion for achieving any known objective; but it remained throughout chiefly in the role of regulator, specifying the character of each improvement, the procedures in effecting it, and the rates and tolls that should be charged. In 1805 it gave the counties permission to authorize private ferries and bridges and to fix toll rates in accordance with customary charges, but it retained power to review such rates and order changes.

2. Influence of War of 1812: A State Program

The stimulus given to internal improvements by the War of 1812 was as evident in Georgia as elsewhere in the United States. But the failure of the Fort Jackson Treaty to secure Indian land cessions in central Georgia served to dampen enthusiasm and retarded the development of an integrated state program. The liberal leaders urged the citizens and their legislators, nevertheless, to make a genuine start on improvement of river navigation and construction of decent market roads. Wilson Lumpkin cited the necessity of improved transportation facilities as one of the chief lessons that the war had taught the American people.[6] David Mitchell, who had fathered the cause of internal improvements before the war, returned to the governorship in 1815 to agitate the movement even more persistently.[7] And an ardent new champion was rising in James Jackson's protégé, George M. Troup, who was to become one of the most powerful figures in Georgia politics during the next decade; removal of the Indians and internal improvements were the major planks in his platform.[8] Equally important no doubt in influencing public action was the appearance of a healthy treasury surplus. Rising tax yields plus federal payments on the western land settlement and other obligations produced a surplus of $168,000 in 1816. Despite the investment of $360,000 in bank stocks and other extraordinary expenditures, a further increase of tax receipts plus additional federal remittances the following year boosted the surplus to

$299,000 by the time the legislature convened in November 1817.[9] The state also could anticipate an early payment of the balance of the western land debt, amounting to $377,000. As Governor Rabun tersely stated in his message to the legislature, the state could not expect "a more favorable opportunity to commence internal improvements on an extensive scale." [10]

A beginning in state support for internal improvements already had been made in 1815 through appropriations of $10,000 each for improvements for the Savannah and Oconee rivers, but sectional and political jealousies had flared up in the following year to prevent a similar appropriation for the Ocmulgee River. By 1817, however, practically all interests in the state were ready to adopt a comprehensive program of river improvements. Sixty-one thousand dollars were voted to be distributed as follows: $20,000 to the Savannah and Tugaloo above Augusta and $5,000 to the Savannah below; $10,000 each to the Oconee and Ocmulgee; $5,000 each to the Altamaha and Broad; and $3,000 each to the Ogeechee and Brier Creek. An additional $5,000 was authorized for the Oconee above Milledgeville, conditional upon relinquishment by the Oconee Navigation Company of its charter and the proceeds of a lottery. A permanent Internal Improvement Fund of $250,000 also was created, which was to be invested in bank or other profitable stock, the income from which was to be used for such internal improvements as the legislature in the future might direct. This was increased in 1821 to $500,000, of which $100,000 was invested in the Steamboat Company of Georgia and the balance in state bank stocks. Additional appropriations of $60,000 for the Oconee above Milledgeville and $5,000 for Brier Creek were made in 1818, and $5,000 for the Altamaha in 1822.[11] The canal fever began to spread shortly thereafter and nothing further was done about river improvements until it subsided in 1826.

The state continued overwhelmingly water-minded until nearly the end of the decade. Roads were viewed chiefly as feeders to the water courses. They were predominantly local, and were deplorably maintained. There were few through roads and travel on them was mainly by horseback and a limited number of stagecoaches.[12] Very little freight moved over them for any distance, because of their bad condition and the prohibitive rates. A revision of the general road law in 1818 did not change the county system materially. However, the counties of Richmond and Jefferson, containing Augusta and Louisville, were permitted to commute the usual labor services to an annual tax and to increase the general levy, up to 50 per cent of the state tax, for road purposes. Work was to be let by contract. This act was extended later to Baldwin County in which Milledgeville was located. These inland cities at the heads of navigation were the centers of a steadily growing wagon trade and they were becoming deeply concerned about the improvement and extension of the road networks in their areas.[13]

3. Turnpike Companies with State Aid

The other important interests in good roads at this time centered among the cotton planters and in the smaller cities in the Cotton Belt above the fall line. This section became enthusiastic in the early twenties over the possibility of constructing turnpikes. Governor John Clark strongly advocated the organization of incorporated companies for this purpose and the participation of both private individuals and the state in subscription of stock. He was a firm believer in the mixed corporation as a mode of providing internal improvements and other public utilities. He thought that such undertakings required the use of both private and public resources in an economy such as Georgia's, and were doomed to failure when attempted on the basis of either alone.[14] The action that ensued in regard to turnpikes largely followed his suggestions.

The Washington Turnpike Company was incorporated by the legislature in 1821 with authorized capital of $300,000 to build a turnpike from Augusta via Washington and Lexington to Athens. The roadway was to be fifty feet wide, of which twenty-five feet in the center were to be of stone, wood, or other base to assure a firm surface. A maximum scale of tolls was prescribed and also rules for the operation of traffic. A year later the state subscribed for $50,000 of the company's stock, to be paid out of the Internal Improvements Fund. Branches were authorized, in 1823, to Warrenton and Clayton, the latter also being intended to complete the Georgia section of the proposed road from Lexington, Kentucky, to Augusta. Three more turnpike companies were chartered in 1822: the Milledgeville Turnpike Company, capital $400,000, with proposed route from Augusta via Warrenton, Sparta, Milledgeville, and Clinton to Fort Hawkins (later Macon) on the Ocmulgee River; the Greensboro Turnpike Company, capital $200,000, to build from Warrenton via Powellton and Greensboro to Madison; and the Eatonton Turnpike Company, capital $120,000, to extend from Sparta via Eatonton to Monticello. Stock in the three companies in the amounts of three hundred, one hundred and fifty, and one hundred shares, respectively, were reserved for state subscription. Had these turnpikes been constructed they would have provided the eastern Cotton Belt with a network of main highways connecting all of the principal centers and leading by direct route to Augusta, as well as connecting the heads of navigation of the principal rivers in middle and central Georgia. But the projects failed utterly in the hands of the private promoters,[15] and the state made no effort beyond its offer to subscribe for stock.

4. The Canal Movement

Canals had received attention in the coastal region since the late eighteenth century, but had never been visualized generally as possible main avenues of commerce in Georgia until after 1820. Gallatin's proposal for a system of coastwise canals had been discussed and the progress of the Erie Canal had been followed, but active interest had continued to center in river improvements.[16] But as population moved into the interior and beyond the fall line, another suggestion of Gallatin's began to receive attention. This was the possibility of uniting the Tennessee River with the waters of the Atlantic Ocean and the Gulf of Mexico. A glance at a topographical map of Georgia and its neighboring states will reveal the apparent possibilities that Gallatin had in mind. The navigable Tennessee River flows around the northwest corner of Georgia. The Oostanaula and Coosa are navigable from almost the northwest boundary southward and then westward within Georgia for 165 miles. The Chattahoochee rises in the mountains of the northeast and flows diagonally southwest across the state and down the western border to the Gulf, with four hundred miles of navigable channel below Coweta Falls. The Flint rises near the banks of the Chattahoochee in northwest central Georgia and flows south to a junction with the Chattahoochee at the southwest corner of the state and is navigable for 150 miles below Albany. The Ocmulgee and Oconee, rising in north central Georgia, join to form the Altamaha and the three together possess 545 miles of navigable water. The Savannah on the eastern boundary is navigable for the 230 miles below Augusta.[17] Gallatin visualized a canal from the Tennessee through northwest Georgia to some point on the diagonal section of the Chattahoochee, thence to one of the navigable Georgia rivers flowing into the Atlantic, and also down the Chattahoochee to its navigable section flowing to the Gulf of Mexico.

The notion lay dormant for a number of years, but several events in the early 1820's served to revive it. Western Georgia was opened to settlement by the Indian treaties of 1821 and 1825. Steamboats were beginning to make their appearance in Georgia waters, and reports were coming in of their rapid increase on the western waters. Then Gibbons *versus* Ogden, in 1824, opened the water courses to all comers. In 1823 the governor of Tennessee approached both Georgia and Alabama about the possibility of connecting the Hiwassee River, a branch of the Tennessee, with the Oostanaula and Coosa, which would have called for a canal across the northwest corner of Georgia and would have joined the Tennessee River with the Gulf of Mexico via Mobile Bay. Governor Troup replied that Georgia was much more interested in connecting the Tennessee and the Atlantic Ocean, and the governor of Tennessee readily agreed to coöperate on the basis of Georgia's proposal. The completion of the Erie Canal in 1825, joining the Great Lakes with the Atlantic, seemed to furnish the spark that enabled Governor Troup and other internal improvement advocates to bring canal enthusiasm to fever pitch in an incredibly short time. It reached its peak during 1825–1826. Gallatin's old proposal suddenly blossomed into a group of proposed canals in northern and north central Georgia which should unite the Tennessee River and the western waters with all of the navigable rivers of Georgia and the Atlantic Ocean. The general notion contemplated a main canal extending from the Tennessee River to the central part of the state, with branches, or a transverse canal with laterals, connecting with the Savannah, Oconee, Ocmulgee, Flint, and Chattahoochee rivers. With improvements on the rivers above the fall line, it was conceived that every part of the state, except the northeast, might be served by water transportation and become joined, through steamboat operations, with every major area in the United States. Here seemed the possibility of creating the most likely parallel and rival of the Erie Canal anywhere in the United States.

A fact that had become glaringly evident to all of the more thoughtful advocates of internal improvements in Georgia was that the most hampering shortage, probably, was the lack of knowledge of the techniques of waterway improvement and road construction. Wilson Lumpkin, admitting his own utter lack of such knowledge, said that all of them were novices.[18] This lack of technical knowledge and skills was blamed generally for the slight accomplishments that had resulted from the efforts that had been put forth in internal improvements. In 1819, the hiring of a state topographical and civil engineer was authorized, but it was not possible to secure the services of such a person for the stipulated salary until 1826, when Governor Troup induced Hamilton Fulton, North Carolina's English engineer, to take the position.

5. The State Board of Public Works

Improvements in administration were as necessary, in the minds of many, as were trained technical advice and direction. Virginia had created a central Board of Public Works in 1816 and given it charge of internal improvements; South Carolina and North Carolina had done likewise in 1819; and reports were being received of gratifying progress with extensive internal improvement programs under such boards. The efforts to establish such a board in Georgia failed in 1821 and again in 1824, but finally, with the enthusiasm for canals at its peak, were successful in 1825. In fact, the vote was nearly three to one in both houses and was almost entirely non-partisan. Of the combined vote by counties, nineteen Clark and seventeen Troup counties voted for the board while nine and three respectively voted against it.[19] The opposition in a group of poor southeastern counties and in the block of northeastern small farm counties rested probably upon their fear of higher taxes and their belief that they would not benefit from programs of internal improvements. The opposition of some counties in the extreme west no doubt rested in part

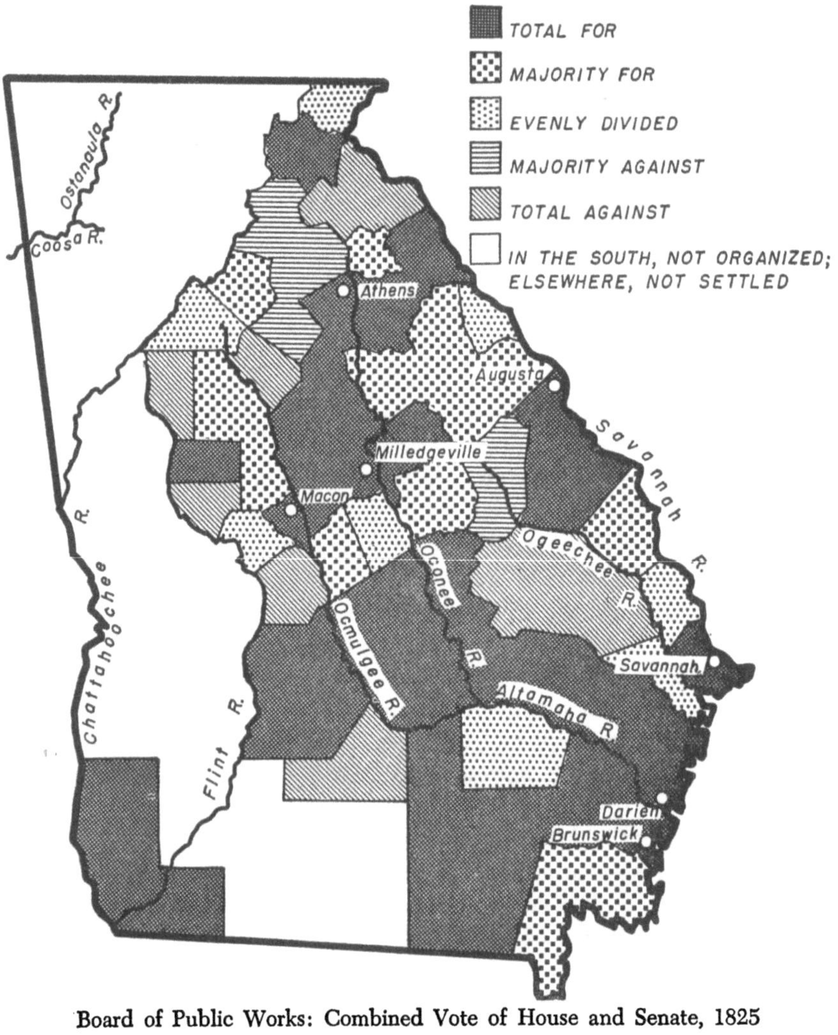

Board of Public Works: Combined Vote of House and Senate, 1825

on recent hard times in that frontier region; though most of them, it would appear, stood to benefit greatly from internal improvements.

The board was comprised of one member from each congressional district and was chosen by the legislature. Like the vote on its creation, the election of its members was non-partisan: three were Clark, and three Troup men, and Wilson Lumpkin might be considered to have been an independent. Governor Troup was *ex officio* chairman of the board. All members were prominent state leaders with long-standing interest in internal improvements. Lumpkin was most familiar, probably, with the physiographic features of the state, particularly in the newer areas, since he had served much of the preceding decade as United States commissioner for the location of Indian land cessions as well as for the settling of the Georgia-Florida boundary line. Another member, James H. Couper, had visited England recently and had familiarized himself with the new railroad developments there.

Three days after the creation of the board, another act required it to devote its first attention to the feasibility of a canal program. It was to study the construction and ascertain the best routes for a system of canals, complete with surveys, models, a definite plan, and estimate of costs. It was requested also to study the possibility of substituting railroads for all or any parts of the proposed canal network. The board was delayed in meeting, because of Governor Troup's illness, until March 20, 1826, and Chief Engineer Fulton did not assume his duties until a month later. The Board divided its task into three sections: Lumpkin and Pittman were to examine the route for the main canal from the Tennessee River to central Georgia, Crawford and Schley the possibilities for a transverse canal from the Savannah at Augusta to the head of navigation on the Chattahoochee or possibly the Flint, and the other members were to survey the possibilities leading to the Atlantic Ocean south of the transverse route. Chief Engineer Fulton made a preliminary survey of the transverse route and decided that a canal was impractical, recommending instead a railroad. Leaving his assistant to survey for a railroad, he joined with Lumpkin and began the survey of the central canal route. Though stopped by the Indian chiefs before completing the survey, they had proceeded far enough with the work to become convinced that a canal from the Tennessee to the Chattahoochee was feasible. Burritt and Fulton then surveyed from the Chattahoochee south to the transverse line, after which Fulton joined the third group for work below the line including an investigation of the possibility of connecting the Altamaha-Oconee-Ocmulgee river system with a suitable harbor south of Savannah.

6. A Plan for a State System of Internal Improvements

Reports of the board and the chief engineer were presented to the legislature in November 1826. The board stressed the importance of the Altamaha-Oconee-Ocmulgee rivers in any waterway system; and the possibility of its improvement and connection with seaports and the balance of the state system it considered crucial to any comprehensive plan of internal improvements. Then it considered the matter of objectives. It had been common, in promoting internal improvements, to stress the desirability of securing the commerce of distant regions and foreign countries; but the board considered this to have been, as a rule, a mistaken notion. The objectives of any system should be determined by the primary interests of the state. In Georgia these were, and for a long time were likely to continue to be, predominantly agricultural, and the state's commercial interest was related primarily to agricultural products. It would be vain therefore to try to invest the state at this time with a commercial character, by trying to induce foreign trade to move through its borders by constructing internal improvements with this purpose in view. It would not be possible for Georgia to divert the western trade from the Mississippi River, because costs would be higher by either canal or railroad through Georgia. And the value of such transit trade was greatly overestimated. But cheapening the cost of conveying the state's products to market produced a vast economy, for the lowering of cost "becomes a profit to the producer and is an absolute accession to the capital of the country." It would attract labor; and thus the state's resources and productive powers would be increased. Public funds invested in transportation facilities that would unlock rich natural resources would never be wasted, even if early operations should be conducted at a loss. An internal system, that is, one designed primarily to serve the interests and needs of the state, had advantages also in construction, in that the most useful parts that served the greatest general interest could be built first, and less urgently needed construction could follow later. It did not require staking a large amount of scarce and valuable state resources on a single grand speculative venture that might fail and lose the entire effort. Three steps were suggested: first, the selection of a seaport; second, improvement of the primary river systems — these should be made fit for steamboat navigation if possible, since steamboats were the most efficient type of transportation at the time; and, third, the building of canals or railroads as rapidly as the state's resources would permit, into those sections that lack river transportation, beginning with the most populous areas.[20]

The important feature of the chief engineer's report was the comparison of canals and railroads. It gave the opinion that railroads were superior to canals except in a level country, and that they offered an especial advantage in the South because of the unhealthy conditions along the rivers and marshes. Fulton recommended wooden rails with iron strips as suitable to the type of traffic that would move in Georgia and as the least expensive. He calculated replacement on a five-year basis. Troup and Couper and Lumpkin shared Fulton's enthusiasm for railroads, although Lumpkin still thought that a canal might be feasible over the main route from the Tennessee River. The board supported Fulton's ideas to the extent of recommending that the state construct an experimental railroad from Milledgeville to the boat landing on the Oconee.[21]

The reports were obviously of a high quality and of great utility in assisting the state to determine upon an internal improvement policy. But strong opposition had been developing to both the board and the chief engineer. Sectional jealousies, a feeling on the part of rival centers that the board's report favored Savannah, and fear of the authority of a central state board caused the legislature to abolish the Board of Public Works after one year of existence. Attempts were made also to secure the dismissal of the chief engineer, but these proved unsuccessful until 1828. A large minority in the legislature for a number of years continued to work for the reëstablishment of the board. The votes on this issue from 1826 to 1829 probably reflected the state of public opinion in Georgia at the time — a bare majority were opposed to reëstablishment of the board and the undertaking of a positive program of internal improvements.

Despite its short life, the work of the board made a contribution of major significance to the development of internal improvement policy. It provided the first thoughtful, comprehensive analysis, based upon actual scientific investigation, of the state's transportation needs and possibilities. And it presented a clear conception of a state system of transportation in terms of the development of the state's primary resources and capacities. This notion was to serve to steer Georgians away from grandiose schemes induced by the siren magic of distant trade on the one hand, and from an excess of wasteful uncoördinated local efforts on the other. Furthermore, the concept suggested a system that would be complementary to the state's land and banking policies. The board's opposition to the proposal to join the Tennessee River and the Atlantic Ocean by canal at that time and its partial approval of railroads undoubtedly killed the greater canal movement in Georgia and possibly saved the state from a debilitating waste of money and effort. In a larger sense, the work of the board and its report had the effect of focusing thinking and discussion upon the total problem and its fundamental issues. In this respect it was another landmark in the democratic process of investigation, planning, and action in Georgia. According to Lumpkin's credo for public officers in a democracy, the board had performed well its functions — to search out all issues diligently, to present and discuss them honestly and objectively, and to submit to the decision of the voters; it was the first duty of a public servant to aid the taxpayers to find out the truth.[22] As a matter of fact, much of the state's later activity, in river improvements, in market road construction, and ultimately in railroad building, covered the same ground that the board and the chief engineer had gone over.

The reports of the board and the chief engineer killed the general canal movement, but not before one ambitious scheme, to join the Atlantic and the Gulf of Mexico, was placed on the statute books. The Mexican-Atlantic Canal Company was chartered on the same day in December 1826, that the act of the previous year to lay out a central canal was repealed. With authorized capital of $2,000,000, its object was to construct a canal, with feeders and outlets, from the Altamaha, or Ocmulgee, to the Flint River. It was a part of the rather ambitious commercial schemes of Darien interests, led by Thomas Spalding; but the prospectus was sufficiently vague, and the canal fever still high enough, to attract support from prominent business and planter interests throughout the state. The legislature even reserved the right to subscribe for half the stock. But the company was never organized and, following the recommendations of the Board of Public Works, Spalding and his associates changed the scheme a year later to a railroad project.

Two major canal projects with the same objective got under way in coastal Georgia during the canal enthusiasm. They were the Savannah, Ogeechee, and Altamaha, and the Brunswick canals, designed to connect respectively the port of Savannah and the deepwater harbor of Brunswick with the Altamaha River. The prize sought was the rapidly growing trade of central Georgia. As noted earlier, the commercial aspirations of little Darien, near the mouth of the Altamaha, had become aroused already by the potentialities of this traffic, but they had failed to materialize, despite the establishment of its bank, for want of adequate natural port facilities. An ever-increasing volume of produce was moving down the Altamaha-Oconee-Ocmulgee river system, but most of it was being transshipped at the coast to other ports for export or sale, much of it going to Charleston. As Georgia's principal port, Savannah quite naturally was becoming concerned about ways and means of capturing this growing "western" trade.[23] Meanwhile, Brunswick appeared as a possible serious rival of both Savannah and Charleston. Located only twelve miles south of the Altamaha, with a good deepwater harbor but no direct navigable connection with the interior, it offered the only genuine possibility — if it could be connected by a short canal with the Altamaha — of becoming the port of central Georgia at the effluence of the state's major river system. Such a possibility had been contemplated both locally and in the state generally for a quarter of a century, though numerous factors had operated against any serious development of the project. But conditions had changed greatly by the mid-twenties, and so, when the investigations and the report of the Board of Public Works emphasized the importance of developing an Altamaha port, the claims of Brunswick became a major consideration.[24]

The Savannah canal project actually grew out of a less ambitious scheme to connect the port with the Ogeechee River, long a sort of back-door water route to the eastern interior. One Ebenezer Jencks, a private promoter of various internal improvement enterprises, secured the right in 1824 to cut a canal from the Savannah to the Ogeechee, with a view to affording the trade of the latter stream easier and more economical access to Savannah. A year later he was permitted to extend the scope of the project to the Altamaha, and the state also granted him a loan of $50,000 in Darien Bank notes. Meanwhile, numerous citizens of Savannah were becoming deeply interested in the possibilities of the Jencks's undertaking, and were organizing a company with a view to taking it over. A large number of shares were subscribed and, in 1826, a charter was obtained for the Savannah, Ogeechee and Altamaha Canal Company.[25] The new company was granted perpetual exemption from taxation and the Jencks's loan of $50,000 was renewed to it; and the state further reserved the right to subscribe one thousand shares at once and to purchase all of the stock of the company on specified terms after sixty years. The state exercised its stock option in 1829 to the extent of $44,000 and later converted all of the $50,000 loan and $400 of interest into stock. The city of Savannah subscribed one hundred shares, but apparently paid in only $7,000.[26] The canal was completed to the Ogeechee in December 1830, at a cost of approximately $175,000; and work was begun, after a brief delay, on the extension to the Altamaha, which it was estimated would cost an additional $625,000.[27] Attempts to obtain further aid from the state failed and by 1836 the project was still incomplete, on the verge of bankruptcy, and the finished sections of the canal were falling into disuse and decay.[28] Traffic on the Ogeechee, the principal demand for the use of the canal thus far, had almost ceased, which was blamed upon the failure of the state to spend any more money upon improvement of that stream. Both state and city were turning to the promotion of railroads and refused to lend any further assistance. An arrangement was entered into with a group of private stockholders, who wished to carry on, to sell the public stock to the latter for one-tenth of its par value.[29] The private promoters assessed the remaining stockholders, received various forms of assistance in kind from adjacent property owners, even obtained loans from the banks, and continued with the work. Savannah was induced to extend a loan of $25,000 in 1839–1840;[30] but the canal was never completed and eventually succumbed, like other waterways in Georgia, to the competition of the railroad.

The Brunswick Canal, like its rival, was chartered in 1826, as an undertaking of the local community.[31] It was granted a monopoly of transportation within twenty miles on either side of its right of way and perpetual exemption from taxation, but no other form of public aid at the time. Work was soon begun, but the slenderness of local financial resources soon brought it to a halt with only slight accomplishments. The project was revived in 1834, however, with a new charter and new promise, under the leadership of Thomas B. King. King was a promoter with broad vision and a comprehension of the financial requisites of the undertaking. It was he who induced a group of Boston capitalists to supply the bulk of the funds. In fact, the canal became primarily a Boston project, as King and his local associates became more interested in the construction of the Brunswick and Florida Railroad, for which a charter was obtained in 1835. Like Lumpkin, Couper, and others, King became convinced that railroads were destined largely to replace waterways in Georgia.[32]

The state contributed $50,000 to the capital stock of the Brunswick Canal Company in 1837.[33] With such ample support from the outside, work was begun in an energetic fashion. Loammi Baldwin, famous Northern engineer of the Union Canal of Pennsylvania, was brought to Brunswick to survey and draw up specifications for the canal. It was designed to be twelve miles long, six feet in depth, thirty-five feet wide at the bottom, and fifty-four at the surface, with a lock at each end and one sluice. Work of digging the canal began in late 1837 with hired Negro labor. Five hundred hands were employed throughout 1838, but the Negroes proved too unused to such heavy labor to be effective, so most were dismissed during 1839 and Irishmen hired in their place. The entire canal was dug but never opened, owing to the shortage of funds to complete the superstructure and appurtenances and the decline in steamboat traffic on the rivers. The Central of Georgia Railroad reached Macon at about this time. An attempt to revive the canal project was made in the fifties, but without success.[34]

The state in 1826, following recommendation number two of the Board of Public Works, returned to its efforts to improve river navigation. An appropriation of $105,000 was distributed among the Savannah, Ogeechee, Oconee, Ocmulgee, Altamaha, and Chattahoochee rivers, to be applied mostly below the fall line. An additional appropriation of $20,000 for the Savannah above Augusta was made contingent upon a similar provision by South Carolina.

Reviewing the progress of internal improvements in Georgia up to 1827, the Joint Committee on Agriculture and Internal Improvements of the legislature concluded that it had been substantially nil. Failure was attributed to lack of interest in, knowledge of, and practical acquaintance with internal improvements on the part of numerous local road and river commissioners and to the want of a common head to counsel, coördinate, and direct operations within and between the various districts. It charged that public spirit in most counties also was so feeble that it seemed unlikely that their representatives could divest themselves sufficiently of local prejudice to legislate for the whole interest of the state. The heavy charges levied by poor transportation upon the products of the state had greatly retarded its development. The state was not lacking in funds and resources to undertake a genuine program of internal improvements. Both the methods and the types of improvement in the past had been wrong. The contracting of work and the hiring of labor had proved no more efficient than the labor service system. Only such river improvements should be undertaken as would afford boatable water at all seasons. Elsewhere, railroads should be built. The latter were to be recommended particularly for the middle and up country. Lastly, a board of public works should be established with powers to disburse all monies that may be appropriated for internal improvements, to employ an engineer and technical staff, to direct all surveys, and to see that the various works were brought to completion.[35] A bill for a permanent system of internal improvements, embodying the committee's recommendations was lost by the narrow margin of two or three votes.

The history of failures and their causes were recounted again by the committee the following year. The state had obtained nothing to show for its expenditure of $321,500 on river improvements over the previous thirteen years, except some eighty Negro slaves and a few tools. Much more might have been accomplished, in its opinion, by the expenditure of that sum on roads. A resolution was offered and adopted, that no further appropriations should be made for river improvements, and that the present work should be terminated, until some better method could be adopted, and the office of state engineer abolished. Fulton was not blamed for the lack of progress, but it was believed that he could be of no service in the existing situation.[36]

The committee returned again in 1829 to its attacks on the river improvement program and cited anew the state's utter neglect of the public roads. It recommended that at least equal attention be given to the latter. Planters had great need for both through roads, because of frequent low water in the main rivers, and market roads leading to main interior centers. It cited the case of the Savannah-Macon road, with its branches to Sandersville, Milledgeville, Clinton, and Columbus, built in 1824 largely by private subscription, which had become a heavily used thoroughfare. Appropriations were urged for further improvement of this road and for the completion of one leading to Clayton and a North Carolina connection.[37]

7. A State-wide Market Road Program

Support for good roads had been gathering momentum for some time, but not without opposition. Waterway backers in some quarters were fearful of the withdrawal of funds from their projects; and some Savannah residents saw in the market road projects of upstate Georgia a plot of Augusta and Charleston to funnel the trade of central Georgia to Augusta and thence to Charleston over the new Charleston and Hamburg railroad when it was completed.[38] Up to that date almost no money had been expended from the state treasury on roads in any form. An Act to Im-

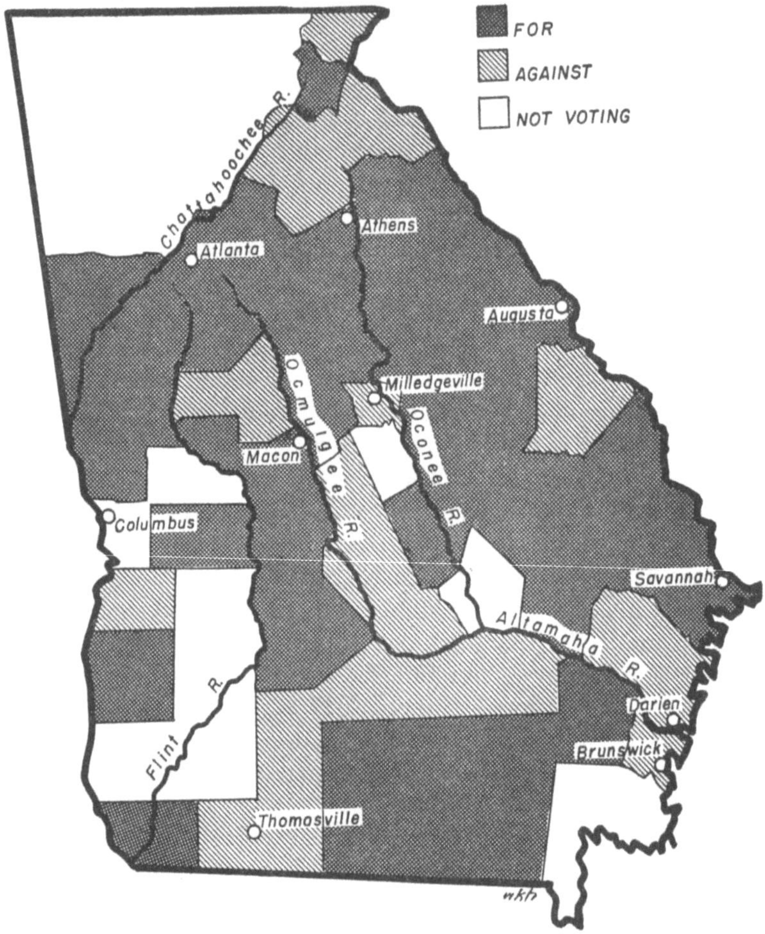

Vote on Market Road Act (Senate), 1829

prove Roads and Rivers finally passed the legislature on December 18, 1829, by almost three to one majorities. Half of the opposition came from counties bordering the Altamaha and Ocmulgee rivers and the balance of it chiefly from the poorer northeastern counties that often were irregular in their support of internal improvements. Savannah and Chatham County voted for the bill. While the statute included river improvement provisions, its primary object was the building of roads, and in its operation it came to be known as the "market road" program. Administratively, the new law represented an effort to secure joint planning, direction, and control by the state and the principal city governments. It divided the state into two major areas and provided for a single state

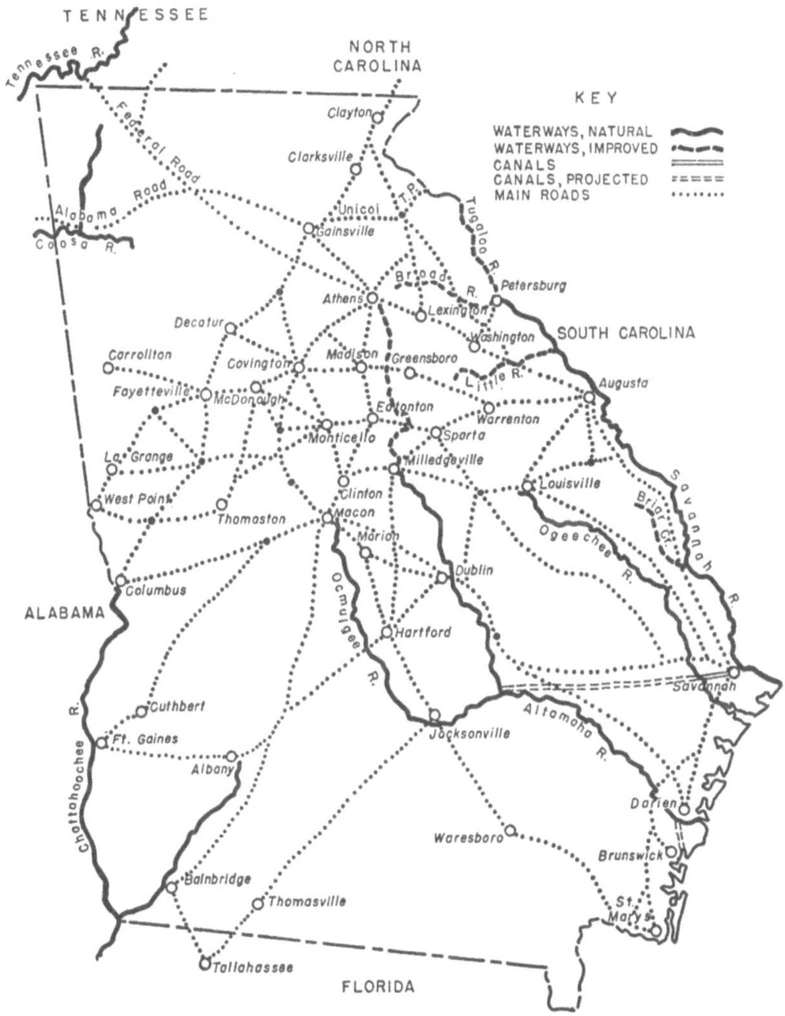

Georgia: Roads and Navigable Waterways, around 1830

superintendent in each, to be the chief administrative officers of the act. The areas divided the state roughly into eastern and western halves. Acting in joint capacity with the state and its two superintendents were to be the municipal governments of Savannah, Augusta, and Milledgeville, in the eastern district, and Macon, Columbus, and the Flint River

Board — a special sub-district board created by the act and representing eight southwestern counties bordering on the lower Flint River — in the western district. Seven overseers were to be selected — two by Augusta and one each by Savannah, Milledgeville, Macon, Columbus, and the Flint River Board — who were to direct the state-owned slave labor force, which was to be increased to 190 slaves. The cities and the Flint River Board were authorized to designate, in their respective sub-divisions, what roads and rivers, or parts of same, should be worked, subject only to such alterations of directions, or otherwise, by the state superintendents as might improve or shorten them. None of the routes worked, however, could lie within the limits of any of the cities. The labor force could not be used on river work more than four months in any year. The superintendents were required to make quarterly reports on the progress of the work to the governor.

The state spent $160,000 under this program, chiefly in building market roads, during the next five years. But again its efforts produced meager results. Little was known about proper road construction, suitable materials often were unavailable, and natural conditions were peculiarly destructive of the type of roads that were built. The roads were turned over to the counties in sections as completed, without adequate provision for maintenance, and soon deteriorated.[39] The state was ready by 1834 to abandon further efforts to construct market roads. The city governments and local groups of citizens already were organizing railroad companies and a strong movement was gaining headway in favor of a state-constructed central railroad.

The state returned once more, after 1835, to river improvements and spent $80,000 between then and 1840. This was the decade of steamboats on the rivers of central and eastern Georgia. Georgia boatbuilders had lessened the draught of river steamboats and remodeled them in other ways so that they could ply the shallow winding streams of the state.[40] Wagoning of produce and merchandise to and from Augusta and Macon, at the heads of navigation, reached enormous proportions during the thirties. But the railroads largely superseded the steamboats in the forties, and the wagon trade of the principal cities declined abruptly, as the planters and farmers discovered that the nearest local railroad station provided a much more convenient point to which to haul their products.

Steamboating continued in western Georgia, however, on the Flint and Chattahoochee rivers and did not even reach its peak until the early fifties. There too, extensive wagon trades developed around the principal river cities, especially at Columbus.[41] Railroads did not reach this section in effective fashion until the mid-fifties. An interesting new "market" road development, allied to this later steamboating period, appeared around 1850 in the form of plank roads. Advocates of plank roads proposed them as a cheap substitute and worthy competitor of railroads. They believed that the combination of the low-cost steamboat carrier and this form of hard surface roadway could meet the challenge of the railway successfully and thus preserve the river traffic and the wagon trade. Columbus was the center of the movement, although it was general in southwest Georgia, and was taken up in Atlanta and northeastern Georgia and by such older cities as Macon and Augusta which entertained visions of recovering thereby their lost wagon trades.[42] Ten plank-road companies were chartered in 1850, eight more in 1852, and three in 1854.[43] The abrupt decline in new companies tells the story. Appeals were made to city governments for public support, without which success appeared improbable. But both public and private entrepreneurship and capital were being attracted irresistibly to the railroads, and the plank road movement succumbed quickly to the competition of the "iron horse."[44]

CHAPTER XI

A STATE SYSTEM OF RAILWAYS

The successful promotion of railroads in Georgia by public and private initiative dates from the incorporation in December 1833 of three companies to construct lines from Savannah and Augusta into the interior cotton belt.

1. Central Georgia Begins a Railroad Movement

Railroads obtained their first widespread support in central Georgia. This region suffered, in comparison with the older plantation areas of the eastern and coastal sections, from long hauls and inferior water communications. It had attempted without success to build turnpikes in the early twenties. A decade later it turned to railroads as promising the solution to its transportation problems. Early in 1831 the newspapers of Milledgeville, Eatonton, and Macon began a vigorous campaign for railroad construction in Georgia.[1] No doubt the steady progress of the Charleston and Hamburg Railroad, under construction to the town of Hamburg, opposite Augusta, had some part in stimulating the movement. Eatonton wanted a railroad built from Augusta west into the cotton belt with branches to the main cities of the interior. This was not a new proposal, since Hamilton Fulton had recommended a railroad along this general route in 1826, and Governor Troup, the Board of Public Works, and successive legislative committees had made similar recommendations. Macon citizens proposed what seemingly was a much more novel idea, a railroad from Savannah to Macon, and pointed out its potential similarities to the Charleston and Hamburg Railroad. The suggestion was novel in that, generally speaking, while Georgians had accepted the notion that the railroad would prove superior to other forms of transport above the fall line, they still clung to the opinion that natural waterways and canals in all likelihood were still the most feasible type in the level-plains region of lower and coastal Georgia. Savannah and Brunswick had accepted this view in launching their Altamaha canal projects; and Savannah had already, in 1824, constructed a direct highway to Macon, with branches to other central Georgia cities, as the usual auxiliary land route to the seasonable waterway.

The town of Eatonton assumed the lead in the central Georgia railroad movement. It sent out a circular to all counties in the state urging

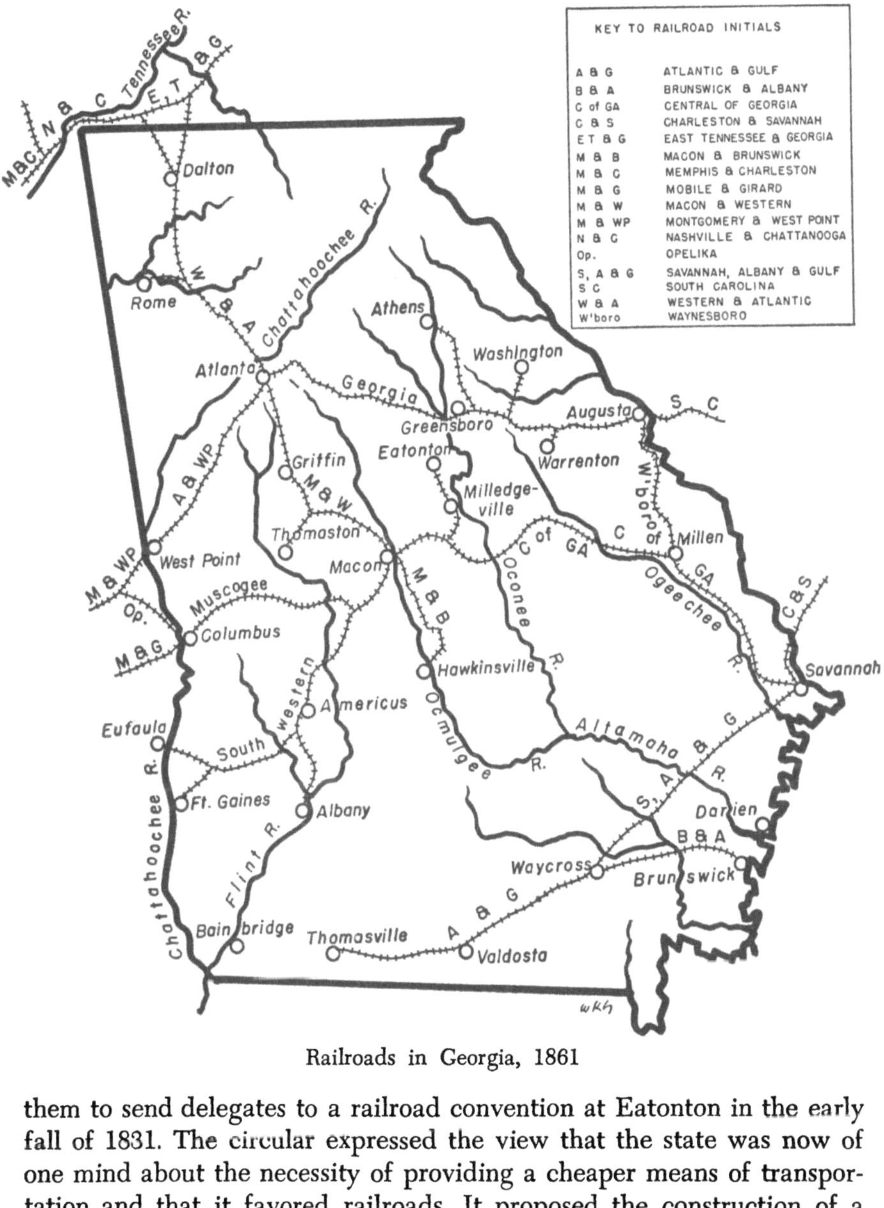

Railroads in Georgia, 1861

them to send delegates to a railroad convention at Eatonton in the early fall of 1831. The circular expressed the view that the state was now of one mind about the necessity of providing a cheaper means of transportation and that it favored railroads. It proposed the construction of a railroad from Augusta westward into central Georgia with branches extending to the various important cities of that region to be undertaken by private enterprise, with the state reserving the privilege of making a stock subscription.[2]

Neither Savannah nor Augusta had shown any interest in railroads thus far. Their trade and prosperity had been built up around the commercial utilization of the Savannah River waterway, and they had been concerned with the construction of roads and canals chiefly as auxiliaries to the Savannah River facilities. Savannah had begun to suffer from the improved steamboat traffic between Augusta and Charleston and had become deeply preoccupied with the construction of the Savannah, Ogeechee, and Altamaha Canal, as a possible means of bringing the growing steamboat traffic of the Ocmulgee and the Oconee from central Georgia to Savannah. The first section of the canal, between the Savannah and Ogeechee rivers, was completed just prior to the railroad agitation in central Georgia and the attention of the city was concentrated upon plans to push the construction on to the Altamaha River, which was the primary objective. When completed, it would cost $800,000, most of which had to be raised in Savannah. Nevertheless, Macon's railroad proposal received a favorable response. The *Savannah Republican* endorsed it heartily, although it expressed surprise at a Macon statement that the state was ready to abandon other internal improvements and concentrate all of its efforts upon railroads.[3] The Eatonton circular aroused rather mixed emotions in the city. Some envisioned a new plot of Augusta and Charleston to divert additional trade from Savannah, but it was decided to send a sizable delegation to Eatonton at the city's expense.

Augusta, as a matter of fact, was less concerned with the construction of railroads than was Savannah. Its interest centered chiefly in the market road program which, it was expected, would extend the wagon trade. The completion of the Charleston and Hamburg would provide a year-round transportation service with the port of Charleston, but this connection was being improved greatly already by the new type river steamboats. It was uncertain how railroads beyond Augusta would affect its trade. Nevertheless, like Savannah, it sent a delegation of prominent citizens to the Eatonton Convention.

Seventy-six delegates from thirty-three counties met at Eatonton on September 26–27, 1831. An unusually large number, certainly, of the prominent leaders in business and public life were among them. The resolutions that were adopted reflected the breadth of views that were represented. The convention recommended: first, a system of internal improvements supported by the state; second, the provision by the legislature of an engineer, who should make thorough studies and surveys of the state and of the relative practicability of canals, railroads, and turnpikes for various lines of communication, the information to be distributed to the people of the state; third, that the following lines should be surveyed: (1) Savannah to Augusta to Eatonton and west to the Chattahoochee River, (2) Savannah to Macon to Columbus, with a connecting line to Milledgeville, (3) Savannah to the head of navigation on the Flint River to Columbus, and (4) Augusta to Athens to the northwest boundary of the state; and four, that, in case the state should decline to assume the work of internal improvements, it should render assistance, by stock subscription, loans, or otherwise, to private companies that might do so.[4] While canals were mentioned, this was obviously a recommendation for a comprehensive system of land transportation, presumably railroads, based primarily upon the port of Savannah.

The convention had taken a different course, apparently, than that anticipated by Eatonton, for, upon the adjournment of the first, the Eatonton delegates called another convention to which were invited all those delegates from counties and localities known to be interested in the railroad from Augusta that had been proposed originally. Delegates attended from Richmond, Columbia, Taliaferro, Warren, Hancock, Greene, Putnam, Morgan, Jones, Henry, and Fayette — two adjoining parallel columns of counties extending across the state from Augusta almost to the western border. This convention recommended the incorporation of a company, with an authorized capital of $1,000,000 to build a railroad, or turnpike, from Augusta to Eatonton. A move of the northern tier of counties to have the project routed farther north and terminated at Kingston, an important road center at the time in Morgan County, was defeated by a three-fifths majority.[5] The proposed company was chartered in December 1831, as the Augusta and Eatonton Railroad Company and $350,000 were subscribed in Putnam and Hancock counties during the following two years.[6]

Elsewhere interest in railroads seemed to subside until the summer of 1833, when a group in Athens, who were ambitious to make that town an industrial and commercial city, organized a movement to build a railroad from Augusta to Athens. Though it received scant encouragement from Augusta, the proposal was enthusiastically received by the wealthy planting communities that lay between the two cities. Eatonton was invited to merge its Augusta and Eatonton Railroad with the new project. Numerous public meetings were held in the various counties and a plan was worked out for a "Union Railroad." It called for a main line from Augusta to a point near Greensboro, with branches thence northwest to Athens, west to Madison, and southwest to Eatonton. The route of the main line and the central branch to Madison was substantially the same as the alternate one that had been rejected by Eatonton and its supporters at the second Eatonton convention. It lay through one of the heaviest cotton-growing regions of the state at the time.[7]

The "Union Railroad" meetings and the approaching completion of the Charleston and Hamburg Railroad served to spur Savannah citizens into action. A large public meeting in October endorsed the immediate construction of the Savannah and Macon railroad, and the city council thereupon promised a subscription of $500,000 and appointed representatives to secure a charter from the legislature.[8] These actions brought assurance from the *Macon Messenger* that central Georgia was strongly in favor of the railroad connection with Savannah.[9]

Meanwhile, a third project was being organized in Forsyth, northwest of Macon, where the citizens of the town and Monroe County were making plans to build a railroad from Macon to Forsyth.[10] This was a significant project for both Macon and Savannah since it would constitute virtually an extension of the proposed Savannah and Macon railroad.

In December the legislature chartered all three projects — the "Union Railroad" as the Georgia Railroad Company, the Savannah and Macon railroad as the Central of Georgia Railroad Company, and the Forsyth project as the Monroe Railroad Company.

During the pioneer years of railway development it was commonly a long time between the incorporation of a company and the completion of its line. Many that were chartered never progressed any farther or expired after a few years of struggle. The small number of such casualties in Georgia, therefore, was unusual and may be attributed mainly to two factors: a sparing creation of chartered companies and the promotion of an integrated system of railroads under the patronage of the state. The above three projects were still viewed by their promoters and the public generally as independent lines rather than potential segments of an interrelated system. The pattern of such a system and its adoption as a positive state policy emerged during the years from 1833 to 1836.

2. Wilson Lumpkin: Railroad Prophet and Advocate

The dominant figure in the development of this policy was Governor Wilson Lumpkin, who served as chief executive of the state from 1831 through 1835. It was largely his quick appreciation of the full significance of railroads and his forceful leadership that led Georgia to the early adoption of railroads and induced it to mold its various particular projects into a functionally integrated whole. He not only saw the technical superiority of railroads but also viewed transportation in general as an instrument of planning a better society. He called attention in his annual message of 1833 to a significant change that must necessarily effect state economic policy: Georgia had come to the end of free land — its frontier was closed; it must now develop the opportunities upon the land that had been settled; and adequate transportation was a *sine qua non* of such development. Railroads had rendered other modes of transportation obsolete in most areas and were certain to have revolutionary effects upon all modern society; by providing numerous routes to the seacoast, they would open up the vast land-locked areas of the interior United States to full production; ports would tend to become equalized and goods to have the choice of a number of routes; the world was on the threshold of a new age — the railroad age.[11]

This vision of the economic and geographic role of railroads provided Lumpkin with his theory of a state system. It should be designed on the one hand to fit into the prospective national pattern and on the other to promote the best interests of the state. He considered these objectives to be complementary, particularly in Georgia where natural advantages were so preponderant. It was reasonable to assume that one of the major lines from the interior of the United States would terminate at a Georgia port. Hence, Georgia should locate the main axis of its system to serve its natural advantages for the western trade and at the same time to promote most effectively its own internal trade and various local interests. Although not favoring federal construction of railroads, he thought that regional and national study and planning by both private and public groups were essential to successful construction by the states and their citizens. State activity during the developmental period was required primarily for two general reasons: the first was pragmatic necessity — there was not enough private capital available to build the railroads and private business operations were typically small-scale and lacking in experience with new enterprises of such great magnitude; and secondly, there was a large element of general, or public, interest involved in planning and constructing a railroad system.

Lumpkin did not deprecate private enterprise in railroad development. In fact, he pointed out that the interest of private individuals and communities had been responsible in most instances for the growing railroad movement in Georgia and believed that they should be encouraged, not checked, by public action. "Every citizen or section should have the lawful privilege of investing their capital according to their views of profit, guarding at the same time the interest of the residue of the community from injury being sustained by any exclusive privilege which may be granted." [12]

He opposed the system of allocation of state funds among all railroad projects, believing that such a policy invited bad planning, political logrolling, waste, and failure. Construction of local and subsidiary lines should be left to private individuals and communities; state funds should be devoted exclusively to a single major project of general interest, namely, the main trunkline of the system. This would assure the completion of the enterprise and afford the greatest possible assistance to the local projects. Furthermore, the state should construct the central line entirely on its own account and under its own management. Past experience, he thought, cautioned against state partnerships with individuals or corporations. There seemed to be something inherently unworkable about such joint enterprises. Misunderstandings almost invariably developed, and private capitalists managed usually to reap the profits, if there were any, or to abandon the project to the care of the state, if there were none. Should the state decide to promote a central railroad, it should start it at Savannah and extend it through central Georgia to the northwest boundary, from whence inevitably others would continue its construction on into the west and northwest.

3. The "Western" Railroad Proposals

Two famous "western" railroad proposals were launched shortly after Lumpkin proposed a central railroad in Georgia. They were the Memphis and Charleston Railroad, suggested in 1834 by General E. P. Gaines, commander of the Western Division of the United States Army, and the Cincinnati and Charleston Railroad, proposed at a railroad convention in Cincinnati on August 15, 1835. Both projects embodied Lumpkin's basic ideas and had significant implications for the future of railroads in Georgia. General Gaines had become interested in the potentialities of railroads in military operations and national defense and had had surveys made by the United States topographical engineers in northern Georgia, Alabama and Mississippi, and southwestern Tennessee, upon which he based the project of the Memphis and Charleston Railroad. It was designed to unite the Mississippi and the Atlantic and to be a key line in a national system that he was projecting.[13] A number of railroad conventions were called in Tennessee, Mississippi, and Alabama, along the route of the proposed line, to promote the project and Gaines wrote to Lumpkin about its construction across northern Georgia to Augusta, where it was proposed to connect with the Charleston and Hamburg Railroad, and also concerning the possibility of aid from the state. Lumpkin's reply expressed general approval of the project, but did not favor public support of a line that would benefit only one section of the state. If the Memphis and Charleston were routed through the center of the state he would gladly endorse state support; but if it were built along the "upper" route, then Georgia's policy likely would be to construct a railroad from Savannah to a junction with it in northwestern Georgia.[14]

A large part of Lumpkin's final message, in 1835, was devoted to the

Cincinnati and Charleston proposal. The Cincinnati Convention had suggested a route through Cumberland Gap in southeastern Kentucky into eastern Tennessee, thence up the French Broad River valley into western North Carolina, through Saluda Gap to Columbia, South Carolina, and thence to Charleston, with a branch from Columbia to Augusta.[15] Lumpkin thought that a more direct and economical route lay farther west, through Rabun Gap and northeastern Georgia, to a connection with the Georgia Railroad by an extension of that line from Athens. Accordingly he recommended state support of any western project that adopted such a route.

This route was well known to Georgians as it had long been contemplated as a means of road or turnpike connection with Lexington, Kentucky, and Cincinnati. The Athens promoters of the Georgia Railroad had it in mind for a possible extension of their line when they drew up the original charter, but they also considered the possibility of an extension to the northwest border. Supporters of the main trunk line, from the Atlantic coast through central Georgia to the northwest border, did not view any connection with the Cincinnati and Charleston, however, as a substitute for their project but only as a possible second connection with the northwest. The central railroad was designed to connect with the northwest by way of Nashville and Louisville, with Memphis over the proposed Memphis and Charleston and with eastern Tennessee by a branch up the valley. It would lie too far west to form a part of the through trunk line of the Cincinnati and Charleston.

Meanwhile the newly chartered companies were progressing variously. The Georgia Railroad Company quickly obtained the necessary stock subscriptions, even with only token help from Augusta. They organized, hired a young Northern engineer, J. Edgar Thomson, who had just returned from the study of railroads in Europe, and began construction early in 1834.[16] The Monroe Railroad was able to start grading in the fall of 1835. The affairs of the Central of Georgia, meanwhile, moved at a slower pace. An attempt was made at the outset to secure the services of the United States topographical engineers to make the preliminary surveys. After six months of unsuccessful waiting, the Savannah City Council paid to have the work done.[17] There followed some controversy with interior communities over the location of the railroad. Solicitation of stock subscription finally began in June 1835. The city corporation subscribed $500,000, and Savannah citizens upwards of $300,000, but subscriptions in Macon and other interior points lagged.[18] By mid-summer scarcely more than half the required capital had been raised and it became evident that some way must be found to increase greatly the financial support of the project.

4. Banking Powers

A somewhat unusual group of circumstances led to the next development in the Central of Georgia's fortunes. The Bank of the United States had recently decided to close its branch in Savannah and this was viewed as likely to create a shortage of banking resources. Consequently, Savannah businessmen and financiers held a series of meetings in the spring of 1835 during which it was decided to apply for a charter for a new bank, to be called the Bank of Savannah. During the course of the summer some of the railroad's supporters offered an alternate proposal, that the Central of Georgia's authorized capital should be increased to $3,000,000 and that one-third of the increase should be devoted to commercial banking, to replace the withdrawn resources of the United States Bank. The business men were inclined to oppose joining banking operations with other business. Past experience had been bad and the state had struggled long to rid itself of "change" notes and other circulating business obligations. However, in view of the strong desire of the citizens of Savannah to have the railroad, it was agreed finally to unite the two projects and apply to the legislature for an amended charter for the Central of Georgia Railroad and Banking Company.[19] In effect it was an amalgamation of two independent projects, neither of which had yet been organized as a going concern, that was contemplated.

Meanwhile, the Georgia Railroad was going forward with its construction without any financial difficulty. But the Cincinnati railroad proposal introduced a new factor, or rather, brought the dream of the Athens group a step nearer reality, in that if a western railroad project were actually launched, the extension of the Georgia Railroad would become a concrete matter of location and physical connection at some definite point on the northern border of the state. Such an undertaking, of course, would require a large additional amount of capital and it was well, in view of the wide interest that the Cincinnati proposal had evoked, that consideration should be given at once to the manner of raising the new funds. It did not seem likely that they could be raised from private sources, especially in view of the indifference of Augusta to the Georgia Railroad. The stockholders were opposed to creating a mixed corporation with state subscriptions, possibly as a result of Lumpkin's influence as a member of the board. Instead, they favored state loans to the company, insofar as funds could not be raised from private sources, in the event of undertaking the work on the extension.[20]

When the respective banking and extension proposals came before the legislature, the differences in views and the mutual jealousies that they aroused, together with the opposition to both railroad companies that already had developed, threatened to prevent any action being taken.[21] A rift developed even within the Central of Georgia group itself. As the banking bill was presented in the legislature, it would have allowed the use of two-thirds of the capital for banking purposes, whereas the original proposal of the railroad supporters had stipulated only one-third. When news of this change reached Savannah it created great indignation among the railroad faction, which accused the bank-minded group of treacherously using its influence in the legislature to reverse the plan and of plotting to sidetrack the railroad project.[22] But the urgent council of coöperation from the more farsighted leaders prevailed, and in the end both companies were granted banking privileges. Their authorized capital stocks were doubled, of which not more than half of each could be devoted to banking until the railroads had been completed — in the case of the Central of Georgia, to Macon, and of the Georgia Railroad, to Athens and Greensboro.

The banking charter provided the boost that was needed by the Central of Georgia. It brought most of Savannah's capitalists wholeheartedly into the project and greatly stimulated subscriptions in Macon and along the proposed route of the railroad.[23] The necessary capital was subscribed quickly and construction was begun early in 1836. The grant to the Georgia Railroad Company was ostensibly to aid it in the extension of its line to the northern boundary of the state. Actually, the Cincinnati and Charleston railroad, with which the extension presumably would join, was still a very nebulous proposal, and the extension therefore a similarly tentative matter. The only immediate effect of the grant was the establishment of another bank and the booming of the stock of the Georgia Railroad and Banking Company. By May 1836, the company's shares were selling at premiums of 15 to 25 per cent on the $50 paid in, although no banking profits had yet been announced and not a single mile of rail had been laid.[24]

Both companies began banking operations early in 1836 and expanded this phase of their business very rapidly. Within a year the Georgia Railroad and Banking Company's loans and discounts reached a peak of $1,100,000 and the Central of Georgia Railroad and Banking Company's, $950,000, which placed them fifth and seventh in size, respectively, among the twenty-one banks in the state.[25] Both were able to pay dividends before the end of the year, and the Georgia company declared 6½ per cent on its entire paid in capital during the first year of banking operations.[26]

Two additional railroad companies were granted banking privileges in 1836. They were the Monroe Railroad Company and the Chattahoochee Railroad Company, and the reasons ascribed were similar to those in the two previous cases — the withdrawal of the operations of the United

States Bank, the need to draw additional investments into the railroad enterprises and the importance to the state of completing the principal lines of the railway network. Both began banking operations early in 1837 and also expanded in somewhat the same fashion, in proportion to their respective capitals, as had the two larger railroad companies.[27]

A rather ingenious parallel to the railroad banks, and undoubtedly something of a product of the same movement, was the statutory relationship between the Brunswick and Florida Railroad Company, incorporated in 1835, and the Bank of Brunswick, incorporated a year later. The charter of the bank permitted it to increase its capital stock *pari passu* with the progress of construction of the railroad. This arrangement may be interpreted as an intention on the part of the legislature either to limit the increase in bank loans and notes to the probable growth of trade, or to stimulate investment in the railroad; both objectives likely were intended.

A moot question arises concerning the element of subsidy, if any, in the granting of the banking privileges to the railroads. Reviewing the history of railroad development, a legislative committee in 1857 claimed that the entire banking profits of the railroad companies, which it estimated to have been $3,000,000 to that date, were in reality a state subsidy; and it proceeded to add the amount to the state's direct expenditures upon railroads to arrive at the total contribution of the state government to railroad development.[28] Now there can be no question about the valuable character of banking privileges, limited as they were by legislative discretion. They were widely sought by investors, including, in previous times, the state itself, but they were always granted in Georgia without an assessment or bonus payment being required by the state.[29] The nearest approach to the latter policy was the practice of reserving the privilege of state subscription to a portion of the stock which was abandoned after 1818. The state's banking policy dictated that a new bank should be incorporated in a community when an evident increase in the volume of trade warranted an addition to the banking facilities. The withdrawal of the United States Bank created an analogous situation, which provided the justification for the railroad bank charters. It was maintained in the chapter which discussed the Darien Bank charter, that an element of subsidy was intended at least, whenever the legislature discriminated, in granting charters, in favor of some place or industry for the avowed purpose of creating trade or profit for a particular group. Such a subsidy was similar to that conferred by a protective tariff and could not be described as a payment from the state government. With respect to the railroad grants we may reasonably assume that they would have been made in any case, either to the railroad companies or to independent corporations; and actual evidence warrants the further assumptions that the grants would have been made in all probability to the same communities and to substantially the same groups of investors. Did the operation of the new banks, as departments of the railroad companies, alter the nature of their income from what it would have been if it had been earned by independent banking companies? The only significant effect appears to have been upon the distribution of the banking earnings. Some of the stockholders in the companies apparently got somewhat increased incomes and the others presumably somewhat decreased ones during the early years, although their positions were reversed in the long run. In any case such a redistribution of income within a group does not indicate that the group as a whole received a subsidy.

Analysis of the facts in the case further weakens the subsidy theory. In the first place, the capital used in banking was additional to that subscribed and used for railroad construction, hence the banking profits were a return on a specific capital devoted to banking, and not an excess return on railroad capital. Nor do they appear to have exceeded the normal return on other banking capital during the period. The legislative committee's interpretation makes no allowance for any return whatsoever to capital and entrepreneurship engaged in the banking departments of the railroad companies. The Central of Georgia Railroad undoubtedly benefited in the beginning promotionally from amalgamation with the Bank of Savannah project. But by 1839 the railroad end was yielding a larger return, and after 1844 consistently yielded several times the rate of return earned on the banking capital. In fact, banking became a minor and steadily declining phase relatively of the company's business after 1840.

The same in somewhat lesser degree was the history of the Georgia Railroad and Banking Company. In fact, with the deepening of the depression, in 1839, the roles of banking and transportation became reversed in both companies. It was the railroad operations that sustained the banking departments between 1839 and 1846. This was particularly true of the Georgia Railroad and Banking Company, which had overexpanded its banking operations and might easily have failed but for the steadily growing earning capacity of the railroad. The depreciation of its bank notes not only embarrassed the company but also the entire region. The poor condition of the bank was a major factor, probably, in the delay for several years of new construction on the road. When the extension to Atlanta was built during 1843–1845 it was done largely with railroad earnings, while during this same period the banking capital of the company showed no earnings whatever.[30] The Central of Georgia contracted its banking operations drastically with the business decline in 1839 and thereafter devoted most of its capital to railroad construction and operation.[31] Its banking business after 1840, relatively speaking, was insignificant.

The extent to which banking privileges aided railroad construction with the other two companies was doubtful in one case and nil in the other. The Monroe Railroad bank was opened in Macon in 1837 and flourished for three or four years. Its notes depreciated rapidly after 1839 and it was certainly insolvent long before the Monroe Railroad Company was forced into bankruptcy in 1845. It is difficult to assess any direct effects of the bank's operations, pro or con, upon the construction of the railroad. The Chattahoochee Railroad and Banking Company was never anything but a bank, since it built no railroad line. Like all other banks in Columbus, it failed during the depression.

The most important factor by far in the development of railroad construction during this first period was the construction of the state railroad. The legislature of 1834, in considering the recommendations of Governor Lumpkin for state action adopted the following resolution: "that the times require, and the resources of the state authorize, a scheme of internal improvements from the seaboard of this state to the interior by railroad on the faith and credit of the State as a great State work." [32] A year later, after pondering the proposal of the Cincinnati Railroad Convention for a northwest-southeast railroad, it authorized the governor to have surveys made to ascertain the feasibility of a route through northwestern Georgia, for a western railroad.[33] It was moving, if slowly, in the direction urged by Governor Lumpkin. Two of the railroad companies undertook surveys of routes through the north Georgia mountain passes. J. Edgar Thomson of the Georgia Railroad surveyed a route through Rabun Gap in northeastern Georgia and made fairly careful estimates of costs of construction through that region. Jacob Scudder of the Monroe Railroad conducted a less thorough survey in northwestern Georgia.

5. The Knoxville Railroad Convention

Meanwhile, Charleston had taken up the Cincinnati and Charleston project in most systematic fashion.[34] The city appropriated $5,000 and the state of South Carolina $10,000 for the conduct of surveys for the railroad. Unsuccessful attempts were made to get North Carolina, Tennessee, and Kentucky to take similar steps. The South Carolina legislature incorporated the Louisville, Cincinnati and Charleston Railroad Company, to build the railroad, and North Carolina, Tennessee, and Kentucky subsequently granted charters also to the company. In the spring of 1836 a call was sent out to all of the states of the South and West, that were interested in the project, to send delegates to Knoxville, Tennessee, to propose, discuss, and devise ways and means of carrying out the ambitious project.

Three hundred and eighty-one delegates, representing Ohio, Indiana, Kentucky, Virginia, North Carolina, South Carolina, Georgia, Alabama, and Tennessee, assembled at Knoxville on July 4, 1836.[35] Fifty-five were from Georgia, a number exceeded only by Kentucky, South Carolina, and Tennessee. The delegates were sent by cities, counties, states, federal departments, and railroad companies. The *Knoxville Register's* statement that it was the "greatest assemblage of talented men ever met in the United States for a similar purpose" was scarcely just an exaggeration induced by local pride.[36]

The convention lasted five days, and the time was consumed largely by reports of surveys, estimated costs, financial plans, and production and trade data. Colonel Blanding of South Carolina presented the charter of the Louisville, Cincinnati and Charleston Railroad. The Georgia representatives, having been unaware of the advanced stage of developments in other states, and especially in South Carolina, had not come prepared with reports. Taking advantage of a recess, however, they met and decided to make up two reports. They were supplied with the engineering and cost data that had been gathered by Thomson and Scudder and also by General Newnan, who had previously conducted extensive surveys in northwestern Georgia. Parkman, of Savannah, presented to the convention the report on the growth of Georgia's production and trade and Chappell, of Macon, the one on engineering and cost data on routes through northern Georgia. The Georgia reports made a deep impression on the other delegates and produced some doubt and confusion about the plan sponsored by South Carolina. In response to the Georgians' request for consideration of a branch of the railroad to be located through Georgia as an equal and coördinate part of the Louisville, Cincinnati and Charleston, the convention finally approved such an amendment to the railroad's charter. The convention also recommended that the states should appropriate their respective shares of the federal surplus revenue, soon to be distributed, for construction of the railroad, which was deemed a fitting use of the funds in view of the national importance of the railroad. It was thought that the amounts received by the states concerned would suffice to build the entire line.

6. The Macon Convention: A State System Projected

The Georgia delegates, before separating after the close of the convention, decided to issue a call for a state-wide railroad convention to be held in Macon early in November. They elected a corresponding committee to circularize every county in the state, urging them to send delegates, equal in number at least to their legislative representations, to the meeting "for the purpose of consulting upon the expediency and the practicability of building a railroad from some point on the Tennessee

River below the Suck, through Georgia, to some point on the Atlantic." [37]

Thirty-eight counties and two railroad companies sent 116 delegates to the Macon convention. The outcome of their deliberations was a report and a set of resolutions to the legislature, just then convening at Milledgeville, recommending: that the state initiate a system of railroad improvements by constructing a railroad, entirely on state account, from a point on the Tennessee line near Rossville in northwest Georgia to some suitable point at or near the Chattahoochee River in the general region of De Kalb County; that existing companies, or ones that should be created where none exist, be authorized to construct branches from the southern terminus of the State Railroad, to Athens, Forsyth, Columbus, and such other places as the legislature might designate; and that the state subscribe one-fourth of the capital required to construct each such branch. The accompanying report stressed the fact that every state and city on the Atlantic coast was bent upon gaining access to the trade of the West; that New York had been the first to succeed, with the Erie Canal; and that Georgia possessed the only other route through the Appalachian Mountain ranges that was comparable to that of New York. In fact, Georgia's route was considered superior, because it was shorter and within effective reach of a more extensive area of western trade. The traffic of the proposed system of Georgia railroads would be of three main types: the trade within the state, which it was deemed unquestionably would be the most important; the large volume of goods of Tennessee and the northwest that would flow into Georgia and neighboring states for consumption; and, finally, the transit export and import trade.[38]

This report reflects one of the earliest instances of general recognition that the railroads were outgrowing their auxiliary relationship to river-coastwise carriers and were soon going to short-circuit the long-distance roundabout waterway system. The ranking of the transit trade as least important was likewise notable. The proposed plan would mold the individual rail lines that were already under construction, and others yet to be projected, into a state system built around a central railroad, which in turn formed a section of a main route to the west and northwest. Lumpkin's conception was bearing fruit. In its basic network the plan reverted to the outlines of the Central Canal scheme of 1824–1825 and followed its routes rather consistently. It placed a great deal of emphasis upon the connection with the Tennessee River near the northwest border of the state. This, it was thought, would possess the double advantage of access to the river's traffic and connections with proposed railroads to Memphis, to Nashville and Louisville, and to southeastern Tennessee. It declared, in effect, the state's independence of the Louisville, Cincinnati and Charleston Railroad project. The only reference made to the latter was a brief comment that, should a connection be made with that line in eastern Tennessee, Georgia would be provided with two routes to the Ohio River.

7. The State as Entrepreneur

The Georgia legislature adopted the recommendations of the Macon Convention almost to the letter. The Western and Atlantic Railroad was

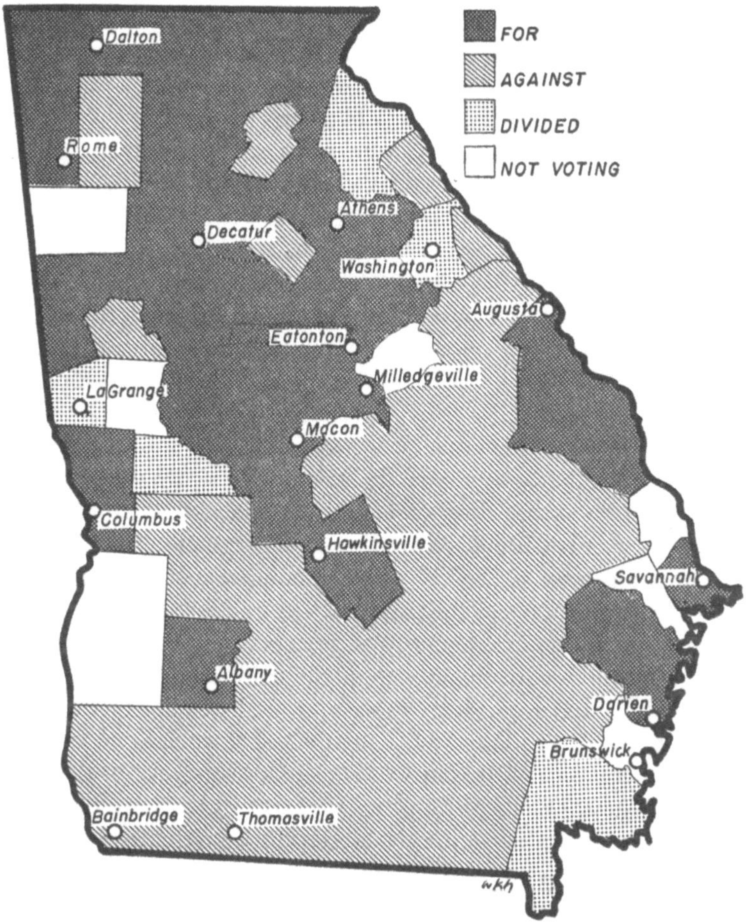

Georgia: Vote on Western and Atlantic Railroad (House), 1836

created by an act of December 21, 1836, which provided that it should be constructed by the state and that it should extend from the Tennessee line, at or near Rossville, to the south bank of the Chattahoochee River at a point most eligible for the extension of branch railroads to Athens, Madison, Milledgeville, Forsyth, Columbus, and other desirable points. Not over $350,000 was to be appropriated annually for construction, although this limitation could be changed by future legislatures. Provision was made also for state aid to the branch railroads as follows: when one-half of the stock in any one of them should have been subscribed, the governor of the state was to subscribe for one-fourth of the capital stock, but not to exceed $200,000 in any one road, and the state was not to be held liable for any payment upon its subscription until the whole amount of the capital stock had been subscribed.

The legislature took steps at once to secure construction of three of the branches, by chartering the Chattahoochee Railroad and Banking Company to construct a line from Columbus by way of West Point to the Western and Atlantic's southern terminus, by granting banking privileges to the Monroe Railroad Company to aid it in securing capital to extend its line from Forsyth, and by chartering the Middle Branch Railroad, to build the link with the Georgia Railroad from Madison.[39] The Chattahoochee Railroad was conceived as a joint project between the city of Columbus and the state. The city was the principal promoter named in the charter, and later subscribed $200,000 of stock of the company. The state reserved the right to subscribe one-fourth of the authorized capital of $2,000,000. The charter of the Middle Branch Railroad was repealed in 1837 and its project absorbed by the Georgia Railroad and Banking Company, when the latter was authorized to extend its line from Madison to the terminus of the Western and Atlantic.

Administration of construction of the Western and Atlantic was vested originally in a superintendent and a chief engineer; but the superintendent was replaced in 1837 by three commissioners, one of whom was designated the president of the railroad. The commissioners were authorized to choose officers and agents and to make regulations for the operation of the business with the advice of the chief engineer. The president was required to make quarterly reports to the governor of the state and to act jointly with the latter on a number of financial procedures. The actual direction of construction was left almost entirely in the hands of the chief engineer. Colonel Stephen H. Long, who had done much of General Gaines's surveying for the Memphis and Charleston project in northwestern Georgia and the adjoining Tennessee section, was employed in this capacity.

Most of the surveying and location work was completed in 1837 and grading of the roadbed begun in 1838. This work was continued steadily, despite the depression, until the end of 1841, when prolonged depression, the straitened condition of the Central Bank, and the collapse of the state's credit forced the legislature to order a suspension of work on the road. Much of the grading had been virtually completed throughout the entire one hundred forty miles, but not a rail had been laid.

The legislature on December 4, 1841, ordered the engineering corps dissolved and the offices of the commissioners abolished. The governor was authorized to appoint a disbursing agent and an engineer, and to take such financial measures as should be necessary to complete approximately the first fifty miles, from the southern terminus. Nothing further was to be done on the balance of the line.

Governor McDonald induced Wilson Lumpkin, who had just retired from public life after a term in the United States Senate, to take the position of disbursing agent and gave him a free hand to carry out the edict of the legislature. Lumpkin has reported that he found the organization ill-devised and much of the personnel inefficient, the methods of work uneconomical and many of the contracts wastefully arranged, to say the least. His judgment of Colonel Long was that he had proved himself a good engineer, but a poor administrator. In particular he thought that Long's policy of grading the entire roadbed, before laying any rails, had added greatly to the costs and largely explained why the outlays already had exceeded by $50,000 Long's original estimate of the entire cost of the road. On the other hand, it had to be borne in mind that building railroads was a new venture, and that this one had been undertaken under exceptionally unfavorable conditions, through a rough and largely uninhabited region, distant from all facilities of transportation. Lumpkin reorganized the personnel situation and instituted rigid economies; but shortage of funds prevented much progress being made during the brief time that he was in charge of operations.[40]

Conditions were somewhat brighter by 1843 and the legislature repealed the suspending act and authorized a gradual procedure with the completion of the entire line. Administration was placed in the hands of the governor and a chief engineer. Wide criticism had developed of the state's handling of the construction and, in fact, of the entire policy of state involvement in railroad building. The new Whig administration was bent upon rigid economy, retrenchment, and debt reduction.[41] However, it was not inclined to abandon the Western and Atlantic, although the governor was authorized to sell it, subject to certain stipulated conditions, for $1,000,000. But there were no buyers on the terms proposed, and work went forward fairly steadily after 1843, supported by additional appropriations in 1845 and 1847. The good progress on other railroad projects within the state and the incorporation of the Nashville and Chattanooga Railroad in Tennessee boosted public morale regarding the Western and Atlantic. It was completed from the southern terminus to Marietta, and train operations were begun, on August 13, 1845.[42] "Terminus," as the settlement at the southern end of the line had been called, received two names about this time — Marthasville, so-named by friends of Wilson Lumpkin, for his daughter, and Atlanta, given apparently by railroad men, possibly on the Georgia Railroad.[43] The latter name attracted general usage and was soon officially recognized by the legislature.

Operation of trains into Dalton, one hundred miles north of Atlanta, began on July 22, 1847; a branch line to Rome was opened in December 1849; and the entire line to Chattanooga was placed in operation with the opening of the tunnel north of Dalton on May 9, 1850. The goal set in December 1836, at last had been reached, but, like most early roads, upon completion the Western and Atlantic found its equipment and rails worn, inadequate, and obsolete and its bridges and other structures already in need of replacement and enlargement. Large additions of capital and five or six more years of effort were needed to make the Western and Atlantic a first-class operating railroad. The financial history of the railroad has been painstakingly summarized by James Houstoun Johnston in his study of *The Western and Atlantic of the State of Georgia* and is reproduced, through 1860, with his kind permission and that of his publishers, the Georgia Public Service Commission, in Table 14.[44]

8. Building Railroads During a Depression

The Central of Georgia was completed in the fall of 1843 and the first train arrived at Macon on October 13. The Georgia Railroad was completed to Madison and Athens in 1841, but the extension to Atlanta was not begun until 1843 and not completed until the end of the summer of 1845. The first train left Augusta for Atlanta on September 11, 1845.[45] The Monroe Railroad Company was the first in Georgia to complete its original line, which was opened from Macon to Forsyth in December 1838. It began work immediately on the extension to the Western and Atlantic, authorized in the amended charter of 1836. The route was surveyed, the entire line located, and all grading contracts were let by July 1839. The heavy costs of the original line and the ill effects of the depression upon the fortunes of the planters who comprised most of its stockholders, brought the company near the end of its resources in 1842. But Savannah came to its aid with a $50,000 subscription and the company was also able later to float some bonds. But in 1845 it defaulted on the bonds and became bankrupt. The road was purchased and reorganized by Northern capitalists, completed before the end of the following year, and train operations into Atlanta were begun on October 1, 1846. The opening of the Western and Atlantic in May 1850, therefore, marked the completion, except for the branches in western Georgia, of the main lines of the state system of railroads, proposed by Governor Lumpkin in 1833, recommended by the Macon Convention, and adopted by the state in 1836.

The greater portions of this group of railroads, which shall be called hereafter the Atlantic and Western system, were built during the Great

Table 14

WESTERN AND ATLANTIC FINANCIAL SUMMARY, 1836–1860

Year	Legislative appropriations	Construction expenditures	Operating revenues	Operating expenses	Payments to treasury	Bond retirement and interest
1836	$ 350,000.00					
1837	850,000.00	$ 17,595.32				
1838	1,500,000.00	229,899.61				
1839		982,653.17				
1840		591,086.14				
1841	474,108.84	360,037.96				
1842		101,437.10				$ 300.00
1843	304,520.12	633,309.12				8,765.00
1844		101,549.35				46,740.00
1845	117,023.48	96,159.92				114,586.44
1846		78,966.54	$ 38,127.22	$ 22,987.13		25,877.59
1847	375,000.00	112,471.39	89,483.86	51,953.07		108,130.00
1848		61,258.15	115,585.30	56,902.91		21,622.96
1849		371,434.78	132,105.70	77,634.58		129,436.82
1850		94,074.98	198,564.34	132,549.74		126,539.64
1851		255,992.62	285,028.44	182,709.00		49,547.92
1852	525,000.00	221,781.09	375,176.62	326,505.63		39,323.36
1853		268,837.70	428,876.06	239,275.87		117,211.22
1854		324,542.34	591,154.78	249,994.63	$ 50,000.00	65,536.30
1855		239,308.08	698,830.56	250,864.84	100,000.00	48,795.14
1856		375,441.76	871,366.53	450,292.25	43,500.00	39,428.75
1857		383,660.44	900,808.95	433,323.40	100,000.00	31,385.80
1858		186,757.87	800,001.29	393,737.84	175,000.00	106,830.74
1859		27,326.70	832,343.80	384,159.90	402,000.00	48,290.00
1860		15,927.51	875,919.55	445,544.30	450,000.00	22,940.00
	$4,495,652.44	$6,131,509.64	$7,233,373.00	$3,698,435.09	$1,320,500.00	$1,151,287.68

Depression of 1837–1844. It is not possible with the data at hand to measure the effects that railroad construction and its supporting fiscal policies had upon the state economy as a whole, but the salient facts will be noted.

The total railroad investment in the eight-year period amounted approximately to $8,500,000, which was equivalent to the entire commercial banking capital of the state at the beginning of the depression and to several times the amount that had been invested in all other forms of internal improvements over the previous fifty years.[46] Of this large investment, $4,060,000 was public. The state spent $3,000,000 on the Western and Atlantic and the cities contributed the balance to the three other railroad projects. Although public investment constituted only 48 per cent of the total, it provided a far greater percentage of the cash investment. A high proportion of the private subscriptions to railroad shares was paid in services and kind, by means of contracts for grading, superstructures, buildings, and equipment, which enabled planters and others to pay their stock subscriptions in the services of managerial personnel, slaves, and equipment and in land and materials such as timber, lumber, bricks, stone, and iron. The customary terms of construction contracts provided for payment of one-fourth in cash and three-fourths in stock in the company.[47] The other chief needs for cash were for railroad iron, engines, and other rolling stock; thus the public cash contribution was the strategic factor. Without it the railroad enterprises for the most part could not have been undertaken successfully. Broadly speaking, it induced, or facilitated, the private investment in labor and kind.

The state pursued substantially the same contract policy on the Western and Atlantic construction that was followed on the other railroads, by making the larger part of the payments in state bonds or interest-bearing scrip. The net result, therefore, was the same, namely, the inducement of private investment through payments in services and kind. The state experienced considerable difficulty with this policy after 1839, owing to the depreciation of its credit and the general deterioration of its fiscal situation. Resort was had to various supporting devices. Interest coupons were made receivable for all debts owed to the state. Scrip was made redeemable in 6 per cent state bonds; and the Central Bank was ordered to buy uncovered scrip, as well as interest coupons, and to pay the principal and interest on domestic and external bank loans as they came due.[48] The Central Bank purchased $680,000 of scrip, interest coupons, and bank loans and paid some $100,000 of interest annually and approximately $156,000 on principal of the external debt.[49] But these burdens depreciated the Bank's currency and otherwise adversely affected its policies, which weakened its support of the public credit. Sale of state-owned bank stocks was then authorized, but the general financial situation prevented sufficient sales to meet the purpose.

It would appear that most of the $8,500,000 of railroad investment represented a net addition to state income, resulting from the employment of otherwise unemployed labor and capital resources. Apparently all of the city and one-third of the state advances were borrowed from the banks. The city loans were obtained from local banks. The state borrowed $700,000 in London, $60,000 from the Georgia Railroad and Banking Company and sold scrip to the Bank of Augusta in the amount of $304,852.76, which was converted later into a sterling loan. All of the remainder of the state advances, some $1,968,000, was paid out originally to the contractors in scrip.[50] Such financing by bank loans and by payments in railroad securities and state bonds and scrip prevented direct drains upon ordinary expendable money incomes. However, there were some indirect drains and offsets. The external payments for iron and rolling stock and for debt service increased the existing adverse balance of payments and the premium upon foreign exchange, and thereby depreciated correspondingly the state currency, thus forcing either an equal amount of disinvestment or a like depreciation in real income. The purchase of scrip by the Central Bank with its notes increased the money supply and facilitated the operation of the investment multiplier, but it likewise may have caused further depreciation of the paper medium and thereby reduced its purchasing power and effects proportionately.

There were undoubtedly other important multiplier and accelerator effects besides the direct ones indicated above. The preference of contractors for state scrip to bonds rested upon its greater convenience in exchange. The scrip and the interest coupons added, in some measure, to the money supply and hence to effective demand. A similar effect was produced by the railroad companies' practice of paying some construction costs in tickets, which were receivable for freight and passenger services. Such tickets frequently enjoyed extensive local circulation as money. The accelerator and other secondary effects were even greater than the multiplier ones, owing to the favorable influence of railroad construction on future expectations. The building of the railroads induced a great number of individual entrepreneurial ventures in self-employment of labor and owner resources. Auxiliary and complementary industries sprang up in considerable numbers along the rail lines. New industries were launched and old ones were extended. This is evidenced by the many new towns and cities. Such investment produced some net addition to state income.[51]

It is not possible with the available data to deduce any quantitative balance of total net addition to income, yet two general conclusions seem clearly warranted: that public investment was a primary activating factor, and that the railroad construction program which it supported was an important countercyclical influence. There is much evidence that Georgia weathered the depression better than most Southern states.[52]

9. Railroad Construction, 1845–1860

A new period of railroad-building opened following the depression. Eighty-five companies were chartered during the years 1845–1860. New incorporations reached a peak of twenty-seven in 1854. In contrast with the previous period was the large number of abortive projects. Many were never even organized. They were either abandoned or replaced by other projects. It was often difficult to raise the necessary capital. Another characteristic of this period was the high percentage of purely local projects.

For the most part those railroads that were undertaken during this period were complementary additions, in one form or another, to the Atlantic and Western system whose foundation lines had been laid in the previous period. Chief among these were: the Southwestern, chartered in 1845 and completed from Macon to Albany, Fort Gaines, and Eufaula (Alabama); the Muscogee, likewise chartered in 1845, which at last linked Columbus, by way of the Southwestern and the Macon and Western (the Monroe Railroad) with the Western and Atlantic; the Atlanta and West Point, first chartered in 1847 as the Atlanta and La Grange, which joined the Western and Atlantic with a line of railroads in Alabama extending to Montgomery and Mobile; the Macon and Brunswick, not chartered until 1857 and completed only as far as Hawkinsville before 1861; and the Waynesboro Railroad, which connected the Georgia Railroad and Augusta with Savannah by way of the Central of Georgia from Millen. These lines rounded out the general framework of the original state system as conceived in the Western and Atlantic Railroad Act of 1836. The remaining projects in this group were local branch-line undertakings, of which some forty-three were chartered and only six or seven completed during this time.

The more significant development of this period, in some respects at least, was the emergence of new trunk-line projects, which contemplated new axes rather than merely additions to the existing network system built around the Western and Atlantic axis. Only one of these new main trunks was actually fully undertaken and substantially completed. This was the Altantic and Gulf Railroad, which was designed to connect the Atlantic ports of Savannah and Brunswick with the Gulf ports of Pensacola, Mobile, and New Orleans. Three others of vast potential importance, that never progressed far beyond the planning stage, were the Northeastern, the Georgia Air-line, and the Georgia Western. The first of these was a revival of the Knoxville Convention project, designed to connect

Georgia's railroads, either from Athens or Atlanta or from both, with the northwest by way of Rabun Gap and the French Broad River route; the second was designed to connect Atlanta with the piedmont Carolinas and Virginia and the railroads of the industrial northeast; and the third was planned to link Atlanta with the prospective new mining and industrial center of north Alabama that was just becoming the focus of attention of a number of railroad-minded groups in the latter state.

Both the Atlantic and Gulf and the Northeastern were descended from earlier projects. Both belonged to the same ancestral vintage, if they did not actually antedate it, as the Atlantic and Western idea. The Northeastern Railroad, as already implied, was part of a revival of the Louisville, Cincinnati, and Charleston scheme, which had been rechartered recently in South Carolina as the Blue Ridge Railroad. The Georgia wing of this system proposed a main trunk over the route in northeastern Georgia surveyed in 1835 by J. Edgar Thomson, which would join the Blue Ridge Railroad in North Carolina and would have branches from its southern end to Athens and Atlanta. Branches were also planned from the main trunk in the vicinity of Clayton to the new copper-mining region around Ducktown, Tennessee, corresponding to similar branches to the same region from the Western and Atlantic in northwestern Georgia. Both the Atlantic and Gulf and the Northeastern, like the Atlantic and Western system, rested upon the basic conceptions of the dominant place of commercial agriculture, ocean-borne commerce, and the Atlantic ports in the Southern economy and of the strategic geographical position of Georgia. The Georgia Air-Line and the Georgia Western, on the other hand, embodied a new conception — of the dominant roles in the modern economy of manufactures, railroads, and inland rail centers. They gave strong evidence that a new center of commercial orientation was rising already in north central Georgia that was scarcely included by Wilson Lumpkin in the effects which he contemplated that the railroads would have, nor visualized by the Georgia legislature when it stipulated that the southern terminus of the state railroad should be located a few miles south of the Chattahoochee River at some point of convenience for building branches to the important cities in Georgia. The citizens of Athens had first glimpsed something of this vision when they launched the Georgia Railroad; but the citizens of Atlanta became the leading champions of it with their two trunk-line projects in the 1850's.[53]

10. The Role of the Cities

Public promotion and financing continued to play a decisive part in new railroad construction, with city activity expanding into the leading public role. It had antedated state action previously, but had become overshadowed, both quantitatively and strategically, by the state's development of the Western and Atlantic. Savannah's record in railroad promotion was particularly impressive. Although slow at first to realize fully the importance of the new mode of transportation, when once aroused it pursued a consistent policy of promotion of rail lines that was designed to link it with its natural hinterland. Its efforts fell into three periods and covered three different areas of development. The first period, from 1833 to 1843, saw the construction of the main line to Macon, to which the city subscribed $500,000. The second, from 1845 to 1852, was linked with the expansion of the Central of Georgia railroad system, in which the city supported the company in promoting the construction of the Waynesboro, the Southwestern, the Muscogee, and the Opelika branch railroads. In 1852 Savannah turned its attention toward its hinterland to the southwest, including all of south Georgia, southeastern Alabama, and middle Florida, with which it possessed no transportation communication of any effective sort. Recent rapid growth in settlement and production was making this region's trade a rich prize, which Savannah undertook to attract through the construction of a trunk-line railroad across the region. Between 1852 and 1860 the city Corporation invested over $1,800,000 in promoting this project.[54]

Augusta's vacillating attitude toward railroads typified more or less the viewpoint of all fall-line cities. Located at the head of navigation, Augusta's commercial position remained impregnable so long as river courses dominated long-distance transportation. Its position was strengthened even further by the development of the shallow draft steamboat, which made it virtually a complementary inland port for Charleston. With these natural and artificial advantages it built up probably the largest wagon trade with the interior of any city in the South. No city in the South grew more rapidly during the 1830's, at the height of the steamboat traffic on the Savannah River. Hence, the city's capitalists were worried rather than enticed by the lavish praises heaped upon the railroad by its early supporters in interior Georgia. Railroads presented a distinct threat to fall-line cities in that they promised to remove the very locational advantage upon which the prosperity of such cities rested. Would the railroads at their inland termini develop great commercial centers, such as the water courses had at their fall-line termini, to take away Augusta's wholesale trade? And would an ever-growing network of rail lines provide local communities with depots and retail stores that would deprive Augusta of its great wagon trade? Faced on the one hand by the possibility that the project might fail and on the other by threatening uncertainties in case it should succeed, Augusta's businessmen gave very little support originally to the Georgia Railroad, and only invested in it later when it gave assurance of becoming an extremely profitable venture and an important weapon in the commercial struggle with Savannah for the trade of northwest Georgia and more distant regions. The city of Augusta eventually subscribed $200,000, on condition that the company should never connect with the Charleston and Hamburg without the consent of the city council.

There can be little question but that, relatively speaking, the railroads affected Augusta's growth adversely and Savannah's favorably. The former's rate of growth dropped sharply with the decline of water traffic, while the latter's forged to the front among Southern cities. The two rivals almost exactly reversed positions, and railroads were largely responsible. Augusta turned to railroad promotion in the fifties to recover its position.[55] First it joined with the state of South Carolina and the cities of Hamburg and Columbia in promoting the Savannah River Valley Railroad, which presumably was expected to develop its trade with northwest South Carolina; but after considerable work on this project, it was abandoned. The city originally had voted a subscription of $500,000. The municipality voted a second $500,000, in 1859, to the Macon and Warrenton Railroad. This plan, also called the Macon and Augusta and the Milledgeville, was projected in the hope that a direct connection with Milledgeville and Macon would divert some of the ever-growing volume of trade that was flowing to Savannah over the Central of Georgia railroad.[56] Baldwin County, in which Milledgeville is located, also voted a subscription to this road as a result of discontent over rates charged by the Central of Georgia.

Columbus' position rather closely paralleled Augusta's, except that it indulged in an early period of enthusiasm for railroads. Later it passed through a similar trial by uncertainty and then finally plunged into railroad-building as a possible means of retaining its commercial position. It had entered wholeheartedly in 1836 into coöperation with the state's Western and Atlantic scheme, in projecting the Chattahoochee Railroad branch. This was before the improved river steamboat had overcome the long voyage down the Chattahoochee River and the lack of a port at the river's mouth. The city mortgaged its Chattahoochee River bridge in order to subscribe $200,000 to the branch railroad;[57] but floods swept away the bridge and, far worse, the depression swept away Columbus' six banks, including the Chattahoochee Railroad bank, and the railroad venture collapsed. Then the forties brought a phenomenal rise of steamboat operations on the Chattahoochee River and a corresponding growth in Columbus' wagon trade. The city replaced Augusta in leadership in the latter. When the enthusiasm for new railroad construction swept over the state after 1845 it met a noticeable lack of enthusiasm in Columbus. Fear of loss of the wagon trade gripped the public.[58] If Columbus helped to build lines to the east, to Macon and Atlanta, it appeared to be inviting all of the cotton from that territory, that now was hauled to Columbus, to move directly to such lines and thence eastward. Columbus easily could lose a half to two-thirds of its cotton trade. Yet if it did not take the initiative in building railroads, other cities would do so, Columbus would be by-passed and the business would be lost, as well as any advantage that location upon an important railroad might afford. It seemed better, therefore, to build its connection with the Georgia railroad system and to locate it where it would do the least harm. The Muscogee Railroad may hold the unique distinction of being the only railroad ever to have been located with a view to avoiding traffic.[59] In this state of mind toward railroads, the city welcomed plank roads in 1850 as a promising defensive measure against the encroachment of railroads upon the wagon trade; but the plank road speedily succumbed to the iron road. Thus Columbus, forced to accept railroads, was never quite certain where it should construct them, or whether it was inviting disaster or insuring future prosperity. To the southwest it was threatened with the same loss of wagon trade to Pensacola and Mobile, and to the north its hopes of expanding its wholesale trade were met by the rising competition of Atlanta. Yet the city invested a considerable sum altogether in railroads between 1848 and 1859.

Macon, though a fall-line city, enjoyed a more favorable position than most as a railroad center in central Georgia. It became the inland pivot of the Central of Georgia railroad system. But like the others, upon the advent of the railroad it lost a large part of its wagon trade. It also embraced plank roads, as they did, in a vain hope of recovering this business. Toward the end of the fifties its citizens became disgruntled over their sole dependence upon the Central of Georgia Railroad and what they believed to be the monopoly rates charged by that company. Consequently, they backed two new railroad projects — the Macon and Warrenton and the Macon and Brunswick — that were designed to give the city independent rail connections with Savannah's two rivals, Augusta and Brunswick. Actually, they could not develop overmuch interest in the proposed line to Augusta, but they became enthusiastic over the Macon and Brunswick and contributed a heavy subscription in addition to that taken by the city.[60]

The closing years of this second period of railroad construction also brought a number of county subscriptions. Generally speaking, Georgia was not hospitable toward the policy of county subscription that was being adopted by so many other Southern states at this time. Hence the extent of county participation was not very great. It appears that each instance in which the state granted permission was viewed somewhat as a special case. For example, in the case of Dougherty County's subscription to one of Albany's pet railroad schemes, for some reason the county government instead of the municipality was chosen as the instrument for public subscription. Incidentally, this action provoked the principal legal action on public subscriptions in Georgia. Three of the county subscriptions involved short branch lines of which the counties were the promoters, there being no cities capable of making subscriptions and little private wealth in these counties. Three other county subscriptions were little more than token ones. The Baldwin County subscription was a part of the movement of cities such as Macon and Milledgeville to secure alternate competing routes in order to obtain competitive rates.

11. The Atlantic and Gulf Railroad

There were two theories concerning state support of railroad construction in the South. One was that the state should assist all projects in some more or less uniform fashion, a policy exemplified most fully in Virginia and Tennessee. The other theory was the one developed in Georgia, that the state should confine its efforts to a single large project that was designed to confer a general benefit upon the entire state and to stimulate efforts widely in private and local construction of complementary and auxiliary railroad lines; and, furthermore, that the state should embark a sufficiently large sum — preferably the entire cost — to assure reasonably prompt completion of the work.[61] There were almost continuous efforts in Georgia, however, to have this policy set aside and state support made general. The provision in the Western and Atlantic Railroad Act of 1836, which bound the state to subscribe a fourth of the stock — under certain conditions — of railroad companies that would build branches to the Western and Atlantic, looked like an entering wedge. The following year an attempt to have this provision extended to all railroad projects was defeated by only a narrow margin. The movement was revived following the depression, when local projects sprang up in such large numbers; and it is surprising that the state resisted it successfully. Other states that had followed policies similar to Georgia's adopted the general state-support system,[62] for the movement seemed irresistible outside of Georgia.

The principal methods of granting state aid in general use were: subscription to stock in mixed corporations, direct money loans, loan of state bonds, and state endorsement of company bonds. Each of these methods received strong backing during the fifties in the widespread efforts to commit Georgia to an all-out aid program. The state credit-loan and bond-endorsement methods were particularly popular. When universal aid programs failed to muster enough votes, an attempt was fostered to secure state support of prominent regional projects. A strongly backed bill introduced into the legislature in 1855 provided for loans of state credit amounting to $3,500,000 to four railroad companies — $500,000 to the Southwestern and $1,000,000 each to the Northeastern, the Savannah, Albany and Gulf, and the Brunswick and Florida.[63] Even this bid for organized support failed. A year later the state reaffirmed its previous policy, when it decided again to back a single "main trunk" project, the Atlantic and Gulf Railroad.

The Atlantic and Gulf undertaking was the culmination of a number of efforts to secure the construction of railroads in southern Georgia. This large section, comprising more than a third of the area of the state, was almost devoid of transportation facilities save in the southwest, where the Flint and Chattahoochee rivers provided a waterway outlet on the Gulf. A sparse population, poor soils, and little production hitherto had offered slight inducements to build roads, canals, or railroads in the region. After 1840, however, settlement and cotton production in southwest Georgia and the adjoining sections of southeast Alabama and middle Florida increased very rapidly. Consequently, the Atlantic ports of Savannah and Brunswick began to cast longing eyes toward the expanding trade of the region and, in turn, south Georgia began to demand a system of transportation patterned after that being developed elsewhere in the state. This railway movement began to take shape immediately after the depression in the following concrete projects: the construction of the Southwestern Railroad under the aegis of the Central of Georgia, and designed to reach the richest section of southern Georgia and southeast Alabama from a connection at Macon; various local railroad projects that were undertaken by such communities as Americus, Dawson, Cuthbert, Fort Gaines, and Eufaula (Alabama), designed to form parts of, and usually undertaken in coöperation with, the Southwestern Railroad;[64] the ambitious projects of Albany — the Georgia and Florida Railroad and the Savannah and Albany Railroad — that were intended to make Albany, at the head of navigation on the Flint River, the transportation center of southwest Georgia;[65] the revival by Brunswick of the Brunswick and Florida railroad scheme with the backing of Northern capital;[66] and finally, the adoption by Savannah of Albany's Savannah and Albany project.

As these various enterprises progressed there were numerous changes of purpose and of routes and frequent conflicts of aims and shifts in support. The situation remained in a considerable state of flux. Savannah early transferred its interest from the Savannah and Albany project to a much more ambitious one.[67] It decided to build a line farther south, that would traverse the cotton-growing counties of Lowndes, Thomas, and Decatur and reach the junction of the Flint and Chattahoochee rivers where it could intercept the waterborne freight of both these streams. Branches could be built from such a central line into middle Florida and into southeastern Alabama, and a connection could be extended from the river junction to Pensacola.[68] The connection with Pensacola was Savannah's ultimate objective. There was an additional reason for the latter desire besides the wish to be the Atlantic terminus of a main route to the Gulf. The Panama Railroad was being planned at this time and Savannah visualized Pensacola as the most likely Gulf port to participate in the transcontinental trade, provided it had rail connections with the Atlantic and other eastern railroads. This new route promised far more for Savannah's future than a railroad to Albany. Savannah would get most of Albany's trade anyway, over this new route or over the Southwestern and Central of Georgia.

There were two disturbing factors, other than the problem of financing the road — probable conflict with Brunswick over infringement of route and difficulties with Florida on account of conflicting railroad plans in that state.[69] Two Atlantic and Gulf projects were being nurtured in Florida, one by south Florida, for a line from the Atlantic port of Fernandina to Cedar Keys on the southwest Gulf coast, and another by east Florida, for a line from Fernandina-Jacksonville to Pensacola. The latter would traverse middle Florida and likewise pass the junction of the Flint and Chattahoochee rivers. Furthermore, its promoters were anticipating a connection with southwest Georgia over the Georgia and Florida Railroad from Albany. Obviously, east Florida and Savannah had designs on the same prizes. Middle Florida probably thought the Savannah project was surer and more advantageous, but found itself in the center of a difficult clash of interests. At a railroad convention in Tallahassee in 1853, middle Florida agreed to raise $800,000 to construct the line from the Flint-Chattahoochee river junction to Pensacola, provided Savannah would route its line through the middle Florida cities of Madison, Monticello, Tallahassee, and Quincy.[70] Savannah accepted this offer and in the following year had the name of its railroad changed to the Savannah, Albany and Gulf, to conform more nearly with its true intentions. Another advantage of this change was that it removed a part of the conflict with Brunswick; and still a further inducement was the movement, that was steadily gaining impetus, to construct a state railroad across south Georgia along the route through Clinch, Lowndes, Thomas, and Decatur counties that Savannah had been contemplating.[71] Should the state construct this railroad, Savannah would have two direct routes to the southwest, as well as the assurance of the connection with Pensacola. On the other hand, Savannah's decision to route its line through middle Florida undoubtedly lent added impetus to the movement to construct the state "main trunk" railroad.

The state's Atlantic and Gulf main-trunk railroad, chartered in 1856, was clearly a replica of the earlier Western and Atlantic Railroad, although organized in a different fashion. It had a parallel historical background, similar objectives, and even much the same physical design. Construction was to begin at a point in southeastern Georgia at or near the intersection of Wayne, Ware, and Appling counties, in the vicinity of the Satilla River, and to extend through an undeveloped region, that was lacking in transportation facilities, into southwest Georgia and thence to the Alabama line, to form connections with projected railroad lines extending to the major southwestern Gulf ports of Pensacola, Mobile, and

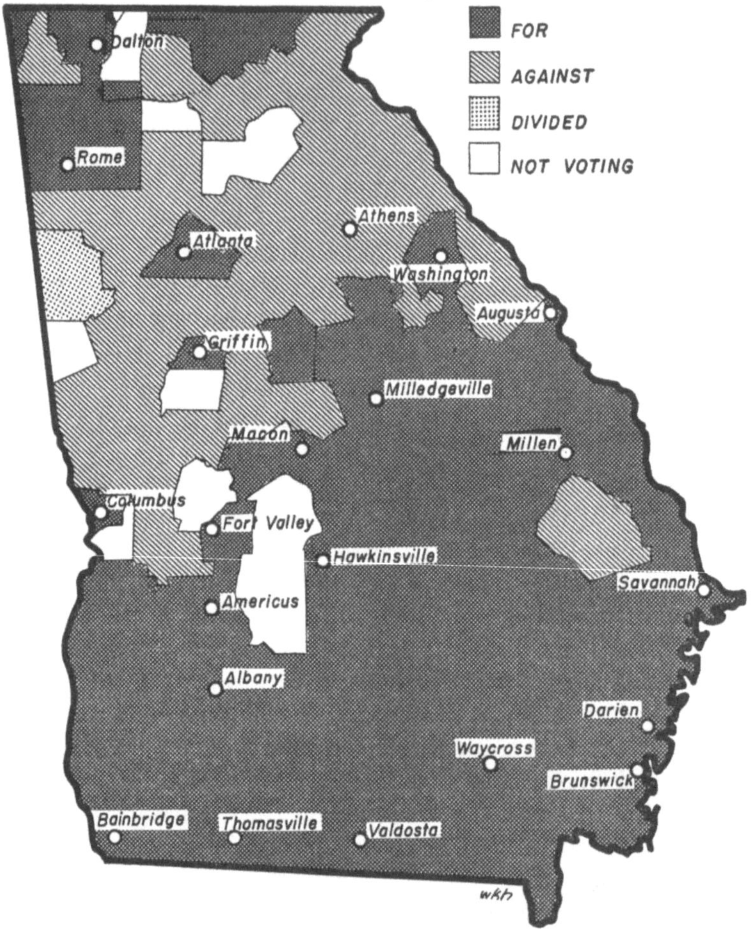

Georgia: Vote on Atlantic and Gulf Railroad Subscription (House), 1855

New Orleans. Both Savannah and Brunswick were expected to connect their Atlantic and Gulf railroads with the eastern terminus of the state-sponsored Main-Trunk.

The Atlantic and Gulf Railroad Company was a mixed corporation, with offices at the capital city of Milledgeville, in which the state agreed to subscribe $1,000,000 of capital stock, payable in two equal installments, provided other guaranteed subscriptions totaling $1,200,000 were secured.

This joint proprietorship venture marked a departure from the earlier policy of the Western and Atlantic financing, but otherwise the state followed the Lumpkin formula rather closely. No rail or superstructure was to be laid on the line until either the Savannah, Albany and Gulf or the Brunswick and Florida had been completed to the eastern terminus. The two companies were to have equal rights in all relations with the Atlantic and Gulf, and all other roads that would form a connection were assured the same privileges, provided they were built with their stockholders' own money. The last stipulation was intended as an inducement to private enterprise, as well as an injunction against seeking state aid.

Although chartered as a mixed corporation, the Atlantic and Gulf became primarily owned by the state and the cities of Savannah and Thomasville. The principal other proprietor was the largely Savannah-owned Savannah, Albany and Gulf Railroad.[72] Private investment was small and contributed chiefly in services and kind. Both the Savannah, Albany and Gulf and the Brunswick and Florida were completed to the eastern terminus of the Atlantic and Gulf, and the latter was finished as far as Thomasville, and much of the grading was done through Bainbridge to the Alabama line, before war prevented completion of the line. Originally the western terminus had been specified only in general terms, but later it was established as a point opposite Columbia, Alabama, where it was expected to form a connection with the newly projected Mobile and Albany Railroad.

The decision of the state to sponsor the Atlantic and Gulf Railroad upheld its established policy of financing a single major project that was designed to produce wide general benefits. The Atlantic and Gulf was intended to provide a main-trunk line that would serve the various local and sectional lines and would promote their development and integration. It was anticipated also that it would provide a common connection with railroads leading to the Gulf ports and the southwest. It upheld the principle of a state system against a multiplicity of uncoördinated, overlapping lines. It gave the state system two axes based upon the Atlantic ports — one extending toward the northwest and the other toward the southwest.

An extended controversy between the state and the Brunswick and Florida Railroad Company followed the chartering of the Atlantic and Gulf. The conflict over the monopoly privilege of the Brunswick and Florida, sidestepped by the Savannah, Albany and Gulf in adopting the Florida route, was transferred to the Atlantic and Gulf. The Brunswick and Florida had finally consented to give up the monopoly privilege; but sought compensation for the considerable amount of grading it had done. It required eighteen months to adjust the issue. The eastern terminus of the Atlantic and Gulf was relocated farther west and the Brunswick and Florida received $75,000 in compensation; and the latter decided definitely to construct its main line as originally planned to Albany, and to build a branch to eastern Florida.[73] Thus a truce, at least, was achieved in the age-old struggle between Savannah and its neighbor port to the south. Both were to have access to the southwest, over their own lines as well as over the state road. Brunswick also was to secure a direct railroad to central Georgia and the northwest over the newly chartered Macon and Brunswick Railroad.

The popular demand for extension of the bases of state aid increased rather than abated after the chartering of the Atlantic and Gulf. Many supported a proposal to sell the Western and Atlantic and allocate the proceeds among the current railroad construction projects. This notion of using public investment as a long-term revolving fund, to be transferred repeatedly from fully developed to new projects, had deep roots in Georgia. It rested upon an accepted doctrine of the innovating role of public enterprise,[74] and had been practiced in town and city planning and development. It had become the established policy of the city of Savannah, which had withdrawn its investments from the Central of Georgia and its controlled lines in order to reinvest in the Savannah, Albany and Gulf and the Atlantic and Gulf.[75]

Individual projects that received especially strong backing for state aid were the Macon and Brunswick and the Georgia Air-Line. It was proposed that the state invest $1,000,000 in each.[76] The state-aid-for-all movement culminated in the Atlanta State-Aid Convention of August 10, 1859, which proposed that state bonds of a uniform amount per mile should be issued to all railroads under construction, for the purchase of railroad iron[77] — a system that had been adopted by neighboring Tennessee. The legislature was deluged with state-aid projects that fall, and Governor Brown gave the policy his approval; yet neither particular nor general aid measures mustered enough votes to pass. The reasons for the defeat seem to have been: the deep roots of the state's established policy; the opposition from the communities in which railroads had been developed; the recent establishment of an educational support program based largely upon the earnings of the Western and Atlantic Railroad; and, finally, the ominous outlook for relations between the North and the South.

12. Financial Summary of Railroad Construction

A financial summary of public and private railroad investments from 1833 to 1860, inclusive, is presented in Tables 15 [78] and 16.

Some additional public assistance was given in property. The commissioners of the Richmond Academy in Augusta and the city of Athens

Table 15

GEORGIA: PUBLIC INVESTMENT IN RAILROADS, 1835–1860

State:		
Western & Atlantic, 1836–1860,		
by appropriations	$4,495,652.44	
by earnings	1,635,857.20	
Milledgeville & Gordon, 1850,		
by stock	20,000.00	
Atlantic & Gulf, 1856–1857,		
by stock	1,000,000.00	
Total State	7,151,509.64	$7,151,509.64
Municipal:		
Savannah:		
Central of Georgia, 1835–1843,		
by stock	500,000.00	
by payment for original surveys	4,774.00	
Monroe Railroad, 1842, by stock	50,000.00	
Ocmulgee & Flint Rivers, 1842,		
endorsed bonds	5,000.00	
Waynesboro Railroad, 1848–1849,		
by stock	251,700.00	
Southwestern, 1849, by stock	150,000.00	
Muscogee Railroad, 1851–1853,		
by stock	100,000.00	
Savannah & Albany, 1852–1853,		
by stock	1,000,000.00	
by payment for original survey	11,019.94	
Montgomery & West Point, 1852–1854,		
by stock	130,700.00	
Atlantic & Gulf, 1856–1857,		
by stock	238,300.00	
Savannah, Albany & Gulf, 1859,		
endorsed bonds	300,000.00	
Total Savannah	2,741,493.94	
Augusta:		
Georgia Railroad, 1835–1839,		
by stock	200,000.00	
Macon & Warrenton, 1859,		
by stock	500,000.00	
Total Augusta	700,000.00	
Macon:		
Central of Georgia, 1835–1843,		
by stock	250,000.00	

Table 15 (Continued)

Monroe Railroad, 1835–1839,			
by stock		50,000.00	
Macon & Brunswick, 1859,			
by stock		200,000.00	
Macon & Warrenton, 1859,			
by stock		100,000.00	
Total Macon		600,000.00	
Columbus:			
Muscogee Railroad, 1848–1853,			
by stock		172,000.00	
by loan		75,000.00	
Mobile & Girard, 1851–1854,			
by stock		450,000.00	
Opelika Railroad, 1854,			
by stock		70,000.00	
La Grange Railroad, 1859,			
by stock		50,000.00	
Total Columbus		817,000.00	
Milledgeville:			
Milledgeville & Gordon, 1847,			
by stock		30,000.00	
Thomasville:			
Atlantic & Gulf, 1857, by stock		500,000.00	
Total Municipal			$5,388,493.94
County (all by stock subscription):			
Morgan	Georgia Railroad, 1834	5,300.00	
Habersham	Habersham Railroad, 1855	50,000.00	
Dougherty	Georgia & Florida, 1855	150,000.00	
Randolph	Southwestern, 1856	10,000.00	
Chatham	Southwestern, 1856	10,000.00	
Terrell	Southwestern, 1857	15,000.00	
Walker	Coosa & Chattooga, 1860	50,000.00	
Chattooga	Coosa & Chattooga, 1860	50,000.00	
Baldwin	Milledgeville Railroad, 1860	60,000.00	
Total County		$400,300.00	$ 400,300.00
Total Public Investment			$12,940,303.58

each conveyed ten acres of land to the Georgia Railroad for terminal uses. All of the cities donated freely of the services of public officials and public buildings to the railroad enterprises, especially in the developmental stages. The federal government remitted duties on railroad iron in the amount of $204,985.21.

Some public subscriptions were voted for projects that either lapsed or were not completed during this period. Columbus' early subscription of $200,000 to the Chattahoochee Railroad lapsed when the project was abandoned. Augusta subscribed $500,000 to the Savannah River Valley Railroad, and some of the money may have been paid in; but the road was given up after some work had been done. The City of Atlanta voted stock subscriptions of $300,000 each to the Georgia Air-Line and the Georgia Western railroad companies, but both projects lagged after the legislature failed to vote them state assistance.

The total investment in railroads in Georgia prior to the War between the States approximated $26,000,000 and was shared almost equally between public and private sources, if all reinvested earnings on lines, other than the Western and Atlantic, are counted as private investment. An attempt is made in Table 16 to provide an estimate of the breakdown

Table 16

GEORGIA RAILROADS: ESTIMATED PRIVATE INVESTMENT, 1833–1860

Individuals, banks, and institutions	
by stock subscription in cash	$ 3,150,000.00
by stock subscription in services and in kind	5,000,000.00
Railroad companies	
by earnings applied to construction	2,000,000.00
by stock subscription in other railroads	2,600,000.00
Total private investment	$12,750,000.00

of the private investment into its principal categories. The amount of investment by the railroad companies themselves was notably large, both in their own properties and in the stock of other railroads. The latter type of investment became very extensive after 1845, when the Central of Georgia and the Georgia railroads engaged in extending their systems and in competing for the freight traffic of northwestern Georgia and adjoining sections of Alabama and Tennessee. Some of the funds thus invested came from earnings, but a considerable portion was raised by stock increases and stock assessments and, indirectly, represented subscriptions by individuals and other shareholders. The estimates are based on numerous data taken from reports of all of the railroads, but they are admittedly rough and can claim only a substantial degree of accuracy. The object in presenting them is to afford a view of private sources that is comparable to that of public investment presented in Table 15.

13. Social Summary of Railroad Construction

Railroad construction in Georgia above all else was a coöperative achievement. It was the result of the combined efforts and resources of individuals, groups, corporations, and governments applied jointly, or, if separately, with common purposes. The conception of an integrated state system of railroads was the first product and the continuing basis of this multiform coöperative activity. No attempt will be made to assess the relative importance of any of the various public and private efforts. Taken as a whole, public and private investments were almost equal, but that does not express the true significance of either type of contribution to the common effort. Generally speaking, the state served as the vehicle for the promotion of the system as a whole, while the private investors and the cities and counties bore the responsibility for the planning and construction of the regional and local branches of the system. The state launched its investments in major trunk-lines that were designed both to promote the common pattern and to exploit the state's natural advantages within the evolving national system of rail transportation. But these investments represented as well the more developmental and hazardous aspects of railroad construction; the trunk lines traversed extensive undeveloped regions of recent land settlement and the benefits of interstate and inter-regional connections were still unknown. The local projects, on the other hand, usually were located in regions of established production and trade and stood to benefit also from their connections with the state-sponsored main-trunk lines.

Coöperation grew out of necessity, tradition, and established principles of social policy. The scale of the railroad construction effort required the use of every possible public and private resource. No single unit of government or group of capitalists possessed the funds or the means of raising the huge sums that were necessary. Furthermore, railroads by their very nature affected a number of communities, and hence almost inescapably took on the character of joint enterprises. The public meeting readily became the means for planning railroad projects and securing participation. Even in those cases like the Georgia and the Southwestern railroads, in which capital was so largely provided privately, promotion and construction were sustained through the quasi-public community meeting method.

The history of the construction of the Muscogee Railroad well illustrates the many-sidedness of the coöperative activities that built the Georgia railroads. Railroad connection with Columbus was one of the primary objectives in the original design of the state's Atlantic and Western system. After the failure of the early coöperative efforts between the city of Columbus and the state to construct the line, the citizens and the city of Columbus, a decade later, undertook the project. It was planned and organized through public meetings — as a matter of fact, public meetings continued to be held for discussion of the affairs and progress of the railroad throughout the period of construction. Columbus subscribed $150,000 initially to launch the project, an action which was considered absolutely necessary to insure its success. Private citizens subscribed some $130,000 in cash and over $100,000 in labor and kind. Numerous artisans in the city were reported to have subscribed to stock in skilled labor time. But the total of these contributions proved insufficient to build the line, and further public meetings failed to raise the necessary additional funds. However, at this juncture the Southwestern Railroad Company, with the financial assistance of the city of Savannah and the Central of Georgia Railroad, agreed to build the twenty-two miles at the eastern end. Still Columbus lacked enough funds to complete the balance of the road. But another public meeting secured the subscription of "155 hands for one-year's work" and thus, with some additional aid from the city, the Muscogee Railroad finally was completed. Similar methods were employed in the extension of the Southwestern Railroad to Albany, Fort Gaines, and Eufaula during the fifties. Not a railroad was built in Georgia prior to the Civil War without such coöperation in greater or lesser degree. Preëminent among all, in scale and persistence of coöperative effort, was the building of the Central of Georgia Railroad during the Great Depression.

The public utility nature of the railroad and the hesitancy on the part of private individuals to venture their capital in early railroad development were considered ample justification for the large role assigned to government in the coöperative undertaking. Such views commanded wide acceptance throughout the state,[79] yet the public role always remained a strategic rather than a diffused one. It was designed to avoid local and institutional interference and to induce a maximum of private effort, to promote active rather than merely passive private participation.[80] The state's policy secured a higher ratio of private participation than the average in Southern states and the virtual completion of the main rail network well in advance of similar progress with railroads elsewhere.[81] Another notable fact was the virtual absence of financial failures among the main projects.[82]

Historians in recent decades have been prone to emphasize the non-coöperative, narrow gauged, self-seeking motives and actions manifested in the course of historical events, and much evidence of such a nature can be and has been found in the past records in Georgia. The railroad construction period is no exception. The Western and Atlantic Railroad had its seamy side. It was always a political issue, and a violent one in later years. But the fact remains that it, and the system of transportation that it evoked, was an outstanding accomplishment of all of the people of the state in their joint capacities as public, quasi-public, and private citizens. The Western and Atlantic's record is a good one, whether in spite of or because of the fact that it was planned, constructed, and operated under the direction of the state's political leaders, and its contribution to the welfare of the state was immeasurable. There were continuous efforts to convert the railroad movement into a political grab-bag, yet the usual logrolling methods did not avail. Public-largess-for-all was defeated in the late 1850's in favor of a second planned experiment in system-building, the Atlantic and Gulf Railroad, patterned upon the conception of the general welfare as embodied in the earlier Atlantic and Western program.

CHAPTER XII

PUBLIC ACTION AND THE GROWTH OF CORPORATE ENTERPRISE

1. Antecedents of the Corporation in Georgia

The general origins of the modern business corporation lie largely outside the scope of this brief introductory survey.[1] We are concerned with a much narrower frontier of corporate background, namely with the ideas and institutions, in particular those of a public nature, that conditioned the introduction and early adaptation of the corporate form in a single, rather isolated, American community.

The early rudimentary notions of corporateness, such as developed in other colonies during the colonial period, were confined in Georgia almost entirely to the public sphere. The government's extensive administration of group enterprises, especially of the all-important land distribution, prevented the growth of any considerable amount of private associative effort; and the fewness of the population and its strictly agrarian occupation and the availability of water transportation further removed the necessity of private projects of a group character. The colony was first operated as a politico-benevolent corporation under the Trustees. The position of the Trust bore a distinct likeness to that of the Church in New England, and its activities within Georgia, carried on through Oglethorpe and other agents, exhibited many similarities to the New England communal activities.[2] The strong emphasis that was placed upon cooperation, community obligations, and group objectives unquestionably left a permanent impression upon the inhabitants in the older settled region; although, as a positive influence upon the growth of the corporation, the effect lay chiefly in the direction of public and quasi-public types of corporate organization. The public administrative board, introduced extensively under the royal governors and continued even more widely by the new state government, embodied the traditions of the earlier period and supplied the link with the later public and quasi-public corporations.

The complexion of settlement in Georgia had changed markedly by the beginning of the incorporation period. In addition to the old European settlements with their principal focus at Savannah, a prosperous community of New England puritans had grown up around Midway and the new port of Sunbury, and a new immigration, chiefly from North Carolina and Virginia, was pouring into middle Georgia at a steadily increasing rate. Differences in background and experience between these three major groups produced a diversity of views regarding the corporation that played a conspicuous part during its early history.

The Savannah colonization took place at a time — between 1732 and 1776 — of especial ill-repute for the corporation in Great Britain;[3] in fact, as already pointed out, the original Georgia colony was a direct product in no slight degree of this antipathy to the corporation and of its rising antithesis, the philosophy of free enterprise. Most of the Savannah leaders shared with Adam Smith the notion that the business corporation was an enemy of a freely competitive society. Their view received expression most forcefully and explicitly from James Jackson in his attack on the proposed charter of the First Bank of the United States in 1791 and in his campaign against the Yazoo land-company acts five years later. This view derived essentially from the legalistic concept of the corporation that had become so widely prevalent in Great Britain during the fifty years prior to the American Revolution, and which perceived the corporation to be a quasi-public body, created by government and endowed with various monopolistic privileges.[4] But it had become narrowed even further until, practically speaking, it would have excluded corporations from the field of private enterprise, limiting them to public bodies, over which the legislature exercised power at all times to alter or remove, or to private organizations of a non-business but public interest purpose such, for instance, as those engaged in benevolent or educational endeavors; incorporations for profit, according to such a narrowed view, presented a threat to a democratic society.

The New England Congregationalists probably were less antagonistic toward the business corporation than their Savannah neighbors, although there is not a great deal of evidence to substantiate the point, other than the fact that they did not take a prominent part in the Jacksonian campaign against corporations and big business. On the other hand, they were the leaders in the movements that introduced incorporation of educational and religious institutions. There seems to be every reason for assuming that their New England background conditioned them favorably toward the corporate form of property-holding for such institutions. A sense of "corporateness," for which the Church supplied the principal medium, continued to prevail among them as a group; although the Church played a lesser temporal role than was customary in New England. Georgia's land policy, for instance, prevented group holding and alienation of public lands, which was a chief feature of "corporate" action among similar theocratic groups in New England; hence the "conception of corporate action" was not given an opportunity to develop in such a form in Georgia.

From the newer communities of Augusta and middle Georgia came the earliest and most persistent support of what may be termed the business concept of the corporation. These new arrivals from the older American communities were imbued with the acquisitive, "business" spirit, that was soon to typify so widely American life. Land speculators among them were responsible in the main for the introduction of the western land company, that leading forerunner of the American business corporation. But this adulterine corporation was short-lived in Georgia. Popular reaction to the collusion of government and landed big business drove the land company permanently from the scene and probably destroyed whatever positive influence it may have had upon the promotion of the corporate form in the state. But upstate business leaders did not confine their interests for long to land companies — as a matter of fact, many had been opposed to them on the grounds of social policy. With the rapidly growing needs for financial credit and improved transportation, following the invention of the cotton gin, they became the first advocates of incorporated banking, internal improvement, and manufacturing companies. They were the first to perceive that such large-scale undertakings required more effective modes of organization than the familiar partnerships and loose voluntary associations.

Thus far we have dealt primarily with concepts and attitudes. What organized units, if any, were there that embodied at least some rudimentary elements of a corporate model? A search of the field of private enterprise reveals a paucity of such. The sole proprietorship predominated overwhelmingly in agriculture and trade, interspersed with occasional partnerships, chiefly in the latter, especially among wholesale firms. And though some of the group trading suggests a possible likeness to corporate activity, it was well suited to various partnership forms and at no time exhibited any tendency to develop into corporate undertaking. However, the mercantile firm is in one respect a parent of corporate enterprises, though scarcely their model: the splitting off of its auxiliary functions of banking, warehousing, and insuring created new enterprises that supplied a most fertile field of early incorporation.

It is rather in non-profit enterprises and in public administrative activities that we must look principally for early crude "models" and precursors of the corporation. There may be found two types of organization — the voluntary association and the public administrative board — that were distinctly forerunners of the corporation.

The non-profit voluntary association typically was a body of citizens joined together to contribute money or services regularly or occasionally for the promotion of some public, benevolent, or mutual purpose. Such groups were numerously prominent in poor relief, welfare, education, internal improvements, fire protection, military training, fraternal and social activities, and literary and scientific pursuits.[5] In the fields of welfare, education, fire protection, and internal improvements they often enjoyed certain quasi-official prerogatives and frequently carried on their work in conjunction with public administrative boards; in fact, the state often appealed to such groups for financial and other support of work assigned to the public units. In time, the voluntary association in such fields was largely supplanted by the corporation. Experience proved that voluntarism frequently needed a more effective vehicle than the loose association, especially if the group were large and its membership at all scattered and if the task entailed the use of any considerable property. Nor did the combination of voluntarism and the public administrative board work successfully in most instances.

Not all voluntary associations were of the non-business type. There were hotel and theater associations, for example, that were private businesses, though affected with an element of public interest. As a rule such associations eventually turned to the corporate form with a view to securing more efficient organization and more responsible administration. It was common practice also to organize business associations as a preliminary step to securing a charter of incorporation. Sometimes the intended stock was entirely subscribed and even partially paid in.[6] This latter type of association should not be considered a model, or forerunner, of the corporation; but, on account of the obscurity of records and frequent delays in securing charters, it is not always possible to distinguish it from the true business association.

The public administrative board, even if not always the obvious prototype of the corporation, was certainly its most frequent predecessor. The usual board of commissioners was an administrative unit created and elected by the legislature and given a mandate for carrying out a designated task or purpose. Its work might involve a single task or the performance of a continuing function, usually the latter. Public boards multiplied profusely under the broad role played by government in early community life. Their growth represented, however, two somewhat contradictory tendencies: on the one hand, the propensity of central political authority to expand its organization with the growth of the area of social action and, on the other, the emergence of a stage of decentralization of authority prior to the establishment of local political autonomy.

Tables 17 and 18 show how numerous were the public boards and how many different functions they performed. Prominent among colonial boards — not included in the tables — were those for laying out and regulating towns, supervising road construction, regulating the hire of

Table 17

PUBLIC BOARDS OF COMMISSIONERS AND INCORPORATIONS, BY SPECIAL ACTS, 1777–1860

	Public boards of commissioners						Incorporations											
							Public			Quasi-public				Private				
	Political	Economic	Educational	Welfare	Regulative	Religious	Political	Economic	Educational	Fire Protection	Military	Welfare	Educational[b]	Scientific[c]	Religious	Social[d]	Business	Business: Mixed
1777		8																
1778		6																
1779																		
1780	2																	
1781																		
1782																		
1783	3	19			1				3									
1784	3	6	1	1														
1785									1									
1786	2	3	1									1						
1787	5	3		1														
1788	2	1							3									
1789							1								3			
1790	3	3																
1791	5								1				1					
1792	5																	
1793	8	2	1	1												1		
1794	2		1						1							1		
1795	1					1												
1796	5	3	1		3				2						1			
1797	4	3	1		1				1									
1798	2	4					1											
1799	6	3			1	1							1				1	
1800	3	2			1								1					
1801	2	1	2										1		2		1	
1802	2	6	1	1			1					1				1		
1803	8		1												1			
1804	2	4	1	1			1	1						1	1			
1805	3	4				1	2						1				1	
1806	10	3	1				2								2			
1807	2	4	1			1	2		1									1
1808	3	2					4					1	1		2		1	
1809	4	2					3		2			1						
1810	6	3		1		1	2					1	1	1			4	2
1811	4	1			1		1								2			
1812	4	2					5									1	1	
1813	1		1															
1814	1	3					1											
1815	2	3		1			2		2				1	1			2	1
1816	4	1					3		3						1	1	1	
1817	2	4					2						1		1			1
1818	1	4					1		2	1			4		2		4	1

Table 17 (Continued)

	Political	Economic	Educational	Welfare	Regulative	Religious	Political	Economic	Educational	Fire Protection	Military	Welfare	Educational[b]	Scientific[c]	Religious	Social[d]	Business	Business: Mixed
1819	3	1					3		1	1		2	2	1			1	
1820	2	2	1				1		1				2	1	1		1	
1821	2	3					3	2	9			1	7				1	1
1822	4	2					2		5			1	2			1	1	3
1823	10	3					4	1	4			1	6					
1824	1	5					2		5	1		1	9		1	1		
1825	7	3	1	1			3	2	2				7		3		2	1
1826	3	10	6	1			2		1				15		4		1	2
1827	3	8	5	1					1				9		5	2	5	
1828	7	1	1				7	1	5	1		1	10		4		2	
1829	3	4					4	1	3	1		1	5		1			
1830	4	1	1				4					1	15		9	1	5	
1831	6	2	1			2	2		1	1		1	14		9	1	4	
1832	5	4					6		2			1	17		7		6	
1833	3	4			1		5		5				32		9	1	4	3
1834	7	2		1			6			1	2		22		13		10	1
1835		4	1				2				6	1	13		5		16	3
1836	7	10					2	1			3		39		18		16	3
1837	4	3					4		1		1	1	67	1	5	3	17	1
1838	6	6					8		3		6	1	46		15	2	17	1
1839	5	1					5			1	3		17	1	5		14	
1840	3	2					3	1					17		10		5	1
1841	1			1			2		1		7		10		17	1	8	
1842	2	3					2					1	18	1	23		7	
1843	1	1					3		2	1	4	1	11		26	1	3	
1844[a]																		
1845	1	1					2			2		2			2	2	8	2
1846[a]																		
1847	1						2			2	3	2	1		2	4	19	
1848[a]																		
1849[a]																		
1850	2	3	1				5	1		3	14		31	1	17	22	33	
1851[a]																		
1852	6	3					11		2	2	3	3	35		20	32	43	2
1853[a]																		
1854	14	5					27	2	3	6	6	5	22	1	31	3	74	3
1855[a]																		
1856	11	4					18	2	2	2	6	4	25		7	7	82	4
1857	6						8	1		4	1	2	9		2	7	30	
1858	1						4			1	4		2	2	4	6	7	
1859	13						20			2	28		11	2	9	5	34	
1860	6						8	4		2		1	12		12	2	17	
	282	214	32	12	9	7	224	20	81	35	97	40	573	14	314	109	509	37

[a] There were no meetings of the legislature. [b] Includes libraries and lyceums.

[c] Includes agricultural societies.

[d] Chiefly lodges, but the early mechanics' societies, certain beneficial societies, and the temperance societies of the mid-fifties are also included.

urban labor, emitting government paper, and operating the Public Loan Office. All of these were continued by the state government, which also created many new ones — for the disposal of confiscated property, the writing of marine insurance, the improvement of rivers, the construction and regulation of ferries and bridges, the marking of Indian land cessions, the settlement of political boundary disputes, the laying out of new counties, the distribution of land, and the establishment and supervision of schools, hospitals, markets, wharves, harbors, pilotages, public wells, lotteries, churches, and burying grounds. Such boards were related to the genesis of the corporation in two important respects: a number of them closely resembled public corporations in both functions and legal status, and in a large number of fields they were the direct predecessors of the corporation.

Table 18

PERCENTAGE DISTRIBUTION OF GEORGIA PUBLIC BOARDS OF COMMISSIONERS, 1777-1860

Type	Number	Per cent
Town development	242	43.5
Transportation	(163)	(29.4)
River improvement	85	15.3
Roads	61	11.0
Bridges	6	1.1
Canals	5	.9
Turnpike	4	.7
Railroad	2	.4
General: treaties, boundary lines, et cetera	40	7.2
Public land administration	(37)	(6.6)
Lotteries, selling, and renting	22	3.9
Confiscated property	15	2.7
Education	32	5.7
Welfare	12	2.1
Finance	9	1.6
Regulation	9	1.6
Religion	7	1.3
Public market	2	.4
Warehouse and levee	2	.4
Manufacture	1	.2
	556	100.00

A few prominent examples will indicate how closely some of the boards approached to being public corporations. The commissioners of the Public Loan Office operated under a law that amounted virtually to a charter for engaging in a public banking business: it ran for a term of years and enabled the commissioners to issue notes, to extend and renew loans, to accumulate a capital surplus, and to distribute net income for such public purposes as were designated by the legislature from time to time. The Board of Commissioners of Confiscated Property, one of the more important of the state-created agencies, carried on an extensive public business for almost half a century. It formulated its own rules of procedure, inventoried and evaluated the various parcels of confiscated property, adjusted claims, instituted suits, conducted sales, levied amercements, arranged payments, and rendered reports to the state. The State Insurance Office, established in 1777 and liquidated at the end of the war, might well be considered the first corporation created by the state of Georgia. It was established to supply marine insurance — when the vicissitudes of war had so greatly increased the shipping hazards and likewise had severed the connections with northern and foreign insurance firms — and was placed under the administration of an independent board of directors who operated it as a public insurance company, although paying premiums into and losses out of the public treasury.[7] Clearly it was a prototype of the later Central Bank and Western and Atlantic Railroad corporations, that likewise were organized and operated on state account. Another distinctly "corporate" board of this early period were the Commissioners of Louisville, created in 1786. This board of three members was authorized to sell the state house and lot in Savannah, to select and purchase a tract of land for the site of a new capital city and the University of Georgia, to plan and lay out the city, to sell lots, and to construct the public buildings of the state and the university. It was authorized to bargain and sell and to accept securities for payment in its own name and, upon receiving full payment, to issue titles in fee simple that should be fully binding in law.[8] Each commissioner was required to give bond and security to the governor of the state in the amount of £6,000 (approximately $26,500). When it was decided, in 1802, to move the state capital farther west, a second board with similar powers and functions was created to establish the city of Milledgeville.

The latter two boards were specialized variants of the ubiquitous town planning and regulating board, described in Chapter VIII, which commonly metamorphosed into the twin public corporations, the town government and the trustees of the county academy. These successor corporations divided the functions carried on previously by the single administrative board and possibly enjoyed a somewhat greater degree of autonomy, derived chiefly from a change in the mode of election. But basically they performed the same functions and in much the same manner as their predecessor, and were equally subject in law to the will of the legislature which at any time might change their structures and functions.[9] A similar direct change of status from board to corporation occurred in a number of other types of public boards. Thus the Board of

Commissioners for establishing an institution of higher learning, created in 1784, was incorporated a year later as the University of Georgia; a whole series of hospital and relief boards in Savannah eventually culminated in the incorporation of the Savannah Poor House and Hospital in 1808; and even occasional instances of a like transformation are to be found among religious institutions.

This close structural-chronological relationship between the public board and the corporation held no less typically in at least one field of private business entrepreneurship, namely that of internal improvements. The first business corporations in Georgia, the navigation companies, took over the task of river improvements around the turn of the century directly from the public administrative commissions. It was hopefully expected that this somewhat novel type of continuing group organization, with share capital, responsible administrative direction, and the opportunity for profit would succeed where public boards and voluntary associations had so generally failed and where the sole proprietorship and partnership — prevalent in ferry and bridge enterprises — were recognized to be inadequate. Actually the corporations achieved no better success than their predecessors and, in 1816–1817, spurred also by a rising public interest in waterways, the state returned to the public board system, supported by what was believed were adequate state appropriations. The new waterway enthusiasm blossomed into a genuine canal movement in the mid-twenties, which in turn led to the incorporation of a number of canal companies. The state also considered seriously the construction of a central canal on state account. The canal mania subsided shortly, however, and there was a return again to river improvements under public boards. The history of roadway improvements followed much the same pattern of alternate trials of public administrative boards and private business corporations. The meager product of the county road-board system, especially in major highways, led the state in the early twenties to transfer its hopes to incorporated turnpike companies;[10] but the complete failure of the latter induced recourse to a state-wide program of market-road construction at state expense under the joint direction of state commissioners and city councils. When both the road and waterway programs undertaken by the state produced disappointing results, they were largely scrapped in the early thirties for a railroad program organized under a number of local and regional mixed corporations and a single public corporation owned and operated by the state. With the advent of railroad construction, the business corporation entered upon the period of its most significant development, and public boards in internal improvements became relegated almost entirely to local levels or to very minor roles. When an attempt was made in the

CHART I Number of Public Boards of Commissioners, by Special Acts, 1777-1860

5-year weighted moving averages of annual data

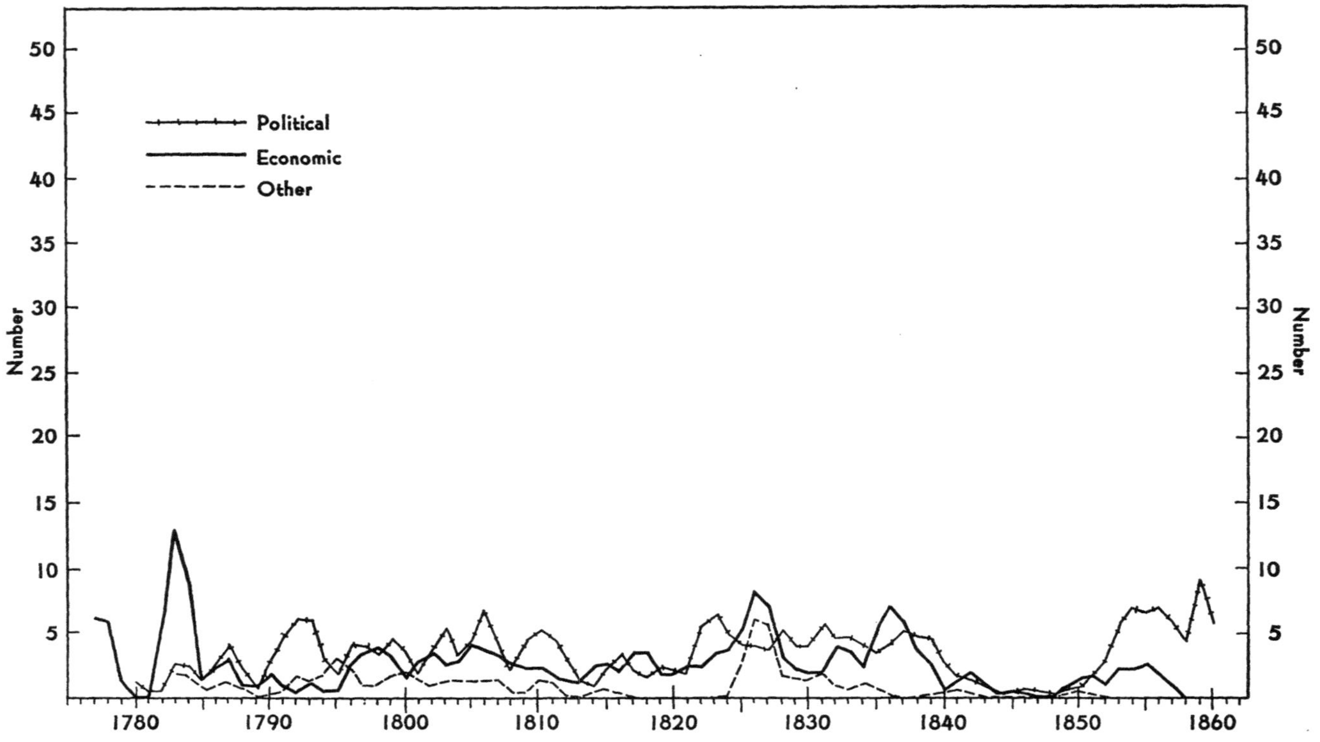

fifties to revive highway development, recourse was had to the incorporation of plank-road and turnpike companies.

Thus it is evident that the origins of the corporation in Georgia were closely linked to the wide exercise of public powers over common economic matters. With the Revolutionary War, public power became democratized and further decentralized, but it continued for some time to provide much of the substance of group activity. Gradually, however, there came an increase in the number and variety of quasi-autonomous groups within the broad gap that separates the state structurally as the unit of total group action from the individual as the single mathematical social unit, and the corporation emerged as an increasingly prominent one among such groups. The relative decline of the public administrative board with the rise of the corporation, as shown by Table 17, is indicative of these changes, as it is also of the close functional and chronological relationships between the two forms of administration.

The early growth of the corporation took place in the non-business spheres, especially in education and religion. Of the twenty-four charters granted prior to 1800, fourteen were to educational institutions, four to churches, and only one to a business group, and that just at the close of the century, on December 14, 1799. Business incorporations accounted for only twelve of the eighty-six charters that were granted by special acts prior to 1815. This relative situation was reversed completely, however, in the closing decades covered by this study, as may readily be observed from Chart II.

How much the numerous non-business corporations that preceded or accompanied the introduction of the business corporation influenced the progress of the latter is impossible to determine or even to conjecture very significantly. They served doubtless to implant the "concept of corporate action" widely in Georgia; but, on the other hand, they may easily have fortified the narrow legalistic doctrine of the "public nature" of the corporation and thus may have retarded its early widespread adoption in business enterprise. It must always be borne in mind, as well, that opportunities for large-scale business enterprise were not very numerous in Georgia even at a much later date, and that they were especially lacking in the early years after the proscription of land companies. The non-business corporation must be numbered among the antecedents and early "models" of the business corporation, but the character of its influence would be difficult to appraise satisfactorily.

2. The Corporate Pattern

Our attention will be directed henceforth almost entirely to the business corporation. Table 21 presents a breakdown chronologically of business corporations by principal industries; Table 22 indicates the nu-

Table 19

GEORGIA PUBLIC AND QUASI-PUBLIC INCORPORATIONS, BY SPECIAL ACTS, 1783–1860

Type	Number	Per cent
Education	(641)	(60.0)
Academies	528	49.4
Colleges	66	6.2
High Schools, free schools, and manual labor schools	47	4.4
Cities and towns	224	20.9
Military companies	97	9.0
Welfare, charity, et cetera	40	3.7
Fire companies	35	3.3
Transportation	18	1.7
Libraries	10	.9
Lyceums	3	.3
Finance	2	.2
	1,070	100.0

merical and percentage distributions for major classifications as well as for particular industries for the entire period as a whole; and Table 23 reproduces the chronological record of authorized capitalizations according to three size groups and for all corporations. The data contained in the last table also are represented graphically in Chart III. It may be observed that charters were confined largely to internal improvement, banking, and insurance companies prior to 1830, but that thereafter they became common to nearly all fields with the conspicuous exceptions of agriculture and trade. New incorporations, particularly in the public service industries, experienced a sharp decline during the worst years

Table 20

GEORGIA PRIVATE NON-BUSINESS INCORPORATIONS, BY SPECIAL ACTS, 1789–1860

Type	Number	Per cent
Churches and religious societies	314	71.9
Lodges	85	19.4
Scientific societies	14	3.2
Beneficial societies	12	2.7
Mechanics' societies	6	1.4
Temperance societies	6	1.4
	437	100.0

Table 21

GEORGIA BUSINESS INCORPORATIONS, BY SPECIAL ACTS, 1799–1860

	Navigation	Canal	Turnpike	Steamboat	Railroad	Plank Road	Other transportation	Public utilities	Banks	Insurance	Building and loan	Textile manufacturing	Other manufacturing	Mining	Lumbering	Miscellaneous
1779	1															
1800																
1801	1															
1802																
1803																
1804																
1805	1															
1806																
1807									1							
1808	1															
1809																
1810	3								2			1				
1811																
1812										1						
1813																
1814																
1815	1								1	1						
1816			1													
1817				1												
1818	1	1		1					1							1
1819								1								
1820															1	
1821			1							1						
1822			3							1						
1823																
1824																
1825		1							2							
1826		2							1							
1827					1				3				1			
1828									1							1
1829																
1830									2	1			1			1

Table 21 (Continued)

	Navigation	Canal	Turnpike	Steamboat	Railroad	Plank Road	Other transportation	Public utilities	Banks	Insurance	Building and loan	Textile manufacturing	Other manufacturing	Mining	Lumbering	Miscellaneous
1831					1				3							
1832												2	1	3		
1833					3							3				1
1834		1	4				1					2		2	1	
1835				3	4			2	4	2		1		3		
1836				4	3			1	7	3		1				
1837				2	4							1	4	2	2	3
1838	1			3	6		1			2					3	2
1839		1			2							3	8			
1840			2		1							2				1
1841			4							1			1			2
1842			3									1	1	1		1
1843			2						1							
1844[a]																
1845			1	1	3							3				2
1846[a]																
1847				1	12		1			4						1
1848[a]																
1849[a]																
1850		1	2	2	4	10		3	3			5				3
1851[a]																
1852	1		1	2	12	7	2	4	4		4	4	2			2
1853[a]																
1854				3	23	2	2	3	8		7	2	3	20	1	3
1855[a]																
1856		1	2	2	17	2	1	4	20		5	2	4	23		3
1857		3	2	2	6		1	3		5		1		7		
1858				1	1					1			2	2		
1859	1		1	1	11		1	2		5	3		2	6		1
1860			1	1	2			1		2	5			5		
	12	11	30	30	116	21	10	24	64	30	24	34	30	74	8	28

[a] No meeting of the legislature.

CHART II Number of Incorporations, by Special Acts, 1785-1860

5-year weighted moving averages of annual data

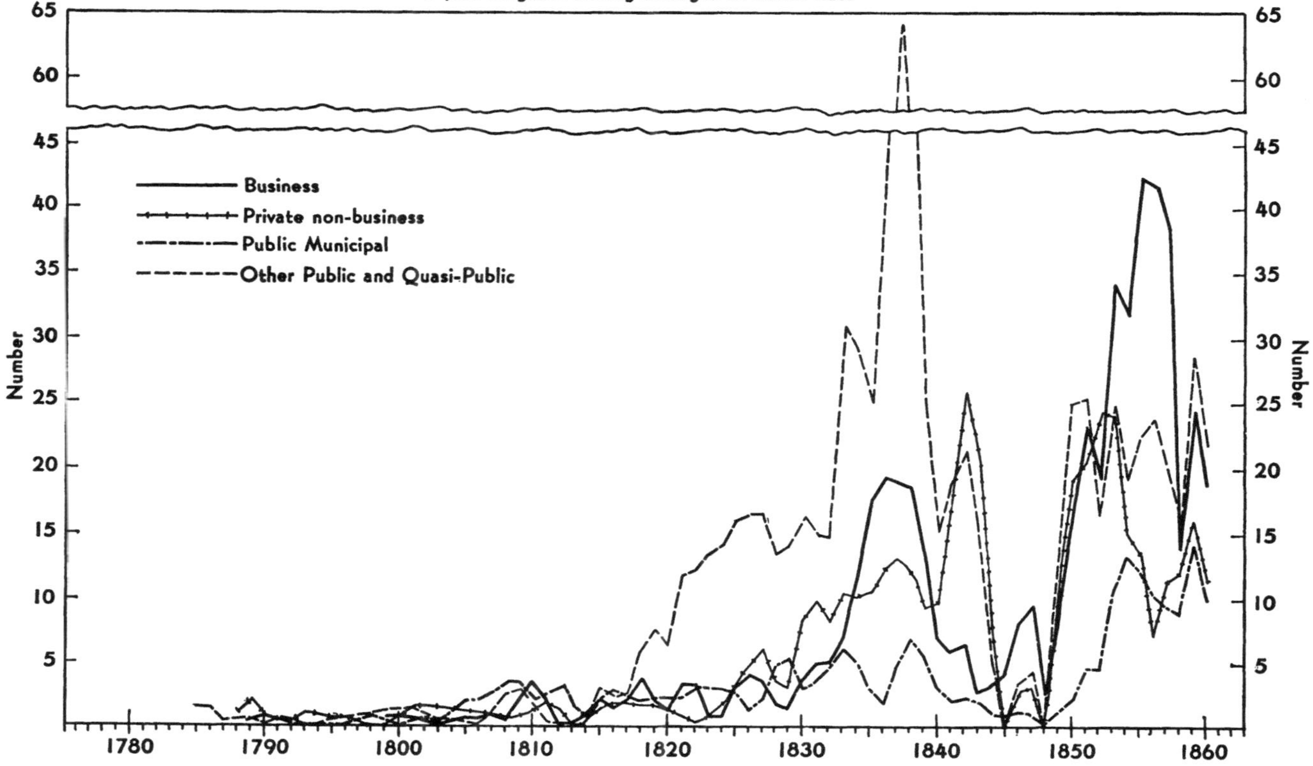

of the Great Depression, but revived more vigorously than ever in the late forties, with transportation companies again assuming the lead. The notable lag in new manufacturing and miscellaneous business charters likely resulted, in part at least, from use of the newly enacted general incorporation laws, which will be discussed later. Fragmentary data indicate that a number of companies secured charters in that manner.

Table 22

PERCENTAGE DISTRIBUTIONS OF GEORGIA BUSINESS INCORPORATIONS BY MAJOR CLASSES AND INDUSTRIES, 1799-1860

Type	Number	Per cent
Public utilities	(254)	(46.5)
Transportation	(230)	(42.0)
Railroad	116	21.1
Steamboat	30	5.5
Turnpike	30	5.5
Plank road	21	3.8
Navigation	12	2.2
Canal	11	2.0
Bridge	7	1.3
Miscellaneous	3	.6
Other	(24)	(4.5)
Telegraph	8	1.5
Gas	8	1.5
Water	5	.9
Miscellaneous	3	.6
Finance	(118)	(21.6)
Bank, commercial	57	10.4
Insurance	30	5.5
Building and loan	24	4.4
Bank, savings	7	1.3
Mining	74	13.5
Manufacturing	(64)	(11.7)
Textiles	34	6.2
Foundry and iron works	10	1.8
Machinery and metal work	4	.7
Ice	3	.6
Shipbuilding	1	.2
Mixed and miscellaneous	12	2.2
Lumber	8	1.5
Real estate	8	1.5
Hotel	6	1.1
Theater	2	.4
Trade	2	.4
Miscellaneous	10	1.8
	546	100.0

Table 23

AUTHORIZED CAPITALIZATION OF GEORGIA CORPORATION CHARTERS, 1799–1860

	Small		Medium		Large		Total	
	Number	Amount	Number	Amount	Number	Amount	Number	Amount
1799	1	$ 40,000					1	$ 40,000
1800								
1801	(1)						(1)	
1802								
1803								
1804								
1805	1	50,000					1	50,000
1806								
1807					1	$ 1,000,000	1	1,000,000
1808	1	50,000					1	50,000
1809								
1810	4	80,000	1	$ 300,000	1	1,000,000	6	1,380,000
1811								
1812			1	300,000			1	300,000
1813								
1814								
1815	1	10,000	1	400,000	1	1,500,000	3	1,910,000
1816	1	6,000					1	6,000
1817			1	200,000			1	200,000
1818	(1)		2(1)	800,000	1	1,000,000	3(2)	1,800,000
1819			(1)				(1)	
1820	(1)						(1)	
1821			2	800,000			2	800,000
1822			4	1,220,000			4	1,220,000
1823								
1824								
1825			2	400,000	1	2,000,000	3	2,400,000
1826			3	1,600,000			3	1,600,000
1827	(1)		3	1,200,000			3(1)	1,200,000
1828	(1)		1	300,000			1(1)	300,000
1829								
1830	(2)		3	650,000			3(2)	650,000
1831			3	1,200,000	1	1,000,000	4	2,200,000
1832	3	100,000	3	400,000			6	500,000
1833	4	150,000	1	300,000	2	3,000,000	7	3,450,000
1834	(7)		4	1,450,000			4(7)	1,450,000
1835	1(1)	41,000	8(3)	2,300,000	5	8,000,000	14(4)	10,341,000
1836	(1)		11(1)	2,925,000	5(1)	5,500,000	16(3)	8,425,000
1837	2(6)	60,000	5	1,150,000	4	5,500,000	11(6)	6,710,000
1838	1(3)	50,000	9	2,420,000	4	6,700,000	14(3)	9,170,000
1839	3	180,000	10(1)	3,100,000			13(1)	3,280,000
1840	4(1)	100,000	1	500,000			5(1)	600,000
1841	4(2)	15,000	2	200,000			6(2)	215,000
1842	7	180,000					7	180,000
1843	2	26,000					2	26,000
1844[a]								
1845	2	35,000	3(2)	1,500,000	3	5,000,000	8(2)	6,535,000
1846[a]								
1847	1(1)	8,000	8(4)	3,350,000	5	8,000,000	14(5)	11,358,000
1848[a]								
1849[a]								
1850	4(3)	140,000	22(2)	5,200,000	2	2,000,000	28(5)	7,340,000
1851[a]								
1852	10(4)	384,150	14(8)	3,700,000	3(1)	3,000,000	27(13)	7,084,150
1853[a]								
1854	12(1)	307,000	35(6)	9,930,000	13(3)	19,800,000	60(10)	30,037,000
1855[a]								
1856	9(5)	305,000	48(10)	12,535,000	8(4)	17,500,000	65(19)	30,340,000
1857	3(3)	112,000	11(3)	2,050,000	7(1)	11,000,000	21(7)	13,162,000
1858	2(1)	95,000	3(1)	1,300,000			5(2)	1,395,000
1859	5	152,300	19(1)	5,900,000	4(2)	6,500,000	28(3)	12,552,300
1860	3	55,000	4(1)	1,350,000	6	8,000,000	13(1)	9,405,000
	91(46)	$2,731,450	248(45)	$70,930,000	77(12)	$117,000,000	416(103)	$190,661,450

[a] No meeting of the legislature.

( ) Numbers inclosed in parentheses represent corporate charters in which no figures for capital stock are given. Based upon the averages for which capitalizations are given, such would increase the total of small corporations to $4,112,190, of medium to $83,800,360, and large to $135,233,760, or the total of all corporations to $223,146,310. The above table does not include incorporated savings banks, building and loan and some of the mutual insurance companies.

General acceptance and continuous growth of the business corporation date from the middle of the first decade of the nineteenth century, as is shown clearly by Chart III. It may be somewhat surprising to observe that the long-run rate of growth of prospective capital investments in corporate enterprises remained almost constant from 1805 until the end of the ante-bellum period. The virtual absence of small corporations during the first three decades reflects the restriction of charters primarily to internal improvements, banking, and insurance, just as their significant appearance in the thirties and fifties indicates the spread of incorporation into other fields. The continued marked growth of medium and large corporations after 1830 represents the development of the railroads and the increasing multiplication of financial institutions. However, the high level attained by the medium-sized firms in the fifties resulted as well from the numerous mining ventures of those years and the growth in size of new enterprises in other non-public-service groups. It is noteworthy that the prospective investments in small corporations maintained approximately their mid-thirties' peak throughout the depression. Their sharp drop after 1843 and slow recovery further confirms the theory of extensive use of the general incorporation laws of 1843 and 1847. Even after allowing for considerable recourse to these general laws, which is not reflected in our tables, it may be concluded that the corporation remained predominantly a medium and large-scale enterprise throughout the period. Not only were the larger corporations three times more numerous, but their authorized capitalizations were proportionately even far greater. The medium-sized group had an average authorized capitalization of $250,000 and the large corporation, $1,500,000, whereas the small corporation averaged only $30,000. The small business enterprise in Georgia, omitting consideration of agriculture, was to be found typically in trade; and the mercantile firm continued to remain almost entirely outside the corporation orbit.

Although Georgia's adoption of the business corporation may have been somewhat tardy, it would appear that it had caught up with other states by 1850, if not before. It seems possible that the state had given the corporate form even wider acceptance than had some of its older neighbors. Comparison with Hartz's study of Pennsylvania shows a somewhat wider dispersion in Georgia than in the northern industrial state.[11] Concentration of corporations in transportation was less than two-thirds the ratio in Pennsylvania, in public utilities about the same, in banking and insurance about one-eighth greater (resulting possibly from the relatively large number of building and loan associations in Georgia), in manufacturing almost twice as great (three times if mining companies are included), and in the remaining business enterprises more than eight times as great. The total number of corporations was far greater in

CHART III Authorized Capital Stock of Georgia Business Incorporations, 1799-1860

5-year weighted moving averages of annual data

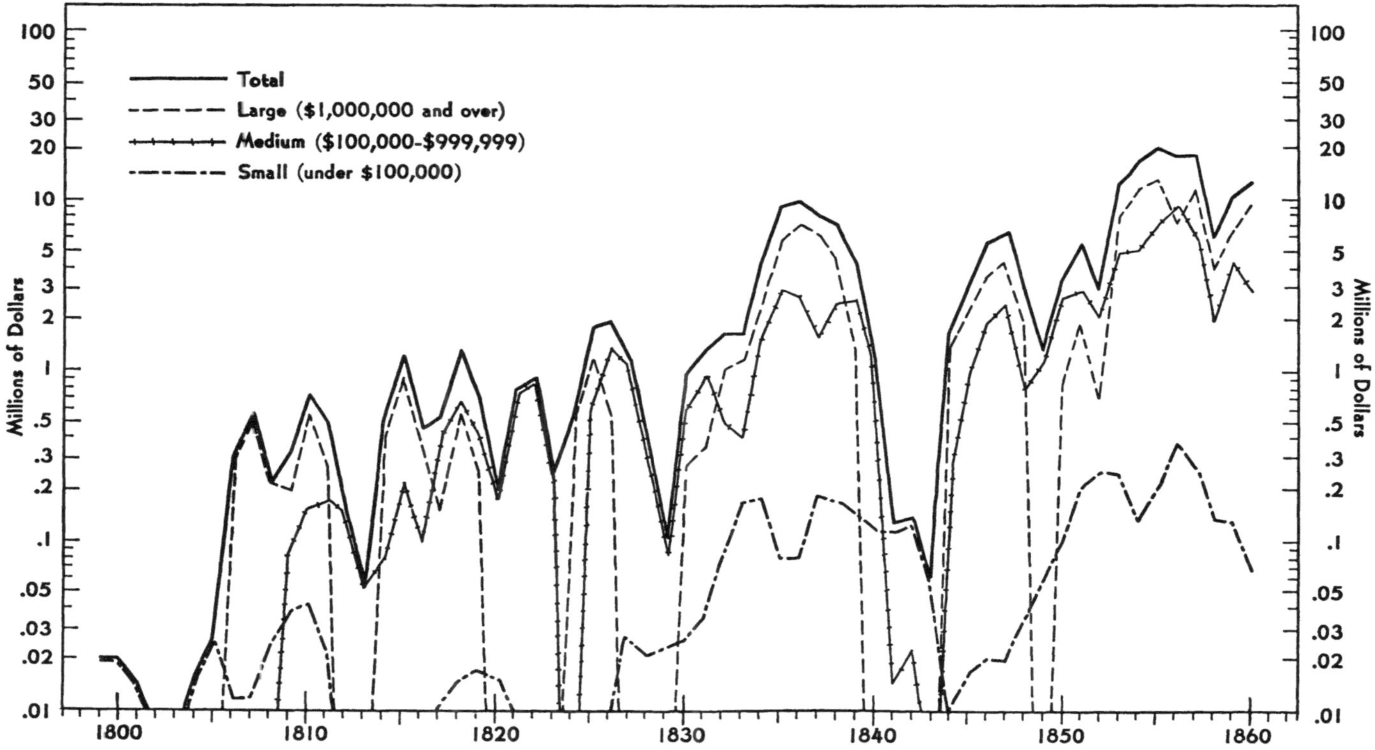

Pennsylvania, as might be expected in an older, wealthier, more populous, and far more highly industrialized state; but the wider distribution among types of enterprises in Georgia at least suggests a more general acceptance of the corporate form in the latter state.

A frequent test chosen by which to measure general acceptance, as well as increasing maturity, of the corporate form is the development of general incorporation laws. No such measure was adopted in Georgia until the decade of the forties, although several acts that were passed during the late thirties may be considered as anticipatory of such a law. The Limited Partnership Act of 1837, while not related to corporations, limited special partners' liability to amounts paid in by them, and thus indicated a trend toward statutory uniformity with respect to one of the common rules of corporate structure. Almost immediately following the Partnership Act, two general acts dealing with liability of corporate stockholders were passed in 1838 and 1841. Also, in 1838, the state adopted a free banking act which provided a uniform mode of forming banking associations.[12] Another general law, to facilitate the organization of joint-stock companies to engage in foreign trade, was passed in 1839.[13] The first general incorporation law was enacted in 1843. It empowered either a superior, or an inferior, court to charter churches, camp grounds, academies and schools, and manufacturing, trading, ice, theater, hotel, bridge, ferry, fire, and volunteer military companies. Under this act the organizers of any business corporation were required simply to file a statement of the nature of the organization and its purpose; shareholders were to be liable for contracts of the company as in partnerships; and the life of the company was to be limited to fourteen years, but might be renewed.[14] A somewhat more liberal act for the incorporation of manufacturing companies was passed in 1847. This required the filing with the clerk of a superior court of a declaration covering the general purpose, the specific kind of manufacture intended, the name of the company, and the amount of capital. The president of the company must make a statement under oath of the amount of capital actually paid in and employed to be published weekly for one month, only specie or notes of specie-paying banks could be considered as paid-in capital, and stockholders should incur unlimited liability only if the statement of the president were false. Maximum term of life was thirty years.[15] The last general law, passed in 1850, was a very liberal one covering macadamized, graded, and planked road companies, which permitted their incorporation by the inferior courts. The court was to be the sole judge of public convenience and necessity, and the companies were to be extended the right of eminent domain and the privilege of charging tolls, for which a minimum but no maximum schedule of tolls was set forth in the law. If return on capital should exceed 15 per cent, the inferior court might order a reduction in rates, but such reductions should not go below the legal minimum schedule. Liability was limited to the assets of the corporation.[16] The latter condition was more lenient than were the special act charters that were granted to most of the small railroad companies at this time. All of these general statutes, it will be noted, provided for the issue of charters by local authorities. None such providing for state issue was enacted prior to the Civil War.

Data are insufficient to estimate the number of corporations that were launched under these various general statutes. The decline of special charters in the covered groups during the forties has been cited already as evidence of a possible considerable number; and the relatively small number of charters issued by special acts during the fifties to manufacturing and road-building companies lends like evidence. The conclusion is also borne out by the surprising number of companies, among those chartered by special acts, that already held charters under the general acts, as well as by several instances that came before the legislature wherein local courts erroneously had granted charters to companies in fields outside the coverage of the general acts.[17] It is an interesting point that the courts held that in the case of a rechartering under a special act such an act did not constitute the creation of a new corporation, but that the special charter was rather in the nature of an amendment to the original one and that the provisions of the old charter were in full force insofar as they were not repugnant to any provisions of the special charter.[18]

Other significant developments in the evolution of the corporation in Georgia came largely within the following areas of corporate structure and policy: (1) the nature and amendability of the corporate charter, (2) the liability of stockholders and officers, (3) the transference of shares, and (4) the financial structure and consolidation.

The important questions of contract and property rights inherent in a corporate charter — involving the right of a state to modify such a charter, which was denied by the Dartmouth College decision in 1819 — were already litigious ones in the Southern states two decades prior to Marshall's famous decision.[19] Charters granted in Georgia around the turn of the century show that that state was fully cognizant of the questions at issue and was disposed to retain some measure of control over its incorporated companies. It had only recently annulled the statute creating the Yazoo land companies and was even then vigorously defending its sovereign right to repeal such contracts under the circumstances of the case. Gratuitous rights and privileges were among the alleged evils most often associated with corporations created by European monarchical governments and it was surmised that corporations all too often had been created in the image of the monarchs themselves; hence institutions with such absolute powers and immunities could have no place in a democratic society. It was inevitable, therefore, that charters should be scrutinized closely and that limiting and safeguarding provisions should be inserted in them. Retention of control over the acts of corporations was sought chiefly in three ways: by strict prescription of corporate behavior through the terms of the charter, with severe penalties including forfeiture of charter for noncompliance, by limiting the lives of charters to short periods, and by reserving to the legislature the right to alter or repeal a charter during its lifetime.

Bank charters furnished the leading example of strict prescription, and almost any charter violation subjected a bank to the possibility of forfeiture and liquidation by act of the legislature. Internal improvement and manufacturing companies were shown somewhat more leniency, although charters commonly specified forfeiture for failure to organize, begin operations, or complete construction within stated time limits. The state also exercised surprising restraint in the issue of charters and sought diligently to avoid having numbers of outstanding inactive ones. Exclusive privileges were hedged about with safeguards designed to protect the rights of other enterprises and the public.[20] Such restrictive charters not only served to deter corporations from actions that might have been inimical to public and private interests but also afforded the state, in the event of extreme abuse of privileges, an opportunity to revoke or secure an amendment to the charter of a corporation.

The limitation of the life of a charter to ten, fourteen, or twenty years, as was usual for several decades, was an effective way of retaining the power of frequent amendment. After the 1830's longer term charters became more common, although they seldom exceeded thirty years.

The insertion in charters of clauses reserving the legislative right of alteration or repeal occurred only occasionally prior to the decade of the fifties. The first charter of a business corporation, in 1799, contained such a clause, but it was not again until 1822, shortly after the Dartmouth College case and possibly reflecting Georgia's reaction to that decision, that the clause recurred in the charter of an insurance company.[21] Nine years later, the charter of the state's first railroad company contained the following proviso: "That nothing in this act shall be so construed, as to prevent the alteration or repeal of any part of the act, should any subsequent General Assembly deem such alteration or repeal expedient." [22]

Such provisions do not reappear, however, in any of the numerous charters of the following years prior to the Great Depression. The corporate failures of the ensuing business recession, particularly in banking, created a widespread demand for stricter interpretation of corporate obligations and a tightening of the rein upon corporations, their officers, and stockholders. Courts became highly critical of the irresponsible acts of some of the banks, although they did not question at the time the validity of the Dartmouth College principle of the sanctity of corporate charters. The principal effects, as reflected in new charters in the years following through the Panic of 1857, were an increase in the liabilities of stockholders and officers and the introduction of much greater uniformity. The latter development eliminated much of the possibility of favored treatment of individual corporations. A popular conviction began to develop in the fifties, however, that mere charter regulation was not sufficient to curb the anti-social practices of corporations, especially of the larger ones. This feeling was first engendered particularly by the growth in size and monopoly position of the leading railroad companies, and then was fanned into a popular storm by the bank suspension in 1857. Demands were made both for remedial legislation against the corporations and for state-sponsored competition. The movement was probably reflected and undoubtedly strengthened by Justice McDonald's supreme court opinion in 1857 in a prominent educational corporation case. While admitting the applicability of the Dartmouth College principle for charters of private corporations, he went on to observe "that a period may arrive when there shall be cause to regret that the Court (in the Dartmouth College Case) placed a construction on the constitutional powers of the States which restricts them from repealing or modifying acts of incorporation of any sort passed by them"; that corporations were entirely the creatures of the state and, while established for the purpose of promoting local interests, were affected also with a public interest; and that there could be no reason to assume that the legislature, chosen by the people, would act arbitrarily and in violation of the rights of private property, or would interfere in the activities of a corporation except when the public interest was jeopardized, and then only with ample provision for the security of private property which had been conveyed under the charter or had been accumulated by the corporation. The judge found sufficient evidence to support the latter views in the practice of the many states that recently, in granting charters, had been reserving "the power to alter or repeal them at pleasure, thus putting them on the same footing they were before the decision (Dartmouth College) of the Supreme Court"; such reserved powers had not been exercised, in any instance that had come to his attention, in a fashion detrimental to private interests; but whenever they had been employed, it had been done with caution "and in no instance except in cases where the misconduct of a corporation (had) made it necessary to the public safety." [23]

The popular judge's *obiter dictum* was a prophecy of things to come immediately in Georgia. During the three closing years of the decade, clauses similar to the following were included in ever-increasing numbers of charters: "That the General Assembly expressly reserve the power, to be exercised at any time within the period (life of the charter), when, in their opinion, the public good may require it, to alter, amend, or totally repeal this charter, and to recall and annul the said powers, privileges, immunities, and franchises."[24] A third of all charters granted in 1860 contained such provisos, extending to companies in manufacturing, mining, building and loan, and turnpike construction and operation. This movement in Georgia, which apparently was shared widely throughout the United States, sheds additional light on the character of the provocations to leading designers of the Fourteenth Amendment to the Constitution of the United States. Georgia's tactics may not have been the proper mode of restraining the growing young corporate giants that were inverting society's free enterprise sanctions and trampling down its defenses, but it was a recognition of the growing problem and an approach to it. But the effort was lost, not only in Georgia and the South but also throughout the country, in the controversy over slavery and the war that followed, and the gates were thrown open to almost unfettered aggrandizement of corporate power and privilege.

No other aspect of corporate evolution in Georgia exhibited as many or as frequent permutations as did the rule of shareholder liability. The state began with the acceptance of the present-day principle of limited liability, namely, that the corporation was liable for its debts, like natural persons, to the full amount of its assets, but that its shareholders were not liable additionally in their persons and property. No mention was made of stockholder liability in any charter prior to 1818. In that year additional personal liability was introduced into banking, in the charter of the Bank of Darien. This innovation was considered justifiable on the grounds of the special element of risk imposed upon the public generally by bank currency. Since banks were allowed to contract and circulate their debts as money, it was deemed expedient to increase the security behind their contractual obligations by making the shareholders proportionately liable in their persons and property to the amount of the capital stock that each held.[25] This principle of "double" liability was followed consistently in banking thereafter. It is an interesting fact that the chartering of the Bank of Darien, in which the state was the principal prospective stockholder, should have been the occasion of the introduction of the double liability rule.[26]

Some uneasiness appears to have arisen following the Depression of 1819 over the possibility, owing to some corporate failures, that the principle of shareholder liability might be extended to all corporations. An attempt was made in 1821 to legislate unlimited liability upon the stockholders of a proposed insurance company; but a year later a second charter was granted which specifically limited liability to the corporate assets of the company; and similar restricting clauses appeared in other corporate charters during the twenties. This was the first period in which limited liability was spelled out in the corporate charters.

A general abandonment of limited liability occurred, however, in the early thirties, caused by the widening range of requests for charters from private business promoters, the experience with corporate failures, the rising sentiment for more effective charter regulation, and the lack as yet of a clear understanding of the proper role and genuine advantage of the corporate form in business generally. Policy swung to the opposite extreme of imposing unlimited liability upon stockholders, as applied to members of a partnership. This rule was first introduced in 1832 in charters granted to two textile and three mining companies, and was included in many others during the years immediately following. Such a rule reduced the corporation to little more than a partnership venture with a fixed term of life and the right of an individual member to withdraw, through transference of stock, without disrupting the organization but not with escape from liability. The new railroad charters, however, preserved the rule of corporate-asset liability, as had been customary with previous internal improvement companies; except that where banking privileges were extended the rule of double liability for banking debts became applicable; but the railroad assets were exempted specifically from the banking obligations.

A recession from the extreme policy of unlimited liability began after 1834 with the increasing adoption of the *pro rata* rule. This rule did not fix *ipso facto* any upper limit to an individual shareholder's liability; it simply freed solvent shareholders from liability for the proportionate shares of insolvent ones. However, three mining charters, as early as 1835, fixed the upper limit of *pro rata* liability as the value of shares held; but whether this referred to par value, or to value actually paid in — an important point that came up later — was not specified. A similar provision was included in the general Joint-Stock Company Act of 1839. Yet numerous charters that were granted during the decade 1835–1845, and which carried the *pro rata* rule, fixed no maximum limits. Following the Great Depression, however, the *pro rata* rule with the limit of the amount of stock held became common features of charters in all fields. It was embodied in the general incorporation law of 1843 for manufacturing and miscellaneous enterprises. Meanwhile, unlimited liability, though making an occasional appearance still, definitely was being discarded from general use. On the other hand, the somewhat middle ground "double" liability principle, in what had become the generally accepted *pro rata* rule, did not immediately displace the rule of corporate-asset liability; in fact, the two principles prevailed about equally for a time. For some reason that is not clear, none of the numerous steamboat company charters carried double liability. Lacking adequate reports of legislative discussions, it is not possible to determine the bases upon which choices were made between the two policies. However, the double liability rule became almost universal after 1853. Every charter that was granted in 1859 included it.

The legislature also developed a second approach to the problem of limiting liability, namely, by placing legal limits upon the powers of corporations to contract debts. It was usual in bank charters to restrict total banking debts to three times capital stock; officers, including directors, were held liable individually and collectively for any excess of debts above such amount. Although creditors of early railroad companies had only the security of corporate assets, they derived additional protection from the rule, included in the railroad charters, that debts must not exceed one-half the paid-in capital. The same provision was included in three textile-manufacturing company charters in 1845, but with the important proviso that, should debts be allowed to exceed one-half the paid-in capital, the stockholders automatically should become liable without limit. The general incorporation act for manufacturing concerns, 1847, required a sworn statement of paid-in capital made in court and published for a period before commencement of operations, and a similar action upon any addition to capital. Any false statement subjected stockholders to unlimited liability; otherwise, the *pro rata* rule with a limit of double liability was to apply, debts must not exceed the amount of capital stock, and officers and agents should incur unlimited liability for any debts in excess of that amount. Such in general remained the rules applicable to manufacturing and miscellaneous corporations, whether chartered under general or special acts, during the remainder of the antebellum period.

Other important aspects of liability which passed through similar evolutionary processes were the questions relating to liability for unpaid balances of stock subscriptions, extent of liability after transference of stock, and legal procedure in the event of corporate insolvency. The question of unpaid subscription balances arose in some of the bank liquidation cases following the recession of 1839. The court ruled that such balances were collectible assets of a bankrupt corporation and that executions could be taken against the persons and properties of the stockholders for the same, even though the company had never called for them.[27] Thus, when a bank had called only 50 per cent of the stock payments, the stockholder's liability would be quadruple — not double — his actual investment. This rule is to be found incorporated in numerous charters of all types during the fifties. For instance, a frequent provision declared that a stockholder's liability should cease upon full payment of the capital stock which indicated that liability was limited to corporate assets, but that unpaid stock balances would be included among such assets in the eyes of the law.

The transferability of shares was considered one of the chief advantages of the corporation and was particularly emphasized in all of the early charters. But, with the introduction of additional, shareholder liability, the question soon arose as to whether transference terminated the shareholder's liability for debts incurred by the corporation. Judicial and legislative opinions inclined to the view that it did not, although it seemed reasonable to prescribe certain limits. To be sure, where charters prescribed unlimited liability the courts conceivably might hold that liability extended to all corporate acts performed throughout the life of the charters, regardless of time of transfer, since the charters stipulated that liability should conform to the rules in partnerships. The question of limitations actually involved three issues: the time at which corporate debts were contracted, the length of time after transfer that liability should continue, and what publicity should be given to the fact of transfer. The legislature first took cognizance of the problem in 1836 in a number of charters, in which it provided that a transfer of stock did not free the transferor from liability for any debts of the corporation, if bankruptcy occurred within six months from the date of such transfer. The issue led two years later to the first general law pertaining to business corporations, which released a transferor from liability after six months unless he received written notice from a creditor during the six-month period following transfer and provided notice of transfer was published monthly during such period in the two newspapers nearest the domicile of the corporation. If public notice were not given, a transferor could be held liable for the corporation's debts no matter when they were contracted.[28] It was not until the fifties that charters generally stated specifically that shareholders' liability was restricted to debts contracted during the time of stock-ownership.

The greatest measure of uncertainty and confusion arose probably over questions of procedure in liability cases. Suits were instituted variously against the corporation and its stockholders jointly and separately. Judgments were frequently sought in the first instance against an individual stockholder, who appeared most likely to be able to satisfy it. Consequently, a general statute, designed to remedy the situation, was passed in 1841, which outlined proper procedure as follows: a single public notice should serve as a legal notice of the institution of an action for debt against both the corporation and its stockholders; but action must first be taken against the property of the corporation; and only in case of insufficient corporate property should executions be had against individual stockholders for their ratable shares of the remaining debts and costs in proportion to stock that each held. The law did not cover all corporations but only those whose charters bound stockholders individually but ratably. It provided no, or insufficient, procedures and remedies in the numerous instances in which charters included no such clauses.[29] However, the above procedural requirements became an express feature in a large proportion of the charters that were granted after 1845.

Railroad bankruptcy presented some special problems of liability procedure: particularly, could creditors proceed individually against a railroad company and could executions be obtained against particular items of corporate property? The state supreme court ruled in the case of the Macon and Western Railroad in 1851 that the entire assets of a railroad company must be sold as a unit to satisfy its debts and that individual creditors might enter the case by filing notice of such intention with the court of competent jurisdiction.[30] This represented a long step forward in common carrier bankruptcy procedure and would appear to have established in Georgia essentially the rules of present day practice. However, the legislature failed to live up to this advanced position in a number of railroad charters which it granted during the fifties, in which it made permissible individual suits for particular parcels of corporate assets as well as suits against individual stockholders. In the main these were charters granted to small local companies, and hence may not have signified an intent to modify the court's rule with respect to major railroad companies.

In most matters pertaining to liability the decade of the fifties witnessed progress in the standardization and unifying of rules that strongly suggest considerable maturity of the corporate form. Liability cases became increasingly infrequent and legislative prescription followed a relatively stable pattern — which indicates that the corporate form had largely completed a cycle of adjustment to the prevailing principles and practices of property rights and business enterprise and at last had attained a distinct role of its own as a mode of business organization and practice. The period of the state's constant experimentation appeared to be drawing to a close.

The flexibility that had been introduced increasingly into the corporate form following the Great Depression further indicates the achievement of a substantial degree of maturity. The right to issue bonds, which had been granted to the railroads in the thirties, was extended to a number of manufacturing concerns in the fifties. No limitation had ever been placed specifically upon corporations regarding ownership of stock in other corporations and this practice became very general among major railroad companies after 1845. Beginning around 1850 a number of acts were passed permitting specific consolidations: by purchase through exchange of stock, by purchase of controlling stock interest, and by lease of lines. This policy resulted in the absorption by the principal roads of most of the local branch lines, or laterals, and also in extensive end-to-end combinations. Yet another prominent trend after 1845 was the granting of charters to multiple-purpose enterprises. These included companies for the combined manufacture of textile, iron, steel, and other metal products, and of flour and wood products, for the conduct of wholesale and retail trade in conjunction with manufacturing, and for mining, manufacturing, and fabricating of copper and other metals. An interesting charter granted in 1859 to the Georgia Internal Improvement Association permitted it to acquire and own extensive tracts of land, to engage in mining, manufacturing, and lumbering, and to lay off lots and build houses. This suggests a pattern for a company-owned community enterprise and may possibly have been the original such project in Georgia. A similar charter — which permitted the Cherokee Manufacturing Company to produce "fabrics of iron and steel, or other metal, or of wood, wool, cotton, grain, or other material or materials, and to vend the products thereof, and to buy and sell such commodities as may be necessary for carrying on their business" — also granted the privilege of owning lots and dwelling houses.[31]

3. Factors Affecting the Growth of Incorporation

The strongest motive of incorporation originally among the non-business groups that preceded the business corporation was the desire to establish firmly the group's ownership of property. Group activity other than of a public nature had been conspicuously lacking in the colony, and scarcely any practice or precedent of group property-holding other than in close partnerships had been developed. Property had been set aside by public authority for the use of the Established Church as well as for some of the dissenting groups; but there had been no growth of church property-holding, with powers of alienation. These had been confined largely to public boards. The property-owning status of groups bound together by religious ties, benevolent purposes, or loose associational bonds had not become very clearly established. Hence arose the desire for incorporation. The first three church charters, in 1789, state as the specific purpose of incorporation the establishment of the right of a group to own property as a church.[32] This was an even more compelling matter with educational institutions on account of their dependence for support largely upon grants and gifts of land. Hence possibly the chief contribution of the non-business corporation toward the general adoption of the corporate form was the firm establishment of the corporate property ownership principle and tradition.

Possibly the strongest continuing inducement to the use of the corporate form arose from the nature of the savings-investment structure in the South. Agriculture and trade supplied the normal channels and insatiable demands for investment. There were practically no investment institutions nor other means whereby the saver, who did not wish to employ some or all of his capital himself in agriculture or trade, could make an investment. Conversely, the organization of agriculture and trade did not lend itself to the assembling of the large sums of capital that were necessary for internal improvements, railroads, and similar enterprises. The corporation, with the device of transferable share capital, offered a convenient vehicle to the saver for investment in other enterprises than his own and also some assurance to the promoters of securing the required capital.[33]

A situation quite similar to the prevailing savings-investment structure existed with respect to administrative organization. The individual-enterprise forms that were prevalent in agriculture and trade were not adapted to large-scale operations nor to the type of group efforts that were necessary in other areas. Attempts to build turnpikes, canals, and railroads by individuals and partnerships either failed or were supplanted by corporate organizations.[34] Attempts to organize group efforts through some form of loose joint-stock or partnership association likewise almost invariably encountered management difficulties.[35] It was found that a more closely knit organization, with clearly defined rights and responsibilities and delegated powers of action, was required for successful and efficient operation. The corporation became recognized as such a type of business unit. For example, it afforded the small merchants and scattered planters of an interior community a means of pooling their small individual surplus capitals, of building a textile factory at a suitable water-power site, and of placing the responsibility of operations in the hand of a competent officer or manager. Such problems of achieving effective entrepreneurship were among the chief reasons that led to incorporation in all enterprises where the participants were fairly numerous, scattered, and engaged primarily in other occupations. They explain in large measure the incorporation of many manufacturing companies in the interior and of numerous hotel and public service enterprises throughout the state. They were the leading considerations in the incorporation of internal improvement companies and they made incorporation of the far-flung, coöperative railroad projects a necessity.

Considerable reference has been made already to the existence in Georgia of the anti-charter doctrine that was so widely current in America and in England at the time. What were its effects upon the growth of the corporation? The anti-charter doctrine flourished in Georgia during a period when economic factors other than the opportunities for land speculation created little need for undertakings that required the corporate form. It lost its dominant force sometime before the outbreak of the War of 1812 and, although it lived on among the poorer sections and groups, it never became the rallying force of any major group and seldom wielded a decisive influence. The expansion of the cotton belt and the rise of commercial cities fostered the "business" viewpoint and inclined men favorably toward any undertaking or form of business organization that promised to advance the primary interests of agriculture and trade. When the needs for improved transportation, banking, insurance, and manufacturing became apparent, the opposition to incorporated companies largely melted away. Navigation companies were chartered as early as similar enterprises in most states,[36] and, although banks came somewhat later, it was the hard-money attitude rather than the anti-charter sentiment that caused the delay, plus the fact that the Branch of the Bank of the United States in Savannah supplied the growing demand for currency during the first decade of the century. Interestingly enough, when banks were established, it was the large, branch-banking type of institution — the one most in disfavor with the anti-charter folk, who had feared the big financial corporation with its ramifying tentacles — that was adopted. Anti-charter sentiment, like the early anti-bank feeling, became transmuted into a regulatory mood, which demanded stricter charter control over corporations rather than their proscription. This attitude is evidenced in the concern about protection of the natural rights of property, contract, and traditional free enterprise, which largely motivated the extension of the rule of stockholder liability by the legislature and the courts. The views were expressed repeatedly that the corporation should not become a device to create special privilege and monopoly, to allow abuse of the rules of free enterprise, or to permit individuals to escape their "natural" obligations.[37] How much this attitude influenced the growth of corporations is difficult to estimate, but it seems likely that it played a considerable part in preventing the mushrooming of corporate charters, such as occurred in many other states. Anti-corporate sentiment was directed rather at particular corporations, such as the big city banks, the Steamboat Company, the Georgia Railroad and Banking Company, and the Central of Georgia Railroad and Banking Company, than at the corporate form as such. Every decade had its special target. Although the old anti-charter arguments were frequently employed, the attackers were inveighing in reality against the "big" businesses of their day, and were often to be found supporting incorporations that served their own interests.

The inherited notion — rather closely associated and sometimes confused with the anti-charter attitude — that incorporation was a public act and that it endowed an enterprise with a public purpose, long persisted in Georgia and unquestionably influenced the growth of the corporation.[38] There can be scarcely any doubt that such a notion was uncongenial to the introduction of the corporate form in the two dominant areas of agriculture and trade, the traditional preserves of private enterprise. This was particularly true with regard to trade, whose "laws" were recognized universally as the backbone of the system of contracts, property rights, and free enterprise. Trade was the bailiwick of "natural" man, so the "public nature" doctrine of the corporation must have constituted a strong presumption against incorporation in that extensive field of business enterprise. Other influences, however, such as the long tradition and practice of individual enterprise and the small-scale, personal nature of business organization in both agriculture and trade, were the primary deterrents to incorporation. Merchants showed no inclination to introduce the corporate form in their business, which would appear to indicate that they did not consider that it possessed any marked advantages in trade. I have been unable to find evidence that established merchants were opposed to mercantile corporations because of the fear of competition. But while the merchant *qua* trader remained an individualist, nevertheless he figured prominently among groups sponsoring and financing corporations in the expanding auxiliary and complementary operations of banking, insuring, warehousing, and transporting. This tends strongly to confirm Livermore's thesis that "side issue" investment was among the chief advantages of the corporate form.[39]

There is some indication after the Great Depression that merchants' attitude toward incorporation was changing. This is suggested by the Joint-Stock Company Act of 1839, and also by the chartering during the fifties, as a result of the "direct trade" movement, of a few large trading corporations to engage in commerce with foreign countries. But these still represented limited special areas and not in any sense the broad field of mercantile activity. It is also conceivable that the element of "public purpose" may have had a lingering influence in the chartering of the foreign trading companies.

Outside of agriculture and trade, the "public nature" doctrine decidedly advanced the growth of incorporation. There can be little doubt that the traditional association of public prerogative with money and transportation paved the way for the introduction of the corporate form in industries that presumed to perform these functions. The early charters of banking, insurance, internal improvement, and public utility companies uniformly emphasized the public interest in such enterprises and also clearly implied that incorporation was expected to greatly facilitate their establishment. Such indeed was the rationale of mixed corporations in internal improvements. So, also, incorporation was extended to mining and manufacturing projects because there was a "public concern" for their development and in order to encourage popular support. Grants of incorporation repeatedly suggested a definite element of "protective" inducement to home enterprise.[40] From 1808 until 1830 almost any new enterprise would have been welcomed as a matter of public interest. After 1830, increasing recognition of the corporation as a legitimate form of organization in industries of a purely private character led to a decline in emphasis upon the "public nature" doctrine.

Finally, there remains the question of what influence other public policies may have exerted, either directly or indirectly, upon the development of the corporation. Did the state's investments in bank and other corporate shares encourage or deter the growth of corporations in such enterprises? What were the effects of public land, internal improvement, banking, and fiscal policies?

The state's investment policy between 1810 and 1828 almost necessarily must have encouraged corporate growth. The recurrent treasury surpluses, the ever-present desire to find a substitute for taxes, the adoption of the policy of bank stock investment, and the establishment of the Educational and Internal Improvement Funds with the requirement that they be invested in bank or other "safe and profitable" corporate shares could not have supplied other than a constant invitation for new charter requests. Numerous bank projects proposing state subscriptions were organized during the second decade and several mixed turnpike corporations were chartered in the early twenties with provision for state subscriptions from the Internal Improvement Fund. If corporate development lagged behind its actual potentialities, the blame lay with the private promoters; for there can be little doubt concerning the state's willingness during this period to invest in almost any corporation that should engage in banking, internal improvements, or transportation. This policy came to an end, however, in 1828 with the establishment of the Central Bank of the State; and thereafter, with the exception of the stock of the Atlantic and Gulf Railroad in 1856, the state's investments were confined primarily to the time discounts of the Central Bank and the construction of the Western and Atlantic Railroad.

Whether the first phase of state investment in the four chartered banks tended to discourage additional bank charters is a question that cannot be answered with entire satisfaction. Protection of the state investment was mentioned frequently in official papers and discussions, but usually in connection with the operating policies of the banks and questions regarding their solvency. The most common criterion for new bank charters was the question of an increase in trade; but the state's investment no doubt encouraged a cautious attitude in weighing necessity in each case, and may have been in some measure responsible for the conservative bank charter policy. On the other hand, the growing enthusiasm for public investment in bank stocks following the War of 1812 unquestionably eased the way for the chartering of the Bank of the State and the Bank of Darien. That the state in each of these instances chose a single large bank with numerous branches instead of several small independent banks was due to the prevailing sentiment for a few large banks rather than many small ones. The big bank policy was supported on the grounds that it provided greater resources, stability, and currency uniformity. The state's investments may have been an added consideration, but it was not a major one. Later banking history confirms this conclusion, as well as the general one that state investment was not a major deterrent to the multiplication of bank charters. After 1828, when the state's investments in the older banks should have become a real consideration, charter policy actually tended to become freer and to slant increasingly in the direction of smaller and therefore more numerous banks. Of course, the small bank policy was an interior movement and the state had become equally interested through the Central Bank in providing long-term capital to the planters and farmers of the interior. Short-term commercial bank accommodation would have supplied a complementary rather than a competing service with the Central Bank's long-term credits. The state's interest in banking investments had become somewhat divided by the thirties. By the time that bank chartering was resumed in the fifties, the state's bank investments had become reduced to a nominal amount.

One of the primary objects of the public land policy after 1800 was to prevent the growth of large land companies. It is doubtful that a charter could have been obtained for a land company from a Georgia legislature prior to the late forties, owing to the deep-seated repugnance to such undertakings that had been created by the Yazoo affair. The several real estate companies that were chartered after 1845 were small urban enterprises which, in some cases at least, obligated themselves to make certain public improvements and to supply some public services.

It has been shown already that the early failures of the public programs in internal improvements led directly to the introduction of the business corporation, first, in river improvements around the turn of the century and in highway construction a couple of decades later. Substantial encouragement was given to these corporate ventures, including, in the case of the turnpike companies, the pledge of state subscription to stock. Their failures, which led to the substitution of a state-financed program, may be attributed to the weaknesses of large-scale private promotion at this time. Disappointments with mixed corporate efforts such as the turnpike projects doubtless influenced Governor Lumpkin strongly at a later date in urging state construction of the main stem of the state's proposed railroad system in preference to a universal policy of mixed corporations with state participation, such as were developed in Virginia and Tennessee. While the adoption of Lumpkin's policy prevented the state-wide multiplication of mixed railroad corporations, nevertheless the vigorous action of the state in launching the construction of a central trunk line contributed more than any other single factor to the successful development of corporate railroad enterprise throughout Georgia and thereby to early development of corporate enterprise generally in the state.

State banking policies, as distinguished from bank stock investments, may be credited in the main with favorable effects upon the development of the corporation. Although early opposition to banks may have held back their introduction at least for a decade, public policy thereafter sought to channel banking operations wholly into the chartered companies. Banking was accepted as necessary and advantageous and the charter was considered to provide a means of its proper regulation. Unchartered banking was frowned upon and many and various measures were adopted to stamp it out. The state's policies prior to the depression of 1837, of favoring large, strong banks with branches and of restricting banking capacity to the "needs of trade," placed a brake upon the multiplication of banking corporations, but on the other hand may have contributed to the development of the corporate form and procedure, in that the resulting general soundness of the banking institutions developed confidence in corporate organizations and the complexity of operations of the large banks tended to result in a greater elaboration of business functions in the charters than otherwise might have taken place.

There was nothing in taxation policies that could have discouraged incorporation. Taxes on bank stocks were levied first in 1813, but were not collected under the law because of its contest by the Bank of the United States. The law was reënacted for all other banks and houses of discount and deposit in 1817. The tax did not constitute any serious element of discrimination or double taxation, since banking capital was scarcely reached at all by the customary taxes on real and other property. A similar tax was placed upon the capital stock of the Steamboat Company in 1820 and for the same reasons. Very moderate special taxes of the general nature of franchise taxes were levied against railroad, express, and insurance companies at the end of the ante-bellum period, none of which could have had any influence upon corporate growth. On the other hand, the general failure of the tax system to reach intangibles other than through the stock taxes on one type of corporations must necessarily have encouraged investment in corporate shares. In any case taxation was not sufficiently heavy to constitute a major influence either one way or another upon corporate growth.

Viewing state policies as a whole, with the possible exception of land policy, it must be concluded that they either were a favorable or were not a deterrent influence upon the development of the corporation. Even land policy indirectly was a major factor in the growth of banks, internal improvements, steam shipping, and railroads. Also the wide distribution of land did much to strengthen the capitalist viewpoint and to develop a hospitable outlook toward efficient types of business organization.

4. Mixed Corporations[41]

The partnership of government and private citizens in corporate enterprise for profit, although widely advocated — particularly in internal improvements — and commonly permitted by charter, was not a frequent occurrence in Georgia prior to the railroad period. Furthermore, state participation in mixed corporate ventures was rather sharply separated from that of local governments. The state joined in relatively few enterprises which, with two exceptions, were confined to the pre-railroad era and chiefly to banking. Conversely, with a single exception, city and county participation was restricted entirely to the later period and to railroad enterprises. Local governments had engaged widely in joint undertakings previously, but these had been either of an unincorporated character such as road and river associations or — if incorporated — of an educational or welfare nature; none had been organized on a stock-ownership, profit basis. There were only three instances — a canal and two railroad companies — of common participation in mixed corporations by the state and local governments.[42]

The state's subscriptions to mixed corporations is summarized in Table 24. Since all city and county participation except Savannah's stock subscription of $7,000 (1826) and loan of $25,000 (1836) to the Savannah, Ogeechee and Altamaha Canal Company, is shown in Table 15, it will not be reproduced here. However, in order to have the general picture before us, it may be recalled that six cities subscribed a total of $5,400,000 to seventeen railroad companies between 1833 and 1861, and nine counties a total of $400,000 to six railroad companies, of which three were among the seventeen city-supported roads; hence a total of twenty mixed corporations resulted from local government participation. Practically every railroad company in the state that completed any line was a mixed corporation, and public subscription to railroad companies with two exceptions was restricted to local governments. The charters of these mixed corporations further indicate that, in nearly every case, the legislature considered some particular city (or county) to be the primary promoter.

Despite the larger number of counties involved, that unit of local government played a relatively minor role. Not being public corporations in the eyes of the law, but actually administrative divisions of the state, they could not subscribe to railroad companies without special provision by the legislature. This was accomplished for each county individually by transforming it into a corporation for the specific and sole purpose of making a designated subscription and holding temporarily the title to the stock. In no instance was a county given the general powers to purchase and own stock in the manner that was enjoyed by the municipal corporations. A county was required to take a popular vote on the question of subscription; if a majority was indicated in favor, it might make the subscription, but it must then levy a special tax for a given number of years to meet the payments on it; and, finally, it must exchange the acquired stock for the special tax receipts whenever holders presented them in proper amounts.[43] The county subscription in essence was a forced subscription to a railroad company's

Table 24

STATE SUBSCRIPTIONS TO MIXED CORPORATIONS

Date	Company	Amount
1812	Bank of Augusta	$ 100,000
1813	Planters' Bank of Savannah	80,000
1815	Bank of the State	500,000
1818	Bank of Darien	325,000
1819	Steamboat Company of Georgia	100,000
1825–29	Savannah, Ogeechee and Altamaha Canal Company	98,500
1836–38	Brunswick Canal Company	50,000
1850	Milledgeville and Gordon Railroad	20,000
1856	Atlantic and Gulf Railroad	1,000,000
	Total stock subscription	$2,273,500
1821	Loan to Unicoi Turnpike Company	3,000
	Total participation	$2,276,500

stock imposed upon all private property owners which was justified primarily upon the principle of increased value of adjacent property, as in cases of special assessments in cities.[44] This argument also was commonly advanced in support of city subscriptions and special taxes frequently were inaugurated for that purpose, but a municipal corporation usually possessed the power to pay subscriptions out of any surplus revenues or to have recourse to loans and to pay interest out of general revenues; furthermore, the stocks remained the property of the city corporation.

Public participation in corporate enterprise in Georgia was motivated principally by profit-seeking and promotional objectives, with some occasional admixture of other purposes. The state's sole motive in the investments in the four commercial banks and the Steamboat Company was profit-seeking. The desire to create a permanent source of revenues other than taxation lay behind the first three bank investments and the creation of the permanent Education and Internal Improvement Funds in 1817 required the governor to invest the principal sums in bank stocks or shares of "other safe and profitable corporations." The Education Fund was increased from $250,000 to $500,000 in 1821 and the whole amount was invested in bank stocks. At the same time it was decided to sell the lands that had been granted to the university and to create out of the proceeds a similar permanent fund for that institution. In fact, the demands of the state's various investment policies outran the opportunities for acquiring "safe and profitable" securities. They led to the investment in the Steamboat Company's stock and strongly influenced the decisions to make the loan to the Unicoi Turnpike Company and to subscribe to four other turnpike companies in 1821–22.

The turnpike subscriptions mark, rather weakly, the first appearance of the promotional motive. It would be more accurate to describe the intent as modest assistance joined with the hope of a return on the investment since it is difficult to discover any very strong promotional bent in the proposed purchase of 10 per cent of the capital stock of each company, contingent upon the payment of 90 per cent by private individuals. Even the term "aid" might be considered an overstatement. The loan to the Unicoi Company has even less suggestion of promotion. The company had been chartered in 1816 and had been promoted entirely by private interests; the state required first mortgage security of twice the value of its loan. In much the same category were the loan and stock subscriptions to the Savannah, Ogeechee and Altamaha Canal Company and the stock subscriptions to the Brunswick Canal Company.[45] The state was not the promoter of either of these canal projects, though neither could it have viewed very hopefully its investment in them from the profit angle. The state actually was doing what was frequently done in the South during the early stages of the internal improvement movement — it was extending aid to municipal and other local projects. It had not as yet assumed the role of primary promoter. When it did so it rejected the policy of mixed corporations at the state level for that of direct construction on state account.

Strong opposition to state participation in mixed corporations developed during the mid-twenties owing probably to the demise of the turnpike projects, the default of the Unicoi Company upon its debt, differences that arose between the state and the management of the Steamboat Company, and, in particular, the financial difficulties of the Darien Bank. Many felt that the gulf between state and private interests was too great for successful operation in partnership and that, where the public interest was imperative, it was better for the state to proceed on its own account. Following this line of policy the state first examined the feasibility of building a central canal, then reverted to direct appropriations for river improvements, and finally undertook the construction of market roads; it liquidated its investment in the Steamboat Company; and, in 1828, it established the Central Bank for the purpose of investing all surplus state funds in direct capital loans to individuals on a state-wide basis. The anti-mixed-corporation sentiment continued to dominate policy as the state turned to railroad promotion in the thirties. It undertook construction on state account of the main trunk of a contemplated state-wide system, leaving mixed corporate undertakings — for the balance of the system — to local communities and their city governments. There was substantial sentiment, nevertheless, for state participation in branch-line construction, and some concession in this direction was made in the provision, in the Western and Atlantic act, for contingent state subscriptions to certain contemplated bridge-line companies, in order to encourage early connections between the state railroad and the various city projects; but the state was never called upon to make any payments on the tentative subscriptions. The construction of the state road proved a sufficient inducement in itself to compel the building of the connecting links without any state assistance.

The Atlantic and Gulf Railroad afforded the single case of state participation in a mixed corporation in which promotion was clearly the primary motive. It was considered desirable to develop southern Georgia and connections with the southwest and the Gulf ports after the fashion in which the Atlantic and Western system had advanced the economy of the balance of the state and its connections with the northwest. The choice of a mixed corporation instead of construction on state account was probably a compromise with the growing faction that sought a program of state-wide subscription to new railroad corporations.

Control of business policy does not appear to have been a significant public motive in any of the mixed corporations in which the state became involved. Although the state was ever jealous of its right to proportional board representation, there is slight evidence that the attitudes of the public directors — whenever they were active — differed from those of the private ones. They did not report directly to the legislature where there were frequent complaints that the public directors gave little attention either to the affairs of the corporations or the public interest, and resolutions were passed from time to time requesting various public directors to take some particular steps with respect to corporation policy or practice. On the whole mixed corporations were operated as if they were entirely private.

Local governments' motives were predominantly promotional. Unlike the state, they enjoyed no surplus revenues, and so were not moved by the same investment reasons. Savannah, the outstanding public partner in mixed railroad corporations, followed the policy of revolving its investments: as soon as the earnings of a new line brought the value of its stock in the neighborhood of par, the city transferred its investment to a fresh project. Its policies, as well as those of most other cities, were always predominantly promotional. Conceivably Augusta's subscription to the Georgia Railroad was partially dictated by the desire to protect local interests, as was reflected in the conditions attached to the subscription; and Macon at times appeared motivated by like considerations.[46] One of Columbus' chief objects was to prevent other cities from building roads over routes that might drain away the city's prized wagon trade. County aims were entirely promotional; in fact, they were almost necessarily so, since the legislature practically limited their role to that function.

The cities, even to a less extent than the state, sought to guide the affairs of their mixed corporations, once the railroads were built and operations were fully established. They often found themselves with little or no representation on the board of directors, since charters did not assure cities a proportionate number of directors, as was customary in cases of state subscriptions. Hence cities could be outvoted on the election of directors by the private shareholders, unless they held a majority of the shares, and even in cases of the latter they did not always possess elective control, as will be shown in a later paragraph.

In conclusion may be noted some of the effects of the development of mixed corporations upon corporate structure. Several early variants in capital structure were related directly to state participation. In 1819 the state subscribed for one thousand shares of the Steamboat Company of Georgia and subsequently, upon call, paid in $60,000. In 1820, when the company encountered difficulty in raising additional funds from private sources owing to the depression, the state agreed to pay in the balance of $40,000 of its subscription on condition that the company guarantee annual payment of 8 per cent upon the entire $100,000 of state-owned stock and agree additionally to the state's participation in any distribution of earnings in excess of 8 per cent.[47] This action was tantamount to a conversion of the state's shares into a special issue of cumulative and participating preferred stock. It was duplicated later in the state's subscription to the Milledgeville and Gordon Railroad.[48] Corporate notes and bonds likewise had their origins in public action. Thus the state loan to the Unicoi Turnpike Company in 1821 was the first instance in Georgia of a corporate mortgage loan; actually it should be classed as a note. Another, to the Savannah, Ogeechee and Altamaha Canal Company in 1826, later was converted into capital stock. The city of Savannah likewise made a loan to the latter company and was the effective agency in several railroad bond issues. Its stock subscription to the Monroe Railroad in 1842 strengthened that company's financial position sufficiently to enable it shortly thereafter to float a bond issue; its endorsement of a small issue of bonds of the Ocmulgee and Flint Rivers Railroad Company in the same year marked the first appearance of that type of corporate security in Georgia; and its endorsement of $300,000 of bonds of the Savannah, Albany and Gulf Railroad in 1859 originated the largest such issue of the period. Thus it appears that the beginnings of differentiation of corporate security structure came from public participation in corporate financing. However, differentiation did not progress as far in Georgia as in some other Southern states, where the policy of universal state participation in internal improvements and railroad construction resulted in a great multiplication of mixed corporations and in innumerable issues of preferred stocks, endorsed bonds, and loans of public bonds.[49] The typical corporate capital structure in Georgia remained a relatively simple one, composed in the great majority of cases only of common stock. This resulted from the state's careful charter policy, its vigorous leadership in the promotion of an integrated railroad system, the extensive payment of railroad subscriptions in kind, as well as from the state's forbearance from mixed-corporate partnerships.

The other important changes that grew out of public participation relate chiefly to voting powers and control. Voting rights, under all of the early charters, were apportioned according to shares, but in a declining ratio with size of individual holding, and ceased entirely beyond a not very large stipulated number of shares, which gave small stockholders a highly preferred position. The state's insistence upon its right to elect public bank directors on a strictly proportional basis in effect broke this rule. By the time of the first railroad charters, voting in proportion to shares owned had become general. An apparently opposite result of public participation occurred at a much later date involving Savannah's subscription to the Savannah, Albany and Gulf Railroad. Originally the charter had provided for proportional voting but, as an inducement to encourage private subscriptions, apparently, the charter was amended in 1859 to reintroduce the rule of small shareholder voting preference with a maximum limit of 120 votes to any stockholder, including the city of Savannah, which owned 80 per cent of the stock. The concession failed to secure additional private subscriptions and the city was forced to commit itself still further by an endorsement of the company's bonds in the amount of $300,000. Nevertheless, a small minority of private stockholders was able to wrest control entirely away from the city. This is a rather curious instance in which the very large element of public participation led to the concentration of control in the hands of a small minority group of private stockholders. To all intents and purposes the amendment secured by the private stockholders transferred the city's huge block of shares into non-voting common stock.[50]

5. Summary

On the whole the corporation developed under reasonably favoring circumstances in Georgia. While the agrarian-commercial economy tended to preclude corporate growth in the two major activities — agriculture and trade — it almost equally encouraged it in other enterprises. Public policy, while discouraging corporate landholdings, was congenial in most other respects to corporate development. The state was predominantly "business-minded." The long reign of the Whigs during the formative period of the first three decades of the nineteenth century and the presence of a strong moderate faction among the Democrats afforded a climate of opinion that was sympathetic to the development of efficient business organization and practice. Corporation baiting, though not entirely absent, was restricted to minor political leaders. The traditional conception of the corporation as a quasi-public instrumentality was deeply rooted in both popular and legal thinking in early Georgia, and tended, especially prior to the 1830's, to restrict incorporation to the broad class of public-service industries and to such other enterprises whose encouragement was deemed in the "public interest." While this viewpoint may have circumscribed somewhat the area of corporate expansion, on the other hand it opened up to incorporation the chief fields — banking, insurance, internal improvements, transportation, public utilities, and even manufacturing — that were most required for the further development of the agrarian-commercial system. Nor was it ever too difficult to find a "public interest" in yet other enterprises whenever the occasion arose. Thus the public nature concept actually facilitated rather than impeded the early introduction and growth of the corporation. During the early thirties the doctrine may have retarded somewhat extension of incorporation to "private" industries, with the tendencies to enforce partnership status upon incorporators in such enterprises. The corporation passed through a transitional period from 1830 to 1850, out of which it emerged as an independent business form, clearly distinguished from public institutions on the one hand and from the traditional private proprietorships on the other. The view had become accepted that the corporation was simply another type of business unit that possessed peculiar advantages in the modern world for certain business purposes. The success of the railroad was a prominent factor in two respects in bringing this about: it proved the efficiency of the corporate form and it embodied within itself a shift in a leading industry away from public and quasi-public toward private status. Both legislative and judicial bodies avoided rather scrupulously all notions of endowing the corporation with natural personality. As corporate law developed, it distinguished rather sharply the rights and obligations of stockholders and officers in their corporate capacity from their personal, or natural, rights and obligations as individual members of the group. The generalization of the rule of "double" liability is a prominent evidence of this distinction. Incorporated companies stressed increasingly over the years the contractual nature of their charters. Following some difficulties with railroad companies over exclusive privileges and exemptions, and with banks over the stoppage of specie payments in 1857, there developed a considerable new anti-corporation movement under the leadership of Governor Brown, which had as its objectives rigorous enforcement of charter regulations, stricter charter limitations, and general regulatory laws. This movement anticipated the later nation-wide granger and anti-trust movements and indicated that Georgia already was experiencing some of the problems of industrial growth and concentration that became associated at a later date generally with the growth of the corporation. Its force was dissipated, however, in the face of the storm of sectional conflict.

CHAPTER XIII

THE STATE AND HUMAN RESOURCES

1. Background

"Work in its best sense, the healthy energetic use of faculties, is the aim of life, is life itself." [1] The words of the eminent British economist, Alfred Marshall, might be interpreted as ascribing a third dimension to the human resource, which is customarily defined in proportions of quantity and skill. These identify all labor with the ends of human activity.

Practical men in the past have considered labor chiefly in its quantitative aspect. Mere population — in particular, the mass of the "able-bodied poor" — has often been accounted a measure of national wealth. The early economists challenged such crude notions, but too often in dealing with labor they too relied upon the quantitative concept. They were cognizant of the importance of qualitative differences, but the latter gave them difficulty in their value theories and usually they abstracted from such inconveniences and then omitted to make adequate allowance for the partial character of their theoretic results. It is only recently, relatively speaking, that economists have begun to recognize that human labor is more than mere numbers and skills, that it is a multiplicity of motives as well, arising out of the personality and environment of the individual laborer.[2] Marshall in particular has assigned a high role to education in shaping this total character of the laborer.[3]

Modern educational policies began to take definite shape in the eighteenth century according to three general patterns. In Great Britain educational policy emerged from a combination of medieval tradition, the new science, puritan benevolence, and *laissez faire* as a program of voluntaryism, in which the state was assigned a minor, if any, part. In France around the middle of the century, and in Germany still later, the outlines of a system to be supported and administered by the state emanated from the Enlightenment and the reaction to parochial education, was fostered by the Revolution, and was firmly established by the Code Napoleon in 1808. Finally, in the last quarter of the century, in America the notion of public-supported education began to take root as an outgrowth of the American Revolution, the new democratic institutions, the relative absence of social stratification, and limitless economic opportunities. The English policy rested upon a theory of education by assimilation from the top, supplemented by benevolence at the bottom; the French and, still more so the German, upon the aim of national unification; and the American upon the philosophy of public coöperation in providing the bases of enlightened political and economic action by the individual citizen.[4]

The British system requires some further elaboration in certain pertinent aspects, since it was an important part of the background of the struggle in Georgia between the principles of voluntaryism and state support. Puritan benevolence — the leading factor in the settlement of Georgia — contributed to British education both a fundamental idea and a prominent institution. The idea was that education could serve as an instrument for training productive labor and the institution was the charity school, in which such education was to be provided free to the children of "the indigent poor." [5] What was considered necessary training was most elementary and general, being divided between virtue and reading, writing, and simple tools of arithmetic. Religious indoctrination received a preponderant emphasis.[6] Secondary and higher education remained almost entirely for the children of those who desired it and who could afford the cost. The charity school was not designed to provide a broad base of universal education. Primary schools in general remained private and instruction optional in quality and amount.

The charity school movement introduced a dualism into the British educational system, that continued to prevail well into the nineteenth century: private schools for those who could afford to pay tuition, and charity schools for those who could not.[7] Both drew their support primarily from voluntary private action. Opposition to state support or direction was almost universal; at most, only public "aid" was considered admissible.[8]

As the colonial labor policies have been described in detail,[9] only their principal features need be recalled. The Trustees' labor policy was broadly gauged for the times and was highly idealistic. It emphasized qualitative as well as quantitative considerations: colonists were to be selected as far as possible on the bases of occupational skills and all possible opportunities for employment in Georgia; and provision was made also for the development of industries and industrial training in the colony, in order to secure maximum utilization of both labor power and natural resources. Consideration even of the cultural dimension was implied in the anticipation that free land and new opportunity would encourage self-development among the colonists. Possibly the Trustees in the latter respect placed too much faith in economic determination. They were dealing primarily with selected adults and hence seem to have undervalued the importance of the education of children and the future human resource supply. Insofar as they developed any educational program it conformed to the English pattern: preachers and catechists were sent over to give religious instruction and a charity, or orphans', school was established at Bethesda near Savannah. Further instruction was left to the initiative of private individuals or groups.

Despite the deficiency in educational policy, labor policy constituted the heart of the Trustees' scheme of colonization; consequently, the admission of slavery, near the close of the Trust period, represented the collapse of their entire strategy as well as the end of their labor policy. However, slavery was the cornerstone of labor policy of the Crown government that followed, and its labor policy was the heart of its colonization policy. Georgia was to become a highly specialized unit of commercial agriculture — a replica of the West Indies sugar islands and South Carolina — in which land was to be distributed in proportion to numbers of slaves owned. Under the royal governors, Georgia became the latest model, so to speak, of the staple system on the mainland of North America. As the planters prospered, the British educational system took a firmer hold. Religious education came more generally under the Established Church, the Orphans' School was expanded, and numerous private schools for the instruction of the more privileged children sprang up in Savannah, Sunbury, and Augusta.[10] Some of the wealthier parents sent their children to England for secondary and higher education and others sent them to Northern schools and colleges.

2. The Educational Policy of the New State

If the Constitution of 1777 may be taken as an indicative expression, the revolution in educational ideas in Georgia was no less complete than was the political revolution it accompanied. Article LIV of the Constitution reads: "Schools shall be erected in each county, and supported at the general expense of the state, as the legislature shall hereafter point out and direct." [11] Initial legislative action in conformity thereto was taken in 1780, while the British still occupied much of the state: it reserved a lot on Broad Street in Augusta "for houses of public simenaries (sic) and schools." Augusta soon became a bitterly contested battleground between the military forces; yet the idea of a school was not numbered among its casualties, for, upon the termination of war, the new state concerned itself at once with education. An act of 1783 not only revived the provision for a school at Augusta but also projected the general outline for a state-supported school system. The Augusta Academy was chartered and made the residual beneficiary of all public lots in Augusta; the Waynesboro Academy was likewise chartered and granted 2,000 acres of land;

provision was made for a free school at Washington, which was to be granted 1,000 acres of land; and the governor was empowered to make additional grants of 1,000 acres to any person or persons, authorized by any of the counties, for the purpose of erecting free schools similar to the one proposed at Washington. A year later the Assembly named a board of trustees and authorized a grant of 40,000 acres for a state college.

The culmination of this early educational movement came in 1785, when a plan for a state-wide system was adopted. The preamble of the creating act reveals its philosophy: "As it is the distinguishing happiness of free governments, that civil order should be the result of choice, not necessity, and the common wishes of the people become the laws of the land, their public prosperity and even existence, very much depends upon suitably forming the minds and morals of their citizens." Such an object cannot be accomplished by "laws and punishments," but "only by religion and education." The act then went on to require specifically that all previous laws providing for free schools, academies, and an institution of higher learning, and allotting land from the public domain, should be "comprehended and made the basis of one general and complete establishment." It chartered the University of Georgia, with a self-perpetuating board of trustees to administer its affairs, and created the Senatus Academicus, to be composed of the University Board of Trustees and an *ex officio* Board of Visitors comprising the chief officers of the state government, which was to determine the policy and to have general supervision of all units of the system. The Senatus Academicus was required to gather information on all schools of the state and, upon the basis of such information, to determine the needs for additional schools of various types, as contemplated by the constitution, to prescribe courses of instruction, and to examine and recommend staff personnel of the various units. The president and members of the faculty of the university likewise were required to visit all schools annually; and all schools instituted or supported by the state were declared to be a part of the University and subject to all the provisions of the act.[12]

The adoption of such a state-supported and state-directed system of universal education was unprecedented, except for the abstract principles of such philosophers as Locke, Montesquieu, and Rousseau and the recommendations of a French public administrator by the name of Louis Rene de la Chalotais.[13] It represented the sharpest conceivable break with the British tradition that had prevailed in the colony. Of the men chiefly responsible for framing it, Abraham Baldwin, Lyman Hall, and Nathan Brownson had been educated at Yale, John and Joseph Habersham and Joseph Clay at Princeton, Noble W. Jones, John Milledge, John and William Houstoun, and Samuel Elbert largely in Georgia, William Few in North Carolina and Georgia, James Jackson and William Gibbon in

England and Georgia.[14] Because of the leading part that is known to have been taken by Baldwin, the program might be adjudged to owe considerable to the educational ideas of New England, except for the rather lethargic and far from democratic state of education within that region at the time.[15] It resembled most the conceptions of the early French writers, though not the later rigid state system of France. The Georgians probably were familiar with the ideas of Montesquieu and possibly with those of Rousseau, but it seems doubtful that they had any knowledge of La Chalotais's plan for a national system of education, which appeared only in 1763.[16]

What then is the likely explanation of the origin of this novel plan of education? Elements of originality and uniqueness it most certainly possessed. In the first place, the political break with Great Britain in Georgia had been radical and complete and had been fashioned almost entirely by very young men. The older generation had remained loyal to the Crown, which had done so handsomely by most of them; whereas the younger had rebelled almost *in toto;* hence the revolutionary movement had been a highly idealistic one. The "new instrument of government" commanded an almost unbounded faith and, furthermore, was practically the only machinery of group action in existence in the state at the time; it constituted the rallying focus of the small, sparsely settled, and separate communities that made up the young state. This significant role of state government was enhanced further in respect to educational matters by the utter destruction that had been wrought by the Revolution upon the Anglican Church, which had become the chief stronghold of private and public education in the colony.[17]

Georgia, at the end of the Revolution, approached as near as is ever anywhere likely to be possible, except for the slaves, to a classless society. With seemingly limitless lands, it appeared possible to maintain its democratic institutions and freedom of economic opportunity, if only a complementary system of universal education were established. The notion of education as a guide to chart the course of a democratic people was a flash of rare insight, and this plan deserves to be accorded front rank among the early projections of the future educational system of the United States. Fortunately, the elements that prompted the program in Georgia were widely common to most of America. Unfortunately for Georgia, its brilliant scheme was destined to remain largely a dream recorded upon the statute books and its initial leadership to be lost to other regions.

The reasons behind the failure of this enlightened program will become more evident as we proceed, although some of the initial difficulties may be recalled such as the state's heavy indebtedness and continuing deficits, its lack of an adequate revenue system, and the prostrated condition of the private economy. Under the circumstances, the state had no means for supporting schools except its landed domain, and effective support from this source necessitated either the inauguration of an income-yielding land policy or the development of a competent method of administering direct land grants. The first alternative was roundly defeated even as the state was planning its elaborate educational program, and the policy of direct land grants succumbed to private land hunger. Lack of leadership was another contributing factor. Baldwin and Milledge, who were among the most competent as well as the most interested, were early sent to Congress to represent the state in the increasingly important area of national affairs, and that move undoubtedly greatly hurt the cause of education. Only the most able and persistently devoted leadership could have carried out the proposed program.

The basic free school section of the program lapsed almost immediately. Any schools that were established soon changed over into academies.[18] The other end of the proposed educational ladder, the university, fared no better for a couple of decades. The academy part of the program, on the other hand, took root through local efforts, aided by state grants of land and other property, and grew steadily until it became the backbone of the state's educational system.[19] The omission of the free schools and the concentration upon academy development appear to have been sanctioned by the new constitution that was adopted in 1798, which made no reference to general education, but only stated that "the arts and sciences shall be promoted in one or more seminaries of learning, and that the legislature shall, as soon as conveniently may be, give such further donations and privileges, to those already established, as may be necessary to secure the objects of their institution," and further enjoined the legislature that it should at its next session "provide effectual measures for the improvement and permanent security of the funds and endowments of such institutions." These provisions were interpreted at the time to refer to the academy system.

The eclipse of the free school idea by the ascendancy of the academy meant the perpetuation in Georgia of many of the features of the British system. The academy was essentially a secondary school for children of parents who could afford to pay, in tuition, books, and other materials, the costs of education. It came to be a three-year college preparatory school for boys, with an added year for girls, which was deemed sufficient advanced study to fit them for their future station in life.[20]

State grants to academies from the public domain were of two types. The policy of making academies residual beneficiaries of the public lots in towns and cities, begun at Augusta and Waynesboro in 1783, was followed subsequently in the laying out of nearly all new county seats in Georgia; and academies that originated in this fashion were known as county academies. The initial town tract was granted from the public domain if such were available; otherwise a state-appointed board of commissioners was authorized to purchase the necessary land. A second policy was introduced in 1788 with the establishment of the Chatham and Sunbury academies, when each was granted the right to purchase, free of payment, £1,000 value of property from the Commissioners of Confiscated Property. This step was adopted originally no doubt because of a lack of available public lots in Savannah and Sunbury or of any valuable public lands remaining in Chatham and Liberty counties. However, this right of free purchase was extended in 1792 to all other existing academies and in 1810 to all new academies that might be established in the future. Of the two types of grants, that based upon city lots proved to be by far the more lucrative. It provided for most of the county academies the original grounds and buildings and some operating funds, and, in some instances, notably the Richmond Academy at Augusta and the Putnam Academy at Eatonton, grew into endowments of sizable proportions. The confiscated property grants, on the other hand, proved disappointing in most cases. Nearly all available property of this kind had been sold before the academy grants were initiated; hence these purchases were made perforce either from properties that had reverted to the Commissioners through default or otherwise and which often possessed doubtful value, or from remote and vaguely identifiable tracts that in several instances could not even be found. Academy trustees could realize little from properties that afforded slight attraction to private buyers.[21] Furthermore, with the opening of the virgin lands in central Georgia, the attractiveness and profitability of the coastal region, where the confiscated properties lay, declined sharply. The great majority of academies prior to 1820 were county academies; thus the rate of growth followed the organization of new counties. These academies legally were public corporations, by virtue of the state land grants upon which they were founded and endowed by the legislature under the constitutional mandate. On the other hand, academies that were incorporated privately by local religious and civic groups, began to spring up with increasing frequency, and, after 1820, came to greatly outnumber the county academies. While only some forty academies were established over the four decades prior to 1820, over one hundred new ones were chartered in the twenties and nearly three hundred in the thirties. There was a sharp drop to around fifty new charters during the depressed forties and only a moderate increase during the fifties when the common school movement began to gain momentum. Reference to Tables 17 and 19, where incorporated academies are listed among all incorporations, will afford a quantitative picture of their growth and also will reveal by contrast the paucity of other educational institutions, or at least of such as obtained to corporate status.[22]

The academy system, under local guidance, was steadily becoming established during the last two decades of the eighteenth century while the Senatus Academicus, though organized in 1786, remained only a nominal body. It did not turn seriously to the question of establishing the university until 1799, and in the meantime had given no real attention to the organization of primary and secondary education. In 1800 it selected a "presiding" professor, although it had not yet determined upon a site for the institution. The present location at Athens was chosen in November 1801, construction of buildings was begun shortly afterward, and the first commencement was held in May 1804.[23] The state loaned the university $5,000 in 1803 to complete its buildings, the loan to be repaid out of revenues from its land grant. It proved difficult, however, to realize income from the lands and, for two decades, the university eked out a poor existence largely from tuition; which led the state in 1817 to decide to sell the university's lands and to set up a permanent endowment with the receipts from the sales. At the same time it appropriated $10,000 of receipts from land fraction sales for new buildings and authorized the governor to use $15,000 of the university land receipts for the same purpose. The sale of the university's lands grossed $127,000 and a permanent fund of $100,000 in bank stocks was created therefrom. As the banks at the time were paying 8 per cent, it gave the university an annual income from endowment of $8,000. When the depression of 1819 finally forced the banks to reduce dividends, the state, in 1821, guaranteed the annual income of $8,000, to be made up from the treasury whenever the fund income fell below that amount.[24] With this assured income the university made rapid strides in expansion of both curriculum and enrollment.

The state added an important unit to higher education in 1833 by the establishment of the Medical College of Georgia at Augusta. It appropriated $10,000 for the purpose, and granted fifty town lots of the Augusta commons and certain bank stock subscription rights. It will be recalled that the state had reserved the right of its proportionate share in any increase in shares that might be voted by the stockholders of the Bank of Augusta. Action had just been taken to double the bank's capital stock, and the state released its rights, resulting from this action, to the trustees of the Medical School.

With this increase in state support and encouragement the two institutions of higher learning assumed leading roles in the development of the state's intellectual and professional life. Whereas the leadership of the first half of the ante-bellum period had been trained largely elsewhere, or self-taught, that of the second half was instructed for the most part in the state's own institutions of secondary and higher learning, thus realizing a primary object of the founders of the academies and the university, to educate their sons and daughters at home.[25]

The Senatus Academicus by law was the chosen instrument of state educational policy. To enable it to perform this function more effectively with respect to primary and secondary schools, county senators were added in 1811 to the *ex officio* Board of Visitors. But, although it made numerous attempts to supervise the academy and free school operations by requiring reports and providing for visitations and inspections, supervision and control remained perfunctory to the end.[26] The academies already had become established under local sponsorship and guidance and ignored, for the most part, the requests of the higher body; the local officers who controlled the disposition of poor school funds were equally unresponsive; and the Senatus Academicus found that most of its available time was fully occupied with the affairs of the university. Accordingly, Georgia's centralized system remained largely a paper one until even this pretense was discarded in 1858, when the Senatus Academicus was abolished and the Board of Trustees of the University of Georgia created.

Meanwhile, during the early years, the provision for primary education, an integral part of the original design, had been dropped entirely. The recrudescence of liberal thought after 1795 did nothing to revive the common school program, despite the fact that James Jackson and his associates all included universal education, along with general land-ownership, free markets, cheap transportation, and efficient government administration, as a necessary guarantee of free economic enterprise and intelligent democracy. But the public and the legislature were lethargic toward education. Possibly the deletion of the revenue principle from the new public land policy doomed any hopes that the liberals may have entertained of securing state-supported common schools. The defeat of the revenue principle was only a manifestation of the overwhelming interest of the average citizen in immediate material development and possibly also of an undue faith on the part of the liberals, especially Jackson, in the all-embracing salutary effects of the new homestead land policy. Primary education too was left to local and individual efforts. The old field schools, like the academies, were organized by local initiative[27] as were dame schools and other private schools, with an occasional "free school" being established through the support of a church or benevolent organization.[28] What was developing was a dual voluntary system resembling the British, but possibly with more state assistance. On the one hand were the predominant group of schools for the tuition-paying children of the higher income groups, while on the other were the charity schools, or schooling, for children "of indigent parents." Free schools were coming to mean "poor schools."

3. The Struggle for a Common School System

This theory of dichotomic education did not go unchallenged. Following the War of 1812 a group of educational liberals, led by Joseph Singleton, Duncan Greene Campbell, and Tomlinson Fort, launched an appeal to the state for the adoption of a state-supported system in which the distinction between rich and poor should be removed, and their voice finally secured the attention of the legislature in 1817.[29] The Senate passed a highly encouraging resolution in which it declared education to be the only certain basis and the first business of a free government; academies and colleges should not be abandoned, but a much more comprehensive system was urgently required; the state should assume the chief burden of providing education for that large proportion of the population whose means were limited; and the House was urged to originate the necessary legislation.[30] The subsequent action fell far short of what was suggested: a free school fund of $250,000 was established from which the income was to be used for the education of poor children; thus the state chose to follow and abet the theory and practice of the dual voluntary system that had grown up. The state added to its aid in the education of poor children in 1818 by including in the Land Lottery Act of that year the reservation of lots 10 and 100 in each surveyor's district and the appropriation of the net proceeds of land fraction sales for that purpose. However, the generally inferior quality of the lands distributed or sold under the Lottery Act of 1818 resulted in small returns for school purposes. Nor was much income forthcoming immediately from the free school fund. The latter was enlarged in 1821 to $500,000 and invested in bank stocks, but actually this represented no increase in the support of free schooling, since the income was to be divided equally between free schools and academies. Wilson Lumpkin urged Governor John Clark to support a proposal to reserve for school purposes a large section of the rich territory that was ceded by the Indians in 1821, but Clark, though a severe critic of the stigmatizing "poor school" policy, appeared lacking in enthusiasm or broad vision toward education.[31] Singleton and Fort led a determined fight in 1822 for a common school system. However, their bill, providing for the allocation of one-half the state tax in each county for school purposes, was defeated by the conservative majority which adopted in its place a "poor school" fund system.[32] Under the provisions of this act, the income from the fund was to be distributed to counties proportionately to censuses of "poor children of indigent parents," the latter being defined as anyone who did not pay over fifty cents in taxes above the poll tax. Annual income available for "poor schools" was expected to approximate $12,000.

The defeat was a bitter one for the liberals, since it forebode a fastening of the "poor school" system upon the state. Although they were unable to get it replaced, they did get the appropriations increased in 1830 to $20,000. Administration of poor school funds was placed in the hands of county officials with the restriction only that such funds were to be used for the education of poor children. Subsequent reports of their disposition were few and the evidence suggests that they were not always effectively applied. Local practice varied widely. Some counties consolidated them with their academy funds, making such provision as they saw fit for the education of poor children at the academies; a few set up free schools for poor children;[33] only one or two attempted to establish a genuine common school system.[34] It would appear that most frequently the officers used the funds to pay tuition of poor children in private schools of one sort or another, sometimes amounting to mere private tutoring. Such practice opened opportunities for waste and abuse.

The coalescence of liberal thought in the new Union Party during the early thirties brought renewed hope to the supporters of common schools. Singleton introduced a bill in 1830 providing for an annual appropriation of $120,000 for a state-supported basic three-month school term and an additional three months to be provided by tuition.[35] Myron Bartlett, the liberal editor of the *Macon Telegraph*, advocated support for the full term entirely by state and local taxation.[36] Governor Lumpkin fought indefatigably for educational reform throughout his governorship, from 1831 to 1835. His ideas deserve careful consideration, because they mark a distinct advance in the liberal theory of education. Earlier liberals had placed emphasis primarily upon the political significance of education in a democracy; Lumpkin reiterated such virtues, to be sure, but also emphasized equally the economic and social — particularly the former — utility of general education. He visualized far more clearly than any of his predecessors the positive role of education in modern industrial society. Free land, plentiful capital, accessible markets, and cheap transportation were insufficient without intelligent farmers, tradesmen, and workers. His conception of the role of education, like his prophecy about railroads, was penetrating and forward-looking and represents the zenith of thinking on the subject by political leadership in ante-bellum Georgia.[37] He thought that the university was fulfilling the purpose for which it was designed, as far as its curriculum extended, but that the academies and poor schools were defective and that the small amounts that the state was spending on them were being wasted. He recommended replacing both types of institutions with a single system similar to that in operation generally in the northeastern states. He regretted that, although a move in such a direction had been started and an investigating committee established by the legislature in 1831, it had been virtually impossible to induce prominent men to work for unification. Unfortunately few were interested in Northern methods and objectives in education; nevertheless the citizens must be aroused to their fundamental importance for a free society.[38] A republican government could not stand upon the education of a few. A sound educational policy in a democracy required the promotion of a general effect upon the whole community; it need not provide a college education for all — nomenclature anyway was an immaterial matter; it was important only that children should "receive adequate instruction in solid and useful branches of science . . . the great object to be effected" was "to give the plain working man an education which (should) make him intelligent, virtuous and useful; and which (should) place him upon the ground of hopeful competition with the professional classes." [39] Lumpkin proposed a leveling-up policy in education to replace that of seepage downward that had come to prevail in Georgia. The future development of the state, he maintained, depended upon the widest possible diffusion of knowledge, which could be effected only through "some general system which (would) place common education within the grasp of every child." The educational system should provide an open road to the top: it should be possible for every child to work his way up, through industry, as far as his ability would permit; education supplied the chief catalytic agent of that free movement of human labor between levels of enterprise, that constituted the *sine qua non* of societal progress. Lumpkin recommended the establishment of professorships in the university for the preparation of teachers who might instruct the youth in all branches of the arts and sciences and, in particular, in manual training and agriculture.[40] He was fearful lest agriculture, the chief dependence of the Georgia economy, should languish without especial attention to the training of talent in that occupation. He was also the leading advocate in public life of manual training in all schools, a policy that was gathering wide support from leading educators at the time. In 1835, his last message vigorously opposed what he considered to be a growing sentiment for control and management of colleges by the churches. He did not think that religious influences of this nature were salutary. "College education . . . in a free government is the consideration of the whole community, and should never be surrendered . . . to the safekeeping of any sect or party." Lumpkin deserves a high place among the pioneer advocates of functional education in the broad sense, from the bottom level to the top. His ideas were far in advance of public opinion and action upon them, as upon his railroad recommendations, came only after his retirement from the governorship.

A move in the direction proposed by Lumpkin was indicated in 1836, when the state earmarked one-third ($350,474.03) of its share of the federal surplus revenue as a permanent Free School and Education Fund and set up a special committee to bring in a plan for a common school system. The report of this committee and the act of 1837 which grew out of it provided the highwater mark in the public planning for education in ante-bellum Georgia. The report began with a description of the educational systems of Europe and the United States — those of New England and New York in considerable detail. It cited the prevalence of state support in Europe and of joint state and local government support, through taxation, in New England; it discussed various methods of instruction that were in vogue; it considered the peculiar problems of administering a general system in Georgia and offered suggestions for overcoming the difficulties; and, finally, it criticized the existing policy which gave the academies, which educated one-tenth of the children, one-half of the funds.[41]

The Common School Law of 1837 provided: for the consolidation of the Academy and Poor School Funds and one-third of the federal surplus revenue into a Common School Fund; for the establishment of administrative divisions — presumably each county was to constitute such a division — and school districts with commissioners and trustees respectively, to be elected annually, and for their separate incorporation; for the distribution of state funds by divisions, and within divisions by districts, in proportion to free white children between five and fifteen years of age; for minimum annual operation of schools for three months; for permissive attendance between the ages of five and twenty-one years; for local tax supplements; for restriction of use of state funds to payment of teachers' salaries and the purchase of books and stationery for children whose parents were unable to furnish them; and for annual reports to the governor by the division commissioners upon all matters pertaining to the operation of schools within their respective divisions. However the law was not to go into effect until January 1, 1839.

A reaction set in almost immediately. Attempts to secure repeal of the act failed for the time being, but the deepening of the depression in 1839 supplied untoward pressures that conservative opponents could not muster; consequently, in 1840, not only the new law but also all laws providing state support were repealed.

During the two decades of the Funds' existence up to this time, annual payments to the poor schools had averaged $10,735 in the twenties and $19,661 in the thirties, and to the academies, $9,556 and $18,908 respectively.[42] Two-fifths of the original Educational Fund of 1821 was lost during the depression through the failure of the Bank of Darien, and $28,000 of the remaining bank shares were applied after 1840 to payment of debts incurred for construction of the Western and Atlantic Railroad.

A "poor school" fund was set up once more, in 1843, to be comprised of the remaining bank stocks owned by the state and any remaining assets of the Central Bank of the State.[43] With the improvement in economic conditions an effort was made, in 1847, to revive the common school law, but a bill failed to pass by one vote. This measure proposed to use half the net earnings of the Western and Atlantic Railroad plus a 25 per cent addition to the state tax rate. Since a portion of the School Fund and of the surplus revenue had gone, directly or indirectly, into the construction of the Western and Atlantic, it was deemed fitting that the railroad should now contribute to the support of education.[44]

The common school movement did not recover any consistent momentum until the mid-fifties. Governor Herschel Johnson offered a plan in 1857 that called for state matching of funds to be raised by local taxation.[45] The chief objection to this was that it favored the wealthier communities. A year later, Governor Joseph E. Brown, a man of the common people and an ardent advocate of general education, proposed a more "democratic" plan: the state should provide schools for every "free white child," a common school, rather than a "poor" school, system; it should establish a large permanent school fund by the issue of school bonds, beginning with an issue of $200,000 and increasing it *pari passu* with the retirement of the state debt until it reached $4,000,000, which would then provide an income of $240,000 at the proposed rate of 6 per cent; and it should also establish a fund of $200,000 — interest to be paid by the Western and Atlantic Railroad — for the support of teacher training at the university, the state military institute, and the state's three denominational colleges.[46] Governor Brown's bond scheme was a rather ingenious one: permanent state 6 per cent bonds were to be issued to the School Fund as the outstanding state debt was retired; thus the schools would be assured a definite and steadily growing income which would require no taxes additional to those then in force, in fact, the growth of the fund would be accompanied by declining demands upon the state in the amount of the amortization of the old debt.

Backed also by the influential Southern Central Agricultural Society,[47] Governor Brown's proposal largely was enacted into law in 1858. The new statute immediately added to the School Fund $100,000 annually as income from the net earnings of the Western and Atlantic Railroad; it provided for further steady increase of the fund by the bond-issue method recommended by Governor Brown, the state's old bonds to be retired from earnings of the Western and Atlantic; school districts were to be created and state funds distributed among the counties on the basis of school population, ages eight (later reduced to six) to eighteen; counties were authorized to levy school taxes for additional revenues and to be permitted to determine school policy, subject only to the requirement that state funds must be spent for the elementary branches of education. The effects of the act during the remaining years before the war can be measured only in terms of income distributed. Funds allotted under the old law had amounted to $36,362 in 1857 and $30,604 in 1858; whereas under the new law they were $130,000 in 1859 and $149,565 in 1860.[48]

4. Labor

Education shared preponderance with slavery in state policy on human resources. Slave policy remained relatively static throughout its history. The act of 1770, which differed little in essentials from the orignal code of 1755, was reënacted by the state following the Revolution and remained with scarcely any substantive changes the basic law of slavery throughout the ante-bellum period. There were a few specific amendments and additions, mostly of a minor nature, during the first two decades of the nineteenth century but scarcely even any minor alterations thereafter.[49] There was a new codification in 1833. Besides the state law, there grew up a considerable body of local legislation, in town and city ordinances, for the regulation of slaves and their occupations within municipalities. The sections of these two groups of laws embodying economic policy dealt primarily with the preservation of the institution of slavery, the slave traffic, the administration of slave employment, welfare, training, and competition between slave and free labor.

The act of 1770 declared all Negroes, Indians, mulattoes, and mestizos, not free by act of law or living in amity with the government, to be "absolute slaves" and hence "chattels personal" within the law of private property.[50] But the slave was also a person, which raised difficult problems of both fact and theory. He might conspire, or seek by various other means, to obtain his freedom, resist his owner or guardian, or run away. Accordingly, a considerable body of legal restrictions were imposed to discourage his indulgence of the human propensity to seek freedom — measures to prevent insurrection and inciting to insurrection, traveling in groups, gathering together, absenting from quarters at night, and carrying weapons. In addition to the authority of the masters and the ordinary machinery of law enforcement, an elaborate patrol system based upon the militia system was provided additionally to assist in the enforcement of the above prohibitions.

The presence of free persons of color within the state was deemed peculiarly offensive to the institution of slavery, and every possible step was taken to discourage their presence or increase. For this reason primarily, manumission was prohibited except by special legislative act.[51] Slaves were forbidden to own property, sell goods, or otherwise secure a profit from their own labor lest they obtain the means of purchasing their freedom; property could not be willed to them, nor could trusts be set up for them.[52]

The conflict in theory between the slave as property and as person remained an unresolved one. Like other property rights, that in the slave was viewed as natural, inalienable, and practically absolute; but likewise were the rights of persons. But a slave could scarcely be property and at the same time enjoy any civil, social, or political rights.[53] Protection of persons, in the systems of philosophy and law of the nineteenth century, inhered so largely in the "natural" rights of free persons that legislatures and courts found it very difficult to define any grounds for the protection of the persons of slaves. It may go far to explain the extreme harshness of punishments meted out for crimes committed against whites; the law gave homage to the principle of equality before the bar of justice, but in practice the unmistakable status of the slave had to be preserved.

The chief sources of supply of slaves were natural increase and importation. Slaves were imported either as the property of immigrant settlers or by merchants for sale. The sources of the latter were chiefly the West Indies, other slave-owning states, and Africa. Natural increase and immigrant importations did not suffice to meet the demands of the state's expanding economy, particularly in boom times, so recourse was had to external slave trade, regardless of the moral regrets that were so often expressed. It was early discovered that slaves from older slave-owning communities were likely to prove undesirable property. "This nefarious commerce," wrote Governor Tatnall in 1802, "empties the jails" of neighboring states;[54] and similar opinions concerning this trade were frequently expressed throughout the ante-bellum period.[55]

Almost from the beginning, prime Negroes from the shores of Africa had been in demand among the colonists. A temporary opposition to the African trade had arisen at the beginning of the Revolution, stimulated in some quarters by a latent opposition to slavery itself, but chiefly as a part of the non-intercourse policy since the trade was in British hands;[56] but importation was not proscribed by the constitutions of 1777 and 1789. In fact, the popularity of African slaves immediately revived after the war. Joseph Clay, writing to the London merchant, James Jackson, in 1784, voiced the strong preference of the Georgia planters for slaves from Africa: " 'tis from the coast (Africa) only that we wish to receive them." And he urged Jackson to obtain for him a share in this business, as participation in this trade was deemed essential to the prosperity of any mercantile firm in Savannah.[57] The opposition of Georgia and South Carolina to the closing of the foreign slave trade is readily explained, as is also the willingness of the other Southern states to see it closed in order to maintain the value of their slave property. Georgia in particular, a new and largely uninhabited region, possessed enormous possibilities for expansion; labor was in very short supply, because of the relatively limitless land supply and because British occupation and loyalist migration had removed a large part of the slave population. Experience had proved that the pure African stock made a superior labor force; and, though the Constitution of 1798 forbade the trade, extensive violations accompanied the prosperity following the War of 1812 and other boom periods down to 1860.[58] Interstate slave trade, on the other hand, was generally frowned upon from the beginning. Originally slaves could be brought from other states only by masters who came to settle. Prohibitory laws were passed and subsequently repealed at least eight times — the trade was illegal more than half the time between 1800 and 1850 — but violations here were also frequent and difficult to prevent in prosperous times.[59]

The master derived command over work performance of the slave through ownership rights rather than the law of contracts. He possessed undisputed right to control conditions of work, assign labor tasks, and direct performance, and to correct and inflict punishments for insubordination, disobedience, shirking of duties, and any other actions injurious to his interests, provided such requirements and punishments were not "cruel and excessive." The preamble of the act of 1770 states as one of the three primary purposes of the act, to settle and limit the powers of owners over slaves and to prevent "unnecessary rigor or wanton cruelty over them." [60] This injunction against cruelty is persistently repeated in later laws, codifications, and court opinions. An act of 1851 probably provides the most specific and forceful statement: "any owner, overseer or employer of a slave or slaves, who shall cruelly treat such slave or slaves, by unnecessary and excessive whipping, beating, cutting, or wounding, or by cruelly and unnecessarily biting or tearing with dogs; by withholding proper food and sustenance; by requiring greater labor from such slave or slaves than he, she or they are able to perform; or by not affording proper clothing for such slave or slaves, whereby the health of such slave or slaves may be injured or impaired, or cause or permit the same to be done, shall be guilty of a misdemeanor, and on conviction thereof, shall be punished by fine, or imprisonment in the common jail of the county, or both, at the discretion of the court." [61] In practice, however, the owner's judgment prevailed, and such laws and judicial opinions amounted to little more than moral injunctions against excessively "cruel treatment." Judges were unable to define "excessive," and juries would not convict even in obviously flagrant cases.

Should the owner wish to do so, for a fee he could have an unruly slave punished by a regular officer of the law. Slaves could be taken for this purpose to some public place of corporal punishment or incarceration. This method of shifting responsibility apparently became fairly general, especially in towns and cities where the services of the constable or town marshal were employed, although the practice was frowned upon by leading citizens.[62]

Closely related to the general legal attitude against cruel treatment were certain statutory provisions that might be classed as welfare measures. Owners were required to give reasonable attention to the health of slaves and to maintain old and infirm ones in a suitable fashion;[63] enforced labor on the Sabbath was prohibited.[64]

Early slave codes were largely silent on instruction of slaves and the training of their skills, but measures restricting such practices were later introduced. It was forbidden to teach slaves to read or write or to employ them in occupations where such skills would be used or would likely be developed by them;[65] city ordinances, in particular, excluded them from numerous occupations. For supposed reasons of the safety of white families, it was forbidden to employ slaves in the handling or dispensing of medicines or drugs.[66]

A growing purpose behind state and municipal restrictions upon training and employment of slaves was their exclusion from competition with white workers, particularly in the semi-skilled and skilled trades. The demand for such protection grew steadily, and resolutions and petitions from local and regional mechanics' societies asking that Negro slaves be barred from white occupations became common in the forties and fifties.[67] These appeals might have produced greater results but for the direct pecuniary interest of numerous owners. The hiring of slaves was a growing practice and the income to be gained thereby bore a direct relation to the skills that they possessed. Nothing was more fundamental to the doctrine of property than the right of the owner to improve and use it freely in any and all occupations, yet the prohibition upon teaching slaves to read and write and the innumerable laws and ordinances designed to prevent slave competition with white labor estopped the slave owner from enjoying both of these property rights. Nevertheless, a steadily gaining sentiment in the press and among political leaders took up the cause of white labor and favored the restricting of slaves to common tasks, primarily in agriculture.[68] This reflected in part the increasing importance of the non-staple areas and cities in the northern section of the state and in part the increasing fears of the slave owners themselves regarding the possible effects of the industrial and commercial training of the slaves upon the institution of slavery.[69] Such a policy, coupled with increasing numbers of other restrictions, could only have the effect in the long run of reducing the slave's relative productivity and his usefulness both to the owner and to society at large.

Free persons of color were the pariahs of the social and economic system. Subject to all of the occupational prohibitions and the civil, social, and political disabilities visited upon slaves,[70] they lacked much of the legal protection and all of the owner's concern enjoyed by slaves and were universally distrusted and resented by the whites. Prior to 1819 they could not acquire property and thereafter only outside the major cities. They were heavily taxed and their activities were restricted in every conceivable manner both by state laws and city ordinances, obviously with the intent to drive them out of the state. Immigration restrictions, as well as anti-manumission acts, sought to prevent any increase in their numbers.[71] A person who had been a "natural" slave, or who belonged to a race that had been ordained by God to be forever the servants of man,[72] could not by the laws of Georgia become transformed into a "natural" free man. Practically speaking, much the same attitude prevailed toward the Indians with whom the equally serious problem of land ownership was involved; but in their case Georgia held a contract with the federal government for their removal from the state.

There was almost no legislation in Georgia dealing directly with white laborers or their services. The original slavery law had required the employment of a fixed proportion of white servants with slaves, a requirement that was revived in the fifties. Another early act sought to encourage the immigration of indentured servants by establishing methods for their protection during the time of indenture.[73] Mechanics' lien laws, to secure the workers' right to receive payments, were passed in the twenties for the chief cities and towns;[74] otherwise the general laws supporting free enterprise apparently were considered sufficient encouragement, except for the protection against slave labor. Actually, the land laws were the most significant legislation in the interest of white labor in Georgia. The land lottery acts afforded the chief opportunity and mode of employment, that of the self-employed laborer and his family in agriculture.

5. Summary

The cardinal importance assigned to educational policy in the early liberal design for economic development is unmistakable. Utilization of the state's vast natural resources was deemed to require an intelligent citizenry as well as to promise the material basis of cultural development. Yet, while the state on the whole pursued constructive policies regarding land, capital, markets, and transportation, it neglected to implement the broad educational plan that was to provide the very foundation of its liberal program. Why did it abandon its forward-looking educational vision? Did it sacrifice it to land hunger or the desire for immediate material prosperity? Or did it become enmeshed in a slave system that was inimical to its development?

The economics of slavery are self-evident. The institution in the Southern states was the outcome of the profitability of commerce and staple agriculture, the urgent need for labor, and a climate that was repellent to the white labor of northwestern Europe. Slavery provided plentiful cheap labor (as well as a profitable commercial cargo) which, under existing techniques, continued profitable as long as the demands for staples were expanding and free lands were available. It was a primary contributing cause of rapid settlement and growth of wealth in the South.

But the profitableness of slavery was relatively short-run, particularly for any given state or region. The cumulative effects of one-crop agriculture, soil exhaustion, increasing land shortage, the competition of fresh soils in other regions, and growing overhead of unskilled labor made it an inefficient system in the long-run. Furthermore, a region whose permanent labor force was composed so largely of common unskilled workers was handicapped by its resulting incapacity to adopt readily the technological improvements of the rising industrial age. The technology of modern industry makes "cheap" labor occupations unable to provide a decent standard of living. And slavery and the Southern attitude toward slave training prevented the competitive adjustment that might otherwise have tended to alleviate the situation. The economics of slavery ultimately ran contrariwise to the predominant trends in both economic and political life, trends which emphasized an ever-broadening of the bases of action and placed a premium upon the development of skills and individual initiative.

Although the inherent weaknesses of slavery were scarcely noticeable as long as free land and a liberal land policy distributed the initial advantages of slavery widely, yet such economic progress as obtained could scarcely transcend the limits of available land that was suitable for staple culture. Such a policy offered slight economic opportunity to those who did not secure lands and slaves. The auxiliary opportunities of a staple economy — in trade, finance, and the professions — were not extensive and were filled largely from the slave-owning class.

Nevertheless, Georgia escaped until quite late some of the prominent evils of the slave system because of its continuous expanding economy. It continued to provide a large proportion of its people with land, banking capital, and cheap rail transportation; and the latter factor in particular added greatly to the effective land supply. Yet the slave economy became increasingly a social system in which slave ownership constituted the basis of group esteem. Non-owners were likely to be considered "poor whites," economically, because they were unable to purchase slaves, socially, because their manual labors had become stigmatized by slavery.

The influence of the slave system is reflected clearly in the evolution of the educational system. Private academies, which developed and flourished throughout the cotton belt and in the commercial cities, met the needs of the slaveholders, while "poor schools" had to suffice for those who did not belong to the slaveocracy. Adult white illiteracy, reported by the census as amounting to 30,000 in 1840 and 42,000 in 1850, actually was increasing at a faster rate than population. There were 38,536 "children of indigents" returned for the poor school fund in 1852, although current estimates placed the actual number at 50,000, and the state's expenditures for the education of those who were returned averaged less than sixty cents per child.[75] Effective education at the primary and secondary levels reached only a small percentage, possibly one-tenth of the white population, or about 5 per cent of the total population. Out of this small group only a fortunate few, selected mostly on the basis of wealth, reaped the benefits of the state's offering in higher education. Thus the aims and effects of the educational system, as it developed, would appear to have been inverse to the actual human resource needs of the society it served based upon the criteria of maximizing economic productivity.

CHAPTER XIV

THE STATE AS REGULATOR

1. Economic and Political Bases of Regulation

Regulation as a democratic process in Georgia began with the rise of staple production, lumbering, trade, and shipping between 1755 and 1770 and had a continuous history down to 1861. The temptation to characterize the early regulatory measures as vestiges of mercantilism should be appreciably diminished by the fact that all of the colonial acts were continued after the Revolution. The laws embodied almost none of the traditional principles of mercantilism, such as the desirability of accumulating specie, the notion of favored commodities, or the theories of favorable balances of trade and labor. Most of the original measures were introduced during the decade of the 1760's, a period of flourishing laissez-faire sentiment in Georgia. Some of the statutes contained "protective" or "developmental" features, but such was only one among a number of aims of the legislation as a whole. The foremost objectives were the protection of the public from monopoly prices, the inspection, grading, and standardization of products in the interests of improved production and marketing, and the provision of adequate physical facilities and services for shipping. Other aims included maintenance of competition, prevention of "unfair" competition, protection of property and property rights, and the elimination of health and safety hazards and public nuisances.

The later supposed "decline" of regulation following the depression of 1819 has some basis in fact; but it is likewise something of an historical illusion. It is true, for instance, that legislatures ceased to be concerned with numerous regulations that had occupied their attention earlier and that many such measures disappeared from the state statutes. The explanation is found primarily in political, economic, sociological, and technological changes which were altering the pattern of public policy but were not abolishing the role of government. Most early regulatory legislation, although locally oriented, was enacted by the state, since the state was practically the sole legislative unit in Georgia prior to 1800. With the rise of local government, however, the state transferred more and more of its legislative, executive, and judicial powers, and in particular the regulation of matters of local concern, to the cities and counties. With the incorporation of first-class cities went most of the rights to regulate taverns, urban transportation, public markets, weights and measures, auction sales, itinerant peddlers, dispensing of liquors, prices of bread, slaughtering, occupation and hire of slaves and free colored persons, health and safety hazards, and public nuisances. With the transfer of responsibility for roads to the counties went likewise the regulation of ferries and bridges and the administration of several of the commodity inspection laws.[1] While commodity inspection is seldom mentioned in the state legislature after 1800, it was practiced locally wherever certain articles continued to be produced throughout the remainder of the ante-bellum period. To be sure, regulations died, or at least fell into disuse, whenever their objects ceased to exist — when articles were no longer produced or economic relationships had become altered. When cotton superseded all other commercial staples, it changed the economic and social position of the average Georgian who became more of an isolated sole enterpriser, producing for distant markets. For one thing, cotton growing, processing, and marketing were relatively simple operations that were equally adaptable to almost any scale of production and with which little government assistance was needed; for another, the primary evils from which the cotton grower suffered had almost no local flavor, but were largely external matters as world-wide price recessions, currency depreciation, multiple handling charges, high transportation costs, and interest charges which far transcended his surroundings and experiences.

The cotton grower was just as anxious as his forebears to regulate the evils that beset him, but he was uncertain how to go about it. He did not understand the emerging new industrial world or its forces of which he was so largely a pawn. The city merchants, bankers, and lawyers preached to him the doctrine of the natural laws of trade and recommended a laissez-faire policy. Blame for all ills was placed upon Northern protectionist policy and its "hothouse" creation, Northern industry. The scope of the regulatory problem had shifted suddenly from the local area to at least a state-wide and, more probably, a nation-wide dimension, and the old instrumentalities of regulation no longer sufficed to cope with the problems. The cotton grower was torn between the impulses to seek insulation from outside forces through state action, to embrace national regulation, and to strike back at his own metropolitan merchants and bankers whom he viewed as probable monopolists and more often than not in league with Northern and European capitalists.

Georgians originally had been strongly pro-federalist, but had lost much of their enthusiasm for the central government as a result of early disagreements with it and disappointment over its state debt assumption policies. James Jackson's hard-money anti-bank policy in part was a phase of this reaction. A growing understanding of the changed pattern of economic life and of the need felt for a strong national regulatory policy was evidenced clearly two decades later in the wide support given to the Second Bank of the United States which Georgians viewed as potentially an effective instrument for the regulation of the currency and, thereby, of prices and business fluctuations. Disappointment in the early twenties over the shortcomings and failures of the Second Bank, however, forced the Georgians once more into the policy of insulation which tended to grow upon them with the unfolding of the slavery controversy.[2] They were not unaware of the nugatory nature of insulationism which explains their vigorous efforts to solve their problems by other methods. In the field of regulation itself this was reflected in the growing efforts of the interior agrarians to control the activities of banks and other large corporations.

It should not be inferred that Georgians relied primarily upon regulation as a means of solving their economic problems. At no time in their history did they go all out for regulation in the narrow sense. The colony had been slow to introduce it in the first instance, then had given it a strong pragmatic flavor; the first post-Revolutionary assembly at its initial meeting had postponed reënactment of the numerous regulatory measures until a second session later in the year; and Georgians continued to look upon regulation as an auxiliary rather than a primary department of public control. They were far more interested in public developmental policies — removal of the Indians, land distribution, currency and capital provision, internal improvements, and railroad construction. Hence, they became increasingly preoccupied with government's role as initiator and promoter. If they appear to have been less concerned with public regulation after 1820 than formerly, it was because they were more concerned with public promotion of land distribution, capital creation, and railroad construction. They favored a more positive, dynamic approach to the problems of competition, monopoly, production, and trade than was comprehended under regulation. Such a dynamic policy harmonized with the prevailing individual psychology, which doubtless largely explains the seemingly paradoxical development of a broad program of public action in a climate of *laissez faire*. Likewise it may explain why a state which developed, in greater degree probably than any other, centralized administration of land, capital, and railroad policies, exhibited no inclination whatsoever to introduce state-level administrative bodies in the area of regulation.

2. Regulation in the Eighteenth Century

The Georgia Assembly on July 31, 1783, declared all regulatory laws, not of a temporary nature nor repugnant to the Constitution of Georgia, and passed before December 29, 1778, to be in full force until repealed.[3] These were enumerated as including the regulation of taverns and liquor retailers, workhouses for the custody and punishment of Negroes, patrols, the services and hire of porters and slaves, purchase and sale of slaves, branding of livestock, pilotage, wharves and wharfmasters, the manufacture and quality of lumber, staves and shingles; the prevention of vessel masters carrying off persons in debt, seamen and marines deserting vessels, running into debt or being harbored, the disposal of ballast, rubbish, and other wastes in harbors and other navigable waters, frauds in selling beef, pork, pitch, tar, and other products; inspection and regulation of the quality of leather; inspection of the quality and handling of tobacco and fixing rates for handling and storage; imposing an export duty on raw hides; and enforcing the assize of bread. Added later were the regulation of interest rates and the mode of calculating interest, the quarantine of vessels and imported slaves, the operation of rice dams, the disposal of indigo weed, and the rates and services of grist mills and ferries.

Little more is heard about some of these regulations that were associated with early local monopolies and pioneer products and activities. Although they may never have been repealed, their effective existence ceased with the passing of the objects and conditions to which they had pertained. The extensive growth of tobacco inspection featured the first two decades following the Revolution, as tobacco replaced rice as the leading staple of the state. The first postwar general statute — covering inspection, grading, stamping, packing, handling, and warehousing of tobacco — was passed in 1785. Successive special acts caused some confusion, until a uniform state act was passed in 1791. Important amendments were enacted in 1798, 1799, and 1805. Meanwhile public warehouses and inspection boards were established throughout the length and breadth of the Savannah River valley and other favored areas as tobacco culture spread over a large part of settled Georgia.[4] But after 1805 nearly all of this elaborate machinery of regulation disappeared even more abruptly than it had come into existence, as tobacco quickly succumbed to cotton.

Two other rather prominent objects of regulation of the same period were lotteries and bread. Lotteries, widely used until around 1820 for raising funds for various public and quasi-public purposes, were objects of legislative authorization and frequent detailed prescription. They afford a significant historical chapter in the state's use for public purposes of men's propensities for "doubtful" pleasures. Private lotteries were regulated otherwise, as pure gambling devices. The assize of bread had a somewhat curious but rather instructive history. A price-fixing device of ancient vintage, it was introduced into colonial Georgia at a time of flour shortages and scarcity bread prices. When similar occasions arose after the Revolution — in 1792, in the embargo year of 1808, during the War of 1812 and in the boom years of 1816–1817 — it was brought out repeatedly to prevent price-gouging by city bakers. All of which suggests that its use was something of an early analogue to our recent practice of reviving public war controls on the occasion of each succeeding economic emergency. Any notion that the assize of bread was merely a nominal archaism that Georgia somehow failed to discard should be dispelled by the record of the long public controversy which it engendered in Augusta and of the strenuous efforts of the city council, with the approval of the state, to make its operation effective.[5] Georgians were not especially prone to hang onto the outmoded legal practices and customs of their English forebears unless they served a definite pragmatic purpose.

3. Old and New Types of Regulation after 1800

A large body of regulation was maintained actively and continuously from the close of the Revolution until the outbreak of the Civil War. Such applied to timber products, shipping, transportation facilities, warehousing, markets, weights and measures, taverns, interest rates, porters, and slaves. Inspection and measuring of timber products figured prominently between 1783 and 1800, then declined into lesser notice for several decades, becoming significant again in the fifties when lumbering enjoyed a considerable revival and extension. The laws governing the physical facilities and services of the ports — including pilotage, use of harbors, movement and anchorage of vessels, wharf construction and operation, weighing, compressing, warehousing, and unloading and loading of vessels — were first revised and extended during 1785–1787. After a succession of amendments and additions during the following four decades, they were revised, unified, and elaborated in much greater detail in the Act of 1829. This act remained the basic law, although later modifications and additions kept pace with the continued growth of commerce and the industrial and technological changes. Regulation of domestic markets continued, but was transferred largely from the state to local jurisdiction, and hence was recorded much less frequently in later years in the acts of the legislature.[6] The same was true of regulation of ferries and bridges, placed under the county courts in 1818. However, the state reëntered the field of transport regulation almost immediately, with the appearance of the new turnpikes, canals, and railroads. The development of regulation of weights and measures followed an opposite course to that of markets, ferries, and bridges. Traditionally the standards for weighing and measuring goods had been controlled by trading custom and had varied widely; municipalities first began regulation in order to establish standards for the settlement of grievances that arose under their jurisdictions. The state began to take cognizance of the problem, first by recognizing officially the standards that had been established in its leading commercial centers and, finally, by establishing a uniform standard that was made applicable throughout its borders. At the same time it took over the control of weighing and measuring operations. Regulation of the use and hire of porters and slaves continued to be a feature of both state and local legislation, taking on increasing rigorousness and significance with the growth of influence of white labor groups in towns and cities.[7] Closely related to, and largely patterned upon, such laws were the measures that were adopted for the governing of free persons of color. The control of taverns in first-class cities was relinquished generally to the municipalities, but a uniform state law, which applied elsewhere, was adopted in 1808.

Continuing types of regulation did not remain confined to established fields. The appearance of new commodities and enterprises often raised problems that became fitting matters for state or local governmental attention. Thus public auction sales in 1794 and peddlers in 1796 came under state regulation.[8] Also in 1796 an act was passed providing for the inspection of cotton, but it was repealed in the following year on the grounds that it was "by no means beneficial to the interests of the state" and constituted "an unnecessary burden on the planters."[9] No attempt was made thereafter to apply such measures to cotton; however, the methods and charges for weighing cotton were placed under state regulations in 1803, as were also the care and disposal of cottonseed dumps around the gins. Cotton warehouse rates, where they affected cotton growers, were sometimes regulated both by the state and by the cities, but on the whole cotton growing, processing, and marketing were subjected to slight public interference at any time. Flour was placed under official inspection in the major cities in 1801 and the law was extended to new cities as they arose throughout the ante-bellum period. Banks, navigation companies, turnpikes, canals, railroads, mutual insurance companies, and building and loan associations all were regulated through their charters. The examination and licensing of physicians, surgeons, and midwives was required in 1821, and the Georgia Medical Society was named the examining body.

One of the most heterogeneous and complicated bodies of regulations was that which resulted from the competition of different groups for the use of streams. The disharmonies of interest among claimants were a perennial source of legislation, as raftsmen, boatmen, fishermen, ferrymen, bridgebuilders, and manufacturers strove for priority. Each was an obstacle to all of the others and also frequently a competitor. The state denied any prior, or absolute, rights from the very beginning, even in cases of non-navigable streams. Most often it tried to effect a compromise solution, but on several important occasions it invoked the overriding principle of the public interest. An early example of this, involving a wide and growing controversy, dealt with the conflict between manufacturers and fishermen. The former were beginning to build dams on several of the principal streams of the state, which resulted in complaints from various quarters that there were "numerous people" who were "anxious to enjoy fishing," but that the dams prevented fish passing up the streams, thereby "adversely affecting this important interest." A responsive legislature adopted a law in 1796 that required that mill dams be kept one-tenth open or be built with a slope that would permit fish to pass. Upon further investigation the legislature changed its mind; two years later it expressed the opinion that the restrictive measure interfered greatly with the construction of certain merchant mills, "and whereas, it is of much more consequence to the community at large, to encourage the manufacture of flour, than the inconsiderable advantage resulting to a few individuals, from the egress of fish in the aforesaid river," it voided the measure's application to one of the principal streams of the state.[10] Disputes among the fishermen themselves over the use of poles, seines, and traps were interminable and the statute books are crowded with acts pertaining to them. The record is similarly voluminous with respect to the other interests enumerated above. It reflects vividly also the course and effects of technological, industrial, and social changes. When, in the fifties, the railroad displaced other forms of transportation and economic maturity largely removed the frontier avocation of fishing, the streams were left at last to the manufacturers and the body of regulations shrank noticeably.

4. Public Utilities

The largest body of regulation was concerned with public utilities. This was a broad category and included taverns, hotels, gristmills, pilotage services, wharves, warehouses, ferries, bridges, stagecoaches, navigation companies, toll roads, turnpikes, canals, railroads, plank roads, banks, mutual insurance companies, insurance agents, and weighing and measuring operations. Even some of the services of public inspection were of a public utility nature. Although waterworks, gas, and telegraph companies belonged to the public utility category and had a large growth during the 1850's, they were not brought under public regulation prior to the Civil War. The characteristics that were most commonly accepted as defining a public utility probably were the common necessity of the service, public charter or authorization, and monopoly. In the case of banks, control of the money supply constituted the most important feature. It was not essential that all of these characteristics be present, nor did the existence of any one or two of them constitute an enterprise a public utility.

The regulation of public utility services dealt primarily with rates, although it covered usually also some features of service and even certain aspects of management. It was largely of the statute or charter type. Rate schedules for taverns, grist mills, and ferries were established by legislative enactment during the colonial period, for wharves, warehouses, and pilotage shortly after the Revolution, for bridges initially in 1790, navigation companies in 1801, toll roads in 1808, turnpikes in 1816 and plank roads in 1850. The most extensive and detailed of these schedules were those adopted for wharfage and storage in 1829. Canal and railroad rates were objects of regulation from the beginning, but the schedules were confined to two or three general maximum rates. The rates of one early canal company could not exceed 33⅓ per cent of prevailing wagon freight rates on the highways, while the usual limits imposed upon the railroads were: ¾ cent per 100 pounds per mile for heavy goods, 4 cents per cubic foot per twenty-five miles for other goods, and 5 cents per mile for passengers. Such maxima remained unchanged throughout the antebellum period. In some instances the only limit imposed upon charges was a maximum rate of return upon the investment, and in a few cases in the late forties it was only a general provision that rates must be reasonable. Regulation of services of public utilities covered extent and time of operations, physical dimensions of facilities, standards of operation, baggage and similar privileges, uniformity, and discrimination. Regulation of management dealt as a rule with liability, public safety, numbers and grades of personnel, and maintenance policies. The regulation of banks has been dealt with already.

The question naturally arises concerning what bases the state used in determining maximum rates and proper standards of service and management. The word "reasonable" recurs throughout the records of regulation but its components are seldom defined. The most common notion is that of a fair return upon original investment, which is stated in substance or implied in practically all transportation charters. Sometimes the words "and repairs" are included; developmental costs, in the form of interest on investment and depreciation during construction, are not infrequently suggested.[11] Canal and turnpike charters of the second and third decades quote both maximum and minimum rates of return, the rates usually being 25 and 8 per cent respectively.[12] The specified maximum rate was lowered markedly and the minimum rate was omitted in later decades. A typical charter of the fifties permitted the company to establish reasonable rates to yield not more than "ten percent dividends after payments for expenses and repairs." [13] This suggests that the legislature was basing its "legal" rate upon the regular 8 per cent dividends and occasional extras that had long been paid by the more successful banks and other corporations. The wisdom of using such dividend payments as a measure of fair return may well be questioned. Little distinction was made by railroad companies between repairs and improvements, hence dividends-paid-out seldom represented actual return upon investment. With respect to local ferries and bridges, where self-employment of the operators rather than capital investment usually constituted the major element of cost, the legislature more often emphasized "customary" rates as a guide for local regulatory bodies. In the regulation of public utility services and management, the state stressed equality of treatment of customers, public safety, and standards of public necessity and convenience — however arrived at — as the usual tests. Such obviously are little more than generalities, though they may have had some customary bases.

A second question concerns the administrative machinery for regulation. Was regulation confined to the usual statutory type of this period, with enforcement lodged in the hands of the regular executive officers and the courts? Generally speaking, yes, though local commissions of a mandatory character were fairly common during the earlier decades of our period. The commissioners of pilotage and of public market were such bodies; also the numerous special boards that were appointed for such purposes as locating and regulating towns and cities, and establishing and regulating ferries, causeways, and other transportation facilities, often were granted powers of a legislative and a judicial character in addition to their executive duties. A typical case was a special board the legislature appointed in Chatham County in 1796 with a mandate to select a ferry site, obtain the private establishment of a ferry, prescribe rules of operation, and fix reasonable rates. Somewhat later, during the first two decades of the nineteenth century, the legislature began to confer broad regulatory powers upon the local inferior courts. Thus in 1801 the inferior court of Burke County was authorized to establish and regulate ferries on the Savannah River. In 1817 the inferior court of Laurens County was empowered to reduce prescribed statutory rates of ferries whenever it might deem such action to be in the public interest. Finally, in the General Road Act of 1818, county inferior courts were granted general powers to establish ferries, to fix tolls on both new and old ones, and to deal with all such other matters relating thereto "which may in their judgement be of public utility," provided only that they required all ferrymen to give sufficient bond and security, according to their judgment, to secure adequate facilities and services and good repair. This growth of the administrative functions of regulation in the local courts was a phase no doubt of the rise of county government. The inferior courts were steadily acquiring administrative powers in all other areas as well. However, as regulation took on more state-wide aspects, with the growth of banks, insurance companies, turnpikes, canals, and railroads, these local administrative forms and procedures were not developed on the state level. The state appeared on the verge of taking a step in this direction in 1859, when it provided for the establishment of a state insurance commissioner with broad powers to obtain information and to regulate the agents of foreign insurance companies, but the act was not put into operation before the war.

5. How Significant Was Regulation?

How successful was regulation in Georgia? A satisfactory answer to this question would require investigation far beyond what has been possible in this study. Much responsibility for enforcement of public utility regulations was placed upon the customer, to lodge complaint with the proper officer, board, or court. This did not augur of effective regulation, especially as new large-scale facilities such as canals and railroads came into existence and problems of reasonableness grew complex. Much emphasis was placed upon publicity of prescribed rate schedules as an aid to the consumer. Laws required that the legal rates for grist mills, taverns, ferries, bridges, navigation companies, toll roads, turnpikes, and plank roads be posted prominently on the premises at all times and places of approach. The regulation of service and management was not suited, however, to such devices, and persistent newspaper accounts and grand jury presentments suggest that laxity in enforcement of such regulation was very general. Among the various types of public utilities it would appear that the railroads felt the hand of regulation least. Considering the generality of the regulatory laws that were applied to the railroads, the high levels of maximum rates, or net earnings, that were permitted, the inaccessibility of the data, the absence of modern accounting methods and practices, the responsibility upon the shipper to initiate complaints, and the total lack of specialized enforcement machinery, it would appear fairly conclusive that the regulation of railroads remained little more than a nominal matter throughout the ante-bellum period. There were widespread complaints during the fifties about the alleged exorbitant rates and profits of the major railroads, which were attributed to their monopoly position, and demands from many quarters for state-supported construction of competing lines. This policy seemed to be favored much over stricter regulation, especially since it coincided with the commercial ambitions of numerous cities.

Public regulation on the whole declined noticeably between 1820 and 1850, despite its unbroken history in many fields and the increase of efforts to control banks following the depression of 1819. Its virtual absence or slight effectiveness in the two primary activities of cotton growing and rail transportation largely accounts for the relative decline. The fifties however brought a considerable revival. Old statutes were remodeled and a variety of new ones added. There was a modest growth for the first time of general legislation covering railroad operations, in such matters as public safety, the handling of baggage, storage, through rates, commodity rates, and freight billing. In 1854, the labor of white persons under twenty-one years of age in cotton, woolen, and other manufacturing plants was limited to the hours between sunrise and sunset, all contracts to the contrary were declared null and void and a fine of $100 was provided for each offense. The same year saw uniform rules for weighing agricultural products. Maximum interest rates were reduced from 8 to 7 per cent and oyster beds were placed under public control in 1856. The local inspection of liquor for injurious drugs was enacted in 1857. Following the panic of 1857, several laws were passed regulating exchange transactions of banks. During the decade, there was also a notable growth of new local regulations, covering the operations of slaughter houses, care of livestock, hunting, fishing, trespassing, and timber cutting among other matters. A step in the opposite direction, possibly, was the repeal in 1854 of the requirement of examination of physicians and the substitution in its place of the presentation of a diploma from any medical college in the United States.[14]

CHAPTER XV

FISCAL POLICY

1. Expenditures and Revenues

Besides constituting an important phase of public activity in itself, fiscal policy summarizes the particular public programs with which we have been concerned as related aspects of the public business as a whole. This chapter does not deal with fiscal history in detail, but with its broader features. The over-all record of expenditures, revenues, and public debts, presented in Tables 25, 26, 28, and 29, includes the operations of the Central Bank from 1829 through 1842 as an integral part of the public business, since it belonged entirely to the state and operated virtually as its treasury and as its fiscal agent. Therefore, additions to the Bank's capital are treated as state investment and subtractions as revenue, and its earnings also are treated as income. Such inclusion creates certain difficulties because of the incompleteness of records both for the Bank and for other financial agencies during the critical years between 1839 and 1843, and also because of the discrepancies and differences of form among such records which exist; but it is thought that sufficient data have been found to recreate with general accuracy the history of the Central Bank period.[1]

The opening decade of the nineteenth century marked the first extended period in which the state consistently enjoyed a balanced budget. Ordinary revenues barely sufficed to meet the expenses of general government and, consequently, no other significant activity was undertaken except the distribution of two land cessions which bore its own costs and netted a modest surplus which was applied upon the public debt.

The second decade produced striking changes in the fiscal balance sheet. The totals were more than tripled, reaching a plateau that was not attained again until the late thirties.[2] While public expenditures as a rule may be considered to be the *raison d'être* of public revenues, this causal order was largely reversed during this particular decade: it was the large federal payments for western lands that made possible the heavy investment which constituted the weightiest addition to the expenditures column, and the state's own land receipts, chiefly from the distributions

Table 25

PUBLIC EXPENDITURES, BY DECADES, 1801–1860

	1801–1810	Per cent	1811–1820	Per cent	1821–1830	Per cent	1831–1840	Per cent	1841–1850	Per cent	1851–1860	Per cent
General government	$474,969.80	65.0	$ 596,087.77	18.7	$1,225,235.39	42.7	$1,961,336.60	26.7	$1,259,728.86	21.1	$1,807,875.04	25.7
Land distribution	98,300.00	13.5	231,215.60	7.2	300,906.14	10.5	195,642.54	2.7				
Roads and waterways	1,769.00	.2	146,900.00	4.6	199,604.44	7.0	209,607.04	2.8	4,424.32	.1	21,999.99	.3
Railroads							1,821,234.24	24.6	2,011,063.59	33.7	1,277,822.72	18.1
Investments, other than railroads			1,173,000.00	36.9	839,031.06	29.3	2,330,745.25	31.6			98,218.78	1.4
Education	5,000.00	.7	12,000.00	.4	169,891.94	5.9	487,802.65	6.6	151,387.65	2.5	488,194.01	6.9
Penitentiary			162,686.77	5.1	72,166.06	2.5	81,700.00	1.1	58,509.38	1.0	104,294.03	1.5
Welfare			8,890.00	.3			41,500.00	.6	160,878.86	2.7	677,628.59	9.6
Military	10,000.00	1.4	224,158.84	7.0	35,373.72	1.2	237,730.20	3.2	38,009.83	.6	66,100.32	.9
Payments to U.S.			332,337.73	10.5								
Interest and debt retirement	140,237.15	19.2	295,144.00	9.3	26,391.44	.9	8,577.58	.1	2,280,992.75	38.3	2,504,284.63	35.6
Totals	$730,275.95	100.0	$3,182,420.71	100.0	$2,868,600.19	100.0	$7,375,876.10	100.0	$5,964,995.24	100.0	$7,046,418.11	100.0

Table 26

PUBLIC REVENUES, BY DECADES, 1801–1860

	1801–1810	Per cent	1811–1820	Per cent	1821–1830	Per cent	1831–1840	Per cent	1841–1850	Per cent	1851–1860	Per cent
Taxes:												
General	$418,786.43	54.3	$ 830,457.29	25.2	$ 872,702.98	28.5	$ 288,505.89	3.9	$2,153,744.01	35.7	$3,654,947.50	49.9
Capital stock, etc.			15,262.12	.5	150,184.17	4.9	86,235.45	1.2	219,020.61	3.7	344,967.59	4.7
Sales	10,797.81	1.4	34,402.09	1.1	27,637.93	.9	16,047.45	.2	1,347.59	—		
Peddlers' license			3,070.00	.1	21,153.00	.7	10,745.00	.1	14,250.00	.2		
Direct (U.S.)			155,059.35	4.7	2,412.63	.1						
Land:												
Fees	69,345.90	9.0	27,970.95	.8	469,099.35	15.3	313,058.50	4.2	36,709.00	.6	23,415.50	.3
Fractions and town lots	194,751.77	25.3	449,607.12	13.6	549,506.00	18.0	311,994.80	4.2	162,810.52	2.7	7,544.60	.1
Miscellaneous			36,752.50	1.1	148,954.70	4.9	26,794.04	.4	11,165.87	.2	19,302.61	.3
Rents	114.25	—	285.05	—	26,941.20	.9	515.37	—				
Dividends, interest, and other earned income	3,408.35	.4	286,497.70	8.7	559,450.00	18.3	1,408,405.07	19.0	225,478.34	3.8	296,496.20	4.0
Western and Atlantic Railroad											1,363,500.00	18.6
Payments by U.S.			1,344,610.94	40.8			1,051,422.09	14.1	62,469.36	1.0	220,425.60	3.0
Disinvestments and capital transfers	34,551.43	4.5			78,947.90	2.6	2,284,336.34	30.7	1,207,666.01	20.0	49,372.07	.7
Borrowed funds							1,424,429.35	19.2	1,870,548.25	31.0	1,281,784.69	17.5
Miscellaneous	20,046.25	2.6	73,372.69	2.2	35,530.74	1.1	13,842.47	.2	16,929.17	.3	2,574.47	—
Balance, beginning period	19,165.55	2.5	40,691.79	1.2	115,618.88	3.8	189,539.29	2.6	49,995.01	.8	67,138.50	.9
Totals	$770,967.74	100.0	$3,298,039.59	100.0	$3,058,139.48	100.0	$7,425,871.11	100.0	$6,032,133.74	100.0	$7,331,469.33	100.0

of the previous decade, that enabled it to retire substantially all of its remaining old debt. An exception was the "direct tax," which resulted from Congress' levy of such a tax upon the several states during the War of 1812. Actually, Georgia paid its allotted share by a transfer of western land credits in the federal treasury, and then levied the "direct tax" upon its citizens only to reimburse itself; however, the tax was discontinued after about half the amount had been recovered.[3] Other significant changes in the revenue pattern during the decade were: the appearance of dividends as a major source of revenue; the permanent introduction of the share-capital tax on banks, that was to be extended later in one form or another to practically all forms of monied investment and to all corporations; and the doubling of the yield of the general tax, reflecting the rapid expansion of the Cotton Belt. Redundant revenues largely made possible the inauguration of the state-supported internal improvement program and the construction of the penitentiary, both advocated persistently by the liberals throughout the previous decade. Expenditures for the support of general government began a relative decline as the state began to broaden its activities, although the unusual amount of investment and war expense exaggerated unduly the amount of the decline during this decade. If such items were omitted the drop would be only to 40 per cent of the total.

The third decade reflected the growing conservatism, with increasing wealth in the Cotton Belt and the commercial cities, of the ruling parties in Georgia.[4] General government reoccupied the leading position among expenditures, partly as a result of the extension of territory and a corresponding multiplication of counties, tripling the expense of legislative sessions and doubling that of the executive and judicial departments, and partly because other expenses remained relatively constant or receded. Despite much talk about internal improvements there was little increase in appropriations for that purpose. The one significant new item in the budget was education, but the expenditures on that account unfortunately averaged less than seventeen thousand dollars annually in a decade that yielded nearly one million dollars of surplus revenue. The state chose to take advantage of its redundant revenue position rather to increase investments and reduce taxes than to build schoolhouses and hire teachers, to distribute capital loans rather than to disseminate knowledge among its citizens. Reduction in taxes took the form of sharing the receipts of the general tax with the counties, which enabled the latter largely to dispense with local taxes. This explains why the yield of the general tax remained practically constant, since the treasury reported only that part of the tax which was retained by the state. Although total state revenues declined 12 per cent from the previous period, income from sources within the state increased 50 per cent, or nearly a million dollars, as a result primarily of substantial increases in land receipts, dividends and interest, and capital stock tax yields.

The fourth decade featured the return of the strong upward trend in public expenditures that had been characteristic of the second decade. Like the previous one, this reflected the strong upward swell in economic prosperity, but in addition a significant broadening of public activities. Public investment for the third successive decade overshadowed all other items. The combined investments, through the Central Bank and in the Western and Atlantic Railroad, accounted for three-fifths of all expenditures. The expense of general government continued to grow absolutely at about its previous pace, but at the same time to decline relatively along a clearly defined secular trend. Reflecting the efforts of the liberals in the new Union Party, education fared considerably better, rising to fourth, though remaining still only the leading one of the minor items of the budget. The rise in military outlays resulted from the necessity of policing the disturbed Cherokee northwest and the introduction of a new voluntary militia system. But it was the revenue pattern that exhibited the most striking changes in this decade. General tax receipts dropped to a minor place as a result of sharp across-the-board reductions in rates and its entire abandonment for state purposes in 1835. The decline in yields from special taxes reflected the depression of the latter years of the decade. Public land revenues fell for the sufficient reason that the state came to the end of its landed domain with the land distributions of 1832. That land receipts amounted to as much as they did, resulted in part from the efficiency of the Central Bank as a collection agency. Its collections of $296,645.08 upon land notes and sales and of $158,195.16 through the disposal of state-owned slaves were added to its capital and therefore are included under State investment.[5] Some $610,000 of the Bank's earnings, which were requisitioned by the legislature for various purposes, helped to swell the item of Dividends, interest, and other earned income. But it was extraordinary sources which accounted for almost two-thirds of the income during this decade. The distribution among the states of the federal surplus revenue accounted for the reappearance of Payments by the United States in the balance sheet. This large sum was added to the capital of the Central Bank for investment in small long-term loans. Borrowing was necessitated chiefly by construction of the Western and Atlantic Railroad. Disinvestment, or what the comptroller general listed as income from State Stock chiefly, represents the liquidation, or transfer, of the capital investment in the Central Bank, which was described fully in Chapter X. Insofar as such legislative requisitions upon the Bank were made for the purchase of canal stocks or the payment for costs of construction of the state railroad, they constituted merely a transference of public investment; but the greater part of such requisitions were to pay ordinary expenses of government, especially following the release of all general tax revenues to the counties in 1835 and the decline of other revenues after the crisis of 1837. Such investment transfers and disinvestments averaged $440,000 annually during 1837–1840.

The early years of the following decade found the state deeply embarrassed by economic depression, increasing indebtedness and a lack of income. It had largely exhausted the active capital assets of the Central Bank by the end of 1840, and hence could make further demands upon that institution only at the certain risk of flooding the state with paper money and involving both itself and the Bank in still greater difficulties. It adopted a number of measures that were dictated principally by immediate considerations and without any view to their long-run effects. It stopped construction on the Western and Atlantic Railroad in order to halt further growth of the debt; it called upon the Central Bank still further, to meet interest payments and maturing principal of the debt, despite the latter's lack of available liquid resources; it abolished the Educational Funds, thereby releasing their income, and possibly their principal assets, for meeting other state obligations; it discontinued all internal improvements; and it reinstituted the general tax without division of receipts with the counties.

The conservatives returned to power in 1843 and instituted further economies, chiefly by the substitution of biennial for annual sessions of the legislature; but, on the other hand, they resumed construction of the state railroad and reintroduced educational support, though on much reduced scales. They also hiked the general tax rate by 25 per cent. Viewing the decade as a whole, the outstanding fiscal features were: the dominant dual position of the related items of railroad construction and debt service, accounting for nearly three-fourths of the total costs of government; the return, after three decades, of the general tax to the primary role of public revenue producer; and the demise of the Central Bank as the instrument of public investment and as a fiscal agency. A somewhat unexpected feature in a program of retrenchment was the notable growth in welfare expenditures. The considerable item of land revenues reflected the state's effort during the second half of the decade to wind up its land business. Thus it may be seen that the fifth decade in many important respects was a turning point in fiscal matters.

The closing decade of our period was one of generally sustained prosperity and of continued economic growth. It was the most stable, or normal, decade probably, from a fiscal point of view, that had been experienced thus far as the balance sheet clearly reflects. Although the item of debt still bulks large, and on balance was being added to, it had been placed upon a manageable basis and no longer represented a heavy burden upon the state's resources. It would appear that the cost of general government had found a new and fairly stable relative level after its earlier downward secular trend. The return of educational expenditures to the absolute level of the thirties resulted from the enactment of the Common School Law in 1858, rather than from the revival of support for the decade as a whole. Much more striking was the advance in welfare expenditures. If expenditures upon education, welfare, and the penitentiary are combined, it may be seen that the state at last was devoting approximately as much financial consideration to its human resources as it was to its material ones.

The revenue side of the picture features the growing dependence upon the general tax, which was changed in 1852 to a general property tax, and the large contribution of the Western and Atlantic Railroad. The latter reflected income-wise for the first time the full significance of the transference of the state's primary investment interest from banks to railroads. Of the investment in the latter, about $1,500,000 represented actual transfer of investment from banking; while the balance represented approximately $2,000,000 of borrowed funds that were still owed by the state, $1,800,000 of plowed-back railroad earnings and $1,350,000 of other state revenues that had been applied on retirement of the railroad-created indebtedness or to the purchase of railroad securities.[6] The rail profits returned to the treasury in 1859–1860 constituted an annual return of approximately 7 per cent upon the state's investment in the Western and Atlantic as of those dates. The increased receipts from the corporation levies reflect both the growth of the corporation and the further extension of this type of tax. The virtual disappearance of land receipts marks the close of one of the most important chapters in the state's business history. The sizable item of Payments by the United States represents the settlement of Georgia's claims for reimbursement for expenses incurred in connection with internal Indian troubles and the Florida War and, with the like item in the previous decade, should be considered as offsets against military expenditures in preceding decades.

2. The Tax Structure

The history of the tax structure of Georgia reflects the dominant features of the private economy, the various other activities of state and local governments, and the conditions of the public treasuries as affected by other flows of public revenue. The tax system comprised a general tax and a number of special ones.

The general tax underwent no actual basic changes in structure and scarcely any major ones in administration between 1784 and 1852. While its rates did not find a permanent level until the mid-1790's and some of its other features underwent some slight revision, or rewriting, between

1798 and 1805, its general framework was not changed essentially until the adoption of the general property tax in 1852. Changes in 1799 were chiefly of an administrative character, in line with Governor James Jackson's efficiency program; specific rates were substituted for ad valorem ones for agricultural lands in 1801; and the law was wholly rewritten, though without any significant changes, in 1804. Thereafter it was simply reënacted by each succeeding legislature, and even this action was deemed unnecessary by some legal authorities. Thus the Act of 1804 came to be accepted generally as the basic tax law, and subsequent changes were looked upon merely as amendments. Although there were almost no changes in basic rates after the mid-1790's, there were occasional annual across-the-board percentage reductions or increases, usually the former.

The general tax was something of an omnibus law: as it stood in 1800 it comprised the following main divisions: (1) an agricultural land tax, (2) a poll tax on all slaves under sixty years of age and on adult white males and free persons of color, (3) a tax on urban real estate and merchandise, and (4) a group of miscellaneous levies — on professions, pleasure vehicles, billiard tables, gambling devices, and legal suits. The act grouped agricultural lands, according to location and quality, into eighteen classes of three grades each and two classes of one grade each, or fifty-six groups in all, and assigned a valuation per acre to each group, ranging from $10.37 for first grade tidewater swamp land to 21 cents for the poorest grade of pine land. The rate was 35 cents per $100 valuation.[7] The poll tax was 31¼ cents for both freeman and slave. The rate on urban property and merchandise was 31¼ cents per $100 valuation. The levy upon professions — chiefly lawyers and doctors — was four dollars each; upon United States stock, 50 cents per $100; billiard tables, $50; gambling devices, $500; two-wheeled carriages, 50 cents; four-wheeled, one dollar; and suits in court, 50 cents to two dollars.

The switch to specific taxes on agricultural lands in 1801 introduced no change in the effective rate, but only simplified the calculation of the tax by converting the ad valorem rate into a specific amount per acre for each grade upon the basis of the old statutory valuations — thus the specific tax on first grade land of the highest class became 3.7 cents per acre and of the lowest, 0.075 cents.

The growing needs of the counties for more ample and regular revenues were reflected in the law of 1821, which permitted them also to levy a general tax. But as the state revenues again became redundant after the depression of 1819–1821 — the treasury reported a surplus of $426,000 in 1823 — a strong sentiment developed in favor of returning a part of the state general tax receipts to the counties. Accordingly, the legislature voted in 1823 to return to each county one-half the amount that had been collected in it, but treasury surpluses continued to grow, owing to a virtual doubling of the yield of the general tax and to the great increase in other revenues. With the conservative elements effectually blocking educational and internal improvement programs and clamoring loudly for tax reduction despite the exceedingly low level of existing rates, the general tax was reduced 25 per cent in 1830 and 1831, 50 per cent in 1832 through 1834, and was voted entirely to the counties in 1835. Thus the

Table 27

DISTRIBUTION OF THE BURDEN OF GENERAL TAXES [a]

Object	Under general tax, 1847 Amount	Per cent	Under general property tax, 1859 Amount	Per cent
Agricultural lands	$ 37,384.50	12.2	$ 97,206.35	24.5
Town lots	32,370.60	11.1	20,884.05	5.3
Stock in trade	18,865.28	6.5	8,795.61	2.2
Money and solvent debt	10,553.35	3.7	62,481.06	15.8
Shipping and tonnage			410.61	.1
Manufacturing plant			2,878.27	.7
Household and kitchen furniture			1,469.59	.4
Undesignated property	15,900.00	5.5	25,554.79	6.4
Slaves	123,900.19	42.5	176,553.33	44.6
White males	28,021.78	9.6		
Free colored	2,121.94	.8		
Professions	7,225.00	2.5		
Pleasure carriages: two-wheeled	250.25	.1		
Pleasure carriages: four-wheeled	11,883.00	4.1		
Stallions	2,537.70	.9		
Others	1,239.42	.5		
Totals	$292,253.01	100.0	$396,233.66	100.0

[a] Levies of the General Tax, that were continued as Special Taxes after 1852, and their yields in 1859 include: white polls, $24,736.25; free colored, $6,065.00; and professions, $14,935.00. Manufacturing plants paid a Special Tax prior to the introduction of the general property tax: the amount paid in 1847 was $441.30.

state in effect consigned all real property and poll taxes to the local governments, leaving only the special business taxes for state purposes. Viewed in the light of later history, the move might be adjudged a sound one, but its wisdom seems to have been doubtful at that early stage in the development of capitalism, and it unquestionably proved inadvisable at that particular juncture for it was soon to bring the state into a precarious financial position. Facing an empty treasury in 1839, the state returned to the policy of half-and-half division of the general tax with the counties and, a year later, reintroduced the identical tax law of 1804 without any division with the counties. Rates were increased 25 per cent in 1842. The distribution of the burden of the general tax was reported by the comptroller general in 1847 as shown in Table 27.

Thoughtful leaders had long been conscious of the archaic and inadequate character of the state's tax structure; but the average citizen had been lulled into contentment about it by the providentially large amounts of extraordinary revenues and by the exceptionally light burden of the general tax. As early as 1827, Governor Troup pointed out that the state had no "rational, coherent financial system"; that the yield of the general tax was entirely insufficient to support the regular functions of government, including education and internal improvements, and hence failed to fulfill the cardinal fiscal requirements of a balanced budget; and that the habit of dependence upon precarious and uncertain sources of income was an unhealthy and dangerous one.[8] He urged the establishment of a genuine financial system, but offered no specifications. Governor Lumpkin in 1834 pressed for revision and consolidation of the existing laws which he deemed had become confusing and highly inequitable in their operation. He suggested that property should be taxed on the basis of income, that being the "true measure of ability" in taxation. "Our present selection of objects of taxation fails in arriving at that true standard of justice and equity which is believed to be attainable." [9] When, four years later, the state sought to borrow funds abroad for construction of the Western and Atlantic Railroad, it found that foreign investors were concerned chiefly about the adequacy of its revenue system. They laid emphasis upon the major importance of taxes and the certainty of their yield. This was quite in contrast to the state's usual reliance upon land revenues and bank stock dividends. Another cogent fact was that the land revenues had practically come to an end.

In 1838 the legislature directed the governor to appoint three commissioners to study the situation and to prepare a plan for a state financial system. What they proposed was the introduction of ad valorem taxes, but the legislature in 1839 simply reintroduced the old general tax which by then had become largely a heterogeneous mixture of specific taxes. The confusion about the true character and effects of the general tax may explain why the legislature in the following year passed again the precise act of 1804. George W. Crawford attempted to forestall that action by introducing a substitute measure calling for a general property tax on all real and personal property with a rate of eight cents per $100 of valuation, but the bill was brushed aside by the overwhelmingly rural representation in the legislature by a vote of more than two to one.[10] The worst inequality in the tax resulted from the slight burden which it imposed upon agricultural lands, and even this nominal burden was unequally distributed among individual landholdings. The state treasurer prepared a compromise measure in 1845 calling for ad valorem taxation of real property, but retaining most of the other specific rates. This was likewise turned down despite the strong support of Crawford, by then governor.

The defeat in 1847 of the Whig candidate, who ran upon the "Crawford principles," might have suggested an end, at least temporarily, to strong opposition to the old tax law, but Governor Towns outdid Crawford in attacking the iniquities of the general tax.[11] He characterized it as "odiously discriminatory," "a patchwork — a capricious, ill-digested and miserable expedient," which violated every principle of a sound and equitable tax system. He was particularly critical of the uniform poll tax on slaves. Although willing to see personal property taxed at a somewhat higher rate than real, he deplored the ridiculous favoritism shown to land under the general tax as it then stood. He also opposed poll taxes on whites, on grounds of their regressive nature, but, if they must be levied, he thought the receipts should be applied entirely to the support of common schools. He reiterated the point that had been made by all supporters of reform, that the primary object was not to increase taxes on the whole but only to equalize the present burden. The equalized rate of eight cents per $100, most frequently suggested, was almost unbelievably low. Governor Towns's oft-expressed view that the common citizen would be entirely willing to support the establishment of an adequate and equitable system, if he were once thoroughly acquainted with the shortcomings of the present one and the character of the proposed reforms, would appear to have been well taken in the light of the noteworthy fact that the Georgia land and slave owners voted in 1852 to install the general property tax, thereby raising appreciably the amount that they were obligated to pay.

The new law provided for the return of all real and personal property, both individual and corporate, including slaves, by owners or official agents under oath to the receivers, who were required to prepare digests of such valuations and file with the comptroller general who was to make an audit of them and to compile a figure of the total value of the property of the state. The legislature was to set the total amount of revenue to be raised — fixed at $350,000 for 1853 — and the law directed the governor, in consultation with the comptroller general, to fix a rate, not to exceed 8⅓ cents per $100, upon the reported total value of property in the state, that would raise the designated amount of revenue. When Governor Cobb expressed doubts concerning the adequacy of such a low rate, the law was amended to permit the chief executive to fix whatever rate might be found necessary. The specified amounts of total revenue to be raised were increased to $400,000 in 1854 and to $600,000 in 1860; however, the rate that was found necessary seldom exceeded 8⅓ cents and, as a result of improved listing of property after 1857, it fell to 7½ cents in 1858 and to 6½ cents in 1859.

The category of special taxes was not always clearly distinguished from the general tax. Originally they were items in the miscellaneous group of the general tax. They became split off in practice, apparently, because of necessities and conveniences of separate administration. This was peculiarly the case with the public auction sales and broker and factor license taxes, which usually were included in the general act, but were administered separately. It remains something of an open question whether these taxes were viewed as supplementary to the state's policy of supervision and regulation, or were designed to assure the collection of the tax revenues. Probably it was the second in view of the fact that some conflict arose between the state and the local governments because the latter were concerned primarily with the regulation of such businesses. The license tax on itinerant peddlers, introduced in 1813, had a similar history. All of these were abolished eventually, in the forties, and such matters thereafter were left to the concern of the local governments.

Special taxes in the main were aimed at reaching productive property and enterprises that did not lend themselves readily to taxation under the general tax law. It was not intended to tax such businesses more heavily than others but only their proportionate share. Chief among such enterprises thus taxed were monied institutions, financial agencies, transportation companies, and larger manufacturing concerns. Special taxes took on an additional purpose in the fifties as the notion developed that a tax upon a corporation's real and personal property was not likely to reach its total assets, or full earning power.

The first move to tax banks was made in 1805 when a levy of 2½ per cent on banking capital and ½ per cent on note issue was introduced. This tax was greatly scaled down a year later, to a single rate of 34¼ cents per $100 of paid-in capital, which, it will be noted, was the same as the presumed rate on agricultural land, though somewhat higher than the rate on other urban property. The Savannah Branch of the Bank of the United States, which was the only incorporated bank in the state at the time, successfully contested this tax on constitutional grounds and it became a dead letter. It was reintroduced in 1813, after the opening of two state banks, but there is no evidence of any collections, and it was not reënacted in the following year. Finally, in 1817, it became a permanent part of the tax structure, with a rate of 31¼ cents, the same as on other urban property. When the Savannah Branch of the Second Bank of the United States, like its predecessor, protested payment, the state exempted it but levied an identical rate upon all shares of the Second Bank owned within the state. In 1827, the tax was extended to all funds employed by banking agents or exchange or money brokers and, in 1839, to all money at loan or discount whatsoever, except the value of book-credit accounts and a few other categories of negligible importance.

A capital stock tax was levied upon the Steamboat Company of Georgia in 1820, but generally transportation companies were not so taxed until more than two decades later. Early railroad companies enjoyed charter exemption from property taxes and most other incorporated transportation companies received exemption below a minimum level of income or upon a percentage of earnings. But in the forties the state began to levy taxes on paid-in capital of bridge, ferry, and turnpike companies and on railroads not exempt by charter or on such parts of their capital not so exempt. A net income tax of ½ per cent — the charter limit — was imposed on the Central of Georgia and Georgia Railroad companies whose charters exempted them from a capital stock tax.[12] Capital investments in excess of $15,000 of manufacturing companies also were subjected to the capital stock tax.

Some of the above taxes — on private loans, bridges, ferries, turnpikes, and manufacturing companies — were absorbed into the general property tax in 1852, but those upon banks, railroads, and agencies of foreign banks and finance companies were continued. However, in 1854, an attempt was made to equalize the tax on railroad capital stock with the rate of the general property tax. Additional special taxes were levied, in 1858, on the premiums of foreign insurance companies, the net incomes of all railroads, and the gross profits of express companies.

The use of special taxes for coercion, or destruction, deserves notice because of its regulatory implications. The amounts levied upon gambling devices were a case in point. The high poll tax upon free persons of color levied continuously from 1807 and the levy of $100 on each such person entering the state — to be remitted in case of departure within ten days — were intended to discourage their becoming residents. The numerous levies upon the circulating obligations of non-chartered institutions, following the incorporation of state banks, were designed to drive such money out of circulation: a tax of 20 per cent was levied in 1815 upon "change bills" of one dollar or less and another of 2½ per cent in 1817 upon all circulating bills other than bank notes. The legislature relented in 1818 and reduced the latter rate to 31¼ cents per $100, but in 1830 it placed a prohibitive tax of 40 per cent on all such bills.

The evolution of the revenue structure of local governments, particularly of the counties, presents a heterogeneous picture. Cities and towns, generally speaking, were given wide latitude to develop their own tax structures, but counties were kept very much under the thumb of the state both in activities, hence expenditures, and in ways and means of raising revenues. Their income pattern often reflected particular state policies as well as the condition of the state treasury. For a long while the revenue pattern was dictated largely by the character of the services rendered by local governments. Most of its functions were adapted to the fee system or the service levy. But as county functions grew, the need for cash funds rose correspondingly. Particular counties were permitted frequently to commute road service obligations into money payments in order to obtain cash for bridges and waterway improvements. Such sources, however, proved increasingly inadequate, and the state began to pass special acts granting to individual counties the right to levy special taxes, usually as an added percent to the state general tax, for given purposes. Such acts multiplied rapidly after the War of 1812. Finally, in 1821, as already noted above, a general law was passed which permitted any county, upon a two-thirds vote of its justices of the peace and the grand jury members, to levy a general tax, up to 50 per cent of the state tax, for county purposes. Little use was made of this law for two decades since the return, after 1823, of half the state tax to the counties served the same purpose, but recourse was had to it after 1839, with the stoppage of participation in the state tax. No further changes were introduced, which may explain the return to the practice, during the last two decades, of passing special county tax acts.

3. The Public Debt

The outstanding debt of the state was estimated in 1803 to be $1,100,245.10, distributed among various types of obligations as shown in Table 28(a).[13] It will be recalled that this was the unpaid balance of the Revolutionary debt and postwar deficits. No serious effort had been made to retire it after 1789. An act of 1802 assigned the remaining net assets of the confiscated property fund to payments on the debt, but this move was largely an idle gesture since that source already had been wrung practically dry. As a matter of fact the public in general, still quite wroth over the western land scandals in which depreciated debt certificates had figured, inclined toward repudiation of the balance of the old debt. It was largely held supposedly by the land speculators and their ilk. Hence an attempt to inject debt retirement into the new land distribution measure of 1803 met defeat.

Settlement of the debt question continued to hang fire until the second land lottery act, in 1806, in which at last a genuine provision for retirement was made. The entire proceeds from the sale of land fractions included in that distribution were assigned to that purpose, but even then no administrative procedure was indicated and it was not until 1808 that the treasury was authorized to accept evidences of public debt in payment of fraction notes at the following rates: audited certificates, at one-eighth of nominal value; governors' warrants issued prior to 1790, at one-eighth of nominal value; accrued interest on the Funded Debt, for seven years only; and all remaining obligations, except the paper medium of 1786 seemingly overlooked by the legislature, at nominal values. The treasury was directed also to use any cash receipts from fraction sales as well, up to $55,000 annually, to retire debt on the same bases. The legislature ignored any claims there may still have been voiced for interest on the non-funded portion of the debt. Actually the measure was a compromise between outright repudiation and payment in full. The rejection

Table 28

RETIREMENT OF THE OLD DEBT, 1800–1840

(a) 1800–1808

	1800	1803	1807	1808 Scaled down
Audited certificates	$ 471,588.64	$ 471,588.64	$ 471,588.64	$ 58,948.58
Funded debt 7 per cents	166,547.94	166,547.94	166,547.94	166,547.94
Accrued interest	180,547.94	216,549.94	251,523.02	81,608.49
Governors' warrants	90,888.14	70,239.25	92,534.43	92,534.43
Presidents' & speakers' warrants	13,799.32	13,799.32	13,799.32	13,799.32
Gratuitous certificates	22,337.77	22,337.77	22,337.77	22,337.77
Paper medium, 1786	11,968.88	11,860.87	11,573.88	11,573.88
Treasury notes	424.50	424.50	424.50	424.50
Creek War bounty warrants	126,896.87	126,896.87	126,896.87	126,896.87
	$1,085,000.00	$1,100,245.10	$1,157,226.37	$574,671.78

(b) 1809–1840

	Retirements	Remaining debt
1808		$574,671.78
1809–1810	$127,980.90	446,690.88
1811–1820	295,144.00	151,546.88
1821–1830	26,391.44	125,155.44
1831–1840	8,577.58	116,577.86

of interest claims and the scaling down constituted, from one point of view, a partial repudiation, but from another, the prevention of speculators from making a profit from depreciation of the debt. The action was not atypical of this period of revived liberalism and emphasis upon social justice.

It soon became evident that the 1806 lottery fractions would not suffice to liquidate the whole of the debt. Since large sums were still owing the state on the fraction sales of the 1803 lottery act, the legislature in 1809 included the 1803 fraction sales under the debt retirement law, thus reversing the action of its earlier predecessor body. Under these measures, three-fourths of the estimated public debt was retired by 1820; and payments over the following two decades increased the figure to approximately 85 per cent. Governor Gilmer's statement in 1838 that the state was free of debt was probably true, since considerable amounts must have become lost permanently and, in view of the inadequacy of early financial records, the estimates of amounts outstanding likely were too high.[14]

After two decades of virtual freedom from debt, during which the state had built up a large credit balance, it found itself once more during the late thirties and early forties becoming a heavy debtor. The construction of the Western and Atlantic Railroad, together with bad fiscal policies, shrinking state revenues, and excessive pressures upon the Central Bank, forced recourse to deficit financing. The interactions of these factors were complicated and not clearly understood and their adverse effects came with a suddenness that produced a great deal of confusion in thinking and action. In 1838 Governor Gilmer, in citing the state's freedom from debt, had called attention as well to its exceptionally sound financial condition and high credit standing that had just enabled it to secure a temporary 5 per cent loan at a 4 per cent premium. The usually conservative Gilmer had even suggested the wisdom of a policy of public borrowing for productive purposes, since capital yields and private interest rates in Georgia greatly exceeded 5 per cent. But within two years from then the state found itself destitute of revenues, unable to negotiate its bonds, and compelled to call upon the Central Bank to pay its current expenses and to service its mounting debts by the issue of bank notes.

The state appropriated during 1836–1838 a total of $2,700,000 for work on the Western and Atlantic and also, in 1837, directed the Central Bank to extend its capital loans to individuals through resort to borrowing in anticipation of the fourth installment of the federal surplus revenue. To meet these commitments it authorized the Central Bank to borrow $900,000, the governor and Western and Atlantic commissioners jointly to issue up to $500,000 of state 6 per cent bonds in any one year and the Western and Atlantic commissioners to sell, hypothecate for loans, or pay directly to contractors and suppliers up to $1,500,000 of interest-bearing, 6 per cent thirty-year state scrip within the limit of $300,000 of maturities in any one year.

The financial record of what transpired during the initial period of new deficit financing, which may be considered to have ended in 1842 or early 1843, following the virtual stoppage of construction on the state line, is fragmentary and far from clear as to timing and detail. The following appears to have been what happened: the Central Bank negotiated two sterling loans through New York, one for $263,000, used primarily to extend the capital loans that had been authorized, and another for $440,000, applied to railroad construction; the Western and Atlantic commissioners borrowed $304,852.76 from the Bank of Augusta on a pledge of scrip, which was subsequently placed in London, and $60,000 for a short term from the Georgia Railroad and Banking Company on a similar pledge of scrip; and the governor and commissioners issued $1,250,000 of 6 per cent bonds and scrip and temporary right-of-way certificates of indebtedness. The Central Bank retired the $263,000 sterling loan and $37,000 of accrued interest in 1841 and, as directed by various acts, it retired during 1841 and 1842 some $419,078.63 of scrip and certificates of indebtedness and $74,607.06 of 6 per cent bonds and paid $184,316.01 of interest on outstanding state 6 per cent bonds. A legislative committee reported that the outstanding debt at the end of 1842 comprised sterling loans of $735,556.33 and state 6 per cent bonds of $821,750.00 or a total of $1,557,306.33.[15] Apparently this does not include some small amounts of scrip that were presented for payment in later years or that may have

Table 29

DEBT OUTSTANDING AT CLOSE OF SELECTED FISCAL YEARS

1840	$1,424,429.35	1849	$1,828,472.22	1857	$2,632,722.22
1842	1,557,306.33	1851	1,724,722.22	1858	2,630,500.00
1845	1,727,760.00	1853	2,265,972.22	1859	2,670,750.00
1847	1,578,875.60	1855	2,644,222.22	1860	2,670,750.00

been taken up by the Western & Atlantic Railroad, but the amounts of such could not be ascertained and it is not likely that they would greatly increase the committee's total, which is reproduced in Table 29. There was also $133,158.33 of interest due at the time.

The close of this first period of deficit financing coincided with the transfer of the fiscal operations from the Central Bank back to the treasury. The treasury thenceforth became responsible for interest payments and retirements, except for the Central Bank's 8 per cent bonds which remained an obligation of that institution in liquidation. The obligation to retire $75,000 annually, earlier placed upon the Central Bank, was continued upon the treasury, but was to be applied specifically to the sterling debt, which had become especially burdensome, as well as a cause of some irritation, as a result of the depreciated exchanges and the generally deranged monetary conditions. After 1843, when construction was actively resumed on the Western and Atlantic, the level of the debt fluctuated with the relative volumes of new bond issues and retirements, but with a general upward long-term trend through 1855, after which it remained practically stationary for the balance of the period. New indebtedness for construction or improvement of the state railroad was incurred after 1843, 1847, and 1852 and the remaining debts of the Central and Darien banks were added in 1855. Important new elements in the debt toward the end of the fifties were the $450,000 of bonds issued during 1858 and 1859 to meet the state's subscription to the Atlantic and Gulf Railroad and the same amount of replacement bonds that were issued in 1859 and 1860 to the Common School Fund. Retirements matched the new bonds, however, making virtually no change in the debt total.[16]

4. Fiscal Administration

Fiscal administration, like the revenue system, had its close ties with various of the state's special programs. Administrative reform was a primary plank in the liberal program that developed around the turn of the century; in fact, Governor James Jackson placed it first, as a sort of necessary framework of procedure. He pointed out in particular the need for greater centralization of responsibility and direction and for the substitution of adequately paid, full-time personnel for the more or less voluntary part-time *ex-officio,* or politically appointed, local officials who then comprised most of the responsible financial officers.

The chief reforms secured during Jackson's administration were: the establishment in the comptroller general's office of supreme supervisory and auditing powers over the tax receivers and collectors, over all warrants issued against the treasury and over the accounts of the treasury as well; and a much more careful delineation of the duties of all fiscal officers and of all citizens liable to the state for taxes or other monies, together with schedules of penalties, which were also increased. However, not too much was done about the local machinery of revenue collection and, except for minor alterations, it was allowed to remain largely unchanged down to the Civil War: local justices of the peace were substituted in 1830 for militia captains in assisting the tax receivers, and numerous counties were permitted during the forties and fifties to consolidate the offices of receiver and collector in the interest of economy and efficiency.

The problem of securing effective operation of the local segment of the fiscal establishment remained a perennial one. It arose from the inherent laxness of the system, abetted by an archaic mode of compensation. The multiplicity of both regular and special agents, responsible frequently for relatively insignificant sums, greatly increased the difficulty of effective central administration and accounted no doubt for the slowness in making returns, the frequent absence or confused condition of reports, and the prevalence of defaulting. Financial delinquency was chronic among both taxpayers and tax gatherers, as the treasury reports of the first three decades amply reveal. It was especially marked during depression periods. Collectors were almost as prone to default as taxpayers. The comptroller general reported in 1814 that collectors were in default of a total of $85,000, or far more than the total of tax receipts of any single year prior to that date. Governor Clark likewise reported a serious situation in 1822 regarding defaulting collectors. It was even worse in the matter of land fees, sales, and rents. Normally grantees were allowed one to four years for making payments and the relatively small amounts were seldom paid within the allotted time. Generous legislatures, however, usually extended the legal time for payments repeatedly. The state suffered heavy losses from all of these delinquencies as well as the expense in litigating over them. A certain contributing factor to inefficiency as well as to some peculation was the mode of compensating financial agents. By long custom they were allowed a percentage of the sums collected. With the splitting up of counties and the growth of wealthy urban communities this system produced wide differences and gross inequalities in rewards. Although Governor Jackson had damned the system before 1800 and its shortcomings were cited frequently thereafter, it was not until 1845 that a graduated scale of percentages was adopted; otherwise the method of compensation was retained.

More important changes, or experiments, were made at the state level. Numerous shifts were made in efforts to obtain more successful prosecution of the various delinquents noted above. The power first had been transferred, in 1799, from the treasurer to the comptroller general; then in 1814 it was given to the solicitor general,[17] and, finally, in 1828, to the newly chartered Central Bank. An added inducement to debtors to make at least a show of payment was included in the last-named move, since the Central Bank was authorized to convert debts to a bankable loan basis. The Bank found the obligation to prosecute defaulters burdensome and requested to be relieved of the duty, but the legislature was not responsive to its plea.[18] With the return of fiscal duties to the treasury in 1843 the problem was thrown upon that agency, but it had ceased by then to be so serious a matter as in earlier years.

The state treasurer, whose role had been shrinking in importance, as a result of transfer of responsibilities first to the comptroller general and then to the Central Bank, was raised again to an important administrative position by the closing of the Central Bank and the passage of an act in 1843 which made him the budget officer of the state. The latter act required the treasurer to prepare in itemized form the biennial estimates of expenditures and revenues for submission to the legislature; and, in case anticipated revenues from established sources should appear to be insufficient, he was to specify new rates and objects of income together with estimates of their probable yield. Whether within the powers contemplated by the law or not, the treasurer's first budget estimates, in 1845, included a proposal for virtually a new tax law, designed primarily to secure equalization of tax burdens by adoption of an ad valorem tax on land and its improvements and of additional special taxes upon productive properties and enterprises that were escaping taxation.[19] As noted previously, the recommendation was not accepted. Governor Crawford supported the treasurer's budget estimates and recommendations in both 1845 and 1847; but his successor, Governor Towns, whether for political reasons or otherwise, criticized the estimates as unreliable and largely perfunctory; however, Towns laid the blame largely upon the archaic and unintelligible tax structure.[20] Shortly thereafter the new method was replaced by the old legislative committee system, which was much narrower in scope and possibly in intent. This early instance of an executive budget is significant of a steady advance in thinking about the administrative problems of determining fiscal policy. No doubt the governor should have been designated the chief budgetary officer. It is rather surprising that he was not, since not to select him for such a task was distinctly contrary to established practice. The action indicates that the legislature still looked upon budget-making as largely a technical rather than a policy matter.

One other practice that bears upon the development of budgetary procedure should be noted. This was the increasingly frequent authorization of executive financial commissions, usually of an interim tenure, with the duty of investigating the state's entire financial condition and policy and of reporting facts and recommendations to the legislature. The one provided in 1838 has been mentioned already. The act of 1843 authorized the governor to appoint regularly an executive finance committee to examine the condition of the treasury and of the state's finances in general during the off year, when the legislature was not in session. This arrangement may be viewed as supplementary to the treasury-budget procedure, as well as investigational and supervisory. Such commissions were discontinued apparently with the adoption of the general property tax; but a similar body was authorized in 1855 for one year to investigate the reported weaknesses that had appeared in the new tax system.

Difficulties in administration of the old general tax were among the leading complaints that led to the adoption of the general property tax in 1852. It was believed that the uniform valuation formula would greatly facilitate administration. But very soon it was discovered that undervaluation could become nearly as prevalent a source of inequity under the general property tax as had been its counterpart and other institutional weaknesses under the previous system. Successive governors pointed out the evidence in the annual comptroller general's report of shocking undervaluation and urged the establishment of some kind of

Table 30

GENERAL PROPERTY TAX VALUATIONS[a]

Type of property	1857	1858	1859	1860
Land	$136,681,959	$138,850,970	$149,547,880	$161,764,955
Slaves	223,939,723	227,468,927	271,620,504	302,694,855
City and town property	30,037,061	30,110,244	32,129,314	35,139,415
Money and solvent debts	83,895,461	89,762,797	96,124,701	107,336,258
Foreign banking capital	1,064,932	773,413		
Merchandise	11,831,899	10,462,511	13,531,687	15,577,193
Shipping and tonnage	856,510	763,235	631,732	943,940
Manufacturing capital[b]	5,750,001	3,868,736	4,428,132	4,034,252
Household and kitchen furniture	2,019,602	2,054,505	2,260,937	2,374,284
Other, not identified	32,850,815	34,928,856	39,315,089	42,427,295
Totals	$528,927,963	$539,044,194	$609,589,976	$672,292,447

[a] Aggregate valuation for 1856, not itemized in comptroller general's report, was $495,478,045.
[b] In excess of $15,000 per establishment.

equalization machinery. Unwarranted differences were conspicuous in land, but were most glaring in slave valuations. Average values of slaves returned varied in some cases, between counties with similar slave compositions, by almost 100 per cent. Publication of the returns and legislative efforts in 1858 to secure better listing resulted, it would appear, in considerable improvement. Valuations were increased nearly $150,000,000 between 1857 and 1860, 50 per cent in slave values, and 20 per cent in land values. Of the balance, 15 per cent was in money and solvent debt. The comparison was not warped by the depression of 1857, since the valuation of that year was completed prior to the business recession, in fact, upon the crest of the previous boom, and was $35,000,000 above the total for 1856. The depression is reflected rather in the valuation of 1858. Since there was no increase in land acreage and only a 5 per cent gain in slave population between 1857 and 1860, the 13 per cent increase in valuations reflected considerable improvement in the administration of the general property tax in the closing years of the decade.

The foregoing financial summary of public activities attests the prominent and many-sided role performed by government in the economic development of Georgia. Although the spirit of *laissez faire* was ever pervasively present and its influence reflected repeatedly, it enjoyed no extended period of ascendancy. The course of public policy instead was cyclical in character, producing a wave-like succession of broad peaks and troughs of public activity. The historical notion of an early "Age of Laissez Faire" is not corroborated by Georgia history. Such an illusion could have been created by the extensive transfer of regulatory activities from state to local governments during the decades following the War of 1812 or, even more likely, by the fact that the promotional activities of government so greatly overshadowed the regulatory ones throughout much of the period.

Public action followed no set role. Like private action it was affected by technological change, new developments in capitalistic organization, and economic growth. As long as unemployed lands, scarcity of capital and labor, and poor organizational facilities presented the urgent economic problems, the role of the state continued to be largely a promotional and entrepreneurial one. But as free lands dwindled, as population and wealth increased, as the business corporation developed, and the internal pressures of a maturing economy began to be felt increasingly, the state's role took on more of a regulatory complexion.

At no time was the state looked upon as a separate entity with ends of its own. Such old world ideas never took root in Georgia. The primacy of the individual remained unquestioned. Yet it was accepted that individual development was a social process, the product of many sorts of group action as well as individual initiative. The state was only one among the former, albeit the most inclusive and potentially powerful. These attributes of the state afforded advantages to be exploited as well as dangers to be avoided. Even the devotees of *laissez faire* seldom scrupled to support the use of the credit and taxing powers of the city or state to establish a bank or cut a canal or build a railroad if any such project promised to benefit their community.

Public action, it needs be further emphasized, was only one among many forms of group action that were employed. There were the countless joint public-private projects and the many and various quasi-public and private voluntary associations. The community open meeting became an important local public policy-making institution as did, likewise, the improvement or trade convention on the state and regional levels. Out of such evidenced needs and types of coöperation in large measure also evolved the corporation.

This broad associative movement, which combined public activities with those of a wide variety of quasi-public and private groups and individuals, appears to have been the product, in part at least, of the exigencies of the times and circumstances in a new country. More broadly speaking, it could be interpreted as the continuation of the mass cooperative movement which had so largely planned and settled the American colonies. Viewed from still another perspective, it might equally well be described as a stage in the evolution of modern enterprise capitalism out of an authoritative politico-economic status into a new democratic juxtaposition of political and economic forces whose evolution is still in process today.

APPENDIX

I. CHIEF EXECUTIVES OF GEORGIA, 1732–1860

Colonial: Trustees, 1732–1752	
James Edward Oglethorpe, Resident Trustee	1732–1740
William Stephens, President	1740–1750
Henry Parker, Vice-President and President	1750–1752
Colonial: Crown, 1752–1776	
Patrick Graham, President	1752–1754
John Reynolds, Governor	1754–1756
Henry Ellis, Lieutenant Governor and Governor	1756–1760
James Wright, " " " "	1760–1771
James Habersham, Acting Governor	1771–1773
James Wright, Governor	1773–1776
Revolutionary, 1776–1782	
George Walton, President of Council of Safety	1776
William Ewen " " " " "	1776
Archibald Bullock, President	1776
Button Gwinnett, President	1777
John A. Treutlen, Governor	1777
John Houstoun, Governor	1778
Interregnum (John Wereat, President of Supreme Executive Council, 1779; George Walton and Richard Howley, Governors, 1779–1780, and Stephen Heard, President of Executive Council, 1780, elected by an upstate assembly.)	1779–1780
Nathan Brownson, Governor	1781
John Martin, Governor	1782
State, 1783–1860	
Lyman Hall	1783
John Houstoun	1784
Samuel Elbert	1785
Edward Telfair	1786
George Mathews	1787
George Handly	1788
George Walton	1789
Edward Telfair	1789–1793
George Mathews	1793–1796
Jared Irwin	1796–1798
James Jackson	1798–1801
David Emanuel	1801
Josiah Tattnall	1801–1802
John Milledge	1802–1806
Jared Irwin	1806–1809
David B. Mitchell	1809–1813
Peter Early	1813–1815

David B. Mitchell	1815–1817
William Rabun	1817–1819
Matthew Talbot	1819
John Clark	1819–1823
George M. Troup	1823–1827
John Forsyth	1827–1829
George Gilmer	1829–1831
Wilson Lumpkin	1831–1835
William Schley	1835–1837
George Gilmer	1837–1839
Charles J. McDonald	1839–1843
George W. Crawford	1843–1847
George W. Towns	1847–1851
Howell Cobb	1851–1853
Herschel V. Johnson	1853–1857
Joseph E. Brown	1857–1865

II. REVENUES AND EXPENDITURES OF THE TRUSTEES

Revenues, 1732–1752[a]
(in pounds — shillings and pence omitted)

	General subscriptions for establishing the colony	South Carolina tax on rum[b]	Special subscriptions for religious purposes	Special subscriptions for agriculture and botany[c]	Parliamentary grants	Totals
1732–33	£3,443		£165	£116		£ 3,724
1733–34	1,338		45	120	£10,000	11,503
1734–35	1,710	£465	47	60	3,135	5,417
1735–36	789	411	900	65	26,000	28,165
1736–37	2,809	334	359	127	10,000	13,629
1737–38	143		400	107	20,000	20,650
1738–39	362		71	40	8,000	8,473
1739–40	55	86	40		20,000	20,181
1740–41	24		10		4,000	4,034
1741–42	10				10,000	10,010
1742–43						
1743–44					12,000	12,000
1744–45						
1745–46						
1746–47					4,000	4,000
1747–48						
1748–49	159[d]					159
1749–50					5,304	5,304
1750–51					3,552	3,552
1751–52	416[d]				4,000	4,416
	£11,258	£1,296	£2,037	£635	£139,991	£155,217
	$50,098	$5,767	$9,065	$2,825	$622,960	$690,715

[a] *Colonial Records of Georgia* (Atlanta: Candler, editor, Vol. III). Thousands of books, mostly religious, and large quantities of clothing, articles of furniture, tools, utensils, seeds, and plants also were contributed by individuals for the use of the colony.

[b] South Carolina levied a 3 pence per gallon tax on rum imports for the benefit of the Georgia colony during the years indicated. This was collected in South Carolina currency which was depreciated between 600–700 per cent at this time. Figures in the table are at specie value.

[c] These were special individual gifts chiefly for the purpose of hiring a botanist and for the expense of collecting botanical specimens in the western semi-tropical regions for transplanting in Georgia.

[d] Receipts from sales of articles made of Georgia silk and of wound silk.

Expenditures, 1732–1752[a]

(in pounds — shillings and pence omitted)

	Office expenses in England[b]	Freights and passage charges	Provisions, and stores for charity settlers[c]	Military expenditures[d]	Public works[e]	General expense in the colony[f]	Public agricultural operations[g]	Silk culture	Indian presents	Religion and church construction	Totals
1732–33	£ 297	£ 629	£1,496	£ 74	£ 167	£ 14	£ 163	£ 149	£ 219	£ 22	£ 3,230
1733–34	422	1,473	6,064	1,096	905	343	298	208	439	30	11,278
1734–35	306	1,056	4,395	1,199	1,107	210	377		1,146	50	9,846
1735–36	928	3,998	5,418	1,116	282	299	122	471	938	57	13,629
1736–37	793	2,128	8,395	1,923	1,083	901	1,001		834	204	17,262
1737–38	968	2,676	9,199	2,641	3,148	802	1,988	175	820	337	22,754
1738–39	881	1,343	4,814	4,725	3,493	1,023	2,603	273	1,486	324	20,965
1739–40	724	940	1,232	851	2,000	1,094	1,251	179	106	297	8,674
1740–41	990	325	1,076		332	378	1,188	30	216	169	4,704
1741–42	1,021	1,889	1,656	195	606	1,082	1,367	304	238	13	8,371
1742–43	812	78	485		172	2,083	749	131	230	63	4,803
1743–44	679	203	306		197	801	97	156	88	60	2,587
1744–45	613	131	50	119		1,023	150		65	22	2,173
1745–46	717	289	36		100	897	427	371	143	27	3,007
1746–47	673	16	64		182	1,397	172	220	73	65	2,862
1747–48	559	6	1,181	157	670	1,580	454	146	17	222	4,992
1748–49	581	402	15		77	418	97	140	166	139	2,035
1749–50	614	298	119	263	109	1,748	255	462		423	4,291
1750–51	635		114	152	150	1,055	200	6	150	54	2,516
1751–52	1,789			139		1,996		1,092	122	100	5,238
	£15,002	£17,880	£46,115	£14,650	£14,780	£19,144	£12,959	£ 4,513	£ 7,496	£ 2,678	£155,217
Per cent	9.7	11.5	29.8	9.4	9.4	12.4	8.4	2.9	4.8	1.7	100.0
	$66,759	$79,566	$205,212	$65,192	$65,771	$85,191	$57,667	$20,083	$33,357	$11,917	$690,715

[a] *C.R.G.*, III. The financial reports of the Trust were not given for identical annual periods in many instances, and they were not always separated clearly according to purposes; hence allocation had to be estimated in these cases.

[b] Chiefly clerical work and stationery; also includes £521 of interest and fees on bills of exchange and £453 for diplomatic correspondence with the Spanish government in Florida.

[c] Charges amounting to £541 credited against Trust servants are included. Financial operations involving servants supplied to colonists do not appear in the reports. Most of the expenses of the Trust servants in other purposes.

[d] Construction and maintenance of forts, supply of garrisons, arms, and ammunition.

[e] Includes construction of roads, public buildings, sawmills, grain mills, botanical garden; clearing and surveying; purchase of boats for public use; lighthouses; and some fortifications of minor sort around Savannah.

[f] Chiefly salaries of executive and judicial officers; also includes an item reported as "Poor Relief and the Execution of Justice" totaling £5132. "Execution of Justice" appears to have referred to police duties.

[g] This column is made up of: purchase and care of livestock herds, 1733–1751, £5,854; operations of the Trust farms, 1737–1743, £5,548; and agricultural subsidies during 1736–1739, 1741–42 and 1745–46, £1,557.

NOTES AND BIBLIOGRAPHY

NOTES AND BIBLIOGRAPHY

The system of reference used herein has been designed with a view to simplicity and economy. Sources that have been employed extensively in any chapter are given in full title at the head of the chapter notes and are cited thereafter only by surname of author or by symbol, unless further identification is deemed to be necessary. Other source references are reproduced by full title upon the first citation and thereafter as above. No note references are made to the annual *Acts of the General Assembly of the State of Georgia* wherever the date of a statutory action is sufficiently obvious from the text, except in certain instances prior to 1825 for which compilations have been used and when the language of a statute has been quoted. The following official publications, compilations, codes and manuscripts and the *Georgia Historical Quarterly*, which have been used throughout all or large sections of the study, will be referred to in all notes by the symbols printed on the left-hand side opposite the titles:

CRG	*Colonial Records of the State of Georgia*, collected and edited for the state by Allen D. Candler. Atlanta, 1911. 26 vols.
RRG	*Revolutionary Records of the State of Georgia*, collected and edited for the state by Allen D. Candler. Atlanta, 1908. 3 vols.
CRMSS	*Colonial Records of the State of Georgia*, in manuscript, State Department of Archives and History, Atlanta.
Laws (Watkins)	R. and G. Watkins, *A Digest of the Laws of the State of Georgia, from its First Establishment as a British Province down to the Year 1798, Inclusive*. Philadelphia, 1800.
Laws (M. & C.)	H. Marbury and W. H. Crawford, *A Digest of the Laws of the State of Georgia from its Settlement as a British Province in 1755 to 1800, Inclusive*. Savannah, 1802.
Laws	*Acts of the General Assembly of the State of Georgia*, 1799–1860.
Laws (Schley)	William Schley, *A Digest of the English Statutes of Force in the State of Georgia*, Philadelphia, 1826.
Laws (Clayton)	A. S. Clayton, *A Compilation of the Laws of Georgia*, 1800–1810. Augusta, 1813.
Laws (Lamar)	L. Q. C. Lamar, *A Compilation of the Laws of Georgia*, 1810–1819. Augusta, 1821.
Laws (Dawson)	W. C. Dawson, *A Compilation of the Laws of Georgia*, 1819–1829. Milledgeville, 1831.
Laws (Foster)	Arthur Foster, *A Digest of the Laws of Georgia*, 1820–1829. Philadelphia, 1831.
Laws (Prince)	O. H. Prince, *A Digest of Georgia Laws to 1821*. Milledgeville, 1822; 2nd edition, to 1837. Athens, 1837.
Laws (T. Cobb)	Cobb, T. R. R., *A Digest of the Statute Laws of Georgia in Force Prior to 1851*. Athens, 1851.

Laws (H. Cobb)	Cobb, Howell, *A Compilation of the Statutes of the State of Georgia.* New York, 1859.
Code (Hotchkiss)	Hotchkiss, W. A., *Codification of the Statute Laws of Georgia, including the English Statutes of Force.* Savannah, 1845.
Code (C. C. & I.)	R. H. Clark, T. R. R. Cobb, and D. Irwin, *Code of the State of Georgia.* Atlanta, 1861.
JGA	*Journal of the General Assembly of Georgia,* 1783–1789 (Manuscript). Atlanta: State Department of Archives and History.
SJ	*Journal of the Senate,* 1789–1860.
HJ	*Journal of the House,* 1789–1860
MED	*Minutes of the Executive Department,* 1790–1860. (Manuscript). Atlanta: State Department of Archives and History.
GLB	Governors' *Letter Books,* 1786–1840 (Manuscript). Atlanta: State Department of Archives and History.
Reps.	Supreme Court, *Reports of Cases,* 1847–1860.
JCC	*Journal of the Continental Congress,* 1744–1789. Washington: S. Hunt, and W. C. Ford, 1904–1928.
GHQ	*Georgia Historical Quarterly.* Savannah: Georgia Historical Society.

Governors' annual and special messages are included in the printed Senate and House *Journals.* The reports of the state treasurers and the comptroller generals are included in the Senate and House *Journals,* 1799–1831; in the *Acts of the General Assembly,* Appendices, 1830–1840; and were printed separately, 1841–1860. There is an incomplete series for the last period in the state library at Atlanta. R. B. Flanders reports a broken series also in the Washington Memorial Library, Macon, Ga. Warrants issued by the treasurer are also included in the *Minutes of the Executive Department,* 1790–1860, in the Department of Archives and History.

Chapter I Planning for Economic Freedom

1. Freedom of choice included freedom of conscience, of religious worship, and of economic and political enterprise. This group of freedoms was sometimes referred to as liberty of person, or personal liberty.

2. Selected references upon the philosophical bases of economic liberalism as presented in this chapter include: Thomas Hobbes, *Leviathan* (1651); Gerrard Winstanley, *Works* (edited by George H. Sabine: Ithaca: Cornell University Press, 1941); James Harrington, *The Commonwealth of Oceana* (1656), *The Prerogative of Popular Government* (1658), and *The Art of Lawgiving* (1659); (all edited with an introduction by John Tolland, *The Oceana and Other Works,* London, 1771); John Locke, *Two Treatises on Government* (1689–90); Baron Montesquieu, *L'Esprit des Lois* (1748); Adam Smith, *Wealth of Nations* (1776); Jeremy Bentham, *Principles of Morals and Legislation* (1780–89); Thomas Paine, *The Rights of Man* (1792); W. L. P. Davidson, *Political Thought: The Utilitarians* (London, 1915); Albert V. Dicey, *Lectures on the Relationship Between Law and Public Opinion in England During the Nineteenth Century* (London, 1941); G. P. Gooch, *Political Thought in England from Bacon to Halifax* (London, 1914–15); L. T. Hobhouse, *Liberalism* (New York, 1911); J. M. Keynes, *The End of Laissez Faire* (New York: New Republic, Inc., 1926); Harold J. Laski, *English Political Thought from Locke*

to Bentham (New York, 1920); H. F. Russell-Smith, *Harrington and His Oceana: A Study of a Seventeenth Century Utopia and Its Influence in America* (Cambridge: University Press, 1914); W. Stark, *The Ideal Foundations of Economic Thought* (New York: Oxford University Press, 1944). References pertaining more specifically to Georgia are included in the body of the analysis in succeeding chapters.

3. Some early economists, notably Nassau Senior, ascribed to man's ingenuity in organization a principle of increasing returns, which operated, especially in commerce and industry, to counteract nature's diminishing returns upon man's efforts upon land. Later, Alfred Marshall gave the principle of increasing returns a central position in his *Principles of Economics* (1890).

4. Hobhouse has pointed out (*Liberalism*, 65–77) that Bentham based his system of social theory upon the principle of utilitarianism rather than upon natural law, but arrived at essentially the same conclusions as the natural law theorists. Actually both concepts are to be found in the works of Adam Smith, who inherited natural law principles from Locke and Newton and social utility from his teacher, Francis Hutcheson.

5. *Wealth of Nations* (Cannan edition), 49, 66–67.

6. The supporters of voluntarism claimed efficiency as a primary advantage of quasi-public activity; the quasi-private nature of the voluntary principle would assure a retention of the self-interest and efficiency of private enterprise. Proponents of outright public activity maintained that voluntarism was likely to be undependable, that it tended to create unequal burdens, and that it could not by its very nature be held responsible for efficient action.

7. The movement had its leadership roots chiefly in Savannah and the idealism of the Revolutionary War. James Jackson had come to Savannah shortly before the outbreak of the war, had taken a militant part in the revolutionary cause, had fought throughout the war and had risen from the ranks to become a brigadier general; John Milledge was the grandson of one of the original charity colonists, the son of a close associate of N. W. Jones in the liberty movement, and had shared personally with James Jackson his most trying experiences as a soldier during the Revolution; Joseph Habersham, son of former Royal Governor James Habersham (who had first come to Georgia with George Whitefield and helped the latter to establish and operate the Bethesda Orphans' House, later became a wealthy merchant and planter and served as governor while James Wright was in England), educated at Princeton, had been a liberty boy, had personally arrested Governor Sir James Wright, had fought through the war, and had been a signer of the protest against the first land company sale in 1789; his brother, James Habersham, Jr., was foreman of the Chatham County Grand Jury that issued the first public denunciation of the Yazoo Companies sale of 1795; Josiah Tatnall, the son of a prominent loyalist, had returned to Georgia after being sent away by his father to keep him out of the revolutionary movement, had fought with great patriotism, and had risen to a prominent position of leadership in the young state; David Emanuel, another of Jackson's associates, was a veteran of the Revolution; and still another, David Mitchell, had come to Georgia after the Revolution to settle the estate of his uncle, a colonial British military surgeon, who had joined the patriot army and served with unusual devotion and had died while a prisoner of the British. Five of these men became governors.

8. George M. Troup had been the political protégé of James Jackson and had inherited his political mantle on the coast. William H. Crawford, who had sided with Jackson in the Yazoo land sale annulment, had become the dominant political figure in the wealthier sections of the cotton belt. Troup inherited much of Jackson's fiery liberalism and was a person of considerable social insight, but was either unable or unwilling to force his party followers to support a liberal state program. He expended much of his energy while governor chiding the federal government for its tardiness in removing the Indians from Georgia according to their agreement in 1802.

9. Clark was the son of General Elijah Clark, the Revolutionary hero of upper Georgia. The Clarks emigrated to Georgia from North Carolina shortly before the Revolution. Both father and son would seem to have had the land fever; and John

Clark's political enemies persistently tried to associate him with the Yazoo land company speculations. Governor Clark moved to Florida in 1828 and his party was left without leadership.

10. Joseph E. Brown was born in Pickens County, South Carolina, and grew up on a small mountain farm in northeast Georgia. Through arduous efforts he was able to obtain an education, including a law course at Yale. He taught school to repay funds that he had borrowed, served in the state Senate and as judge of his circuit, and became governor at the age of thirty-six.

Chapter II Poverty and Benevolence

This and the following chapter, dealing with the colonial period, have drawn most heavily upon two primary source collections: Allen D. Chandler, editor, *Colonial Records of the State of Georgia,* 26 vols., and the *Diary of John Percival, First Earl of Egmont* (Historical Manuscript Commission, 3 vols., London, 1920–1923), hereinafter cited as *Egmont.* There is a wealth of secondary literature, both general and special, on the colonial period. Those of a general nature that have been most helpful are: Walter G. Cooper, *The Story of Georgia,* I (New York, 1938); E. Merton Coulter, *Georgia, A Short History* (Chapel Hill, 1947); Charles C. Jones, *The History of Georgia,* I (Boston, 1883); Lucian L. Knight, *A Standard History of Georgia and Georgians,* I (Chicago, 1917); James R. McCain, *Georgia as a Proprietary Province* (Boston, 1917); Hugh McCall, *The History of Georgia,* 2 vols. (Savannah, 1811–1816; reprinted, Atlanta, 1909); Albert B. Saye, *New Viewpoints in Georgia History* (Athens, 1943); and W. B. Stevens, *A History of Georgia,* 2 vols. (New York, 1847). Although more specialized in subject matter, John P. Corry, *Indian Affairs in Georgia, 1732–1756* (Philadelphia, 1936) supplied helpful suggestions on other aspects of colonial life; and M. G. Jones, *The Charity School Movement in the Eighteenth Century* (Cambridge, 1938) gave invaluable background information on the Georgia colonial venture. I am much indebted to Professor R. H. Tawney for calling my attention at an early point in the progress of this study to this latter work and to other of the less publicized English studies of early eighteenth-century liberal benevolence.

1. There are numbers of analyses of the personnel of the Board of Trustees. See especially Saye, *New Viewpoints,* chs. I–II; by same author, "The Genesis of Georgia: Merchants as well as Ministers," *GHQ,* XXIV, 191–206; Verner W. Crane, "The Philanthropists and the Genesis of Georgia," *Amer. Hist. Rev.,* XXVII, 63–69; Leslie F. Church, *Oglethorpe: A Study of Philanthropy in England and Georgia* (London, 1932); McCain, *Proprietary Province,* ch. II. Much may be gained from Egmont's *Diary* and from the Journal of the Trustees and Minutes of the Common Council, *CRG,* I–II; also of the backgrounds of various members in Jones, *Charity School Movement;* W. O. B. Allen and E. McClure, *Two Hundred Years: The History of the Society for Promoting Christian Knowledge* (London, 1898); C. F. Pasco, *Two Hundred Years of the S.P.G.: An Historical Account of the Society for the Propagation of the Gospel in Foreign Parts* (London, 1901); and Benjamin Rand, editor, *Berkeley to Percival: The Correspondence of George Berkeley, afterwards Bishop of Cloyne, and Sir John Percival, afterwards Earl of Egmont* (Cambridge, 1914).

2. McCain, chs. IV–V; Saye, *New Viewpoints,* ch. III; *CRG,* V.

3. *CRG,* especially vols. I–II, VII–IX, in land grants report origins of nearly all colonists.

4. Egmont's *Diary* sheds most light upon the motives of the Trustees, especially if studied with the Journals and Minutes of Trustees and Common Council. See: *Egmont,* I, 370; II, 133, 222–247, 320–321, 342–365, 498; A. Saye, "Was Georgia A Debtor Colony?" *GHQ,* XXIV, 323.

5. Max Weber, *The Protestant Ethic and the Spirit of Capitalism* (English trans., 1930); John Locke, *Concerning Human Understanding; Thoughts Concerning Education; On Civil Government,* II, ch. 5.

6. *Egmont,* I, 370–9; II, 436. Bernard Mandeville was a severe critic of the philanthropists and their theory of human behavior; see *Fable of the Bees* and *Essays on Charity and Charity Schools.*

7. M. G. Jones, chs. I, IX.

8. *Ibid.,* 3; *Egmont,* I, 44–45. John Wesley, a founder and teacher of charity schools, was sent as an Indian missionary to Georgia; and Thomas Coram, an original Trustee, was probably the leading British proponent of the theory of Indian and Negro education summarized above. Indian conversion and education were given by William Penn as the primary reason for the settlement of Pennsylvania. James Vernon, another original Trustee and the most active and influential one throughout the period of the Trust, was a leader in the relief of German Protestant minorities.

9. M. Beer, *A History of British Socialism* (New York: Harcourt, 1921), I, 76, 80.

10. M. G. Jones, 11–12.

11. The secular liberal outlook was especially pronounced in the Georgia enterprise: *Berkeley and Percival,* 270; *Egmont,* II, 222–247.

12. M. G. Jones, 340–342. Abundant evidences in Egmont's *Diary* and in Minutes of Trustees.

13. *Egmont,* I, 45–46; *Berkeley and Percival,* 270, 276. Oglethorpe's original plan resembled closely a proposal by Joshua Gee, *Trade and Navigation of Great Britain Considered,* 1729, ch. XXVII. See also Saye, "Genesis of Georgia," 196; Verner W. Crane, *The Southern Frontier* (Durham, 1928), 316.

14. *Egmont,* I, 273–274, 373–379; II, 126, 135.

15. *Ibid.,* I, 193; II, 45–46, 124, 200, 320–321, 457; III, 2. Oglethorpe was not interested in Indian missions; nor were any of the Trustees except Egmont and possibly one or two others concerned with Negro education. The Trustees never officially engaged in the latter, although some were members of another trust that did. *Egmont,* II, 193; Saye, *New Viewpoints,* 14–19.

16. *Egmont,* I, 44–45.

17. *Ibid.,* II, 119, 127, 279, 419; III, 207–208; *CRG,* I, 77, 87, 181–187, 195; II, 46.

18. The principal ones were: Thomas Coram's Royal "Province of Georgia" (1717), to be located in Nova Scotia (Coram was an original Georgia Trustee), *Calendar of State Papers, Colonial Series: America and the West Indies,* 1716–1717, pars. 576–577, 582–584; Keith, Ocks and Staubers' "Province of Georgia," to be located in western Virginia and to be settled by foreign Protestants, *ibid.,* 1731, XXXVII–XXXVIII, pars. 342, 399; Sir Robert Montgomery's "Margravate of Azilia," to be located to the south of South Carolina (1717); and Jean Pierre Purry's scheme to colonize in southern Carolina with foreign Protestants, emphasizing particularly the opportunities for silk culture (1721). Saye, "Genesis of Georgia" gives an excellent summary of these other schemes. Saye credits Purry with the first use of the name "Georgia" for the region south of the South Carolina colony.

19. *Economic Writings of Sir William Petty* (C. H. Hull, editor); John Bellers, *Proposals for Raising a College of Industry for All Useful Trades and Husbandry* (1696); Sir Josiah Child, *Discourse of Trade* (1699); Sir William Temple, *Works* (1720). The ideas contained in these and other works of a similar vein are summarized in: James Bonar, *Theories of Population from Raleigh to Arthur Young* (London, 1931); and Beer, *British Socialism,* chs. IV–V.

20. Such works as Thomas Mun, *English Treasure by Foreign Trade.*

21. See Appendix I.

22. It explains also, probably, the increasing royal preoccupation with Indian policy and its support of Oglethorpe's unusually successful early moves in that area. Some of the Trustees, notably Percival and Digby, enjoyed great personal influence in Crown circles; and at least three of the church officers among them were in the personal service of members of the royal family. It seems clear that Oglethorpe became increasingly interested in the military features and came to view the project finally almost as a part of a vast military operation against Spain and France. The other leading Trustees broke with him over this issue and practically removed him

from participation in the colonial enterprise. The more our attention is centered upon Oglethorpe as the guiding genius and spirit of the Georgia enterprise, particularly after the initial phase, the more likely the project will appear to have had strong imperialistic and militaristic designs.

23. *Egmont,* II, 286, *passim.*

24. Some of the Trustees, notably Shaftsbury, supported vigorously the position that the Trust was wholly a public agency, and that the Trustees should be recognized as occupying an administrative position in the government.

25. *Egmont,* III, 19–20, 117; *CRG,* XII, Pt. I, 314, 326, 364; XXIV, 190, 205; XXV, 100, 341, 354, 389.

26. Saye, *New Viewpoints,* ch. III.

27. A. Saye, "Was Georgia a Debtor Colony?" *GHQ,* XXIV, 331–332; E. M. Coulter, "A List of the First Shipload of Georgia Settlers," *GHQ,* XXXI, 282–288, indicates character of early charity colonists.

28. *Egmont,* I, 370, 376; *CRG,* II, 12–19; III, 411–413.

29. *Ibid.,* I, 391; II, 25, 205, 320–321; III, 54–57, 77, 195–197.

30. *Ibid.*

31. *Ibid.,* I, 370, 376. See also land and labor laws: *CRG,* III, 373; I and II, *passim.* There was a strong desire also not to incur the opposition of manufacturers and others at home who feared colonial competition.

32. *Egmont,* I, 151.

33. *CRG,* II, 12–19; III, 411–413.

34. *Egmont,* III, 57, 77.

35. *Ibid.,* 67; *CRG,* IV, *passim.*

36. All of these activities generically were quasi-public, but they are treated herein as public, since they were owned and controlled by the governing powers of the colony and operated in a public as distinct from a private manner. The Trustees were fully aware of the large role of conducting public business in the colony that would devolve upon them. *Egmont,* I, 227, 293.

37. *CRG,* IV, 213–218; XXII, Pt. II, *passim.*

38. *Egmont,* III, 44; *CRG,* II, 318.

39. *Egmont,* III, 44.

40. *CRG,* II, 429.

41. *Egmont,* III, 93; *CRG,* II, 231–232; XXII, Pt. II, 163.

42. *CRG,* III, 86. Purchases were made in South Carolina; they were chiefly of cattle, but there were also some of horses, swine, and poultry.

43. *CRG,* IV, 314–315.

44. *CRG,* XXIV, 66; XXV, 133.

45. *CRG,* II, 507.

46. *CRG,* III, 14, 51, 83, 112, 141, 166, 195.

47. *CRG,* I, 276–277; II, 5–6; XXI, 68, 191–195, 281, 491.

48. *CRG,* IV, 44; V, 630; VII, 101.

49. *CRG,* II, 275–278; XXII, Pt. I, 245–246.

50. *Egmont,* I, 272–273; II, 436; *CRG,* II, 104, 231–232, 249.

51. *Egmont,* II, 407–408; *CRG,* II, 73–74, 76–77, 98, 249–252.

52. *Egmont,* II, 473.

53. *Ibid.,* 275–282.

54. *Ibid.,* 119, 193; *CRG,* XXII, Pt. II, 170.

55. *Egmont,* II, 221; III, 38.

56. *CRG,* XXIV, 93.

57. *CRG,* XXII, Pt. II, 170.

58. *CRG,* II, 407.

59. *Egmont,* II, 320–321; *CRG,* I, 265–266, 278–279; II, 192.

60. *Egmont,* II, 184, 195–196, 230–253.

61. *CRG,* XXII, Pt. I, 90, 103, 291; *Egmont,* III, 48.

62. *CRG,* II, 476; IV, 84, 172–173, 285–287.

63. *CRG,* II, 407.

64. These included besides one year's subsistence and an iron pot and frying

pan, passage money, a hatchet, hammer, handsaw, shovel or spade, broad hoe, narrow hoe, gimlet, and drawing knife. *CRG,* III, 407–409.

65. Innumerable references to these experiences: *CRG,* I, II, IV, XXV, 100; *Egmont.*

66. *CRG,* II, 164–167; XXII, Pt. II, 93. Petty capitalists taking one servant to Georgia were given free passage, bedding, clothing, and one year's subsistence for the servant: *CRG,* III, 411. All colonists were supplied mulberry trees free.

67. James Habersham to H. Verlest: *CRG,* XXV, 100.

68. *CRG,* III, 409.

69. *CRG,* II, 72–7, 95–99, 110, 141, 166–167, 200; XXII, Pt. I, 55, 59–64, 282; Pt. II, 163.

70. *CRG,* XXV, 397, 441.

71. *Egmont,* I, 391; II, 25, 205. There were attempts also to select foreign Protestants for desired skills: *CRG,* II, 54, 66, 69.

72. *Ibid.,* 20–27.

73. *Egmont,* II, 194.

74. *CRG,* II, 420, 428, 492; XXIV, 413.

75. *CRG,* II, 420, 428, 491, 507–511.

76. *Ibid.,* 437, 447; XXII, Pt. II, 244; XXIII, 100, 150.

77. *CRG,* II, 12–79, 128, 218, 228, 241; III, 87, 118, 146, 192, 211; XXII, Pt. II, 162, 244.

78. *CRG,* III, 195, 404.

79. *Egmont,* I, 373.

80. *Ibid.,* 151.

81. *CRG,* III, 377–8; *Egmont,* III, 109–111.

82. *Egmont,* I, 339–340.

83. Appendix I.

84. *CRG,* XXV, 182, 362–382, 469, 491.

85. *Egmont,* III, 54–57, 77.

86. *CRG,* II, 90, 100, 109.

87. *Ibid.,* 44–45.

88. *CRG,* III, 64–69, 101, 135–136, 206.

89. *CRG,* II, 116. Its value fluctuated widely. At this time it was worth about seven to one in terms of specie.

90. *CRG,* IV, 25, 242.

91. *Ibid.,* 213–218.

92. *CRG,* II, 114 ff.

93. *Egmont,* II, 186.

94. *Ibid.,* 189; *CRG,* II, 113.

95. *Ibid.*

96. *Egmont,* II, 189.

97. *CRG,* II, 113–114, 207, 362.

98. *Ibid.,* 184.

99. *Ibid.,* 128, 178, 223–227, 476.

100. *Ibid.,* 217, 235–236, 262–284, 410–421.

101. *Ibid.,* 318.

102. *CRG,* XXV, 2; Proceedings of President and Assistants, June 18, 1746.

103. *CRG,* XXIV, 331; XXV, 362, 389, 397.

104. *Ibid.*

105. *Ibid.,* 397.

106. *CRG,* II, 249; IV, 239, 673.

107. *CRG,* II, *passim.*

108. *Egmont,* I, 370; II, 320–321.

109. Recent reductions in the sizes of land grants had been introduced into South Carolina with the intent of developing a higher proportion of small landholdings. Since the Georgia limitations were similar and had much the same purpose, it seems likely that the South Carolina laws were the immediate model. The Pennsylvania laws preceded both. W. R. Smith, *South Carolina as a Royal Province, 1719–1776*

(New York, 1903), chs. 1–3; A. S. Salley, Jr., editor, *Commissions and Instructions from the Lords Proprietors of South Carolina to Public Officials of South Carolina, 1685–1715.*

110. W. R. Shepherd, "History of Proprietary Government in Pennsylvania," *Studies in History, Economics and Public Law* (New York: Columbia University Press, 1896), VI; W. R. Smith, *South Carolina;* A. S. Salley, Jr., *Commissions.*

111. The extensive land grant abuses, particularly the growth of vast individual holdings, were receiving an airing in England at the same time that the Trustees were planning the Georgia colony. The legality of the baronial grants was being threshed out in the courts. These occurrences must have influenced the actions of the Trustees.

112. *CRG,* I, 17–18, 67, 418; II, 11–26; *Egmont,* I, 154, 277, 313. South Carolina notified the Trustees immediately that some grants had been made already within the territory.

113. Text of treaty is reprinted in *GHQ,* IV, 12–16.

114. *Ibid.,* 5–8.

115. The king held right to only seven-eighths part of the quitrents, since Lord Carteret still held one-eighth share in Carolina territory: *CRG,* I, 418.

116. *CRG,* III, 373–380, 404–413; *Egmont,* I, 370; II, 104. The Trustees' conception finds similarities in some of William Penn's ideas for Pennsylvania, and it may also reflect the influence of the seventeenth-century writer, James Harrington. It clearly somewhat anticipates Thomas Jefferson's ideal agrarian society. Oglethorpe referred to the Georgia plan as one of "agrarian equality" (*CRG,* XXII, Pt. II, 163). Servants' grants were increased to fifty acres in 1741. This action became necessary because it was found that most servants emigrated as soon as their time was up, if not before, for they could obtain at least fifty acres in South Carolina: *CRG,* II, 361; IV, 238; *Egmont,* III, 150.

117. *CRG,* I, 77–79; II, 49–50; III, 409. Residence and garden lots were sometimes combined and, in small village settlements, all three lots were combined in a single unit.

118. *CRG,* III, 375–376, 412.

119. *CRG,* II, 7; *Egmont,* II, 70, 104, 184.

120. *CRG,* III, 422–431; P. Tailfer, H. Anderson, D. Douglas, *et al.,* "Narrative of Georgia," *Force Tracts,* I, No. IV.

121. *CRG,* IV, 239.

122. *Egmont,* II, 104, 184, 199.

123. *Ibid.,* 70, 103–104, 147, 184, 405, 478–479; *CRG,* III, 373–375; XXII, Pt. II, 163.

124. *CRG,* II, 227–228; III, 422–427; IV, 11–12, 29–30; *Egmont,* II, 428–429; III, 152; McCain, *Proprietary Province,* ch. VIII.

125. *CRG,* III, 394.

126. *CRG,* I, 359; II, 300–302, 393–401; III, 397–398; IV, 390–391.

127. *CRG,* II, 340, 393–401; III, 400.

128. *CRG,* I, 398, 433.

129. *Ibid.,* 544.

130. *Egmont,* II, 274, 493; *CRG,* I, 389; II, 240.

131. *CRG,* II, 349; III, 376; IV, 59–60, 200–201, 266, 282, 307–315, 335–336.

132. *Egmont,* III, 201–202; *CRG,* XXIV, 434.

133. *Egmont,* I, 272–275.

134. *Ibid.,* 293–295; II, 405, 478–479; III, 108; *CRG,* I, 85; II, 47–50.

135. D. Ricardo, *Principles of Political Economy* (Everyman's Edition), 52.

136. *CRG,* II, 72–73, 95, 119, 164–167, 192; IV, 77; XXII, Pt. I, 10–32, 135, 361; XXII, Pt. II, 163; *Egmont,* II, 389–391.

137. *CRG,* IV, 175, 201–208, 278–282, 305–306, 671–672; XXII, Pt. I, 171, 361.

138. *Ibid.,* 22, 53; *Egmont,* III, 181–182.

139. *CRG,* IV, 293–294.

140. *Ibid.,* 673; XXII, Pt. I, 10, 19–22, 53, 185, 220; XXIII, 148.

141. *Egmont,* III, 136, 193; *CRG,* IV, 672–673.

142. *CRG,* II, 24, 175.

143. *Egmont,* I, 379; II, 436. Oglethorpe, however, strongly urged sending child servants.

144. *CRG,* XXII, Pt. I, 171, 359–361; XXIII, 148. Oglethorpe gave the first lot to his soldiers as wives to relieve the Trust of further expense. William Stephens, secretary and later president of the colony, tried three female servants. The first two turned out to be prostitutes and the third, a housewife, in an advanced state of pregnancy; after these experiences Stephens decided to get along without a female servant.

145. *CRG,* IV, 59–60, 200–201, 307–315, 335–336; XXII, Pt. I, 67, 82, 256, 270, 342, 361; XXII, Pt. II, 93; XXIII, 150; XXIV, 258, 372; XXV, 12, 133; *Egmont,* III, 73, 134, 154. Yet indentured servitude continued longer in Georgia than anywhere else: H. L. Osgood, *The American Colonies in the Eighteenth Century* (New York, 1924), II, 486.

146. *CRG,* IV, 203, 266, 307; *Egmont,* III, 150–155, 200–202.

147. *CRG,* XXIV, 93, 182; XXV, 343–346, 424–427.

148. *CRG,* III, 422–434; IV, 11–12, 59–60, 242–244, 264–265, 491; XXIV, 434; XXV, 282, 290; *Egmont,* III, 188.

149. *CRG,* I, 506–507; XXIII, 160; XXV, 225, 290.

150. *Egmont,* II, 141, 171, 205, 493; III, 55–58, 60–61, 108–111, 133–140, 150–155, 188–189, 200–205, 229, 242.

151. *CRG,* 506–507.

152. *Ibid.,* 530–531; XXV, 347–351; I, 56–62.

153. *Ibid.,* 430–437; XXIV, 347.

154. *Ibid.*

155. *Egmont,* III, 202.

156. *Egmont,* II, 429; III, 18–19, 47. On previous occasions some of the original Trustees had favored withdrawing the colony in preference to abandoning their fundamental policies.

157. *CRG,* VI, 198 ff., 247–248, 304.

158. *CRG,* I, 77–79; II, 6–7, 49–50; III, 409; Stevens, *History,* I, 99–100; Coulter, ch. III.

159. *Egmont,* I, 295.

160. *CRG,* XXIV, 93.

161. *CRG,* I, 93; III, 409; XXI, 115.

162. *Egmont,* II, 16–18, 160–166, 226–227.

163. *Ibid.,* 293, 320–321, *passim; CRG,* IV, 671–672.

164. *Ibid.,* 286–292, 313–315, 339–341; XXI, 115; Amos A. Ettinger, *James Oglethorpe: Imperial Idealist* (Oxford: Clarendon Press, 1936). What relative weight is attached to military objectives in the Georgia project will depend upon the weights given to the attitudes of Crown and Parliament, Oglethorpe's later activities, and to the proceedings and discussions of the Trustees. It is not inconsistent, of course, that the British government which put up most of the money may have harbored different aims from those of the Trustees who contributed most of the labors.

165. *Egmont,* II, 251–252, 284–295.

166. *Ibid.,* 289–291. Oglethorpe had begun the operations before learning of the Trustee action.

167. *Egmont,* III, 293.

168. *CRG,* XXIII, 160.

169. *CRG,* II, 109; III, 86, 116; XXI, 228, 289.

170. *CRG,* III, 255; XXI, 116.

171. *CRG,* VI.

172. *CRG,* III, 145; XXII, Pt. I, 59, Pt. II, 20, 236.

173. *CRG,* III, 169, 191, 210.

174. *Ibid.,* 211; IV, 25; XXII, Pt. II, 236.

175. *CRG,* IV, 314.

176. *Egmont,* II, 70, 104, 147, 184, 478–479; *CRG,* III, 373–375, 431–432.

177. *Egmont,* II, 103, 405.

178. *CRG*, I, 25, 43, 93; III, 44–45, 151, 171; IV, 59–60, 179, 250–266, 307, 312, 461, 502–503; XXII, Pt. I, 67, 103; XXV, 354.

179. *CRG*, I, 31 ff., 548; II, 120–123, 509; Saye, *New Viewpoints*, 72–75.

180. *CRG*, IV, 239; XXII, Pt. I, 161, 361; XXV, 166, 322, 354, 389. The Trustees were exceedingly anxious to avoid any implications of trading ambitions — they did not aspire to be another East India Company. Merchants were among their chief supporters in Parliament (Saye, *New Viewpoints*). They were sufficiently unpopular already — among manufacturers, raw silk importers, and some publicists like Mandeville. Oglethorpe in particular was adamant against any change, feeling that existing policies gave sufficient encouragement to trade (*CRG*, XXIII, 332). Possibly the Trustees were also influenced by the existing frictions aroused by the trading activities of the other American colonies.

181. Shaw Livermore, *Early American Land Companies* (New York: Commonwealth Fund, 1939), 46–48. The poor success of this venture in Pennsylvania may have deterred the Trustees from undertaking not only similar ventures but any others as well.

182. J. Clay, *Letters of Joseph Clay of Savannah, Ga., 1776–1793* (Savannah: Georgia Historical Society, 1913), 194–195, to James Jackson, Feb. 16, 1784; also 33–40, 240–259; *Land Grant Books of the Colony of Georgia*, 1758–1772 (Secretary of State, Atlanta), *passim; CRG*, VI, 25, 242–244, 373–396; XXIV, 331; XXV, 112, 389–97; Leila Sellers, *Charleston Business on the Eve of the American Revolution* (Chapel Hill: Univ. of N. C. Press, 1934), particularly ch. 3, is an excellent study of the Southern colonial merchant.

183. *CRG*, IV, *passim;* XXIV, 434.

Chapter III Imperialism and Agrarian Capitalism

1. Saye, *New Viewpoints*, ch. III.

2. The power to make new grants was transferred from the president and assistants to the governor with advice of council: three letters from the Lords Commissioners for Trade and Plantations, August 16 and December 22, 1752 and August 12, 1753; eight letters from Benjamin Martyn who served the Board of Trade as secretary for Georgia during 1752–1754.

3. *Acts of Privy Council*, Colonial Series IV, 296–299; *CRG*, VII, 295–298, 600–611; VIII, 577–579.

4. References to quitrents in Georgia: *CRG*, I, 400–407, 467, 570; IX, 90, 110; XIII, 687; XV, 552; XVI, 428. On the recommendation of Trustees, all quitrents were forgiven for the Trust period. There were continuous efforts during the Crown period to have them reduced or abolished, but no action seems to have been taken. Governor Wright estimated that arrears totaled over £2,000 in 1767, but indicated in 1773 that it was a principal source of revenue.

5. *CRG*, XVIII, 743–748. An appropriation of £1,815 of paper money, to be retired in six years from general tax revenues, was made to cover these expenses.

6. *CRG*, VIII, 125, 204, 520, 563, 762, 790. It should be noted that Governor Wright's slave holdings entitled him to more than twice the acreage of land grants that he received.

7. The scale provided: field officer, 5,000 acres; captain, 3,000; subaltern or staff officer, 2,000; non-commissioned officer, 200; private, 50. *Laws* (Watkins), 742; *CRG*, IX, 121. Comparison of this scale with the bonuses granted later by the state to Revolutionary veterans shows some democratic tendency to be found in the modification of the head-right grants: the upper ranks were scaled down and the lower increased notably. Soldier bonuses began in Georgia with Oglethorpe's troop during the Trustee period. *Acts of Privy Council, Colonial Series*, V, 295–296.

8. *CRG*, IX, 225–261; X, 747–748, 788; XI, 146.

9. *CRG*, VII, 869; VIII, 70, 345, 639–643, 697–698, 717–762.

10. *CRG*, VI, 225–230; VII, 102–103; XIII, 93, 390; XVIII, 588–598.

11. *CRG*, XIII, 687; XVI, 428.

12. E. B. Greene and V. D. Harrington, *American Population before the Federal Census of 1790* (New York: Columbia University Press, 1932) 180–182.

13. Slave ownership of immigrants is indicated fairly clearly by land-grant records. *CRG,* VI–XI.

14. *CRG,* XVIII, 102–144; *Letters of James Habersham* (Savannah: Georgia Historical Society, *Collections,* 1904); R. B. Flanders, *Plantation Slavery in Georgia* (Chapel Hill, 1933) ch. II.

15. *CRG,* XVIII, 225–235, 462–464; XIX, 75–82.

16. *Ibid.,* 558–560, 799–802.

17. *Ibid.,* 649–688; 760–762, 792–794; XIX, 76, 209–249.

18. *CRG,* XVIII, 277–282.

19. Flanders, ch. III, is a good treatment of the large plantation.

20. Coulter, *Georgia,* 103.

21. *CRG,* VI–XI, delineate the records of the accumulation of the lands of the large plantation. Land holdings were usually far in excess of lands actually under cultivation.

22. *Letters,* 38–39, 101.

23. Estimates are based on commercial and other records and given in Spanish milled dollars.

24. The *Letters of Joseph Clay of Savannah, Ga., 1776–1793* (Savannah: Georgia Historical Society, *Collections,* VIII, 1913) and the *Letter Books* of the mercantile firm of Clay, Telfair and Company, 1783–1791 (unprinted manuscript collection in the Library of the Georgia Historical Society, Savannah), though dating only from the outbreak of the Revolution and later, give the most adequate picture of the commercial system in Georgia at the end of the colonial period; and they also contain a great deal of data on the colonial period. See also Leila Sellers, *Charleston Business on the Eve of the Revolution;* John G. W. De Brahm, *History of the Province of Georgia.*

25. "Letters from Sir James Wright" (Savannah: Ga. Hist. Soc., *Collections,* III, 1873), 165; Amanda Johnson, "Georgia, 1774–1777," *GHQ,* XVI, 253–273.

26. *Augusta Chronicle,* "Georgia: Situation and Extent," Feb. 15, 1817. These were pound sterling figures, presumably, converted into dollar equivalents at par of exchange.

27. George White, *Historical Collections of Georgia* (New York, 1855), 107.

28. Wright, "Letters," 165–167. The figures have been converted into the equivalent of Spanish milled dollars of the period for comparability.

29. *CRG,* XVIII, 87–101.

30. *Ibid.,* 182–188.

31. *Ibid.,* 505–507, 583–586; XIII, 562, 582, 609–616, 692.

32. *CRG,* XVIII, 717–742.

33. *Ibid.,* 794–796.

34. *CRG,* XIX, 3–11.

35. *Ibid.,* 59–67.

36. *Ibid.,* 253–288.

37. *CRG,* XI, 36; XVIII, 80–86, 218–224, 494–501, 570–577, 706–708, 751–752.

38. *CRG,* XIX, Pt. II, 8–23.

39. *CRG,* VI, 430; XVIII, 515–525, 769–773.

40. See Internal Improvements, above.

41. *CRG,* XVIII, 430–432, 797–799.

42. *Ibid.,* 774–780; XIX, 93–95; Pt. II, 38–44, 243–248, 290–292.

43. *CRG,* XIX, 70–71, 204–208.

44. *CRG,* XVIII, 86–87.

45. *Ibid.,* 335–337.

46. *CRG,* XIX, 14–22.

47. *CRG,* XVIII, 73–74, 303–307, 353–357.

48. *CRG,* XIX, Pt. II, 33–35.

49. *Ibid.,* Pt. I, 14–22.

50. Coulter, *Georgia,* 91–92; *CRG,* VI, 147–148; Percy S. Flippin, "The Royal

Government in Georgia, 1752–1776," *GHQ*, VIII, 87–88; J. P. Corry, *Indian Affairs in Georgia, 1732–1756*, gives much of the background of these treaties.

51. Coulter, *Georgia*, 98–100.
52. *Laws* (Watkins), Appendix.
53. *CRG*, XVIII, 48–63.
54. *Ibid.*, 235–240.
55. *Ibid.*, 308–313.
56. *Ibid.*, 420–426.
57. *Ibid.*, 435–455. An interesting feature of the act was a provision that deeds of mortgage should be drawn in a short, concise and substantial form, which should have the full power of conveyance as "any deeds of feoffment with livery and seizin or deeds enrolled in any of His Majesty's courts at Westminster may or can do." The object of the shortened form was to reduce expense to the minimum. This was a typical attitude of the Georgians toward the verbiage and costly procedures of the English law of property. Brevity became almost an obsession with them and some of their later property instruments are incredibly succinct.
58. *Ibid.*, 639–648. An earlier effort to obtain an issue for building forts, to be sunk by special taxes upon deerskins, was defeated by the Savannah merchants. *Ibid.*, XIII, 616–619.
59. *CRG*, XVIII, 743–748. See Land Policy, *supra*, for more details of the immigrant program.
60. *CRG*, XIX, 83–89.
61. *Ibid.*, 147–151.
62. *Ibid.*, 418–426.
63. *Ibid.* Counterfeiting was made a felony punishable by death without benefit of clergy, in 1773. It was feared that counterfeiters of other colonies' monies were locating in Georgia.
64. *CRG*, XIX, Pt. II, 3–8.
65. *CRG*, XIX, 415–418.
66. *Ibid.*, 449–470.
67. *CRG*, XVIII, 240–247, 685; XIX, 100–113, 161–175, 449–470.
68. Wright, "Letters," 170–179. It has been estimated (Saye, *New Viewpoints*, 135) that Parliament expended £4,000 annually, on the average, in Georgia. The colonial records indicate somewhat less, but some items may not appear in them.
69. *CRG*, XVIII, 66–73. The average value of a slave was about £40 at this time, which also was considered generally the approximate value, on the average, of one hundred acres of land. Consequently, the rate of 2½ shillings per £100 value on slaves and land was only about one-third the rate on urban property. The actual rate was very much lower on improved rice and indigo plantations of the best grades of land.
70. *Ibid.*, 240–247, 337–350.
71. *Ibid.*, 656–657, 685.
72. *CRG*, XIX, 100–113.
73. *Ibid.*, 161–175.
74. Wright, "Letters," 170–179.
75. *Ibid.*; *CRG*, XIX, 449–470.
76. *CRG*, XVIII, 75–77, 159–160, 164–171, 484–489, 636–639, 691–703; XIX, 83, 147–151, 359–406, 439–449; XIII, 640–643, 692.
77. These conditions are reflected in the tax laws and in the minutes, proceedings, and journals of the governing bodies. *CRG*, VII–XIX.
78. Wright, "Letters," 170–172; *CRG*, XIII, 688.
79. Coulter, 103.
80. Records of land grants: *CRG*, VI–XI.
81. *Letters*, 160.
82. De Brahm, 51.
83. Flanders, *Plantation Slavery in Georgia*, ch. III.
84. Coulter, 101.
85. Governor James Jackson, who came to Georgia as a young man during the

years immediately preceding the Revolution, stated that a majority of Georgians were not in favor of the American cause at the outbreak of the struggle. Quoted in footnote: W. O. Foster, "James Jackson in the American Revolution," *GHQ*, XXXI, 249.

86. Coulter, 112.

87. Saye, *New Viewpoints*, 149. Henry Laurens of South Carolina may have exercised the greatest influence for the patriotic cause of any single person outside of the colony. He was particularly close to men like Joseph Clay, Edward Telfair, and Lachlan McIntosh.

88. Allen P. Tankersley, "Midway District: A Study of Puritanism in Colonial Georgia," *GHQ*, XXXII, 149–157; Reba C. Strickland, *Religion and the State in Georgia in the Eighteenth Century* (New York, 1939), 115–116.

89. Louise F. Hays, *Chronology of Georgia* (Atlanta: State Dept. of Archives and History, 1943). It is doubtful whether these frontier settlers exerted a major influence in initiating the Revolution, but unquestionably they played an important role in maintaining armed resistance and in winning the struggle in the Georgia sector. Letter of Peter Tarling, to John Houstoun (?), Oct. 24, 1775 (Manuscript, Library of Ga. Hist. Soc., Savannah).

90. It is notable that the first leader of the democratic movement against the Crown in Georgia was Noble Wymberley Jones, son of one of the original settlers who came over with Oglethorpe. The father had become a wealthy planter and a Crown officer. It should be pointed out, however, that several of the ablest younger leaders who later came to the fore were either students or ardent admirers of President Witherspoon of Princeton, a Northern "Liberty Boy" and later an independence stalwart. This was notably true of Reverend John Joachim Zubly, John and Joseph Habersham, and John Houstoun. Rev. J. J. Zubly, Manuscript Journal, 1770–1781 (Library of Ga. Hist. Soc., Savannah). On N. W. Jones, see Coulter, 115–124.

91. Records of Commons House of Assembly, 1770–1773.

92. Peter Tarling's letter (note 89) reflects the thinking of the young leaders, as well as the apathy of the rank and file and the militant attitude of the opposing royal sympathizers. Clay, *Letters*, to Josiah Smith, May 15, 1777, describes the fervent, self-sacrificing attitude of patriot leaders like John Wereat and James Jackson. Jackson, who came to Savannah in 1774, studied law with Wereat. See Tankersley, "Midway District" on Jackson.

Chapter IV The Public Domain and Early Land Policy

1. Estimates are based upon: *Abstract of the U. S. Census; Colonial Records of Georgia*, VII–XI; *Revolutionary Records of Georgia*, I–III; Watkins, *Digest of the Laws of Georgia;* Evarts B. Greene and Virginia Harrington, *American Population before the Federal Census of 1790* (New York, 1932), 17–18, 180–186; Stella H. Sutherland, *Population Distribution in Colonial America* (New York: Columbia University Press, 1936); Walter S. Cooper, *The Story of Georgia* (New York, 1938); E. M. Coulter, *Georgia: A Short History* (Chapel Hill, 1947); S. G. McLendon, *History of the Public Domain in Georgia* (Atlanta, 1924).

2. Based upon the number of head grants (Sutherland), population records (Greene and Harrington), the family right laws and the records of sales of timber lands (*CRG*).

3. *RRG*, II, 449–453.

4. *Ibid.*, 62.

5. Sutherland, map at page 222 indicates 1,052 persons in 1775, in what is now Lincoln County.

6. *CRG*, XIX, Pt. II, 201–215; *RRG*, II, 237–42; Absalom H. Chappell, *Miscellanies of Georgia* (Atlanta, 1874), Pt. II, ch. 1.

7. *RRG*, II, 556 ff; *U. S. Census*, 1790.

8. *Laws* (Watkins), 763–766.

9. *RRG*, III, 207–213, 229–230, 404, 530; Joseph Clay, *Letters of Joseph Clay of*

Savannah, Ga., 1776–93 (Savannah: Georgia Historical Society, *Collections,* VIII, 1913), 46, 54; *Laws* (Watkins), 767–768.

10. Chappell, Pt. I, chs. 1–4.
11. *Laws* (Watkins), 769, 779–781.
12. *JCC,* V, 682. Three departments of Indian Affairs had been established already, by act of July 12, 1775. *Ibid.,* II, 174–177.
13. *JCC,* XXIV, 264; XXV, 681, 684, 693.
14. *JCC,* 681.
15. *JCC,* XXX, 396; XXXI, 507, 759–760; XXXII, 365–369, 454–463.
16. *Laws* (Watkins), 770-778.
17. *Georgia State Gazette,* Oct. 28, Nov. 4, 18, 1786; June 9, 16, 1787; *Laws* (Watkins), 384; Governor Edward Telfair, "Letters," *GHQ,* I, 145, 147–153.
18. *JCC,* XXXIII, 666, 707–711.
19. *Laws* (Watkins), 782–785; Clay, *Letters,* 214, 236; Stevens, *History of Georgia,* II, 443–444.
20. Cooper, II, 126–127.
21. Clay, *Letters,* 213–215, 236–239; Stevens, II, 399–405; "Trans-Oconee Republic," *GHQ,* XXVII, 285–289; E. M. Coulter, "Elijah Clarke's Foreign Intrigues and the Trans-Oconee Republic," *Bulletin of the University of Georgia,* XXII, 4.
22. *Laws* (Watkins), 791–797; Benjamin Hawkins, *Letters of Benjamin Hawkins, 1796–1806* (Savannah: Ga. Hist. Soc., *Collections,* 1916) amply supports the claims of the Indians. Hawkins was Indian Agent. *Correspondence of Governor John Milledge* (edited by Harriet Milledge Salley, Columbia, 1949), 47–49, 97, reveals Georgia's side.
23. Thomas P. Abernethy, *Western Lands and the American Revolution* (New York, 1937), chs. 13–21.
24. *Laws* (Watkins), Appendix.
25. Clay, *Letters,* 213.
26. *Ibid.,* 212; Abernethy, 260–261, 288, 331–335.
27. *JCC,* XXXI, 507; XXXII, 365–369, 454–463, 690–692.
28. *Laws* (Watkins), 756–757; *JCC,* XXXIV, 188.
29. *JCC,* 320–326.
30. Treaty of San Lorenzo. *Laws* (Watkins), 759–761.
31. *Laws* (1799), 106–109, 127–132; (1800), 16–17; (Prince, 1822), 525–6; *U. S. Statutes at Large,* I, 549.
32. *CRG,* IX, 215; *Laws* (Watkins), Appendix.
33. *RRG,* I, 308–315.
34. *Laws* (Watkins), 752–755; *CRG,* XIX, Pt. II, 528–532; *JCC,* V, 681; XXXII, 466–474.
35. *SJ* (1809), 6, 36; (1811), Governor Mitchell's Message; (1818), 14; *Laws* (Clayton), 682–683.
36. *CRG,* IV, 562; Egmont, *Diary,* II, 287–295; *RRG,* I, 306, 324; *Laws* (Watkins), 759–761; *Laws* (Dawson), 740; *SJ* and *HJ* (1818-1861); *SJ* (1866), 129, 331, 440, 449; *HJ* (1866), 217, 416; *Fla. v. Ga.* (1854), 17 Howard 478–525.
37. *SJ* (1823), 10; (1826), 11–12; (1833), 17; (1839), 17; *HJ* (1824), 21; (1825), 20–21; (1828), 10; (1840), 16.
38. *Ala. v. Ga.,* 23 Howard 505.
39. *HJ* (1852), 61; *SJ* (1853), 37; *Laws* (1856), 552; *South Carolina Reports and Resolutions* (1853), 263–264; *South Carolina House Jour.* (1853), 28–29.
40. *CRG,* XIX, Pt. II, 152–162; *RRG,* I, 326–348, 373–397, 414–607, 611; III, 286, 365–570.
41. *RRG,* I, 279–280.
42. *JCC,* V, 763, 788, 945; XVII, 726–727.
43. *RRG,* II, 580–581; III, 561.
44. *RRG,* II, 50; *JCC,* XII, 1117, 1337.
45. *RRG,* II, 96.
46. *Laws* (Prince, 1837), 521.
47. *RRG,* II, 687, 699, 700, 747, 770; III, 298–299.

48. *RRG*, II, 587–588, 628–629.
49. *Ibid.*, 587–588; III, 73–74.
50. *Ibid.*, 73–74, 385.
51. *CRG*, XIX, Pt. II, 53–58.
52. *Ibid.*, 70–72, 130–141.
53. *Ibid.*, 208–211, 248.
54. *RRG*, II, 225–226, 237–243.
55. *RRG*, I, 326–347.
56. A section of the second attainder act (1782) states that some sales were made and that the terms of sale in some instances had not been complied with. In the latter cases the sales were declared void and the property reverted. *Ibid.*, 395–396.
57. *RRG*, II, 77, 215, 253, 264, 276, 285–286, 304; III, 17–18, 116–117.
58. *CRG*, XIX, Pt. II, 147–151.
59. *RRG*, I, 326–348, 373–397.
60. *RRG*, I, 231–235; II, 304–312, 337–338, 491–492, 506, 567, 570–573, 639; III, 17–18, 107–108, 112, 119–120, 150, 155.
61. *RRG*, III, 89–90, 155.
62. *Ibid.*
63. *Ibid.*, 70.
64. *Ibid.*, 108.
65. *Ibid.*, 107–108. These became known as the "Gratuitous Certificates." Those not exchanged for confiscated property were recognized later as a part of the state debt.
66. *Ibid.*, 21, 116, 124, 165–166.
67. *Ibid.*, 171, 228. Count D'Estaing, the French naval commander, was voted later 20,000 acres in Franklin County. *RRG*, II, 639–640, 717.
68. *Ibid.*, 137.
69. *RRG*, I, 214–251, 265, 305–308; II, 633–637; III, 108, 114–115, 138. See also note 62.
70. *RRG*, I, 279; II, 542–543, 549–552, 635–637; III, 569–570.
71. *RRG*, II, 487, 636–637, 643, 657; Governor Samuel Elbert, *Letter Book* (Ga. Hist. Soc., *Collections*, V), 212–213.
72. *CRG*, XIX, Pt. II, 183–200, 216–236, 442–443. Since these acts and the subsequent operations under them are described in Chapter VI, further discussion will not be included at this point.
73. *Ibid.*, 216–236, 443–447; *RRG*, II, 554; III, 74, 78; *SJ* (1813), 92; (1815), 50.
74. *Journal of the House of the Assembly of Georgia*, Feb. 14, 1786.
75. *Laws* (Watkins), 388.
76. *Ibid.*, 400.
77. *Laws* (Clayton), 497, 671–672; (Prince, 1837), 17.
78. *Laws* (Lamar), H. Res. 213; (Dawson), 37, 59, 75, S. Res. 225; *SJ* (1813), 36, 68–9, 71.
79. *Laws* (Dawson), 22.
80. Chapter VI, below.
81. *RRG*, I, 326–347; II, 323–324; III, 11–13; *CRG*, XIX, Pt. II, 100–103; *Laws* (Watkins), 252.
82. *RRG*, I, 373–397; *Laws* (Watkins), 534, no. 502.
83. *RRG*, II, 303–305, 317–320, 341, 405–450; III, 71.
84. *RRG*, I, 414–607; III, 365–376, 404–412, 554–570.
85. *RRG*, I, 286–291, 483; II, 328, 352, 529–530, 547–548, 610; III, 21, 70–71, 202–203, 545–554, 568–572.
86. *CRG*, XIX, Pt. II, 53–58. Enoch M. Banks, *The Economics of Land Tenure in Georgia* (New York: Columbia Univ. Press, *Studies in History, Economics and Public Law*, XXIII, No. 1, 1905) contains little information on the years before 1865.
87. *CRG*, XIX, Pt. II, 70–72, 130–141.
88. *RRG*, III, 206–208, 219, 233–237, 267–280, 492, 511.

89. *RRG,* II, 449–453, 628; III, 267, 452–453.
90. *RRG,* III, 267; Clay, *Letters,* 171.
91. *RRG,* II, 449–453.
92. *RRG,* II, 509–514; III, 388–389.
93. *RRG,* II, 81; III, 303; *Augusta Chronicle,* "Judge Walton's charge to Jury," Sept. 15, 1792; "Governor George Mathews to Edward Watts," Apr. 16, 1795.
94. Clay, *Letters,* 46, 54, 194–195, 205, 214–215, 236.
95. See Reba C. Strickland, *Religion and the State in Georgia in the Eighteenth Century* (New York: Col. Univ. Press, 1939), 152–166, for an account of the growth of Baptist and Methodist churches in Georgia.
96. *Georgia Land Grant Archives,* 1784–1789. Dept. of Archives and History.
97. *RRG,* III, 267, 278–280, 303, 359–360, 388–389; *Laws* (Watkins), 474.
98. The two-hundred-acre headright, however, was made free.
99. *CRG,* XIX, Pt. II, 201–215.
100. *Ibid.,* 280–284. There was not as sharp division of opinion on some of the provisions of this act.
101. *Ibid.,* 292–304; *RRG,* III, 359–360.
102. *CRG,* XIX, Pt. II, 434–441.
103. *Ibid.,* 516–517; *Laws* (Watkins), 422, 438, 474–475, 515, 571, 615.
104. *RRG,* III, 359–360.
105. A state supreme court was not established until 1846.
106. Greene and Harrington, *American Population; U. S. Census,* 1790, 1800.

Chapter V Soldiers and Speculators

1. Georgia was authorized to raise one artillery and two infantry battalions in Virginia and North and South Carolina because of the small numbers of its own citizens available and the urgency of the military situation. Most of these troops served for one year during 1776–1777. Resolutions of the Continental Congress, July 5, 1776 and February 6, 1777: *Journals of the American Congress* (Washington, 1823), I, 399; II, 345; Lucian L. Knight, *Georgia's Roster of the Revolution* (Atlanta, 1920), 7.
2. *CRG,* XIX, Pt. II, 299.
3. Knight, *Georgia's Roster;* Mrs. Howard H. McCall, *Roster of Revolutionary Soldiers in Georgia* (Atlanta: Ga. Soc., D. A. R., 1941); Clay, *Letters,* 190.
4. *RRG,* III, 73–74, 385.
5. *RRG,* II, 605–606; III, 281; *Laws* (Watkins), 289; *CRG,* XIX, Pt. II, 292–304.
6. *Ibid.,* 302–304.
7. *Ibid.,* 450–452.
8. Chapter IV; Ruth Blair, *Revolutionary Soldier Receipts for Bounty Grants* (Atlanta: State Dept. of Archives and Hist., 1928); Knight, *Georgia's Roster.*
9. *Laws* (Prince, 1837), 530.
10. *RRG,* II, 667–668, 787–799; Stevens, *History of Georgia,* II, 355–359.
11. *RRG,* II, 556–785.
12. Knight, *Georgia's Roster;* McCall, *Revolutionary Soldiers.* Knight is taken as the basis for the estimates of numbers of veterans and amounts of grants. While admittedly incomplete, its coverage does not appear to omit any considerable percentage of the actual figures. I have been unable to substantiate the much larger figure of 4,381 veterans given by Stevens (II, 358–359) and so often repeated by later historians.
13. Knight, *Georgia's Roster;* McCall, *Revolutionary Soldiers; CRG,* XIX, Pt. II, 299. There is an interesting reference in the *Journal of the House of the Assembly of Georgia,* Feb. 11, 1785, that indicates that the state of Connecticut was interested in acquiring lands in Georgia with which to pay off its Revolutionary War land bonus. Georgia offered to make the sale, if Connecticut would pay by assuming a

part of Georgia's Continental debt quota. Nothing came of the matter apparently. Georgia extended an invitation, however, to Connecticut soldiers to take up lands under the headright law.

14. *Laws* (Watkins), 384; Telfair, "Letters" (Ga. Hist. Soc. *Collections*, I), 145–153; *Georgia State Gazette*, "Proceedings of the Convention in the State of Franklin," July 14, 28, 1787.

15. *Laws* (Watkins), 390.

16. *SJ* (1808), Treas. Rep., 47–48.

17. *Laws* (Watkins), 520.

18. *Ibid.*, 567.

19. *Ibid.*, 626; *Laws* (1799, 2nd. sess.), 11–15.

20. Treas. Rep., 47–48.

21. *Laws* (1806), June 26; (Clayton), 434, 445; (Lamar), 171.

22. *Laws* (1806).

23. *Laws* (1808).

24. See Chapter VIII.

25. Reba C. Strickland, *Religion and the State in Georgia in the Eighteenth Century*, 162–163.

26. Clay, *Letters*, 47; *RRG*, I, 318–319.

27. *Ibid.*, 167–171.

28. *Ibid.*, 212.

29. *RRG*, III, 397–398.

30. *RRG*, II, 556.

31. *Ibid.*, 667–682, 707, 763–766.

32. Clay, *Letters*, 223.

33. *Land Grants*, 1787 (Office of Secretary of State, Atlanta).

34. *RRG*, II, 556–787.

35. *Land Grants*, 1788.

36. Mrs. Grace G. Davidson, *Early Records of Georgia* (Macon: J. W. Burke Co., 1932), I, 296.

37. *Ga. State Gazette*, Jan. 27, 1787; Jan. 31, 1788.

38. *Augusta Chronicle:* Supplement, No. 356, Aug. 10, 1793; No. 407, Aug. 2, 1794; E. M. Coulter, *Georgia*, ch. XV.

39. S. G. McLendon, *History of the Public Domain of Georgia*, 40–66; W. G. Cooper, *Story of Georgia*, II, ch. LXXIII.

40. McLendon, 46–58.

41. Joseph G. Baldwin, *Flush Times in Alabama and Mississippi* (New York, 1853).

42. Arthur P. Whitaker, *The Spanish American Frontier: 1783–1795* (Boston: Houghton Mifflin, 1927), 1–122; Carl S. Driver, *John Sevier, Pioneer of the Old Southwest* (Chapel Hill: Univ. of N. C. Press, 1932). Thomas P. Abernethy, *Western Lands and the American Revolution* (New York, 1937), portrays in detail the activities of American western land speculators. This work supplies the best background, probably, for an understanding of speculative operations in Georgia, although it contains little information on Georgia, since it stops before the heyday of speculation in the latter state. (Refs. in Abernethy to Georgia, 260–269, 288 ff., 331–335). Theodore Roosevelt, *Winning of the West* (New York, 1889), II and III, gives a general account of the forces behind the southwestward thrust.

43. Whitaker, 10–13.

44. *JGA*, Jan. 27, 1786.

45. Whitaker; *Correspondence of Governor John Milledge* (edited by Harriet Milledge Salley, Columbia, 1949), 32–34, shows Georgia's perilous position regarding Spain.

46. Clay, *Letters*, 213–215, 253; Telfair, "Letters," 145–153; Whitaker, 25–26, 36–46, 56–59, 113–114, 131–138; *Correspondence of Governor Milledge*, 27.

47. Whitaker, 24.

48. Adams, *History of United States*, I, 303.

49. Driver gives a full account of this project; also Whitaker, 54–55, and by the same author, "The Muscle Shoals Speculation," *Mississippi Valley Historical Review,* Dec. 1926; Coulter, *Georgia,* 199; *JGA,* 1784–1789, gives the Georgia legislative record on the District of Tennessee.

50. Driver, 70–73; Abernethy, 260–261, 288–295, 331–335.

51. *RRG,* III, 525–526, 536. Connecticut's veterans were offered land in the Great Bend on the same terms: *JGA,* Feb. 19, 1785.

52. *JGA,* Feb. 22, 1785.

53. Driver, 70–73; Abernethy, 260 ff.; Roosevelt, II, Pt. II, 191.

54. *JGA,* Jan. 19, Feb. 10, Aug. 12, 14, 1786; Louise F. Hays, *Chronology of Georgia* (Atlanta: State Dept. of Archives and History, 1943), 82.

55. Cox was the chief promoter of the Tennessee Yazoo Company in 1789 and 1795.

56. *GLB,* Mathews to Sevier, Nov. 12, 1787; Sevier to Mathews, March 3, 1787; *GHQ,* I, 151; *JGA,* Feb. 3, Oct. 25, 1787; James R. Gilmore, *John Sevier as a Commonwealth Builder* (New York, 1887), 100.

57. Gilmore, 149.

58. Driver, 73. Georgia ratified the federal constitution unanimously on January 2, 1788, being the fourth state to ratify.

59. Gilmore, 126–219.

60. *JGA,* Dec. 2–3, 1789.

61. *JGA,* Jan. 20, 1785, Feb. 19, 1785; J. C. Parish, "The Intrigues of Doctor O'Fallon," *Miss. Valley Hist. Rev.,* XVII, 230–263.

62. *CRG,* XIX, Pt. II, 371–375; *Laws* (Watkins), 296, 386.

63. *JGA,* Feb. 11, 1785.

64. Whitaker, 55–58.

65. *Laws* (Watkins), 386.

66. Clay, *Letters,* 194; Whitaker, *Spanish American Frontier.*

67. It was not any part of Georgia's policy, however, to pursue other than a circumspectly just attitude about its claims, debts, and Continental quotas. It was most meticulous concerning its obligations to carry its full share of the common financial load.

68. See Abernethy, *Western Lands and the American Revolution.*

69. Charles H. Haskins, "The Yazoo Land Companies," *Papers of the American Historical Association,* V, 61–80; *JGA,* Dec. 8, 16, 1789; *Laws* (Watkins), 418; Driver, 74–78; Cooper, II, 145–157; Coulter, 200.

70. *Augusta Chron.,* Dec. 19, 1789. For converse view, July 9, 16, 1781.

71. Haskins, 80–103; *Laws* (Watkins), 530; Cooper, II, 157–202; Coulter, 201–206; McLendon, chs. III, VIII, XI; A. H. Chappell, *Miscellanies of Georgia,* 56–137; *Augusta Chron.,* Oct. 29, 1796.

72. Coulter, 202.

73. *Augusta Chron.,* Feb. 28, 1795.

74. *Ibid.,* Mar. 14, 21, 28, 1795; Governor Mathews to Edward Watts, May 9, 1795.

75. An intrepid Revolutionary soldier, Jackson had achieved a degree of popular acclaim shared only with General Elijah Clark. Hot-tempered and impulsive, he was sometimes over-hasty in action; yet he possessed remarkable candor and a willingness to admit mistakes. He had practiced law in Savannah after the war, and had served frequently in a public advisory capacity before entering actively into politics. He had once declined the governorship on the grounds that his abilities were unequal to the duties. He was an ardent defender of the rights of the common citizen and of the principles of integrity in government.

76. There is a paucity of data on this period and no recent published study of James Jackson's life. T. U. P. Charlton's *The Life of Major James Jackson* (Augusta, 1809) is brief, incomplete, and somewhat eulogistic, although a seemingly faithful picture by an able and intimate associate. Chappell's *Miscellanies* also contains something on Jackson. Mrs. Harriet Milledge Salley has rendered great aid to scholarship

in editing and publishing her great-grandfather's correspondence (*Correspondence of Governor John Milledge*, Columbia, 1949), which contains the most revealing information extant upon the two central figures, James Jackson and John Milledge, of this revival of democratic liberal thought and policy. Other references: *Augusta Chronicle*, "Contested Election of 1791," Nov. 5, 26, 1791; Gov. Jackson, annual messages, *HJ* (1799, 1800); *Columbian Museum & Savannah Advertiser*, "Senator James Jackson" (Reprinted, *GHQ*, III, 174); William E. Heath, "The Yazoo Land Fraud," *GHQ*, XVI, 274–291; Coulter, 203–205, 239–241.

James Jackson's social philosophy resembles more that of James Harrington in the *Oceana* than that of Locke in *Treatises on Government*. Tolland's edition of Harrington's works was published in 1771 and it seems more than likely that Jackson was familiar with its contents. However, Jackson was a vigorous independent thinker whose ideas were always strongly grounded in experience and shaped with a view to policy and action. Jackson also resembled Harrington in other respects. What R. H. Tawney has said of Harrington, that "the civic temper . . . burned strongly in him," (*Proceedings of the British Academy*, XXVII, 202), might have been said as truly of James Jackson.

77. *Augusta Chron.*, Apr. 23, 1796; "Report of Committee of Nine," Feb. 19, 1796.

78. Jackson at this time might be grouped as a militant "Jeffersonian," if the label is not understood to mean than he was a follower of Jefferson. He, Milledge, Baldwin, and other Democratic Republicans in Georgia were among the prominent originators of "Jeffersonianism." *Correspondence of Governor John Milledge.*

79. Message, *HJ* (1800); Heath, Yazoo Land Fraud. The ultra-conservatives were referred to at the time as "Aristos," *Correspondence of Governor John Milledge*, 68.

80. *Laws* (Watkins), 543.

81. Article I, Sec. 23.

82. Jackson as the founder of the first genuine political party in Georgia — the party led by William H. Crawford and George M. Troup after Jackson's death — has tended to obscure Jackson as leader of resurgent democratic liberalism during the years 1795–1805. The *Correspondence* of Governor Milledge presents a firsthand, intimate view of Jackson's motives and guiding principles as well as the close relationships that existed between the members of the Jackson group in most all of their political actions. Coulter, 238–242, provides an excellent summary of Jackson's role in party politics.

83. *Fletcher v. Peck*, 6 Cranch 87–148; McLendon, ch. VIII.

84. E. B. Greene and V. Harrington, *American Population before the Federal Census of 1790*, 17–18, 180–186; *U. S. Census*, 1790, 1800.

85. R. B. Flanders, *Plantation Slavery in Georgia*, ch. III; *JGA*, Treas. Reps., 1783–1800.

86. There is a possibility, of course, of errors in any estimates of the population for 1783. Nevertheless, the evidence is fairly convincing that white population increased at a considerably more rapid rate than did slaves during the first postwar years.

87. Bureau of Census, *A Century of Population Growth, 1790–1900* (Washington, 1909); Flanders, 70; *U. S. Census*, 1790, 1800.

88. *Ga. State Gazette*, "Georgia's Exports," Apr. 4 to Nov. 15, 1788; *Augusta* Chron., Apr. 25, 1795; July 16, 1796; Mar. 14, 1801; Mar. 6, 1802; "Georgia Situation and Extent," Feb. 15, 1817.

89. Flanders, 63.

90. Chappell, *Miscellanies*, Pt. II, ch. VII. Absalom H. Chappell, 1801–1878, prominent lawyer of central Georgia, Congressman, publicist, and railroad advocate, was among the first apparently to perceive the true significance of the Yazoo land company affair in the development of Georgia land policy. James Jackson, with his instinctive sense of the public will, described the true nature of Georgia's action in a letter to John Milledge in 1797. *Correspondence*, 50.

Chapter VI Fiscal Problems and the Currency

1. "Proceedings of the Provincial Congress," Ga. Hist. Soc., *Collections*, V, 1–13.
2. "Proceedings of the Council of Safety," Ga. Hist. Soc., *Collections*, V, 15–24, 63.
3. *Ibid.*, 24, 30–31.
4. *Ibid.*, 21–22, 103–106.
5. *Ibid.*, 32 ff.; Clay, *Letters*, 36, 52–55, 71–78, 112–117, 139–140.
6. *Ibid.*, 112–117.
7. *Georgia State Gazette*, "Report of Committee on Finance, Georgia Assembly," Feb. 24, Mar. 3, 1787.
8. Of this amount, $100,000 was borrowed from Georgia out of the $500,000 paid to the state for currency and debt retirement. There is no record of repayment; hence the amount paid to Georgia is shown herein as $400,000. *JCC*, Aug. 1, 15, 1777; Aug. 24, 1779; Clay, *Letters*, 120, 140, 150.
9. Ga. Hist. Soc., *Collections*, V, 38; *CRG*, XIX, Pt. II, 58–60.
10. Joseph Clay implies that no collections were made. *Letters*, 52.
11. *CRG*, XIX, Pt. II, 87–99.
12. *Ibid.*, 237–242; Clay, *Letters*, 52.
13. *CRG*, XIX, Pt. II, 237–242.
14. *Ibid.*, 152–162; *RRG*, I, 611; III, 173–179.
15. *RRG*, II, 509–514; III, 205–206, 219, 254–255.
16. *RRG*, III, 349–355.
17. *CRG*, XIX, Pt. II, 263–279; *RRG*, III, 355, 391, 403, 501; *JGA*, Feb. 4, 1789, reports small yield of this early tax.
18. *RRG*, II, 526–527.
19. *Ibid.*, 539–540; *CRG*, XIX, Pt. II, 398–416.
20. *Ga. State Gaz.*, Feb. 10, 17, Mar. 10, 1787.
21. *Ibid.*, Nov. 11, 1787.
22. *Laws* (1788), Feb. 1.
23. *Ga. State Gaz.*, Feb. 28, Mar. 7, 1789.
24. *Laws* (1790), Dec. 10.
25. *Laws* (1791), Dec. 22.
26. *Laws* (1792), Dec. 20.
27. *Laws* (1794), Dec. 29.
28. Laws (1796), Feb. 2.
29. *Laws* (1797), Feb. 11; (Watkins), 590.
30. *Laws* (1798), Feb. 2; (Watkins), 623.
31. *Laws* (1799), Feb. 13, Dec. 4.
32. *RRG*, III, 22, 301–302.
33. *CRG*, XIX, Pt. II, 312–340.
34. *Laws* (Watkins), 474.
35. Governor's fees were an important exception.
36. *RRG*, I, 373–397.
37. *Laws, supra.*
38. *RRG*, I, 413–607, contains accounts of most of the original auction sales. The operations are described in detail in Chapter V above.
39. Clay, *Letters*, 95–96, 102, 139–140; *RRG*, III, 80–81.
40. *JCC*, Aug. 1, 15, 1777.
41. Clay, *Letters*, 71–74; *RRG*, II, 85–86.
42. *Statutes at Large*, I, 138.
43. Clay, *Letters*, 55, 75–78, 107, 140.
44. *Ibid.*, 77–78; *RRG*, II, 85–86.
45. Clay, *Letters*, 102.
46. *Ibid.*, 75, 95, 102; *RRG*, II, 155–159, 280, 316, 476, 480, 509–514; III, 182.
47. Considerable supplies were captured from the enemy during this period.
48. *RRG*, III, 28, 114, 182. Amount shown in table is an estimate.

49. *CRG*, XIX, Pt. II, 147–151.
50. *Ibid.*, 183–200; *RRG*, III, 264, 287–291, 336; *JGA*, July 22, 1786; "Report of Committee on Finance of Assembly," *Ga. State Gaz.*, Feb. 24, Mar. 3, 1787.
51. *CRG*, XIX, Pt. II, 216–36; William G. Sumner, *The Financier and the Finances of the American Revolution* (New York, 1891), II, 56–58, 132–133.
52. *Ga. State Gaz.*, *loc. cit.*; *Aug. Chron.*, "Georgia Public Debt," Aug. 25, 1792; *RRG*, III, 292–295, 305–308, 568–569, 572–573; *JGA*, Jan. 18, 1788; Jan. 19, 1789.
53. *Laws* (Watkins), 349. Only $135,000 were issued. It soon became unpopular and ceased to circulate after a few months; it was mostly retired by 1790, when it ceased to be legal tender by law.
54. *SJ* (1804), 47–48.
55. *Ibid.*; *Laws* (1799, 2nd. sess.), 11–15; (Watkins), 626.
56. *SJ* (1804), 47–48.
57. *RRG*, II, 85–86.
58. *RRG*, I, 326–347.
59. Actually, a very minute value was given to them by an act of Feb. 22, 1785, which offered redemption at one-tenth cent on the dollar.
60. *CRG*, XIX, Pt. II, 183–200; *RRG*, III, 58–59, 181, 264, 271, 280–291, 336, 348–355.
61. *CRG*, XIX, Pt. II, 442–443.
62. *Ibid.*, 216–236.
63. See Chapter V; also *RRG*, I, 305–308; II, 635–637.
64. All of the figures are estimates, based upon various official reports that are incomplete, often fragmentary, and sometime contradictory. Principal sources of data: *JGA*, 1784–1789; *Ga. State Gaz.* and *Augusta Chron.*, previous citations; Governor Telfair's "Messages," *Aug. Chron.*, June 12, Aug. 10, 17, 1790; Nov. 12, 1791; Nov. 10, 1792; Stevens, *History of Georgia*, II, 392–395; Cooper, *Story of Georgia*, III, 188; *RRG*, III, 515–518, 537–538. $560,000 of old Treasury certificates were converted into $230,000 of audited certificates in 1789; *JGA*, Feb. 3, 1789; see also *ibid.*, 1787, appendix, 198–222.
65. *CRG*, XIX, Pt. II, 443–447; *JGA*, Feb. 8–9, 1786; Jan. 11, 1788; *Ga. State Gaz.*, "Speculators," July 26, 1788; *Laws* (1788), Res. of Jan. 11; (1790), Res. of June 11; Clay, *Letters*, 212.
66. Clay, *Letters*, 52; Governor Edward Telfair, "Message," *Augusta Chron.*, Aug. 10, 17, 1790; Nov. 12, 1791.
67. *Augusta Chron.*, "Message," June 12, 1790; Aug. 10, 17, 1790; Nov. 11, 1791.
68. *Ibid.*, Nov. 10, 1792; Nov. 7, 1793.
69. *Laws* (1793), Dec. 20.
70. "Financial Report of Governor Edward Telfair," *Augusta Chron.*, Nov. 5, 11, 1792; Nov. 7, 1793.
71. *SJ* (1804), 47–48.
72. *Laws* (1799, 2nd. Sess.), 11–15; (Watkins), 626.
73. Clay, *Letters*, 52.
74. *Ibid.*, 27, 30.
75. *Ibid.*, 36, 41, 52.
76. *Ibid.*
77. *CRG*, XIX, Pt. II, 341–347; *RRG*, III, 158, 180–181, 349–355, 483–496, 512, 537; Stevens, II, 394–395.
78. Stevens, 537–544; *Laws* (Watkins), 373.
79. *CRG*, XIX, Pt. II, 237–242; *RRG*, II, 645; *JGA*, Jan. 18, 1788, Feb. 4, 1789; *Augusta Chron.*, Mar. 7, 1807; *GLB*, Feb. 21, 1801.
80. Message, Jan. 27, 1798; *GLB*, to Richard Wall, Apr. 20, 1800; and *passim.*
81. *Laws* (1796), Feb. 2.
82. *Laws* (Watkins), 590.
83. *Laws* (1799), 1–8; (1799, 2nd. Sess.), 33–56.
84. *Laws* (Watkins), 626; (1799, 2nd. Sess.), 11–15; (Prince, 1822), 390–391.

Chapter VII The State Recharts Its Land Policy

The primary data upon which this chapter is based are contained chiefly in the *Laws*, 1800–1860, the various *Compilations* of laws and the legislative and executive journals and documents listed in the bibliographical note at the beginning of this section. Other helpful sources have been: *Reprint of the Official Register of the Land Lottery of Georgia*, 1827 (Martha Lou Houston, 1929); *The Cherokee Lottery* (New York, 1838); Absalom H. Chappell, *Miscellanies of Georgia;* Wilson Lumpkin, *The Removal of the Cherokee Indians from Georgia*, 2 vols. (Wormsloe, 1907); *Correspondence of Governor John Milledge* (Harriet Milledge Salley, editor: Columbia, S. C., 1949); and the following newspapers: *Augusta Chronicle and Gazette*, 1787–1810; *Augusta Chronicle*, 1810–1819; *Chronicle and Sentinel* (Augusta), 1836–1860; *Federal Union* (Milledgeville), 1832–1860; and the *Savannah Republican*, 1821–1860. Secondary works: E. M. Coulter, *Georgia: A Short History* (Chapel Hill, 1947); Ralph B. Flanders, *Plantation Slavery in Georgia* (Chapel Hill, 1933); and Ulrich B. Phillips, *Georgia and States Rights* (Washington, 1902).

Note on Georgia's policy on Indian land cessions. It passed through four phases: (1) Oglethorpe's benevolent policy, 1733–1772, which sought to obtain for actual white settlement only such lands as were not required for use by the Indians and was based upon the notion of peaceful neighborly relations between whites and Indians and mutual economic and social development; (2) Governor Wright's commercial, or purchase, policy, 1773–1781, under which Indian territories were transferred to the colony to satisfy trading debts; (3) the war indemnity policy, 1782–1792, under which Georgia secured Franklin and Washington counties and laid claim to large additional areas; and (4) the policy of complete extinguishment of all Indian titles within Georgia, 1793–1835, under which the federal government finally assumed, in 1802, the obligation to remove the Indians as a part of the price of the transfer of the western lands.

1. Art. I, Sec. 23.

2. Abraham Baldwin, father of public education in Georgia, also was a member of this group of liberal leaders although not a member of either legislative body, since he was in the U. S. Senate at the time. John Lumpkin, father of the great liberal statesman Wilson Lumpkin, sat in both the rescinding legislature and the constitutional convention. The son entered the state legislature in 1804 and was greatly impressed by the ability of most of the members and their devotion to the common interest; he became a staunch believer in Jackson's social philosophy, which remained his fundamental creed throughout his forty-odd years of public life.

Under Jackson's leadership this group of liberals founded the first genuine political party in Georgia. George M. Troup at this time was a young protégé of Jackson. Troup and Crawford succeeded to co-leadership of the party upon Jackson's death in 1806, and Troup became virtual head of it in the state after Crawford transferred his public activities so largely to Washington. The party has been described as Jeffersonian; but actually the label fits very loosely. There were always two points of view in the party. Jackson, Tatnall, Milledge, Baldwin, and Lumpkin represented the positive liberal wing and their views gave the "Jeffersonian" tinge; their social philosophy was a product of the spiritual and military experiences of the Revolution and of the study of Harrington, Locke, and later eighteenth-century liberal writers, particularly Adam Smith. William H. Crawford and many of the Virginians were "Washingtonian" in leaning. There was also a strong Whig element in Savannah and the coastal area, represented by such able men as the merchant, Joseph Clay, and the state's leading lawyer, T. U. P. Charlton. George M. Troup was something of an enigma, a radical liberal in his youth, always retaining much of the progressive spirit at least in word of mouth, but gradually moving into the leadership of the more conservative elements of the party and also carrying the party with him. Thus under the Crawford-Troup leadership the party later turned quite conservative and eventually became the Whig Party. It was this trend away from its early principles that led to the defection of John Forsyth, Wilson Lumpkin, and others and to their alliance with the Clark democrats to form the Union Party. The most intimate view of the personalities and philosophies of these men and of their mutual relationships is afforded in the *Correspondence of Governor John Milledge*. Coulter, ch. XVIII, gives an excellent brief summary of political parties in Georgia during this period. Longer works, dealing chiefly with the second quarter of the nineteenth century, are: Arthur C. Cole, *The Whig Party in the South* (Washington, 1913); and Paul Murray, *The Whig Party in Georgia, 1825–1853* (Chapel Hill, 1948). See Ch. I, footnote 4.

3. See Ch. VI.

4. *MED,* Jan. 8, 1799; Messages, Nov. 5, 1800 and Mar. 3, 1801. See Ch. IV, for a summary of the history of Georgia's western lands.

5. *Augusta Chronicle,* "Legislators and New Land Cessions," Aug. 7, 14, 21, 28, 1802.

6. Annual messages, *HJ* and *SJ,* 1799–1801.

7. *Augusta Chron.*, Dec. 4, 1802; *SJ* (1802), 4.

8. *Ibid.*

9. Message, *SJ* (1803), Apr. 18. *Correspondence,* especially 64–69, shows the liberal governor's views.

10. The law provided for the removal of all squatters and declared all squatter rights invalid.

11. *SJ,* 80–82.

12. *SJ,* 68–79.

13. The larger area of the squares in Wayne was intended to compensate for the poorer soils in that section.

14. Lots in South Georgia were 490 acres as in Wayne county.

15. *Laws* (Clayton), 279.

16. Treas. Reps., *HJ* and *SJ*.

17. Governor Irwin, message, *SJ* (1809), 5–9; Governor Mitchell, message, *SJ* (1811).

18. *Laws* (Dawson), 1821, Sen. Res., No. 9; House Res., No. 27.

19. *Augusta Chron.*, Aug. 20, 1808.

20. *Ibid.*, July 30, 1808; *SJ* (1808), 160, Appendix, 119–172.

21. *SJ* (1825, Extra Sess.), 79–127.

22. *Laws* (Lamar), 313–315; *Laws* (1843), 67–68.

23. *Augusta Chron. and Sent.*, Aug., 28, Sept., 11, Oct. 2, 1845.

24. *CRG*, XIX, Pt. II, 133.

25. *Ibid.*, 248–256.

26. *Ibid.*, 560–561; *Laws* (Watkins), 599; Dorothy Orr, *A History of Education in Georgia* (Chapel Hill: Univ. of N. C. Press, 1950), 22–23.

27. *CRG*, XIX, Pt. II, 466–468.

28. *Ibid.*, 419–433; *Laws* (Watkins), 464, 579; *Laws* (1799), 110–114, 144; (Clayton), 124. The town of Lincoln afforded an interesting case, where a single person was created a commissioner to lay out a town on his own lands: "Whereas it is necessary and will be greatly conducive to the general convenience of citizens . . . that a town be laid out, and a tobacco inspection established . . ." one Zachariah Lamar was authorized to lay out the town and convey titles in fee simple and use the revenues therefrom for the construction of a tobacco warehouse for the reception and inspection of tobacco. Tobacco warehouses were important public utilities in sections of Georgia at this time. *CRG*, XIX, Pt. II, 489–491.

29. Treasurers' and Comptrollers' Reports, 1805–1840.

30. *Ibid.*, and Reports of Central Bank, 1829–1840.

31. *Laws* (Dawson), 1432.

32. The commissioners of Eatonton in Putnam county were a notable case.

33. *Ibid.* $25,000 of receipts from public lots were spent on the Macon bridge, but this was recovered by the state through sale of the bridge to Macon.

Chapter VIII Banking Theories and Policies

The substance of this chapter and Chapter XIII is drawn almost entirely from primary sources, chiefly the following:

A. Official Documents: *Acts* of the General Assembly of Georgia, 1782–1861; *Journals* of the House and Senate of the General Assembly, 1806–1861; *Minutes of the Executive Department,* 1790–1860, (bound manuscript) and *Governors' Letter Books,* Department of Archives and History, Atlanta, Georgia; *American State Papers, Finance I–V* (Washington, 1832); *State Papers,* 15th–21st Congresses; *House Documents,* 18th–19th Congresses; *Senate Documents,* 22nd–29th Congresses; *Executive Documents,* 21st–29th Congresses. The federal document references are chiefly to the reports of the Secretary of the Treasury. M. St. C. Clarke, and D. A. Hall, *Legislative and Documentary History of the Bank of the United States* (Washington, 1932).

B. Contemporary works: J. N. Cardozo, *Notes on Political Economy,* Charleston, 1826; Thomas Cooper, *Lectures on the Elements of Political Economy,* Columbia, 1826; William M. Gouge, *History of Paper Money and Banking in the United States,* Philadelphia, 1833; Eleazar Lord, *Principles of Currency and Banking,* New York, 1829; Wilson Lumpkin, *Removal of the Cherokee Indians from Georgia, 1827–1838,* Wormsloe (Savannah): Privately Printed, 1907; John McVickar, *Outlines of Political Economy,* New York, 1825; Daniel Raymond, *Elements of Political Economy,* 2 vols., Baltimore, 1823; Adam Smith, *Wealth of Nations,* edited by Edwin Cannan, London, 1904; Francis Wayland, *The Elements of Political Economy,* New York, 1837.

C. Newspapers and Periodicals: *Augusta Chronicle and Gazette,* 1787–1810; *Augusta Chronicle,* 1810–1819; *Chronicle and Sentinel* (Augusta), 1836–1860; *Southern Banner* (Athens), 1835–1853; *Columbus Times,* 1845–1851; *Southern Sentinel* (Columbus), 1852; *Times and Sentinel* (Columbus), 1853–1860; *De Bow's Review,* 1846–1860; *Georgia Telegraph* (Macon), 1826–1860; *Federal Union* (Milledgeville), 1832–1860; *Georgia Journal* (Milledgeville), 1821–1839; *Georgia Gazette* (Savannah) 1789–1803; *Columbia Museum and Savannah Advertiser,* 1800–1803; *Savannah Republican,* 1821–1861; *Sumpter Republican* (Americus), 1854–1858.

There is scarcely any reference to banking in Georgia in the wealth of American secondary works and journal literature on the history of money and banking in the United States. One study by Thomas P. Govan, *Banking and the Credit System in Georgia* (unpublished Ph.D. Thesis, Vanderbilt University, 1936) has been summarized in *The Journal of Southern History, IV,* No. 2, May 1938. The following secondary works have been found most useful for suggestions and purposes of comparison: *Banking Studies,* Washington: Federal Reserve System, 1941; Ralph C. H. Catterall, *The Second Bank of the United States,* Chicago, 1903; E. Merton Coulter, *Georgia, A Short History,* Chapel Hill, 1947; Davis R. Dewey, *Financial History of the United States,* New York, 1934; Bray Hammond, "Long and Short Term Credit in Early American Banking," *Quarterly Journal of Economics,* XLIX, 79–103; John T. Holdsworth, *The First Bank of the United States* (Washington: National Monetary Commission, 1910); Sister M. Grace Madeleine, *Monetary and Banking Theories of Jacksonian Democracy* (Philadelphia: The Dolphin Press, 1943); Harry E. Miller, *Banking Theories in the United States Before 1860* (Cambridge, 1937); Paul Murray, *The Whig Party in Georgia, 1825–1853* (Chapel Hill, 1948); Paul Murray, "Party Organization in Georgia Politics, 1825–1853," *GHQ,* XXIX, 195; William G. Sumner, *History of Banking in the United States* (New York, 1896).

1. *Ga. Gaz.,* Sept. 2, 1902.

2. *Augusta Chron.,* Mar. 31, 1810; Mar. 8, 1816; Jan. 11, 1817; *SJ* (1816), 37–38.

3. Clarke and Hall, 37–56, 467–471; Governor Clark, Message, *SJ* (1823); Governor Gilmer, Message, *SJ* (1831); Governor Lumpkin, Messages, *SJ* (1832–1835); *HJ* (1840), 51–54, 309–311; *Augusta Chron. and Sent.,* Nov. 18, 1840;

Governor McDonald, Messages, *SJ* (1840–1842); Governor Brown, Message, *SJ* (1857); *ibid.*, Veto Message, *HJ* (1857), Dec. 22.

4. Clarke and Hall, 307–315, 437–456; *Augusta Chron.*, Mar. 31, 1810; *Exec. Docs.*, 2nd Sess., 25th Congress, IV, No. 79; *Augusta Chron. and Sent.*, Nov. 16, 1840; Mar. 31, May 1, 1841; Governor Johnson, Message, *HJ* (1855); *Federal Union* (Milledgeville), Dec. 1, 1857; *Savannah Republican*, "The Banks and the People," Jan. 1858; *Laws* (Dawson), 641.

5. Clarke and Hall, 437–456, 664–665; *Augusta Chron.*, Sept. 1, 1840.

6. *Laws* (1835), 36–42.

7. Bray Hammond, "Long and Short Term Credit in Early American Banking," *Quart. Jour. of Econs.*, XLIX, 79–103, is an excellent brief treatment of this tendency in the country at large. There was not as much "hybridization" in Georgia, however, as Hammond suggests was the case generally in America.

8. James Madison's statement on Smith's doctrine, that paper money enabled a country to ship specie abroad for the purchase of valuable goods, indicates that Miller (*Banking Theories in the United States Before 1861*, 40–41) was in error in supposing that this phase of Smith's doctrine was overlooked in America prior to 1809. Madison recognized that advantage, but thought that Americans would exchange the specie for consumption goods and so would reap no permanent advantage, whereas the probable losses from paper money, which would replace the specie, would be greater and more lasting. Clarke and Hall, 39–45.

9. Clarke and Hall, 37, 54–56.

It has been assumed that Jackson's economic philosophy had a Jeffersonian origin, and there are grounds undoubtedly for such a thesis. But study of his life and of all of his documents tends to show that his views were largely developed out of his early associations with the Savannah liberal revolutionaries, his trying experiences as a soldier during the Revolution, his deep consecration to the Revolutionary cause, his extensive association with the common people during the war, and a considerable study of English liberal literature. His creed was ever the principles of the American Revolution as espoused by the common people. He is really the forerunner of the much more famous Jackson, who destroyed the Second Bank of the United States which James Jackson's younger associates so largely established. On no other issue does James Jackson so fully anticipate the position of Andrew Jackson as on banking. The hard-money theories of (Andrew) Jacksonian Democracy (See Madeleine, *Monetary and Banking Theories*) had become fully developed in Georgia four decades before President Jackson penned the famous veto message. Jacksonian democracy, which had a deep root in colonial reform liberalism, was established solidly as a political creed under James Jackson's leadership during the last decade of the eighteenth century.

10. *MED*, Jan. 12, 1796.

11. Chapter V, above.

12. *Columbia Museum and Savannah Advertiser*, Feb. 16, 1802; *Georgia Gaz.*, Sept. 2, 1802.

13. Clarke and Hall, 437.

14. *Augusta Chron.*, Mar. 12, 1810; Mar. 29, 1819.

15. Clarke and Hall, 308–315, 436–456.

16. *Ibid.*, 467–471.

17. Lumpkin, 21–25; *HJ* (1841), 381.

18. *Augusta Chron.*, Oct. 29, 1808; *SJ* (1813), 6; *Augusta Herald*, Apr. 21, 1841.

19. *SJ* (1814), 33, 36–38, 40–49; *Augusta Herald*, Dec. 1, 1814. Governor Early was an intimate friend of W. H. Crawford and shared the latter's views on financial matters.

20. *Augusta Herald*, Jan. 19, 1815.

21. *Ibid.*, Apr. 6, May 4, June 8, 1815.

22. *HJ* (1815).

23. Madeleine, 32–35.

24. *SJ* (1815), 17, 22, 58–63.

25. Branch-banking, however, was fairly common in the South.

26. Such a bank, on a national scale, was first suggested in this country apparently by Robert Morris in 1786. (Madeleine, 68). Whether the lineage of this idea in Georgia traces back to Morris cannot be established. There were ample indigenous roots.

27. *SJ* (1813), 13, 17, 70–71; *HJ* (1813), 49–50.

28. *SJ* (1814), 48–49.

29. *SJ* (1815), 14–19.

30. *SJ* (1814), 5.

31. *Laws* (Lamar), Sen. Resol. No. 140.

32. *SJ* (1816), 5–6. This action was rather typical of bank practice during suspension periods. Specie payments often were made to public or private note holders in limited amounts to meet emergencies or dire need, when exchange could not be supplied or was unsuitable.

33. *Exec. Docs.*, 2nd Sess., 24th Cong., II, No. 65.

34. Clarke and Hall, 481–665.

35. *Ibid.*, especially 664–665.

36. *Ibid.*, 481–483, 582, 607, 649.

37. *State Papers*, Reports of Secretary of Treasury of United States.

38. *HJ* and *SJ* (1817–1818).

39. *Augusta Chron.*, "Prices of Bank Stocks," Mar. 29, 1819; Governor Mitchell, Messages, 1816–1817; Governor Rabun, Message, Nov. 3, 1818.

40. *Ibid.*; *HJ* and *SJ* (1818); *Augusta Chron.*, Mar. 4, 18, 1818.

41. *HJ* (1818), 32.

42. See Chapter XI, below.

43. *Darien Gazette*, Jan. 4, 1819; *Augusta Chron.*, Jan. 9, 1819; June 13, 1818; *Laws* (Lamar), 231.

44. *SJ* (1851–52), 297–300; State Treasurer, Annual Reports.

45. It was the general practice for country notes to be discounted by the city banks through the endorsement of local merchants, and this method was generally required. The practice produced widespread complaint: it was thought to give the city merchants and the banks undue power over the borrower and to lead to discrimination in the granting of credit. It will be noted that this provision was contained also in the agricultural bank bill.

46. *HJ* and *SJ* (1818).

47. *Laws* (1821), Sen. Resol., Dec. 19; Governor Clark's Messages, 1821–1822.

48. *State Papers*, 18th–20th Congresses, Sec. of Treas., Reports and Correspondence.

49. *Ibid.*; *House Docs.*, 18th–19th Congresses; Governors' Messages, 1820–1824; *Laws* (Dawson), Rep. of Joint Committee of Legislature, Sen. Resol. 65, 218.

50. Notably William M. Gouge, *History of Paper Money and Banking in the United States* (1833), 142–143.

51. Secretary of Treasury, United States, Reports, contained in: *State Papers*, *Exec. Docs.*, *House Docs.*, and *Senate Docs.*, 19th–25th Congresses.

52. *Laws* (Dawson), Rep. of Joint Com. on Banks, Nov. 18, 1824, H. Resol. 324.

53. An interesting question is, how much did the Darien Bank's liberal loan and note issue policies offset the monetary contraction policies of the other banks and hence retard deflation? It would appear that the state, through its subscription to the Bank's stock, unintentionally supplied credit and monetary relief in this time of depression.

54. This practice had furnished one point of issue in the U. S. Bank controversy. The Savannah banks asked the Branch of the Bank of the U. S. to accept half of their clearance balances in Darien notes, because they did not believe that they should bear the entire cost of obtaining specie from Darien.

55. *State Papers*, 1st Sess., 18th Cong., VIII, 436. The Treasury also had entered into such an agreement with the Bank of Augusta and with the Milledgeville Branch of the Bank of the State. Furthermore, with these institutions Secretary Crawford agreed to draw drafts only between October and May 1st, when they would have

available exchange. These various agreements were made with the three other banks at the same time that Crawford, and the Bank of the U. S., were refusing to make such an agreement with the Planters' Bank in Savannah and were insisting on its paying specie to the Branch of the Bank of U. S. Admittedly Crawford was in an embarrassing position over the Savannah situation; but the Planters' Bank had just reason to feel that it was the object of discriminatory treatment. *Ibid.*, 286–287.

56. Governor Troup, Messages, *HJ*, May 23, 1825; Nov. 8, 1825; Nov. 7, 1826.

57. *Laws* (1823), Sen. Resol., Nov. 21, 1824; H. Resol. 205.

58. Treas., Rep., 1825.

59. *Laws* (Dawson), H. Resol. 324; *SJ* (1825, *Special Sess.*) 23–24; *Laws* (Dawson), Rep. of Com. on Finance, Nov. 16, 1826, S. Resol. 439; Treas. Rep., 1826.

60. *Laws* (Dawson), Special Jt. Com. Rep., H. Resol. 517.

61. *SJ* (1851–1852), 297–300.

62. Governor Troup, Messages, 1825–1826.

63. *HJ* and *SJ*, 1825–1828.

64. *Laws* (1827), 217–218; Governor Forsyth's veto message, *SJ* (1827), 122–126; Central Bank, Annual Reps., 1829–1835; *Laws* (1829), 23–24.

65. *Laws* (1829), 204–205.

66. *Laws* (1830), 271–272.

67. Governor Forsyth also had argued repeatedly that the bank had neglected its paramount obligation to the state in favor of a very minor one to private parties and the desire to make profits. See especially the veto message, *op. cit.*

68. *Laws* (1831), 281–282; (1832), 296; (1833), 410; *SJ* (1834), Rep. of Sen. Com., Dec. 19.

69. *Laws* (1834), 44.

70. *Exec. Docs.*, 2nd Sess., 24th Cong., II, No. 65; *Senate Docs.*, 1st Sess., 24th Cong., IV.

71. There was a surprising uniformity among bank charters in most respects, which was not true regarding charters of other corporations. This uniformity continued down to the Civil War.

72 *Laws* (Dawson), S. Resols. 7, 12, Dec. 19, 1820.

73. *Laws* (1823), Dec. 10., S. Resol. 226.

Chapter IX Banking Policies

See footnotes to Chapter IX for statement regarding sources.

1. Governor Clark, Message, *SJ* (1823).

2. *State Papers*, U. S., Sec. of Treas., Reps.; *HJ and SJ* (1825–1837), Bank Reports.

3. *Laws* (Dawson), 198.

4. Governor Clark, Message, *SJ* (1823).

5. Special Message, *SJ* (1828).

6. *SJ* (1829), 9–19.

7. James Camak, Report on Central Bank, Nov. 2, 1929, *SJ* (1829), Appendix.

8. *Laws* (Dawson), Sen. Resol. 641; James Camak, Statement on Operations of Central Bank to Legislature, Dec. 6, 1829.

9. *Ibid.*, 242–246.

10. Camak, Report, *SJ* (1829), Appendix.

11. Central Bank, Reports, 1829–1836; *Laws* (Dawson), 641; *SJ* (1829), 223–227, 235–248; *Laws* (1831), 280–281; (1833), Appendix; (1834), 274–275; (1835), 36–42; (1836), Resols. 4–6.

12. *HJ* (1839),.410–412.

13. *Laws* (1836), Resols. 4–6.

14. Governor Lumpkin, Message, 1833; Central Bank, Reps., 1832–1834.

15. See Chapter XIII, on the nature of public corporations. Since funds in pos-

session of the Bank, other than current state deposits, were considered to be a part of its capital, the comptroller general lists the source of revenue from deficit drafts as "state stock."

16. *SJ* (1829), Appendix. (Italics mine.)

17. *Laws* (Dawson), Sen. Resol. 641 — Rep. of Jt. Com. on Banks, Dec. 16, 1829.

18. The Bank of Macon, chartered in 1825, failed in July 1832, and the Merchants and Planters Bank of Augusta, chartered in 1827, failed in May 1833. Both were relatively large banks, with capital of $300,000 each, with extensive circulations. Reports of special investigating committees presented circumstances and causes — peculiar and exceptional in both cases — of the failures: *Laws* (1832), 279–295; (1833), 399–408.

19. *Laws* (Dawson), Reps. of Jt. Com. on Banks, 1829, 647, 651; *Exec. Docs.*, 2nd Sess., 25th Cong., IV, No. 79; *Augusta Chronicle*, Sept. 1, Nov. 12, 18, 19, 1840.

20. Governor Gilmer, Message, *SJ* (1831); Governor Lumpkin, Messages, *SJ* (1832–1835); Governor Schley, Messages, *SJ* (1836–1837).

21. *Laws* (1832), 29–31.

22. *Exec. Docs.*, 2nd Sess., 24th Cong. II, no. 65.

23. *Ibid.*, 1st Sess., 26th Cong., V, 172.

24. Governor McDonald, Message, *SJ* (1842).

25. *Laws* (1854).

26. Message, *SJ* (1839).

27. Governor McDonald, Message, *SJ* (1842).

28. Augusta *Chronicle and Sentinel*, Sept. 26, 1840.

29. *Ibid.*, Nov. 10, 18, 1840; Apr. 6, May 10, June 12, 1841; *HJ* (1840), 51–54.

30. *HJ* (1840), 309–311.

31. Augusta *Chron. and Sent.*, June 12, 1841.

32. *Ibid.*, "Crisis of the Country," Sept. 1, 1840; "Smith," May 1, 1841.

33. *Ibid.*, Oct. 29, Nov. 12, 20, 1840.

34. *Ibid.*, "Georgia," Nov. 16, 19, 21, 1840; "Suspension of Georgia Railroad and Banking Co.," Mar. 1, May 10, June 12, 24, 1841.

35. *Ibid.*

36. *Ibid.*, Mar. 30, 1841.

37. *Exec. Docs.*, 1st Sess., 29th Cong. VI, no. 226.

38. *Laws* (1842), 29–31. The Darien Bank was liquidated by the Central Bank.

39. *SJ* (1836), Nov. 24.

40. *Laws* (1837), 38–45.

41. *HJ* (1841), 15; *SJ* (1842), 195–197, 238–239.

42. *SJ* and *HJ* (1838).

43. *HJ* (1840), Rep. of Finance Com., 190–193, 250–252, 309–311.

44. *HJ* (1839), 410–412.

45. Central Bank, Annual Rep., Nov. 2, 1840; Governor McDonald, Message, *SJ* (1840).

46. *Ibid.; HJ* (1840), 250–252; Augusta *Chron. and Sent.*, "Memorial," Nov. 10, 1840.

47. Augusta *Chron. and Sent.*, Editorial on Locofocos, Sept. 26, 1840; *ibid.*, Oct. 1, 7, 15, Nov. 12, 19, 1840; May 19–20, 1841. Statements from Crawford's "protest" were repeated widely in the press and in the legislature. *Ibid.*, "Review of the History of the Democrat's Handling of Finances," July 30–31, 1842; Governor Crawford's Message, *SJ* (1845).

48. Governor McDonald, Messages, *SJ* (1841–1842).

49. Augusta *Chron. and Sent.*, "Morgan," Apr. 15, 1841; "Bank Reports," May 6, 1841.

50. Except that it might change notes of large denominations for $1 and $2 notes. This latter provision of the act, presumably intended to remove the dearth of money of small denominations, was attacked severely by both hard-money and commercial banking groups as a "change-bill," a "rag money" device.

51. Governor McDonald, Message, *SJ* (1843).

52. Governor Crawford, Message, *SJ* (1845).

53. Reprint of Report of Committee, Augusta *Chron. and Sent.*, Sept. 25, 1845.

54. *Laws* (1847, 1850, 1854, 1856); Governor Crawford, Message, *SJ* (1847); Governor Towns, Messages, *SJ* (1849–1851); Governor Cobb, Messages, *SJ* (1853–1855).

55. The table is derived from data contained in the following: Annual Reports of Treasurer and Comptroller General, 1829–1860; Annual and Special Reports of Central Bank to Legislature, *HJ* and *SJ* (1829–1841); Governors' Messages, *HJ* and *SJ* (1828–1860); Special Reports of Committees of the Legislature, *HJ* (1841), 15; *SJ* (1842), 195–197, 238–239; *HJ* (1847), 208–212; *HJ* (1849), 659–661. Practically all statements made after 1847, relative to what transpired prior to 1847, simply repeat the House Committee Report of that date. There are very important omissions in all of the summary reports as well as discrepancies on particular items. For example, the amount of the state's deficit withdrawals, 1831–1841, is reported somewhat greater by the comptroller general during the years in which it took place than it is by the House Committee in 1847. It is not possible to determine which is the correct amount, if either. I have used the sum of figures reported annually by the comptroller general. The difference in the amounts is not significant. The item of bond issue is a duplication of a like amount of notes and appears in both the debit and credit accounts. The 8 per cent bonds were refunded into 7 per cent ones during 1848–1849. An important item lacking in the table is operating expense. All of the available reports are net of such expense.

56. William B. White, cashier of Ruckersville Bank, in Augusta *Chron. and Sent.*, June 23, 1841.

57. This long drawn out controversy supplies an early pattern of some of the prominent issues of the Great Depression of the 1930's that were raised by the federal budgetary deficits.

58. Message, *SJ* (1839).

59. *Laws* (1841), 23–24; (1843), 181; (1854); *SJ* (1851-1852), 297–300; Governor Crawford, Message, *SJ* (1847); Governor Cobb, Message, *SJ* (1855), Nov. 6.

60. They were distributed among: Albany, Athens, Bainbridge, Brunswick, Cuthbert, Dalton, Ft. Gaines, Greensboro, Griffin, Hamilton, La Grange, Madison, Morgan, Ringgold, and Rome. Atlanta was the important new metropolis of this period, as a result of having become the hub of the railway system, not only of the state, but likewise of much of the southeastern United States; but it had not become important as yet in the banking world. Its first bank, the Atlanta Bank, capital $300,000, was chartered in 1852, and its second, the Bank of Fulton, capital likewise $300,000, was chartered in 1856. Both of these banks were rated as country banks by the banks in Savannah and Augusta.

61. Augusta's rate of growth, which had been greater than Savannah's between 1830 and 1850, slackened markedly after 1850, whereas Savannah's increased.

62. Americus *Sumpter Republican*, Dec. 10, 1857.

63. Brown's veto message was reprinted in the *Federal Union*, Dec. 29, 1857. To override the veto, the vote in the House was 68–34, in the Senate, 61–22.

64. *Federal Union*, "Suspension," and also an article reprinted from the *Charleston Mercury*, Oct. 20, 1857; *ibid.*, Oct. 27, 1857; *Savannah Republican*, "The Banks and the People," Jan. 1858.

65. *Federal Union*, Jan. 26, 1858.

66. *Ibid.*, Mar. 16, 1858.

67. Clarksville *North-East Georgian*, Dec. 30, 1857; *Federal Union*, "One of the People," Nov. 3, 1857, Jan. 12, 1858; Governor Brown, Message, *SJ* (1857), Nov. 10; *Federal Union*, "Calhoun," Dec. 1; *ibid.*, editorial, Dec. 29, 1857.

68. Jan. 19, 1858.

69. *Federal Union*, Jan. 26, 1858.

70. Veto Message, *SJ* (1857), Dec. 22.

71. *Federal Union*, Jan. 26, Feb. 9, 16, 23, 1858

72. "One of the People," *loc. cit.*

73. *Ibid.*

74. *Federal Union,* Jan. 26, 1858.
75. *Ibid.,* "Calhoun," Dec. 1, 1857.
76. *Ibid.,* July 27, Aug. 10, 1858.
77. *Ibid.,* Oct. 26, 1858.
78. Message, *SJ* (1838).

Chapter X Waterways and Roadways

Chief sources have been the following:

A. Official Documents: see bibliographical note at beginning of this section.

B. Contemporary works: Loammi Baldwin, *Report on the Brunswick Canal and Railroad* (Boston, 1836); J. S. Buckingham, *The Slave States of America* (London, 1842); George R. Gilmer, *Sketches of Some of the First Settlers of Upper Georgia, of the Cherokees and of the Author* (New York, 1855); *Capt. Basil Hall,* Travels in *North America in the Years 1827 and 1828* (London, 1829); Frances A. Kemble, *Journal of a Residence on a Georgia Plantation in 1838–1839* (New York, 1863); Wilson Lumpkin, *Removal of the Cherokee Indians from Georgia, 1827–1838* (Wormsloe, 1907); Charles Lyell, *A Second Visit to the United States of America, 1845–1846* (New York, 1849).

C. Newspapers: Augusta *Chronicle and Gazette,* 1787–1810; *Augusta Chronicle,* 1810–1819; *Chronicle and Sentinel* (Augusta), 1836–1860; *Columbus Times,* 1845–1851; *Southern Sentinel* (Columbus), 1852; *Times and Sentinel* (Columbus), 1853–1860; *Georgia Telegraph* (Macon), 1826–1860; *Federal Union* (Milledgeville), 1832–1860; *Georgia Journal* (Milledgeville), 1821–1839; *Savannah Republican,* 1821–1861.

D. Secondary Works: The best study of the internal improvement movement in Georgia prior to the railroad period is by J. C. Ward, Jr., *Internal Improvements in Georgia, 1817–1843* (unpublished manuscript, 1934, Emory University Library, Atlanta). Others: J. C. Butler, *Historical Record of Macon and Central Georgia* (Macon, 1879); E. M. Coulter, *Georgia: A Short History;* Thomas Gamble, Jr., *History of the Government of Savannah* (Savannah, 1901); John H. Goff, "The Steamboat Period in Georgia," *GHQ,* XII, 236–254; Milton S. Heath, *Public Cooperation in Railroad Construction in the Southern United States to 1861* (unpublished Ph.D. thesis, Widener Library, Harvard University, 1937); John H. Morrison, *History of American Steam Navigation* (New York, 1903); Ulrich B. Phillips, *History of Transportation in the Eastern Cotton Belt* (New York, 1908); Henry V. Poor, *History of Railroads and Canals of the United States* (New York, 1860). Numerous county histories have been consulted for local information and also innumerable articles in the *Georgia Historical Quarterly.*

1. Augusta *Chronical and Gazette,* numerous articles, letters, and grand jury presentments, 1786–1810.
2. *Augusta Herald,* Aug. 1, 1799; *Augusta Chronicle,* Aug. 22, 1801; Aug. 22, 1802.
3. Annual Message, *SJ* (1805).
4. *SJ* (1810, 1811).
5. *GLB,* Dec. 2, 30, 1802; Dec. 15, 1803; Aug. 7, 1804; Annual Message, *SJ* (1805).
6. Lumpkin, I, 22–24.
7. Messages, *SJ* (1815, 1816).
8. Annual Messages, *SJ* (1823–1826); *Savannah Republican,* Oct. 27, 1824.
9. State Treasurers' Reps., *SJ* (1815–1817).
10. *SJ* (1817), 7.
11. *Laws* (Prince, 1837), 709.
12. The first regular stage coach line was established between Savannah and Augusta in 1786. Operated weekly, it required three days each way and the one-way fare was $12.50, or ten cents per mile for lesser distances; fourteen pounds of baggage

were allowed. The stage was operating twice weekly in 1799, covering the distance in two days easily, and charging $8.00. *Georgia State Gazette*, Nov. 4, 1786; *Augusta Herald*, Oct. 30, 1799.

13. More than one-fourth of Augusta's budget in 1806 was being spent upon roads, under various provisions of the city's ordinances, and this policy was maintained apparently at least until the county acts were passed. *Augusta Chronicle*, Apr. 8, 1808; July 7, 1810; *Laws* (Lamar), 656.

14. *HJ* (1821), 6–14.

15. Ward, 78–81.

16. Albert Gallatin, Report on Roads and Canals April 4, 1808, *American State Papers*, Class X, Miscellaneous, I, 724–741; Carter Goodrich, "National Planning of Internal Improvements," *Political Science Quarterly*, LXIII, 16–44.

17. Other navigable internal waterway distances include: Ogeechee, St. Marys, Satilla, Ocholocknee, and Ohoopee, 150 miles, and coastal waters, 200 miles. Figures are reproduced from Goff, 251, and refer to waters navigable to steamboats at any time. There were many additional miles, on lesser rivers, the larger creeks, and the major rivers above the fall line, that were navigable by boxes, rafts, and small boats; but the many efforts to improve these sufficiently for general steamboat traffic were largely a failure.

18. Lumpkin, I, 39.

19. *HJ* and *SJ* (1825). Comparison is made of votes with returns of the gubernatorial election of 1825 as reported by Ulrich B. Phillips, *Georgia and States Rights*, 104–107.

20. *SJ* (1826); reprinted in the *Savannah Republican*, Nov. 17, 1826; summarized by Ward, 41–54.

21. A considerable controversy developed later over what had been the respective attitudes of members of the board toward railroads. Lumpkin states in *Removal of the Cherokees* that, while making the survey with Fulton and discussing the characteristics and advantages of railroads with him, reading his manuals, and investigating the terrain, he became convinced that railroads would be superior to canals in middle and upper Georgia and that he had been a railroad advocate ever after. He says further that he conveyed this opinion to Governor Troup. James Couper, writing in 1858, states that he, Couper, was in a minority on the board in favor of railroads, but that finally, with the aid of Fulton and Governor Troup, he secured the favorable recommendations regarding railroads that is contained in the report. Ward, 52–53. No doubt most members of the board were waterway-minded; but Lumpkin's continuous labors thenceforth to secure the adoption of railroads seems to suggest that Couper may have misunderstood his position.

22. Lumpkin, I, 29–30; Inaugural Address, *SJ* (1831), Nov. 9.

23. *Savannah Republican*, Jan. 23, Mar. 19, 1824; May 14, 1825. "Western" trade in Savannah referred to that of central Georgia, as distinguished from the Savannah River commerce. Savannah citizens contributed heavily to the construction of a through road to Macon, with branches to other central Georgia cities, in 1824.

24. *Ibid.*, May 5, June 22, Aug. 12, Dec. 15, 1824; July 18, 1826.

25. *Ibid.*, Feb. 15, 28, Mar. 11, 28, 1826.

26. *Ibid.*, Mar. 23, 1827; Aug. 14, 1828; July 19, 1833.

27. *Ibid.*, Dec. 4, 1829, Mar. 31, Dec. 23, 1830.

28. *Savannah Georgian*, Nov. 10, 1836.

29. *Savannah Republican*, Dec. 5, 1836; Mar. 24, 1837.

30. *Ibid.*, Apr. 17, 1839; July 16, 1840.

31. The leading spirit in this first, purely local effort was William Brunswick Davis.

32. I am deeply indebted to Mr. Edmund Steel, graduate student in History at the University of North Carolina, who is writing a study of the life of Thomas Butler King, for most of the information concerning King and his connection with the Brunswick canal, the Brunswick and Florida Railroad, and other projects of that area. Mr. Steel most graciously permitted me to read chapter II of his study, which deals most extensively with King's role in the internal improvement movement. King

and his associates transferred extensive land holdings at Brunswick to the Boston capitalists, who organized the Brunswick Land Company as a part of their promotion ventures in the Brunswick area. King became a prominent figure in public life in Georgia, possibly the most influential person in his region.

33. The subscription was paid by the Central Bank of Georgia. *HJ* (1847), 208.

34. Margaret Davis Cate, *Our Todays and Yesterdays* (Brunswick: Glover Bros., 1930), 208–210; Loammi Baldwin, *Report on the Brunswick Canal and Railroad.* Baldwin's father, Loammi Baldwin, Sr., had been superintendent and a principal owner of the Middlesex Canal in Massachusetts, which was an earlier counterpart of the Brunswick Canal in most important respects. His brother James was also a famous engineer, who, in the same year that Loammi was drawing up the plans for the Brunswick Canal, was performing the same task for the Boston and Albany Railroad.

35. *Laws* (Dawson), S. Res., 499.

36. *Ibid.*, 607; H. Res., 1828, 219–220.

37. *SJ* (1829), 101–103; *Savannah Republican,* May 19, 1824.

38. *Savannah Republican,* Nov. 23, Dec. 9, 1829; Jan. 22, 1830.

39. *Ibid.*, Jan. 24, 1831; Governor Lumpkin, Message, *SJ* (1832), Nov. 6.

40. Goff, 236–254; Ward, Chap. V.

41. *Columbus Times,* Feb. 18, 1846; Jan. 11, Feb. 22, 1848.

42. *Ibid.*, Jan. 15, Apr. 2–9, 1850; *Southern Sentinel* (Columbus), Mar. 19, 1852. Four plank road projects were launched in Macon with a view to recovering for that city the lost wagon trade, but efforts to enlist the city's aid proved unavailing. *Ibid.*, Apr. 2, 1852.

43. *Laws* (1849–50, 1851–52, 1853–54).

44. Steamboat and wagon trade interests dubbed the railroad the "Iron Boa" in the 1840's. *Columbus Times,* Nov. 4, 1846.

Chapter XI A State System of Railways

Some of the investigations that have contributed to this chapter reach back a quarter century or more to my early researches upon my doctoral project. Then and since I have paid innumerable visits to libraries and other repositories of historical information in Georgia pertaining to its railroads. Naturally some of the sources have become vague. However, the following represent the chief sources and those studies that have been most helpful in the collection of the materials for this chapter:

A. Official Documents: in addition to those listed in the bibliographical note at the beginning of this section, the following — City of Savannah, Annual Reports of Mayor, 1827–1861; City of Savannah, Annual Reports of Treasurer, 1827–1861; *American State Papers,* 1832–1859; U. S. Department of Agriculture, *Soils of the United States,* 1913; *Affairs of Southern Railroads,* House Docs., No. 34, 39th Congress, 2nd Session.

B. Railroads' Annual Reports: almost complete for Georgia, North Carolina, and South Carolina, and numerous ones in Tennessee, Florida, and Alabama.

C. Contemporary Works: J. S. Buckingham, *The Slave States of America* (2 vols., London, 1842); J. C. Butler, *Historical Record of Macon and Central Georgia* (Macon, 1879); Charles Cist, *The Cincinnati Miscellany, or Antiquities of the West* (2 vols., Cincinnati, 1845–46); William Gregg, *Essays on Domestic Industry, or an Inquiry into the Expediency of Establishing Cotton Manufactures in South Carolina* (Charleston, 1845); Wilson Lumpkin, *Removal of the Cherokee Indians from Georgia, 1827–1838* (Wormsloe, 1907); Sir Charles Lyell, *A Second Visit to the United States of North America, 1845–46* (2 vols., New York, 1868); Frederick Law Olmstead, *A Journey in the Seaboard Slave States, 1853–54* (New York, 1856), and *A Journey in the Back Country* (New York, 1860); H. S. Tanner, *A Description of Canals and Railroads of the United States in All the States* (New York, 1840); John S. Toof, *Trade and Commerce of Memphis* (Memphis, 1861).

D. Newspapers and Periodicals: *American Railroad Journal,* 1832–1861; Athens *Southern Farmer,* 1835–1853; *Atlanta Republican,* 1855; *Atlanta Examiner,* 1857; Augusta *Chronical and Sentinel,* 1836–1860; *Charleston Courier,* 1827–1840; *Columbus Inquirer,* 1841–1847; *Columbus Times and Sentinel,* 1845–1860; *De Bow's Commercial Review of the Southern and Western States* (New Orleans), 1846–1860; Macon *Georgia Telegraph,* 1826–1860; Milledgeville, *Southern Recorder,* 1851–1852; Milledgeville *Federal Union,* 1832–1860; Nashville (Tenn.) *Republican Banner,* 1837–1841, 1849–1861; *Nashville Union,* 1844–1848; Knoxville (Tenn.) *Standard,* 1845–1848, 1855; Savannah *Daily Georgian,* 1832–1856; *Savannah Republican,* 1826–1861; *Sumpter Republican* (Americus, Ga.), 1854–1858.

E. Secondary Works: James Houstoun Johnston, *Western and Atlantic Railroad of the State of Georgia* (Atlanta, 1931) is the definitive history of the State Railroad; Ulrich B. Phillips, *History of Transportation in the Eastern Cotton Belt* (New York, 1908) is the standard work on early railroad development in Georgia; E. Merton Coulter, *Georgia: A Short History* (Chapel Hill, 1947) provides the best treatment of the railroads in the setting of general history; Thomas Gamble, Jr., *History of the Government of Savannah* (Savannah, 1901) contains a summary of the financial efforts of that city in railroad construction; and Mary S. Cumming, *Georgia Railroad and Banking Company* (Augusta, 1945) supplies useful information that is not otherwise readily available. Other works: Samuel M. Derrick, *Centennial History of the South Carolina Railroad* (Columbia, 1930); Fairfax Harrison, *A History of the Legal Development of the Railroad System of the Southern Railroad Company* (Washington, 1901); Milton S. Heath, *Public Cooperation in the Construction of Railroads in the Southern United States to 1861* (Harvard, Widener Library, unpublished manuscript, 1937); Interstate Commerce Commission, *Valuation Reports,* Regular Series, vols. 125, 130, and Special Series, vols. 29, 38; J. C. Ward, Jr., *Internal Improvements in Georgia* (Emory University Library, unpublished manuscript, 1934); William Way, Jr., *History of the Clinchfield Railroad* (Chapel Hill, 1930).

1. *Savannah Republican,* June 9, 1831.
2. *Ibid.,* July 19, 1831.
3. *Ibid.,* July 28, 1831.
4. *Ibid.,* Oct. 4, 1831; Ward, 142–146.
5. Ward, *Internal Improvements.*
6. *American Railroad Journal,* Sept. 7, 1833; Phillips, 225.
7. Athens' promotion of this railroad is described in detail by Phillips, chapter V, and a brief summary is given by Peter S. McGuire, "Athens and the Railroad," *GHQ,* XIX, 145.
8. *Savannah Republican,* June 28, Oct. 15, Nov. 1, 1833; *Savannah Georgian,* July 27, 1833.
9. *Savannah Republican,* Nov. 11, 1833.
10. *Ibid.,* Nov. 28, 1833.
11. Message, *SJ* (1833). Lumpkin's ideas are contained chiefly in: *Removal of the Cherokee Indians;* inaugural address and messages, printed in House and Senate *Journals* and also included in *Removal of the Cherokee Indians;* and in his *Letter Books* while governor.
12. Message, 1833.
13. General Gaines submitted a memorial to Congress, December 31, 1839, which outlined his entire plan. It called for seven key railroads: (1) Lexington, Ky., to Buffalo or Plattsburg, N. Y., with branches to Detroit, Albany, and Boston; (2) Lexington, via Nashville, to New Orleans; (3) Memphis, Tenn., to Charleston, S. C.; (4) Memphis to Sabine Ridge, Ark., with branches to Ft. Towson and Ft. Gibson, Ark.; (5) Knoxville, Tenn., to Norfolk, Va., or Baltimore, with branches to Richmond and New Bern, N. C.; (6) Louisville to Mobile, with a branch to Pensacola; and (7) Louisville, or Albany, Ind., to St. Louis, and thence to the mouth of the Big Platte, with branches to Chicago and to the upper Des Moines River crossing. It was to be double-tracked and mileage was estimated at 4,200 miles and total cost

at $64,000,000; and construction was to be done by the Army at federal expense. Lines when completed were to be transferred to the states, with the single condition that United States troops, munitions, supplies, and mails should be carried free forever. Gaines was a Virginian whose memorial is reprinted in *Amer. RR. Jour.*, July 1–15, 1840.

14. *GLB*, II, Letters to General E. P. Gaines, Dec. 10, 1833, Mar. 3, 1834.

15. Reports and Resolutions of the Cincinnati Railroad Convention, Aug. 15, 1835, are reprinted in *Amer. RR. Jour.*, Dec. 5, 12, 1835. This was not the first suggestion for a railroad over this route. Western North Carolina had been trying for several years to interest the southeastern states in a transmontane road or railroad by way of the French Broad River valley. Governor Lumpkin was a resident of Athens and a member of the first Board of Directors of the Georgia Railroad, but such fact seems not to have altered his position in favor of a Central State Railroad from Savannah to northwest Georgia. The Athens group believed that Rabun Gap was a more economical and logical route than Saluda Gap to the east for a transmontane railroad through western North Carolina. They probably considered northwest Georgia, on the other hand, too far west for such a railroad.

16. *Amer. RR. Jour.*, Mar. 12, 19, Aug. 2, 1834; June 27, July 4, Sept. 26, 1835; *Augusta Sentinel*, June 5, 1834; Jan. 26, 1835; Phillips, 227–230. J. Edgar Thomson's father built the first experimental railroad in the United States, in 1809, at Leiper's stone quarry, Delaware County, Pa. J. Edgar was a member of the engineering corps that laid out the Philadelphia and Columbia Railroad in 1827 and was assistant engineer of the Camden and Amboy Railroad in 1830 before going to Europe to study. He left the Georgia Railroad in 1847 to go to the engineering department of the Pennsylvania Railroad Company and later became its president. Probably no one has left a deeper imprint upon American railroad practice.

17. *Savannah Republican*, Jan. 10, June 2, Nov. 14, 1834; July 3, 1835.

18. *Ibid.*, Apr. 3, May 14, June 4–26, Sept. 9, 1835.

19. *Ibid.*, Nov. 12, 1835; Mar. 14, 1836.

20. *Ibid.*, Nov. 9, 1835.

21. Some politicians already were referring to the Georgia Railroad as a monopoly.

22. *Savannah Republican*, Nov. 18, 1835.

23. *Ibid.*, Feb. 11, 12, 15, Mar. 29, 31, 1836; *Macon Messenger*, Feb. 18, 1836.

24. *Augusta Sentinel*, Apr. 26, 1836; Phillips, 231–232.

25. *Exec. Docs.*, 24th Cong., 2nd Sess., II, No. 65.

26. Phillips, *History of Transportation.*

27. The record on railroad banks is confusing on one or two points. The United States Treasury reports for 1837 list a small bank under the title, Branch Railroad Bank. This might be the Chattahoochee Railroad Bank, which is omitted under that name, or a branch bank of either the Central of Georgia Railroad or the Georgia Railroad, or a bank of the Middle Branch Railroad, assuming in the latter's case that its charter privileges, which were defined as identical with those of the Georgia Railroad, included banking. The title of the Washington Railroad and Banking Company, chartered in 1839, suggests that this small company, which built a branch of the Georgia Railroad, possessed banking privileges; but there is no mention whatever of banking in the text of the charter and no reference could be found that such a bank ever existed.

28. *HJ* (1857), 229. I included, I now think mistakenly, the legislative committee's figure in the state's contribution in my early study, *Public Cooperation in Railroad Construction.* Federal Coordinator of Transportation, *Public Aids to Transportation,* II, 64–65 (Washington, 1938), reduces the committee's figure to $1,000,000. But I doubt that the lower figure has any sounder basis than the higher one.

29. There was one apparent minor exception. See Chapter X, footnote 82.

30. Phillips, 244–245.

31. *Exec. Docs.*, 27th, 28th, 29th Congresses, Reports of Secretary of Treasury.

32. *Laws* (1834), Sen. Resolutions.

33. *Laws* (1835), 314–318.

34. *Amer. RR. Jour.*, Mar. 19, 1836; Reprint from *Charleston Courier, Amer. RR.*

Jour., May 21, 1836; Reprint from *Columbia Telescope, Amer. RR. Jour.*, Apr. 9, 1836.

35. Phillips says that the number exceeded four hundred before the Convention adjourned.

36. The entire "Reports" of the Knoxville Convention, including reports of members of the Georgia delegation to their own group, were reprinted in the *Georgia Messenger* from the *Knoxville Register* and also were reprinted, from the former, in the *Amer. RR. Jour.*, Aug. 6, 20, 27 and Sept. 3, 1836.

37. Reprinted from the *Miners' Record* in *Amer. RR. Jour.*, Sept. 3, 1836.

38. "Minutes and Resolutions" of the Convention, reprinted in *Amer. RR. Jour.*, Dec. 10, 1836.

39. It seems likely that the Middle Branch Railroad Company enjoyed banking privileges, since the other two branch projects were so favored. See footnote 27, above.

40. *Removal of Cherokee Indians*, II, 265–295.

41. Augusta *Chron. and Sent.*, "Review of History of Democrats' Handling of Finances," July 30–31, Oct. 4, 6, 1845.

42. *Marietta Helicon*, reprinted in Augusta *Chron. and Sent.*, Sept. 6, 1845. Johnston, page 29, fixes a different date, which quite likely may be the correct one, from that stated in the *Marietta Helicon*.

43. The *Marietta Helicon*, discussing operations of trains from the terminus on September 3, 1845, uses the name Marthasville; and five days later, the Augusta *Chronicle and Sentinel* speaks of the Georgia Railroad's announcement of its intention to operate trains to Atlanta the following week.

44. Johnston, 106–107.

45. Augusta *Chron. and Sent.*, Sept. 11, 1845. The Company had been operating trains to Decatur, within six miles of Atlanta, for some time.

46. It would be impossible to ascertain the amount of investment upon roads, rivers, canals, and turnpikes. The only known figure is the approximate $500,000 expended by the state. Cities, voluntary associations, and private capitalists may have expended an equal amount. The total value of the compulsory services devoted to county roads and bridges could only be conjectured. But actual money costs of state construction of main through roads averaged from $50 to $100 per mile. The costs of railroads built during the depression varied from $12,000 to $30,000 per mile. Furthermore, a large part of the annual service in labor rendered on the county road systems was applied to maintenance.

47. Georgia Railroad Company, Engineer's Report, 1836; Central of Georgia, Engineer's Report, 1840; *Columbus* (Ga.) *Times*, Oct. 24, 1848.

48. The Central Bank purchased $419,078.63 of "cash" scrip, that was issued to contractors by the Western and Atlantic commissioners without any covering 6 per cent bond issue. *SJ* (1842), 195–197; *HJ* (1847), 208–212.

49. The exact amount of the Central Bank's purchase was $680,001.70, composed of "cash" scrip, $419,078.63, interest coupons on 6 per cent bonds, $186,316.01, and redemption of six per cent bonds, $74,607.06. *HJ* (1847), 208–212; Governor McDonald, Message, *SJ* (1841).

50. *SJ* (1842), 195–197, 238–239; Savannah City Treasurers' Reports, 1834–1843; Macon City Council Reports, 1835–1843.

51. This was not entirely net, of course, since migration from other localities reduced somewhat the productiveness and value of capital in the latter places.

52. Railroad construction was not the only contributing factor. Other important ones were: the land policy, which developed small proprietorships and kept down land speculation; the conservative policy of commercial bank expansion; and the Central Bank's relief credit policy.

53. James Camak and his associates in Athens had visualized that city's becoming the industrial-commercial center of Georgia, with rail lines radiating eventually in every direction — connecting Athens with the west, the northwest, the northeast, the south Atlantic and the Gulf. What they were invisioning actually was to come to pass later in the city of Atlanta; Athens' location was too far east.

Atlanta's Georgia Air-Line Railway project (now the main line of the Southern Railway between Charlotte and Atlanta) was considered by most Georgians at the time as an idiotic notion — it would be a railroad without any traffic in either direction!

54. These financial activities of the city are recorded in the issues of the *Savannah Republican*, 1845–1860. They have also been summarized by Thomas Gamble, Jr., in *History of the Government of Savannah*.

55. Minutes of Public Railroad Meeting, Augusta, Jan. 6, 1860.

56. Columbus *Times and Sentinel*, Apr. 2, 1856, Jan. 7, 1860; Butler, 289–290; Phillips, 224–225, 288–291.

57. Ward, 162.

58. Columbus Railroad Meeting, July 18, 1846, reported in *Columbus Times*, July 26, 1846; *ibid.*, Apr. 29, 1857.

59. *Ibid.*, June 17, July 26, Nov. 4, 1846; Jan. 11, Feb. 22, 1848; Feb. 5, 1850; Columbus *Southern Sentinel*, Jan. 8, 1852.

60. Butler, 589–590; Columbus *Times and Sentinel*, Jan. 13, 22, 1859.

61. I have analyzed these theories and described the practices based upon them, in the South, in "Public Railroad Construction and the Development of Private Enterprise in the South Before 1861," *Journal of Economic History:* Supplement X — 1950, *The Tasks of Economic History*.

62. Kentucky did not adopt any general state aid policy for railroads. During this period the state was devoting almost all of its internal improvement funds upon river improvement. However, the aid policy for railroads was applied universally in the state on a county and city basis. Tennessee adopted the general public aid policy on both the state and local government levels, as did several other states in a lesser degree.

63. *Savannah Republican*, Nov. 28, 1855; Columbus *Times and Sentinel*, Feb. 3, 1856.

64. Lumpkin, *Georgia Courier*, Mar. 4, 1853; *Albany* (Ga.) *Courier*, Dec. 24, 1853; Americus *Sumpter Republican*, Apr. 1, 1853; Sept. 30, Oct. 19, Nov. 2, 1854; July 9, Aug. 8, 1856.

65. *Albany Courier*, May 8, 1847, Apr. 29, 1854; *Albany Patriot*, Oct. 28, 1849; *Sumpter Republican*, Nov. 9, 1854; June 18, 1856; Albany *American Standard*, Nov. 8, 1855.

66. *Sumpter Republican*, May 21, 1856. The president and four of the six directors of the Brunswick and Florida were from New York City.

67. *Savannah Republican*, Report of Town Meetings, Nov. 12, 1852; July 2, 1856.

68. *Ibid.*, May 12, 29, June 1, 1853.

69. The original charter of 1835 prohibited any competing line being built within twenty miles of the Brunswick and Florida. It was the identical provision that had been in the Brunswick Canal and Railroad Company the year before. When the Brunswick and Florida Railroad charter was revived in 1847, presumably this monopoly guarantee again became valid. Likely it was an oversight on the part of the legislature.

70. Tallahassee Railroad Convention, June 6, 1853, Report in *Floridian and Journal*, reprinted in *Savannah Republican*, June 23, 1853.

71. Columbus *Times and Sentinel*, Mar. 4, 1853.

72. The city of Savannah and its Savannah, Albany and Gulf each subscribed $200,000 of the $600,000 necessary to secure the first state installment of $500,000. Later the Thomasville subscription of $500,000 and the additional Savannah subscription were advanced to secure the second state installment. The subscription of the Savannah, Albany and Gulf was tantamount to a city subscription, since the city had to endorse the railroad company's bonds to enable it to do the financing. Furthermore, the railroad was virtually a city project, even though its charter permitted it to be controlled by its private shareholders: of its capital, the city had supplied $1,300,000 and private individuals $310,000.

73. Columbus *Times and Sentinel*, Jan. 23, May 20, June 26, July 8, Nov. 28, Dec. 5, 1857; *Savannah Republican*, Nov. 25, 1858.

74. Heath, *Public Cooperation in Railroad Construction*, 40–43.
75. Gamble, 225–227.
76. *Savannah Republican*, Nov. 25, 1858; Oct. 19, 20, 1859.
77. *Ibid.*, Aug. 14, 1859.
78. There are minor discrepancies between the totals in this table and those shown for Georgia in Table I-A of my paper, "Public Railroad Construction and the Development of Private Enterprise in the South Before 1861." In the latter, I carried the construction account of the Western and Atlantic Railroad only to 1857, when investment was virtually complete; but in the present study I have extended the period through 1860, to make it somewhat more comparable with available investment statistics of other roads. I found a small error in my previous city figures and also have omitted one item because of the doubtful character of the reference. The small subscription of Morgan County had escaped my notice until recently. There may well be other imperfections in the record as given herein. There are a few items that I have never been able to verify to my complete satisfaction. But it is my belief that the table is substantially correct.
79. Heath, *Public Cooperation in Railroad Construction*, 40–43.
80. It would appear that in some instances this principle was carried almost to extremes. The city of Savannah supplied 80 per cent of the capital of the Savannah, Albany and Gulf Railroad, yet private shareholders with the remaining 20 per cent held the entire voting power in the company. Gamble, 220–223.
81. Heath, "Public Railroad Construction and the Development of Private Enterprise in the South Before 1861," 46–52.
82. The Monroe Railroad Company was the only case of bankruptcy. This company failed financially in 1845 when it was within sight of completion. It was purchased by Northern capitalists and soon completed. The failure actually had relatively little effect upon the progress of construction of the railroad.

Chapter XII Public Action and the Growth of Corporate Enterprise

1. Selected references on the history of the corporation: in Great Britain — W. R. Scott, *The Constitution and Finance of English, Scottish and Irish Joint Stock Companies to 1720*, 3 vols., Cambridge, 1910–1912; C. T. Carr, *Select Charters of Trading Companies, 1530–1707*, London, 1913; A. B. Du Bois, *The English Business Company after the Bubble Act, 1720–1800*, New York, 1938; B. C. Hunt, *The Development of the Business Corporation in England, 1800–1867*, Cambridge, Mass., 1936; W. S. Holdsworth, *History of English Law*, London, 1922, vols. III, IX. In America — J. S. Davis, *Essays in the Earlier History of American Corporations*, Cambridge, 1917; Shaw Livermore, *Early American Land Companies*, New York, 1939. General — R. L. Raymond, "The Genesis of the Corporation," *Harvard Law Review*, XIX, 350– .
2. Livermore, Editor's Introduction, by Julius Goebel, Jr., vii–xxvi.
3. Du Bois, ch. I; Hunt, 6–13; Livermore, 38, 61–66.
4. Du Bois, ch. I; Livermore, vii–xxvi, 61–69.
5. There are frequent references in the current newspapers to existing or contemplated voluntary associations, but little specific information about them. They are also mentioned in statutes whenever, as in the case of the Savannah Seamen's Hospital, use of public property or lottery was granted. *RRG*, III, 534. Also *Laws* (Clayton), 287.
6. A leading case was the Bank of Augusta: *Augusta Chronicle*, Mar. 31 and May 12, 1810; preamble of bank's charter, *Laws*, 1810.
7. *RRG*, I, Act of Sept., 16, 1777; *RRG*, III, 362; J. Clay, *Letters of Joseph Clay of Savannah* (Savannah, 1913), 27. This method of public insurance has something of a counterpart today in the Federal Veterans' Insurance Bureau.
8. *CRG*, XIX, Pt. II, 466–468.
9. A notion was prevalent, at least among some sponsors of the county academies, that those institutions were private corporations and, consequently, were protected

from legislative interference by the Dartmouth College decision. But the Georgia courts held that, since they were established under the mandatory provision of the state constitution and drew their support from public land grants, they were public corporations; and hence that they could be regulated and their charters altered at the will of the legislature. Charlton (1823), 250; *Ibid.* (1830), 342; *Young vs. Harrisons,* 16 Ga. Rep.; *Cleveland vs. Stewart,* 3 Ga. Rep. 283; *Dart vs. Houston,* 22 Ga. Rep. 506; *Board of Education of Glynn County vs. Mayor of Brunswick,* 72 Ga. Rep. 353; *Trustees of Academy of Richmond County vs. City Council of Augusta,* 90 Ga. Rep. 634. The far greater proportion, approximately six-sevenths, of the academies were private corporations. See Table 17, wherein the private academies are classed as quasi-public.

10. The state built two roads — one through Cherokee Territory to the Tennessee line and another through uninhabited south Georgia to the Florida line — and voluntary groups, with some assistance from local governments, constructed a through road from Savannah to Dublin.

11. Louis Hartz, *Economic Policy and Democratic Thought.* (Cambridge, 1938) p. 38.

12. *Laws* (1838), 33–43. To secure legal existence, a banking association had to file a certificate of organization and compliance with the clerk of the superior court in its county, and to deposit securities or mortgages with a state board as the basis of note issue. The state board (composed of the comptroller and two appointed members) held the collateral and issued bank notes much as the Federal Reserve Agent does today. The act was in effect a general incorporation law for banks. Only two banks were chartered under the act, owing to the severe business collapse and long depression that followed immediately.

13. A minimum of $250,000 capital was required, of which 10 percent had to be paid in and the balance fully secured before the commencement of business. A certified statement of the nature of the intended business, names of shareholders and amounts subscribed by each had to be filed with the clerk of the superior court in each county in which a company intended to do business.

14. *Laws* (1843), 108–109.

15. *Laws* (1847), 219–221.

16. *Laws* (1850), 262–265.

17. *Laws* (1856), 480–481.

18. *Johnston vs. Crawley,* 25 Ga. Rep. 316.

19. M. Hutcheson, "Virginia's Dartmouth College Case," *Va. Mag. of Hist. and Biog.,* LI (July 1943); Edgar W. Knight, "North Carolina's 'Dartmouth College Case,'" *Jour. of Higher Educ.,* XIX, No. 3 (March 1948). Professor Knight's article provides an excellent brief summary of this early litigation and the Jeffersonian point of view. See also C. A. Beard, *Jefferson, Corporations and the Constitution,* Washington, 1936.

20. *Laws* (1835), 192; (1847), 122.

21. *Laws* (1822), 52.

22. *Laws* (1831), 198.

23. 22 Ga. Rep.

24. *Laws* (1859), 242.

25. 8 Ga. Rep. 468, 527; 11 Ga. Rep. 459; 16 Ga. Rep. 289; 19 Ga. Rep. 325.

26. The state subscribed one-half the capital stock, but the withdrawal of private stockholders following the depression of 1819, by relinquishment of stocks in satisfaction of debts to the bank, left the state as the owner of four-fifths of the shares. The failure of the bank in 1839 and its subsequent liquidation involved the state in a sizable payment of its proportionate share of the remaining unpaid obligations of the bank.

27. *Hightower vs. Thornton,* 8 Ga. Rep. 486. The Court cited a number of American precedents: 2 *Stor. Eq. Jur.,* Par. 1252; *Nevitt vs. Bank of Port Gibson,* 6 Smede and Marsh, 513; *Vose vs. Grant,* 15 Mass. R. 505; Spear vs. Grant, 16 Mass. R. 9; *Wood vs. Dummer,* 3 Mason's Rep. 308; *Briggs vs. Perminan,* 8 Cowen 387; *Slee vs. Bloom,* 19 Whet. Rep. 456; *Allen et al. vs. Montgomery Railroad Company*

et al., 11 Ala. Rep. N. S., 437. Stockholders of a bankrupt corporation were not liable at common law.

28. *Mason and Fields vs. Force Brothers and Company,* 30 Ga. Rep. 99.

29. *Force Brothers and Co. vs. Dahlonega Tanning & Leather Co.*, 22 Ga. Rep. 86.

30. *Macon and Western Railroad Company vs. Parker,* 9 Ga. Rep. 377.

31. *Laws* (1859), 242.

32. *Laws* (Watkins), 424, 425.

33. Livermore stresses this "side-issue" opportunity of participation in business ventures as a major factor in the introduction of the corporation: 2, note 2; 44 ff; 222.

34. Cases in point are the attempts of Ebenezer Jencks and Thomas Spaulding and their associates to build turnpikes, canals, and railroads in southeastern and southern Georgia, which either failed or were supplanted by chartered companies. See *Acts* and *Journals,* Georgia, 1820–1835.

35. This problem is stated concisely in the preamble of the charter of the Eagle and Phoenix Hotel Company, *Laws* (1833).

36. George Heberton Evans, Jr., *Business Incorporations in the United States,* 1800–1943, New York: National Bureau of Economic Research, 1948, ch. 3.

37. 8 Ga. Rep. 486; 19 Ga. Rep. 325; 30 Ga. Rep. 99.

38. *Cleveland vs. Stewart et al.*, 2 Ga. Rep. 283.

39. Livermore, *Land Companies.*

40. The preambles of charters frequently cited the nature of the general interest in the prospective project, the need to encourage useful skills, the manufacture and use of machinery, the development of products and of the resources of the state, and the desirability of freeing the state from the exorbitant charges and discriminatory practices of out-of-state concerns. Typical examples: *Prince's Digest,* 353, 382; *Laws* (1827), 75; (1839), 116–117.

41. The term is used to signify any combination of public and private stock-ownership in a corporation. See Hartz, *Economic Policy,* ch. III.

42. The projects were: Savannah, Ogeechee and Altamaha Canal Company, 1826 (state and city of Savannah); Milledgeville and Gordon Railroad Company, 1850 (state and city of Milledgeville); and Atlantic and Gulf Railroad Company, 1856 (state and cities of Savannah and Thomasville).

43. *Laws* (1855–56), 118, 123; (1860), 199–204.

44. Such a tax was levied generally in county subscriptions to railroads throughout the South and was much more frequent and important in most other states than in Georgia. The tax was sometimes graduated downwards with distance from the right-of-way and ceased to apply at all beyond a stipulated distance (Mississippi *Laws,* 1852, ch. 57). M. S. Heath, "Public Railroad Construction and the Development of Private Enterprise in the South Before 1861," *Jour. of Econ. Hist.*, Supplement X (1950), 49, and *Public Cooperation in Railroad Construction in the Southern United States to 1861,* Widener Library, Harvard University, 1937.

45. The state first loaned the Savannah, Ogeechee and Altamaha Company $50,000 of Darien Bank notes in 1836, by virtue of continuing a loan that it had made a year previously to Ebenezer Jencks, who had not used the notes; then it subscribed $44,000 in stock; and finally it converted the loan and $4,500 of accumulated interest into stock. It sold the $98,500 of stock to the promoters of the company for $10,000 in 1836. The total investment of $50,000 in the Brunswick Canal Company was lost with the ultimate failure of that project.

46. *Augusta Sentinel,* Jan. 26, 1835; U. B. Phillips, *History of Transportation in the Eastern Cotton Belt,* New York, 1908, 224–225, 294; Central of Georgia Railroad, Seventh Report of Chief Engineer, Nov. 1, 1841; Thomas Gamble, Jr., *History of the Government of Savannah,* Savannah, 1900, 172–173.

47. *Laws* (1819), Sen. Resol. 247; Governor John Clark, "Message," *SJ* (1820), 5–7; Dawson, Nos. 15, 228, 277.

48. *Laws,* Feb. 8, 1850; *ibid.*, 1851–52, sec. 74; *ibid.*, 1859, sec. 320.

49. Heath, "Public Railroad Construction."

50. Gamble, 220–223.

Chapter XIII The State and Human Resources

I am deeply indebted in this chapter to the comprehensive information and scholarly insight of two excellent studies: Dorothy Orr, *A History of Education in Georgia* (Chapel Hill: Univ. of N. C. Press, 1950) and Ralph Betts Flanders, *Plantation Slavery in Georgia* (Chapel Hill: Univ. of N. C. Press, 1933). These studies have removed any necessity on my part of presenting detailed accounts of the history of education and slavery in Georgia. Although I had collected most of the data for the present chapter before Miss Orr's book appeared, I have leaned very heavily upon her exhaustive research and competent judgment. Professor Flanders and I have examined the same legal sources relating to slavery, but his extensive investigations of all other aspects of plantation slavery in Georgia have produced a breadth and solidity of interpretation of public policy that I could not have obtained from my own much briefer researches. The general factual outline of the present chapter necessarily follows closely the accounts given by these two studies, and I have made free to refer to them extensively for fuller treatments of subject matter. Other general works that have been most helpful are: Elbert W. G. Boogher, *Secondary Education in Georgia, 1732–1858* (Camden, N. J.: I. F. Huntzinger, 1933); Charles W. Dabney, *Universal Education in the South* (Chapel Hill: Univ. of N. C. Press, 1936); and Edgar W. Knight, *Public Education in the South* (Boston, 1922).

1. Alfred Marshall, "Future of the Working Class," *Memorials of Alfred Marshall* (A. C. Pigou, editor), London, 1925, p. 115.
2. Charles Horton Cooley, *Human Nature and the Social Order* (New York, 1902); John M. Clark, *Preface to Social Economics* (New York, 1936), and *Social Control of Business* (New York, 1939); John R. Commons, *Labor and Administration* (New York, 1913); Alfred Marshall, *Principles of Economics* (London, 1920), Bk. IV, chs. 4–6, Bk. V, ch. 13; Elton Mayo, *The Human Problem of an Industrial Civilization* (New York, 1933); Carleton H. Parker, *The Casual Laborer and Other Essays* (New York, 1920).
3. Marshall, *Principles of Economics.*
4. I. L. Kandel, *Comparative Education* (Boston, 1933) and *History of Secondary Education,* 1930; F. Paulsen, *German Education Past and Present* (New York, 1908); M. G. Jones, *The Charity School Movement in the 18th Century* (Cambridge, 1938), ch. IX.
5. Jones, *The Charity School Movement.*
6. *Ibid.,* 343–347.
7. *Ibid.,* ch. IX.
8. *Ibid.,* 341.
9. Chapter II.
10. Orr, 12–16; Reba C. Strickland, *Religion and the State in Georgia in the 18th Century,* 133–134; H. S. Bowden, *Two Hundred Years of Education, 1733–1933* (Richmond, 1932), chs. II–III.
11. *RRG,* I, 296.
12. *CRG,* XIX, Pt. II, 363–371.
13. Locke, *An Essay Concerning Human Understanding,* 1690; Montesquieu, *L'Esprit des Lois,* 1748, Bk. IV; J. J. Rousseau, *Emile,* 1762; Louis Rene de La Chalotais, *Essai d'Education Nationale, ou Plan d'Etudes pour la Jeunesse,* 1763 (trans. by H. R. Clark, with introductory essay, under title, *Essay on National Education,* London: Edward Arnold & Co., 1934); Paulsen, *German Education;* Jones, 339–341.
14. Brief biographies of these men are contained in: William J. Northern, *Men of Mark in Georgia,* 6 vols. (Atlanta, 1907), I. See also Bowden, 71. Joseph Clay, a cousin of the Habershams and the leading merchant of Savannah during the Revolution and for two decades afterwards, probably was the strongest supporter of voluntaryism in education among this early group. He feared the incompetence and "politics" that were likely to be associated with state operation. *Letters of Joseph Clay of Savannah, Ga* (Savannah, 1913), 40, 47, 171, 229, *passim.*

15. Aubrey A. Douglass, *The American School System* (New York, 1934), p. 115, *passim*.

16. The political leader in Georgia whose educational ideas resembled most closely those of LaChalotais was Governor Wilson Lumpkin. The backgrounds of the two men, of long public service and of opposition to existing private schools, also were similar.

17. Strickland, 161–163. Meanwhile, the other churches, while rapidly replacing the Anglican, had not developed any particular strength in educational policy or practice.

18. Orr, 20–24.

19. Orr, ch. II; Knight, ch. IV; Aubrey A. Douglass, *Modern Secondary Education* (New York, 1938), pp. 18–36.

20. Orr, ch. III.

21. *Laws* (Dawson), H. Res. 36, 1820, Report of Jt. Legis. Com. on Education; *Laws* (1826), 492–497, Report of Com. on Public Education and Free Schools.

22. The incorporation record would appear to afford a reasonably accurate picture of the situation, since incorporation had become so universal among non-business enterprises. See also Orr, 35–38.

23. Orr, 30–32; Stevens, *History of Georgia*, II, 362–364.

24. *Laws* (Dawson), No. 1472; *Laws* (1826), 492–497.

25. The churches began to enter the field of higher education, for the training of ministers in particular, during the 1830's, and to contest increasingly the dominant position of the state institutions. The denominational colleges of Oglethorpe, Emory, Mercer, and Wesleyan soon expanded beyond ministerial training and exercised a steadily widening influence upon the culture of the state. Orr, ch. VII.

26. Orr, 32.

27. Orr, ch. III.

28. Orr, 72.

29. Orr, ch. IV.

30. Senate Resol. quoted in *Augusta Herald*, Nov. 29, 1817.

31. Orr, 70; Robert P. Brooks, *History of Georgia* (New York, 1913), 171 ff.

32. Orr, 73–74.

33. Orr, 72–73.

34. An act of Dec. 19, 1823, authorized Baldwin County to establish a common school system, to elect school commissioners, lay off school districts, build a school house in each district, appoint trustees for each school, levy a tax for school purposes, and allow free tuition and books to children whose parents were unable to pay for same. Tomlinson Fort represented Baldwin County in the state legislature from 1818 through 1825, and the above act no doubt reflects his influence.

35. Orr, 82–83.

36. *Ibid.*

37. Lumpkin's educational theories and views are contained in his annual messages, 1831–1835, his *Letter Books* while governor, and in his *Removal of the Cherokee Indians*, 2 vols. (Wormsloe, 1907). See also Note 16 above for comparison with La Chalotais.

38. Message, 1832.

39. Message, 1833.

40. Message, 1834.

41. Orr, 88–94, contains a summary of the report.

42. During the decade of the twenties, the poor schools received payments in five years only and the academies in seven.

43. The bank stocks comprised 1,744 shares of Bank of the State and 890 shares of the Bank of Augusta, both with par value of $100.

44. Orr, 156–157.

45. Message, 1857.

46. Message, 1858.

47. Orr, 172.

48. State Treasurer, *Annual Reports*.

49. *CRG,* XVII, XVIII, 102–144, *passim,* 649–688, XIX, 75 ff., XXV; *Laws* (Prince, 1837); *Laws* (T. Cobb); *Laws* (H. Cobb); *Code* (C. C. & I.); Flanders, chs. II, X, XI.

50. *Laws* (H. Cobb), 595.

51. *Laws* (Prince, 1837), 787, 794–8; Flanders, 249–251.

52. *Laws* (Prince, 1837), 784–785, 788, 794; *Myrick v. Vineburg,* 30 Ga. 161.

53. We may observe here something of a precedent for the Supreme Court's interpretation in the twentieth century, in the famous yellow-dog labor contract case, of the right to work as a property right.

54. Annual Message, 1802.

55. Governor Rabun, Message, 1818; *Augusta Chronicle,* Oct. 11, 1817.

56. Flanders, 37–38, 53–54; Clay, *Letters, passim.*

57. Clay, *Letters,* 194–195.

58. *Laws* (Lamar), Nos. 236, 510, 513–515; *Laws* (Dawson), Nos. 323, 326; Flanders, 182–183; *Augusta Chronicle,* Oct. 11, 1817.

59. *Laws* (1783–1860); Flanders, 183–184, 253.

60. *Laws* (Prince, 1837), 777; *Laws* (H. Cobb), 595.

61. *Laws* (H. Cobb), 635–636.

62. Flanders, 263–264.

63. *Laws* (Prince, 1837), 791; *Laws* (H. Cobb), 635–636.

64. *Code* (Hotchkiss), 770; *Laws* (T. Cobb), 827, 981; Prince, 786.

65. *Laws* (Prince, 1837), 658, 785.

66. *Ibid.,* 779–780, 811–812.

67. Flanders, 205–207; Augusta *Chronicle and Sentinel,* Sept. 22, 1845.

68. Flanders, 205–207.

69. Richard Harrison Shryock, *Georgia and the Union in 1850* (Philadelphia, 1926), 24.

70. Their status was defined in the slave code and nearly all prohibitions and punishments applicable to slaves were likewise applicable to them.

71. *Laws* (Clayton), 277, 348; *Laws* (Lamar), 512, 516; *Laws* (Dawson), 1270, 1272–1273, 1279–1281, S. Res., No. 270; *Augusta Herald,* Oct. 16, 1799; June 30, 1814; Mar. 3, 1819; Flanders, 34–35, 233–239, 249–252.

72. 9 Ga. 582.

73. *Laws* (1796), Feb. 6.

74. *Laws* (Dawson), 851, 881–882, 1023, 1353, 1395, 1412.

75. Orr, 163–164; U. S. *Census,* 1830–1860; Shryock, 24–25, contains a map showing the geographical distribution of illiteracy.

Chapter XIV The State as Regulator

1. City ordinances dealing with these matters in Savannah and Augusta were printed regularly in the *Savannah Republican* and *Augusta Chronicle* until the mid-twenties.

2. Their vigorous anti-nullification stand in the early thirties testifies to their distaste for insulationism. Paul Murray, *The Whig Party in Georgia,* 28–34, 57–64.

3. *CRG,* XIX, Pt. II, 243–248.

4. From tobacco warehouses located at the junction of the Broad and Savannah rivers mushroomed the city of Petersburg, one of the earliest cities to be incorporated in Georgia and, for a brief period, one of the most flourishing and important trading centers in the state. Its growth and prosperity rested entirely upon tobacco and, with the passing of that crop as a staple, Petersburg declined as suddenly as it had arisen and eventually disappeared entirely.

5. *Augusta Chronicle,* Jan. 10, 1801; Sept. 10–12, 1801; Aug. 20, 1808; *Augusta Herald,* June 7, Aug. 18, Sept. 29, 1814; Jan. 12, Feb. 2, June 8, 1815; Oct. 11, 1817.

6. Acts Regulating Savannah and Sunbury, Feb. 21, 1785, *CRG,* XIX, Pt. II, 419–433; Incorporating Augusta, Jan. 31, 1798, *Laws* (Watkins), 609; St. Marys, Nov.

26, 1802, *Laws* (Clayton), 59; Ordinances Regulating Augusta Public Market, June 4, 1814, *Augusta Herald*, June 30, 1814.

7. Chapter XIV.

8. A difference of interest developed between state and local governments over both of these matters. The former viewed control in both these cases primarily as a means of levying taxes, whereas the latter were concernd chiefly about the quality of wares and competition with local merchants. In the end the state shared its authority, devoting its attention solely to the collection of sales and license taxes and permitting the local governments to impose such regulations as they deemed proper.

9. *Laws* (Watkins), 556, 576.

10. *Ibid.*, 541, 602, 618, 622.

11. Ogeechee and Savannah Rivers Canal, 1824, *Laws* (Dawson), 203; Ocmulgee-Flint Rivers Canal and Railroad, *SJ* (1827), 69–72.

12. *Laws* (1822), Milledgeville Turnpike Co.; *Laws* (1826), Mexican Atlantic Canal Co.; Savannah, Ogeechee and Altamaha Canal Co.

13. *Laws* (1854), 407.

14. The legislature enacted a number of special acts after 1854 licensing individual physicians to practice, who apparently could not produce a college diploma.

Chapter XV Fiscal Policy

Primary sources for this chapter include most of those used throughout the study. The quantitative data have been taken largely from the annual reports of the state treasurer and comptroller general. Occasional gaps in these financial reports have been filled in from other sources, such as the reports of legislative committees and state institutions, the annual appropriation and revenue acts, the *Minutes of the* Executive Department, the Governors' *Letterbooks* and messages, the newspaper publications of official documents and the reports of the Secretary of the Treasury of the United States. It was necessary to use estimates in some instances, but fortunately annual totals of both expenditures and revenues were obtainable for all years and considerable evidence was available for missing individual items, hence it is thought that whatever degree of error there may be in a few items of the tables is not significant.

1. The various loans and other deficit transactions and their purposes are described in the governors' messages, 1837–1843, in such annual reports of the Central Bank as are extant, and in legislative committee reports, particularly *House Journal* (1841), 15; (1849), 659–561; and *Senate Journal* (1842), 195–197, 238–239.

2. Expenditures averaged $480,000 annually during 1817–1820, reaching a peak of $578,877.58 in the last year.

3. Immediate payment, out of the state's credit account with the U. S. Treasury, enabled Georgia to secure the discount offered by the federal government for prepayment of tax allotments.

4. Expenditures dropped precipitately in 1821 to $231,000, and averaged only $170,000 per annum during the succeeding five-year period. The level rose again slightly during 1827–1830; although the rise was accounted for by the investment in the Central Bank in 1829–1830, which amounted to one-third of total expenditures for the entire decade.

5. The purchase of slaves under the market road and river improvement program during 1830–1831 has been included already under expenditures for Internal Improvements, hence the sale of the slaves by the Central Bank does not represent actual net income to the state. The purchase and sale could have been treated as Investment and Investment Transfer respectively. Some slight duplication has seemed warranted in order to present a full picture of the state's financial operations.

6. Governor Brown made the last payment of $50,000 on the Atlantic and Gulf Railroad subscription out of surplus cash in the treasury; but he issued $50,000 of

new state bonds to the School Fund on the grounds that the cash payment was a retirement of state debt, owed to the railroad company.

7. This classification of lands had been set up originally in 1784 and the valuations and rates had been expressed in British money of account until 1795, when they simply were translated into dollars and cents, which accounts for the odd figures. From 1784 until 1795 the rate had varied between 6/0 and 8/0 per £100 of valuation, or, in terms of cents, roughly between 30 and 40 cents per $100; hence the state in fixing the rate at 35 cents had adopted the average of the preceding rates.

8. Annual Message.

9. Annual Message.

10. *HJ* (1840), 375–378.

11. Various annual and special messages, *HJ* (1847–1852).

12. The usual tax exemption granted to early canal and railroad companies in Georgia was that taxes should not exceed ½ per cent upon their annual net income. This did not apply to their banking operations. On such they were taxed as other banks.

13. *HJ* (1807); Appendix; Treasurers' Abstracts and Reports, 1804–1828; Comptroller Generals' Reports, 1828–1840; governors' messages. The figures for the 1800 column are estimates. Complete records for individual types of debt are lacking after 1808, hence the use of Table 28 (b) for the history of the debt after that date. For the origin of the gratuitous certificates see Chapter IV.

14. Gilmer, annual message. It was not possible to discover what part of the governors' warrants was issued prior to 1790, and so all were counted at full value, which may account for some of the apparent balance of debt still outstanding.

15. *SJ* (1842), 238–239 and other references in note 4 above. J. H. Johnston's table of expenses of construction of the state railroad (*Western and Atlantic Railroad*, 106–107) has been an invaluable aid in arriving at the estimates given here and in Table 29 for the years 1837–1843.

16. Governor Brown, annual messages, 1859–1860.

17. Governor Early, annual message, *H* & *SJs*.

18. Central Bank, reports, May 5 and November 2, 1829.

19. Governor Crawford, annual message, 1845.

20. *SJ* (1847), 445–447.

INDEX

Bei Fragen zur Produktsicherheit wenden Sie sich bitte an:
If you have any questions regarding product safety,
please contact:

Walter de Gruyter GmbH
Genthiner Straße 13
10785 Berlin
productsafety@degruyterbrill.com